Peter FitzSimons is a journalist with the *Sydney Morning Herald* and *Sun-Herald*, and has interviewed everyone from President George Bush Snr to Sir Edmund Hillary. He is also a popular after-dinner and motivational speaker and the only Wallaby sent from the field against the All Blacks – unjustly, he swears.

Peter is the author of twenty-seven books – including the number-one bestselling military history books *Kokoda* and *Tobruk*, and biographies of Nancy Wake, Kim Beazley, Nick Farr-Jones, Les Darcy, Steve Waugh, John Eales and Charles Kingsford Smith – is one of Australia's biggest selling non-fiction authors.

In 2011 Peter was named a Member of the Order of Australia for service to literature as a biographer, sports journalist and commentator, and to the community through contributions to conservation, disability care, social welfare and sporting organisations.

He lives with his wife, Lisa Wilkinson, and their three children in Sydney.

ALSO BY PETER FITZSIMONS

Basking in Beirut

Little Theories of Life

Hitchhiking for Ugly People

Rugby Stories

Everyone But Phar Lap

Everyone And Phar Lap

Nick Farr-Jones: The Authorised Biography

FitzSimons on Rugby

Beazley: A Biography

Nene

Nancy Wake: A Biography of Our Greatest War Heroine

The Rugby War

John Eales: The Biography

The Story of Skilled Engineering and Frank Hargrave

Kokoda

Steve Waugh

Tobruk

The Ballad of Les Darcy

A Simpler Time

Charles Kingsford Smith
and Those Magnificent Men

PETER FITZSIMONS

HarperCollins*Publishers*

Harper*Collins*Publishers

First published in Australia in 2009
This edition published in 2016
by HarperCollins*Publishers* Australia Pty Limited
ABN 36 009 913 517
harpercollins.com.au

HarperCollinsPublishers
Macken House, 39/40 mayor Street Upper
Dublin 1, D01 C9W8, Ireland
Harper*Collins*Publishers
Level 13, 201 Elizabeth Street, Sydney NSW 2000, Australia
Unit D1, 63 Apollo Drive, Rosedale, Auckland 0632, New Zealand
A 53, Sector 57, Noida, UP, India
1 London Bridge Street, London SE1 9GF, United Kingdom
2 Bloor Street East, 20th floor, Toronto, Ontario M4W 1A8, Canada
195 Broadway, New York NY 10007, USA

National Library of Australia Cataloguing-in-Publication data:

FitzSimons, Peter, author.
Charles Kingsford Smith and those magnificent men / Peter FitzSimons.
978 1 4607 5190 9 (paperback)
978 0 7304 9278 8 (ebook)
Includes bibliographical references and index.
Kingsford-Smith, Charles, 1897-1935.
Air pilots – History.
Aeronautics – History.
Air travel – History.
629.13

Cover design by HarperCollins Design Studio
Author photograph by Marco Del Grande / Fairfax Photographs
Cover image by National Archives of Australia (A1200), photographic negatives and prints, L96364, Sir Charles Kingsford Smith, an Australian pioneer of long distance flying, 1934
Back cover image from the collection of the Air Force Museum of New Zealand
Drawings by Brian Caldersmith
Maps by Demap www.demap.com.au
Typeset in 10.5 on 12.5pt Bembo by Kirby Jones
Printed and bound in Australia by McPhersons Printing Group

To my wife, Lisa

If any one man typified the Australian character at its best, with all its great qualities, as well as some of its faults, he was Charles Kingsford Smith. No other Australian was ever so worshipped by the average man and boy. He still figures in most Australian minds as the greatest native son ...

STANLEY BROGDEN, *THE HISTORY OF AUSTRALIAN AVIATION*, 1960[1]

He had greatness as a pilot and as a man. As the fundamental urge to his flights he had the enlightened spirit of the born pioneer whatever the risks, the way into the unknown was always an irresistible invitation to him. His rugged appearance hid a sensitive finely balanced personality upheld with a smile throughout his adventurous life by an inner structure of fine steel, that was the extraordinary combination of Smithy. It was this unusual combination of qualities which made him the great airman. He could see, feel, and predict the air vividly and accurately with his sense of personality, but whatever the conditions his steel structure had the strength to deal with any situation ...

BILL TAYLOR ON HIS LONG-TIME FLYING COMPANION, SIR CHARLES KINGSFORD SMITH[2]

HIGH FLIGHT

Oh! I have slipped the surly bonds of earth
And danced the skies on laughter-silvered wings;
Sunward I've climbed, and joined the tumbling mirth
Of sun-spilt clouds — and done a hundred things
You have not dreamed of — wheeled and soared and swung
High in the sunlit silence. Hov'ring there
I've chased the shouting wind along, and flung
My eager craft through footless halls of air.
Up, up the long delirious, burning blue,
I've topped the windswept heights with easy grace
Where never lark, or even eagle flew —
And, while with silent lifting mind I've trod
The high untrespassed sanctity of space,
Put out my hand and touched the face of God.

PILOT OFFICER JOHN GILLESPIE MAGEE, RCAF[3]

Contents

FOREWORD

BY CHARLES KINGSFORD-SMITH JNR

Author Peter FitzSimons begins this eminently readable book with a quote from my father: 'I came into the world of flying at its dawn, and what a glorious dawn …'

Everyone knows how the 'world of flying' has brought about enormous and profound changes affecting almost every person on the planet. As one beneficiary of these changes, I'm solidly enthusiastic about flying, its technology and the technical skill called piloting.

But for me, there is an aspect of flying just as important as the benefits it has brought. I suppose I could call it the *romance* of flying. The quote above from my dad hints at what this is. From the earliest days — and extending to the present — aviation has exerted a tremendous hold on its practitioners: designers, builders, pilots etc. There is a fascination, both intellectual and emotional, which captures an individual, often for a lifetime. My father is a prima facie example of this total involvement.

How I would have loved to talk long hours with him about his passion, to gain more insight into what captivated him and his flying generation, and to experience vicariously his exciting adventures. But it was not to be; he was lost just before I turned three.

So how do we, in the present, experience something of that 'glorious dawn'? The pioneers are gone and what few airplanes are left sit silently in museums. As always, when we yearn to recapture something of the spirit of the past, our best resource is a good book by a skilful author. When Peter sent me a copy of his manuscript, I read it avidly, hoping that it would turn out to be just such a book. I was not disappointed! For that reason, if you are intrigued even slightly with the 'world of flying', I recommend it for your insight and enjoyment.

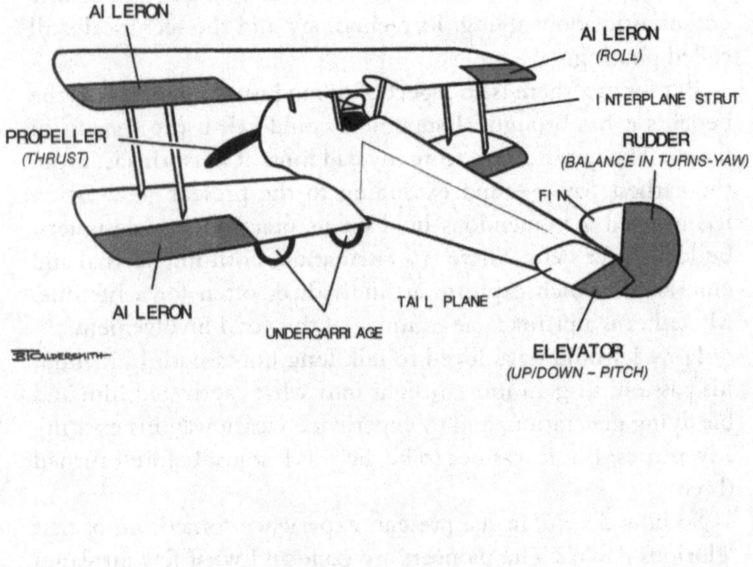
AILERON
AILERON
(ROLL)
INTERPLANE STRUT
PROPELLER
(THRUST)
RUDDER
(BALANCE IN TURNS-YAW)
FIN
TAIL PLANE
AILERON
UNDERCARRIAGE
ELEVATOR
(UP/DOWN – PITCH)

Introduction

In March 2007 I was asked to have a cup of coffee with a couple of blokes who wanted to make a documentary about Charles Kingsford Smith. They had a few extraordinary revelations they felt they could make in the doco — were gung-ho on the whole subject — and wondered if I was interested in writing a book on the aviator that might come out at roughly the same time.

The idea grew on me. For me and most Australians of my age and older, Sir Charles Kingsford Smith was an iconic figure, although that was mostly through his long-time appearance on our $20 bill and the fact that Sydney airport was named after him. Too, I dimly remember my parents and grandfather speaking reverentially about him.

But who *was* he? What was the legend actually built on? After some preliminary research, the best of all possible things happened to me. I — as we writers say in the trade — got into it and was consumed by the wonder of the story.

Certainly there were many accounts of his life to learn from, foremost of which was the outstanding 1999 book by the New Zealand writer Ian Mackersey, *Smithy: The Life of Sir Charles Kingsford Smith*; and many other biographies dating back to the 1930s. I did indeed find Kingsford Smith a fascinating man the more I found out about him and yet, apart from the wonders of Smithy's own life, I also became intrigued — my wife would say obsessed — by other aviation people of those early times. I found I loved the stories of Lawrence Hargrave, the Wright brothers, Lord Northcliffe, Louis Blériot, Harry Hawker, Anthony Fokker, Roland Garros, Charles Nungesser, the Red Baron, Sir Ross Smith, Lawrence of Arabia, Bert Hinkler, George Wilkins and Charles Lindbergh among many more.

They were all, of course, august names — at least in their own time — but even in such exalted company, Kingsford Smith could more than hold his own.

I was fascinated to find, in the course of my research, that no-one less than Charles Lindbergh himself had dipped his lid to Kingsford Smith personally, saying that what Lindbergh had done in crossing the Atlantic could not be compared to Kingsford Smith's feat with the Pacific.

As well, when I came across the stories of the 1919 air race from England to Australia, the formation of Qantas, the saga of the *Kookaburra*, the loss of the *Southern Cloud*, the 1934 Centenary Air Race, the story of P.G. Taylor's wing-walking in 1935, I was stunned both by what wonderful sagas they were and by how little those stories were known by the wider public outside the aviation community, which certainly included me.

The book that I offer now, thus, is not the book I intended to write ...

Starting with the narrow parameters of looking at Smithy's life, bit by bit it morphed into the story of his life and *times,* and of the other extraordinary figures who occupied those times. I have never enjoyed working on a book so much, from finding out more and more about these figures long gone, to travelling all over the world in pursuit of their tales. All through San Francisco, New York, Washington, London, Paris, Calais, Wellington, Christchurch and, of course, all around Australia, I traipsed through museums, over abandoned airfields, into old hotels, and regularly buried myself under piles of dusty newspaper cuttings and old letters, trying to get the feel for the times that were and the place that Kingsford Smith and those magnificent men had in them.

It is, of course, for the reader to judge whether or not I have managed to pull this off, but at least let me state my aim at the outset — that was to have Kingsford Smith and his companions *fly* again. I wanted to take the thousand points of light represented by endnoted fact, and, by judicious and occasional use of the poetic license I keep in my wallet, to put enough colour in between that the book would have the feel of a novel, even while remaining in the non-fiction genre. This is the approach I have employed since coming under the influence of the American writer Gary Smith in the year 2000 — most particularly in my books *John Eales, Kokoda, Tobruk* and *The Ballad of Les Darcy.*

In terms of ensuring that my endnoted fact was indeed *fact*, allow me to say, it was not easy. I have never worked on a subject with such an extraordinary amount of technical detail, nor with such a vast body of archival material to trawl through. Nor, might I add, have I ever worked on a story where accounts of the same episode have been so different, sometimes from the same writer who was there at the time!

In order to do everything possible to get the detail in this book to be as accurate as possible, I was fortunate to be able to call on the expertise of many people, and draw on their scholarship in particular fields. In this regard, I warmly thank Michael Adams for help with the story of Lawrence Hargrave; Simine Short on Octave Chanute; Andrew Moore on the New Guard; Simon Nasht on Sir Hubert Wilkins; Ron Cuskelly on the saga of the *Lady Southern Cross* and on details of other people and planes — extending even to photographs of the manufacturer's plates on the engines of the *Southern Cross*; Mark Day on the Red Baron; Neil Cadigan on the pilot Lester Brain; Dick Smith on the saga of the *Kookaburra*; Ron Frew and Matthew Higgins on the fate of the *Southern Cloud*; and Howard Jones on what happened to the *Uiver* when it found itself in trouble over Albury.

The remaining family of Sir Charles Kingsford Smith were good to me, led by Sir Charles's only son, Charles Kingsford-Smith Jnr, and I warmly thank him — including for his fine foreword. Early in the writing of this book, I had lunch with John Ulm, the only son of Charles Ulm, and I thank him equally for the help he gave me thereafter.

Soon after I started the project I was blessed to find exactly the person I needed: an aviation researcher with knowledge as deep as it was wide, powered by a passion that would kill a brown dog. His name is Peter Finlay, and he proved to be a godsend in terms of ferreting out fresh detail and endlessly tapping old detail on the head with a hammer to see if it sounded tinny or not. And while, of course, all mistakes that remain are my own, I cannot thank him enough for his work and dedication to the cause.

My long-time researcher Sonja Goernitz was a great help across the board, liaising with libraries, newspapers and museums around the globe, as well as using her own prodigious writing skills to give much salient advice as my manuscript took shape.

I record my appreciation to my other long-time researcher Glenda Lynch for her efforts in working the wonderful resources of the Australian War Memorial and National Library for me; Henry Barrkman in London for the research work he did for me there, most particularly with the British Museum and gleaning crucial, minute detail by trawling through newspaper archives around the world; David Wiseman in Israel; and my friend Dr Michael Cooper, who helped me a great deal with medical research.

I hope in the thousand or so endnotes and bibliography to have acknowledged all other writers whose work I have drawn from, but there are several in particular I wish to cite here. In his book *The Wright Brothers*, the aforementioned New Zealand writer Ian Mackersey recounts how, as soon as he began writing it, everyone in the field said if you're doing Orville and Wilbur, then you have to talk to Tom Crouch, who had himself done a biography of the brothers and is the acknowledged leader in the field. My own experience was similar except that when it comes to Kingsford Smith, it is Mackersey who is the equal authority on Charles Kingsford Smith. His book *Smithy* is, and will remain, the benchmark for research on the great pilot, and the notes of his book were also particularly valuable pointers as to where the diaspora of Kingsford Smith treasure-troves of information could be found.

Ted Wixted and Pedr Davis are two other writers who have done particularly valuable work over the years. Beyond *Smithy*, I found John Gunn's book on the history of Qantas, *The Defeat of Distance*, another absolute treasure trove of fascinating material — with equally valuable notes. (I was impressed with Gunn's book after just reading it, but when I saw the Qantas Heritage Collection, and the truckloads of archival material that he had to trawl through, I was in awe.) And, though Percy Cogger's book on

Charles Ulm — *Wings and the Man — the Private Papers of Charles Ulm, Aviator* — was never published, I found the manuscript held by the Mitchell Library of Sydney immensely helpful, most particularly when it came to the machinations of the Air Inquiry Committee hearings, after the Coffee Royal affair.

I also cite Scott Berg's masterwork on the Lone Eagle himself, *Lindbergh*, and note that Robert Wohl's book, *A Passion for Wings*, was a wonderful pointer to early aviation history. In 1990, the Australian academic Dr Leigh Edmonds wrote a paper titled *Problems of Defence, Isolation and Development: What Civil Aviation Could Do To Help*, which I have subsequently sucked dry for information in that field.

I found the wider aviation community and descendants of particular characters in the Kingsford Smith story to be wonderfully helpful.

My thanks for their contributions to this manuscript go to: Ashlyn Macfarlane, Ivor Davis, Warwick Finlay, Jo Beresford (NZ), Dave Homewood (NZ), Brian Caldersmith, Mac Job, Frank Cuttell, John Laming, Cam Spencer, Aub Pop, James Oglethorpe, Pauline Curby, Terri McCormack, Stewart Wilson, Tom Sonter, Kenneth Hope-Jones, Helen Wilder, Millie Cooper, Cynthia Balderston, Jack Eyre, Glenn Pettit, Eta Varani-Norton, Mr Tukana Rainima, Ken Garling and Rob Garling and my great friend, the late Matt Laffan.

From particular institutions, I thank Megan Wishart and Allan Rudge, Walsh Memorial Library at Auckland's Museum of Transport and Technology; all the fast, friendly, reliable and rotating staff at both the National Library of Australia and the State Library of New South Wales; David Watmuff and Matthew O'Sullivan, Air Force Museum of New Zealand, Wigram; Bob De La Hunty, Historical Aircraft Restoration Society; Ian Debenham, Powerhouse Museum; Val Carpenter, Cowra and District Historical Society and Museum; Dace Taube, Doheny Memorial Library, University of Southern California; Karen Harrigan, Sydney Airport Corporation; Cecilia Ng, Alexander Turnbull Library, New Zealand; Rebecca McConnochie and Toni Kasch, Brisbane Airport Corporation; Lex Rowland, Hinkler House Memorial Museum; Richard Breckon, Australia

Post Historian; Roger Meyer, Airways Museum, Essendon; Richard Chenoweth, Santa Maria Valley Historical Society; Hans Holzer, Deutsches Museum, Aviation Department; Hayden Hamilton, APT Collectibles; William Edwards, Reference Officer, National Archives of Australia; John Blanch, Bondi Surf Bathers' Life Saving Club; Peter Dobson, New Plymouth Aero Club; Des Sullivan, Qantas Heritage Collection, Kingsford Smith Airport; Guy Tranter, ABC Document Archives; Michael Nelmes, Curator, Narromine Aviation Museum; Sarah-Donna Philips and Lynette Riquelme, Supreme Court of New South Wales; Nancy Meddings, Allan Hancock College, USA; David Whatmuff, Wigram Aviation Museum, New Zealand; Di Davies, Bank of England; Meg Reilly, Sydney Technical High School; and Professor Sean Brawley, University of New South Wales.

For her help in all things to do with the form and texture of the book, I offer, as ever, my deep appreciation to my treasured colleague at the *Sydney Morning Herald* Harriet Veitch, who put many weekend and evening hours into the project. I also record my appreciation and professional respect to everyone I worked with at HarperCollins, most particularly Shona Martyn, Mel Cain, Mary Rennie, Glenda Downing, Kylie Mason, Graeme Jones, Matt Stanton, Jessie Borkan and Tracey Gibson.

Finally, my thanks to my wife, Lisa Wilkinson. In fact, Lisa was not only supportive of the project from the beginning, but also did a wonderful job once again of applying her long-time professional editing skills to — in my opinion — making it sing where it sometimes was only warbling. I have always loved that line from Jack Nicholson to Helen Hunt in *As Good As It Gets*, when he says: 'You make me want to be a better man.'

Lisa does that for me, too, but she also makes me write better books.

I hope you enjoy this book.

Peter FitzSimons
Sydney, April, 2009

One

In the Beginning ...

I came into the world of flying at its dawn, and what a glorious dawn ...
Charles Kingsford Smith, 1935[1]

Bliss was it in that dawn to be alive,
But to be young was very heaven!
William Wordsworth[2]

In my mind, the flying machine will tend to bring peace and goodwill to all; it will throw light on the few unexplored corners of the earth and it will herald the downfall of all restrictions to the free intercourse of nations.
Lawrence Hargrave, speaking to an audience in Sydney in the late 1890s[3]

January 1894. A soft, snowy kind of day ...

Before a roaring fire in the study of his stately Chicago home, the respected French-American scientist Octave Chanute was seated at his oak desk, putting the finishing touches to the manuscript of his book which he intended to publish under the title *Progress in Flying Machines.* It was a work that had been a long time in coming.

After retiring from a successful and prosperous career as a railway engineer, the robust 62-year-old with the white and well-groomed spade beard had recently returned to a passion that had first engaged him some forty years earlier. As a young man, he had become so absorbed in documenting the history of man's quest to fly that it threatened to derail his paying job and he had been obliged to put it aside. Now freed from that daily burden of work, he had been able to re-enter the field with gusto and had been quick in publishing many learned treatises on the remaining riddles of successful flight.

As he put it in a letter to a friend: 'My general idea is to pass in review what has hitherto been experimented with a view to accounting for the failures, clearing away the rubbish, and pointing out some of the elements of success, if I can ...'[4]

Chanute's book covered everything from the Greek mythology of Icarus and his wings of wax to the genuine vision of Leonardo da Vinci that man would be able to fly. He took particular interest in the eccentric English baronet George Cayley, who in 1809, at the age of thirty-six — after examination and experimentation with the theories of flight dating back to 1792 — had published a treatise, 'On Aerial Navigation'. In this work, Cayley had stated as firm principles that 'lift', 'propulsion' and 'control' were the three key elements that had to be resolved before successful flight could take place. For the next forty years Cayley had continued refining his gliders to the point that, by 1853, the then 80-year-old had been able to press-gang his coachman into sitting in a fixed-wing machine as it glided serenely for several hundred yards across Yorkshire's Brompton Dale. Cayley was immensely impressed, but the coachman was *not*.

'Please, Sir George,' he had shouted to him. 'I wish to give notice. I was hired to drive, not to fly!'[5]

There was also in Chanute's towering work detailed examination of the various experiments in the possibilities of flight that were being conducted around the world. Much of his writing was heavily scientific in nature, with complex diagrams and long mathematical calculations tougher than Chinese calculus. And yet, a warm man, he was also keen to acknowledge many of those scientists, engineers and inventors around the world with whom he had engaged in such extensive correspondence, helping him to become the world's foremost authority on the subject.

And so now, on this cold and snowy day, he came to the warmest, most heartfelt passage of all, and penned it in his elegant longhand ...

> *If there be one man, more than another, who deserves to succeed in flying through the air, that man is Lawrence Hargrave of Sydney, New South Wales. He has now constructed with his own hands no less than 18 flying machines of increasing size, all of which fly, and as a result of his many experiments (of which an account is about to be given) he now says, in a private letter to the writer, that 'I know that success is dead sure to come'.*
>
> *M. Hargrave takes out no patents for any of his aerial inventions, and he publishes from time to time full accounts of them, in order that a mutual interchange of ideas may take place with other inventors working in the same field, so as to expedite joint progress . . .*[6]

•

Stanwell Park is a tiny strip of beach, clinging like a crab to a coastal cleft just south of Sydney. On this morning of 12 November 1894, the local eccentric, Lawrence Hargrave, who was known in those parts for his obsessive belief that it was possible to build a machine that would fly — no, *really* — was going about his business with the help of the property caretaker, James Swaine. People down that way had noticed the newly arrived bearded one with the wild eyes, long-suffering wife and gaggle of kids. They knew he was forever pottering in the workshop he had set up on the northern veranda of his house on the hill, and was always muttering about 'air flows', 'thrust', and 'curved surfaces' but few knew what he was on about.

Lawrie Hargrave had always been regarded as a bit odd since, as a young man, he outraged local Rushcutters Bay churchgoers up in Sydney Town by 'walking on water', courtesy of some 'elongated flotation shoes' that he had designed and built. But look, what on *earth* was he up to now? Flying kites? But what curious-looking kites they were! Three-dimensional kites!

'Cellular kites', he called them — like two open-ended boxes, with upwardly curved top surfaces, joined and strengthened by thin struts. And instead of flying around all over the place, diving and bobbing and soaring like normal two-dimensional kites, these strange things were amazingly stable. Somehow, they were built in such a way that as the air flowed over the curves, they were perpetually tugging upwards ever upwards and so seemingly defying the law of gravity, which had ruled the physical world since Eve ate one apple and another fell on Isaac Newton's head.

First, as a couple of his kids sat at a safe distance watching, Hargrave got one kite in the air and then attached the rope beneath it to the next kite, which went up. And then he and the caretaker Swaine did the same thing twice, then three times more, until four of the contraptions were in the air, all connected to one rope tethered to … to … to what? What was he doing now? Sitting in a kind of sling? Yes, a sling!

And now came the celebrated moment, just before eleven o'clock — a stray puff of wind rising off the majestic Pacific Ocean from the south-west gave a silky surge and then, as it flowed over the curved shape of the box kites, the upward pressure on the rope attached to the inventor increased to the point that … suddenly the 44-year-old broke free of the 'surly bonds of earth'[7] and was propelled upwards. It *was* possible! Before the awed Swaine, Lawrence Hargrave was momentarily lifted 16 feet above the ground and would have gone higher still if not for another rope that kept him tethered to heavy bags of sand on mother earth — and even then it was only just, as Swaine had to desperately wrestle with the block and tackle to hold him down. A 'Eureka!' moment, if ever there was one! The key fact he had demonstrated was that when air moves at pace over *curved* wings, there is enough upwards pull to *lift* a human off the ground.

As to the problem of propulsion, Hargrave had already put in an enormous amount of work on that vexing question. His view was that the only way forward was to develop a very light-weight yet powerful engine to which could be attached an especially designed propeller, or 'screw' as he called it, which could bite upon the air and pull the machine forward in the same way that a ship's propeller did in water. If it worked, then this would always pull the plane forwards and the speed of the wind over the wings would be able to lift a man.

It was with this specific aim that seven years earlier Hargrave had created, and since refined, the world's first rotary engine. This was a revolutionary departure from most existing engine designs whereby, instead of the cylinders (and their pistons) being in a fixed position providing force on the whirling crankshaft, it was the cylinders and pistons which rotated around a stationary crankshaft. Hargrave's idea was that, by attaching the propeller to those whirling cylinders, they would be kept cool with their own flow of air instead of the cumbersome and leaky water-cooled systems. This would only leave control as the key issue ... and then a man could even, genuinely, fly like a bird.

Of course, Lawrence Hargrave was not a man working in isolation, for all over the world in the last gasp of the nineteenth century, people were busily trying to solve the riddle of how to fly — just as they had been for centuries. But, crucially, Hargrave was also a man keen to share his knowledge — with no interest whatsoever in patents — and he had no sooner been borne aloft by the power of wind moving swiftly over curved cells in a kite than he wrote a full report of it, complete with diagrams, which he sent off to Octave Chanute, just as he had previously put into the public domain notes on the design of his rotary engine.

No, this was not powered flight, which was the grand quest, but it was a significant breakthrough, one of the key riddles solved, and as Chanute spread word among other researchers around America and the world, the reaction was immediate.

Only a couple of years later, in 1897, in one of the many letters Octave Chanute wrote to his Australian correspondent, he noted: 'Mr Millet has put a Hargrave kite on the market and I am told the skies in our eastern States are red with them.'[8] Another of his admirers was the famed American inventor of the telephone, Alexander Graham Bell, who was then getting very interested in the problems of flight. Bell considered Hargrave's 'box kite', as it had become known, as 'a very sound design'.[9] The two corresponded and became such close friends that Bell would later visit Australia, just to meet with Hargrave, and noted, amazed, that 'Mr. Lawrence Hargrave is better known in America than in his own country'.[10]

And it had always been thus. In the mid-1890s, Hargrave had written to Chanute that, 'The people of Sydney who can speak of my work without a smile are very scarce; it is doubtless the same with American workers. I know that success is dead sure to come, and therefore do not waste time and words in trying to convince unbelievers.'[11]

•

It was at this time of great excitement in the nascent world of modern aviation that, some thousand and a bitty miles to the north of Lawrence Hargrave, wee Charles made seventh, and last, in the Smith family when he was born on the 9th day of February 1897, in a rather unprepossessing house on Riverview Terrace in the leafy Brisbane suburb of Hamilton.

It was not that Charlie was necessarily a 'mistake', but the fact that his next oldest sibling, Eric, was a full ten years older than him, and that the first five of those seven children had come in the space of just six years, was a fair indication that he was at least a surprise. (Another indication was the fact that his father was forty-five years old when he was born, and his mother forty.) Still, the key thing was that 'Chilla', as he soon became known to his own flesh and blood, was loved, as much by his four brothers and two sisters — Harold, Winifred, Wilfrid, Elsie, Leofric and Eric — as by his parents. As it was, though, in the first few days of his life they felt they pretty much *had* to love him, as no-one else except the family possibly could, so unsightly did he seem to their eyes.

Bald at birth, terribly wrinkled and with a mashed nose, he looked as though he had been bashed in the face with a shovel, and there was some discussion in the family that he resembled nothing or no other person so much as 'Yorkey', an extremely old and battered-looking Aboriginal man who used to do chores around the house for the family when they had lived in Cairns.[12]

And yet, what a transformation! In just a short while this baby, born with a face like a dropped pie, began to develop before their very eyes and look like an advertisement for mother's milk, with — to use his sister Winifred's words —

'golden hair, blue eyes, rose-leaf skin, and the reddest lips imaginable curling over pearly teeth ...'[13]

Both sisters thought such good looks were wasted on a boy, but they didn't stop pampering him for all that, and the sunny-tempered toddler happily soaked up all the attention from them and the rest of the family.

And a very tight family it was, as in part registered by the fact that each of the children had their mother Catherine's maiden name of 'Kingsford' for their middle name, to go with the 'Smith' surname inherited from their father, William. Generally, the maternal weight on the family scales was greater than the paternal. Catherine was warm-hearted, strong-willed and deeply involved in all her children's lives, the sun around which they revolved. She combined great femininity with a strong constitution, and was up at five o'clock every morning, sweeping the kitchen, preparing breakfast, sorting the washing, getting the kids off to school, doing the shopping and myriad maternal things until late into the night. A born hostess, she ran an open house where there were frequent visitors and they were always welcome — at the dinner table if they needed a feed, or on the couch if they needed a place to stay. For his part, William was a loving father, and a hard worker who left the house early and didn't return until late, but he was also a little detached and definitely deferential to his wife.

Brisbane was Catherine's home town, with her father no less than a former lord mayor of that metropolis, while William, a relatively humble bank manager, had started his life in Sydney and, as an adult, was posted through his working life here, there and everywhere — and it just so happened that 'here', when Charles was born, was on Riverview Terrace. By the time Charlie was two, however, the whole family had moved to 'there', Sydney, to live first near Manly Beach and then to the inner harbour-side suburb of Longueville.

Each day, William would head off to work in the city with his older sons, while the other siblings would walk to school and Charlie would stay at home to play, with his mother never more than a quick scold away. Generally, he was a boisterous child, confident from the first, and despite his angelic looks, never minding a bit of rough 'n' tumble or taking a scrape. Ah, the stories the family delighted in telling each other of what Chilla, their 'engaging little sinner',[14] had got up to *this* time.

What about when he put the house-help Ruby's hat through the laundry wringer, only to have it emerge as flat as *two* pancakes? Knowing that he was in real trouble this time, Chilla trotted out to the rose garden, broke off the thorniest branch he could find, and brought it to his mother, gravely announcing: 'Here's a pwickly stick to whip him wif, he's been a naughty boy to put poor Wooby's hat froo her mangle ...'[15]

Catherine did not whip him with the prickly branch or anything else on this occasion, not that she was above administering the odd bit of corporal punishment. (Still, as one who stood just over 5 feet tall, and weighed only 6 stone, she was never one to pack much of a wallop even on a bad day — it was her emotional power that guided her children to adulthood, not her physical force.)

While she was close to all her children, the bond between her and her youngest child was a particularly strong one from the beginning. With the rest of the family gone for the day, it was frequently just the two of them spending time together. One way Catherine kept him occupied was to set him up with a pencil and huge sheets of butcher's paper, encouraging him to draw, which he delighted in doing, frequently focusing on drawing those mechanical things he could see from their garden, like ships, ferries, paddle-steamers, bridges and trains. Not for nothing would Chilla's first note to Santa Claus read when he was four:

> *Dear Santa,*
> *Will you bring a train with piston rods to make the wheels go round? Will you make Christmas come quick?*
> *Sincerely,*
> *Chilla.*[16]

Of course, it was Catherine who would arrange with Santa to bring exactly that, and then delight in playing with him and the train while Father was at work. And it was also Catherine who tended his many wounds when Chilla, convinced that he could *fly*, jumped from the roof of their shed holding nothing but an open umbrella.[17] Turned out he couldn't fly after all …

Generally, however, Chilla's favourite times were when the whole family was together, particularly on Sundays, when he was more often than not the centre of attention. One of his show-stoppers — at this time when the Boer War was in full swing — was to sing out with great passion the words of Rudyard Kipling's poem 'The Absent-Minded Beggar', as best he could. With all the family around him, egging him on, Chilla would stand on the enormous polished dining-room table and belt out …

Duke's son — cook's son — son of a hundred kings —
(Fifty fousand horse and foot goin' to Table Bay!)
Each of 'em doin' his country's work
And who's to look after the things?
Pass the hat for your credit's sake,
And pay —PAY— PAY![18]

Again, Chilla, *again!* they would urge him. And he would give another rousing rendition. Whenever there were guests over, young Chilla would take centre stage with some kind of performance or other and the entire family thought the little showman something of a prodigy for his capacity to memorise words and sing them well, and as he got a little older to quickly teach himself the musical instruments they were playing on, including the piano and the ukulele.

Even when Sunday began to ebb away there was still a little more fun to be had, albeit of a slightly more pious nature, as the family would gather round the piano and lustily sing hymns together, before Father would read a chapter from the Bible. This last was less because they were particularly religious than because it was just a nice, communal family thing to do.

All up, there might have been happier kids than Chilla as the twentieth century dawned, but probably not many …

•

'Is that man your dad?' asked the small boy down at Stanwell Park of the young girl who sat gazing at the man on the beach with all the kites.

'Yes, he's my father,' replied Nellie Hargrave, barely repressing a sigh and throwing a 'here-we-go-again' glance at her sister Hilda and younger brother Geoffrey. She more or less knew what the young tousle-headed lad was going to say before he said it.

'Is he … is he really a *wizard*?'

'No,' replied Nellie firmly, 'he's a scientist discovering how men can fly.'

'Fly! That means he must use magic,' said the boy with wide eyes.

'No magic,' said Nellie with some conviction. 'One day men will fly in machines with wings like those.'[19]

In fact, many men around the world had been trying to do exactly that, and her father's initial breakthrough with box kites was just part of a great burst of experimentation in aviation, as the conviction had grown that it really might be possible for man to fly. No-one had been more active than Germany's Otto Lilienthal, who for many years had been pioneering gliders, including an 1894 model designed to have the two wings flap in the manner of a bird. Lilienthal established that a key component to successful flight was for the pilot to be able to react while in flight to changing wind conditions, and he was able to fashion a primitive rudder on his gliders, attached to a piece of string, which he could control by backwards and forwards movement of his head. Alas, on 9 August 1896, while he was soaring from the hill he had constructed just outside Berlin, he was caught by a gust of rising air, causing the glider to stall and he fell to the ground from a height of more than 50 feet. Just before he died the next day in a Berlin hospital, celebrated legend has it that he uttered his last words on the subject of flying experimentation: '*Kleine Opfer müssen gebracht werden* …' (Small sacrifices must be made …)

Lilienthal's work went on. His greatest disciple was a Scottish marine engineer by the name of Percy Pilcher, who as well as being a devotee of building gliders believed that powered flight was possible. In 1897, after building a glider called the

Hawk, which sailed a breathtaking 820 feet, he began to build a triplane — with three levels of wings — which he intended to get into the air by virtue of a 4-horsepower engine. And yet, like his mentor Lilienthal, Pilcher was to discover the perils of leaving mother earth's close embrace.

On the afternoon of 30 September 1899, after it had turned out that his engine did not have enough power to get his triplane into the air and Pilcher used real horses to drag himself and the *Hawk* into the air, the flimsy, single bamboo link to the crankshaft broke. Pilcher fell 30 feet and landed in a crumpled heap, his broken legs being the least of it, and passed away two days later. Small sacrifices had to be made ...

As always, however, there were others ready to come forward and take over where Pilcher had left off.

Percy Pilcher's 'Hawk' glider.

•

The morning of 17 December 1903 dawned cold and windy on the sand dunes of Kill Devil Hills, near a town called Kitty Hawk on a small island off the coast of North Carolina in the United States. This was the place where Wilbur and Orville Wright — two bachelor brothers in their early to mid-thirties, who owned a bicycle store in Dayton, Ohio — had been staying over the previous couple of months. It was too windy, Wilbur thought, for them to try out the machine they had been working on for so long. Maybe they should wait until the wind dropped?

Maybe ... But in the end neither brother could bear to wait any longer, whatever the wind, and just after ten o'clock they brought their strange contraption out from its hangar and into the open.

They were hoping to do nothing less than *fly* in it. They had picked Kitty Hawk at the suggestion of Octave Chanute, whose book *Progress in Flying Machines* they had devoured before entering into correspondence with him. It was he who had suggested that what they most needed was a place with open space, a frequent steady breeze and, perhaps most importantly, a soft landing ground should they actually succeed in getting off the ground.

Which last, of course, was no certain thing.

Over the previous few years the brothers had built various unpowered versions of their current machine, and through trial, error and scientific experiments, together with close study of the work of the likes of Lilienthal and Pilcher, and with a great deal of material from Chanute, determined what worked and what didn't. There had been moments of despair, as on one occasion in August 1901, when a hoped-for breakthrough had proven to be a dud and Wilbur had exclaimed to Orville, 'Not within a *thousand* years would man ever fly.' And there had been times of elation, as when they had realised that the secrets of lateral control of their craft, of maintaining balance, could be discovered by studying the way birds shaped their wings when soaring, turning and descending. Through it all, they had simply kept going, solving the problems that presented themselves one by one and incorporating all their successes into this machine.

Built out of spruce, ash and muslin, they called their plane the *Flyer*, in a show of faith that would make their father, Bishop Wright, very proud. (And he was a bishop, for the record, who believed that if his sons could invent something capable of flying long distances, it might be useful in helping to spread the word of Christianity to far-flung corners of the world.)[20]

Their bizarre-looking machine had a two-tiered wing of some 40 feet across, with a curved shape that Lawrence Hargrave would have recognised as bearing a great similarity to the curve of his box kites. So, too, would Hargrave have felt at home in the windy environment of Kitty Hawk, which was not at all unlike that of Stanwell Park, where he had first proved that air flowing fast over curved wings could lift a man off the ground. Though the *Flyer* had many points of difference with other attempts to build a plane that would fly in a *controlled* fashion, one in particular was revolutionary — and the Wrights had established that it worked by long testing.

The *Flyer* had evolved from a series of gliders with movable surfaces, so that as the pilot flew he could control the plane's movement around the lateral, longitudinal and vertical axes in 'pitch', 'roll' and 'yaw' respectively. That is, the pilot could use a front-mounted 'elevator' to point the plane's nose up or down to gain or lose altitude; he could control a specially designed and patented wing-twisting system to roll the plane on its axis from stem to stern to bank, so that either the right wing or the left wing lifted to encourage the plane to turn left or right.

The 1902 glider's wings had proven to be somewhat too enthusiastic to obey the pilot's control inputs and, as the plane banked, it fell into a 'side slip', winding itself into a death spiral to the sand. The glider's fixed tail fins contributed to this effect.

It was Orville who, wrestling with the dynamics of flight late one night in bed, managed to bring that particular demon to the ground. What if, he wondered, while staring at the cracks in the ceiling, the rudders were to be altered so that they could swing from side to side and the pilot could then perhaps *balance* the turns. Carefully, he suggested this proposal to Wilbur at breakfast the following day. Wilbur drew on his pipe, just long enough to recognise his brother's proposal for the enormous breakthrough that it was, and then all but instantly matched it with a breakthrough of his own.[21] Yes, he replied, and why not build it so that when the pilot, already lying prone on the lower wing with his hips in a cradle attached to the wing-warping wires, could *simultaneously* turn the movable rudders?[22] Orville liked it and deleted the second rudder for good measure and simplicity. Two breakthroughs, and they were not even on to their second cup of coffee for the day!

Now, the *Flyer*'s propulsion was provided by two enormous counter-rotating propellers on shafts just behind the wings and

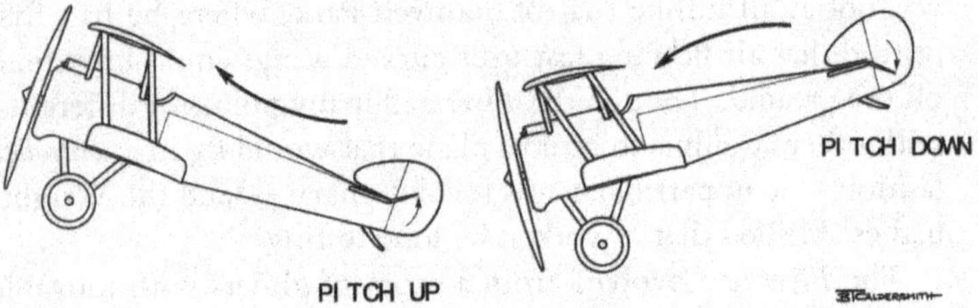
PITCH UP
PITCH DOWN
BT CALDERSMITH

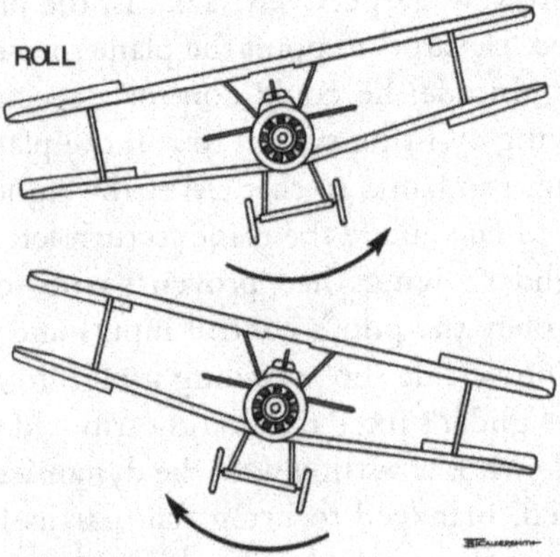
ROLL

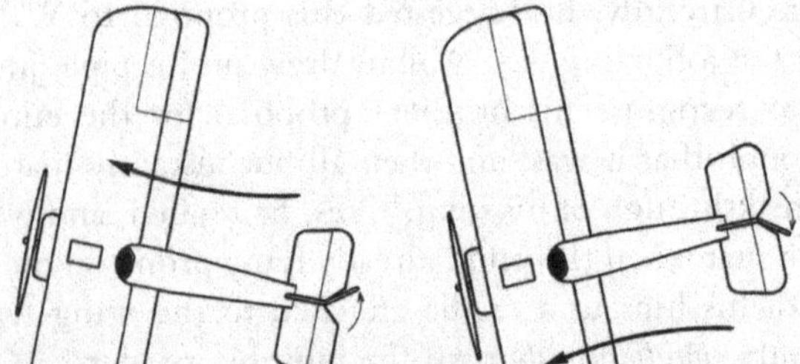
AILERON INDUCES ROLL
RUDDER BALANCES TURN-YAW

turned by chains, one of which was contained in a metal tube. These were powered by a 12-horsepower engine the brothers designed and had built in their bicycle shop by their mechanic, Charlie Taylor, in six weeks, after it had emerged that existing manufacturers were too busy to produce a small gasoline engine with the power-to-weight ratio Orville and Wilbur required to generate sufficient thrust for man-carrying flight. The whole machine weighed 605 pounds without the pilot.

But would it all work? Would it even be able to get off the ground?

To reach sufficient speed to take off, the *Flyer* was placed on a single rail of two-by-four laid in the sand, nicknamed 'Junction Railroad' by the pair. Once the craft was launched along that rail, the speed of the air flowing over those curved wings, aided by the thrust of the propellers, would lift man and machine off the ground and they would proceed in a forward direction — in the air! And the pilot would be able to control the machine once it was flying, reacting to changing air conditions by changing the shape of the plane as required, and so stay aloft! That, at least, was the theory.

Upon an earlier coin toss, it was Orville who had the honour of being the first to attempt to fly that day, lying prone on the lower wing as the prevailing headwind continued to come straight at them in freezing gusts of about 25 miles per hour.

The engine was started and the propellers whirled. Orville released the catch of a restraining rope and the *Flyer* tore down the 60-foot track, with Wilbur running alongside holding onto the right wing for as long as he could to keep the whole thing steady. Faster and faster it went until ... until ... until ... then came the moment. As Wilbur dropped back, he was stunned to see the *Flyer*, with his brother Orville on board, lift off the ground some 10 feet into the air, sail forth in a slightly awkward bound, and return to earth at a point level with the commencement of the flight in a *controlled* fashion, some twelve seconds and 120 feet later.

Success!

Then it was Wilbur's turn and, taking a couple of tips from his brother about what he had learnt, he managed to go a little further still, up to 175 feet. Just as they once had to learn to ride a bicycle, they were now trying to learn how to fly this plane they had built together.

Next, Orville Wright, now the world's second most experienced pilot, nudged the distance up to 200 feet and was once again the world's most experienced. Oddly enough, neither brother at this point was overwhelmed with exultation — they just weren't the type. And nor was either overwhelmed with trepidation at watching a beloved brother put himself in harm's way in this fashion. Fact was, they had been working long enough on this flying machine, and hard enough — and most crucially, glimpsed enough signs indicating they were on the right track — that they expected nothing less than success. So when it came, it was good, but not absolutely stunning. Such, it seems, are many iconic historical moments, at the time. The brothers kept going.

Just before noon Wilbur took off, as before, but this time … this time, instead of coming almost immediately back to earth, the plane majestically kept going … and going. Two hundred feet! Three hundred! *Five* hundred! *SEVEN* hundred! At about 850 feet, the machine suddenly darted down — in fact so suddenly that on impact a part of the plane's elevator supports were broken, and then a sudden gust of untimely wind flipped the whole thing over several times, breaking it so badly that it would never fly again.

In one morning, aviation had recorded its first powered flight, broken four records and had its first crash …

•

In Australia, the news of the extraordinary feat didn't so much hit like thunder as like the sound of a walnut dropping onto parched earth some distance away. That is, while the American newspapers did, after a fashion, fête the brothers — still with one eyebrow raised because no journalist or photographer had witnessed their triumph, and the brothers didn't release their own photos — the news did not immediately reach Australian shores. The first flicker of what happened at Kitty Hawk came via a letter from Octave Chanute to Lawrence Hargrave, who by this time had moved back to Sydney from Stanwell Park, and was living in the salubrious eastern suburb of Woollahra.

'It is possible,' Chanute wrote to his trusted and admired Australian colleague, 'that your newspapers have reproduced the sensational report that the Wright brothers have flown three miles in a dynamic machine. This is erroneous — the real facts are set forth in the enclosed statement issued three days ago.'

Despite the fact that he was suffering from typhoid fever, Lawrence Hargrave devoured the report in nothing flat and, excited beyond measure, soon took up a pen himself. First he wrote a letter of sincere congratulations to the Wright brothers: 'I have just read of your flight on the 17th December 1903. My heartiest congratulations. May the caution you have hitherto exercised not be relaxed for an instant. I hope Mr Chanute was with you and took plenty of snapshots ...'[23]

And then Lawrence Hargrave penned a letter to the editor of Sydney's *Daily Telegraph*:

> Sir,
> In the *Chicago Daily News* Jan 6th, you will find an account of the successful experiments of Mssrs Orville and Wilbur Wright with a power-driven man-carrying aeroplane. These are the first practical results that have ever been attained by the numerous workers in this branch of aeronautics. Lest you think it only a yarn the facts are vouched by Mr O. Chanute the Past President of the Western Society of Engineers who writes to warn me of the sensational reports that had previously been published. Should you not have the *Chicago Daily News* on your files your reporter is at liberty to copy that in my possession.[24]

The *Daily Telegraph* editor dispatched a reporter immediately and published a story the following day. In Australia, as elsewhere, the news was getting out. A new age really was upon the world, and it seemed that with these extraordinary machines, all things were possible.

•

They were crossing the mighty Pacific Ocean! From horizon to horizon, there was nothing but sparkling water as far as the eye could see, in every direction a vast panorama …

While, in that first part of the twentieth century, for most Australians the Pacific was an almost unbreachable blue barrier separating them from everywhere else in the world, that was not the case for six-year-old Chilla and his siblings and parents. For at much the same time as those hardy inventors from Ohio, the Wright brothers, were demonstrating that the Wright stuff was just what the aviation world was looking for, the sprawling Australian family had upped sticks once again, marched up the gangplank of a ship called RMMS *Aorangi*, and sailed off to settle in Vancouver, on the west coast of Canada.

Sadly, this was less a case of the family seeking adventure than one of simple need, as Vancouver was the place where father William had at last found work. It was a long and horrifying story, but in essence the family patriarch had gone guarantor on a loan to a trusted friend who, after being unable to pay, had shot himself as a result. William had lost his job, his self-respect and a lot of money in one fell swoop. The family had just been able to stay afloat, with the financial help of Catherine's businessman father. To raise the fare for Canada and give them start-up money, they had been obliged to sell all the family furniture, including the piano.

Not that young Chilla was aware of any of that, of course. In fact, for a young lad of his adventurous disposition — already excited beyond measure at the thought that he would soon be throwing real snowballs in Canada[25] — shipboard life was heaven on water, though hell for the family trying to keep track of him. Under the captain's table, in the engine room, hiding in the lifeboat, running around the funnel, climbing onto the backs of laughing sailors, hanging out the porthole …

Hanging out the porthole? This time he had gone too far and after a few whispered words between Catherine and the ship's captain it was all organised. In no time Chilla and the young friend he had been doing it with were hauled before Captain Phillips, who gravely informed them that if there was one more instance — just *one more*, do you hear me? — then the two terrors would have to be placed in chains for the duration of the voyage, if not keelhauled first. Was that *absolutely clear*?!?!

Yes, Cap'n. Sorry, Cap'n. Terribly sorry, Cap'n. It will not happen again, Cap'n.

Not to worry, there was soon plenty of excess excitement aboard the *Aorangi* anyway, as the ship crossed the equator. There had long been a tradition among English-speaking seafarers that all who crossed the equator for the first time should be initiated into the Solemn Mysteries of the Ancient Order of the Deep and such. Those who were yet to 'cross the line' were derisively referred to as 'pollywogs', whereas, once they had crossed and thereby entered into the domain of His Royal Majesty *Neptunus Rex*, otherwise known as King Neptune, they could henceforth be known as 'trusty shellbacks' ...

At the age of just six, thus, Chilla had crossed the line, and — after going through a fun ceremony consisting of having mud and whitewash smeared over his face, and being dumped backwards into a tank of water[26] — was now a trusty shellback.

•

Although William's new job as a humble clerk with the Canadian Pacific Railway company wasn't a particularly well paying one, it was certainly better than being unemployed in Australia, and the family settled down to make the best of it. For at least they had each other and at least Vancouver provided a whole range of fresh outdoor pursuits for them to engage in. On the weekends they would go camping in the great Canadian outdoors, skiing in winter, sailing in summer, salmon fishing any time. The best part of the fishing, apart from the marvellous moment when you first felt the tug on the line, was that it did a lot to put free food on the table, which was a great bonus given William's humble wage. And somehow, too, Catherine always managed to make that wage go a long way. Generally, William was in his wife's considerable thrall, acutely aware that he had not turned into the great provider she had thought he would be when they married, and yet also deeply appreciative that she did not rub his nose in it for that fact. A sensitive, retiring type, he was a good father, and that was something ...

By this time the 'Smith' family had become known as the 'Kingsford Smith' family, by virtue of the fact that they were living on a street in Vancouver where two other families named Smith lived, and it was just easier that way. For many families, living in a foreign land would have been daunting, removed as they were from all things familiar including wider family and friends, but not for the Kingsford Smiths. They were entirely self-contained, enjoying their own company enormously and always looking out for each other. Of the children, Harold was perhaps the most serious, feeling the responsibility of being the oldest brother, while Winifred was a deputy mother to Catherine in her relations with the younger ones. Wilfrid, Elsie, Leofric and Eric all had the charming combination of being hard-working but fun-loving types, while the most carefree of the lot was young Chilla — sure as he always was that he only had to stumble and there would be a dozen hands instantly reaching down to lift him up again.

•

The Wright brothers kept working, as indeed did other aviation inventors around the world. On 20 September 1904, just a little less than a year since their first flight, *Flyer II* hit the launch rails at the nearby prairie cow paddock owned by Dayton banker Torrence Huffman and lent to them *gratis.*

Made of fragile white pine, instead of spruce, their new flying machine was equipped with a stunningly powerful 16-horsepower engine and a more efficient wing shape. In the absence of reliable winds of the required strength, the Wrights had developed a catapult launch system consisting of a tower from which a cable was attached to 1600-pound iron weights. With the motor running and poised to launch, the pilot released the weights, which had been winched to the top of the frame and attached to the plane by a cable.[27]

It worked, first time.

Older brother Wilbur managed to take off and pilot *Flyer II* in a complete circle of a distance of just over 4000 feet and remain aloft for a full minute and a half! A couple of months later, the distance covered had grown to 3 miles and they were able to stay aloft for over five minutes. With each flight the brothers were growing in understanding what modifications their machine needed to get better control in the air, and also *feeling* that air better, how it was filled with eddies, pockets and currents, which were not necessarily apparent to an observer on the ground. And, of course, other intrepid aviators from all parts of the developed world kept doing their utmost to get aloft and replicate what the Wright brothers had done. Nowhere were they trying harder than in France, where, with its long tradition of trying to thwart the laws of gravity in balloons and gliders, the nation was positively beside itself with enthusiasm for flying ...

•

For the French, the great breakthrough came on 12 November 1906, when a Brazilian-born man by the name of Alberto Santos-Dumont took off from the Parisian park Champs de Bagatelle, within the Bois de Boulogne, in a machine built in secret by the *frères* Voisin — two brothers who operated what was later acknowledged as the first commercial aircraft factory in Europe. The plane, christened *14-bis Oiseau de Proie* (bird of prey), but colloquially dubbed *Canard*, was an enormous version of Lawrence Hargrave's box kite, based directly on his still unpatented designs, with an engine and propeller attached. In this strange contraption the foundation member of 'the beautiful people' — with his always fashionable dress, bowler hat and impeccable suit set off by his gaily billowing red scarf and perpetually preened moustache — succeeded in tearing across the ground like an 'infuriated grasshopper',[28] and then taking off to fly *un magnifique* 239 yards in less than twenty-two seconds! *Victory!* The first real flight in Europe!

Santos-Dumont, alternately laughing and crying with joy, was carried around the field on the shoulders of his many admirers. Paris was agog, and its immense excitement was manifested by the wall-to-wall coverage in the French newspapers the following day. To this point the 33-year-old Santos-Dumont had been famous in Europe as a rather foppish pioneer of the lighter-than-air dirigibles, and he had been a

Model of Santos-Dumont's *14-bis*.

frequent and famous sight above the streets of Paris in a basket beneath his elongated balloon, elegantly floating along. He was a trendsetter, as witness the fact that once, over dinner at Maxim's — celebrating his victory in a balloon race around the Eiffel Tower — he had complained to his jeweller friend Louis Cartier how difficult it was to check flight times on his pocket watch while flying, so Cartier had invented something called a 'wristwatch' for his friend. And now *everyone* was wearing them!

But nothing Santos-Dumont had ever done had attracted attention like this. Clearly, he had abandoned balloons and was now going for heavier-than-air planes. And whereas the Wright brothers had needed a rail and derrick and weights to launch their plane — and it only worked when the wind was blowing in the right direction — the thing about Santos-Dumont's aeroplane was that it had needed none of that. He had wheels to launch himself along the ground, and an engine to provide propulsion, and he had flown. *Le tout Paris* had seen it!

One observer who was present at the flight and keenly interested in the press reports the following day was Britain's Lord Northcliffe, the proprietor of the *Daily Mail*. Immediately upon reading his own newspaper's coverage of the event the outraged Lord Northcliffe — who had begun his serious journalistic career by becoming editor of *Bicycling News* — got his editor on the phone and put his views in the strongest terms.

'The news,' he said deliberately, 'is not that Santos-Dumont flies 722 feet, but that England is no longer an island. There will be no more sleeping safely behind the wooden walls of old England with the Channel our safety moat. It means the aerial chariots of a foe descending on British soil if war comes.'[29]

The implications of flying were huge, they were going to change the world *and* sell a lot of newspapers. The *Daily Mail*, Lord Northcliffe told his editor, had to be at the forefront of this coverage and he further instructed that the man he had recently appointed as the world's first specialised aviation correspondent, Harry Harper, be immediately dispatched to Paris to interview Santos-Dumont. From that point on, the indefatigable Harper, with his owl glasses, quizzical but distracted manner, and mania for taking notes in his notably large copperplate script, became a perpetual presence at airfields around Europe. If it 'appened, 'Arry was there. Or at least heard about it.

One such aeronautical event that Harry Harper covered early in his new job was a flight by a British Army soldier, Sapper Moreton, who, attached to an extraordinary collection of Hargrave box kites, was borne aloft to an altitude of 2600 feet above Sussex, and stayed there for over an hour! With just such a system, the British Army intended to be able to easily discern enemy movements well before they reached the men on the ground.[30] A veritable revolution was under way.

•

'The kindness of parents to their children,' Lawrence Hargrave wrote to a friend, at a time when he was not only crook but going through familial turmoil, 'is like presents to savages. Both are incapable of appreciating a gift. Whatever love you feel for your offspring, be careful of not showing it, be stern, and give as you would a bone to a dog.'[31]

It was, of course, a severe statement from an occasionally severe man, and yet the truth of it was that the older Lawrence Hargrave became, the more difficult he found it not to show his love for his children. He and his long-suffering wife, Margaret — who had no interest in his wretched experiments, and only wished they wouldn't so dominate their lives — had had seven children, of whom five had survived, and Hargrave was always very conscious of his duty to his offspring. As to which ones he was closest to there was little doubt. His first-born daughter, Nellie, and his only son, Geoffrey, were the sole members of the family who really took an interest in his endless experiments. And after Nellie and one of his other daughters, Margaret, moved to England to study art and subsequently marry, the relationship between father and son became closer than ever. This led to the quietly spoken Geoffrey even becoming his father's scientific collaborator after the young man began attending Sydney Technical High School. One of Geoffrey's great passions would become the modifying and refining of his father's original rotary engine design — whose first version had run on compressed air — by building a petrol-fuelled rotary engine. 'If he develops a little ambition,' the proud father had written to a friend, 'I think he will outstrip the ruck ...'[32]

Of course Geoffrey was not the only person to become interested in his father's engines. Lawrence Hargrave was soon approached by some German professors visiting Australia, with the offer to display his kites and engines in Munich's Deutsches Museum, where his work could be readily accessed by all interested workers in the field. Given that none of the Commonwealth government, New South Wales government, Melbourne Museum, Smithsonian Institution, or any of the British museums had previously shown any interest in displaying them, Hargrave agreed, and it was not long before European engineers were all over them, paying particular attention to his revolutionary — in both meanings of the word — rotary engine.[33] And well before that, almost as soon as he had invented it, Hargrave had provided notes on the concept to *Railroad and Engineering* journal, an English publication, and it was this that had first attracted Chanute's attention to him. Thus, while the Wright brothers continued to zealously guard their every breakthrough and take exhaustive legal action against everyone who they felt tried to copy them, Hargrave's approach, from the beginning, could not have been more different.

•

It was a current that was surely going to kill him. On the hot afternoon of 2 January 1907, the ten-year-old Chilla — on a brief holiday back home in Australia with his mother, paid for by Catherine's father — was swimming out beyond the breakers with his cousin Rupert Swallow at Bondi Beach when the two boys were suddenly gripped by a strong rip that carried them further out to sea.[34]

Chilla was almost immediately in trouble, as was Rupert. Try as they might to swim towards the shore, the land quickly receded and they were soon exhausted, their arms feeling like lead. Both began to flounder, and Chilla to swallow water, as a haze of blackness began to envelop him.

So easy ... now ... to stop ... thrashing ... to let go ... to sink down ... just a little ... letting go ...

Suddenly a strong hand descended into the water and gripped him, probably at the last possible instant. The hand belonged to a man by the name of Warwick Wilce, of Croydon, and he was in turn attached to what was known as a lifeline, a long rope stored in a box on the beach which allowed the lifesaver to stay connected to the shore.[35] Back on the beach, the surf lifesavers of the about-to-be-formed Bondi Surf Life Saving Club began to haul on the line, and both Chilla and his rescuer, Wilce, were quickly brought back to the shore, just as Rupert Swallow was, by other lifesavers. Rupert quickly recovered from the ordeal, but not Chilla. Once back on the sand in the middle of the crowd that had gathered, he not only looked dead, but probably was.

To most of the bystanders it was obvious that his rescuers had got there too late and he was *gone*. And yet even as some people, mostly women, began to wail at the tragedy of his loss — and young Rupert, wrapped in a towel, gazed dully at his seemingly lifeless cousin, trying to comprehend the magnitude of what had just happened — a short, angular woman with a no-nonsense attitude about her strode forward and took charge. Her name, with title, was Nurse Sweeney. (Her Christian name was Sadie, but no-one ever called her anything other than Nurse Sweeney. She really looked as though she had just been *born* a 'Nurse', and there had never been any need to call her anything different.) She was from Quirindi, a bit over 200 miles north of Sydney, and was visiting Bondi to get some sun and fresh air, as she had herself been poorly from an undiagnosed illness. Luckily Nurse Sweeney had been trained in the modern method of resuscitation — the Sylvester Method.

Turning the young lad over on to his back, she kneeled at his head, pulled his tongue forward to clear a passage to his throat, and then grabbed both his arms at the wrists and pulled them out and upwards until they were above his head, pulling his ribs up and sucking air into his lungs. She then pushed his arms back down and applied a gentle pressure on his ribs to force the air back out again — and repeated the process between fifteen and twenty times a minute.[36] A persistent woman, Nurse Sweeney. Even when a quarter of an hour had passed and there was still no response from the lad, she didn't give up. She had made a career of beating death back from the door and if, in this case, death was in fact already through the door and halfway down the hallway before she caught up with it, well, it was just going to have to be dragged out again. For some onlookers in the crowd it was so obvious that she was wasting her time that they began to drift away, some of them even returning to the surf. And then suddenly, after nigh on half an hour, the kid coughed. He coughed!

It was true.

Somewhere from the darkest depths where death lurked, Chilla, or the thing inside him that still stood for life, was slowly, slowly, agonisingly making its way to the surface, and when he finally did burst through, coughing furiously and expelling the last gulp of water from his lungs, it sounded almost like a spluttering motor …

Though shocked and trembling when he at last came to, there was nothing physically wrong with him that a shaky night in bed, with his calm and caring mother watching over him by candlelight until dawn, couldn't fix. Emotionally, it might have been another question …

Sadly, in the case of Nurse Sweeney, death would have its ultimate revenge when — though still fighting it to her last breath — just a few weeks later she succumbed to her illness and passed away.[37]

•

And finally it had come to this.

After endless experimentation and modification mixed with many test flights — nearly all of it well away from the public eye and journalists — the Wright brothers' latest version of *Flyer I* and *II*, *Flyer III*, had magically grown and changed shape from its previous incarnations. The propellers were still driven by a single 16-horsepower engine, but the elevator and rudder were twice the size of the earlier models and extended back twice as far from the wings, which now had a slight upward tilt from the fuselage. Flights of up to 24 miles in figures of eight and of thirty-nine and a half minutes' duration had been accomplished.

The new version of *Flyer III*, in which they had hoped to interest the US Army Signal Corps, was powered by an improved engine producing between 30 and 40 horsepower, and the pilot sat upright for the first time, exerting control by virtue of twin 'joysticks' variously connected to the wing-warping cables, elevator and rudder.

Despite a shocking setback when the plane had crashed during a demonstration for the US Army, breaking Orville's left thigh and several ribs and killing his passenger, Lieutenant Thomas Selfridge (a member of the official army board, who now had the disastrous distinction of being the first fatality from a powered flight), the brothers still felt that they were at last ready to demonstrate their flying machine to an international audience. Specifically, they wanted to show it in France, which — absurdly, in the Wrights' view — considered itself the centre of world aviation. Ideally, the brothers wished to make it clear that anyone buying a plane in Europe should buy a Wright plane from either them or one of their European agents, otherwise they would not be getting the *best*.

So it was that at Hunaudières racetrack, about 7 miles from Le Mans and 132 miles south-west of Paris, on the Saturday afternoon of 8 August 1908, Wilbur Wright continued to fuss about the machine that he had personally and oh so methodically assembled over the previous two months, as the impatient, sceptical crowd waited. No matter that these spectators from the French aviation community were there at Wilbur's specific invitation, he was oblivious of the expectations of others, and kept to his own schedule — just as he had done since arriving in France — leaving nothing to chance, and doing everything personally to ensure that every last tiny detail was looked after, under his own hand and done absolutely perfectly to *his* satisfaction.

'LE BLUFF CONTINUE', a Parisian newspaper had trumpeted in a headline the day before, as Gallic impatience had boiled over into irritation and frustration at the continued delays to the flight. Yes, they had read all the stories about these Wright brothers and knew that flight in some form was possible — as witness the wondrous leap of Santos-Dumont — but could this strange, gaunt little man in his dusty, dark grey suit with a starched white wing collar, all 'neath a ludicrous green cap really do what he claimed and fly this awkward-looking thing wherever he wanted? He seemed so odd, so disdainful of all around him, so charmless, so *unfashionable* — especially when compared with their own incomparable Santos-Dumont — it was inconceivable that one so ordinary could accomplish something so miraculous. He really must be a *bluffeur* ...

'Even if this man sometimes deigns to smile,' the French aviator Léon Delagrange, there for the occasion, would write of first meeting with him, 'one can say with certainty that he has never known the sweetness of tears. Has he a heart? Has he loved? Has he suffered? An enigma, a mystery.'[38] The French were accustomed to visitors to their shores raving about the wonders of their country, the wine, the food, the women, the Eiffel Tower, but this strange one barely said a word.

On this afternoon, Wilbur Wright continued his preparations regardless, entirely untroubled. His every move was calculated and even, yes, rather bird-like, in the kind of twitchy way he did things — tightening nuts, checking struts, using a screwdriver on the carburettor — but that was the only thing that remotely resembled flying.

Suddenly, however, Wilbur straightened, smiled, yes, *smiled*, and spoke. 'Gentlemen,' he said, to no-one in particular among those standing around, 'I am about to fly.'[39] With which, and with absolutely no fanfare for the common man, he climbed aboard the aeroplane, gave the signal for the engine to be started up, and moved into position as the twin propellers whirled.

As the crowd pressed forward and positively crackled with excitement, Wilbur pulled the release mechanism, causing six large discs of iron to plummet from the derrick, and the plane accelerated along its rail until, four seconds later, the strange American was airborne! What followed was nothing less than extraordinary. While some in the crowd had previously witnessed flying of some sort — and two of them in Léon Delagrange and Louis Blériot who had themselves flown, a little — the vast majority of the flights witnessed or executed had been of a few seconds in duration, or perhaps a minute, and all of them in a roughly straight line.

Now, though, before their very eyes, Wilbur Wright took the plane twice around the field in an almost perfect circle — several consecutive arcs of triumph — before executing a perfect figure eight. Around the racecourse, many local children — boys and girls both — who had climbed trees in lieu of an invitation, cheered Wilbur to the echo and waved their caps at him as he passed overhead. He then brought the plane in for a precisely executed landing, 107 seconds after take-off.[40]

Uproar. Complete pandemonium. Cheering, whistling, crying. All those who had been critical and sceptical had now been definitively proved wrong. The Wrights really *could* fly, and superbly at that. With such control! Such *finesse*! Bravo! Bravo! Bravo!

Even Wilbur himself seemed moved by the crowd's reaction and gave a small cheery wave upon alighting from the plane. He was particularly pleased at the stunned reaction of some of the French flyers, who had come to see him perform.

'*Cet homme a conquis l'air*,' voices in the crowd exclaimed. '*Il n'est pas bluffeur*!'

'*Nous sommes battus*,' cried Delagrange, while furiously pumping Wilbur's hand. '*Eh, bien. Nous n'existons pas*!'

For his part, Blériot — a tall man with sad, hound-dog eyes and a perpetually sleepy moustache — was equally congratulatory.

'For us in France and everywhere,' he told a reporter, 'a new era in mechanical flight has begun. I am not sufficiently calm after the event thoroughly to express my opinion. My view can best be expressed in these words — *c'est merveilleux*!'[41]

Quietly pleased at the reaction of the French aviators — for his personal view on their own attempts at flight was that they were only capable of 'hopping from the ground, or fluttering along like a hen chased by a dog!'[42] — Wilbur told them he could have stayed up there for an hour if he had liked. And yet Wilbur was less circumspect in his letter that night to Orville, who was holding the fort back in Dayton: 'Blériot and Delagrange were so excited they could scarcely speak, and Kapperer could only gasp and could not talk at all. You should have seen them.'[43]

The following morning, the Parisian newspaper *Le Figaro* set the tone: 'It was not merely a success but a triumph; a conclusive trial and a decisive victory for aviation, the news of which will revolutionize scientific circles throughout the world.' And so it did. Over the next few days, Wilbur continued to fly at the racetrack, making progressively longer flights before ever larger crowds, as more and more people made their way there to witness *le miracle*.

Afterwards there were many banquets in Wilbur's honour and great celebrations. At all of them he was asked to speak, but he declined, noting on one famous occasion: 'The only birds who speak are parrots and they can't fly very high.'[44] (*Quel bon mot!*)

No matter. The feats of the Wright brothers spoke for themselves, and now that they had demonstrated their plane's capability in Europe, they had unleashed an entire new wave of energy towards aviation in general.

•

In Canada, young Chilla Kingsford Smith continued to prosper, at least mostly. At the Queens School in Vancouver, which he was attending, a particularly perceptive teacher noted of young Charles's conduct that while he was 'Good', he was also 'Silly at times'.[45] A young man of strong abilities in many areas, the general view of his teachers was that he was a good egg with the only real worry being that he lacked the maturity to focus and grind down if a subject didn't interest him. At least he was adjudged 'Excellent' at writing, 'Very good' at arithmetic and drawing, and 'Good' at geography — a subject he was no doubt helped in by the fact that he had already seen a fair chunk of the world that his fellow students only knew of from books.

•

In London, on 5 October 1908, Lord Northcliffe announced that the *Daily Mail* was offering a prize of £500 for the first successful flight across the Channel, a distance of 22 miles at its narrowest point. The *Mail*'s nearest equivalent publication in France, *Le Matin*, sniffed that this was nothing but a cheap publicity stunt, as there was no chance that the paper would have to pay up for many years. For its part, the widely read satirical publication *Punch* offered its own handsome prize for the first man to swim across the Atlantic, and an even bigger prize for someone who could fly to Mars and back in a week.[46]

Untroubled, Northcliffe was so satisfied with the publicity the offer generated that he doubled the prize to £1000.

He had two motivations. Firstly, it was obvious that the level of public interest in flying was enormous, and by offering such a prize, and corralling much of the subsequent story to his own paper, he would easily make that money back. But secondly, he had been appalled to see that his own British government had not realised that planes were going to change the world — most particularly when it came to the colossal effect they would have on a war — and he was determined to do what he could to awaken some interest. After all, Lieutenant B.F.S. Baden-Powell, the President of the Aeronautical Society of Great Britain, was in no doubt about the significance of mechanical flight, after observing some of Wilbur Wright's first flights in Europe, and even going aloft *with* him on one occasion. He had been quoted: 'That Wilbur Wright is in possession of a power which controls the fate of nations is beyond dispute.'[47]

Exactly! And yet to this point, the British government had done nothing to get possession of that power. Lord Northcliffe's view was that once a plane flew across the Channel, the government would realise that Britain's much vaunted navy was now superseded as a military force, and would begin to pour resources into ensuring the nation was at the forefront of this new, overpowering weapon of war.

•

William Kingsford Smith had tried. He had really tried.

After the disaster of the defaulted bank loan, which had destroyed his banking career, he had been glad to make a fresh start in Canada, and now, after a couple of years working as a humble clerk, he had decided to try his hand at business once again. With his brother-in-law Arthur Kingsford and his oldest son, Harold — who had now married a Canadian girl, Elsie, with whom he had two children in quick succession — he had decided to begin a real estate business. Vancouver was growing, money was flowing in, and it stood to reason that there would be many opportunities to make money if they did it right. But somehow it just didn't work. Maybe it was because for something so personal as the buying or selling of a home, Canadians preferred dealing with their own, or maybe it was because they were entering into a business of which they had absolutely no first-hand knowledge ... but one way or another the venture failed. In the end, after nearly six years in Canada there was nothing to do but sell up and head home. While the Canadian experience had been physically invigorating, it had been financially debilitating. And at least Australia was warm. In ones and twos, then, the Kingsford Smiths began to head back across the Pacific throughout the last half of 1908, until William, Catherine and young Chilla were the last to leave in January 1909.

William found work sorting mail at the Neutral Bay post office, on Sydney's lower North Shore, and the Kingsford Smiths now based themselves in a modest rented home in that suburb, at 68 Yeo Street.

•

Scribbling again.

Ever since her husband Louis Blériot had seen Monsieur Wilbur Wright fly, his wife Alicia had been driven *mad* by his constant distraction, up to and including his endless scribbling of plans and drawings on the tablecloth while she was trying to feed him and their five children dinner![48] The children would finish dinner and ask to be excused, and her Louis would still be sitting there, jotting down notes, working out sums, and frequently he would have entirely forgotten to eat! More often than not, Alicia — mightily annoyed, much as she loved him — cleaned up and left him to it. He talked about nothing else, thought about nothing else, did nothing else but continue to build his plane in his workshop with the help of another designer, by the name of Raymond Saulnier, incorporating all the best features of the Wright *Flyer* he had seen at Hunaudières racetrack.

For this plane owed no little inspiration to what Louis had closely observed on that wonderful day he'd seen Wilbur Wright take to the air, including wing warping, which the Frenchman recognised would give him greater control. Louis' great departure, however, was to embrace the concept of a *monoplane*, a plane with just one set of wings, which he was convinced would give him greater speed and less drag. In fact, it was something he had been working on even before he'd seen Wilbur Wright fly, and had even built some monoplanes with mixed success — read disastrous and just passable — but *Flyer III* had given him the clue as to how to make it really work.

This plane, he decided, would be built of oak and poplar wood, with its cockpit and flying surfaces covered with canvas, save for the uncovered rear fuselage. It incorporated the Wright's wing-warping system, and also had a steel tube tower above the cockpit to provide a firm anchor for the flying wires needed to support the monoplane's 25-foot 4-inch wings. A matching frame underneath the cockpit gave a handy attachment for wires to resist the lifting forces. The main undercarriage consisted of two bicycle wheels which were free to swivel, with another bicycle wheel supporting the tail.

For propulsion, Louis decided, after experimentation, to give it a 25-horsepower Anzani 3W cylinder radial engine, with a 6-foot 10-inch twin-bladed wooden Chauvière Intégrale propeller, turning at 1200 revolutions per minute. And, just as he had done in his recent designs, he put that engine with the propeller right at the *front* of the plane, not too far from the wings, while he put the elevator and rudder well back at the end of the tail. Oh, and one more thing, *ma chèrie*. Developing a system he had tried in previous incarnations of this plane, he would link the control to the wing warping and elevator to one central *manette*, a joystick, while he would control the rudder of the plane by a bar at his feet. If he wanted to go up, he pulled the joystick back. If he wanted to go down, he would push the joystick forward. So elegant. So simple. If he pressed the right rudder while banking, it would turn right, and if the left rudder, it turned left. Louis, as he never tired of telling Alicia, was absolutely *sure* that this would be his best plane yet …

•

One man in Australia who had come to the same conclusion as Lord Northcliffe about the potentially huge military significance of aeroplanes was an engineering disciple of Lawrence Hargrave, an intense fellow by the name of George Augustine Taylor. He had variously worked as a builder, journalist and cartoonist; had been a leader in Sydney's literary set and bohemian movement; was a successful businessman and nationalist; and was now possessed by two passions — how important both aviation and wireless communications would be to the future of Australia.

Convinced that Australia would soon no longer be isolated, and therefore safe, from the rest of the world, Taylor was determined that the Australian government should be prepared. With that in mind, on the late afternoon of 28 April 1909, he met other leading figures — including Lawrence Hargrave — to discuss the formation of the Aerial League of Australia in Sydney.

This meeting was held at the salubrious Hotel Australia, on Castlereagh Street in downtown Sydney. While other men caroused downstairs discussing such banalities as cricket and football, matters of great moment were being discussed upstairs. Taylor himself began, opining that the conquest of the air changed entirely Australia's position in the world. Not for much longer, surely, could the nation depend on the all-powerful British naval fleet for its protection, when that fleet could so soon be flown over. There were also many commercial considerations, as the advent of the aircraft would likely change entirely the way nations interacted with each other commercially. Both ways, it was important that Australia be at the forefront of this aerial revolution, and the Aerial League of Australia would devote itself to that end. He then moved a motion to that effect!

Hear, *hear*! Hear, *hear*![49]

The motion was seconded by one Major Charles Rosenthal, who noted that while it had long been difficult for Australia's enemies to get battleships to such distant climes, the same could not long be said of flying enemy planes here, and it was urgent that Australia get prepared.

Hear, *hear*! Hear, *hear*![50]

By meeting's end it was done and the Aerial League was formed, immediately receiving much positive comment from the press and public alike. 'While the utility of the airship or aeroplane is little understood,' the Sydney *Daily Telegraph* noted the following day, 'its possibilities appeal strongly to the imagination. One scientist avers that a voyage to the moon would be possible, could we once "get a kick on the ether".'

It went on, 'The development of the aerial ship, in warfare, may yet mean much to Australia, and the new league begins a useful and patriotic work ...'[51]

Two

DISTANCE

What we early designers did we did under the stress of necessity, that ancient mother of invention. We were not university trained. Rule of thumb inventors taught in the school of experience, we used our necks as measuring sticks of success.

ANTHONY FOKKER[1]

There was a young man of Mark Lane
Who constructed an aeroplane,
It flew, so we heard,
Like a beautiful bird,
His tombstone is pretty but plain.

POPULAR LIMERICK AMONG THE ENGLISH PUBLIC IN THE EARLY 1900S[2]

[The first seafarers] had it easier. They could practice first in pools, then in ponds, then in streams, and not venture out to sea until much later. For this man there is only the sea.

FRANZ KAFKA DESCRIBING HIS FIRST VIEW OF LOUIS BLÉRIOT FLYING AT BRESCIA[3]

In Europe, things moved quickly in the aviation world from the moment that word of Lord Northcliffe's prize for crossing the Channel got out. There had already been several failed attempts before the 37-year-old Louis Blériot decided that he and his plane were ready. For years he had been fascinated by the concept of powered flight and had poured all his resources into building planes of his own design. The key feature of this latest wood and canvas monoplane, the *Blériot XI*, he called it rather grandly, was that it was the first one he had built that hadn't actually — *comment ça se dit?* — crashed. As a matter of fact, Blériot had crashed so often in so many different planes that he had developed a theory that his survival had all to do with 'the elasticity of the aeroplane'.

'What happens when an aeroplane strikes the ground,' he had written in 1907, with surely more authority than any pilot in the world, 'is this: first some wooden rod or strut breaks, and then another, until half the machine has been either crushed or beaten in. The breaking of these parts, one after the other, absorbs the shock of the impact with the ground. One feels … as though … the machine was telescoping upon itself.'[4] As to how one must comport oneself in a crash, he was equally clear: 'One must not try to save both the machine and oneself. I always throw myself upon one of the wings of my machine, when I have a mishap, and although this breaks the wing, it causes me to alight safely.'[5]

Blériot also had a very relaxed attitude to injuries sustained while flying, never allowing them to interfere with getting back into the air. At the present, for example, he was unable to walk without crutches because of a deep burn he had sustained to his left ankle when it had been pressed hard up against an exhaust manifold while he had been flying the previous week. Never mind. Maybe he really would get over *La Manche* and win the prize offered by Lord Northcliffe. True, that morning when he had been awoken at 2.30 am to be told the weather across the Channel was clearing and he could make an attempt at dawn when the wind would be calmest, he had received the news in his own cloud of blackness, all but certain that he was now on the edge of yet another heroic failure, and perhaps this time a catastrophic one. There would be no throwing himself on the wing this time, not if he hit the water. There would be no point. In that pre-dawn darkness, jostled awake to be told his hour was now, he had wished that the weather would turn bad again, so that he wouldn't have to go, but could stay there, snuggling into his wife Alicia.

But then he felt better! Stronger. Maybe, just maybe his *jour de gloire* had indeed arrived.

And now, as the dawn of Sunday morning 25 July 1909 broke over Les Baraques just west of Calais — not far from the abandoned late nineteenth century workings of the Channel Tunnel project — and he breathed in the fresh air, he even felt strangely confident, the more so after he made a quick test flight to ensure that all was in order. At his take-off for that trial flight the spectators had wildly applauded and cheered. The fuel tank was topped up again and all was in readiness, as the crowd of hundreds of villagers, awoken by the stunning noise overhead as Blériot did his test flight, pressed close, *pulsing* with excitement.[6]

Without further ado, Blériot's manager and great friend, Alfred Leblanc, started the 25-horsepower engine of his frail-looking mechanical dragonfly. The plane, still caked in mud from its last flight and looking very weather-beaten, instantly came to life and now the intrepid pilot, dressed in the ubiquitous blue overalls of the French workman, replete with oil stains, adjusted his goggles and did up his top button. Blériot had just one last question for Leblanc, and he shouted it over the sound of the engine, even as the *Daily Mail*'s aviation correspondent, Harry Harper, faithfully recorded it in his notebook.

'*Au fait, ou* est-ce *exactement, Douvres?*'[7] (By the way, where exactly *is* Dover?)

The insouciant Leblanc pointed rather vaguely over the misty waters in a more or less north-westerly direction, and with that Blériot gave the order: '*Laissez aller!*' (Let 'er rip!)

With this, the chocks were removed from in front of the plane's wheels, whereupon the machine lurched forwards across the rough paddock towards the cliffs, the air poured over and beneath the curved wings, providing that magic upward lift … and in no time at all he was *flying* towards England!

Behind Blériot on the cliffs of Calais, there was no wild applause or cheering as he took off, the tension was simply too strong.[8] At the instant of take-off, Alfred Leblanc and other support crew, together with reporters and the hundreds of spectators, at this early hour, rushed up the nearby sand dunes so they could watch the plane for as long as possible. And it was going well! The fact that it was 60 metres high already was incredible; as no-one had seen a plane at that altitude before.

'Gradually,' ran the account of one eyewitness, 'we lost sight of the tiny little black spot which carried our fervent hopes, and nothing remained except the luminous sheet of water and the radiant sun. We were truly overcome by the disappearance.'[9] Between them there was a mixture of excitement, wonder and fear. They had either just witnessed a man flying to his death … or an historic triumph.

Quickly they jumped onto bikes and into cars and headed to the Marconi wireless hut a couple of miles away, which had been installed by the *Daily Mail* and was in contact with another wireless station installed on the roof of the Lord Warden Hotel at Dover. It was from here that Harry Harper's reports to the *Daily Mail* had been transmitting all morning, and now, if there was news, this would be the place to hear it.

With just 17 gallons of petrol on board, it was imperative that Blériot cover the 22 miles to England in as direct a manner as possible. And, not to forget, every three minutes he had to furiously pump a hand-plunger atop an oilcan, to prevent the engine from seizing up. Strangely, because there was an endless expanse of water beneath him, with no rushing landmarks, Blériot had the sensation that he was travelling distinctly and unnervingly slowly, whereas on land it was *merveilleux* the rapidity with which everything passed beneath. And yet, travelling at just a little over 40 miles per hour, at an altitude of around 250 feet, the Frenchman quickly outstripped his naval escort, the destroyer *Escopette*, which, with his wife Alicia on board, had been sent out by the government for his possible salvation. Alicia saw her husband go overhead, flying just to the left of the smoke from the destroyer's funnel, and waved furiously, but couldn't help wondering if she would ever see him again. (She wished that sometime in his busy but not always glorious life to this point her husband had learnt how to swim. *Merde!*)

As it happened, Blériot was also soon wondering if he would ever see his wife again, as his remaining petrol reduced to *très peu*, and *Angleterre* refused to show. Only a few minutes after passing over the *Escopette*, he looked behind to check its position and found that both it and the French coast had disappeared! No shoreline behind … none in front … no boats in any direction.[10] He was totally, *totally* alone, if one did not count the ghosts of the Norman invasion of 1066 and all that, looking up in amazement as he passed over.

Adding to his worries was that the wind, which had been blessedly mild to this point, was now starting to buffet him and his tiny machine from side to side and up and down. Where, oh *where*, was England? It was all very well to just head roughly north-west and hope to hit it, but which way was north-west, anyway? He had neglected to bring a compass, and as a matter of fact, didn't even have a watch. He simply continued to point his nose in the direction that Alfred Leblanc had indicated, trying to keep his shadow on the water just forward and out to his left as it had been when he had set off, and felt he must still be on track. Well, at least he hoped so.

Just as he began to feel the rising bile of panic, Blériot was at last relieved to see a thin grey line in front of him that *had* to be England. But, *hélas*, where were the fabled white cliffs of Dover? Of them, no sign at all … What he did see *however* were three small ships, all pointing in the same direction — surely towards a port — and he decided to follow their aquatic arrow. As he passed over the ships, the sailors took off their hats and waved at him, cheering all the while, which was heartening. And if he had spoken a word of English he might even have swooped low and asked them which way was Dover. Still, he felt, he *must* be getting close.

Sure enough, just a few minutes later, which was to say thirty-seven minutes after he had left France, he saw not just the white cliffs, but beyond them Dover Castle, where he intended to land. Blériot flew in over Dover Harbour, where by pure happenstance the suddenly puny-looking toy warships of the Home Fleet were anchored, and headed to the castle.

Not far away, an English writer by the name of H.G. Wells gazed, stunned, as what had been just a tiny speck on the horizon turned into an extraordinary flying machine soaring over his head. The English Channel had been conquered! On that feat alone, the possibilities of the future were astounding and, in that instant, as he would often later recount, his writer's mind leapt forward to the days when the entire world was girdled by huge aerial fleets taking people hither and thither across the globe.[11]

For Blériot, Dover Castle now loomed large, and there, on a meadow just before it, was a friend waving a French flag! As it turned out, an enterprising French journalist, Charles Fontaine, had crossed the Channel by boat the previous day, having packed the French flag in the hope that he would be able to do precisely what he was doing as Blériot flew over.

Blériot swirled around to come in for something that was a lot less than a 'landing', and — some habits died hard, no matter how much improved his plane was — a lot closer to a 'falling'.

'*Merde, pas encore*,' he murmured to himself, just before impact, but the main thing was that once again he survived intact — enough for a weeping Fontaine to immediately wrap him in the flag, bury him in kisses and shower him with many a heartfelt '*Bravo! Bravo! Bravo!*'

Within minutes, police, press and the people of Dover — many of them still getting dressed — had started to crowd onto the little field, all eager to shake the hand of the amazing Frenchman. Can you believe it? He flew here from France!

Blériot's own English was restricted to 'good morning' and 'sank you, ver' much', but at least he was able to get that out to everyone who congratulated him.[12]

Back in Calais a short time later, the large crowd gathered outside the Marconi hut was ravenous for information. They could hear the endless beeps of Morse code coming from within, but what was happening!? Had he made it? Crashed? Disappeared? Been rescued? What? What? *What?!*

At long last an elderly Englishman emerged from within, a veteran journalist from the *Daily Mail* with an upper lip so stiff you could hammer a 4-inch nail with it, and spoke to the assembled people displaying much the same emotion as he might have in reading a grocery list, not his own. 'I am informed by the wireless station at Dover that an engineer of the Ecole Centrale de Paris, Monsieur Louis Blériot, born at Cambrai … piloting a flying machine of his invention … a monoplane, with an Anzani engine of 25 horsepower, equipped with a Chauvière propeller … who at 4.52 this morning left Les Baraques near Calais … has landed safely in a field at Dover Castle and …'[13]

And that was as far as he got. For the rest was drowned out in cheers, tears and wild yells of exultation. Blériot's team collapsed into each other's arms in tears of joy and relief. And above it all, English voices could be heard, rousing the crowd to three cheers for Blériot! Yes, he was French, but his feat belonged to the world, and now so did he. *Man* had now flown across the Channel, and Blériot was that man.

But wait! Back in Dover, amid all the festivities, one thing had to be attended to. Through the throng and pressing towards the airman, came a very solemn, officious immigration officer, intent on doing his duty. First he wished to interrogate Blériot, as the 'master' of a 'vessel' that had arrived at the port of Dover, and then he gave him his official clearance papers.

'I hereby certify that I have examined Louis Blériot, Master of a vessel called the Monoplane, lately arriving from Calais, and that it appears by the verbal answers of the said Master to the enquiries put to him, that there has not been on board during the voyage an infectious disease demanding detention of the vessel, and that she is free to proceed.'[14]

Blériot was free to go! And so was his plane.

Which was to the good, as although the Frenchman was very pleased with his survival and his *grand exploit*, he had decided that where he really wanted to be was back in France with Alicia, with whom he had just been tearfully reunited on the Dover dockside, once the French destroyer *Escopette* had berthed. With that in mind, the French couple went back across the Channel on the *Escopette* that very afternoon, Louis thinking that his feat would bring him perhaps a little renown. He had no idea …

As Alicia later noted in her own memoirs, '*C'était le commencement de la gloire*'.[15] Within a day, Blériot had been prevailed upon to return to England, by boat across the Channel this time, where he found that he was the front-page news across the land — no newspaper selling more copies than Lord Northcliffe's *Daily Mail*, which broke circulation records with its coverage, beginning with the enormous headline on the front page, 'BLERIOT FIRST MAN TO FLY THE CHANNEL'. An editorial inside, penned by Northcliffe himself, was emphatic that 'As the potentialities of the aeroplane have been proved, we must take energetic steps to develop a navy of the air'.[16] For its part, the *Daily Express* put its finger on the nub of the military significance of his feat with its own front-page headline: 'GREAT BRITAIN IS NO LONGER AN ISLAND'. German journalists had pursued a similar theme, with *Berliner Lokal-Anzeiger* beginning its own coverage almost with martial glee: '*England ist keine Insel mehr*' (England is no longer an island).[17] And right there on the *Figaro* front page: '*Depuis aujourd'hui on peut dire que l'Angleterre a cessé d'être une île*' (From today, one can say that England is no longer an island).[18] After all, what price a mighty navy of Britannia ruling the waves, if there was now an entirely different realm above it which Britannia did *not* rule?

As Blériot alighted at Victoria Station from the saloon carriage specially attached to the regular train for the exclusive use of him and Madame, he was stunned to see an enormous crowd waiting for him, and all these people applauding and calling out his name in that strange accent they had — 'Mind the foot!'[19] someone shouted as he limped along, a little dazed — even as Madame Blériot was presented with a massive bouquet of carnations![20] And thus it continued all through the streets of London. People cheered at his very sight, as they proceeded along Buckingham Palace Road and entered The Mall, before going through Trafalgar Square, the crowd swelling as the couple neared their destination.

At a massive luncheon banquet held at the Savoy Hotel, situated on the Strand, and hosted by Lord Northcliffe, Blériot — who two days earlier had been more anonymous than a lost dog in the Bois de Boulogne — found himself seated right beside Sir Ernest Shackleton, whose own fame had been built on two journeys towards the South Pole, covering a combined distance of 35,000 miles and lasting a total of three years. The climax of the lunch was when Lord Northcliffe presented the Frenchman with a gold trophy and a cheque for £1000 — or at least would have presented both things, had not Alicia stood up and reached forward at that precise moment to grab the money and crisply put it in her purse.[21]

In response, Monsieur Blériot made a simple, elegant speech in French, which was translated to the crowd. Holding a glass of wine in his right hand he said, 'I am deeply touched by your welcome, a welcome which is altogether out of proportion to the feat which I have accomplished. I hope that France and England, already united by water — by the Channel that was below me during my flight — may now be still closer united by air. I drink to England and to her King, and as you say in English, "your good health".'[22]

With which, Blériot raised his glass and then sat down, beaming at his wife, as she beamed back at him, and all around that massive ballroom — resplendent with French and British flags awash in the glorious light of so many candles refracting through all the crystal glassware — a spontaneous standing ovation took place as lords and ladies, cabinet ministers, industrialists, magnates and many of the good and great of the day expressed their deepest admiration.

One who watched from afar the stunning reaction to Blériot's feat was the famous magician Harry Houdini, who decided on the instant that he needed to incorporate flying into his own shows. And if France was where Blériot was from, well, then that was where he would go to get lessons …

And still, the reaction to the Frenchman's cross-Channel dash was just warming up! For as soon as both the thrust and the detail of the feat had spread across two lands, it really was *tout le monde* that was caught up in celebrating it. That, at least, was how it seemed to Blériot when, on his return from London the next day, he arrived at Gare du Nord station to find a stunning 100,000 wild Parisians waiting to cheer him to the echo. '*Vive Blériot!*' they cried. '*VIVE Blériot!*' There were so many people, and so much tumult, that the five goggle-eyed Blériot children who had been taken by their nanny to the station to meet their parents, simply couldn't get near them.

Songs had been penned to Blériot's greater glory, street peddlers were hawking his image, and the now great man was taken by open horse-drawn carriage up the Champs Elysées to another luncheon, where the Aéro-Club de France awarded him a gold medal.

Just two days later, Blériot was visiting the offices of the great French newspaper *Le Matin* — which had so overcome its scepticism of the previous year that it now had the successful aviator's plane suspended outside its window for all the world to see — when the editor asked him if he would step out onto the balcony to greet the crowd gathered there to acclaim him. Blériot obliged, only to be near deafened by the almost aggressive, *hungry* roar of the multitude that sprang forth upon his first sight. There were people as far as the eye could see, along the boulevard, straining out of windows, clambering over the top of each other, just to get a better look at him. Roaring, and roaring, and roaring. On and on and on …

'It's too much,' the bewildered Blériot murmured to the editor, his once sleepy moustache now wide awake and quivering. 'Never, ever, not even the other day in London did I feel anything like this. It's wonderful and it's frightening …'[23]

Just what was going on? It was a question worth contemplating as he waved at the crowd, glancing a little at his frail plane, its fin now covered with the signatures of the English people who had been in front of Dover Castle that morning and had decided to leave their own mark on history …

Other men, most notably the Wright brothers, had already covered much greater distances than his 24 miles (flying off course added another few miles to the Channel crossing), and had stayed in the heavens for much longer than his mere thirty-seven minutes. And yet even the famously taciturn Wilbur Wright himself, when woken in the middle of the night by a reporter to be told of the news, had professed himself impressed, and thanked the reporter for telling him! Wilbur couldn't resist, however, adding a rider: 'Mr Blériot is very daring in his work, too daring, really, for flying. His feat is the greater when the machine he used is considered.'

Do you think it would have been less remarkable if he had used a Wright aeroplane, the reporter asked.

'Well, of course,' replied Wilbur. 'We think we have the best aeroplane in the world.'[24]

Which was as may be, but the fact that Blériot had vaulted such a famed natural barrier between two countries in one magnificent hop had so totally captured the imagination of both populaces that it was felt nothing would ever be the same again, either for him, or the world.

And it never was.

Within a couple of months, a survey of French schoolboys found that the man they most admired, well ahead of someone called Napoleon Bonaparte, was Louis Blériot.[25] Suddenly Blériot was awash in the money he needed to make a lot of planes, and the fame he needed to sell them.

As to forthcoming changes to the world, some of these were picked early by journalists rhapsodising over the significance of Blériot's flight. Gaston Calmette in *Le Figaro* posed the question: 'What will become of men's laws, their customs, barriers, the vain efforts of their industrial protectionism, their commercial exchanges, their defences, their relation, their intercourse, on the day when man can, by the action of his will alone, pass in a few hours beyond all horizons across all the oceans and above all the rivers ...? Within the foreseeable future, the conditions of human life will be profoundly changed ...'[26]

Even in faraway Italy — although now, suddenly, a lot less faraway than it had been before — an ambitious journalist by the name of Benito Mussolini wrote in a regional paper that there was only one word that could possibly sum up this new century: '*Moviménto*'. 'Movement towards the icy solitudes of the poles and towards the virgin peaks of the mountains; movement towards the stars and towards the depths of the seas. Movement everywhere and acceleration in the rhythm of our lives ... The dream of Icarus, the dream of all the generations, has become a reality.'[27]

In Australia, a keen observer of the leap forward made by aviation was George A. Taylor, the Hononary Secretary of the Aerial League of Australia, who, just two days after Blériot's feat, wrote an appeal in the columns of the *Daily Telegraph* for greater effort to be made towards 'the aerial defence of Australia'. Among other things he noted, 'To England is credited the steam railway engine, to France belongs the honour of producing the automobile, to Australia belongs the credit of giving the world the key to the problem of flight, by inventing the aeroplane fifteen years ago, and leaving it for the rest of the world to develop.'[28]

As to Lawrence Hargrave, he made no public pronouncement, but was quietly thrilled at the progress that was being made in the field of aviation, and certainly felt a great deal of satisfaction. That satisfaction was lifted a few notches further when, at the Reims International Air Meet held in France, the star of the show was Henri Farman's eponymously named *Henri Farman III*, which won the distance competition by flying 111.8 miles in three hours, four minutes, and fifty-six seconds using a 50-horsepower air-cooled Gnome Omega rotary engine, which owed its inspiration to the design of the rotary engine Hargrave had released into the public domain many years before. A veritable revolution in aviation had begun — and again, it had Hargrave's name on it.

•

It was a pleasure to be back in Australia. It felt like home, and was home, even if young Chilla, whose language had not been fully formed when he went to Canada, had returned with an accent strong enough that the other kids would razz him a bit about it, not to mention his weird haircut, rather reminiscent of a Mohawk. No matter, it was just good to be home. On weekends and holidays the family would frequently go camping and sailing on the Hawkesbury River, with Chilla, particularly, delighting in how the wind, coming from any direction, could still propel them in almost any direction, just so long as you understood the way it worked ...[29]

•

All Europe was now plane crazy. Newspapers seemed to cover little else. Science had become obsessed with understanding the laws of flight, while industry and then commerce had devoted themselves to first building flying machines and then refining them. Influential people within the establishment were agitating for Britain to develop a 'navy of the air', and similar movements were afoot in continental Europe, particularly France and Germany.

There were, yet, small hold-outs against all this aviation craziness. In a grand mansion in the thriving Dutch city of Haarlem, near Amsterdam, a heavily moustachioed man by the name of Herman Fokker had no doubt that the whole flying fad would pass and things would return to normal. In the meantime, he would be *damned* if he stood by and watched his wastrel son Anthony continue with his obsessive compulsion to build flying machines. For days on end, over months, and then *years*, Anthony had been in the family attic, building models of aeroplanes, devouring everything he could read about the Wrights and Blériot and *totally* wasting his time. The young man, who *Mijnheer* Fokker was sure would come to nothing, seemed to think of nothing else, talk of nothing else, do nothing else. He had even convinced himself that he knew better than some of the aircraft designers how a plane should be built — saying that, for starters, he felt the lateral stability of the Wright brothers' plane could be vastly improved — and the precocious one had tried to demonstrate this fact to his father by virtue of his models! Well, Fokker the elder was having none of it. A practical man who had made his fortune carving out a coffee plantation in Java, he felt he had earned the right to enjoy his prosperous retirement, and wanted his son to head off into something useful in turn. He had hoped that young Anthony would grow out of his *idée fixe*, but if anything it had become worse all through his teen years until now when he was almost twenty. The boy was obsessed.

Within the British Empire, Fokker's nearest equivalent was perhaps a young marine engineer by the name of Alliot Verdon Roe, who had also become fascinated by the mechanics of flight and was endlessly throwing paper gliders from a window in the top storey of the family home.

He did this so often that he eventually commanded the attention of an inmate in the mental hospital next door, who gravely informed his doctor, 'I am afraid there's another one like us in that house.'

When the doctor carefully informed him that he was mistaken, for that was a private home, the inmate was not put off.

'No,' he said. 'I've been watching that house. A man opens a top window and throws out a lot of bits of paper. Then he runs down into the garden and picks them up. And he keeps on for hours at a time!'[30]

•

Bother Bess.

Ehrich Weiss, aka Harry Houdini, loved his young wife all right, but she never seemed to have the first clue about the kinds of pressures and strains that he was under. Or, if she did know, it didn't seem to concern her unduly. In Paris, for example, just before they had left on the long voyage to Australia — where he intended to be the first man to fly a plane — he had spent all day, every day, out at the Voisin factory, getting the plane that he had purchased properly packed and put in a box, together with all the requisite spare parts, while she spent all her days amusing herself.

'Bess out early and shopping,' he wrote in his diary. 'Buys dresses and hats, happy as a lark, her trunks full to overflowing. She has no worries.'[31]

And then, on the trip aboard the steamer to Australia, his wife had both drunk and danced up such a storm with the captain of the vessel during one of the interminable formal balls that she had collapsed, and Houdini had been obliged to carry her back to their cabin and put her to bed.

And where was Bess on this morning, the very morning he was to risk his life by attempting to be the first person to fly an aeroplane in Australia, at a place called Diggers Rest? Safe and sound, and no doubt asleep, back in Melbourne's luxurious Hotel Windsor, 20 miles to the south-east. It was just the way things were between them. They had fallen in love at first sight, and been married within a week, but it hadn't always been easy, least of all now.

But to work. Always to work …

The night before, Houdini had performed his magic show to a sold-out audience at the Melbourne New Opera House and had not got to bed until midnight. And yet, on this fine morning of 18 March 1910, he had risen well before dawn to be in this large flat paddock, talking to his French mechanic, Antonio Brassac — a man who had formerly been in the employ of none other than the great Blériot — just as the golden Australian sun began to appear.

The firm rule of flying at this point was that it was only safe to take off if the wind wasn't strong enough to blow out a match. Nigh on three weeks earlier, on this very field, in his eagerness to be the first man aloft in Australia, an American by the name of Ralph C. Banks had ignored that rule and promptly crashed straight after take-off, but on this clear morning, for Houdini there was not a breath of wind and conditions seemed perfect.[32]

Houdini's plane, a Voisin, looked remarkably like a couple of Lawrence Hargrave's box kites of fifteen years earlier, for the simple reason that it was essentially just a larger version joined by thin struts, with an engine and propeller attached, atop five small wheels. In fact, so greatly did the Voisin brothers admire Lawrence Hargrave that their first commercially available aircraft had been christened *Le Hargrave*, and Houdini's plane was simply a more refined version of this.

The small crowd of aviation enthusiasts who had been gathered for many days waiting for an attempt, now leaned respectfully closer to get a better look. The wings spanned 33 feet from tip to tip, with a 'chord' — the width from the front of the wing to the back — of 6½ feet, while the distance from the front of the plane to the back was just over 35 feet, the whole thing powered by a 60-horsepower ENV engine. Most interestingly, in terms of advances on previous aircraft, was that the Voisin brothers had made a leap forward from the Wright brothers' system of 'wing warping' to bank left and right, and had installed the first primitive system of *ailerons* — 'little wings', in French. By moving these ailerons up or down on the respective wings, Houdini could alter their shape and so make the wing rise or fall on the appropriate side.

After taking the little plane up and down the paddock a couple of times without attempting to take off, Houdini had Brassac make some adjustments to the rudder and then steeled himself. He was not crazy about the whole flying caper, but its pull on the public was undeniable, and that was the business he was in. Besides, the contract on which he had come to this continent stipulated that if he made ten flights in Australia, each of more than five minutes' duration, he would receive no less than £20,000 — so he may as well get started now. (Not that this day's endeavour had been promoted. Rather, this attempted flight was in the manner of a trial, to make sure everything worked, before getting the paying public in.) The Australian promoter who had brought Houdini out for that money was the sleekly moustachioed impresario Harry Rickards, but the tour had been in part organised by George A. Taylor of the Aerial League of Australia. Taylor was still determined to press the Australian government into investing in a 'navy of the air', to thwart the likes of Japan which had become notably militaristic of late.

At last Houdini signalled to Brassac that he was ready, and the wizened French mechanic moved in to grip the propeller, while the others present — a couple of Houdini's theatrical assistants, the chauffeur who had driven him the 20 bumpy miles from Melbourne, and a small group of young Australian men who had been camping nearby to await this very moment — stepped back.

'*Un, deux, trois*,' the mechanic muttered, before giving the great 8-foot-long blade the powerful heave it needed. In an instant the engine caught and throbbed into noisy life. Houdini gunned it, and within seconds was accelerating down the paddock.

All seemed well until, just 50 yards on, the plane suddenly careered sharply to the left and headed straight for a tree. If only the plane had brakes he might have applied them, but that was not an option. So, instead of slewing to the left or right, Houdini kept 'er straight, gunned the throttle and, as the onlookers held their breath … lifted off and managed to clear the tree by just a few feet![33]

'I love you! I love you!'[34] the mechanic yelled in English, though this was to the aeroplane — which he had so lovingly worked on for the previous few months that he had slept beside it most nights — and not Houdini, whom Brassac only tolerated so long as he didn't crash his beloved plane.

And now, about 50 feet above the ground, Houdini circled the paddock just once and then came in for a good landing, only a minute after he had taken off. Two more flights followed in quick succession, each one a little longer than the first, and at the conclusion of the last one, the magician landed and was overcome with elation.

Climbing out of his craft he yelled with uncharacteristic exuberance: 'I can fly! I can fly!'

At this moment a black bird, probably a raven, landed on the wing above Houdini's head and squawked loudly. 'He's telling me,' Houdini laughed, 'that I can't fly worth a cuss.'[35]

Ah, but he really could, as the handful of men present attested in written statements. One who had witnessed the whole thing — and was simply beside himself with the wonder of it all — was a 21-year-old Melburnian mechanic by the name of Harry Hawker.[36] With several others he had been living at the Diggers Rest railway station over the previous few days in the hope of seeing precisely this, and he had not been disappointed.[37] For from the moment Hawker saw Harry Houdini fly at Diggers Rest, he knew that whatever happened, however it happened, he simply *had* to fly himself.

When Houdini landed after his first stunning flight, he exulted to journalists, 'I am the first man to have flown in Australia, and I have fulfilled my greatest ambitions. I shall never forget my sublime and enthralling sensations, and I only hope that my success will encourage other aviators to persevere and conquer the air. They will find aviation a pastime providing new and wonderful sensations, such as no other pastime can afford.'[38]

(In fact, Englishman Colin Defries briefly left the ground in a Wright Flyer three months earlier in Sydney, as did L.J.R. 'Jack' Jones at Emu Plains,[39] while two South Australians, Bill Wittber and Fred Custance, also fleetingly lifted off the ground near the town of Bolivar in a Blériot aeroplane, the latter, reportedly, just the day before Houdini — although there is no doubt Custance crashed the machine. But it would be some time before these feats became widely known, and it is certain that the man who captured the public imagination as the first man to fly in Australia was Harry Houdini.)

That night Houdini performed his last show at the Melbourne New Opera House, and over the next few days — frequently before crowds of up to 200 open-mouthed spectators as the stunning news made the Melbourne press — went up another fourteen times, including a crucial flight that lasted two minutes more than the contracted five minutes.

All of this, however, was merely a preliminary to Houdini's real attempt to make huge money out of flying, above and beyond the already fabulous money promised by Rickards. For now that he felt he had properly learned to fly the machine, after those first few tentative lessons in France and then practice at Diggers Rest, he and Rickards agreed it was time to take the whole show to Sydney and charge people to watch!

And it worked a charm. For a week from 18 April 1910, Houdini flew before stunned crowds at Sydney's Rosehill racetrack, each person paying one shilling for the privilege of watching and being part of it. As reported in the *Daily Telegraph* on 19 April, on the moment Houdini first became airborne, 'men tossed up their hats, women grew hysterical and wept for sheer excitement. A hundred men rushed towards the biplane, pulled the happy aviator from the seat, and carried him, shoulder-high, mid deafening cheers and salvos.'

Watching with great satisfaction was George A. Taylor. He was deeply satisfied with the impact that Houdini was making, and the demonstration of what the advent of aviation must mean for military power. No paper put it better than the *Daily Telegraph*, which wrote: 'People who scoff at the idea of warfare in the air, ought to have been at Rosehill racetrack on Sunday. Shortly after noon, when, with a roar like a thousand maniacs released, the Voisin biplane, which had been tugging at its moorings for a week in vain endeavour to break away, was released by command of the pilot, Harry Houdini.'[40]

For its part *Melbourne Punch* commented: 'When Houdini's great machine was circling and whirring round like a gigantic bird, the great thought was "What of the future?" We in Australia are remote from the great world centres. We are peculiarly exposed to attack … We are building ships and training men … We are making no provision to defend ourselves against an enemy in the air. Yet the battles of the future will go to whoever is strongest in the air.'[41]

There was a great deal of such reaction, and in an effort to consolidate and keep it going, Taylor and the Aerial League of Australia held a reception for Houdini at Sydney Town Hall with an array of speakers celebrating the magician's feat, and focusing on its military implications.

Taylor himself thundered to the theme he had already written on copiously. 'Australia, at the crash, will be like a rabbit in a trap. It will watch the blow fall and be powerless — for the crash will come from the sky. You, O brother, may rush the fighting line with bare fists if nothing else. But what of your wives and children? Some, at first thought, will rush the great buildings till they are shattered. Others, more desperate, will crowd and fight and tear at the manholes of our sewer shafts and will mass in huddling mobs in the darkness, safe from the aerial terror that is smashing their menfolk above. And this day will come as sure as tomorrow's sun, unless Australia is prepared to meet aerial invasion with aerial defence.'[42]

The upshot was that the government got the message and it wasn't long before Australia's defence minister, George Pearce, was on his way to London to sort out the beginnings of an Australian 'navy of the air'.

As to Houdini, he and Bess returned to the United States shortly after his successful week at Rosehill racetrack — Bess laden down with the shopping she had done in Melbourne. Despite the tremendous financial rewards he had received, Houdini was never to fly again. Though immensely satisfied with that week in Sydney, he did have one regret.

Lawrence Hargrave, whom he knew all about, had not been there to see it. When Houdini had formally written to him before arriving in Sydney, inviting him to come out to the racetrack as his guest and watch him fly his plane, Hargrave had replied rather crisply, perhaps disapproving of his science being presented by a mere magician: 'Why should I do that? I invented it …'[43]

•

The King. The *King*. The King, he is dying …

In his bedchamber at Buckingham Palace, King Edward VII — Sovereign of the United Kingdom and the British Dominions, Emperor of India, Supreme Governor of the Church of England — just shy of his allotted 'three-score years and ten', was clearly close to breathing his last rasping breath. Beside him throughout sat the Prince of Wales, willing his father to go on, but acutely conscious that the last beat of his father's heart would be followed by the first beat of his own reign. At one point when King Edward surfaced from his nearly comatose state the prince was able to inform him that his horse Witch of the Air had won at Kempton Park that very afternoon.

Slowly, agonisingly, the King replied, 'I am very glad.' And then he spoke no more. A short time later, just before midnight tolled on this sixth day of May 1910, the King did indeed breathe his last breath, with his son, formerly the Prince of Wales and now King George V, embracing his father's still warm body.

When the bells pealed the news the following morning, the people wept, first in London and then throughout the entire British Empire. For its part, the *Sydney Morning Herald* claimed, 'death has clutched at the heart of the Empire with a grip of ice'. In Australia the populace immediately moved into a period of official mourning, where many officials wore black, and large parties, public balls and any public exuberance were severely frowned upon.

Even as King Edward's body lay in state in Westminster Hall — and the good and the great of Europe, including the German Emperor, the kings of Greece, Spain, Portugal, Denmark, Norway, Belgium and Bulgaria, and Archduke Franz Ferdinand of Austria gathered in London for the funeral — so too were services being held all over Australia, packed with loyal citizens wishing to pay their final respects.

One such service was held at St Andrew's Cathedral in Sydney's George Street, presided over by the Anglican Archbishop of Sydney, John Charles Wright, and commencing with angelic choirboys slowly walking down the aisles singing a favourite hymn …

Praise, my soul, the King of heaven,
To His feet thy tribute bring;
Ransomed, healed, restored, forgiven,
Who like me His praise should sing?
Praise Him! Praise Him!
Praise Him! Praise Him!
Praise the everlasting King …

Their glorious voices soared surely to the heavens above, though many people were weeping at the sadness of it all. Still, on this most solemn of all occasions, the smallest of the choirboys, the one at the front of the procession, who had been singing with fervour like all the rest, was seen to turn to his mother in the pew just to his left … and *wink*.[44]

At this moment, that good woman, Catherine Kingsford Smith, could have wished that the stones of the cathedral floor would simply open up and swallow her, so mortified was she by her boy's levity …

But on the other hand, that wink from her Chilla was simply him all over. *Nothing* was to be taken too seriously and no convention too solemn that it couldn't be broken. There was fun to be had in everything, even the death of the King, and she couldn't really hold it against him. He was just that kind of child, and she adored him regardless.

And, truth be told, it was only in his singing and his long white smock that Charles Kingsford Smith had much of the 'choirboy' about him in the first place. Despite the religious belief of his father particularly, Chilla himself was neither pious, nor quiet and withdrawn, nor meek, nor even particularly humble. As a matter of fact, his personal taste in songs was far less hymns harmoniously sung than bawdy ballads belted out. But, and this was the important part, singing such hymns was at least helping him to get an education. The cathedral school had been established a couple of decades earlier, by the third Bishop of Sydney, Dr Alfred Barry, for the purpose of providing 'the choristers with a high-class, free education on Church principles, in addition to a musical training', and, noting that Chilla had a very strong singing voice, Catherine had applied to get him a scholarship, whereby in return for his singing prowess being placed at the service of the church on Sundays and special occasions, her lad would be privately educated.

Generally, Chilla was very happy at the school, notwithstanding its rather strict regime, and the fact that four afternoons a week he and his fellow choirboys had to head to the cathedral after school to participate in evensong, and do the same as often as three times on a Sunday. Every morning he would rise just after six o'clock, dress in his formal uniform — white shirt with high Eton collar, jacket, shorts, straw boater, black stockings — and head off to the city, via the ferry at Neutral Bay, across the harbour to Circular Quay, and then take the tram up George Street until he made his way into the rather dour grey stone building on Pitt Street.

As in most private schools of that time, there was a fair measure of 'fagging', with older students using younger ones as their 'fags' — running errands, shining shoes and so forth — but young Kingsford Smith was tough enough that he coped well and was very popular with his peers. Generally, his intellectual ability was regarded by his masters as being of the top rank, without necessarily being matched by a level of application to his studies. *Charles is talented but must work harder.* As to sport, he excelled most at the physically robust games such as rugby, where he was a bustling back.

Now thirteen years old, he was fascinated by all things mechanical, and enjoyed his trip to school in the city principally for the fact that it afforded him a chance to get a really good look at how both a ferry and a tram worked. By 1912, that tram trip was taking a little longer still as, once his voice had broken and he could no longer hit the high notes for the choir, Chilla moved on from St Andrew's to Sydney Technical High School, which was one more stop down the line, near Central Station at Ultimo. Here, effectively changing his white collar for a blue collar, he began study to secure an engineering apprenticeship, and now, instead of spending such an inordinate amount of time singing hymns, the fifteen-year-old was able to do such things as help experienced mechanics dismantle and reassemble engines, clean carburettors, change brake shoes and repack ball bearings. Among his classmates he was known as being a lot of fun if slightly wild and shambolic, reflected in the nicknames they gave him: 'Mouldy Tooth', 'Buccaneer', 'Pirate' and 'Mad Yank'. In the classrooms and corridors, he was noted for a particular ability to perfectly imitate the sound of a buzzing bee — in a bottle, in an old lady's shoe, on a cat's tail — as desired. Ah, how they laughed, as Pirate went through his repertoire.[45]

Graded in the C class, with classes being graded from A through to H according to intellectual ability, his results in that first year were solid, if not spectacular. His annual report read: *Conduct: very good, Punctuality: excellent, Homework: very good, Classwork: very good, Notebook: good; one day absent.* He finished twelfth in his class of about thirty-four students.

Outside of school, he remained an amazingly self-assured and high-spirited kid, spoilt by his adoring parents and older siblings, and sometimes teetering on the edge of going off the rails … without ever quite getting there. What he was mostly, was a young man with an enormous zest for life, a small blond ball of energy riding too fast on the footpaths with 'look-no-hands-mum!' bravado, immensely enjoying most things, constantly surrounded by friends, laughing easily and getting into and out of scrapes ridiculously easily. Once or twice the police even showed up on the Kingsford Smith doorstep when his antics went just that bit too far, as when he dropped bungers off a cliff onto a courting couple below, but it was never anything *too* serious.

•

A win for Lord Northcliffe, at last …

On 13 May 1912, by Royal Warrant of King George V, the military wing of the Royal Flying Corps was created, and quickly began to expand from the eleven qualified pilots with which it began. By the end of that year it had 133 officers in its ranks, flying a dozen manned balloons and thirty-six aeroplanes, all of which had been manufactured by the Royal Aircraft Factory.

Yet it was not a birth without pain. Less than two months after its formal beginnings, a tragedy occurred. On Salisbury

Plain near Stonehenge, No. 3 Squadron's Captain Eustace B. Loraine and his observer, Staff-Sergeant Richard Hubert Victor Wilson, were flying their Nieuport monoplane at about 1000 feet when one of the strange arrangement of struts and wings and wires, which so worked on the laws of physics that they kept a plane aloft, suddenly snapped ... and the flimsy craft plummeted to the ground, killing both men. The entire Flying Corps was devastated, but a great tradition was born that afternoon, as a Memorandum for All was issued by the corps commander, stating flatly: 'Flying will continue this evening as usual ...' The show must go on, come what may, and it was up to the men of the corps to put on a jolly good one, what? Come ... what ... may. The corps' official motto was *Per Ardua Ad Astra* (Through Adversity to the Stars), and they meant it.

•

In the wee hours of the morning of Wednesday, 30 May 1912, a single wan light burned in an upstairs bedroom of the Wright family home in Dayton, Ohio. For three weeks Wilbur had been vainly struggling against a fever, and in the last twelve hours his condition had deteriorated drastically. Now, as Bishop Wright said his prayers, and Orville held Wilbur's hand and sister Katharine mopped her ailing brother's brow, Wilbur ever so slowly passed from this world. That evening, the devastated Bishop Wright carefully wrote in his diary: 'This morning at 3.15, Wilbur passed away, aged 45 years, 1 month and 14 days. A short life, full of consequences. An unfailing intellect, imperturbable temper, great self-reliance and as great modesty, seeing the right clearly, pursuing it steadily, he lived and died. Many called — many telegrams. (Probably over a thousand.)'[46]

•

His name was Tom Sopwith and, at Kingston-on-Thames, he was running one of England's first factories devoted to building aircraft, the Sopwith Aviation Company, with a flying school attached. On this day in mid-1912, a young Australian mechanic whom the factory had recently hired as their fifteenth employee, a rather capable chappie by the name of ... of ... what was it again ...? Harry, yes, Harry Hawker, came up to him. And just like that the slight Australian with the confident manner asked Sopwith straight out, 'Will you teach me to fly, sir?'

The *cheek* of the lad! Still, amused by the question, Sopwith asked him what would happen if he broke the aeroplane he was learning in.

Without hesitation, young Hawker dug into his sock and retrieved his life savings, all of £50. 'This,' Hawker said evenly, in an Australian accent so broad that Sopwith could only just understand it, 'should help to pay for any damage.'

Waving the money away, Sopwith agreed that Hawker could receive flying tuition.[47] It was to be the beginning of a strong association between the Sopwith organisation and Harry Hawker.

•

Though flying remained a dangerous activity, there continued to be a veritable army of engineers, designers and inventors across the world working passionately to develop every aspect of it, to make planes that flew faster and higher with better stability and more control. One of those designers was none other than the Dutchman Anthony Fokker, who by this time was at the forefront of world aviation design.

The young Fokker had — after attending an engineering school in Germany, where study was of the more practical nature in which he excelled, and not academic, which withered him — built and tested his first plane just before Christmas 1910. The fact that he hadn't broken his neck was as good an indication as any of his success, and by squeezing dribs and drabs of money out of his still reluctant father, he was able to build another plane, and then another one, with successive modifications to make them fly even better.

Fokker's endless experiments and modifications had led him to the belief that the key to stability in aircraft was to have a high centre of gravity and *not* have the wings coming straight out from the fuselage. Instead, Fokker believed, it was better to sweep them back and to have the tips pointing slightly upwards from the horizontal.

On 31 August 1911, in the best moment of his life to that point, the young Fokker was able to demonstrate his latest plane, the *Spin III*, to the good burghers of his own town, by flying around the spires of the sixteenth century cathedral of Haarlem, on the occasion of Queen Wilhelmina's birthday. And *that* showed his father something! So thrilled was *Mijnheer* Fokker, in fact, that Fokker junior later recorded, 'we held our only extended conversation in which I wasn't asking for money'.[48]

As Anthony Fokker's ability to build planes grew so did his ambitions, and he soon embarked on many journeys to try to get one European government or another to back him in setting up a major factory. His preference was for his native Holland, but in the absence of any real interest — his own country preferred Farman planes from France — he tried successively England, Italy and Russia.

One country, however, was really very interested indeed. And that was Germany. Fokker soon set up a factory there, in the town of Schwerin, and by 1913 Fokker Aviatik Gesellschaft, as he called his company, had begun to make a profit.

•

Free at last!

It was not that young Kingsford Smith's time at school and Technical High School had been unhappy, by any means. It was just that nearing the end of his described formal education he was more than ever conscious that what he most wanted was to be liberated from the artificial strictures of the classroom and get into the *real* world, with a job, a salary and freedom. In May 1913 that opportunity arose when he was taken on as an apprentice at the engineering workshops of the Colonial Sugar Refinery (CSR) in Pyrmont, in Sydney's inner west, right by the harbour foreshore.

For some people working in such a place, so full of grinding, noisy machinery, would have been unpleasant and perhaps intimidating. But not for Charles Kingsford Smith. He loved being in such a busy place as Pyrmont to begin with — a thriving industrial hub full of workers, steam engines shunting into sidings, ships coming into dock, and the endless hustle and bustle of heavily laden horse-drawn drays. He particularly loved working at CSR, a place where frantic and oft-exhausting activity was countered somewhat by the lovely, languorous smell of molasses and sugar that permeated everything. Most importantly for young Charles, it was a place where he could earn money, learn things and become physically stronger, as he engaged in hard daily labour. After three months of working with the refinery's massive machinery he was able to move into the electrical workshop and so begin to develop skills in an entirely different field …

Yet he still had time to amuse himself, and one of his favourite ways was fighting. This was never in the manner of picking on smaller blokes, as for a start there were few smaller fellows than him, but he did like a good scrap.

One day while walking along in downtown Sydney with his friend Terence Trousdale, he pointed out a big lad coming their way, with a smaller companion. 'Trousers, you see that big chap coming along? Well, I'm going to have a bit of him.'[49]

And, sure enough, as they passed, Charles knocked the chap's boater off. The said chap was not very happy about it, though his companion seemed more amused, telling Trousers that his aggrieved friend was actually a boxing champion and 's-a-matter-of-fact, they were off to do a training session together.

Not to worry, Charles invited him to a nearby park to ''ave a go' if he liked, and the two went at it, with Charles at least holding his own until the police came and they all scarpered.

•

What on *earth* was going on?

One Saturday night when her parents were out with friends and all her brothers and sisters bar young Chilla were otherwise engaged, Winifred Kingsford Smith returned home unexpectedly. And what did she find? Seemingly every light in their Neutral Bay house ablaze and the whole place rocking to the sound of music and singing. Winifred crept up to the front window and looked in. Through the billowing clouds of cigarette smoke she could see her youngest brother at the piano, bellowing out the verses of bawdy songs, with his mates laughing hysterically and joining in on every chorus. She could, she supposed, storm in and make a scene, but to what point? They were having such a lovely time, she wrote in her memoirs, 'that it seemed a great pity to spoil it ...'[50]

Fact was, wherever Chilla was, there was usually a crowd around him as he held court, always with a lot of laughter and high-jinks and frequently raucous singing and carrying-on. He had such naturally high spirits, and such an easy charm, it was impossible to be angry at him for long. It was also a charm that, mixed with his exceptionally good looks, many teenaged girls found hard to resist, notwithstanding the fact that in terms of dress sense he could look like something that had been dragged through a hedge backwards. Not surprisingly, the young engineering apprentice developed something of a reputation as a ladies' man. Yet the object of his most ardent affections remained a woman he had never even met.

Her name was Nellie Stewart, and she was one of the most accomplished actresses and theatre performers in the country. One day, he dreamed, he would meet her. One day!

Still, if there was one thing to rival his passion for Nellie Stewart, it was a passion for his motorbike. Now that he was earning the princely sum of five shillings a week as an apprentice, he could almost afford to run it, and given that his father had kindly agreed to make up the difference — from the meagre wage he was on himself — the teenager became a constant sight, and an even more constant *noise*, around and about the streets of Neutral Bay and Mosman on his powerful 'one-lunger', as his motorbike was known.[51] Around the big loop of Kurraba Road, he would lean into the corner as his wheels angrily spat out loose gravel, before going up and over the hill, hanging a left on Wycombe Road and dropping a gear to get across the Harriette Street dogleg. Then tearing up Bannerman Street, he was soon getting close to his favourite part of all, the downhill 'S' bends of Rangers Avenue. The speeds he got up to! The gravel he threw! Always aiming to go about 1 mile per hour slower than an accident, he would lean into each corner, his heart racing, as he powered up, changed gears, gripped the handlebars and screamed past oft-appalled pedestrians staring open-mouthed at this noisy larrikin making such a dreadful peace-shattering noise. Not for nothing was he known locally as the 'Terror of Mosman' … Then one day, he went 1 mile per hour *faster* than an accident, and straight through the wall of a dairy went he and his bike, mercifully only completely wrecking the latter.

Three

WAR!

Rally round the banner of your country,
Take the field with brothers o'er the foam,
On land or sea, wherever you be,
Keep your eye on Germany.
But England, home and beauty have no cause to fear;
Should auld acquaintance be forgot?
No! No! No! No! No! Australia will be there …
Australia will be there …

POPULAR SONG IN AUSTRALIA, 1914–18[1]

At 10.15 am on 28 June 1914, Archduke Franz Ferdinand, heir to the Austro–Hungarian throne, and his wife Sophie, Her Highness the Duchess of Hohenberg, were in an open-topped limousine bathed in bright sunlight, magisterially progressing down a street in Sarajevo, Bosnia–Herzegovina, when a young Serb by the name of Gavrilo Princip ran towards them with a pistol in his hand and fired two shots.[2]

A thin stream of blood spurted instantly from the Archduke's mouth, whereupon the Duchess cried out to her husband of fourteen years, 'In heaven's name, what has happened to you?' And yet, no sooner had she said that, than she too reeled, bleeding from a grievous wound in her abdomen. As she weakened, the Archduke gurgled to his beloved but stricken wife, 'Sophie, Sophie, don't die. Stay alive for the children!'

Tragically, both the Duchess and the Archduke passed away shortly afterwards.

Although the assassination in Sarajevo represented to most Australians nothing more than a tiny rumble of dirty thunder on the northern horizon, it was not long before a storm the likes of which no-one had ever seen before, broke out. In a matter of a few weeks, after an outraged Austria–Hungary declared war on Serbia for its failure to take action to quell the subversive organisations that nurtured the likes of Gavrilo Princip, Europe's two armed blocs were drawn into action against each other. Russia lined up beside her Slavic brothers in Serbia and was joined by France, while Germany stood four-square with Austria–Hungary.

When, on 4 August, Germany invaded neutral Belgium to get quickly to the French infidels, Britain declared war on Germany and the Great War had begun. Across most of Europe, men, munitions and the machinery of war were mobilised.

At his Fokker Aviatik Gesellschaft factory in Schwerin in north Germany, the struggling young manufacturer Anthony Fokker suddenly received a telegram informing him that his entire stock of aeroplanes would be purchased by the German Army, only shortly before the German Navy tried to do the same thing.[3] Price was no object for either military arm, and a similar injection of funds was apparent across much of Europe, put towards anything that might intensify the war effort.

There were, however, exceptions. In France, on the same day that Fokker received his telegram compelling him to work his factory around the clock, the hero of the cross-Channel flight, Louis Blériot, received a delegation of French government officials at his aircraft factory, Blériot Aéronautique, situated just outside Paris. No matter that in the last six years since his Channel triumph, he and his workers had built more than 800 monoplanes of his design, and that he was the most successful aircraft manufacturer in all of France — he was now to stop work *immediatement*. He and all his men of military age were to at once join the French Army.

Blériot had no choice but to comply, just as factories around the country, bar those staffed mostly by women, had to follow suit for the same reason. It was a week before some form of sanity prevailed and Blériot and his men were released to re-open the factory — just as other key factories were also granted exemption — but even then the reason was not to produce planes at all possible speed. No, the view of the French government was that as the war would be over in six weeks, further orders of planes and munitions would be pointless, and the country would have to focus on fighting with the resources it already had. Flying schools were shut down so that would-be pilots could immediately be shipped to the front line where they would be needed.

•

In Australia, meantime, things were also moving.

Even before Britain had formally declared war, there was never any doubt where its most loyal offspring stood, right down to its bootstraps: with the British Empire! Speaking at a political meeting at Horsham in Victoria on the last day of July, Australian Prime Minister Joseph Cook made clear his position in reference to the deepening European crisis: 'Whatever happens, Australia is a part of the Empire right to the full. Remember that when the *Empire* is at war, so is *Australia* at war. That being so, you will see how grave is the situation. So far as the defences go here and now in Australia, I want to make it quite clear that all our resources in Australia are in the Empire and for the Empire and for the preservation and the security of the *Empire*.'[4]

Just five days later, when Britain did indeed declare war on Germany, Prime Minister Cook was as good as his word, and within twenty-four hours had committed Australia to fighting beside Britain against Germany.

'It is our baptism of fire,' the *Sydney Morning Herald* enthused the following day. 'Australia knows something of the flames of war, but its realities have never been brought so close as they will be in the near future.'[5]

Borne along by this sudden surge of patriotism, and the desire to fight for what many saw as 'the Mother Country', able-bodied men from Sydney to Perth, from Darwin to Hobart, began to flood into recruiting centres to become part of the Australian Imperial Force, which Cook had promised Great Britain would be 20,000 men strong.

One who felt the call, despite his advancing years, was the ageing Lawrence Hargrave. Just two days before war had been formally declared, the 64-year-old had turned up at ten o'clock in the morning at the headquarters of the Coast Artillery at Sydney's South Head, clutching a faded letter which dated from December 1877. Addressed to Mr Lawrence Hargrave Esq, it read:

> *I will be glad if you will consider yourself an honorary member of the No. 5 Battery V.A.*
> *Signed,*
> *W. Gore Beverley, Capt., 5 Volunteer Artillery.*

'I have come to report myself,' the old man told the bemused sentry as he handed him the letter. In Hargrave's view this letter, given to him some forty years earlier, entitled him to an immediate position with that branch of the artillery. The commanding officer, no doubt equally bemused, took down Hargrave's name and address and told him they would be in touch.

There was no such problem for Hargrave's beloved son Geoffrey, however, and the young man was able to join up immediately, soon finding himself a long, long way from his father's workshop and part of the 3rd Brigade of the Australian Imperial Force.

As to young Charles Kingsford Smith, he, too, wanted to join up immediately, and was only prevented from doing so by the outright refusal of his parents to co-operate. He was just seventeen years old, and Australian law had it that it was only males at least eighteen years old who could sign up *with* parental permission, and 21-year-olds and older who could join without it. Chilla wasn't at all worried about his age; he knew of plenty of blokes who simply told fibs about their age and got in. (As a matter of fact, his own plan, developed with his cousin Rupert Swallow was for them to turn up to the recruiting station while wearing shoes with the number '18' painted on the soles. That way, when they were asked 'Are you over eighteen?' they could truthfully reply that they were indeed! And yet the plan was no sooner discovered by their respective parents than it was crushed like a grape.[6])

Now, Catherine Kingsford Smith, firmly supported as ever by her husband, simply wouldn't hear of her last-born engaging in any kind of subterfuge. No. No. *No*. Though it went against the grain for Charles to argue strongly with the mother he adored, on this occasion the young man was so infuriated he threatened not to speak to her for six months unless she relented. After all, his brother Eric had joined up with the merchant navy two years previously and had now transferred to the Royal Australian Navy, so there was already a noble precedent! Yes, dear, but Eric is twenty-seven years old, so it is quite different.

No, it is *not*!

In the end, so passionate was Chilla about joining up that Catherine did relent, a little. She and William agreed that Charles could join up when he turned eighteen, the following February, so long as he promised not to join the infantry,[7] and the young man was more or less happy to settle with that. Impatiently, he continued with his work at CSR and followed as closely as he could what was happening with the war, hoping fervently that there would be enough of it left for him to fight in by the time he got there.

•

An interesting bloke, George Hubert Wilkins. As the thirteenth and last progeny of a struggling pastoral family of South Australia, he had become fascinated with the natural world while spending time as a child with the local Aboriginal tribe, before becoming equally absorbed in things mechanical and scientific via his education at a technical school in Adelaide. At a young age he had formed a theory that the world's weather was connected, and that if mankind could achieve an understanding of climate patterns in the polar regions, it might enable accurate predictions to be made as to when the devastating droughts he was growing up with in South Australia would hit.

Put together, his theory had sent him on a peripatetic course around the world, which had seen him stow away as a seventeen-year-old on a ship bound for Africa in 1909, only to be kidnapped in Algeria in 1910, before making his escape and heading to London to become a pilot and work as a photographer in the company of a journalist from Yanovka in the Ukraine by the name of Leon Trotsky. He then found work as a war correspondent in the Turkey–Bulgaria war of 1912, where he was captured and nearly killed by firing squad and finally became a member of what was intended to be a five-year expedition to the Arctic regions way north of Canada … which … was where he was now, asleep in an igloo just inside of the Arctic Circle and dreaming of an easier way to do such an exploration. By aeroplane![8] By flying *over* the beautiful white wonderland, free as a bird, instead of endlessly trudging through it with ice-cold feet in snowshoes, fighting frostbite as yapping husky dogs hauled sleds through the eternal whiteness. True, in a plane there would the risk of great turbulence in a blizzard and being heavily shaken by the buffeting winds, shaken … shaken …

Oh. He was actually being shaken awake. It was a trapper, someone he'd never seen before, a stranger who had just made his way into camp. An enormous man with snow still on his beard and the squinty eyes of one who has spent too much time trying to shield himself from snowblindness. And he had a couple of very interesting bits of news.

The first, after a bit of chitchat, was that, 'that damn fool *scientist* Wilkins has died after shanghaiing his crew'.[9] Not at all offended, Wilkins was overjoyed to have been called a 'scientist', and didn't bother to reveal either his identity or the fact that he had shanghaied no-one.

Which was as well, because the second bit of information was even more stunning … 'By the way,' the fellow asked him, 'have you heard the news?'[10]

What news?

War. A big one. The last thing the trapper had heard was that the British were advancing through Germany towards Berlin at a rate of 20 miles a day, so the show was no doubt over.

A *war,* involving the British Empire and hence Australia, too, and he, George Wilkins, wasn't part of it? Wilkins was stricken. It didn't seem right. A feeling that the Arctic was not the place for him to be was compounded shortly afterwards when he received word that his father had died after a long illness, leaving his mother a widow. Despite his contract with Vilhajalmur Stefansson to stay in the Arctic for another year,[11]

Wilkins resolved to briefly return home to Australia, see his mother and join up to the war effort at the first opportunity. He too only hoped that it might still be going by the time he could get there …

•

In fact, after the first few months had passed there was still plenty of war to go around for everybody who wanted a part of it. And rather than British forces advancing through Germany towards Berlin, as Wilkins had first heard, it was close to the other way around. The troops of Kaiser Wilhelm II had stormed across the Belgian border in early August 1914 and, following their plan, were soon well on the road to Paris. Then, however, a combined British and French force had stopped them, in part because of the superb defensive capabilities of the newly invented machine gun together with the overwhelming power of modern artillery. It had been discovered that machine guns particularly, set up in well-defended positions and covering open ground, could halt even the most ferocious army, and that is exactly what had happened. Of course, the Germans had discovered the same thing when it came to stopping the Allied counterattack. The only way for both sides was to dig in to hold the positions they had, then try to outflank the other, whereupon the other would dig in some more to hold what *they* had and …

And within bare months, a 500-mile-long system of trenches had been dug by both sides, stretching from France's border with Switzerland near Basel in the south all the way up across northern France to the Belgian coast, with a million soldiers manning the barricades and 100 yards or so of vicious no-man's-land between them — the whole muddy mess, replete with minefields, barbed wire, machine-gun nests and pillboxes, being pounded by some 10,000 artillery guns. It was warfare on a scale unseen before, and the way forward was not apparent to either side, other than to keep pouring in fresh recruits to replace the tens of thousands of soldiers killed or wounded every month the bloody war blazed on. Every yard gained was paid for with blood.

One bold proposal to break the impasse emerged in late November 1914, from the First Lord of the Admiralty, a man by the name of Winston Churchill. Frustrated that, to this point, Britain's previously supreme naval power was having little sway on the conflict, he had come up with a plan for the navy to help strike a massive blow. Why not, he put to the War Council, have a powerful squadron steam up through the narrow straits of the Dardanelles and strike at Constantinople, which lay at the heart of Germany's new ally, Turkey?

If done on a large enough scale, it would mean the Germans would have to bleed soldiers from both the Western Front in France and the Eastern Front in Russia to fight on a third front in Turkey.

In the meantime, as the whole war effort became bigger by the week, with more and more resources pouring in, and more soldiers from both sides killed, it had become ever more obvious that Baden-Powell's observation of six years earlier that Wilbur Wright was 'in possession of a machine that could alter the destiny of nations' was being proven correct. This was apparent even in those early days of the war when the primary use of aeroplanes was to dissipate the fog of war, by acting as far forward scouts, with planes carrying pilots and observers over the enemy to report on upcoming terrain and enemy troop movements and positions. They could also occasionally report on how well targeted their own artillery was. But it would not be long before the nature of the struggle for air supremacy was moved up several notches.

One day shortly after the war began, a young French flyer by the name of Roland Garros — who was already famous in France as the first man to fly across the Mediterranean in 1913 — was cruising with an observer at 5500 feet above the town of Saarbrücken, on the German side of the French–German border, when suddenly he saw it. A German plane! Complete with its own observer, the plane marked with large black crosses on its wing was clearly heading towards French lines to do its own bit of spying. What to do?

The obvious — take a shot. While Garros manoeuvred his plane on a close parallel course to the German, his observer took out the carbine he had with him and did his best to draw a bead on the target, just 300 feet away. To Garros's frustration, this was

German Taube hunted down by a French plane equipped with a machine gun over France in 1914.

not a 'shot that rang around the world'. In fact, in all likelihood not even the German pilot who was the target heard it. To the amazement of the Frenchman, after the carbine was fired there was no sign whatsoever of a hit having been registered and it was obvious that the observer had completely missed. Cursing wicked fate that had given him a flying companion so hopeless with a gun in his hand, Roland Garros returned to base and planned his next move.[12]

At much the same time, the German aristocrat and cavalry officer Manfred von Richthofen was concluding that the air war might be important, and in fact the best part of the war to be fighting in. No matter that in the first days of the war, on horseback with the rest of the Uhlan Regiment No. 1, he and his fellow officers had looked at the planes overhead with such complete contempt that they fired on them *all*, regardless of whether they were friend or foe — for who knew which was which?

Then one day von Richthofen was on duty near Verdun when he saw an aerial battle between a German Taube and one of the new French Nieuport fighters. Actually, it was less a battle than a killing, as the Taube was only an observer plane while the Nieuport had a newly installed Hotchkiss machine gun firing 8-millimetre solid brass bullets. Though the Taube dived, darted and dipped to get away — as a sparrow might try to escape a hawk — in the end, the German plane was shot down, exploding into a ball of flame before it hit the ground, not 500 yards from where von Richthofen stood. Despite the death of his countryman, the sheer wonder of the chase took von Richthofen's breath away. As a lad he had loved to hunt prey with his brothers on the family's huge estate in Silesia. What must it be like to hunt *men*?

He decided on the spot to seek a transfer, to get away from trying to fight this war on horseback — a method that was obviously outmoded — and see if he, too, could not become a war pilot.[13] Perhaps then he could avenge the unfortunate German pilot who had died before his very eyes.

•

Roland Garros was not the first pilot of either side to be frustrated by the lack of ability to do damage to the enemy. On one celebrated occasion an English pilot had been so angered that he had thrown his empty, impotent revolver at the propeller of a German plane in the hope that it would bring the bastard down.[14] But Garros was the first to take matters into his own hands by trying to invent something better.

Voila! Within a week Garros had organised as his observer a man who was reported to be one of the best shots in the French Army. *Maintenant* they would see what they could do to a German plane! And sure enough, just an hour after taking off, as the French pilot and his observer were nearing the town of Lunéville, with the majestic Meurthe River ribboning away below to the far horizon through the quilted patchwork of farmlands, they spied a German reconnaissance plane, an Albatros BII. *Aux armes, citoyens!*

Bringing his plane in much closer this time, Garros was able to provide an easier shot for his companion. And it might have worked, too. But after the observer had indeed fired two careful shots at the Albatros for no visible results — careful, because all observers with guns had to be very sure not to fire forward anywhere near the propellers of their own plane — suddenly the German observer pulled out a machine gun and started spraying them! Happy just to make an escape from the fusillade of bullets, Garros returned to base, his mind whirring with both frustration and an idea he was forming on the next leap forward in aerial warfare. Certainly, most, when they heard of his idea, would say it was completely crazy, but with the right mechanic helping him, Garros thought he just might be able to make it work. That mechanic, Jules Hue, was extremely capable and together they began to work on Garros's plan.

•

At last the day had come.

On 9 February 1915 Charles Kingsford Smith turned eighteen, and — with the written consent of his parents in his pocket — his first act was to present himself at the recruiting office at Sydney Town Hall, not even half a stone's throw from his old school of St Andrew's, to enlist. With whom, though, was he going to join, if not the infantry, as he had promised his mother?

Until this point Kingsford Smith had been so keen to 'join up' that he hadn't actually focused on just what he would do, so one thing was as good as another. Just a little more than a week later, 1017 Private Charles Edward Kingsford Smith — all 5 foot 7½ inches for only 10 stone and 7 pounds of him — found himself on the western outskirts of Sydney at the Ingleburn Army Camp, learning both how to be part of a disciplined army and how to fire big guns. Neither was easy …

Fact was, Charles Kingsford Smith and discipline — both self and imposed — simply didn't quite fit together. As his parents and teachers could attest, while he was a lad of many talents, these did not include such basic things as punctuality, punctiliousness, knuckling down, knuckling under — or doing anything he didn't really want to do — most particularly following orders he didn't like, which were … let's see … most of them.

Similarly, it was obvious to the young man from the first that artillery was not his thing. After all, there really wasn't a lot to firing big guns, apart from getting the shell properly into the breech, pulling the lanyard and then coping with the noise of the massive explosion, which could make your ears ring for hours afterwards. Perhaps he'd be better in another division of the army? Something perhaps involving … motorbikes?

Exactly! As it happened, the army did have a need in the Signal Corps for young men who could drive motorbikes fast. The idea was that in the heat of battle, the dispatch rider would be useful in taking messages back and forth from the front lines. The moment the opportunity to be a dispatch rider came up, just a few weeks after he had begun at the Ingleburn camp, Kingsford Smith grabbed it and was soon transferred to a camp at Broadmeadow, on the southern outskirts of Newcastle, to train with the 4th Signal Troop of the 4th Divisional Signal Company.

There was, frankly, little the army could teach Chilla about how to ride a motorbike fast, after his already intense training around the streets of Neutral Bay, though it was an absolute joy to have the official brassard of a dispatch rider on his arm when in traffic, because it signified that he was given special leave to disobey road rules. Beyond that, he engaged in lessons about such basic things as rifle drill, bayonet practice, correct method of dress, how to salute officers and specific signalling skills, such as the operation of field telephones, flag signalling, and how to send and receive Morse code. The key to learning Morse code, he found, was memorising which configuration of dots and dashes went with what letters of the alphabet, and then practising over and over again, until he could instantly recognise letters and then whole words and even whole phrases.

At least it was something to occupy his time until he could do what he wanted to do most, which was to get back on the motorbike.

•

One day, about a month or so after her Chilla had departed for the Broadmeadow camp, Catherine Kingsford Smith was just finishing off the washing-up after lunch when their street was suddenly filled with the sound of roaring engines, as though twenty motorbike riders were trying to outdo each other over who could make the worst cacophony of deafening sound. Like everyone else in the quiet leafy street, she rushed outside to see what on *earth* was going on … only to find her laughing youngest child on his massive army motorbike — a Bullock Precision Big Four machine with a 4.25-horsepower engine — tearing up and down the street, and around and around, waiting for her to appear. *Oh, my dear, my dear!* On his arm, the brassard of a dispatch rider; on his face, a grin as wide as Sydney Heads. All up, a devastatingly handsome young man in uniform, her boy. He was home on a couple of days' leave and couldn't wait to show his mother — and, yes, everyone else in the neighbourhood — his new mount. Wasn't she a beauty?

Yes, Chilla. And in all the excitement and carry-on, Catherine clear forgot about the appointment she had in town, and now it would be too late to catch the ferry, but a still laughing Chilla told her not to worry; he would race her along to the car ferry, riding pillion, at double speed. And to her amazement, she agreed …

Had the time of her life, too.

Yes, sir, there was just something about her youngest son …

While Chilla adored his mother in turn, still Nellie Stewart ran a close second in terms of his affections. Having seen her perform on several occasions, Chilla was completely smitten by her talents and beauty, though in a completely reverential and respectful sense. He was so taken with her that his sister Elsie, who had embarked on a theatrical career and knew Nellie Stewart slightly, arranged a brief meeting between the two, during which Miss Stewart handed her younger brother a signed photo.

The inscription read:

Dear Charles Kingsford Smith
May you live for those who love you; for the work
God has assigned you; and the good you can do.
Nellie Stewart[15]

From the moment he received it, Chilla treasured the photo to such an extent that his mother had it framed for him. Thereafter,

Chilla, about whom it was said would have misplaced his head if he hadn't had it screwed on, always knew *precisely* where his photo of Nellie was — and that was, always within arm's reach.

•

Nearly there now … Garros and his mechanic had succeeded in working out a rough system to fire their weaponry through the propeller of their plane. The obvious key was to ensure that the one in thirty bullets that would hit the propeller would, instead of shattering it, be deflected harmlessly away. To accomplish this, they modified a previous system developed by Raymond Saulnier — the same aircraft designer who in 1909 had helped Louis Blériot design and build his *Blériot XI* — and positioned the Hotchkiss machine gun close to the stem of the propeller. Then onto that stem they attached strong, angled steel.

By 1 April 1915, Garros was finally ready to test his system. While cruising over the town of Bruges, in Belgium, at a height of 4500 feet, he spied four German Albatros planes, 1000 feet higher than him on his starboard quarter. Quickly, he nosed his plane upwards so it was heading straight at the Germans and tightened the pressure of his finger on a piece of wire he had attached to the trigger. What was certain at this point, he knew, was that very soon one plane was going to be tumbling to earth, and he could only hope it wasn't his own, with a shredded propeller.

Steady … steady … steady … *now*!

Just 100 feet away from the nearest German plane, an Albatros BII, Garros fired off four bursts of twenty-five 8-millimetre brass bullets, and was satisfied to see them peppering all along the fuselage of the German plane. From below, German and Allied troops watched what was happening with morbid fascination. It was strange, but they could *swear* they saw flashes of fire coming from the *nose* of the French plane!

High above the ground, the shocked German observer on the first plane that Garros aimed at responded by firing his Mauser rifle carbine at the French attacker, even as his pilot desperately dived to get away from the chattering guns. But Garros followed him down, waiting for the moment. Again the German plane crossed directly in front of Garros and again he fired his machine gun through the propeller, his own plane juddering a little as some of the bullets were deflected off his propeller. Suddenly, a shooting flame burst from where the German aircraft's petrol tanks were situated, then engulfed the entire aircraft. Garros followed the flaming hulk down and, despite his savage exultation, coolly noted with surprise that the German machine didn't simply fall out of the sky as he had assumed it would, but spiralled down to destruction. As it hit the ground the Frenchman was close enough to hear, despite the howl of his own engine, the final explosion which completely incinerated the plane and its two occupants. A new force in aerial warfare had just been unleashed … and in the next fortnight, Garros shot down four more German planes.[16]

•

So it was done. Churchill's plan to send a powerful naval squadron through the Dardanelles to shell Constantinople had been adopted, and all that was necessary to see it through was to secure the land from the Turkish forces that were dug in on either side of the straits.

As the destroyers approached the shores of Gallipoli, in the graveyard hours of 25 April 1915, many an Australian soldier of the 3rd Brigade, AIF — including 23-year-old machine-gunner Geoffrey Hargrave, known as 'Stirrups' to his comrades — was fervently calling upon a higher being to protect him in the coming hours, not knowing just what it was that awaited him. Now the order came through to stop smoking, and maintain complete silence. All that Geoffrey could hear was the gentle throb of the engines … all that he could see was the slightly darker blobs of other destroyers carrying other comrades to the same fate, whatever that may be.[17]

And now it was time. The hissed command went out. '*Prepare to man the boats* …'

Just 200 yards from the beach, the destroyers hove to and, as silently as possible, the ships' boats were lowered to the waters below, followed by the soldiers who quietly clambered down the ships' sides and into them, before they began to pull away towards the shore.

And *stroke.* And *stroke.* And *stroke.* Carefully, quietly, floating phantoms on the water, gliding to their goal …

Then they heard it. Distant gunfire, as scattered as a light rain falling, followed by surprisingly melodic splashing as bullets hit the water all around. The Turks were waiting for them.

And then one of the men in the first boats slumped forward, lifeless, a bullet through his head. And then another man groaned and slipped sideways. And now the scattered rain of bullets had become a heavy shower, before turning into a full-blown storm, and they were right in the middle of it. As soon as the bow of their boat touched the Turkish shore, Hargrave and the other Australian soldiers of the 3rd Brigade jumped into the water and began scrambling forward, eager to get to grips and look for the 200 yards of open land they knew awaited them before they reached the first steep incline. But where was it? There was no open land, just a small beach tucked into near-cliffs, from the top of which fire was now pouring down on them! They had been landed at the wrong spot.

Everywhere now, in this first dull glow of dawn, soldiers were falling, screaming, clutching their stomachs, or legs, or the end of a bloody stump where their other arm should have been. Forward! Fight!

And upwards …

For the survivors of that first assault, the only way forward was straight up and right into the withering fire coming directly down upon them — all of them betrayed by the rising sun, whose rays picked them out on the cliffs and made them progressively better targets. And *still* they climbed, managing, somehow, to fire back and make headway. At least some did …[18]

In just the first twenty-four hours, 2000 Australian soldiers were killed or wounded. Mercifully — for both Geoffrey Hargrave and his family — Stirrups was not among them and was able to dig in with the other survivors. A preliminary assessment was that it looked as though they would not be marching on Constantinople in just a couple of weeks, as had been first planned, and it might take a little longer.

•

It was a Tuesday afternoon in late April and Anthony Fokker had just received an urgent summons from German High Command to travel from Schwerin to Berlin to solve a technical problem. A day earlier, he was informed, a French pilot by the name of Roland Garros had been forced down and captured, and it had quickly been discovered that he had a machine gun firing *through* the propeller of his plane at the rate of 600 bullets a minute, though some bullets were in fact being deflected off. This meant that Fokker's own planes were hopelessly outdated. He *must* come down — *Schnell! Schnell! Schnell!* — and work out the secrets of the captured plane. Fokker began that very afternoon and continued to work into the night on the German air-cooled Parabellum machine gun.

Never mind that in his entire life the young Dutch engineer and designer had never even held a machine gun in his hands. The technical problem was a fascinating one, and he knew immediately that he could do far better than Garros's primitive system. He was working with a two-bladed propeller that revolved 1200 times a minute, meaning that the muzzle of the machine gun would have a blade in front of it 2400 times every sixty seconds.

How to work it? The solution came to him in a blinding flash. The only way to have the gun shoot through the whirring propeller was to have the propeller effectively fire the gun.[19] Fokker quickly rigged up a synchroniser system whereby every time one blade of the propeller was at a certain point in its revolution, it would trigger the firing of a bullet from the muzzle of the machine gun. To imagine, for a moment, the revolution as a clock face, he set it up so that the muzzle was at twelve o'clock, and it would fire every time one propeller blade hit the nine o'clock position — allowing maximum room for the bullet to fly through. It worked a treat, and it would ever afterwards be Fokker's proud boast — although others would claim he was exaggerating, as previous work had been done upon the problem — that just forty-eight hours after the problem had been presented to him, he was able to demonstrate his new system to the stunned German generals. What is certain is that they could barely believe their eyes. Within weeks, aerial warfare was truly revolutionised, with tens of thousands of bullets soon bursting through the propellers of both sides at every turn of the blades. Planes had now, effectively, been turned into flying machine guns.

•

No-one knew quite what happened to the 23-year-old Geoffrey Hargrave. One minute he was making his way back from trenches under heavy fire, and the next he wasn't. When Turkish shells achieved direct hits you never found anything, and that is likely what happened to him on the grey morning of 4 May 1915. In one catastrophic moment his life was over and he lived on only in the memory of those who had known him.

Nowhere, perhaps, did that memory burn as intensely as in his father Lawrence Hargrave. For the news, once the cable arrived at the family home in Woollahra, hit the inventor horrifyingly hard, and the death of his wonderful son and collaborator near consumed him with grief. Their time spent together was all he could think about, talk about and dream about. The things they had done together, built together, refined together. And now Geoffrey was *dead*. Ultimately, and sadly, the news proved to be the death of Lawrence Hargrave as he became bed-ridden and seemed to lose the will to live. He died, still lying there, a short time later.

Geoffrey Hargrave was only one of the many Australian soldiers who died during those first horrendous weeks on the Dardanelles, and with the Allied commitment to remain at Gallipoli seemingly as strong as ever, it was obvious that reinforcements would have to be sent for. They would come from camps in Egypt, as well as in raw recruits in Australia …

On the bright, clear morning of 31 May 1915, Charles Kingsford Smith, with the 4th Signal Troop, which was now attached to the 4th Light Horse Brigade, sailed through Sydney Heads, aboard the *Ajana*. The troopship headed down the coast of New South Wales and then Victoria, before heading west, first across the Great Australian Bight and then on the long haul to conquer the Indian Ocean.

Certainly Kingsford Smith had been on ships before, most particularly back and forth to Canada as a young lad. But this was nothing like that. This was thrilling. An enormous *adventure*. War!

Though army discipline did not sit any better with him now than it had at the beginning, life was a lot easier, principally by virtue of the fact that he had made so many close mates in his section. The way they were living, cheek by jowl by towel, sleeping on hammocks hanging tightly together in the mess — so as to make room for the horses on the other decks — you pretty much *had* to form close bonds with your fellow soldiers, or life would have been untenable. In the many shipboard concerts that the Light Horse commanders organised to relieve the tedium of drills, parades, vaccination shots and endless soundings of the bugle to indicate when the soldiers should get up, go to bed, to church services, have breakfast, lunch and dinner, Kingsford Smith more than came into his own, and was a particularly popular member of the corps. When the *Ajana* crossed the equator and the ship's crew set up a large canvas bath on the deck to baptise into the realm of King Neptune those who had ceased to be 'pollywogs' and would now become 'trusty shellbacks', Kingsford Smith was one of the handful of soldiers who could claim to have already been initiated into the sacred realm. Him and King Neppy? Practically best mates! He, hence, had the right to help initiate the others in scenes of high hilarity.

And yet it wasn't long before the eighteen-year-old was in scenes of terrible, terrible slaughter. Bodies were cut to pieces, axes and knives cutting through flesh, blood everywhere. It was the horses. Quite why they were dying in such numbers was not absolutely clear, only that it was ghastly. Every morning would bring more dead or dying nags, dragged up from the holds and cut up on the deck into quarters before being slung over the side, their dismembered bodies floating momentarily in the wake of the *Ajana*, bobbing up and down in the Indian Ocean before disappearing.

Forever …

Were they themselves, also, going to die? It was the question that bubbled under the thoughts of most of the soldiers, if not all of them. And the answer was almost universal. No, they were not going to die. Some of their mates would die, no doubt, and that would be tragic, but there was a general sense among them that they personally would be spared death's scythe.

The ship sailed on, and, at least nominally, none of the men on board knew any better than the Germans where they were heading as it was a military secret. Still, given the well-publicised events in Gallipoli in recent months, none of them would be too surprised if they were heading in that general direction, and so it proved.

After six weeks' sailing west across the Indian Ocean they turned north-west to the cleft in the landmass that was the Gulf of Suez before disembarking at the town of Suez itself, to board a train heading to Egypt's capital, Cairo. As they stepped down the gangplank, fully laden with their kit, the men were easy targets for the seemingly hundreds of young Arab urchins begging them for '*baksheeeesh*, George, *baksheeeesh*', or their older brothers offering to sell them carved elephants, cushion covers, scarves or their own sisters for a short time — 'very clean, very hi-jean' — and if not her, what about at least some '*feeeelthy* pictures'? Cheap!

Yeah, yeah, yeah ...

Kingsford Smith and his comrades of the 4th Light Horse Brigade were quickly installed in a blazing hot camp, a veritable tent city, in the desert at Heliopolis on the north-western outskirts of bustling Cairo, with all its teeming population and extraordinarily exotic smells. Just before Chilla arrived, a journalist from the *Egyptian Gazette* had written an evocative description of what that camp was like: 'The men seem cheerful and at home. Large wood fires burn beneath and around oval iron pots of tea; toast too, seems a great favourite, baked and often sadly burned in the wood ashes. The many lines of beautiful and much loved horses strike the onlooker immediately; they have practically constant attention night and day.'[20]

For his part, Kingsford Smith had little to do with the horses, as his focus remained on his motorbike, and his task was to be a constant traveller delivering messages between the Heliopolis camp and another camp near the pyramids, dashing along the

8 miles of dusty road. In short order, in fact, he had established a new record for the journey — of seven minutes and forty seconds.

It was an exhilarating, amazing thing to race a motorbike at over 60 miles per hour — over a mile a minute! — past the local peasants on camels, and he didn't particularly mind that neither the peasants nor the camels were too happy about it. The young Australian could not have been more pleased. As ever, he simply loved speed, and was constantly trying to work out ways to go even faster, perpetually tinkering with his engine, experimenting with different tyres, and taking ever greater risks in his desperate dashes, much as he had done when racing along Kurraba Road at Neutral Bay.

Between such trips there was more intense training to do with field telephones, which were being extensively used at Gallipoli, with route marches on which they took their Lee-Enfield .303 rifles with attached Pattern 1888 bayonets slung over their backs, and with such basic fare as sentry duty and digging fresh latrines. Generally it was so hot, with temperatures rising as high as 125 degrees Fahrenheit during the day, that the only way the men could cope was to rise at 4.30 am, work from 5 am till 9 am and then knock off till 4 pm, when they would go about their business for another two hours. From this point the evening was theirs, to either get some grub, write letters, or go into Cairo proper and amuse themselves as much as their army pay would allow.

The Australian soldiers frequented all kinds of places, and were common sights everywhere in the city — being pulled through city streets in horse-drawn gharries, or patronising the American Comosgraph picture theatre, the Cairo British Recreation Club and the Obelisk Hall on Emad al-Dine Street. They were also frequent visitors to the brothels in the Birket district off Ezbekiya gardens, where, for just a few piastres they really could sleep with the sister of one of the urchins. Back to the camp for some kip, and then it was all on again the following morning from reveille at 4.30 am.

Giving some focus to their training, and the fact that they really were in the middle of a *war*, was the constant stream of severely wounded Australian soldiers coming back to Cairo from Gallipoli.

As Chilla wrote to his parents:

> *There are hundreds of men in the hospitals here who have been wounded in the Dardanelles. One poor devil was despatch-running for some weeks and in heavy shell fire all the time; he got out without a scratch, but is now totally blind — shell blindness it is called — due to the fumes and concussion. He is only about 19 years old and quite cheerful over it. Other chaps have arms and legs blown off and no face left perhaps, but none of them seem to regret having gone ...*[21]

And yet Kingsford Smith, like most of his comrades in the Light Horse, was desperate to go Gallipoli too, to get to the front line, see the action, to fire and be fired upon, to test himself.

•

Her name was Muriel Peaty, and on a spring day nearly as beautiful as her, as she was driving with a long-time school friend through London's magnificent Richmond Park, their car stopped — just like that! And it wouldn't go again, no matter how many times she stared at the thing called the carburettor, tried to turn the crank, stamped her foot and said 'bother!' or *willed* it to start. And then this rather good-looking fellow with this frightfully broad Australian accent came along in his own car and asked if perhaps he could help?

Muriel's mother had always been very firm about speaking to strangers, whatever the circumstances, even an extremely good-looking one who took the trouble to introduce himself — 'Harry Hawker', he said his name was — and so Muriel reluctantly declined his offer. But when he drove by half an hour later and she and her friend were still there, he insisted on helping, and she accepted his offer with thanks.

'Was it petrol, after all?' he asked brightly as his opening remark, which rather stunned the eighteen-year-old Muriel, because by this time she had worked out that it was indeed that. But how on earth had he worked that out so quickly, she asked.

'If a girl breaks down,' he said cheerily, 'she will invariably take everything down that is detachable, before she looks into the petrol tank.'[22]

Charmed, she was sure.

And yet she really was charmed only a short time later when this fellow had sorted everything out, using his own tin of spare petrol. So charmed, in fact, she was very happy to exchange cards with him, before she and her friend went on their way. Nice card it was, too — even if he'd had to use a friend's card. Apparently he worked at Sopwith's at Kingsford-on-Thames, where they made all those planes. She liked the cut of this man's jib. And she rather felt that he liked hers too, from the warm but still very respectful way that he looked at her and spoke to her. Quite made her feel all funny inside, it did, Mother …

•

Charles Kingsford Smith could smell death all around. As in really *smell* it. He was right in the middle of the mightiest pyramid of them all, King Cheops — a treat for many but this Australian hated every moment of it. He wrote to his parents:

> *It is all built out of fine granite, and it looks as if it has been recently cut, instead of 6,000 years ago. All this in pitch darkness when the candles go out, and to stand there and smell the faint dead sort of smell, and feel cold draughts of air from somewhere, and realise that you are surrounded by 200 feet of stone every side, is enough to give you the horrors.*[23]

He was not, he knew, a man for confined spaces. He needed air, movement, freedom, horizons stretching unimpeded in every direction.

Back in Neutral Bay, Chilla's letters were eagerly awaited and devoured by the family, usually after Catherine had asserted her maternal rights to read them first. The youngest of her brood was chatty and enthusiastic about his experiences of the war so far. One letter, which he sent in August 1915 was of particular note:

> *You will be interested to know that I have a chance of joining the Aviation Corps and am going to make close enquiries as to the time of training, etc. before I could be bomb-dropping on German troops. If by joining the Corps I could get to the front within a reasonable time, I will do so and let you know immediately. There would be no trouble to get in, as I was offered a place by a Captain in the job ...*[24]

For if riding his motorbike fast was a pleasure, how much more fun would it be to fly a plane? When the local planes were buzzing around and about over Cairo and the pyramids, the young soldier estimated they appeared to travel about twice as fast as a motorbike and, no doubt, were even more thrilling. Still, less a conversion on the road to Damascus than one on the road to Cairo, he didn't mind *re*-converting, and only a fortnight later his parents received another letter, announcing a change of heart: 'I have chucked the idea of transferring to the Aviation Corps, because I wouldn't get to the front for months, and anyway I want to stick to the O.C. and the troop after being with them for so long.'[25]

For Kingsford Smith getting to the front — specifically to Gallipoli —remained the priority. And from the moment that the eighteen-year-old discovered that if he did join the Aviation Corps it would involve at least four months of training, and therefore seeing no action for at least that period of time, he decided to put the whole flying thing on hold. He *had* to get to the front.

•

At that front, the killing went on. In the early hours of 7 August 1915, four waves of soldiers from the Australian Light Horse, with 200 men in each, were ordered to run, two minutes apart, 30 yards across open ground with bayonets fixed and no bullets in their rifles, straight at entrenched Turkish machine-gun positions.

The first wave was cut to pieces, and fell back upon the second wave, which nevertheless, scrambled out when the whistle blew and was equally mown down. As the third wave of Australians prepared to go, a strange, *pleading* call could be heard from the Turkish lines. '*Dur*! *Dur*! *Dur*!'[26] (Don't! Don't! Don't!) Do not keep running into our guns, slaughtering yourselves.

But they did as soon as the whistle blew, and the third wave was slaughtered.

Finally, some semblance of sanity prevailed, and the fourth whistle did not blow. But the queue of those in front of Charles Kingsford Smith waiting to get to Gallipoli began to move quickly …

Four

In the Trenches

They're sticking at it still, incomparable heroes, all. We are lousy, stinking, unshaven, sleepless … I have one puttee, a man's helmet, another dead man's bayonet. My tunic rotten with other men's blood and partly spattered with a comrade's brains.

Lieutenant Alec Raws, from Melbourne, writing to a friend, about conditions in the trenches on France's Western Front[1]

At last, the longed for news came through to Charles Kingsford Smith and his comrades. They were going to Gallipoli! True, they would have to leave their motorbikes behind, at least for the moment, but hopefully if they were able to break through against Johnny Turk and get into the open country leading to Istanbul, then the bikes could follow them over. The main thing was, they were going …

Kingsford Smith set about packing his kitbag, with his main worry being whether to take his photo of Nellie Stewart or leave it safely behind in storage with his other effects.[2] In the end, he decided to take it.

In the wee hours of a desperately cold morning in the last week of September 1915, the eighteen-year-old devotee of all things mechanical wearily waded the last few yards through the waters and onto the shores of Gallipoli. It had been something of a harrowing voyage aboard the HMT *Melville*, and while the first view of their destination — with flames and shell-bursts all around — was a little shocking, at least they were there. As they landed, an enemy Albatros plane tried dropping bombs on them as a welcome, but fortunately did little damage.

Though Kingsford Smith was excited to finally be in the middle of actual combat, it did not take long for that excitement to wear off. What he saw all around him and what he experienced hour by hour, day by wretched day, had nothing to do with excitement, glamour or even adventure, and everything to do with screaming men, severed limbs, dead bodies and unremitting terror. For the first ten days Chilla was there, he was under heavy fire around the clock. Sleep came in tortured snatches, meals in much the same manner, and performing his ablutions was a nightmare. Certainly the trenches — more or less an elongated grave without end — gave some protection, but that was no guarantee of survival, particularly when his role in the war was to leave those trenches and scurry like hell back and forth with messages. Sadly for him, on these rugged slopes, without his motorbike, all that was left was to take 'shanks's pony' at full gallop, hopefully fast enough that an enemy sniper — of whom there were many — couldn't draw a bead on him and pick him off.

And *now*, up and out of one trench, with his written message tucked securely in his pocket, he would suddenly be in open ground and running as fast as his legs could carry him, his lungs burning, his heart bursting, as spurts of dust kicked up around him followed an instant later by the crack of the sniper's rifles, as they tried to nail him. Like the rugby winger he once was, he would run, trying to step to the left and right as he went, to throw their aim off, until up ahead he would see the 'try-line', another safe trench he could dive headfirst into, to deliver his message. Such was his daily chore, perhaps as often as six times a day.

There was also the sprayed fire of the machine guns to contend with. At one point Kingsford Smith had come under such sustained fire from one sniper atop Hill 971 — a Turkish stronghold that dominated the area they were in — that any previous certainty he would survive the war wavered. Finally he scrambled to safety with only a bullet hole in the edge of his cap.[3]

And yet, while snipers and machine gunners were a real problem, the danger they presented simply didn't compare to the Turkish artillery. For if Kingsford Smith hadn't liked big guns sending large projectiles back in Ingleburn Army Camp, he positively hated it *now* ...

Always it would be the same thing. There would be a distant boom, and shortly after its sneering cadences had rolled over the men would come a whistling sound ... followed by a massive explosion. If the shell landed right on you, you wouldn't have known anything — it would have been immediate blackness and your mates would be lucky to find your tooth fillings. But if it was a near miss, the next thing would be a shower of shit and mud and sometimes the body parts of your fallen comrades thrown everywhere from the point of impact, mixed with searing, scything pieces of deadly shrapnel. Time and time again Chilla nearly lost his life, if not from bullets hitting the ground all around him, then from a piece of shrapnel whizzing by so close he could hear it.

And all for what? Far from having brought Turkey to its knees, all the Allies could claim to hold was a narrow patch of ground approximately one mile wide by half a mile deep. It was ground so poor that, in the words of one Australian soldier, one square mile 'wouldn't feed a bandicoot ...'[4]

The general sense of hopelessness deepened as winter settled in on the Gallipoli Peninsula. Night after night the creeping cold came up from the depths of the Dardanelles, stole across the battered landscape and into the trenches, where it would stealthily begin turning flesh to ice, laying siege to the soul, and start seeping into men's very bones. At the beginning of winter the tepid sunlight of dawn would just manage to chase the cold away, at least a little, and at least for those who had made it through the night, but then not even the sunshine could do it and the best one could hope for was numbness to relax its agonising grip. Frostbite was common, with men losing fingers and toes to its deathly, icy grasp.

Everyone was affected by the cold, and personally, Charles Kingsford Smith came down with such crippling rheumatism that he could barely move, let alone run between trenches as he had done. To keep himself useful he became a cook's assistant and then a clerk in the Signal Office, though even those two fairly sedentary activities were an agony for him. So obvious was his disability that his commanding officer presented the opportunity to him to go back to Egypt, but Kingsford Smith declined for much the same reason that he had decided not to pursue becoming a pilot. That is, the great solidarity he felt with the men in his corps and the fact that it was bred into him to see things through. He did not want to leave Gallipoli before they did, and refused to scarper until the job was done.

And yet sometimes, lying in his trench, shuddering, aching, trying vainly to take his mind off the agonising pain of it all — telling himself that at least he was *alive*, as opposed to so many of his comrades who had been lost — Kingsford Smith would find himself gazing up at the daytime skies, where Allied planes would whizz about and occasionally engage their Turkish counterparts. From the first days of the Gallipoli action, both sides had used land-based planes and seaplanes — with the Allies using a prototype aircraft carrier, HMS *Ark Royal*, as their base — in reconnaissance missions, bombing runs, antisubmarine and shipping strikes. And aircraft activity had only increased as the months had passed.

Whatever else, to Kingsford Smith sheltering in his ditch, it was clearly a different existence up there. Not for those pilots, the mud, the muck, the wretched trenches. They were *free*. Before the war Kingsford Smith had never seen a plane, but he was fascinated by the mechanics of the machines, the wonder of how on earth they managed to stay aloft, and he began to ponder again the possibilities of a change in his military career and becoming a pilot.

•

Back in sunny Sydney, Catherine Kingsford Smith did not like it one bit. By the closing months of 1915 there was a tone in her son's letters that she barely recognised. Gone was the enthusiasm, the joy, the sense of adventure, the sheer cheekiness that had previously characterised his letters. Everything now seemed to be downbeat, glum, occasionally even bordering on fearful, which was so unlike him.

'Snipers are pretty bad at the foot of our gully,' he had written to them on 27 November, 'and get our chaps fairly often. One has to do a sprint, or else have a bullet after him.'[5]

For Catherine, the image of her son in Turkey, pursued by bullets with his every move, was enough to keep her awake at night, tossing and turning, worrying about him. And yet the happy circumstance was that by the time the family had received the troubling letter, the evacuation of Gallipoli — along with her son Charles — had already been successfully completed.

In late October, the decision had been taken by the newly arrived Major General Sir Charles Monro that the only sane thing to do was to withdraw and, despite sneers from Winston Churchill about Monro — 'He came; he saw: he capitulated.' — things moved quickly from then. After the worst winter storms in forty years hit the peninsula in late November, with hundreds of Allied soldiers getting frostbite, in early December the evacuations of the 136,000 men began. Each night more and more shivering soldiers were moved onto ships, with those who remained instructed to be as active, conspicuous and noisy as possible to make it appear to the Turks that the Allied presence was undiminished. By day, hostile Allied aeroplanes patrolled the skies in heavy numbers to keep Turkish reconnaissance planes from spotting any telltale activity at Anzac Cove.

Kingsford Smith and his men of the 4th Light Horse got out on the night of 11 December, and by 18 December there were just 40,000 shivering soldiers left. Over the next two nights, every man jack of them got away, with the Turks stunned to find on the morning of 20 December that the invaders had gone. Gallipoli had been successfully evacuated, with not a single casualty — a stunning military feat.

For Kingsford Smith, as for his fellow Australian soldiers, while there was disappointment that their campaign had not succeeded, there was also relief to be out of there — 'I really am glad to see the last of it,' he wrote to his parents. 'No doubt there will be mixed feelings at home about this great retreat, but in everyone's opinion it was the only thing to be done as advance was impossible, and to continue there meant the loss of valuable lives every day which could be ill spared. One thing everyone agrees is that the Turks are honourable and clean fighters and have never been guilty of anything to earn the name "Unspeakable".[6]

The most wonderful thing of all was to be back in Egypt. Fresh meat! Vegetables! Children! *Women!* People going about their daily lives without being plastered with shot and shell. And, from freezing to his very core in the Turkish trenches, the eighteen-year-old was now back in the Egypt's Sinai Desert where, on a hot day, the temperature could reach as high as 120 degrees Fahrenheit *in the shade.* At least it would have been that hot in the shade, if there had been any shade to be in. But there wasn't. There were just vast tracts of endless desert, and the Australian soldiers were the only living things silly enough to be in it, burning up in the heat. The first package Chilla received from his parents upon his return contained a wonderfully warm sheepskin vest that would have been a godsend just a couple of weeks earlier.[7]

In this brief respite from the war, Kingsford Smith and his comrades frequently went swimming in the Suez Canal in the heat of the day, and often paddled out to passing steamers in the hope that some kind soul would throw them a tin of cigarettes or some other luxury. Both Australia, and the war, seemed far, far away …

The lassitude of the desert notwithstanding, in March Smithy was able to proudly write to his parents that after a promotion he was now Corporal Charles Kingsford Smith, and could eat in the Non-Commissioned Officers' Mess. No more washing up!

•

Among British pilots, a rather different version of the Psalm 23 was gaining favour, most particularly among those who flew the rather unreliable BE2 planes. Known as the 'Pilots' Psalm', its rhythm was simple.

The BE2c is my 'bus, therefore I shall want.
He maketh me to come down in green pastures.
He leadeth me to where I will not go.
He maketh me to be sick, he leadeth me astray on all cross-country flights.

Yea, though I fly over no-man's land where mine enemies
would compass me about I fear much evil,
for thou art with me,
thy joystick and thy prop discomfort me.
Thou preparest a crash before me in the presence of mine
enemies,
thy RAF anointeth my hair with oil,
thy tank leaketh badly.
Surely to goodness thou shalt not follow me all the days of my
life,
else I shall dwell in the House of Colney Hatch forever.[8]

•

Oh, the sheer pleasure of it!

After six months in the dirty dust-bowl of North Africa — the hazy horizons, sandstorms, surly Arabs, shiver-me-timbers nights and boiling hot days — to be in Europe was not far short of paradise. After a slightly nervous jaunt across the Mediterranean — looking out for German subs the whole way — Charles Kingsford Smith, with the rest of the men of his Signal Corps, arrived in Marseilles on 8 June 1916 and exulted in the wonder of being back in the very hub of western civilisation.

Trees in the boulevards! Cafes! Pubs! People waving at you in the streets! Arriving in France after well over a year in Turkey and Egypt was like coming home, exciting a feeling like you were back among your own people. No matter that only shortly after arriving in the Mediterranean city they were entrained to the town of Bailleul, a little east of Armentières in the north-west of France — it still felt like civilisation once more.

The thing that Chilla most enjoyed about being in Europe? The French girls. How beautiful they were! As he gushed to his parents in one enthusiastic letter: 'Some of them would turn the head of a statue.'[9]

But to business — the business of war. Only a short time after arriving in France, Chilla was promoted to the position of sergeant in his motorbike section of the 4th Divisional Signal Company, meaning another slight rise in pay, and a lot more responsibility. To this point there had been no doubt about his ability to lead men — or at least to be the most dominant one in a group of friends — it was just that the army was now giving him a chance to demonstrate that such ability could be useful in war.

As it happened, Chilla had landed in France at a particularly difficult time in the terrible saga of the Western Front. The Battle of the Somme had started on the first day of July 1916, as the Allies tried to punch through the German lines on a 12-mile front, north and south of the Somme River. On that first day the British — attacking heavily defended German positions across open ground — suffered 57,470 casualties, including 19,240 dead. Just under three weeks later, as part of the same battle, it was Australia's turn …

On the warm evening of 19 July, the Australian 5th Division attacked across a boggy 400 yards of open ground the entrenched German positions atop Fromelles ridge, at the behest of a British general for whom it seemed like a good idea at the time. It wasn't. One survivor, W.H. 'Jimmy' Downing, later recorded what happened. 'Stammering scores of German machine-guns spluttered violently, drowning the noise of the cannonade. The air was thick with bullets, swishing in a flat criss-crossed lattice of death … Hundreds were mown down in the flicker of an eyelid, like great rows of teeth knocked from a comb … Men were cut in two by streams of bullets [that] swept like whirling knives … It was the charge of the Light Brigade once more, but more terrible, more hopeless.'[10]

At rollcall after just the first catastrophic night, the 5th Australian Division had lost 5533 killed or wounded. Nevertheless, three more Australian divisions were thrown into the fray over the next few weeks, and another 23,000 Australian lives were lost or shattered.[11]

Into just such a scene of carnage and devastation did Kingsford Smith enter, when he arrived at the front on an evening in late July. If Marseilles had been a different world from Cairo and Gallipoli, *this* was a place beyond his previous imagination, even for one of his already horrifying experience. From the moment of his arrival on the front line, the air was riven by the man-made thunder of devastating artillery fire, and the muddy, bloody ground — where green meadows once had been — was torn apart as shells landed. Men screamed and died around him, while others sobbed openly, simply unable to go on. In his own dug-out on that first black night, Kingsford Smith lay, vainly hoping to catch some sleep, but it was soon apparent that this would be impossible, and he switched instead to trying to survive through the night, pressing himself tightly into the embrace of a mother earth that was herself shuddering with every fresh outrage of artillery fire that landed upon her. The dawn, the dawn, the dawn … would he ever see one again?

Somewhere near 4.30 am, the German artillery loaded their weapon of choice for killing Allied soldiers on the Western Front, a *Minenwerfer* — literally, mine thrower — capable of hurling across a short distance a 220- pound shell, of which 110 pounds were explosive, with devastating results. Following their strict routine, the German officer yelled above the cacophony of battle, '*Feeertig*!' (Reeady!) and then '*Feuer*!' (Fire!)

An instant later the gun erupted like an angry volcano, with the shell disappearing in a searing streak of flame into the darkness, as it was lobbed towards the Australian lines. Of course the Germans didn't know exactly where it would land, only that it would be right among those who had been sending exactly the same kind of devastation on them and theirs.

This particular shell, however, reached its peak perhaps some 500 yards ahead of where Charles Kingsford Smith lay, and then began its descent. Did it have his name on it? Too early to tell …

With every gust of wind and reverberation of air around it, the shell's descent slightly changed direction — every tiny such change making a huge difference as to exactly where it would land and detonate. In his dug-out, Kingsford Smith lay wide awake — *Had he really been so naïve as to think of war as simply an adventure? What on earth had made him come to the conclusion that nothing could be worse than Gallipoli?* Even over the sound of so many other exploding shells all around, he now heard a whistling, getting louder, screeching now, squealing … *was this it?* … and involuntarily flexed his whole body and covered his ears, as if that might possibly save him.

The shell landed in the soft, bloodied mud just 20 yards away from him and detonated an instant later, hurling earth and bodies everywhere. Much of the former and parts of the latter landed on Kingsford Smith and, for a split second, everything was indeed blackness, precisely as he feared death might be. But then he took stock. The fact that he wanted to breathe meant he wasn't dead. He was still alive, despite the weight of muck now upon him. Somehow, barely, he moved, and struggled to push his head up to the surface, managing to burst through to the open air once more to take big, gasping breaths, almost as though, *in extremis*, mother earth had given birth to him once more.[12]

Welcome to the Western Front.

Kingsford Smith did make dawn of that day, not that it provided much relief. And then he could actually see what he had only imagined the night before. It was all so much worse — mud, blood, barbed wire, grotesquely shattered corpses with eyes staring to eternity, men weeping, explosions near and far, and nothing, absolutely *nothing* resembling the world he once knew.

If there was one saving grace, it was that his job at the front allowed him periodic release from it, as he carried messages back and forth between headquarters and the front lines. (As a general rule, he loved the 'back' from the front lines part, and was less enamoured about the 'forth'.)

After all those years of hurtling his motorbike around the corners of the streets back home and the constant dashes between the pyramids proper and Cairo, now Charles Kingsford Smith came into his own, roaring from the front lines to various military headquarters usually at least a mile or two behind the fighting, and then back again. For one of the keys to being a good dispatch rider was *speed*, pure and simple, and given going fast was something he had always been interested in, during war or peace, he excelled from the first.

And yet, as good as he was at tearing along on his motorbike, dodging trenches, bunkers, bomb craters and the like to get the message through, danger was all around him. One afternoon, just a couple of weeks after arriving, he was tearing along when perhaps 30 yards in front of him a shell landed, throwing up an enormous wave of billowing mud and muck, not to mention whistling, scything shrapnel. There was no time to take evasive action and all he could do was to try to hold on as he headed into it, careering from one side to another … and then … finally … . across the road and into a ditch. Although shaken, the main thing was that he had survived by the barest of margins. And, as he was acutely aware, many didn't.

On another occasion that he would never forget, when intense artillery fire rained down upon a bit of earth which had recently served as a mass grave for German soldiers, their stinking, decomposing bodies were thrown to the surface, their death's-head grimaces scarring into his consciousness forever more. When the artillery stopped, a few Australian soldiers overcame their disgust long enough to dash forward to souvenir some of the buttons and other items from the German corpses, but Kingsford Smith was among those who simply couldn't stomach it.[13]

Surely, *surely* there was something better in this war than this?

Just maybe … For while Kingsford Smith and his mates had been in the trenches over the last two years in Gallipoli and on the Western Front, other Australians had been making a name for themselves in the air with the Australian Flying Corps. This antipodean version of the Royal Flying Corps had begun at Point Cook, just outside Melbourne, a couple of years earlier, on the strength of a pair of Royal Aircraft Factory BE2a two-seater biplanes and a duet of British-built single-seat Deperdussin monoplanes, two English flying instructors and a request for military volunteers who wanted to learn how to fly.

The first Australian pilots to see action had aided the Indian Army against the Turks in Mesopotamia from April 1915, and it had grown from there. No. 1 Squadron Australian Flying Corps had been formed in early 1916 and had operated with great success from, first, Egypt, and then the wider Middle East, and two more squadrons had been formed. As well as supporting the actions of the Australian Light Horse, some Australian pilots would go on to fly directly in the service of Colonel T.E. Lawrence, better known as 'Lawrence of Arabia'

— fomenting revolution among the Arabs, to attack the Turk's Ottoman Empire from within — and generally the Australians were regarded as 'top-drawer'. The work of these pilots was at least matched by Australians flying for the Royal Flying Corps in action against the Germans in France, and Whitehall wanted more of them.

So much so, that just before Kingsford Smith's unit had arrived at the Western Front alongside the British Expeditionary Forces, the Secretary of the War Office had written to AIF Headquarters in France, to the effect that, 'in view of the exceptionally good work which has been done in the Royal Flying Corps by Australian-born officers, and the fact that the Australian temperament is specially suited to the flying services, it has been decided to offer 200 commissions in the Special Reserve of the Royal Flying Corps to officers, non-commissioned officers, and men of the Australian Force ...'[14]

And so it was that on the fine morning of 21 September 1916, the sergeant major of Kingsford Smith's 4th Divisional Signal Company announced that applications were invited from those who wanted to transfer to the Royal Flying Corps.[15] This would entail going to Britain to train, before likely coming back to France as a fully fledged pilot going at the Hun. The option of applying was not something that the nineteen-year-old Kingsford Smith considered at all, if 'considering' can connote at least a small amount of time spent pondering.

'It was the chance of a lifetime,' he later recounted. 'It proved to be the chance of my flying life, and it was a decision I made without a moment's hesitation.'[16] He sent off his application that very afternoon.

Hundreds of others, of course, had the same idea, but for whatever reason Kingsford Smith's application was accepted within a week — the prevailing view that dispatch riders made good pilots would have helped — and before he knew it he and nearly 150 other Australians had been pulled from the front lines and sent by train to Flanders in Belgium, where they were to undergo further assessment.

For despite what Kingsford Smith had thought, he and the other applicants had not yet been fully accepted into the Royal

Flying Corps; they were still just a mere part of a wider squad and had to prove they were made of the right kind of stuff to grace His Majesty's Flying Corps. That much was apparent from the kind of questions they had to answer soon after arriving in Flanders.

Have you attended university?

Do you play polo?

What musical instruments do you play?

Do you sail?[17]

Now quite how being able to play polo was going to help you to fly a plane was not immediately apparent to any of them, but the Royal Flying Corps seemed to think it was important, so most of the Australians were happy to play along.

Polo? Of course! Who *didn't* play polo?

Did he play any musical instruments? Here, Kingsford Smith could be truthful and say that he played the piano, guitar, ukulele and harmonica.

Sailing? As a matter of fact, Captain Cook had been his grandfather, and he had been taught personally by the great man.

One way or another, Charles Kingsford Smith really did sail on through in a manner that would have made Captain Cook proud — Chilla's rather aristocratic, double-barrelled name wouldn't have hurt — and he was soon on his way to England. Immediately upon arrival at his first training base, on 16 November 1916, he proudly cabled his beloved parents to that effect:

> Address now, RFC Cadet Battalion. Denham, England. Well, love Smith.[18]

In fact, however, there still remained a fair way to go before he would be judged as the right stuff to get into the cockpit of an aircraft and begin to learn how to fly it, as was made clear by the commanding officer on the first day after he had formed the Australians up for a parade in the courtyard.

'You are,' the officer said, with only a small sniff of distaste, '*Australians.*'

So far, so good …

'You come to me from France, very fit, but — ahem — you want to forget all about flying. You are to be prepared as officers and — ahem — I trust, gentlemen. Good afternoon — er — gentlemen!'[19]

And so began ten weeks of studying everything from military law to hygiene, to types of German aircraft, to French customs, to topography and infantry training. (True, not all of the courses were related to flying, but one couldn't be a pilot unless one were an officer, what? And one couldn't be an officer unless one bally-well understood how the military worked at all levels, what?) They were to be prepared as 'officers and gentlemen', and would at least look the part, after being issued with their cadet uniform, which included a double-breasted tunic and a Glengarry cap with white puggarees.

Most of their training was hard work, often tedious, and deeply frustrating, in the sense that it was all just so many *preliminaries* and very far removed from what they had all signed up to do, which was to fly aeroplanes. And yet there was no way around it — if they didn't pass each and every exam that would be set for them, they simply wouldn't be allowed to go on to the next stage. More to the point, this would mean that their likely next port of call would be back in the trenches of France, whence they came. (It was amazing, how that could concentrate a man's mind when it came to memorising reams of dull infantry statistics, the essential contours of an Albatros, as opposed to a Fokker or Taube, and just what angle of ascent a Sopwith could manage before it would stall.)

There were other things to do besides study, of course. Many times, at the end of a long day's instruction, there would remain just one lonely figure pacing up and down the courtyard, his gasping breath making regular puffs of white in the cold night air as he kept going, hour after hour. That man, of course, was Charles Kingsford Smith. It always was. And his punishment was nearly always for the same transgression. While it was permissible to go into town on a pass, to have a drink and perhaps a carry-on with some of the local lasses, it was *not* permissible to return in the wee hours of the morning, no matter how clever you thought you were, or just how beautiful she was.[20]

Still, 'Smithy', as he was now known, always seemed to take it in fairly good cheer, on the reckoning that the odd punishment simply went with the fabulous territory he was in. On other nights the air cadets would sneak away and poach pheasant, and if successful, cook them so they could eat, drink and make merry, all in the comfort of their own barracks. Much of the 'making merry' involved standing around the piano and singing bawdy songs — an activity where, again, Smithy shone, much as he ever had, and he was one of the most popular men in the squadron.

Altogether, roar it out with Smithy!

Here's to the Kaiser, the son of a bitch,
May his balls drop off with the seven-year itch,
May his arse be pounded with a lump of leather,
Till his arsehole can whistle Britannia for Ever [21]

•

Meanwhile, at the Sopwith factory at Kingston-on-Thames, Harry Hawker was busy as never before. A small part of that busyness, true, was taking the delightful, the wondrous, the absorbing Muriel Peaty out for Sunday afternoon drives and the odd supper — at least when her rather conservative parents would allow it — but most of it was developing the new plane he had been feverishly working on. From his first days at Sopwith, Harry had prospered, and had gone from being a humble mechanic to a pilot, then test pilot, then *the* test pilot, then designer, then everything wrapped into one, to the point where no-one was sure if he was Tommy Sopwith's right-hand man or Tommy Sopwith was his. What was certain was that the Allies were in desperate need of a new plane to counter the Germans' Albatros and Fokker models — both of which were faster, more manoeuvrable and lethal than the Sopwith Scout — and Harry was pouring his heart and soul, his expertise and energy, into providing exactly that. Most days, between continuing his test flights, he worked at the drawing board in the company of a designer by the name of Herbert Smith trying to create a biplane that would embody every refined feature he had learnt from his years of flying and testing aeroplanes — as well as encompassing the things that fighter pilots were telling him they needed.

To enable the plane to climb quickly it would need to be light, in fact just half the weight of its contemporaries. For greater manoeuvrability the bulk of that weight — the engine, fuel, ammunition and pilot — had to be tightly packed near the centre of gravity, just forward of the cockpit. Hawker and Smith decided on a tiny fuselage that would be just 7 feet in length, while the wingspan would be a relatively short 28 feet. Power would come from a 130-horsepower Clerget 9B rotary engine. And then there were the guns. Two forward-mounted Vickers .303 machine guns would do the trick — making it the first British twin-gunned plane of the war — and the bulk of the Vickers would be contained within the body of the plane, directly in front of the pilot. That gave the otherwise clean lines of the plane forming up beneath their pencils something of a hump to rather resemble a camel, indeed a Sopwith camel …

•

In France, the war in the air was getting progressively bloodier. In August 1916, the *Oberste Heeresleitung*, the German Supreme Army Command, had embarked on a different tactical approach with its war planes. Instead of sending out patrols of two or three planes at a time from a generally fixed base, they decided to have their best fighters patrol together in packs of fifteen and sixteen planes. These larger squadrons — called *Jagdstaffeln*, for hunt squadrons, *Jastas* for short — were not attached to particular ground units; rather their charter was simply to engage in 'aggressive aerial warfare', to go where they could do the most damage, to roam along the front line, find the enemy planes and hunt them down. Most highly prized was when you could make an enemy plane crash after diving so steeply that it went into a vertical wreck, or *Fliegerdenkmal*, an aviator's memorial, as they laughingly called it.

The first *Jasta* was organised by Germany's greatest fighter ace, Oswald Boelcke, who had toured all over the front to hand-pick *die Besten der Besten*, (the best of the best), and then trained them to fly the way he flew. Of those selected, it had soon emerged that *the* best was the same Manfred von Richthofen who had previously looked upon all aircraft with contempt, but was now such an accomplished war pilot that he had shot down eighteen planes in his first four months in the air. A man of particular, if ruthless, style, after his first enemy 'kill' von Richthofen had arranged for a jeweller friend in Berlin to have a silver cup engraved with the date and the type of machine downed, and he had kept this practice up afterwards, to the point that he soon had to buy an additional cabinet to hold all the cups.

So successful was von Richthofen, and clearly such *ein geborener Führer* (a born leader), that he was given his own *Jasta* to command, and had immediately made his mark, both in terms of the numbers of Allied planes he and his squadron had shot out of the skies, and, again, in terms of his personal style.

For now that he was totally in charge, he decided to have whole sections of his plane, an Albatros DIII, painted glaring red. One reason was it just looked better, and he felt better flying around in it than in the rather drab olive-green and brown it had been when it came out of the factory. More practically, the new colour helped to make him instantly identifiable to his own ground forces, so as to minimise the risk of being shot down by them, and to his flying comrades when they were in dogfights. If it was equally true that the enemy would also come to know him well, then so be it. One way or another, he was soon a familiar figure in the hottest dogfights of *der Front im Westen* (the Western Front). The Germans came to call him *der rote Kampfflieger* (the red battle-flyer); the French to call him *le petit rouge* (the little red one); while in British, Australian and Canadian circles and in popular folklore for most of the next century, he would come to be known rather reverentially as — so stunning was his success — 'the Red Baron'.[22]

In England, where Charles Kingsford Smith continued to engage in his studies to become a fighter pilot himself, of course he and his fellow students soon came to hear of the Red Baron and his exploits. This was just as they had heard, and even studied, other German flyers such as Boelcke. Boelcke had established the *Dicta Boelcke*, a list of eight fundamental tactics of aerial warfare which ranged from 'try to keep the sun behind you' to 'always attack from the rear'. (Not that these helped to save Boelcke. On 28 October 1916, he was killed when he collided with one of his comrades, occasioning the RFC to drop a laurel wreath over his base with the message: '*To the memory of our brave and chivalrous opponent, from the British Royal Flying Corps.*'[23])

Then there was Max Immelmann, who had invented and perfected the 'Immelmann turn', an aerial manoeuvre to change direction by 180 degrees in as quick a time as possible. For their part, the French boasted great aces including Charles Nungesser and René Fonck, while on the English side there were the likes of Albert Ball, Mick Mannock, Billy Bishop and Jimmy McCudden. All of these men were legends of the skies, 'aerial knights', in the popular imagination. Though they were engaged in an activity that had only been effectively invented a couple of years earlier, somehow their exploits struck rapturous chords with all who contemplated them from whichever country, because their activity entailed everything: nationalism, daring, danger, adventure, technological wonder, individual combat, courage and derring-do. And so many men died in the battles of the skies it lent added glamour to those who survived …

Desperate to be of these heroes' number, Kingsford Smith kept studying hard, notwithstanding his continuing nocturnal activities, and after passing his exams at Denham, was sent with the other cadets to Oxford University where the next stage of instruction took place. Here he renewed his study of Morse code — a course he breezed through given his previous experience — as well as engaging in studies on aeroplane construction, army co-operation, reconnaissance, scout flying, the internal combustion engine, wireless operations, ground artillery, bomb-dropping, formation flying and patrol, Vickers and Lewis guns and so forth. Essentially, he and his fellow trainees were to learn everything there was to know about flying an aeroplane in wartime — how the fire of anti-aircraft artillery (known as 'Archie' to the pilots after a well-known British music hall sketch about Archie, 'a dog that didn't bite') couldn't really go above 3000 feet; what signals your squadron leader would give you if he wanted you to attack or withdraw; how to work out which way was east if your compass was broken and you couldn't see the sun; and so on — without *actually* flying. Would that day never come?!

Finally, yes.

One day in mid-March 1917, Catherine and William Kingsford Smith were beside themselves with joy to receive a cable with just a one-word message on it — *COMMISSIONED* — from their son Second Lieutenant Charles Kingsford Smith of the Royal Flying Corps. And yet, they were likely nowhere near as thrilled as Smithy himself.

That joy was compounded by an event that occurred when Smithy was in London on leave a few days later with a fellow trainee, Percy 'Skip' Moody. The two, in uniform, were just walking down Whitehall past a Life Guard in full regalia when they heard a sudden bang and bash, and were stunned to see the fellow raise his sword to *them* in a formal salute. It was then that it hit them. The Life Guard was doing that because they were no longer anonymous footsloggers from the trenches — they were dinkum *officers*![24]

And still there were many pleasures to come, for, shortly afterwards, the great day came when Smithy was posted to No. 8 Reserve Squadron, just outside the village of Netheravon near Salisbury Plain in the county of Wiltshire, where he was to receive his first practical instruction. On a slightly misty morning in March 1917 he turned up to meet his personal instructor, and immediately snapped off a smart salute. 'Good morning,' the young Australian greeted him. 'Can we start now?'

The instructor, old well beyond his tender years, who had been training up men to head off to their deaths for most of the last eighteen months, sighed wearily. If only these young pups had the first clue as to what their likely fate was, perhaps they wouldn't be so all-fired enthusiastic to get on with it.

'What's your name?'

'Kingsford Smith, sir.'

'Ever flown before?'

'No, sir, never …' Which was true, apart from a very brief flight he had had a few months before when a Flying Corps officer had broken regulations to give him a quick lift to Hendon, though Smithy had been nowhere near the controls.

'Well, listen carefully, Smith. You've been given all the ground instruction necessary, and by now you should know the important principles of flight.

'These things,' he continued, as they walked towards a particular Maurice Farman S.11 Shorthorn, 'are so noisy that we can't talk in the air …'

For the first time in his life, Charles Kingsford Smith climbed into the cockpit of a plane with intent, glorying in the feeling of putting his fingers around the joystick, the instrument by which the entire plane was controlled — a plane design which still owed much to the genius of the Wright brothers.

'This is the control column,' the instructor explained, quite unnecessarily. 'Pull it back and the nose rises; push it forward and the nose falls. Over to the left and the machine banks to the left. Got that?'

'Yes, I think so.' In fact, Kingsford Smith knew it all backwards, as for months now he had been studying the basic flight concepts and practising for this very moment by imagining a simple chair was a seat in the cockpit, and the walking stick he tightly held in his right hand was the joystick.

For another fifteen minutes or so, the instructor insisted that they remain stationary on the airfield while the Australian observed with his own eyes how the Farman changed its basic 'shape' depending on what he did with the controls. By pushing the joystick to the right, for example, he extended the ailerons on the right wing upwards and on the left wing, reciprocally, downwards, and so encouraging the machine to bank that way. The pilot's feet, resting on the rudder bar, could make the rudder at the back of the plane swivel to the right, meaning that the nose of the plane would be pushed to the right to balance the turn by counteracting the drag of the down-going aileron. And so it went.

At last they were ready. The instructor waved to a mechanic hovering nearby, who came and gripped the huge, two-bladed wooden propeller.

'Switches off,' the mechanic called.

'Switches off,' the pilot affirmed.

The mechanic pulled the propeller backwards a few turns to suck petrol vapour into the combustion chamber.

'Contact!'

'Contact!'

With which, the mechanic gave the propeller a mighty heave in the direction it needed to go. A cough, a gurgle, and then the engine caught! In an instant the motor gave the roar of a lion going in for the kill, blowing angry blue-white smoke out of its nostrils, and Kingsford Smith and his instructor were caught in the blast of air drawn over them by the whirling propeller. A wave from the instructor and the chocks in front of the wheels were removed, allowing the plane to roll forwards. Kingsford Smith could just hear the instructor's words over the howling motor behind them: 'Remember! Only make very slight movements on the controls. Nothing too jerky. I'll take off, and then you try and follow my movements while I fly straight and level …'[25]

The propeller continued to whirl, flashing in the soupy morning light and the whole machine began to vibrate — either from the pounding engine itself or perhaps Kingsford Smith's thundering heart, he wasn't sure. One way or another, the vibration lessened as the instructor allowed the plane to do what it clearly wanted to do, which was to get faster, and faster still, with the air now flowing over the wings with such speed that they began to vibrate and hum and *sing* and lift and … and then came the moment.

Some 150 yards down the field, first the nose started to lift and then the rattling and bumping stopped and … then …

Quickly Kingsford Smith looked down to find that the earth was falling away and even as the suddenly fierce cold wind slapped his face, flapped the sides of his loosely strapped helmet, pulled on his scarf and blew into every crevasse of his uniform … they were flying. *Flying!*

It was at just such a point that some of his fellow cadets had frozen with fear and gurgled a half-strangled request to be taken back down … please … *now*! Others had experienced such discomfort that they knew that flying was not for them, and resolved to get away from it as soon as possible. For Kingsford Smith, however, the primary emotion, even as he experienced a slightly uncomfortable popping sensation in his ears, was pure, unadulterated *joy*. Flying was an exhilaration such as he had never known — not even racing his motorbike full pelt along the curves of Rangers Road in Mosman, or breaking the speed record on the trip from the pyramids to Cairo. That, in retrospect, was mere tiddlywinks. This, *this* was an entirely different world, a world of billowing white clouds that you could simply zoom through or over, of a sun shining more brightly than he had ever seen it, of the landscape below looking like a patchwork of fields, farms, towns and tiny laneways, in which, as he wrote to his parents, 'roads and streams are just weak streaks of light, houses are tiny squares, and forests patches of moss';[26] below him lay a vast map upon which seemingly little earth-bound pygmies called people were making their way … and Smithy and the pilot soared back and forth above them, free as birds.

And if it was this wonderful just to be a passenger in a plane, how amazing would it be to have command of one of his own, to actually be the pilot himself? The young Australian couldn't wait and, once back on the ground, began to count the hours, the days, until he would be able to receive instruction to learn to fly solo.

Thinking back on that first instructional flight afterwards, he would long be struck by just how *secure* he felt high in the sky. Somehow, it had seemed like the place he was meant to be, and he felt quite safe in the cockpit, and for Kingsford Smith, by the middle of April 1917, the time had come — after little more than a dozen hours' dual instruction — to take a plane skywards under no-one's control but his own.

Into the cockpit. Flying helmet fastened. Gloves on. A waggling of his joystick to ensure that all was as it should be. And then the polite, ritualised exchange with the mechanic …

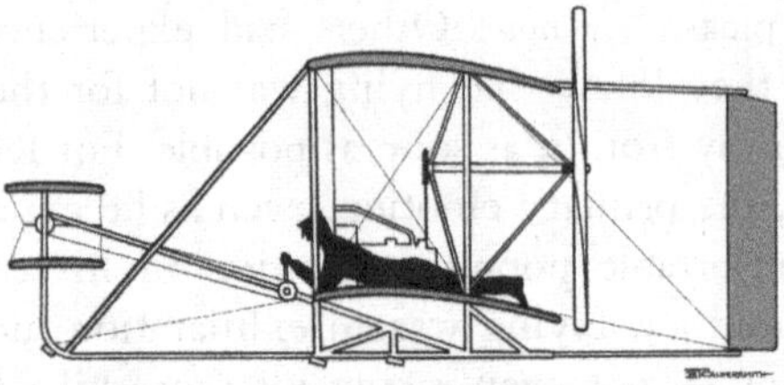

1. Wright Flyer (1903): biplane, centre-mounted engine, twin pusher propellers driven by chains, pitch control by front-mounted canard surface, short tail with twin rudders, roll control via wing warping.

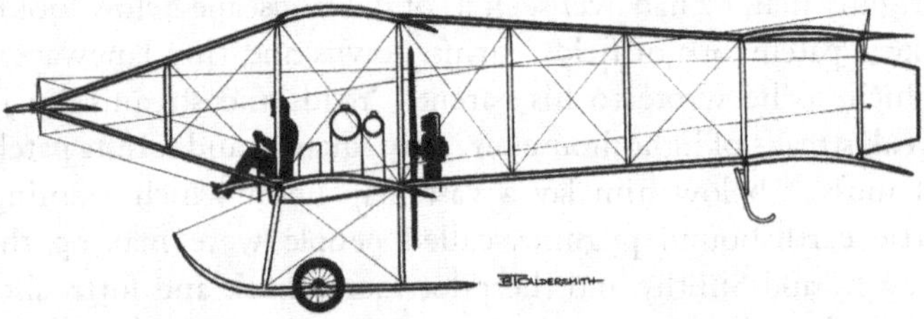

2. Box-kite type Voisin, Farman, Bristol (1908–1910): biplane, single pusher propeller, direct drive, pitch control by front-mounted canard surface, long tail with multiple rudders, control roll evolved to ailerons by Henri Farman.

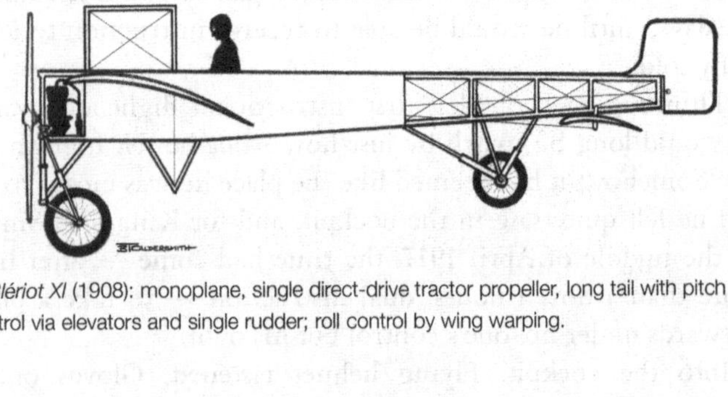

3. *Blériot XI* (1908): monoplane, single direct-drive tractor propeller, long tail with pitch control via elevators and single rudder; roll control by wing warping.

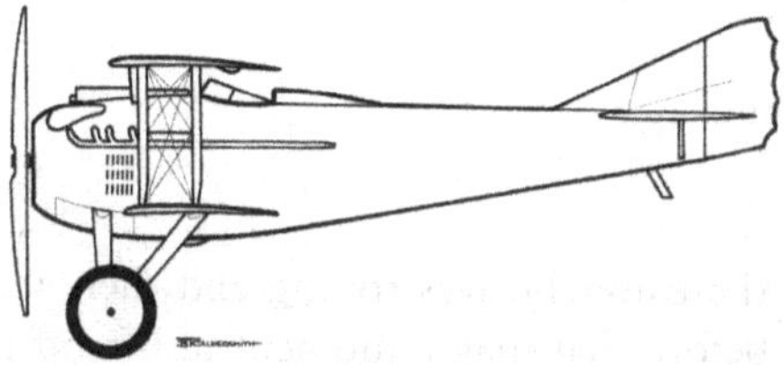

4. SPAD (1916): biplane military fighter, single tractor engine, single machine gun, long tail with pitch control via elevators and rudder; roll control by ailerons. Flown by Smithy in RFC No. 19 Squadron World War I in France.

5. Sopwith Camel (1916): biplane military scout, single tractor engine, twin machine guns, long tail with pitch control via elevators and rudder; roll control by ailerons. Flown by RFC and RNAS squadrons during World War I in France.

'Switch off.'
'Switch off.'
'Petrol on ...'
'Petrol on ...'
'Suck in ...' and ...
'Contact, sir!'
'Contact!'

And shortly thereafter he was rolling and then accelerating down the strip before that magic moment of lift-off in a plane under solely his own control.

For this first solo flight — beginning at 7.15 am on 15 April 1917 — Charles Kingsford Smith followed his instructions the best he could, and after take-off circled the field twice before easing the throttle back to come in for a landing. At least he tried to throttle back. And he also tried to come in for a landing. Somehow, though, it was less than a 'landing' and more of a 'crashing', as his wheels collapsed beneath him and he skidded his screeching way to a stop.

Into his logbook that evening Kingsford Smith wrote enthusiastically 'FIRST SOLO', and beneath that, with apparent good humour, 'CRASHED!' No matter: the saying among pilots at the time was that 'no pilot is any good until he has broken wood',[27] and, as it happened, Kingsford Smith was not the only subsequently famous aviator to have a rather unprepossessing beginning on his first time solo. As a matter of fact, Baron von Richthofen himself had also had a difficult time of it. On his own first solo flight he had neglected to throttle back enough and made his approach to the landing field far too fast, with his left wing too low. The result was that instead of gliding smoothly back to earth on a gentle enough angle that the plane's wheels could caress it, he smashed into the ground and everything gave way in a scream of wrenching steel, torn struts and flying bits and pieces. What had been a plane was now just a mess. Remarkably, a devastated von Richthofen was still able to walk away from it.

Not to worry, his commanding officer had told him, smiling wryly. '*Üb weiter.*' (Keep practising.) Which von Richthofen did, although he was to fail his first examination a fortnight later.

Alas for the Allies, those days of failure by the Red Baron were long gone. And while Kingsford Smith's April solo made it a great month for him personally, it was a grievously bloody month for the Royal Flying Corps, far and away their worst on record. The cynical press called the pilots and their BE2c craft 'Fokker Fodder' and it was in no small part because of the Red Baron.

As the Allies launched a two-pronged offensive on the Western Front, with the British attacking at Arras and the French on the Aisne, British forces relied on their air arms to do heavy reconnaissance and artillery spotting work, providing superb hunting for the likes of the Red Baron and his *Jasta 11*.

By this time, Manfred von Richthofen's younger brother, Lothar, who was also in *Jasta 11*, had convinced him that having the only plane on the Western Front painted red made him a target like no other, and that as his fame grew the Allies would seek him out and destroy him at any cost. The solution was for all pilots in von Richthofen's *Jasta* to have their planes painted red, with some minor variations on each one. Lothar's red plane had yellow trimmings; Schäfer painted the back of his fuselage and rudder black; while Karl Allmenröder had a daub of white on his plane's nose; Kurt Wolff used green and so on.[28] Soon, other *Jasta*s followed suit with different colours, most particularly those that came under von Richthofen's command, for with his continued success he was quickly given control of other squadrons.

Only the Red Baron's Albatros remained insolently in all red, quickly identifiable to his flying comrades, but no longer the sole target that he had been. And so was born von Richthofen's 'Flying Circus', so called by the Allies because of the bright colours that were now flying around all over the skies of France, before returning to their canvas hangars at night, not unlike circus tents. Wherever the fighting was heaviest, so would be the Circus, with von Richthofen in the lead.

In the month of April 1917, alone, von Richthofen's *Jasta 11* shot down eighty-nine Allied planes, of which the Red Baron personally accounted for twenty-one.

•

Some of those shot from the skies would, of course, live to fly again. One such survivor was a big bear of a man, a West Australian by the name of Norman Brearley, who had achieved great renown within his squadron of the Royal Flying Corps for his daring manoeuvre to bring down a heavily defended German observation balloon. Soaring way above it, he had intentionally stalled his plane by lifting its nose with insufficient throttle, pushing his foot down hard on the rudder bar at the exact moment the engine stopped and then, with his joystick pulled back, steeled himself. Sure enough, in an instant his plane was spinning earthwards as if it had been hit, and was now out of control and not worth wasting any more ammunition on. Only at the last second, still above the balloon, did Brearley kick the rudder again and then push forward on his joystick to bring the plane back under control and level out a little, just in time to fire his machine guns on the balloon from close quarters and blow it out of the skies. The force of the explosion shook his plane frightfully, but he survived.

Only a few short weeks later, however, Brearley took a bullet from ground fire through both of his lungs, and this sent him into a crunching crash-landing in the middle of no-man's-land. Crawling out of the wreckage more dead than alive, the 26-year-old was saved by a brave Scottish soldier who crawled under fire to retrieve him, and upon medical examination was told he would never fly again.

Well, he'd see about that. Sent home as an invalid, at every port that his ship stopped at on the way back to Perth, he dived over the side and swam back and forth alongside the vessel, and underwater for as long as he could, determined to strengthen his lungs ...[29]

Instruction continued. By May 1917, Kingsford Smith was training in a SPAD S.VII, a single-seater biplane fighter from the Sociéte Pour l'Aviation et ses Dérivées, Blériot's factory in the 15th arrondissement of Paris. It was a plane that had already achieved great success on the Western Front, most particularly in the hands of the French hero Georges Guynemer. (Guynemer was, in fact, such a hero that when he died, French school children were taught that he had flown so high that he simply could not come down again.) True, it was said of the SPAD that if ever you lost engine power it had 'the gliding angle of a brick', but while so ever the engine worked it could be a very effective weapon.

Now that Kingsford Smith and his fellow cadets could actually fly a plane, the next thing they needed to learn was how to shoot down the enemy. In subsequent weeks they were taught how to fly in staggered formation (six planes, for example, would usually fly in two Vs, with one above and behind the other); how to follow the signals of the squadron leader as in, when he waggled his wings once it was a signal to attack, twice and it was time to withdraw, and so forth.

As to how to manoeuvre so as to best shoot down other planes, this was most particular. The essential idea was to be able to swoop down on your opponent from above, in a position where the enemy pilot would be powerless to see you approaching and you could simply shoot them out of the skies. If the enemy plane had an observer with a machine gun then the same thing applied — if you came at it from the tail, the observer wouldn't be able to fire at you for fear of shooting off his own tail. There was also, of course, instruction in how to prevent exactly the same happening to you, and how to take evasive action when one found oneself under attack.

The key to a lot of the manoeuvres was *speed* and *height*. If in doubt, the pilots were advised to go fast and go high. The faster and higher you went the less likely it was that the enemy 'dog' could get up behind you. And the higher you went the more you could see, and your height could always be converted to even more speed. If you spied anything below, you could dive down upon it 60 per cent faster than the speed of level flight. If you needed to get away when under attack yourself, diving down would gain you maximum velocity.

Now, whatever else happens, '*Beware the Hun in the Sun!*' Remember that just as you will want to swoop down from on high, so too will the enemy want to do the same, so as you fly, keep glancing skywards for any sign of them. Their preference will be to attack you with the sun directly behind them, making them effectively invisible in the glare.

There were so many things to learn, and so little time to learn them in, and yet, though studying hard was not really in his nature, Kingsford Smith applied himself as never before. This was not some dull conjugation of Latin verbs; this was perhaps the difference between life and death.

Chaps, if you are hit and find yourself spinning towards earth, one thing is extremely important: a pilot's instinct when in a spin is to *pull back* on the joystick to try to bring the nose up and flatten out, but you mustn't do that. When spinning downwards, you must understand the wings are no longer producing sufficient lift, and the aerodynamic forces on your plane have changed to the point where the correct response to get out of it is counterintuitive. Indeed, back in 1914, an Australian chap by the name of Harry Hawker risked his own life in a Sopwith Pup over Brooklands to prove that when you are in a spin you must push the joystick *forward* (after applying pressure on the rudder opposite to the direction in which you are spinning), and that is your best chance of bringing the plane back under control. As a matter of fact, if you really master the art, you could even use it as an evasive manoeuvre to lose height rapidly so that any enemy plane that tries to match your spin and follow you will be incapable of drawing a bead on you, and the current reckoning was that the German planes were likely to experience structural failure when diving at high speed if the pilot chose not to spin with you, so you were a winner every way.

And so it went. The course was not easy — in fact it was so arduous and dangerous that over one-third of Kingsford Smith's class did not complete it through failure, injury or death.

Nevertheless, finally, after all the training was done, the great day came in early June 1917 when Smithy was posted to No. 23 Squadron and was on his way to the Western Front to actually fly against the Germans! True, there would be still a little more training to do once they got there, but the main thing was that No. 23 Squadron was initially based by an airstrip next to la Lovie Chateau, on the beautiful flat farmland, just 8 miles to the north-west of the Belgian town of Ypres, where the battles on the Western Front were at their most vicious. Initially, No. 23 Squadron's role — commensurate with their official motto

'Always on the Attack'[30] — would be to fly over the lines to attack both German troops and observation balloons, as well as whatever enemy planes they came across.

Was Smithy perhaps a little unrealistic in his expectations of what awaited him? Perhaps. At the very least, the commanding officer of the squadron, Major Wilkinson, decided it was necessary to take him in hand before he went on active duty and tell it to him straight.

'Now listen, young fellow,' the old man said, in words that Smithy would never forget. 'You're going to die. In fact, you're as good as dead now. Do you know that we are losing three men a day from this outfit, and every one of them are young fools like you? You can't fly. You know nothing of aerial warfare and you are due to go out like a lamp. The ones who live are the ones who obey orders. Get this, and get it once and for all. Obey your patrol leader always. If you lose your patrol mates in the air, turn and fly straight back here. Do that for weeks until you know something about your machine and something about this bloody business we're at, and then you might have a chance of doing some good in the squadron.'[31]

Oh yes, and welcome to France.

Though of course he was slightly anxious about what might await him, one thing that continued to give Kingsford Smith confidence and a curious kind of faith that he would be okay, whatever the major said, was his treasured photo of Nellie Stewart, which he was careful to put as a talisman in every plane that he flew. Others, of course, in the Royal Flying Corps and in the Australian Flying Corps had their own good luck charms, which included everything from small boomerangs, guaranteed to make sure they would return, to models of 'lucky' black cats to rabbits' feet.

Similarly, German pilots had very strong beliefs in the protective powers of things such as four-leaf clovers, small models of pink pigs and of chimneysweeps complete with a brush and ladder. Others still believed in toys of poisonous red mushrooms with white dots, while still more thought that carrying a one *Pfennig* coin in your pocket could help keep the bullets from your plane.

Manfred von Richthofen did not believe in any of them. In fact, when once someone suggested a charm, he was quick with his reply. 'I have a most effective talisman,' he said sharply. 'My Spandaus …'[32]

And when it came to using those Spandau machine guns, he also had very specific ideas, often in sharp contrast to those of his compatriots. Other pilots would no sooner see an enemy plane than their guns would start chattering, sending out a spray of bullets in the hope that one or several would strike a devastating blow. Not the Red Baron. Habitually, he held his fire until right upon the enemy and only squeezed the trigger when he was all but certain of hitting the petrol tank, which was his usual target, and certainly what he taught those in his *Jasta* to do. He had no interest in spraying the whole plane and hoping that it would be disabled when just one bullet in the petrol tank was a near guarantee that it would be a blazing wreck and victory would be his.

The *Jasta*s commanded by the Red Baron continued to exact a terrible toll on the Allied pilots, and Kingsford Smith had arrived on the Western Front at a particularly bloody time. In many squadrons, including that of the still only twenty-year-old Australian, the casualty rate — in terms of pilots killed and wounded — was running at 25 per cent *a week*. A 'veteran' was anyone who had managed to survive for longer than a month.

Five

ACES AT DAWN ...

We were a carefree, cigarette smoking, leave seeking lot of young devils, who feared nothing; except being brought down behind enemy lines ...

CHARLES KINGSFORD SMITH[1]

The glorious thing in the flying service is that one is a perfectly free man and one's own master as soon as one is up in the air...

THE RED BARON, FREIHERR MANFRED VON RICHTHOFEN[2]

Showtime ...

More specifically, it was time for 'dawn show', as the pilots called early morning missions over enemy lines. In his French-made SPAD plane Kingsford Smith went out on this, his first mission on the early morning of 14 July 1917, flying through air so thick and warm it could have been fresh cream. Certainly he was excited to be a part of the mission but also a bit nervous, as he streaked above the flashes of khaki uniforms he could see below which were the men in the muddy, bloody trenches of their own lines he knew so well from his own experience, and then an instant later glimpsed the grey uniforms of the Germans. As he passed over the enemy, puffs of black smoke appeared all around and his plane was briefly buffeted by the explosions of 'Archie' just below, the Hun's way of saying welcome to this part of the war. (A curiosity of the anti-aircraft artillery fire, he soon discovered, was that while the German 'Archie' exploded with puffs of black smoke, the Allied puffs were generally white.) Doing his best to stay in formation with the rest of his squadron of seven planes, he was also scanning the horizon for enemy aircraft and quickly learnt his first lesson. That was that no matter how carefully you scanned every cloud and the far horizon for any sign of the Hun, it was no guarantee that you would get fair warning of being under attack. For suddenly, seemingly out of nowhere, as No. 23 Squadron cruised at 11,000 feet, a circus of German aircraft was all over them, firing and manoeuvring to get into position to shoot them down without exposing their own *Rückseiten* (backsides), as targets. A mad scramble of twisting, turning planes ensued, rolling, looping, diving, climbing and slipping away. Kingsford Smith did his best and even fired his guns at one German plane that momentarily came into his sight. But when his guns jammed, there was nothing for it but to race away from the rising sun and head west, back to his own lines, pursued by three German planes the whole way. Mercifully, the Germans didn't want to continue the pursuit once the Australian was above his own 'Archie', and Kingsford Smith was able to return safely to base, notwithstanding the fact that he had bullet holes all over his SPAD, with around a dozen near where his head had been.

Now 'blooded' for battle, a little more experienced and relieved to be still alive — there were many, many pilots who didn't even survive their first day on the Western Front — the young Australian pilot was slightly more confident when he went out the following day. This time he was with seven other planes and he felt a surge of bloodlust when they saw twenty German planes coming directly for them at an altitude of 8000 feet. The squadron leader waggled his wings in the manner that gave the signal to attack and in an instant they were again in the thick of it.

It was an exceedingly odd thing that despite everything happening in a blur of movement, time almost seemed suspended, with each second passing like the slow dripping of honey. In one such moment of suspended time, a German aircraft appeared right before him. Kingsford Smith zeroed in, squeezed the trigger and fired perhaps fifty shots straight at the pilot. He then had the satisfaction — and it really was that — of seeing the Hun pilot throw his arms in the air and fall back, as his plane began to tumble out of the sky. Going down, getting faster, until the German plane was billowing black smoke in a sickly corkscrew for the ground. Had the pilot been alive after those first few seconds, there was no chance whatsoever he could have survived the crash.

Strangely, although Kingsford Smith had just killed a man, it didn't feel like that, as though he had just ended the life of some mother's son. Rather, he had 'bagged my first Hun',[3] as he proudly put it in a letter to his own mother the following day. True, his gun had jammed immediately afterwards, and he had had to 'tootle off home', but it had been a great beginning.

Day after day, the squadron went out on sorties and returned an hour or two later. Sometimes the men would be intact, with as many returning as had gone out. Other times they would be missing a few men. Night after night they would sit at the dinner table in the mess hall and where the evening before someone had been laughing and joking and singing and telling riotous stories, there would now be an empty chair. Those chairs would fill up soon enough as freshly trained pilots arrived from England, and now America, but many of these men would quickly be gone too. Killed. Shot out of the skies and frequently plunging to their deaths in the middle of flaming wrecks.

How did the survivors cope in such circumstances? Only just. Generally, they drank a lot of alcohol. After all, they were the key players in a game in which the stakes could not be higher. They were playing for both their lives and often the destiny of entire battles and the lives of many men below. When their friends played that game and lost, or they played that game and won, one way or another did they not deserve a drink, or ten? Kingsford Smith certainly felt that way. You flew, you fought, you returned to earth and you could scarcely credit that you had survived. You found out who of your comrades had been killed — often gazing to the east as the twilight deepened, *willing* a particular plane to appear — you drank the better part of the night away, and the following day you did it all again.

The carnage went on and the only place where it was worse than in the air was on the ground, where artillery shells continued to land and bullets fly and men died on a daily basis in numbers never before seen in warfare — with a total of

2250 troops being killed on all sides on an average day on the Western Front.

•

On the last day of July 1917, just a few short weeks after Kingsford Smith had arrived in France, the Battle of Passchendaele began, with the Allies making a concerted effort to break through the Western Front, shatter the German lines and push on to the German submarine bases in Belgium. (Part of the urgency to do this was the fear that after the Russian Revolution in February, it would not be long before the Russian war effort collapsed, enabling all the German soldiers on the Eastern Front in Russia to return to the Western Front, whereupon the war would be lost for the Allies.)

All five Australian divisions in France were thrown into the assault to capture the key Belgian village of Passchendaele, which heavily armed veteran German troops defended from the top of a series of ridges on which they had constructed many thick concrete pillboxes. On the front side of the ridges were trenches manned by more German soldiers. Behind the ridges lay heavy German artillery, ready to lob high-explosive shells into the valleys of thick mud soaked with the blood of those who had already died trying to make the breakthrough. Over days, and then weeks, and then months, the Allied soldiers continued their assault. On a good day only hundreds of them were killed. The conditions were straight from Dante's *Inferno.*

In the middle of it all, one man particularly stood out — George Wilkins. His route to the Western Front had been a circuitous one. Returning south from the Arctic Circle on foot over 600 miles, he eventually came around Alaska by boat, landed in Ottawa, thence travelled overland to New York before boarding a ship to cross the Atlantic. En route the ship was sunk by a German U-boat. Rescued, Wilkins got to London, and then took the long haul home, by ship down the West African coast to Cape Town and thence across to South Australia. After seeing his mother and settling his father's estate, Wilkins journeyed to the headquarters of the Australian Flying Corps at Point Cook, just outside Melbourne, and applied for a position based on his previous flying experience.

Though nearly excluded because of his colour blindness, the intervention of a kind senior officer saw him quickly receive his commission as a second lieutenant, albeit in a non-operational flying position. Once back in England, when he had presented himself as ready to fly, there had been a big problem. Courtesy of a touch of frostbite from his years in the Arctic he walked with a pronounced limp.

'Your feet are in a hopeless condition,' he was informed gravely by one of the military doctors. 'You did not have medical attention in time, and now it is too late. Nothing can be done. You will never be able to walk properly again.'

Wilkins quietly retorted that his faithful feet were good enough to get him 600 miles across Arctic ice at the rate of 15 miles a day, so he didn't think they would be a worry, but the Australian Flying Corps doctor would not be moved. Regulations were regulations.

In the end, not to worry. His unique background and set of skills had quickly seen him recommended for service as an official photographer with the Australian War Records Section of the AIF to record the Australian experience from right in the heat of the battle — and it was possible he could do a bit of flying as a part of that. So it was that, in the company of two other men who were quickly establishing themselves as legends in their field — the journalist–writer Charles E.W. Bean and the photographer Frank Hurley — Wilkins had turned up at Passchendaele and quickly got to work. While Hurley's job was to capture iconic photographs that could be used for propaganda purposes, Wilkins's task was to record photographically what *actually* happened on the front lines. There could have been few men better equipped to do it, though Wilkins was shocked by what he was seeing and recording.

'It seemed like a trip into hell,' he later recounted. 'That black night lighted by flames of guns and by signal flares, the air shaking with noise, and the earth shaking underfoot. Human beings seemed insignificant in the midst of all this. It didn't seem possible that men could go through it and live.'[4]

And maintain a sense of humour, to boot. On that first night Wilkins was stunned to hear a Digger tell the story of a wounded, mud-covered Tommy, who was said to have told his comrades, 'I wish I could go back to Blighty and work in a munitions factory. Just think of those blokes getting five bob a day for making those shells — and us getting only one bob for stopping the gorblimey things!'[5]

Within hours, as he recorded, Wilkins knew exactly how the Tommy felt, and yet his own courage never wavered. He was to become a familiar figure to the troops over the following weeks, always with a camera in hand, traipsing along trenches, limping blithely across no-man's-land as shells burst around him. He visited field hospitals, slipped into dugouts and rambled respectfully through freshly dug battlefield graveyards, capturing it all on film. Sometimes he would hitch a ride on a plane to get aerial shots of the trenches, but more often he was with the troops in the mud and blood, the death and destruction. Twice he found himself in action so thick he had to put down the camera and get involved himself, and on both occasions he won the Military Cross for his trouble. The commanding Australian of the campaign, General John Monash, called him, 'the bravest man in my command'.[6]

Only once, by Wilkins's own reckoning, did he come close to losing his nerve. One night he was with six soldiers moving towards the front line along a wooden 'duckboard' above the sucking mud. Shells were exploding all around, and bullets flying, but they kept going. And then a shell exploded a little way in front of them, hurling shrapnel into the night. One piece of shrapnel hit the leading man in Wilkins's party right in the neck and so neatly took off his head that it plopped atop the post that had been right beside him when he died. That head now stared back at them.

'All the rest of us roared with hysterical laughter to see his head there, stuck upon the post. At the moment it seemed hilariously funny.'[7]

•

In his time in France, Kingsford Smith met many famous pilots, but few impressed him as much as France's most famous ace, Charles Nungesser. The blond 25-year-old, known as 'the fighting pilot's fighting pilot', and a lady-killer to beat them all, had about him an aura, a *savoir-vivre* on the ground, and *savoir-faire* in the air, that was simply mesmerising.

Stories about him and his plane — famously decorated on both sides with a drawing of a coffin flanked by candles, atop a black heart resting on a skull and crossbones — were the talk of Paris. What about the time he took on three German planes at once, and shot down two of them before taking on the third in such an amazing fashion? As his own undercarriage had been shot to pieces, the fearless Frenchman had manoeuvred the surviving German Albatros close to the ground and then *driven* his plane down on top of it, effectively bulldogging it to the ground! Then, when the German had jumped out and tried to set fire to both planes, Nungesser had run towards him and felled the Hun with just one punch.

'What kind of madmen do you Frenchman have as flyers?' the German flyer asked once he was safely in custody, seemingly more outraged by the punch than being shot down.

'Some say,' the smiling French officer is said to have replied, 'that he is completely mad. Others call him a genius. I think he is a little of both.'[8]

Whatever he was, Nungesser continued to bring down German planes at an astonishing rate, and yet he was equally famous for his nocturnal activities on the ground. He was the embodiment of the swaggering 'knight of the air' and his conquests were legendary. He had taken Mata Hari to bed before her arrest for espionage, and managed to feed her a story about a new French plane under construction with *eight* supercharged engines, which she had duly passed on to Berlin. He could drink any man under the table in the sweet Parisian night, and still be on the airstrip at dawn, ready to take down another vicious German, if not two.

Once, early in his flying career, he had disobeyed orders, leaving his post on the ground to go skywards and take on eight German planes which were reported to be approaching Nancy in north-eastern France. As it turned out, he threw himself into the fray with such gusto that he brought one plane down and made the others scatter.

The following day, he was hauled before his commanding officer. 'Lieutenant Nungesser,' the colonel said. 'What would you do to an officer who deserted his post?'

'Sir,' Nungesser replied evenly, 'if he destroyed an Albatros with a primitive Voisin, and made seven others run for their lives, he deserves the Croix de Guerre.'

'I agree,' the colonel had replied. 'The Croix de Guerre — plus sixteen days' arrest.'[9]

Nungesser famously bowed low and replied: '*Mon colonel, vous êtes trop genereux.*' Another fifteen decorations were to follow his aerial conquests — with decorations unknown for his even more outstanding amorous conquests — and though he frequently took outrageous risks, and had many crashes which resulted in shocking injuries, somehow he survived them all, to keep climbing skywards and taking on the Germans.

•

Kingsford Smith had arrived in France with a squadron of sixteen pilots, and after one month there were only three of them left. Under that kind of pressure, many a surviving pilot lost his nerve and mentally collapsed, certain that to take to the skies would mean his own demise. Kingsford Smith did not, and though in letters home he sometimes referred to problems with his 'nerves',[10] he kept going.

And on this occasion, on the early morning of 10 August 1917, when Smithy was flying back towards the safety of his own lines, keeping an eye out for potential trouble, he spotted something interesting …

On his starboard quarter, about a mile ahead and as far below, he could see a German plane just coming into Allied territory. Nudging his joystick forward, the Australian pilot quickly swooped and aimed towards the spot where he judged the German would be in forty-five seconds. It turned out he had judged it almost perfectly and opened fire before the poor bastard knew what hit him. Certainly, Kingsford Smith took some peppered flak from the German Archie as they tried to save their man, but it was to no avail. Smithy had the great satisfaction of seeing his quarry hit the ground and turn over. It was a confirmed 'kill'.

No matter the slight damage inflicted by the Archie, Kingsford Smith was in the mood to continue, and he flew on, looking for other enemy planes he might attack. Shortly thereafter, well into German territory, he noticed something strange about a particular section of road. It was oddly sunken, with the shattered remains of massive poplar trees lining both sides. But what was that black stuff on it? He looked closer …

Could that be a black mass of humanity? Soldiers, in full kit, resting? *German* soldiers? Nosing down, he realised it was exactly that — German soldiers on their way to the front, having a brief rest — and made an instant decision. He would attack! Cutting the engines so he could glide in quietly closer before they were fully aware of his presence, his ears were suddenly filled with the pleasant sound of the wind rushing over his wings.[11]

And then Charles Kingsford Smith, a twenty-year-old Australian flyer, became a veritable angel of death. At a velocity of just over 100 miles per hour, he swooped down on the Germans and held his fire until he was so close he simply couldn't miss … *Now!*[12]

The instant his fingers tightened on the triggers, his two machine guns started spitting lead, and before him dozens, upon *dozens*, of German soldiers were simply flung every which way by his bullets.[13] Many of them tried to run out of the way, but they were too densely packed upon each other in the culvert and there was no room to move. He couldn't miss! And he didn't.

Screaming now — some kind of primeval shriek that came from deep within him — he kept his guns furiously spitting death for the entire length of the culvert, even as angry flashes from below indicated that some of the soldiers were firing their rifles back at him. Kingsford Smith didn't care. Perhaps it was his own experience of trench warfare that possessed him — and the knowledge that every one of these Germans he killed might mean one fewer to kill his mates — but *something* got into him at this moment that he would never quite be sure of.

Perhaps bloodlust …

Executing a tight turn and swooping even lower, he came back for a second run and, shrieking all the while, did exactly the same from the opposite direction. The dozens of prone blobs on the road that didn't try to scramble to safety clearly marked the results of his previous run, but still the Germans were packed so tightly against the unforgiving walls of the culvert that there remained plenty of targets, and he had no hesitation in emptying his chambers upon them, still possessed by an unearthly joy all the while.

Die, you bastards.

And die they did. For good measure, the young Australian pilot then dropped some incendiaries on huts and set fire to them ...

Still possessed by a kind of incandescent and bloody joy which he had never experienced before, Kingsford Smith flew back to his base, landed ... rolled to a stop ... and turned his engine off. Suddenly, all was silent on this bright, beautiful day, apart from the distant rumble from artillery shells exploding on the front lines, which was so constant you barely noticed it. Birds were singing. Somewhere in the distance he could hear men laughing and talking, one of the mechanics in the hangar over yonder was whistling as he worked on the engine of a nearby SPAD ...

What had he done?

What had he done?

Had he really just taken the lives of dozens of men, been the cause of dozens of death-knocks on dozens of doors across Germany, families being told that their husband, father, son, brother, nephew, cousin was dead? Had *he* really done that?

He had.

Whatever deathly mania had possessed him was now entirely gone, leaving in its place revulsion, sheer revulsion for his act. Climbing shakily out of his plane, he leant against the fuselage and vomited. And vomited some more. And kept vomiting until he was dry-retching, trying to expel the last of this thing that had taken hold of him.

Barely out of his teens, he had just killed many men and hadn't the *faintest* idea why. For those few minutes he must have gone completely insane, and now he felt utterly miserable because of it; hated his own weakness for doing what he had done.[14]

In Dayton, the granddaddy of aviation, Orville Wright, was equally appalled. 'What a dream it was,' he wrote, 'what a nightmare it has become.'[15] While Lord Northcliffe, who had maintained a correspondence with Orville's sister, Katharine, wrote ruefully, 'I do not suppose that Wilbur and Orville realised the part their work would play in modern warfare. You have probably read of the harrowing experiences of flying men. A great many have been killed ...'[16]

•

While the business of being a war pilot was clearly a bitter and bloody one, as well as most likely fatal, still the number of those wanting to join the ranks of the 'angels of death' were legion. So exciting was the notion of flying, some men were impatient to get through all the proper channels. One of these was a young Gallipoli and Western Front veteran from Sydney by the name of Charles Ulm, who, though twice wounded in battle and sent home, had returned to England when his father had said to him, 'What are you doing back here when you still have two arms and two legs?'[17]

No matter, Ulm had already decided there was more for him to do in this war, and by the latter months of 1917 was training in England, where he had become fascinated with flight. This fascination had compelled him to finagle several flights with some friendly military pilots, during which he had taken the opportunity to observe closely everything they did to get airborne, control the plane while in the air, and then get back down. Fancying that he probably had it mastered, he decided to have a go himself on an aeroplane that had been left unattended.

So it was that one day in November 1917, he found himself behind the controls of a plane for the first time. Ulm had no formal training, no pilot's licence and no authority to be in the plane, but that didn't bother him. Nor did he care that he risked a court martial if he was found out. After all, he would have to survive the flight to be court martialled, which meant that the worry about what his military masters might think was only a secondary concern.

He gunned the plane forward and only a hundred yards or so onwards, his magic moment came and he was airborne.

Despite the fact that he was proceeding on instinct mixed with observation, he somehow managed to circle the field twice before bringing it in for a 'landing' — read 'bouncing'.

And like so many who had been blessed with the experience of being in control of a plane, he had returned to the ground a different man. An aphorism among pilots was that your first time flying was better than orgasm, and who could argue? Nothing Ulm had done in his life to that point compared to the thrill he had just experienced and he resolved then and there that, whatever else, flying would be a big part of the rest of his life.

•

14 August 1917. Despite what they were about — looking for men in other planes to kill — there was something fantastically beautiful about the French countryside, even from this height of 7000 feet, and Charles Kingsford Smith enjoyed it keenly as its green, hazy endlessness stretched magnificently before him. In terms of enemy planes, however, there was no sign and after half an hour or so, their squadron leader fired a Very light from his cockpit signalling to the squadron to return to base. Smithy was about to do exactly that, swivelling his stick to the right to make a graceful turn along with the others, when he saw that one pilot in the squadron had instead turned left, and was now about to fly towards German territory. Thinking that perhaps this pilot had spotted something, Kingsford Smith decided to follow him. Alas, just a few clouds later, Smithy couldn't find him anymore and suddenly realised he was on his own, except for the irrepressible hobgoblin called Archie now popping all around.[18] Was it him, or was it getting a little warm? Deciding it might be a good idea to head back to base after all, he now turned his plane firmly towards the safety of the western horizon and then he spotted them.

Down there!

Some 1000 feet below him, two Hun two-seaters were cruising eastwards with clearly no idea that he was above them. Nudging his plane down and getting ready to rain hell upon them in a death swoop from on high, Kingsford Smith got himself into position — 800 feet and closing ... 700 feet ... 500 feet. His airspeed indicator registered that he was descending at the wonderful rate of 220 miles per hour and the two planes, which had looked liked toy models far below, were now looking larger with every passing second.

Now! With grim satisfaction he pressed the trigger to unleash a deadly fusillade upon the nearest of the planes.

Only a second after firing though, it was, bizarrely, his own plane that was vibrating, shaking itself to bits. Around him pieces of the cockpit were flying all over, as splinters cut into his face and blood ran down his chin. It was an instant before he understood what was happening. He was under attack!

Even higher than Kingsford Smith had been when he spotted the two German planes, a third Hun fighter had been lurking in the clouds, and while he had been stalking the pair below, he was being stalked himself. Instinctively, Kingsford Smith stamped his feet to hurl his rudder to the left and right to enable his plane to swerve but the fighter above had his measure. It seemed that whichever way he turned, nothing stopped the bullets that kept pouring into his plane. In the midst of the maelstrom the Australian was dimly aware that he had been hit in the left foot, and that ... from nowhere ... a fog of blackness ... was ... filling his cockpit ... no ... maybe just ... his head ... Must ... turn ... and get back ... have another go ... at the ... bastard ... who had ... got him ... *Must.* His nostrils filled, as he later recounted, 'with the unmistakable odour of the German tracer bullets as they streamed past like a jet from a hose',[19] even as he was also dimly aware that his left boot was all sticky and wet.

From above, the German pilot, satisfied to see the Allied plane tumble off into a death roll and spiral down towards the earth, stopped firing. From 4000 feet on high, Kingsford Smith's plane, travelling at a rate now of around 220 miles per hour, had barely a few seconds before it would hit the ground and ...

Suddenly the fog cleared a little. Kingsford Smith opened his eyes to see a crazy quilt of beautiful French countryside spinning like a top and hurtling up towards him. Instinct took over. Not quite knowing what he was doing, but doing it anyway as he dimly remembered something from his training in England, he *pushed* on his joystick, and somehow, almost impossibly from the point of view of observers on the ground, his plane pulled out of the spin and flattened out just a bare 100 feet above the ground, caressing mother earth with an air kiss, instead of slamming into her.

The fog in Kingsford Smith's head didn't lift entirely, but at least enough that the wounded airman was able to make it back to base and land, whereupon he again lost consciousness and was unable to climb out of the cockpit. After base medical staff had carefully lifted him out and rushed him to hospital, mechanics set to work on his plane and were astonished that it had been able to fly at all. They counted over 180 bullet holes in the fuselage; including dozens in the spot where the pilot's head would have been had he not lost consciousness and slumped forward. How on *earth* had he managed to survive such an attack?

When Kingsford Smith came to, he was in a local French hospital, groggily aware that his foot was heavily bandaged. Apart from a massive loss of blood, he was missing two toes and a rather large chunk of his foot. Now, for some pilots, such a wound would have been a godsend, providing an honourable exit from all the carnage and likely ensuring their survival until the war was over. This, however, was not Smithy's primary emotion. Mostly what he felt was severe disappointment that, for the moment at least, his flying was over. All he wanted to do now was to recover as quickly as possible and get back into the air

•

God he hated this job. It had been great, at first, a fairly cushy job, riding all over Sydney's lower North Shore, frequently being the bearer of glad tidings, of congratulations for births, news of engagements, weddings and varied great achievements. Before 1915, it had only occasionally been news of terrible deaths, but now …

Now, being a telegraph boy was a long-running nightmare, with people trembling at his very sight on their doorsteps, because they *knew* what a fellow in that uniform of the Telegraph Office meant in most cases.

And the worst of it was he never knew until they tore it open just what it said, whether it was good news, or bad news. On this occasion he had to deliver a cable to a family in Neutral Bay, and he had no sooner knocked on the door than it was opened by a rather elderly woman whose right hand flew to her mouth at his very sight, then her left hand took the envelope from him, shaking. In an instant she had opened it ... and seemed to relax a little, which was merciful. Whatever it was, it surely wasn't the death of her loved one.

In fact, in her hand, Catherine Kingsford Smith held the following cable:

> August 21. Regret to inform you that 2nd Lieutenant C.K. Smith, RFC 23 Squadron was wounded August 14 and admitted No.2 Stationary Hospital Abbeville with gunshot wounds foot. Condition satisfactory. Further news sent when received.
> Secretary War Office.[20]

Though of course deeply upsetting, the main thing was that he was alive, and Chilla's parents were further pleased to receive a letter shortly afterwards, from their youngest son's Commanding Officer, a Major Wilkinson: 'As you have probably heard by now, your son was wounded in an aerial combat yesterday. It was rather a nasty wound in the foot, and necessitated the removal of two of his toes; but it should not permanently affect him in any way. I went to the hospital yesterday and found him very cheerful. He goes to England tomorrow. We are most awfully sorry to lose him. I am especially sorry as he was one of the very best fighters I have had, full of grit and a splendid fighter pilot. He hasn't been here with us for very long, but had done a lot in that short time and was universally popular. He hopes to be flying again in a few months' time. There is no one I should welcome back more warmly to the squadron. Believe me, there was only one opinion of him out here, and that was "one of the best".'[21]

And clearly, Major Wilkinson was one of many who thought so, as Smithy received the news in hospital that he was to be awarded the Military Cross for his valour against the enemy. The young pilot was thrilled.

•

In the Schwerin aircraft factory north-west of Berlin the workmen could sometimes be heard to whisper, '*der Alte kommt*' (the old man is coming), at which point there would be a furious burst of activity all around. No matter that the old man in question was only twenty-four. Somehow, Anthony Fokker, their boss and paymaster, came across as being mature way beyond his years. Perhaps this was because of what he had achieved — now running a factory that was producing eight planes a day, every day, even on Sundays — or maybe because he looked so very, very tired. For as well as running the factory, hiring and firing, and ensuring that everything was as it should be, he was also extremely busy designing better, faster, more powerful planes, capable of being more and more lethal weapons in the air.

And on this day, 28 August 1917, he was unveiling a beauty — the Fokker Dr.I — to Germany's most celebrated air ace, Manfred von Richthofen. This pilot had fascinated Fokker from the time they had first met, on New Year's Day 1916. Other pilots he met in the course of his travels swaggered, chased women madly and were chased in turn, and smoked and drank as if there were no tomorrow — as for many there wouldn't be — but not the Red Baron. Even at New Year, Fokker found him courteous, slightly aloof without being arrogant, and entirely sober, as he was not a drinker or smoker of any note. In Fokker's eyes, he was calm, cold and ambitious. 'A born leader of men,' he thought.

Well, Fokker felt he had just the plane for von Richthofen to fly in — perhaps the perfect one to counter the plane the English called the 'Sopwith Camel', which had so recently been cutting a swathe through the German squadrons. (In fact, unbeknown to Fokker, the Camel had also cut a swathe through novice pilots, as the torque caused by the tremendous centrifugal momentum of its rotary engine, which made it so manoeuvrable in the hands of an expert, was hell itself for the inexperienced.)

The Dutchman's new machine was a triplane with three stubby wings extending from an open cockpit, behind an Oberursel UR.II nine-cylinder air-cooled rotary 110-horsepower engine, atop which sat twin synchronised Spandau machine guns. The fact that it had large ailerons on the upper wings enabled it to turn on a *Pfennig*, and that the fuselage was made from welded steel tubing, rather than the usual timber, gave the plane enormous structural integrity and capacity to withstand strain.

And, of course, it was all painted in pure, glaring red.

The most important thing was that von Richthofen loved the plane from the first moment he tried it, saying, in a moment of uncharacteristic public enthusiasm that the Dr.I had '*geklettert wie ein Affe und wie der Teufel manövriert*' (climbed like a monkey and manoeuvred like the devil).[22]

•

Back in London still recovering, Smithy was finding the going tough, and not just physically. Emotionally and spiritually, he felt more than a little fragile, jumpy, panicky, teary, and among all that haunted by the horrifying things he had seen and done in the war, from the trenches of Gallipoli to the Western Front, to flying in the air war and, particularly, the killing of dozens of Germans in the culvert lined by the shattered poplars. He just couldn't get it all out of his head, no matter how hard he tried.

'My nerves have gone to the pack,' Chilla wrote home to his parents. 'I am afraid I am in for a breakdown if they get worse.'[23] More than ever, he felt homesick, and longed to be with his parents and family once more, in the heat of a Sydney summer where death and destruction were absent and the sun's rays might burn from him the worst of the memories.

•

King George V, himself!

In a spacious chamber at Buckingham Palace, Charles Kingsford Smith, in full military dress, and other airmen who were to receive medals had been standing around drinking tea and making polite conversation with each other and scattered generals, admirals and commodores. Suddenly there was a rustle, a murmur, and an immediate discharge of electricity into the atmosphere. Everyone looked up, and there was His Majesty, George V, appearing slightly smaller than in the portraits of him that abounded all over the British Empire, but certainly every bit as regal and more. As one, every military man in the room removed his cap and bowed deeply.

It was 10 am sharp on the morning of 12 November 1917, and an extremely significant day in the young Australian's life. Charles Kingsford Smith was to receive his Military Cross for conspicuous gallantry and devotion to duty. The citation said: 'His efforts and fine offensive spirit and disregard of danger have set a very fine example.'

When the time came for Kingsford Smith to shuffle forward on his crutches, he was careful to follow strict protocol, just as he had been instructed, taking three small steps towards His Majesty, before bowing again, the best he could. As he straightened up, he was thrilled when the King even said a few words while pinning the medal on his chest: 'Your mother will be proud of you, today.'

The pilot murmured his thanks and tried to take the requisite three steps back from the King when disaster struck. Somehow his legs got tangled with his crutches, he lost his balance and went down, in the classic Australian lingo, 'like a sack of spuds'. King George V himself rushed forward and helped him to his feet, whispering as he did so, 'Just get out the easiest way.' Which Kingsford Smith did, breaking all protocol, but giving him a story he could tell ever afterwards.

'I was the only man there,' he would say, 'who could turn his back on the King …'[24]

In his account of the ceremony to his parents, the young man made sure to playfully note: 'Don't forget to put Lieut. C. Kingsford Smith M.C. on letters!!!'[25]

Not long after receiving his Military Cross, Kingsford Smith was granted medical leave to return to Australia until 5 May 1918, and boarded a ship for home shortly thereafter …

•

And what a great pleasure it was particularly for Catherine, now the grey-haired matriarch of the Kingsford Smith clan, to have her youngest child once more nestled in the bounteous bosom of the family. Chilla was, just as always, making everyone laugh, telling stories, recounting something of his adventures and, as ever, acting as a magnet for friends and family from all over. True, it had been a bit of a shock to see him hobbling down the gangplank of his ship when it berthed at Circular Quay. But the injury to his foot was as nothing when you knew, as Catherine did from scanning the death lists every day in the newspapers, how many of his colleagues of the air had been killed outright, how many other mothers had nothing coming down that gangplank but haunted memories for the rest of their lives. (A bereaved mother in Sydney's Glebe by the name of Mrs Pyke, wearing nothing but a faded white petticoat, would become locally famous for traipsing down Glebe Point Road, and heading to Circular Quay rain, hail or shine, every day for the rest of her life to see if her only son had finally returned from the war.[26] Alas, he never did.)

As it was, Chilla seemed to have every chance of making a complete recovery and Catherine could just enjoy him being home for as long as she could possibly keep him there. Other sons in the same circumstances might have felt that they had done their bit for the war effort and have stayed put, but her lad had made it clear pretty much from the moment of his arrival that he was home only to recuperate, and then he intended to get right back into it. That was just the way he was.

And he was quietly ecstatic to see his return to Australia noted in two daily Sydney newspapers, in small articles entitled 'AUSTRALIAN AIRMAN RETURNS' and 'FIGHT IN THE AIR — ODDS AGAINST AUSTRALIAN'. Such fame![27]

It was wonderful to be home ...

•

Zu Hause, endlich zu Hause! Home, finally home! He was home!

And yet Baroness Kunigunde von Richthofen simply didn't recognise her son, now the greatest hero in Germany, when he returned for a brief spot of leave in the first weeks of 1918 to the family's ancestral estate near Breslau in the famed pine forests of Silesia. Whereas he once had been a man full of life and love, radiating happiness and warmth, he was now morose, aloof and distant — wounded in his soul and still bleeding. When she looked into his eyes there was something in them she had never seen before, something harsh and agonised, as though he was being tortured. When she would try to talk to him about his future, about what he might do *nach dem Krieg* (after the war), he gave the impression that he wasn't even sure if there would be a *nach-dem-Krieg* for him. He was exhausted, depressed and deeply, deeply pessimistic, though still trying to shield her from the worst of it.

One morning she managed to see some of the photographs he had brought home with him. One showed him in uniform, laughing with other pilots. Baroness von Richthofen, a gentle woman, pointed to a beaming young flyer, and asked where he was now.

'Fallen in combat,' Manfred replied morosely.

'And this man?' she asked, pointing to another one.

'Also dead,' her son replied, before suddenly appearing to lose patience and putting the photo away. 'Do not ask any more. They are all dead.'

Then, seeing the alarm in his mother's eyes, he softened and tried to reassure her. 'You do not need to worry. In the air I have nothing to fear. In the air. We are ready for them, even when there are many of them. The worst that could happen to me would be to have to land on the other side ...'[28]

And yet, despite this assurance, it was not long after this that she overheard him on the phone, batting off someone who had wanted him to attend a dental appointment that afternoon. 'A dental appointment?' he had replied with a mixture of extreme fatigue and outright irritation. 'Really, there is no *point* ...'[29]

•

It was a heady thing for Charles Kingsford Smith to find himself so celebrated in his home town. People made a huge fuss of him.

After all, here was a man who had left Sydney only a couple of years earlier as a humble acting corporal in the Signal Corps, now returned as a decorated fighter pilot, wounded in an air battle, and just about the only man in the whole country in the highly prestigious uniform of the Royal Flying Corps! (Most of the other Australians who were a part of the RFC were still in England, or dead.) Kingsford Smith found that pretty much wherever he went he was hailed as a hero.

This way, Charlie! Over here! *This way!* Make room for him, please, you fellows. Come and have a drink with us, Charlie! You remember me from school? Barman, drinks all round, please. Now, Charlie, about the war, and this flying game …

Not that it was easy to get him to wear his uniform, replete with all its insignia and heavy gold braiding. Initially, he declined to wear it at all, but was eventually prevailed upon to do so by an achingly beautiful girl he had asked to afternoon tea. She said she would accompany him and wear her best dress so long as he wore his uniform and … things went from there. The reaction from everyone was so positive, so enthusiastic, that he began to wear it more often.

Still, it was true that not everyone was appreciative. One day he was dressed in his uniform and getting onto the Mosman ferry with his brother Leofric, when he happened to overhear two rough-nut youths making fun of his finery, jeering about his 'pretty, pretty uniform …'[30]

Oh, *really*? A veteran of Gallipoli, *and* the Somme, *and* the war in the air, wounded in battle and decorated by King George V himself, and he had to put up with that kind of insolence from young punks who wouldn't know one end of a rifle from another? He thought not.

Without saying a word, or interrupting the flow of conversation with his brother, the Australian pilot, though earth-bound, simply stepped forward, banged the heads of the two 'gilded youths' together with a resounding thud and dropped them at his feet.[31] And that was the end of that. Though Charles Kingsford Smith was not a big man, there was a physical force within him — particularly on those rare occasions that he was moved to rage — which was simply overpowering.

And yet, whatever the joys of being home in Australia, seeing all his friends and family again, he was in no doubt where he wanted to be: back in the war. It was still raging in Europe and his squadron was still heading out on daily sorties against whatever the Germans could throw at them — although that was apparently a lot less, lately, as the weight of the British Empire and her newly powerful American ally was brought to bear, pouring resources into the war effort as never before, and the Axis powers began to wilt.

So it was that despite an offer from the Australian military authorities for him to remain safely in Australia to make speeches about the war and sell war bonds to those members of the public impressed with the urgent need for capital to keep it going, he decided it was nearing time to head back to his squadron, strap himself in, and get back into the air war again.

•

On the crisp, clear morning of 21 April 1918, George Wilkins was driving north on the Bray–Corbie road not too far from Villers-Bretonneux on the Western Front to do his usual daily rounds of taking photos in the trenches. The last months had been intense, and in the course of them he had sustained no fewer than nine wounds about his body — courtesy of bombs, bullets, shrapnel and gas — but somehow he had survived the lot, and was still as passionate and fearless as ever, to capture everything possible on film. On this morning, he was fascinated to see suddenly break out right ahead of him a dogfight so intense — with five … six … hang on, ten, no … fifteen … and now as many as *thirty* planes involved! One of the planes, he noted, was an entirely red triplane …

Could it be?

It was. The day before, Manfred von Richthofen had shot down two Allied planes in the skies above Villers-Bretonneux — to bring his total to eighty — and today he had led his squadron back to this El Dorado of English flyers, where he could almost guarantee they would be swarming thickly. He had been patrolling over the Somme River that morning with nine other German planes under his command when they had been engaged by two squadrons of Sopwith Camels, totalling fourteen. In the course of the furious dogfight that followed, the German *Rittmeister* spied something well below that pleased him greatly. It was a lone Sopwith, breaking from the pack and scuttling to make for the safety of the Allied lines. Therein lay a story ...

At the briefing back at base that morning, a novice Canadian pilot, Lieutenant Wilfrid 'Wop' May of No. 209 Squadron, Royal Air Force, had been going out on his first ever patrol, and been ordered not to get involved in any serious fighting. Are we clear, Lieutenant? Very clear, sir ...

No matter that the man giving those orders, the commander of No. 209 Squadron, Captain Roy Brown, was an old school friend of May. This was a formal military briefing, in front of their military peers, and form had to be followed.

In fact, however, once the German planes had come at them in such numbers, Lieutenant May had felt justified in breaking those orders and getting involved. This was fine until his guns jammed, and he realised that in this situation, discretion really was the better part of valour and it was time to get away. In an instant he had spun out of the battle, and was racing to the west to get back to his own lines. Alas, the young Canadian had not yet learned enough to know that a plane of his type, flying at that speed and altitude, on its own away from a dogfight, was like a fat chicken in a farmyard waddling away from a ravenous wolf ...

Manfred von Richthofen moved in for the kill. The Sopwith was so low that there would barely be space to use his preferred method, which was to come up at his targets from behind and below, where the enemy pilots could not see him. Instead, the German decided to swoop down and chase the Sopwith before blowing it out of the sky. He pushed the joystick forward and in an instant his red triplane Fokker responded, darting downward and accelerating all the while as the Sopwith loomed large, fat and ready over his gun-sights ...

Unbeknown to von Richthofen, however, disengaging from the dogfight at that moment just above him was his quarry's flight commander, Captain Roy Brown. Vastly experienced, Brown summed up the situation in an instant, and now, in his

Sopwith Camel, hurtled down after the Red Baron in the hope that he could prevent the certain death of his compatriot and old school friend, Lieutenant May.

Rally, school!

Ruhig … ruhig … ruhig … Steady … steady … steady …

Just a few hundred feet from his target now, the Red Baron was doing what he always did in such circumstances — holding his fire until he just couldn't miss. Other pilots were satisfied if they hit any part of an enemy plane but not him. He always shot straight for the enemy plane's fuel tank knowing that with just one bullet in the right spot, he would win — 500 feet away … 400 … 300 … 200 …

As ever, his finger tightened on the trigger and his twin Spandaus suddenly leapt into life, his plane vibrating in a pleasing fashion. Amazingly, however, this time his first burst of fire didn't bring his quarry down. And what was worse, the Sopwith pilot, now aware that he was under attack, began evasive action, twisting and turning from side to side and going ever lower while still racing like a scalded cat for the Allied lines with every ounce of speed that the terrified Canadian could muster from his tortured engine. In terms of performance capacity, in some ways it was a fair fight, as both the Sopwith Camel and the Fokker Dr.I had maximum speeds of about 113 miles per hour, and while all else being equal the Camel was marginally more manoeuvrable than the Dr.I, in this case the fact that Lieutenant May was so inexperienced probably meant that advantage was neutralised.

The Red Baron, embracing the chase, followed closely, endeavouring to anticipate every move the Sopwith pilot made before he made it. And yet, he got it wrong! Time and again von Richthofen fired where the young Canadian pilot *would* have been, had he been experienced only to find that his target had moved an instant earlier in an entirely unexpected direction.[32] Worse for the Red Baron, the two planes had now flashed over Allied lines — pushed along by a strong tailwind — meaning that the German pursuer was now the intruder, not the Canadian. At this point, it is surprising that von Richthofen continued the fight. Just days before, he had completed and submitted to Supreme Headquarters his Air Combat Operations Manual, essentially a textbook for all German pilots to follow based on everything he had learnt, and one principle he had spelt out in clearest terms was:

> One should never obstinately stay with an opponent who, through bad shooting or skilful turning, one has been unable to shoot down, when the battle lasts until it is far on the other side of the front and one is alone and faced by a greater number of opponents.[33]

Ignoring that entirely, the Red Baron stayed on the tail of Lieutenant May, as the Canadian twisted and turned up the valley of the Somme River, just 50 feet above the surface of the water.

Oh ... *God*.

Though May momentarily thought at one point that he had shaken the German, he became suddenly aware that his pursuer had hopped over a hill on a river bend, and was now coming down on him. This time, there was no escape. This time, *trapped* by the narrow valley sides, he couldn't dart to the left or to the right. He was as good as dead.[34] He tensed, waiting for the blast he knew was coming, and wondered if he should end it himself by jamming the stick forward and hitting the river.

As it turned out, however, von Richthofen was just coming in to fire off his final deadly burst, when ...

Suddenly the German's aircraft began to shudder and shake and splinters of wood filled his cockpit. Exactly as had happened to Charles Kingsford Smith a few months earlier, the Red Baron was under attack from above! Taking instant evasive action himself, he twisted the red Fokker triplane away, which as fate would have it took him towards a hill held by the AIF's 53rd Australian Field Battery, 5th Division.

Atop this particular hill, an Australian gunner by the name of Robert Buie — an oyster farmer before the war, from Brooklyn, just north of Sydney — had watched the whole distant dogfight with fascination and was now amazed to see the red plane heading in his rough direction. It was soon only a few hundred feet away from him, at an altitude of just 50 feet or so! This was too good an opportunity to miss, and Buie was not prone to missing a target that close, ever since those days growing up on the Hawkesbury River, when he had honed his shooting skills by knocking sea eagles out of the sky as they tried to steal fish from his net.

Pointing his Lewis gun upwards, he fired at the plane, while from a nearby hill Sergeant Cedric Popkin of the Australian 24th Machine Gun Company fired his Vickers machine gun … while still another soldier fired a Lee Enfield .303 at the plane … and yet *another* Australian, Gunner 'Snowy' Evans, fired a burst from his Lewis gun.

In the end there was no doubt that a blizzard of bullets was whizzing up, and into the Fokker. Nevertheless, Robert Buie, for one, was absolutely certain that his bullets hit right where the German was sitting, as he could see the fragments from the cockpit flying around as he kept shooting …[35] Sergeant Frank Wormald, standing just 4 yards from Robert Buie, was also sure that it was Buie's bullets that hit the red plane, and later recounted that he could see, 'plain as daylight … the Baron sort of shrug and sit up. I could *see* him'.[36]

An instant later, the Red Baron's plane — for so long a bright red streak of death, the terror of the western skies — staggered in the air, slowed, and then turned, beginning a rapid descent.

Unfortunately, George Wilkins missed this final part of the action. Still back on the Bray–Corbie road, it had been a few moments earlier that the red Fokker had 'side-slipped' downwards behind a hill, momentarily obscuring the photographer's view. Wilkins did not witness, therefore, the Red Baron's plane coming to ground 'like a wounded bird', right in front of the men of the 53rd Australian Field Battery of the 5th Division, who were dug in on the high ground of Morlancourt Ridge, and peeping over their sandbags. As soon as they were sure there were no more German planes coming their way, spitting death, some of the Diggers rushed forward to find the pilot slumped in his cockpit, barely alive. The German legend managed to get out just one last word before expiring: '*Kaputt*.'[37]

It was 10.50 am, on a cool, windy day.

Well before George Wilkins arrived at the scene to take photos of the crashed plane, the Diggers had the pilot's only slightly bloodied body out and, going through his papers, realised who he was.

Stone the bloody crows ... the bloke himself! Von Richthofen! They had got him at last!

For all the excitement at their achievement, however, the body of Manfred von Richthofen was treated with elaborate respect. They carefully laid him on his back on the ground, closed his eyes, and joined his hands in the supplicatory biblical pose that von Richthofen's mother surely would have wanted. Shortly thereafter, the commanding officer of the Australian Flying Corps No. 3 Squadron, Major David Blake, took responsibility for the body and began to organise a full military funeral. That very afternoon an autopsy was held, which showed that the German pilot who had personally caused the deaths of eighty Allied airmen confirmed and possibly another twenty, had himself been killed by a single bullet that had entered his body below his right armpit towards his back, gone through his heart, and exited next to his left nipple.

That evening the Red Baron effectively lay 'in state', in an open coffin in one of No. 3 Squadron's hangars, as a long line of his former opponents and their ground crew came by and paid their final respects. Yes, he had killed many of their comrades, but he had been an honourable opponent and had only done to the Allied pilots what they had been trying to do to him. In their deadly common calling, he was the best.

To bear his coffin the following afternoon, Major Blake chose six captains of the Australian Flying Corps — the same rank as von Richthofen. Too, an honour guard from the other ranks was chosen, comprising twelve Australian soldiers in full dress uniform, and each of these men used spit and polish to be absolutely impeccable for the occasion.

Wreaths were presented by other Allied squadrons, and von Richthofen was buried in the overgrown cemetery of the village of Bertangles, with the propeller of his plane serving as the initial cross at the head of the grave. As a final salute, each man in the honour guard fired three shots into the air. Photos were taken, and copies of these were dropped by an English pilot above a German air base, together with a note confirming von Richthofen's death:

> *To the German Flying Corps,*
> *Rittmeister Baron Manfred von Richthofen was killed in aerial combat on April 21st 1918. He was buried with full military honours.*
> *From,*
> *British Royal Air Force.*

In a later note, the German pilots were further advised that if they wished to, they could fly, unmolested, over his grave on the following day between 3 pm and 6 pm, to drop their own wreaths — an opportunity that many of von Richthofen's fellow pilots availed themselves of.

So ended an extraordinary saga, albeit with a noteworthy addendum …

Von Richthofen's place as commander of his 'Flying Circus', was taken initially by *Oberleutnant* Wilhelm Reinhard, until he crashed three weeks later, at which point the new commander was a German ace with eighteen kills to his credit, one *Oberleutnant* Hermann Göring …

•

'No longer fit for combat duty.'

He was *what*?

No longer fit for combat duty, son.

That was the phrase used by the English doctors, and nothing the Australian said could change it. In response, Charles Kingsford Smith was disgusted, *bristling* with indignation. Now mostly recovered, he believed, from his wounds of the previous year, he had returned to England via the usual six-week journey by ship — this time going on the *Orontes* across first the Pacific Ocean via Wellington, Tahiti, the Panama Canal, New York, then the Atlantic Ocean. Only to be told by medical officers that they would no longer give him clearance to fly! Kingsford Smith could have understood their reasoning if part of flying had been pedalling like mad with your feet, but as the only use for his feet was to operate the rudder, and he was fully capable of doing that, even with his injured foot, it simply didn't make sense.

Do you hear me?!

Accustomed to such indignation from brave men, and trained to counter it regardless, the military doctors simply closed his folder and refused to change their determination.

The role he was offered now was as a flying instructor with No. 204 Training Depot, at Eastchurch on the Isle of Sheppey. And as a matter of fact, he would no longer be part of the British Army's Royal Flying Corps, as that had ceased to exist from 1 April 1918, when it had merged with the Royal Naval Air Service to become the Royal Air Force. A job as a flying instructor wasn't remotely what the Australian had in mind when he had returned to Great Britain, but at least he would be back in the air once more and besides that most crucial feature, his time there was not without its pleasures. Kingsford Smith was able to keep more than busy when not instructing, attracting local women to his bed, and was so successful his fellow officers referred to him as 'King Dick'.[38] At one point, on a course at Shoreham, his colleagues were stunned when they were billeted at a hotel where two girls were resident, one of whom was the hotelier's daughter. In the space of just two days, King Dick had bedded them both, while simultaneously having an affair with an Italian violinist playing in an orchestra up in London.

'He just seemed to hypnotise women,' one of those colleagues, James Cross, would recall to author Ian Mackersey many years later. [39]

Whatever Kingsford Smith's activities, by this stage of the war the truth was that there was quite likely more action to be had between the sheets than in the air. Simply put, the combined industrial might of the Allies was now so strong that Germany and its fellow Central European powers — Austria-Hungary, Bulgaria and the Ottoman Empire — couldn't keep up and that most definitely applied to the war in the air. Things were so bad that from the middle of 1918 onwards, German

Supreme Army Command tried to keep its planes out of the air as much as possible, to reduce opportunities for *den Engländer* to shoot them down.

This was deeply frustrating for the Allied pilots, particularly Australia's premier air ace, Captain Arthur Harry Cobby of the Australian Flying Corps No. 4 Squadron, who was then credited with kills of twenty-five enemy planes and thirteen balloons. In an effort to get the Germans to come out and play, Cobby and the men under his command began to engage in the practice of swooping in low over enemy aerodromes, to drop, yes, old boots upon them!

Inside the boots would be messages addressed to 'the footsore aerial knights of Germany', inviting them to quit their cowardly ways and come up and have a go. More than a few German pilots, seething with rage, did exactly that, and were shot down for their trouble, allowing Cobby to take his tally up to twenty-nine.[40]

•

Elsewhere, other Australian pilots were also making outstanding contributions to the war effort, none more so than a charismatic chunk of a man by the name of Ross Smith, who had begun the war with the Light Horse in Gallipoli and Palestine before training to become a pilot. A swashbuckling larrikin as a soldier, he was known as a fearless, born leader in the air, with a notable capacity to fly well beyond the realms of regulation — not particularly caring what the higher-ups thought so long as he did damage to the Germans. (It was also said of him by one of his pukkah British colleagues that, 'For an Aussie he had a fine command of English and an unusually impressive diction …')

On one legendary occasion Ross Smith and his observer, Stan Nunan, came up with a plan to attack a newly established German aerodrome in northern Palestine. On their first pass over it, they dropped some of their bombs near the hangars to ensure that all the German mechanics would scramble to their trenches and give them an empty canvas on which to execute their own brand of artistry. Then Ross Smith practically dropped out of the sky, so quickly did he bring his Bristol Fighter down onto the runway.

Let the fun begin. As the plane came to a halt, Nunan jumped out with a revolver in one hand and a Very pistol in the other, while Smith manned the Bristol's Lewis gun and trained it in the direction that the German soldiers and mechanics could be expected to come from. Sure enough …

Nunan fired first the revolver into the petrol tank of one German plane, causing fuel to gush forth, and then the Very pistol at the resulting puddle, whereupon the plane exploded with force enough to singe his eyebrows and wake the dead. And then another and another! Smith, in the meantime, ensured that the motor of their own plane was kept at fair throttle, ready for the getaway, even as he kept the Lewis gun firing at the Germans, who were now gathering themselves.

Of course, it couldn't last. Suddenly, twenty German soldiers appeared running towards them, all with rifles, all firing. Nunan, unfortunately, was having a great deal of trouble getting the fourth German plane to explode and couldn't bear to leave before the job was done. Smith, understanding perfectly his desire to destroy the plane above and beyond the desire to get away, taxied the plane up behind Nunan and between them they were able to throw their remaining bomb at the German plane and destroy it before taking off *in extremis*, with bullets whistling around their ears and into the fuselage of the plane.

Smith was just that kind of man and if fortune favoured the brave, it positively *adored* him, notwithstanding the scars he bore on both cheeks courtesy of a bullet having passed through his face, taking a couple of teeth with it. A scar on his forehead bore witness to how close another bullet had come to ending his life in the same engagement.

In fact, it was a measure of how highly regarded both Ross Smith and Lawrence of Arabia were that when the latter needed to be transported somewhere in the swirling desert, it was the former who was sent for.

On one occasion, on 22 September 1918, the two were having breakfast in the desert with some others when an enemy plane came over.[41] In an instant, Smith had put down his plate of porridge, got into his plane and, with his observer, 'climbed like a cat into the skies', as Lawrence described it, followed by another Australian pilot and his observer. When a third one of their compatriots looked to Lawrence in the manner of, 'Well, are you going to come, too?', the Englishman's response was such that he later felt bound to record his feelings. 'No, I was not going to air-fight,' Lawrence wrote, 'no matter what caste I lost with the pilot. He was an Australian, of a race delighting in additional risks, not an Arab to whose gallery I must play.'[42]

No matter. Within five minutes, Ross Smith brought the German plane down in flames close to the nearby railway and then returned to take up the porridge which had been kept warm for him, all with nary a word … until half an hour later another plane came over. Despite Smith being about to put marmalade on his toast and take some coffee, he was gone once more, again followed by the second Australian pilot, and this time it was the latter who did the honours.

A strange bunch these Australians, and Lawrence of Arabia could never quite fathom them, though he admired them enormously.

•

His name was George Price and on this crisp morning, the Canadian conscript from the town of Moose Jaw, in the prairie province of Saskatchewan, was with a patrol of A Company of the 28th Battalion, advancing on the small Belgian town of Ville-sur-Haine, then held by the Germans. He was in the lead of this ground force and had entered two houses looking for a Hun machine-gunner who had been firing on them a short time before. The Canadians had just left the second house and returned to the street when a single shot rang out from a German sniper, and Price immediately fell to the ground.

Dead.

It was 10.58 am, on 11 November 1918. Two minutes after his death, the war was officially over and Germany had surrendered under the terms of an armistice which had been signed six hours before in a railway carriage in the forest of Compiègne.

Sadly for George, there had not been time to inform all units of the armistice before it occurred.

Six

Apres la Guerre

[Being a pilot] is the only first-class thing that our generation has to do. So everyone should either take to the air themselves, or help it forward.

Lawrence of Arabia, on why, after leaving behind his celebrated life in the Arabian Desert, his next step was to join the Royal Air Force as a humble aircraftsman under an assumed name[1]

My mind was filled with aviation to the exclusion of everything else.

Charles Kingsford Smith, writing in his autobiography, on his state of mind in 1919[2]

The last few tragic deaths notwithstanding, the celebrations in Allied countries were heartfelt and overwhelming. In Paris the news burst up the Champs Elysees, swept around the Arc de Triomphe, and hurtled down every boulevard and avenue, instantly turning everyone it touched into a dancing, singing ball of delight. Guns were fired in the air, Parisians waved flags and stormed into the streets even as beautiful girls kissed strangers — most particularly those in uniform — and the whole city resounded throughout the rest of the day and into the night with the sound of cheering and singing, most particularly 'La Marseillaise'. As *The Times* correspondent in Paris noted after close observation throughout the day:

> ... the chilliest-hearted mortal could not miss the significance of the fact that the only colour in the crowd is provided by uniforms and flags. Practically every woman

> is in deep black. But today it was as if the dead themselves had told us to consider their sacrifice as redeemed and rejoice for them, as well as for ourselves. Women veiled in crepe, with red eyes and pale faces were radiant among the rest, as though sorrow had never touched them. For four years the hysteria of sorrow has been sternly repressed; it is but right the hysteria of joy should be expressed ...[3]

So too in London, where from 11 am people gathered in front of Buckingham Palace and began calling for the King, the King, the KING!

And there he was! At a quarter past eleven, a joyous cheer rang out as His Majesty King George V, wearing the uniform of an admiral of the fleet, stepped regally out onto the balcony, accompanied by the Queen, Prince Arthur and Princess Mary as the guards in the courtyard presented arms, and the band crashed out the chords of the national anthem, officers stood at attention, civilians removed their hats, and everyone cheered. And this was just the beginning. Union Jacks sprang out everywhere, together with, most notably, the Australian and American standards. Work ceased, the crowds swelled, people sang both 'God Save the King' and 'Rule Britannia' until they could sing no more, and Australian soldiers distinguished themselves by climbing all over the Victoria Memorial as everyone laughed and screamed out their approval. And on into the wild night they went. The war was *over*![4]

Sadly for him, Kingsford Smith was unable to participate in the celebrations. He had become so crook with the flu and pneumonia then sweeping desperately cold Britain that he had been admitted to the Royal Naval Hospital in Chatham, and at one point when one of his lungs filled with fluid it had even looked like he was going to die.[5]

Though very pleased that the war was over — at least sort of pleased, as he had hoped to fly against the Germans again before it finished — it was a terribly demoralising thing to be stuck in a hospital feeling like death warmed up, while everybody else was celebrating wildly. Still, at least in the quiet of it all, he was able to take time to contemplate the question that millions of other servicemen were also dealing with — that is, what now? Some men, certainly, were able to return home and pick up where they had left off — on the farm, in the factory, with their families. For many, though, the places they had left simply no longer existed, while others, like Kingsford Smith, were no longer the same men.

When he had joined the war he had been little more than a kid working in a factory. Now, he was a veteran of hideous trench warfare in two theatres, no less than a war pilot, and a decorated one at that. Return to the tight little world of the Colonial Sugar Refinery in Pyrmont as a glorified grease monkey? Out of the question! Most pilots felt exactly the same way. Once you knew what it was like to fly, to take wing into the clouds and sail before the sun, you never really wanted to do anything else.

'Of course,' he wrote to his parents on 22 November 1918, 'I am going to continue flying if possible, so long as it doesn't come down to the level of being a chauffeur, which I don't think is highly likely. Anyway, there are lots of openings for starting schools for aviation, etc ...'[6]

Once out of hospital and strong enough to plan his next move, Kingsford Smith wasted little time. As soon as he could, he left his position as an instructor at the Royal Air Force station at Eastchurch, to be 'demobbed', the term used for those who left the services. After an attempt to gain the agency to sell Avro planes in Australia came to nothing — despite at first looking promising — the 21-year-old tried a different tack.[7] Together with an enormous and robust 27-year-old wartime flying friend from Perth by the name of Cyril Maddocks, he formed a company called Kingsford Smith–Maddocks Aeros Ltd.

The two young aviators made plans to buy several new or surplus Royal Aircraft Factory BE2e (Blériot Experimental) reconnaissance biplanes, with the intention of eventually shipping them home to Australia and starting a flying school. To finance his share of them, Kingsford Smith was counting on the £300 'demob' money that was coming through, plus another £150 he was to be paid to remain part of the 'Special Reserve', essentially a standby war pilot who could be called on if the need arose. In the meantime, he and Maddocks would conduct a few joy flights at country fairs and the like around England, taking paying passengers aloft, to earn some more money.

•

In the history of the world there had never been such a gathering of the good and great as was assembled in the glittering Hall of Mirrors in the Palace of Versailles for the Peace Conference during the early months of 1919. The series of meetings involved representatives from the twenty-seven victorious nations of the Great War, gathered to decide everything ranging from the reparations that Germany must pay to who should take over the former colonies of the defeated Axis powers. And yet, though the defeated Germans had no seat at the conference, this did not prevent there being disputes. For there were many …

One of the matters fiercely debated was the proper fate for the former German territory of New Guinea. President Woodrow Wilson of the United States was passionate in his advocacy for Japan, which had fought on the side of the Allies in the war, to take it over, while the irascible Australian prime minister, Billy Hughes, was equally insistent that it should be Australian territory — in part, as a buffer against what he suspected might be Japan's future territorial ambitions across south-east Asia and into the South Pacific.

When a frustrated Wilson said to Hughes that in his role as Australian prime minister, 'after all, you speak for only five million people', Hughes cut him short with: 'I speak for 60,000 dead. For how many do you speak?'[8]

At this table, in this forum, Australia had made a far greater sacrifice than America had, and it *would* be heard. In the course of attending the Peace Conference, Billy Hughes was constantly flying back and forth between London and Paris. Journeying by aeroplane set him to thinking …

If travel in a plane could cut down a one-day trip to just an hour, what would it mean to Australia if an air-route could be established between, say, London and Sydney? If instead of a six-week trip by sea, the whole journey could be cut down to a matter of just a week or two? After all, England was awash with Australian pilots, some of whom Hughes had met while visiting recuperating servicemen at Cobham Hall in Kent, men who had come to the war by ship — but, now it was time to go home they wanted to do the obvious and *fly* back!

The first clue as to which way Hughes was thinking came in a cable he sent from Paris to the Australian cabinet, on 18 February 1919:

> Several aviators are desirous of attempting flight London to Australia in Handley-Page machine. They are all first class men, and very keen.[9]

And things began to move quickly from there …

•

Have you heard?!?! In March 1919 the Australian government announced a prize of no less than £10,000 for the first all-Australian crew, or solo Australian pilot, who could fly all the way from England to Australia in a plane of British make!

£10,000!

In a world where the average working wage was less than £10 a week this was an astronomical sum. Yet Hughes considered it absolutely appropriate as a means of encouraging aviation, which would in turn lessen Australian isolation and bind her ever tighter to Mother England — close to the furthest country on earth from her shores. And yet, the path between them, across four continents, remained relatively squarely within the British Empire.

Certainly it was a risky venture, with even the *New York Times* commenting that 'Christopher Columbus did not take one-tenth the risks that these bold air pioneers will have to face … They will be throwing dice with death'.[10]

The fact was, however, that most of those entering the race were veterans of the air war in France and had thrown dice with death most days before breakfast, and so far they had won every time. So what was another roll?

Kingsford Smith, for one, was absorbed in the idea of the race, and determined to win it. Excited, he wrote to his parents: 'Should we be chosen by any chance, and pull the job through, it will mean that we are made for life, because look at the big advertisement our own little venture would get out of it, to say nothing of the part of the £10,000 that would come to us.'[11]

And while he didn't have remotely the money necessary to finance such a venture, he was convinced this was most definitely a problem that could be overcome. Now that the war was over, interest in civil aviation was just beginning to take off and there were any number of companies eager to associate themselves with whomever they thought might possibly win such a race.

One company of precisely that description was the Yorkshire-based Blackburn Aircraft and Motor Company — owned and run by Robert Blackburn — which was organising for one of its long-range bombers to be entered. (The particular plane chosen was called a 'Kangaroo', because when the 75-foot wingspan, 4-ton twin-engine biplane bomber had first come off the drawing board there was a small 'pouch' below the cockpit where a machine gunner hovered in the belly of the beast.) Blackburn had already secured one pilot in the form of an Australian chap by the name of Val Rendle, and after meeting Kingsford Smith and Maddocks, he affirmed that he was happy for them to join Rendle's crew and fly the Kangaroo to Australia.

Kingsford Smith was thrilled. It was *exactly* the kind of venture he wanted to embark on in those immediate post-war days, when finding something to fill the void was not easy. Certainly, he was acutely conscious that the competition from other pilots would be tough, but on the other hand, he backed himself against them in having the requisite resilience, skill, hunger and ... perhaps crucially ... charm, to find the sponsors necessary. For whatever it was that generally placed the young, easygoing pilot at the centre of any group of men, could be devastating when focused on just one man and, in short, Smithy had personally helped to arrange for the Rolls-Royce company to provide both its best engines and the expert necessary companions to help install them. As well, the Shell Oil Company agreed to contact all its agents along the path between England and Australia — particularly in the Dutch East Indies — to organise for petrol to be supplied to the Blackburn plane when it passed through. Making everything all the sweeter was that Robert Blackburn had told the crew that if they could get the Kangaroo to Australia, and win the race, they could keep the plane. As to the two planes Kingsford Smith and Maddocks had purchased for their company, these were disassembled and packed away, in readiness to be sent to Sydney by ship — while they, of course, would bloody well be *flying* there!

All to the good and full steam ahead ...

•

Maybe it *was* all over. When the final signature was put on the Treaty of Versailles, an edict came into force — backed by the most powerful nations in the world — which effectively shut down Anthony Fokker's four factories and threw his 6000 workmen into Germany's growing unemployment queues. For while a part of the armistice agreement had been an enlightened move to regulate civil international aviation by requiring all signatory nations to set up their own civil aviation authorities, there was one specific article aimed directly like a dagger at Anthony Fokker's heart. Article IV dictated that all of Germany's military aeroplanes and engines should be immediately destroyed, and '*in erster Linie alle Apparate D. VII*' (first of all, all machines of the D-7 type),[12] which were those aeroplanes made by Anthony Fokker. In the treaty, this was the only armament singled out for specific and immediate destruction, meaning that, with effectively just the slash of a few pens, it was now as illegal for the Dutchman to continue to make planes in Germany as it was for anyone to buy them. There was to be no compensation, no nothing.

Just ... shut down.

What was he to do? In the end, Anthony Fokker decided that if the rules demanded that he cease production and hand over everything he had, then those rules would simply have to be broken. Taking an enormous risk, he gathered a group of loyal workers around him whom he felt he could count on, and organised to get as many of his tools, machines and *materiel* — including many disassembled planes — onto a particular train of sixty cars as could possibly fit. And then, after bribing certain officials along the way, he 'smuggled' the whole lot — lock, stock, barrel, engines and wings — back to his homeland of Holland to start again!

In fact, that first attempt proved so successful that Fokker repeated it — five times — on each occasion filling sixty carriages and then clearing a bribed path all the way from Schwerin to Amsterdam. The bribes were not always money, but frequently such things as sewing machines, bicycles and models of Fokker aeroplanes for the officials' delighted children. For many Germans, helping Fokker in this subterfuge was a pleasure in any case, and one in the eye for the wretchedly victorious Allied occupiers.[13]

After most of the machinery was transported, together with 400 engines, 120 D-7s, sixty two-seater observation planes and more than twenty D-8s, Fokker quickly established new premises just outside Amsterdam and proceeded to rebuild. The difference now was that his focus had shifted from making military aircraft for killing and maiming, to designing and building civilian aircraft, capable of travelling long distances reliably, and bearing as many passengers as possible.

•

On the veranda of her home in Neutral Bay, Catherine Kingsford Smith smiled ruefully. Her baby boy just could not sit still, be it in war or in peacetime. Now, in May 1919, he had written to his parents about where his new venture was up to, and as ever he was bubbling over with both impatience and enthusiasm:

> *Dearest Mother and Father,*
> *We're hurrying like mad to get away before the first of next month in order to beat the monsoons around East India which would hold us up for weeks ... When we arrive (if we succeed), we'll go straight ahead and open an aerodrome. We have Blackburn's agency for a year to go on with.*[14]

In his letter, Chilla also spelled out the route he intended to take from the other side of the world home to Australia. After consultation with all members of the crew and other pilots who had flown in various parts of the world, and sending endless cables back and forth, it had been decided that from England to Australia they would hop via Leeds, Lyon, Brindisi, Salonika, Nicosia, Allepo, Baghdad, Bushehr, Chabbar, Karachi, Baroda, Benares, Calcutta, Rangoon, Penang, Singapore, Batavia, Benjawan, Kupang and finally … Port Darwin! Certainly there remained a lot of work to do to really make it happen, but the men were up for it.

•

In the meantime, another Australian pilot had decided to go after a different prize, and either make his mark by flying in the other direction to Australia, or die in the attempt. His name was none other than Harry Hawker, now thirty years old and one of the most highly regarded aviation men in Great Britain, having the year before been anointed as Member of the British Empire for his work developing such Sopwith aeroplanes as the Camel, the Tabloid, the Pup, the Triplane, the Dolphin and the Snipe. After such a glorious career, he announced that he was going out to win the £10,000 prize that had been offered by Lord Northcliffe's *Daily Mail* for the first man or men to fly the Atlantic.

As good as his word, Hawker left St Johns in Newfoundland in a highly modified Sopwith B1 christened the *Atlantic*, at 3.40 pm on 18 May 1919. His navigator was Navy Lieutenant Commander Kenneth Mackenzie Grieve, and from the moment the news broke that they had managed to get off the ground — the first time they had attempted it with a full load of fuel — America and much of Europe held its collective breath, waiting for news. In the absence of any new flight information, a lot of the press focus was on Hawker's beautiful wife, Muriel, and their two-month-old baby, who were waiting patiently in London. As the papers delighted in recounting, Hawker had met Muriel four years earlier, when her car had broken down in London's magnificently sprawling Richmond Park, and out of the blue he had stopped and repaired it for her.

But now …

Where was he? It was hardly surprising that nothing had been heard from them after one day, but after two days the alarm was raised.

Then came news! A report came through that 'er 'Arry and his co-pilot had plopped their plane down 40 miles west of Ireland's Shannon River, had been picked up by a ship and they were safe! There was wild rejoicing — no, they hadn't won the prize, but the main thing was that they were safe — until a follow-up message destroyed everything. It was a false report.

A crushing silence descended once more. Day … after day … after day.

In faraway Australia, Banjo Paterson penned a poem in the widely read journal *Smith's Weekly* eulogising the presumed dead aviator:

Though Hawker perished, he overcame
The risks of the storm and the sea,
And his name shall be written in stars of flame,
On the topmost walls of the Temple of Fame,
For the rest of the world to see.

King George V also was of the view that Hawker and Grieve were dead, with his aide-de-camp sending a telegram to Muriel Hawker:

> THE KING, FEARING THE WORST MUST NOW BE REALISED REGARDING THE FATE OF YOUR HUSBAND, WISHES TO EXPRESS HIS DEEP SYMPATHY AND THAT OF THE QUEEN IN YOUR SUDDEN AND TRAGIC SORROW.[15]

For his part, Lord Northcliffe announced that although the Atlantic had not been successfully crossed, he had decided that £5000 of the £10,000 prize money would be handed over anyway, to be shared between the two airmen's next of kin as a consolation prize.

This prompted a letter from Muriel Hawker to Lord Northcliffe, filled with a gentle reproach: 'While appreciating this as a very noble offer, I cannot, and will not, as you know, believe that my husband is not alive. I am sure that he will return to hear of the generosity of the *Daily Mail* and your personal kindness to me at this time.'[16]

Muriel continued to pray for her husband's salvation, and as it happened, she was in church, on the morning of Sunday, 25 May, doing exactly that when there came a sign that perhaps, just perhaps, her prayers might have been answered. For it was on that morning off the west coast of Scotland that a small Danish tramp steamer, SS *Mary*, had appeared off one of the islands of the Outer Hebrides.

It was a ship without a radio, so as soon as it neared the coastguard station of the Butt of Lewis, it hauled up signal flags, spelling out: 'SAVED HANDS SOPWITH.'

The coastguard immediately replied: 'IS IT HAWKER.'

Came the reply: 'YES.'[17]

The wonderful news was spreading across the land even before the ship had berthed and the captain could tell the story. A week earlier, the *Mary* had been bobbing about in a fierce storm in the middle of the Atlantic when she was suddenly buzzed by a plane with a very sick engine. It was Harry Hawker and his navigator who, at the height of the tempest, with their capacity to remain airborne rapidly running out, had, by miracle, spotted the ship and knew they had only one chance of survival. After firing three distress signals from the cockpit, they ditched the plane ahead of the ship, and were indeed saved.[18] Fortuitously, the plane's near-empty fuel tanks helped to keep it afloat until a lifeboat from the ship could reach them. And, a week later, here they were.

Here they were! Astonishing things happened from the moment the two intrepid aviators made landfall. No, they had not succeeded in flying all the way across the Atlantic, but by God they had tried! And survived against the odds. And that was enough for wild celebrations, with even the sober *Times* recording, 'No event since Armistice has so stirred the popular imagination'.[19] Put on a train to London, the two initially bemused airmen were soon completely stunned at their reception, besieged as they were at every station along the way, through Inverness, Perth, Edinburgh and Newcastle, by cheering crowds and civic receptions. Flags were waved, women wept at their very sight, just as mayors were moved to flights of oratory, and hordes of children ran beside their carriage, laughing, waving and carrying on until they ran out of platform. Along the route to the next station, thousands of people stood on either side of the railway line, fluttering handkerchiefs of welcome and celebration.[20]

Both Hawker and Grieve, in the former man's words, 'completely agreed that the whole of this business was utterly undeserved and out of all proportion to what he had tried, and utterly failed to do.'[21]

Meanwhile, Thomas Sopwith and his wife accompanied Muriel Hawker to Grantham Station, two and a half hours north of London. Beside himself with joy and unable to contain it any longer, the redoubtable Sopwith threw open the door of Hawker's compartment and cried: 'Hello, Hawker!'[22] And so very good to see you, too, Thomas … but it wasn't his employer that Harry had been hoping to see when the door had burst open.

At last, Muriel — oh, blessed Muriel! — met up with her husband in a private room at that station, away from the madding crowd. Himself bursting in, Harry was instantly embracing her and their baby.

'He just said,' Muriel later recorded, 'the sweetest and most wonderful thing I could ever hear, and added, just as the people started to crush in, "Don't cry."'[23]

When finally Hawker arrived in London at Kings Cross Station, the plan was to give him a civic reception on the spot, and yet the mass of Australian Diggers who had assembled for the occasion had other ideas and they were no more disposed to take 'no' for an answer than they previously had been at Gallipoli and on the Western Front.

As reported in *The Times* the following day: 'Mr Hawker is an Australian, and Australia took his reception into her own hands. Other people were there, of course — a multitude of other people — but it was the Australian soldiers who predominated in the crowd, distinguished it from ordinary crowds, and contributed with gentle force to keeping it safe from harm. The force of organisation they brought to bear was perhaps a trifle irregular and unconventional, but had a great deal to do with preventing any very serious accident to one of the biggest, most excited, but one of the best-tempered throngs that has ever gathered in a London railway station.'

The crowd consisted of middle-aged ladies, nine-to-five workers who had missed their train just to see the great man, British sailors and soldiers, and young ladies who were alternately screaming and giggling. Just off-centre, an enormous woman with large brass earrings and an absurd sealskin coat was selling from the tray beneath her bounteous bosom, 'working models' of Hawker's plane. The tide of the crowd swelled and then surged around her island of flesh, trying to get to Hawker himself.[24]

The Times continued: 'More than once the broad shoulders of Australian soldiers were set against ugly rushes, and their quick hands upheld those who had slipped and ran the risk of being run over in the hurly-burly. They finished their conquest by taking bodily possession of Mr Hawker and Commander Grieve, and delivering them to the acclamations of the populace outside in the road.'[25]

First they placed Hawker and Grieve in a car set aside for the occasion, and then they decided to carry the car — with him still in it — on their shoulders. Singing, clapping, cheering and carrying on, Harry was one of theirs and he had done well! As to Commander Grieve, they decided to make him one of theirs just on principle. As also recounted in *The Times*, 'a few thousand voices more or less melodiously sang "Australia Will Be There"', and the two airmen 'were immediately "crowned" with two Australian slouch hats, which Captain Thompson of the 30th Australian Battalion had in readiness. This "crowning" is a ceremony by which Australia recognises men as "Diggers", whether they be her own sons, or children by adoption. Commander Grieve was a son by adoption.'[26]

Someone handed Hawker a newspaper, where it was reported that at the Paris Peace Conference, Australian Prime Minister

Billy Hughes was clearly beside himself with joy. 'The world will not forget his plucky attempt,' he was quoted as saying. 'Australia, whose soldiers have done things the world will not forget, is proud of Harry Hawker, and the Australian delegation hails him as a worthy son of the great land which gave him birth. The flight was for the purpose of testing the ability of an airplane to cross a great space in a new way. Technically, the airplane has yet to be proved, but Hawker's attempt has more than proved the ability of the men who operate those machines. It is a great thing to know we can still produce brave men.'[27]

At Buckingham Palace several days later, King George V presented Harry Hawker and Kenneth Mackenzie Grieve with the newly inaugurated Air Force Cross.

•

If that was the response for men who hadn't covered the distance, and hadn't won the prize, what would it be for someone who actually did fly the Atlantic, or do something comparable by winning the England to Australia race?

Kingsford Smith was keener than ever to win it, but was also frustrated as the date for departure kept being put back. With so many pilots wanting to try their luck it had been decided that some structure had to be placed upon the competition, and so, to give everyone a fair go, it was announced that to be eligible to win the prize all crews would have to leave England after 8 September 1919 and arrive in Australia before New Year's Day 1920. In addition, no more than thirty days could separate the time of departure and the time of arrival. Impatiently, Smithy and his crew wondered what to do with themselves over the summer, as they waited for 8 September to roll around. In the end, there really was only one possible choice. The only thing they wanted to do, the only thing they could do, and love, and make money out of was to unpack the crates, put the BE2s back together and go barnstorming all over England.

And then things *really* started to go wrong. Or right, depending upon which way you interpreted it.

No sooner had the crew uncrated one plane and taken it to the air than a weird succession of disasters began. After one flight just a few days into their new venture, Smithy was landing the plane in a thick fog on a clear field in dead still conditions when suddenly an enormous oak tree jumped in front of the plane, which in turn insisted on wrapping itself around said tree. Or that was the way it seemed. Still, if there was an upside to the accident — *and there certainly was!* — it was that they had insured the plane for more money than it was actually worth. So they were soon able to replace the destroyed plane with an even better one. After all, Britain was awash with war planes that she no longer needed, so it was really no problem to get another one. Kingsford Smith and Maddocks continued on their tour, through such towns as Aylesbury, Oxford, Abingdon, Burnley, Blackburn and Nelson.

The next crash was a little different in calibre. One afternoon after they had been barnstorming together, Kingsford Smith and Maddocks were heading home in their plane when a strong difference of opinion arose between them. Maddocks wanted to get straight back to the aerodrome that was their base, while Smithy much preferred to land in a farmer's field, where he knew the farmer's daughter would be waiting for him, sweet as a peach. Had it been a verbal argument only, the outcome of the disagreement would have been merely raised voices. But in this case they were in a plane with joint controls, and as Maddocks hauled with all of his might one way on the controls, Smithy hauled with all of his strength in the opposite direction and what gave way — with a sudden and sickening *twangggggg* — was a control wire.

The thing about plane crashes, Kingsford Smith was discovering with some regularity now, in much the same way as Louis Blériot had discovered a decade earlier, was an unearthly sense of time suspended … and then rushed … as the once so distant scenery below … slowly floats up … towards … you … and.then.comes.hurtling.right.at.you!

Belting down onto the fields below, they were at least able to avoid trees this time, but nothing could stop them from first breaking off one wing, then the other, then the undercarriage … until all they were left with was the fuselage … bursting over a ditch and into a thick hedge. Never mind, neither of them was hurt and in any case the insurance company would pick up the cost, what?

Yes, albeit reluctantly, and the company was increasingly reluctant when only a short time later a third plane flown by Kingsford Smith had a disaster. This one burst into flames in midair, and he was able to practise a technique he had long heard about — keeping the flames under control by 'side-slipping', banking left with ailerons, while simultaneously applying lots of right rudder to keep the plane straight. The lateral relative wind blew the heat and flames away from the cockpit and at least he was able to get the plane on the ground before running for his life, just seconds before it exploded. Somehow, the insurance company did not seem as joyous as he was that he had lived.

When Kingsford Smith subsequently crashed a *fourth* plane — after a lovely nurse he had taken aloft suffered a panic attack and gripped the controls as if her life depended on it — things had really gone too far and, in some ways, it was perhaps Oscar Wilde who enunciated the principle best: '*To lose one parent, Mr Worthing, may be regarded as a misfortune; to lose both looks like carelessness.*'

One lost plane might be merely misfortune; two lost was carelessness; three destroyed was cause for pause, and four …? Four was cause for serious examination as to just what was going on.

One day shortly after the fourth crash, Lieutenant Colonel Richard Williams, the Australian government's chief organiser of the England to Australia race, based in London, a distinguished war veteran, received an odd phone call in his office at Australia House from the manager of the Blackburn Aircraft Company. Would Lieutenant Colonel Williams mind popping around for a little chat?

Not at all, not at all …

After polite formalities, the manager got to the point. Would the Australian government have any objections if this chappie Charles Kingsford Smith was replaced as a pilot for the Blackburn Kangaroo, which was already entered into the race?

'So long as the replacement is an Australian,' Williams replied, a little bemused, 'it is no business of mine or the

Australian government to say who should or should not be the pilot of a competing aircraft.'

Still, Williams could not resist asking why they wanted to replace Kingsford Smith?

The manager, in turn, was frank.

It's like this: the pilot concerned is purchasing aircraft from government disposals and going barnstorming around the country, ignoring civil air regulations and landing in fields not approved for the purpose. It seems he has also found that he can insure his aircraft for an amount in excess of that for which he can replace them and there have been some crashes …

He paused.

The bottom line? The view of the Blackburn Aircraft Company was that such behaviour was undermining not only civil aviation control, but also damaging aviation insurance, which was just in its early days. So, if the Australian government had no objections, Kingsford Smith was out.[28] And Cyril Maddocks too, for that matter …

And out, they were. Blackburn would simply have to find some others to fill his crew.

•

Back in Sydney, another Australian pilot from the Great War, Nigel Love, had finally made his decision. Like Smithy, he was convinced that there was going to be a quid or two to be made in aviation in peacetime, and with that in mind he had, along with a couple of his mates, formed the grandly titled 'Australian Aircraft and Engineering Company Ltd'. Their key asset was the licence to make and sell in Australia the Avro aeroplane — those constructed by the major British industrialist Alliot Verdon Roe, who had first learnt the principles of flight by throwing paper planes out the second storey window of the family home — and it had fallen to Captain Love to find a spot to build an airfield from which they could operate. After scouring Sydney, and then following up on a tip from the real estate firm of Raine & Horne, he knew that he had the perfect spot.

It was a paddock of 160 acres on the northern edge of Botany Bay, in a suburb called Mascot. The paddock had been used by a local abattoir to fatten cattle before their slaughter, but as the company was going out of business the land was available to initially lease from its owners, the Kensington Racing Club.[29]

The key feature for Love was that the land was flat, fairly well drained — though it had originally been a swamp — and it was covered in buffalo grass that had been kept low by the cattle. The area had clear approaches from every direction for planes to land. All that, and it was only a little bit more than 4 miles from downtown Sydney.[30] And so it was with great enthusiasm that Love sealed the deal and followed it up by also securing premises on nearby Botany Road, where he established a workshop to maintain aircraft and began to fabricate the Avros for customers.[31]

•

But what about the rest of Australia? In the immediate post-war days there was a growing awareness of the need for more aerodromes around the country, as the England to Australia race drew closer. How were those planes that made it to Darwin or to Wyndham in the north-west, to proceed to the east coast, to the likes of Brisbane, Sydney and Melbourne? Where could they land in the Australian outback? Where could they stock up on petrol and supplies? Clearly, someone was going to have to find the right spots, and then follow up by clearing trees, mulga bushes and the like for a good airstrip.

In an attempt to do exactly that, the government of Prime Minister Billy Hughes commissioned two veteran war pilots, Paul McGinness and Hudson Fysh, to reconnoitre the far north of Australia from Longreach to Darwin — an overland trip through vast swathes of land never penetrated before by vehicles of any description. 'From Cloncurry to Katherine River,' their instructions read, 'you will obtain fullest information about the air route proposed, and if possible traverse it by car. Places suitable for aerodromes and for forced landings will be marked and field sketches made of the surroundings to facilitate identification from the air.'[32]

They were just the men for the job, and they were also used to working together. In the Great War, both had served with distinction, first landing at Gallipoli with the Light Horse. 'Ginty' McGinness, as he was known, a burly knockabout knock-'em-down kind of man from Victoria had won the Distinguished Conduct Medal in an action at Pope's Hill, and gone on to consolidate his reputation as a fine soldier from there. Fysh, too — a slight and quiet man by nature, whose uncle had been Tasmanian Premier — had been handy with a rifle, and was commissioned as an officer after his own section officer, none other than Lieutenant Ross Smith, had left to join the Australian Flying Corps. When, not long afterwards, McGinness and Fysh had decided to follow Smith and also join the AFC, McGinness had quickly proved himself a fine pilot, with Fysh as his observer. Together they saw a lot of action in Palestine where 'Ginty' registered seven confirmed victories,[33] and Fysh, just before the war ended, gained his own wings.

Though both intrepid aviators had wanted to enter the England to Australia race themselves, they had failed to get the necessary finance when their chief backer died just before writing the cheque and his family had decided they didn't want to go on with it. Still, just being involved in the race was honour enough for them, and they pursued the plans enthusiastically, organising to get a Model T Ford packed with provisions to the railhead at Longreach, and for another war friend, a mechanic by the name of George Gorham, to accompany them. (The reckoning was that if it had wheels and an engine, then George could fix it — with his bare hands if necessary.)

•

It is an ill wind that blows no-one any good, and the fact that Blackburn withdrew its sponsorship of Charles Kingsford Smith opened the way for none other than George Wilkins to take his place. Wilkins had just returned from the ghostly haunting silence of Gallipoli, where he had been engaged by Charles Bean to document precisely what had occurred there four years earlier, and he had spent many weeks traipsing with his camera around and about such spiritually troubling places as Lone Pine, the Nek and Hill 971, where the tattered bits of cloth and bleached bones of dead Allied soldiers and Turks were still scattered across the bloodied landscape. Back in London, Wilkins wasn't sure if he wanted to be part of the venture to race to Australia when initially approached, but the more he looked at it, the more he liked it.

The money didn't attract him particularly — he had never been motivated by money — but it was a challenge, an adventure, and he could see that it really would help the land of his birth, to open up an air route between Australia and England, so he accepted a position on the Kangaroo. Most importantly, for him, it was an opportunity to continue on his life's quest of scientific discovery, and he was careful to pack all kinds of equipment that enabled him to record temperatures, humidity, air pressure and so forth, in the course of the journey.

In the final structure, Wilkins became both the commander and the navigator on the flight of the Kangaroo and it was a measure of the respect in which he was held within the London establishment that at the crew's departure from London's Hendon aerodrome at 10.37 on the morning of 21 November 1919,[34] he was carrying the cabled best wishes of no less than the future King of England, Prince Albert and the former First Lord of the Admiralty, the Right Honourable Winston Churchill. Which was to the good. All their 'good lucks', 'bon voyages' and 'tally-hos' were very much appreciated. But could the crew actually do the job they had set out to do …?

•

Trouble. Big trouble. After a problem-plagued trip that had taken them only a quarter of the distance to Australia in two and a half weeks, George Wilkins and his Blackburn Kangaroo crew suddenly had the spectre of death riding along with them. Eighty miles south-west of Crete — with the North African coast ahead about the same distance again — Wilkins looked out his window to see the plane's lifeblood pouring away. Just off the back of the port-side engine, an oil pipe had burst and was spraying the black gold into the waves of the Mediterranean Sea, some 2000 feet below. After an agonised, grinding growl to indicate how unhappy it was to go in such a tortured fashion, pilot Val Rendle quickly switched the port engine off to preserve it.

This left the Kangaroo with one engine to make it to the nearest land, and meant going back to Crete — their calculations showed that on one engine from that height, the greatest distance they could hope for was 30 miles. Still, reasoning that it was better to be 50 miles from land in the middle of the ocean than 80 miles, they turned the plane and did their best.

And were favoured a little by providence … as a propitious wind blew up, and helped them on their way.

Paradoxically, as they edged along past 30 miles, 40 miles, 50 miles, then 60 miles, the crew members began to show increasing signs of fear. Somehow, with a growing chance of survival, they all began to feel afraid of dying.[35] At last, at last, Crete came into view, but still they were not safe. For where could they land? Everywhere they looked, all they could see were cliff faces, rugged rock and yawning, hungry canyons, each one clearly happy to swallow them whole without burping.

In vain did they search the terrain beneath them for some flat ground where they could attempt a smooth landing … or at least land flat enough on which they could get down intact. Finally, it was obvious that they were going to have to take their chances on the flattest handkerchief of land they could find. Rendle dropped the throttle back, and began to bring the plane down on the impossibly small clearing that now presented itself. And while it was reassuring to once again be close to mother earth, and in some rough kind of control, the problem was that they were still moving in far too quickly and … and … after clipping the tiles on a farmhouse roof, a solid stone wall, which had been a good distance away when they first made contact with the soil, had now grown legs and was rushing towards them with unseemly haste. As the entire crew held their heads in their hands, in an instinctive effort to provide some protection, the plane rushed over a ditch, up a bank and came to rest against the wall, with its nose in the ground and its tail high in the air.

Now, given how many people thought that only lunatics would enter such a race in the first place, it was perhaps appropriate that the wall they had hit belonged to Crete's largest lunatic asylum. Still, at least they were alive to fight another day!

And, truth be told, George Wilkins was not at all perturbed about not winning the race. As he had made clear from the beginning, he was only interested in competing for the opportunity to collect a lot of scientific data. His major concern after the crash was to ensure that his notebooks were secure, and that his varied equipment — barometers, thermometers, hygrometers, wet and dry bulbs and density meters — was all intact.[36]

•

Kingsford Smith, meantime, was discovering his own new worlds, albeit in rather different circumstances. After Blackburn had so hurtfully pulled the rug out from under him, he had tried to interest other sponsors, but to no avail. He had even written to his prosperous brother Harold in California asking for money, with a similar result. Chilla's sister Elsie, then staying with Harold, wrote something of a telltale letter to their parents:

> *Harold had rather a pathetic letter from Charles … telling all about their troubles (re England–Australia flight) & saying he will not return to Australia unless he can fly back — after all that fuss and publicity made. Incidentally, he hoped that Harold might be able to finance him to the extent of a couple of thousand pounds so that he could get his own machine.*[37]

Harold, though a faithful brother, wasn't particularly interested, and Smithy, with increasing desperation, was obliged to continue looking elsewhere for money.

•

Anthony Fokker was now going well, expanding his aircraft manufacturing premises in North Amsterdam and focusing on building fast, reliable planes capable of carrying the maximum number of passengers and goods the greatest distance — while his old wartime rival, Tom Sopwith, was fading fast. As soon as the Great War finished, the impoverished British government had immediately cancelled all of its orders with the Sopwith firm, with no recompense, and then pursued Sopwith vigorously for a great deal of back taxes!

What could Tom Sopwith do? The only thing he could — allow the old firm to go bust and form a new one with himself and new partners Harry Hawker, Fred Sigist and Bill Eyre, each contributing £5000. This new company bore the name H.G. Hawker Engineering. Sopwith didn't mind that his name was not on the new firm. After all, he told everyone, 'Harry Hawker was largely responsible for our growth during the war.'[38] In no time at all they were making Hawker planes and H.G. Hawker two-stroke motorcycles, while Harry soon personally added to his fame by being the first man to drive a 1500 cc car — whose engine he had personally modified — faster than 100 miles per hour.

•

It was possible there were more inhospitable terrains in the world to take a car, but notwithstanding the fact that both Hudson Fysh and Paul McGinness had flown planes in Syria, Palestine and Egypt, neither had ever seen anything like this. For it wasn't just the endless sand dunes that confronted them as they tried to make their way from Longreach, Queensland, to the Katherine railhead in the Northern Territory, 1354 miles distant. It was also the sucking black plains of western Queensland, which just a few points of rain would turn into a muddy glutinous mass and make them all but impassable. It was the oppressive heat, 'neath a sun that did not so much shine as *beat*. It was the lack of any kind of roads except scratched tracks, and the lack of bridges to get them over constant raging torrents. It was the fact that the population was so sparse that when you did get into trouble there was likely no-one to help in any direction for 100 miles, even if you knew where to begin to look for them. Nevertheless, McGinness and Fysh persisted, in the company of their long-suffering mechanic, George Gorham, who somehow managed to keep his straw boater intact, perched atop his head through everything.

Slowly, painfully, the three men continued to edge their way forward, as the general *put-put-put* and sometimes angry snarl of their overloaded Model T Ford melded with the thick, sweltering buzz of the Australian bush. As they went, it was Fysh who meticulously sketched and mapped the landscape documenting possible places for airstrips to be built. McGinness, never one for details, focused on finding ways to just keep them moving, come what may.

Occasionally they would argue, such was the strain they were under, and mostly it was McGinness who would have the last word. He was a sometimes domineering rough diamond of a man who cared little for correct form — an extrovert Australian original who believed that there was no problem so great that enough elbow grease and fencing wire couldn't fix it. Fysh, on the other hand, was a lot more laid-back, an introvert of a far more cerebral nature.

Somehow, between them — with George the mechanic nearly always in tow but also pushing, too, as well as taking his turn at driving — they continued to make their way roughly west, shooting parrots and the like for food when their supplies ran out. On a bad day they would make only 4 miles. On an average good day they could go as far as 15 or 20 miles. What was soon abundantly clear, through their own observation and through talking to the few people they met, was that this was a part of the world that desperately needed an airline, as land travel was just too damn difficult. The only transport infrastructure that existed in a few parts were the railways, and they terminated at Charleville, Longreach, Winton and Cloncurry, with no connections between.

The only people who seemed to move easily in this kind of country were the Aborigines, whom they would occasionally see flitting away in the distance — and they had had thousands of years to acclimatise. (And for the most part the white men were glad not to make too much contact, as they had been told by locals, 'The blacks are bad, and Murdering Tommy is out in the Turn-Off Lagoon area.'[39])

•

As to the race itself, Ross Smith and his quietly spoken older brother Keith, a former RFC and then RAF flying instructor, were considered by many judges to have the best chance of winning it. With two mechanics, they had left Hounslow Heath at 9.05 am on 12 November 1919 and flown, on average, ten hours a day. Every night, as the mechanics worked feverishly on the engines, the brothers carefully put such petrol as they could find into their machine, being very careful to strain it through cloth to remove whatever local impurities it might contain. Eschewing a radio, as at 100 pounds they had decided that it weighed too much to carry, their one concession to safety was to take a fishing line and a few hooks, on the reckoning, as Ross Smith described it, that they might be useful, 'in case we should land on some small uninhabited island and have to do the Robinson Crusoe act for a time'.[40]

And coming down unexpectedly in strange country was certainly a common experience. In Yugoslavia, a Sopwith Wallaby piloted by Captain George C. Matthews — formerly of the Light Horse and then of No. 4 Australian Flying Squadron — with Sergeant Tommy D. Kay of Ballarat as mechanic, had been obliged to land in bad weather just 100 miles out of Belgrade. This part of the world was still in a state of post-war upheaval, and it had not yet been definitively determined just who were the patriots and who were the traitors. And yet those in temporary power where the plane had come to earth had only taken one look at the Australians before they knew exactly what they were — *Bolsheviks!*

Therefore, for the Australians' trouble, they were immediately arrested and thrown in a room so tiny and dark it was little more than a vertical coffin, just capable of holding the two of them. For four days they were fed only enough of the local delicacy — black bread topped by pig fat and swarming flies — to keep them alive. Until … Until they managed, in the middle of the night, when their captors had fallen into a drunken stupor, to make a break for it … run like mad things for their plane, get it started and fly away … all of it in the company of myriad bullets winging around them.[41]

See yers!

In a highly creditable performance, over the next few weeks Matthews and Kay managed to hip-hop all the way to Bali —

practically in sight of Australia, just a hundred horizons ahead! — before they crashed into a banana plantation on the island on 17 April. But at least they survived. Not all were so lucky …

Sadly, just 6 miles after take-off from Hounslow Heath near London, the *Alliance PZ Seabird*, named after Cook's ship, flown by Captain Roger Douglas and navigated by Lieutenant J.S. Leslie Ross, crashed into a Surbiton orchard, killing both men. Only minutes before, when the plane had been wheeled out of its hangar at Hounslow and the sun had burst through the clouds with an unexpected brilliance, the onlookers had broken into loud applause at such a good omen for a wonderful trip.[42] Quite what went wrong was never established, though it was noted by some that the plane had excessive emergency provisions, which would have weighed it down — as would the leather upholstered armchairs both men were sitting in.

As to another plane, a Martinsyde, flown by the Australians Cedric E. Howell and George Henry Fraser, which crashed into St George's Bay off Corfu in the Adriatic Sea while flying at night on 9 December, its demise was equally tragic. Villagers on Corfu saw distress rockets go up in the night, and could even hear Howell and Fraser yelling for help, but in the middle of a terrible storm it proved impossible to reach them. Then the shouting stopped. A few days later the wreckage washed up on the beach, and two weeks after the crash, Howell's body was also washed ashore.[43]

•

Finally, with no finance forthcoming and all hope of entering the race abandoned, Charles Kingsford Smith and Cyril Maddocks were to find that even trying to sell their joyriding concern was a very lugubrious endeavour because no-one was remotely interested. So it was that, devastated and humiliated in equal measure by his failure to be part of the race, Smithy decided to go home to Australia by alternative means.

Owning only the clothes he stood up in, which was by now his rather threadbare uniform — to make up the fare he had sold his one and only proper civilian suit — Kingsford Smith took a ship to New York, where his first true port of call was the Alien

Immigration Hospital on Ellis Island, courtesy of the return of the same kind of flu that had laid him so low a year previously. Overcoming that, he took a train across America and, living on a solid diet of oranges and more oranges — the only food item he could afford — arrived in California six days later.[44]

There, the 22-year-old had expected to be met at Oakland Station by his 40-year-old brother, Harold, but instead received a wonderful surprise. Besides Harold and his wife and their teenage daughter, Beris, he was greeted by his sister Elsie and brother Wilfrid who, unbeknown to Chilla, were visiting Harold too. In a blizzard of hugs, kisses and pumping handshakes, it was all 'hail brother well met', and back to the bosom of his family in Harold's large and stylish home at Menlo Park, just south of San Francisco, to kill the fatted calf.

Though his siblings were more than a little shocked at his ragged appearance, broken finances and rather fragile health, he seemed to revive quickly in their presence and the old Chilla soon re-emerged, laughing, telling them of his adventures over the dinner table and a few drinks afterwards in front of the fire, and of course gathering them around the piano to sing songs and make merry into the night …

Harold, of course, had to rise early the following morning to go to work in his executive position with the American-Hawaiian Steamship Company, leaving Chilla and the others to sleep in, but that was no problem. Someone in the household had to work …

•

It was one of the greatest thrills in Hudson Fysh's life. After fifty-one days of crossing the central north of Australia, followed by six weeks of overseeing the building of a small aerodrome on the edge of Darwin at Fannie Bay, Fysh was at that very spot at 3.40 pm on the steaming tropical afternoon of 10 December 1919, with a crowd of two thousand people or so, awaiting what seemed like a miracle. News had come to the Darwin wireless station from Timor to say that Ross and Keith Smith should be arriving some time soon, and yet, in truth, no-one was going to believe it until they saw it.

And then the most wonderful thing happened.

Far to the north-west, out over the sparkling sea, they saw the tiniest speck just above the horizon. *There!* As one the crowd focused on it, straining their necks forward and squinting their eyes against the glare. A seagull? An albatross, maybe? No! It was a plane! A plane was coming their way. And not just any plane. This, they knew, was the plane flown by Ross Smith, with his older brother Keith as navigator, both distinguished veterans of the Australian Flying Corps. The flyers had left England just a little less than four weeks before, and at the moment they landed they would be the official winners of the England to Australia race, in the first plane to arrive in the Great Southland under its own power. Hurrah!

As it happened, Fysh would have been delighted to see any Australian pilot now reaching the end of the race, but given their common service with first the 'Emma Gees' — the 1st Machine Gun Section of the 1st Light Horse Brigade — and then the AFC, it was a special thrill to see the Smiths.

And now here it was! An enormous howling beast, like an ungainly flying hippo, a Vickers Vimy bomber with the civil registration of G-EAOU marked in huge letters upon it, which, it later turned out, the crew insisted stood for 'God Elp All Of Us!'. At the moment the wheels touched Australian soil, a cheer went up, and when the plane finally trundled to a stop, the crowd surged forward — brushing aside the two zealous customs and health officials keen to examine the new arrivals — and marvelled anew at the journey the men had made.

Can you believe it? Close up, it was obvious the whole plane had been held together by prayer for the last part of the trip. A small branch of a tree lodged in the plane's undercarriage told how close they had come to disaster on their last take-off, from the airfield at Timor.

Over the previous twenty-seven days and twenty hours the plane and crew had overcome obstacle after obstacle, been through storms, howling winds and cascading rain; had broken down, fixed themselves up; been nearly knocked out of the skies by lightning; come close to crashing; become bogged; dug themselves out; become bogged again, dug themselves out again; taken off *in extremis* and flown over lands where natives had cowered at their very sight, thinking that they were evil spirits of the dead come back to earth,[45] and somehow, *somehow* managed to keep going through it all. Indeed, there was so little fuel left in the plane's tanks when it landed that one of the mechanics on board, Wally Shiers, later noted, 'We almost fell into Darwin'.[46] But look at the time! In 1788, the First Fleet had done the trip in eight months; by 1849 that had decreased to ninety-one days; and there had been a leap forward in 1854 when it had been cut to sixty-three days. But under twenty-eight days? It almost beggared belief.

The race was over, the £10,000 won and, as Ross Smith recorded, 'shoals of telegrams and cables arrived in fifteen minute lots from every corner of the globe',[47] including one from Prime Minister Billy Hughes, addressed to him:

> You have covered the name of Australia with fresh laurels. You have broken all world records, and you have shown the world once more what manner of man the Australian is. You have given your country world-wide advertisement, and proved that, with relays of machines and men, Europe can be brought within 12 or 15 days of Australia.
>
> W.M. Hughes.[48]

For his part, Winston Churchill, the British Secretary of State for Air, cabled: 'Well done. Your great flight shows conclusively that the new element has been conquered for the use of man.' And even His Majesty King George V honoured them by sending a message noting, 'Your success will bring Australia nearer to the Mother Country.'[49]

•

Ross and Keith Smith became almost instantly the two most famous Australians who had ever lived, with no less than Sydney's *Daily Telegraph* opining that: 'Only one achievement in the history of Australia was as great — the arrival of Captain Cook. It took Captain Cook three years to make his voyage to Australia and go back. Captain Ross Smith made the journey one way in 28 days.'[50]

The Smiths and their crew had flown home from the other side of the *planet* — can you believe it? — and the Smiths were, quite rightly, not long in receiving knighthoods! For *Sir* Ross Smith, particularly, it was just one more honour to go with the two Military Crosses and three Distinguished Flying Crosses he had received for his derring-do during the war. True, upon arrival in Darwin, he, his brother and their two mechanics were so exhausted they could barely stand up — not one of them had had more than five hours of sleep on any night during the whole trip — but it had all been worth it. As to the £10,000 they had now won, both Ross and Keith Smith insisted that it be shared equally with their two mechanics, who had taken equal risks with them.

And, as they all slept soundly that night, the printing presses of newspapers around the country were humming along to their fame. The banner headline in the following day's *Daily Telegraph* set the tone. Crossing half of the page it blared:

ROSS SMITH REACHES AUSTRALIA

ARRIVAL AT DARWIN
A THRILLING RECEPTION.
PRIZE CONDITIONS COMPLIED WITH.

Captain Ross Smith, the paper reported, had replied to the welcome by saying, 'He was proud, as an Australian, to be back in Australia, and receive such a rousing welcome from real Australians'.[51] And yet that welcome had only just begun, as all was put in readiness for them to fly on, first across the top of Australia and then down through the major cities of the east coast, before they made their way home to Adelaide.

To that end, Hudson Fysh's partner, Paul McGinness, was over at Cloncurry in far north-western Queensland, putting the finishing touches to the construction of the airstrip there. If all went well, the Smith brothers and any subsequent competitors who made it to Australia — not to mention future generations of aviators and maybe even air travellers — would be able to land and refuel on their way to the east coast. Since mid-October, when McGinness and Fysh had arrived in Darwin, two months had gone by. The trip had convinced both of them, as well as the Federal government that the country in the far-central-north of Australia was fundamentally unsuited to the construction of airstrips. On the instruction of the government, therefore, McGinness had headed back towards their starting point on a much more inland route, getting rough airstrips built along the way, at Newcastle Waters — where he paid a group of Aboriginal women with two bags of flour, 20 yards of red material and twenty-four sticks of tobacco, to do the bulk of work[52] — Brunette Downs and Camooweal. This Cloncurry airstrip would be his last.

It was hard, backbreaking work, in hideous heat, and yet not without respite on the odd occasion. For on the Sunday after the Smith brothers had landed in the north, McGinness was overjoyed to have organised for that early afternoon to go on a picnic with a nice local girl he had met, a real beauty, little knowing what lay ahead …

•

And wouldn't that be a *bastard* of a thing?

Fergus McMaster, a wealthy and well-bred grazier, who had just returned from serving with the AIF himself, was on this hot Sunday early afternoon crossing the sandy, rocky bed of the Cloncurry River, trying to get back to his vast station, Moscow, when the damn stub axle on his car broke.

McMaster had not the tools, nor the spares, nor the skills to fix the car himself and he was on the kind of road where hours might pass before someone else would happen along. The only option was to use shanks's pony and walk the 3 miles back into Cloncurry in the hope that he could get some help there. And yet, when he arrived, it was only to find the place all shut up and practically deserted, as everyone was going to some picnic.[53]

It was while he was trudging exhaustedly up the main street, trying to keep in what scant shade was offered by the low buildings, that McMaster was hailed by a man coming the other way.

Paul McGinness recognised the 6-foot frame as belonging to local station owner McMaster, whom he had met on a couple of occasions. Now, McGinness was the kind of man who would have helped anyone in such circumstances, but for McMaster — a fellow Digger and said to be a good bloke — he certainly went the extra mile. For greater mateship hath no man than he who should arrange for another mate to take a beautiful girl to a picnic so he could help a maybe future mate fix his car. After sorting the girl, McGinness, with McMaster under his wing, carefully broke into the back of a shut-up garage to get the gear they would need, including a spare axle. McMaster left an IOU for the amount, while McGinness left a note for the proprietor explaining why they had been obliged to break in, but noting that they had nailed the corrugated iron they had prised from the rear of the shed back on.[54] (Cloncurry was that kind of place.)

Now, you didn't come through the kind of country that McGinness and Fysh had got through without the capacity to fix just about anything, and McMaster's simple axle replacement — once they had driven back out there in the Model T Ford — was a comparatively easy thing to sort out. Profuse in his thanks, McMaster, in his thick Scottish burr, asked McGinness to look him up if ever he was in Brisbane, where the station owner also spent a lot of time, and perhaps he could find a way to repay his kindness.

Will do …

And then each went about their business: McMaster to get back to his station, and McGinness to more fully explain to the enraged local girl why he hadn't been able to make the picnic. And then, of course, McGinness had to get back to putting the finishing touches to the Cloncurry airstrip. While he worked, his thoughts kept returning to something he and Fysh had talked about intermittently over the previous few months of crossing the top end of the country — the possibilities of forming a company to engage in commercial aviation. One episode in particular had convinced him that there was a need for it. At an enormous cattle station south of Katherine, where he had accepted bush hospitality for a spell, McGinness had been stunned at how tough things were for the station wife, who had a tiny newborn baby. She had explained to him that if the baby — or anyone else for that matter — got sick, they pretty much had to make do, because in the wet season, particularly, no-one could get in or out. Post was always a big problem, and if you wanted anything, it could take up to twelve months to arrive! These people needed, and could afford to pay for, an air service, but there simply wasn't one. And the top end of Australia was full of people exactly like them.[55] It was a huge area, with a fair sprinkling of population, substantially uncrossed by roads. Of course an air service would prosper there, and Hudson and McGinness might be just the men to provide it!

All they needed was the capital to start it. Maybe, just maybe, McMaster might be the man to approach about organising it? It was certainly worth consideration, and McGinness resolved to seriously talk to Fysh as soon as they caught up with each other again.

•

Before leaving Darwin, Ross and Keith Smith were fully briefed by some stockmen on how best to navigate their way to Cloncurry, a thousand miles to the south-east. Just do in reverse what the stockmen had done with their mob of cattle a few months previously, see? First, you hafta follow the telegraph line south, until you get to Newcastle Waters station, and then turn south-east. Do not leave that telegraph line, or you'll dinkum get lost, as everything looks the same, and you'll be rooted. Now follow that line for, oh, about a hunnert miles or so, and then from the air you should see two big patches of scrub that kinda meet in a 'V'. Now, go down low and look hard at the scrubland below. If you look real close, you'll see the tracks of where we drove the cattle — don't worry, there's been no rain to wash them tracks away — and all you'll have to do is follow them for a few miles, and you'll get to a real bush track and if you follow that, you'll get to Cloncurry. Got that?

Yes, no worries.

And so it proved! When Ross and Keith Smith and their two mechanics landed in Cloncurry a couple of days after leaving

Darwin — they had had to spend one awful night on the ground on the way, where it turned out they had been invited to a surprise mosquito banquet and they were the main course — it was to receive the usual accolades and rapturous welcome, and one other thing besides. From Sydney, Nigel Love's Australian Aircraft and Engineering Company sent a telegram, which finished with:

> Should you decide to honour Sydney with
> a visit on your way south, this company
> wishes to extend an invitation to land
> at the aerodrome at Mascot. Position,
> north bank George's River, close to mouth.
> Extreme northern corner Botany Bay.
> Landing ground marked with white circle.[56]

The brothers decided to do exactly that and when they arrived at Mascot a couple of weeks later, were received in the manner to which they had so recently become accustomed: as conquering heroes, men who had managed to fly from one side of the planet to the other!

Seven

HOMEWARD BOUND

Pilot after pilot was featured on the sporting pages of the newspapers as he succeeded in remaining aloft five minutes longer than the hero of the month before, reached an altitude fifty feet higher, or somersaulted his vibrating little kite once oftener. And with deadly regularity pilot after pilot was killed — his effort to find out how far he could stretch the capacity of his machine being successful …

KENNETH CHAFEE MCINTOSH, IN THE *ATLANTIC*, SEPTEMBER 1921

Riding on horseback is always cheaper than travelling by rail or hiring a car. But what would we think of the man who preferred that mode of transport for a journey of any length? In time, people will realise that aerial travel at 90 miles per hour will practically always pay them.

HUDSON FYSH, WRITING IN AN ARTICLE IN *THE GRAZIERS' REVIEW*, EARLY 1920S[1]

Poor Chilla.

News of the triumph of the Smith brothers in winning the England to Australia race was not long in reaching California, and he could have been forgiven for thinking that had things gone differently, their victory might have been his. And that prize money! While the celebrated brothers — with their *knighthoods* — were now splitting £10,000 between them, the rather down-and-out Chilla remained dependent on the familial generosity of his brother Harold and his wife, Elsie.

How to keep body and soul together?

It wasn't immediately apparent. Ideally, it would be by finding people who would pay him for the only thing he wanted to do — fly. Rather inconveniently, however, at that time in California there simply weren't flying jobs to be had, at least not for 'aliens', as non-American citizens were charmingly known.

Clearly, what he most needed was to learn a skill apart from flying, and as ever, Harold came to the rescue, arranging for the baby of the family to take a course as a radio man, which proved to be extremely hard yakka. His family, both in America and Australia, worried about him greatly. Sister Elsie wrote home in mid-February 1920:

> *Poor old Charles is taking up wireless as there seems to be nothing doing in the flying game for him — beyond a couple of rather indefinite offers. The trouble is that Chilla is so very stony he can't wait, so Harold is going to send him away on one of his ships to South America in a few weeks time. Now he is studying hard to get thro' — in the meantime hoping madly that something more congenial will turn up. His whole heart is in flying and nothing else seems to interest him — except a pretty girl and the banjo — and as the former require a certain amount of dollars to be entertained he has had to fall back on the good old banjo and spends all his spare time practising. I don't think [Harold's wife] Elsie is fearfully keen on the banjo though!*[2]

As it turned out, being Australian also prevented Chilla from working as a deckhand on one of Harold's ships, and nor did he have whatever it took to continue his radio studies. The one thing that really worked his spirit, apart from banjos and a succession of pretty girls, was news of a prize that had been put forward, rather like the England to Australia race prize, except this was for a far bigger amount, and for a much bigger task. Smithy had first spied a report of it in the San Francisco *Examiner*. A rich silent-film producer and director by the name of Thomas Harper Ince — known as 'the father of the Western' — had put up $50,000 to the first aviator or team of aviators who could fly across the Pacific Ocean. At 7000 miles, it was the longest stretch of water in the world.

But US$50,000! Well over double the prize for the England to Australia race.

There, *there* would lie his redemption. From the moment of reading about it, Charles could think of little else, talk of little else, dream of little else. Flying across the Pacific Ocean would be a feat like no other, simply because there was no other ocean as vast. And what could he do with US$50,000!

Still, it was not just about the money, as broke as he was.

'If only,' Smithy wrote to his mother, 'I could manage to do that job, I would be able to justify myself in the eyes of the Australian people with a vengeance.'[3]

Now, obviously the youngest of the Kingsford Smith clan didn't have the money himself to mount such a flight, but Harold was able at least to lend a hand in introducing Chilla to people from the Californian business community who might have it and be prepared to back him. For weeks on end, thus, Charles Kingsford Smith did the rounds, trying to interest, variously, aviation manufacturers, fuel companies and assorted others in the imperative to back him ...

The plan he submitted to potential backers at this early stage was fairly simple, and he presented it initially in written form, the whole project predicated on him having a Junkers-Larsen JL-6 all-metal seaplane.

Route:
San Francisco to Honolulu — 2048 miles (refuel at sea)
Honolulu to Fanning Island — 1215 miles
Fanning Island to Enderbury Island — 950 miles
Enderbury Island to Pago Pago — 850 miles
Pago Pago to Levuka — 1101 miles
Levuka to Noumea — 894 miles
Noumea to Brisbane — 913 miles
Total distance — 7971 miles[4]

If he could get the financial backing he needed, the sponsor would receive half the net profits — being outgoings less estimated receipts.

Outgoings:
Cost of machine 16,500 dollars
Preliminary expenses 1000 dollars
Cables, fuel, etc 500 dollars
For return of navigator 500 dollars
Life insurance (approx) 4000 dollars
Total — 22,500 dollars[5]

Estimated Receipts:
Moving picture rights 25,000 dollars
Sale of machine 25,000 dollars
Magazine stories 10,000 dollars
Prize monies 30,000 dollars
Lecturing in US & Australia 25,000 dollars
Total 115,000 dollars
Estimated profit — 92,500 dollars[6]

Now, there are many ways to be told NO, and in those weeks he discovered most of them. In the parlance of the time — if interest in his plan had been dynamite he wouldn't have received enough to blow his hat off.

At least part of the problem, he felt, was, once more, that he was not an American. Another large part was that he might as well have been talking about flying to the moon. To fly the *Pacific Ocean*? Are you goddamn *crazy*, boy? Do you have a suicide wish? If so, there has to be a cheaper way of doing it.

For most people, flying across the Pacific Ocean was beyond the realms of imagination, let alone known possibility. Why, to that day, no-one had even flown to Hawaii!

Never mind. Kingsford Smith continued to believe the journey was feasible and kept trying to convince people of exactly that, until there was simply no-one else left to interest whom he hadn't met and been knocked back by. For the moment he decided to shelve the plan, if not the dream.

One benefit of all the running around was that he was able to secure work back in aviation, though it wasn't quite the work he had been hoping for. Only three years previously he had been decorated by His Majesty the King of England for flying against the Germans, and now he was flying against … against … well, now he was flying against ducks.

It was a time when rice farmers near Sacramento in northern California were trying out a new method of keeping wild ducks off their crops and Smithy accepted a position whereby every morning just after dawn he would roar over the rice fields in a tiny Curtiss Jenny aircraft, often at an altitude — if you could call it that — of just a couple of feet, and straight into the flock.[7] More often than not he would come back two or three hours later with bits of mangled duck hanging from the struts of his plane, all blood, gristle and feathers. A bit of a wash-down for both himself and his plane, perhaps a sleep, and then he'd be ready to go again in the late afternoon.

At least it was a job; though, as Kingsford Smith noted drily many years later, 'It was a sort of anti-climax to shooting down the *Boche* over the Western Front.'[8]

Not so many dead ducks later, he decided to leave this job as a glorified scarecrow and try his luck at the airman's staple when the times were grim — barnstorming. Within a day of being hired by an aerial impresario by the name of Moffett, he was on his way. In something that was close to the peacetime equivalent of the Red Baron's 'Flying Circus', Moffett and Kingsford Smith would move from town to town and, after performing a series of stunts above the main street guaranteed to get everyone's attention, set up their tents in a flat spot just outside the town, usually on a farmer's field — often near a barn, hence the origin of the activity's name. Then they would take off again and leaflets would soon afterwards come fluttering down on the town …

Air Thrills
Moffett-Starkey Aero Circus
Featuring
Chas Kingsford Smith
RAF Ace
Fingleton's Farm.
From Thursday 10 a.m.

And Thursday at ten o'clock, it would begin. The townsfolk would come pouring in, usually paying a base rate of $2 for a simple joyride, $4 to fly all over the town, and then additional fees of a few dollars apiece if they wanted Smithy or Moffett to do particular stunts, like loops, barrel rolls or dives. The pilots would fly all day, filling their pockets with the cash, until night-time would make flying no longer possible and they would retire to work on their planes and get them in shape for the following day. Once the flow of paying customers stopped, usually after four or five days, they would move on to the next town where, hopefully, word would have already spread that they were on their way.

It was a wild, peripatetic life, full of thrills and spills, and the main thing was that Smithy was flying again. True, most of the money went to Moffett, but on his base rate of $150 a month plus 10 per cent of the overall takings, Smithy earned enough to carouse at night, which remained one of his great pleasures. No matter that California, like the rest of the United States, was living under the laws of Prohibition, forbidding the consumption of alcohol, there was a loose system of 'speakeasies' in every town they went to, establishments where you could get illicit alcohol. While a lot of that drink tasted like rat's piss because it frequently came from very dubious stills, it was alcohol all right and Kingsford Smith had at least his fair share, and probably then some. When, at a later point, Chilla and his sister Elsie visited a winery in northern California and wondered out loud how they could possibly sell so much wine — 40,000 gallons of it — when each bottle carried a sticker saying it was '*Only to be Sold for Medicinal and Sacramental Purposes*', the answer was quick. They were told that because it was all made in Sacramento County that it was qualified to be sold for 'Sacramental Purposes!'[9]

•

Seven months after they had left Hounslow, near London, in a quest to win the £10,000 prize for being the first to Australia, on 2 August 1920, Lieutenant Raymond Parer and his mechanic, Lieutenant John C. McIntosh, finally made it to Fannie Bay, Darwin, in their de Havilland DH.9 biplane, G-EAQM, with just a minute's fuel left in its tanks. It had been a brutal trip, with so much ill-luck — crashing and mechanical malfunctioning, all of which they had battled through to make good and keep going — that Parer had become known far and wide, as 'Reparer'.[10] He was not amused. Not even mildly.

All up, eighteen men had set off in seven aircraft. After many adventures, six of them, in two planes, made it to Australia. Eight men, in three aircraft, crashed en route, and though not seriously injured, were unable to continue their flights. Four men, in two aircraft, were killed.

•

So it was settled then, sort of, over a few drinks.

The propitious crossing of paths the year before of Paul McGinness and Fergus McMaster had led to a meeting in the lounge of Brisbane's Gresham Hotel, during the town's Exhibition Week, in August 1920. With the warm smell of beer all around, McGinness and Hudson Fysh were able to put to the wealthy station owner their plans to form an aviation company that would operate in outback Queensland. What they needed, they explained, was some serious financial investment. The two of them had a bit of money put together, but nowhere near enough to buy a couple of planes and launch an airline. They were wondering whether, perhaps, McMaster and some of his friends might like to invest in such a company …?

As a matter of fact, McMaster would. He had not forgotten the sterling service provided to him eight months earlier by McGinness in Cloncurry, when he had rolled up his sleeves and found a way to get his car going again, and McMaster thought those same qualities of getting the job done come-what-may, would stand a new airline in good stead. He shook hands with both men and promised that he would look into it and talk to some of his friends.

And there was one now! Across the smoky lounge, he spotted a wealthy woolgrower from Longreach, A.N. Templeton, whom he knew well. Could he have a chat? It's about those two blokes you might have seen me with just a few minutes ago, a couple of chaps by the name of Paul McGinness and Hudson

Fysh. They were pilots, had done great work for the Australian Flying Corps in Palestine, and now they wanted to start up an aviation company in the outback. Would Mr Templeton maybe think about putting some money up? As a matter of fact, Mr Templeton would, and on the spot agreed to match any money that McMaster decided to put in.

Greatly encouraged, McMaster wandered over the road to where John Thompson, another mate of his from the war, was running a bookshop. Thompson, too, soon said that he was happy to buy into the company to the tune of £100. Out the door, McMaster went to another well-heeled friend working nearby, Alan Campbell, who also stumped up, and then he ran into yet another wealthy bloke in Queen Street, T.J. O'Rourke, whom he knew to be the biggest shopkeeper in Winton.

Now, ol' T.J. was known to be a very careful man with a pound, but McMaster had no sooner explained the proposal than the shopkeeper insisted he accompany him back to his hotel, where he presented him with a cheque for £250, and told him he would be happy to double it up later if the grazier needed it. In just one afternoon, Fergus McMaster had come up with the bulk of the backing he needed, and he soon advised Hudson Fysh and Paul McGinness to that effect.[11]

Not long afterwards, McMaster arranged another meeting with the pilots and the new investors in the Gresham Hotel. Something that impressed the financial heavyweights was that McGinness was going to put up his life's savings of £1000 to the venture, while Hudson Fysh also committed everything he had, which was £500.[12] A few handshakes later and it was done. They would indeed form a company, buy a couple of planes down in Sydney and release prospectuses to attract more investors. Generally, those who could afford it were amenable, though Fysh couldn't help but notice that one of the investors wrote '*Donation*' on his cheque stub as he paid for the shares.[13]

Only a short time after releasing their prospectus they had enough investors, and enough capital — at £6850 — to lock the whole thing down legally. After some to-ing and fro-ing, including a period where they came up with the name of Western Queensland Auto Aero Service Ltd, they decided to call their new company Queensland and Northern Territory Aerial Services Ltd.

It was McMaster who, noting how the Australian and New Zealand Army Corps had become the universally revered term 'ANZAC', decided that they might do the same for their company and call themselves 'Q.A.N.T.A.S.' on all documentation ... which was certainly a lot better than what it would have been, had they stuck to their previous name, making it W.Q.A.A.S.

As to what planes to fly, they soon began negotiation with Nigel Love, down in Sydney, who had the A.V. Roe (Avro) agency in Australia, and was already manufacturing the Avro 504K plane, with specially modified engines for Australian conditions.[14]

•

The next job that hove to on Smithy's aviation horizon in California was flying stunt planes in an amazing place called Hollywood, where they were making moving pictures with stunning women frequently known as 'movie stars'. Heaven on a stick. Smithy's job was to perform acts of derring-do in his plane as the cameras rolled, filming scenes for the many movies then featuring aeroplanes. It wasn't long before Smithy noticed that the stuntmen were getting paid a lot better than he was. Perhaps it would be a good idea to try a few stunts himself, while someone else flew the plane?

Yes and no ...

'So what we want you to do,' a director explained to him on one occasion in August 1920, 'is hang upside down from the wing, with your leg curled round one of the struts. Do you think you can do that?'

In for a penny, in for a pound, in it for the dollars ... Smithy thought he probably could do that and had a go, first, while the Avro plane they were planning to use was parked on the tarmac. True, when the plane was actually airborne it took a great deal of courage to do the same thing, but courage was always something that he had in strong supply, so that wasn't the problem.

The *problem*, after dangling with his arms outstretched, furiously buffeted by the wind, was getting himself back up again! On the ground that had been easy, but now, flopped over the front of the wing, he had 90 miles per hour of wind belting at him and restraining him from righting himself. So it was that for fifteen shocking minutes he stayed there, contemplating what would happen to his head if he was still like that when the plane landed. Finally, blessedly, with the last ounce of strength he had in him, and acting out of desperation pure, he was able to get back up, hugging the strut for dear life and sucking in huge gasps of air.

The following day, still shaken, Kingsford Smith was on site when a fellow he had become friendly with, the greatest Hollywood stunt flyer of them all, Lieutenant Ormer Locklear, was filming the climactic scene for *The Skywayman*, being shot for William Fox Studios.[15] It required Locklear to dive from a great height with flames billowing from his plane, and then dramatically bring the plane under control just before he hit the ground. At 10 pm, Locklear dropped a flare to indicate to the cameramen and directors that he was ready, and then, after his aide and long-time flying companion Lieutenant Milton 'Skeets' Elliott activated the device to get some impressive flames going in a spot where they would do no actual damage to the plane, they began what was meant to look like a death dive towards the ground.

Perfect … perfect … lovely … lovely … the director and cameraman were both ecstatic as the plane came down, looking for all the world as if it really was on fire and about to hit the ground when …

When just at the point where they expected Locklear to pull out of the dive, it was apparent that something was wrong. Very wrong … Pull out, Ormer, *pull out*! And the American pilot tried, he really tried. At the end, he was so close to the camera crew that they could see him hauling back on the stick, trying to get the plane to flatten out. Before their horrified eyes the plane hit the ground not 100 yards away from them, with a sickening *whump*, a split instant before the whole thing exploded with flames shooting into the night sky.

During the war, Kingsford Smith had seen, and been responsible for, similar deaths. But somehow this was different.

Sick to his stomach, he saw up close the results of such flaming crashes, the charred remains at the bottom of the deep hole caused by the impact, and gagged on the stench of burnt human flesh. This wasn't the 'bagging' of a German and another notch on your bragging belt, this was the real deaths of men he *knew*, and it was appalling. And yet it *was* no different because the deaths of all the pilots in the war had been equally appalling — it was just that he hadn't known them personally, or seen their deaths up close. Again, revulsion at what had happened in the war came to him, as the visions of the men he had killed in the air and on the ground returned.

In the there and then, however, the tragic deaths of Ormer Locklear and Milton Elliott confirmed for Kingsford Smith that he no longer wanted to fly for Hollywood.

And so it was back to the barnstorming with Moffett. This time, however, it wasn't his plane that crashed, but the whole flying circus itself. One morning Kingsford Smith woke up to find that Moffett had hopped it during the night, taking his plane with him and, more importantly, all the money that the Australian was owed. For his second stint, the 24-year-old Kingsford Smith had not yet received a dime.

As ever, he retreated to his brother's house and dulled the pain by carousing in the speakeasies and drinking far too much. Sister Elsie, particularly, worried about him. She wrote home to her mother:

> *I really think his experiences are beginning to somewhat daze even his doughty heart. As he remarked after the last discouraging letter from his lawyer, re Moffet — 'Oh d---. I'll be glad when all this knocking about is over, and the flight accomplished so I can settle down in Australia to a good steady job.' ('And get you a wife,' I added, and he grinned.) You see, Mum, after nearly a year here, Chilla is no better off than when he arrived, excepting for the increased experience, so the sooner he can go back and get a settled job the better, and quit rushing around the country with sundry weird gangs ...*[16]

And yet if the decorated war pilot had thought at this point that he had hit rock bottom, he was most definitely mistaken. That would come a few weeks later when, in an effort to muster the money to buy a third-class fare home, he was forced to take a job painting signs for a petrol company at the rate of US$15 a week.

Normal work that was nothing to do with aviation? He hated it, absolutely *hated* it. The sheer tedium of it! The brain-sapping, soul-destroying boredom of it all. He might have been able to do that kind of menial work when he was a young lad, back at the Colonial Sugar Refinery in Pyrmont, but that was before he had discovered flying, before he knew how to live. He stuck it out for as long as he could — about three weeks — but then he could simply bear it no more.

Chilla knew in these first weeks of 1921 that it was time to head home. 'Funds will not permit me to travel as a passenger,' he wrote to his parents, 'so I am going to have to work my way over. You know, it's too bad that I haven't got lots more money than I have.'[17]

Indeed. In the end, his brother Leofric cabled him the money he needed to get home. To get there he took a circuitous route, catching the good ship RMS *Tahiti* from Vancouver, which he thought was heading straight across the Pacific just as it had when he had been a young lad returning to Australia from Canada, but no ...

For some unaccountable reason, the ship sailed down the west coast of the American continent and stopped at San Francisco, which had been his starting point! Though generally Kingsford Smith was not a man prone to panicking, on this occasion he did so and then some. Convinced that the sole reason the *Tahiti* had diverted to San Francisco was because he was on board and the American tax authorities were after him, he stayed in his cabin for the entire two days the *Tahiti* was in port.[18]

Finally, the steamer weighed anchor and headed out of the magnificent San Francisco Bay through the 'Golden Gate', the name the San Franciscans had given to the spectacular narrow strait that separated the bay from the Pacific Ocean, and headed home, home to Australia. Only then did he breathe easy.

•

And so it was done. Following the dictates of the Versailles Treaty to which Australia had been a signatory — and the subsequent Paris Convention where the fine detail had been worked out in October 1919 — in December 1921 the government of Billy Hughes set up a Civil Aviation Branch to administer flying around the country. Of course, it was a part of the structure of the Department of Defence, as it was the view of Hughes and his like-minded individuals that aviation was to be encouraged, primarily because of its defence potential. No less than £100,000[19] was set aside for the encouragement of civil aviation — to set up and maintain airfields as well as subsidise important air services — and it wasn't long before contenders came forward. Foremost among these was a pilot by the name of Norman Brearley, who wanted to set up an air service in the great north-west of Australia, a place where there were no railways and the very area where the government felt the country was at its most vulnerable to invasion from the 'yellow peril' — the 750 million Asians who lived on the country's doorstep.[20] To have pilots and planes operating in the area therefore, to bolster defensive capacity, was viewed as a matter of urgency — with the bonus that it would help the local population by carrying sick patients and doctors in emergencies.[21] Previous government estimates were that it would cost £86,000 a year to have military planes based in that area. But if they were to subsidise Brearley's service, or one set up by a competitor, they could have planes there for as little as £25,000 a year.[22] The choice seemed obvious, and Defence Minister George Pearce was not long in making it known in Federal parliament.

'If we can encourage civil aviation,' he told the Honourable Members during debate over the Air Navigation Bill, in the parliament's last sitting in 1920, 'it will doubtless relieve the Commonwealth of a large expenditure on military aviation.'[23]

•

At Sydney, as ever, the Kingsford Smith clan turned out in force to greet their prodigal pilot when he arrived on the morning of 11 January 1921. There was Catherine on the docks, dressed in her Sunday best. William, as pleased as punch to have his boy home, was beaming like a lighthouse on a dark night, and there were his brothers and sister and some of their own families. In an instant, after coming down the gangplank of the *Tahiti*, the youngest son — dressed in a tatty suit and straw boater and carrying an old grass-woven suitcase[24] — was awash in hugs and kisses and hearty handshakes.

In the time that Chilla had been away, his parents had moved from Neutral Bay and settled into the place that would be their long-time abode, a gracious home called Kuranda at 73 Arabella Street in nearby Longueville, while Leofric Kingsford Smith and his wife, Elfreda, were practically next door, across a side street at No. 75.

Despite all the bonhomie, however, and all the subsequent welcome- home dinners at Kuranda and piano-playing and songs led by Chilla who continued to be the life of the party, the family was in fact quite shocked at their boy's appearance and demeanour. It was not simply that he was so much thinner and more worn than the lad who had left two and a half years earlier, and had come home owning only the clothes on his back and the two American dollars he had in his pocket. It was that between the laughter and jokes and songs there were so many thousand-yard stares, sudden silences and small bubbles of misery that seemed to pop to the surface at odd moments, suggesting a deep well of great unhappiness inside him. Bit by bit, the family became aware that their beloved youngest member was bearing scars beyond the ones on his foot, and that mentally he was still suffering the effects of the punishment he had undergone during the war.[25]

Little by little they were to learn more of what ailed him, some of the things that had happened to him, what life in the trenches both in Gallipoli and on the Western Front had been like, the men he'd killed while flying, and the narrow escapes he'd had, the friends he'd lost and still mourned, together with the great disappointments he had experienced since the war. He'd wanted to fly in the England to Australia race, but that had been denied him. He had wanted to fly the Pacific, but that, too, had failed to elicit any interest from anyone to back him. And despite his ongoing passion for flying — nothing else came remotely close — he'd only just been able to keep body and soul together by doing it since the war had finished. So of course all was not well. What had he achieved? What had he done? Where was he going?

The answers to these questions weren't obvious, either to Chilla or to his family, so for the moment he tried to settle down, hoping something would turn up. In the meantime, the residents of Arabella Street were able to note in subsequent months a rare phenomenon — maudlin banjo playing. For hours the youngest Kingsford Smith would sit in his room plucking at strings to make chords that would occasionally assemble themselves into a recognisable tune, but more often meandered mournfully along. In the evenings, when he could scrape enough money together from family and friends, he would sometimes go into downtown Sydney to catch up with wartime cobbers and do some drinking. And, in fact, it was this activity that was to provide him with his first employment since arriving home …

One evening in early February 1921, Kingsford Smith was getting a rather positive beer perspective by drinking heavily at the Carlton Hotel in Castlereagh Street — it was amazing how much better everything looked when you'd drained a few schooners — when he fell in with a wartime comrade, Lionel Lee, a bloke he'd come to know very well as they had been on the same courses at Denham and Oxford, before they'd flown together with the Royal Flying Corps. And Lionel had news. A few blokes were getting together to form the 'Diggers Co-operative Aviation Company', which would do taxi trips and barnstorming all through country towns. It was going to be funded entirely by them, and everybody working for it would be a part owner, no matter how small a percentage that might be.

In short order, Smithy had done his calculations and worked out that if he put all his combined capital together he could afford to have a small ownership of the business amounting to … *let's see* … £1's worth, so long as Lionel would lend him that pound … which Lionel did!

The main thing was that it was work, and flying work at that. Whatever his woes, he was determined never again to be reduced to wielding a paintbrush or the like, as he had been back in

California. Nothing of his experiences to that point had lessened his love of flying by one jot. In his wartime service he had logged 800 hours in the air, and since that time another 900 hours. It was a part of him, and he couldn't imagine life without it.[26]

•

There was a big buzz in the Queensland town of Winton on the sunny Monday afternoon of 7 February 1921. Two planes from the new aviation company of Qantas were due in after a long journey from Sydney and, in two shakes of a burnt stick, there they were! To hearty clapping from the crowd, McGinness landed first on the bit of flat ground next to the artesian bore in an Avro 504K, and he was followed shortly thereafter by Hudson Fysh in a Royal Aircraft Factory BE2e, a modified two-seater reconnaissance type, with an RAF-1a engine of 90 horsepower. Both planes could go as fast as 65 miles per hour, though it certainly wasn't as simple as dividing long distances by that speed to work out how quick the journey would be. As a matter of fact, the journey of 1200 miles from Sydney had taken six days with seventeen hours and thirty minutes of flying time at an average speed of 68.5 miles per hour, and quite a few unscheduled stops along the way.[27] No matter. The town turned on a hearty welcome, and that evening at the North Gregory Hotel packed to capacity with locals and good cheer, Qantas was toasted three times, as was King George V.

Ladies and gentlemen, the King!

The King … the King … the King …

In a towering voice, Fergus McMaster, who had arrived as the sole passenger in McGinness's plane, made a resounding speech, noting that this was not just a great day for Qantas, but for 'the defence of Australia', which was now dependent on aviation.

'Australia,' he warned, 'lies open to all from the air. The only reason that Australia is held by us today, gentlemen, is because we are fortunately a part of the greatest empire in the world.'

Hear, hear! Hear, hear! *Hear, hear!*

'This commercial aviation company,' he continued when the enthusiastic rumbling had subsided a little, 'should get your support as Australians, not investors; not for the dividends it is likely to bring in, but for the great influence it must have in the administration, development and defence of Australia.'[28]

Bravo! Hurrah!

In any case, they had made a start and were soon in operation, flying through every district of western Queensland, where the need for Qantas's services was greatest. A sure source of revenue was joy flights, where a member of the public would be taken aloft for ten minutes and £3 and 3 shillings, or £5 if they wanted to do a 'loop-the-loop'.[29] If, on the other hand, they wanted to be taken to an outlying station or another town, the basic rate was 'two shillings per mile flown'. Though not yet ready to begin taking passengers on scheduled services, Qantas kept working towards that day, spreading the word and setting up airfields in the towns they intended to fly to. Leaflets were distributed saying such things as:

> The person who has not been in the air has not yet started to LIVE. Fly in the famous B.E.2e, second in the Sydney Aerial Derby. Have you ever had a flight in a British War Machine?[30]

The people flocked to it in their droves.

•

For Charles Kingsford Smith, a wild, wild time in various country towns around New South Wales followed his employment with the Diggers Co-operative Aviation Company. Under the terms of his contract, he was to be paid £12 a week as a base rate, with a further commission of 10 per cent of gross after he had made a certain amount. First-class accommodation in each country town was also to be provided by the company.

In return, Kingsford Smith was expected to 'fly in' around £80 a day, and his first job was to take one of the company's Avros from Mascot and drop into the small New South Wales country town of Oberon to work the local show. And Kingsford Smith intended to do exactly that, and would have, if not for a small crash on landing due to an unexpectedly boggy paddock.

The question then was: to tell the company or make his own arrangements?

Typically, Smithy decided to make his own arrangements, and managed to get the local blacksmith and undertaker to fix the undercarriage and wing. (And if that made the plane resemble a little more a flying coffin, then so be it, and maybe he was dipping a lid to his old French wartime comrade Charles Nungesser, with his famed symbol of a coffin flanked by candles painted on the side of his plane.)

From there Smithy went to Dubbo for a picnic of railway workers, men widely renowned for their thirst and ability to pack beer away as if there was no tomorrow. Even they, however, would likely have had to acknowledge Smithy as their master when it came to drinking.

On this rather warm day, what Smithy did was to take a couple of paying passengers skywards for about ten minutes, then bring them back down and have a bit of a beer while another pilot took the next pair, whereupon he would take over again to take another pair up. Then another beer, before taking another pair up. And another, and another, and another. Beers, cheers, pairs, planes, flying, Dubbo, up, down, over, under, beers, in the end it's all a blur, arr … duzzenmatter.

What was certain was that late that afternoon, and with the beer goggles so firmly attached now that *everything* seemed like a good idea at the time, he decided to take this particular couple, young Oliver Cook and his fiancée, Dulcie Offner, on a couple of loop-de-loops.

As the crowd below watched open-mouthed, Smithy did indeed manage to pull off a spectacular version of the aeronautical loop. 'S matter of fact, it wash sho good, he decided to try another! This time, alas, he was only halfway through when there was a sudden loud crack like a gunshot, as either the work of the undertaker or blacksmith gave up the unequal struggle, and now it was the plane that began to drunkenly lurch.

Only a master pilot could possibly have wrested the machine back under control in such circumstances, and Smithy almost did just that. Somehow he managed to get the whole thing back on the ground with his passengers intact but shaken, in a plane that nevertheless had its nose partly buried in a hillside, with a broken undercarriage and snapped propeller.[31]

•

Up there! For the people in the Queensland coastal country town of Bundaberg on the sunny afternoon of 11 April 1921, it was an amazing thing to look up and see a plane, a real *plane*, buzzing around overhead. Most of the town was completely mystified as to who it could possibly be, but not John Hinkler, nor his wife, Frances. They both knew it had to be their boy Bert, who had left town nine years ago to become first a mechanic with Sopwith and then a pilot with the Royal Naval Air Service, making no fewer than 122 flights over enemy territory. He had always said that when the time came, he wanted to *fly* home, as a 'real dinkum pilot',[32] to the ones he addressed as 'my beloved parents' in his many letters home.

John Hinkler — always distinctive because of his enormous Ned Kelly-like beard — was down town when he saw the plane and, knowing only too well where his boy Bert would head to, immediately crossed the bridge to the north side of town and headed home. Out in the garden, a teary Frances watched as the plane circled lower and lower, and then she saw him, her Bert, waving furiously from the cockpit of his tiny white biplane, as he zoomed low over his childhood home and she waved furiously back before rushing inside to put the kettle on. Banking sharply, the pilot came in for a perfect landing on the Bundaberg Foundry Green and then, as stunned people rushed from everywhere, he taxied it up Gavan Street to his home — blessed home! — as locals on bikes and horses kept pace, and others ran alongside tried to keep up. And there, inside the lattice-enclosed front veranda was his now grey-haired mother waiting for him, soon joined by his father, who was fit to bursting with pride and happiness. Bert was home. In a new Australian record — not that the self-effacing Bert cared, as he was simply flying his Avro 543 Baby home from Sydney, where he had unloaded it from the good ship *Ascanius*. Yet Bert Hinkler had flown 700 miles non-stop in eight and three-quarter hours.[33]

There was much hoopla, many headlines and numerous civic receptions to honour his achievement, the first of which was held the following evening in Bundaberg Town Hall, with Bert and his beaming parents seated at the table of honour. After an overwhelming speech from the mayor, which went on for some time, Bert stood up and simply said: 'Thank you. I'm glad to be home.'[34]

•

In the end, perhaps this result was inevitable, such were the risks that he took and in such flimsy aircraft. Just after 6 pm on 12 July 1921, Harry Hawker was flying his Nieuport Goshawk biplane above the Burnt Oak and the RAF Hendon airfields in preparation for the aerial derby in just four days' time, when on this wonderfully balmy early evening in England the amazing luck that had always characterised his survival despite everything, suddenly began to waver.[35] Witnesses saw his plane catch fire and begin to spin towards earth almost immediately afterwards, with Harry fighting it all the way down …

Oh, blessed Muriel … Oh, my daughters!

On the moment of impact the plane exploded with such force that the broken body of Hawker was found 50 yards away. At their home at Hook, in Surrey, only a short time later, Muriel was informed that there had been 'an accident', and departed immediately for the aerodrome, leaving her two young daughters in the care of a neighbour. While driving there she reminded herself of the Atlantic flight, and how when everyone else had given up hope, she hadn't, and had been proven right, and Harry had returned to her more alive than when he left.

Alas … alas …

When she arrived, it was to find that Harry was dead.[36]

A day later, no less than King George V himself was to write in a letter of condolence to Muriel, noting that 'the nation has lost one of its most distinguished airmen who by his skill and daring has contributed so much to the success of British aviation'.[37] This time, there was to be no miraculous reappearance of Harry.

•

On this dreamy afternoon down Cowra way in western New South Wales, the Lachlan River was flowing as sweetly as ever, the birds were singing and the only other sound on Cowra Bridge was the pleasant clip-clopping of hooves, as a big wheat wagon drawn by twelve horses was heading homewards. In the opposite direction at a slightly faster clip came a sulky in which a farmer was rushing his heavily pregnant wife to the maternity ward of the local hospital, because she had had stirrings, she said. It was a bucolic, perfect scene, one that could well have been painted by Tom Roberts.

But do you hear something? What? That *bzzzzzzz* buzzing sound … getting louder and louder …

THERE!

From out of the blue, literally, and seemingly making straight for the Gates of Hell, suddenly descended the plane of one Charles Kingsford Smith, who had been drinking heavily, and was intent on having some fun. Flattening out above the river, he gunned it straight for the bridge, while those upon the fragile structure stared at the fast-approaching machine in horror! Was he …? Is he …? Can he …?

Yes, or die in the attempt, perhaps taking them with him. The stanchions below the bridge stood 70 feet apart at their widest point, while the Avro stretched 36 feet. This gave the pilot 17 feet of clearance on either side, while a gap of 15 feet separated the bottom of the bridge from the water, just enough, perhaps, to allow the Avro's 10 feet 5 inches height through. Only one of the best, most confident pilots in the world, or the most foolish, or the most drunken, would attempt such a thing. As it happened, on this day Smithy was all three of those things.

The plane continued to hurtle towards the bridge at just under 100 miles per hour, as the three people on the bridge watched, completely terrified … And he made it!

Still, he wasn't done. After emerging on the other side, Smithy pulled back on his stick hard and executed a perfect 'Immelmann turn', just as he had learnt to do in the Great War, which meant that after a tight loop an instant later he was hurtling back over the bridge at a very low height.

On that bridge, of course, total pandemonium had broken out. As Kingsford Smith had roared underneath, the horses hitched to the wheat wagon had bolted like scalded pigs and driven the oncoming sulky hard into the side of the bridge, which precipitated the pregnant farmer's wife falling out and landing heavily on the roadway. Her baby came into the world there and then, on the bridge outside of Cowra, as a plane piloted by a seeming madman screamed off in one direction and flocks of terrified cockatoos raced off in every other.

And still Smithy was only warming up ...

Oblivious of the devastation he had left behind him, he flew on. His job on that late afternoon, after going back to the Cowra airstrip, was to take two local men out to distant Riverslea station to celebrate the christening of the station manager's son and heir. (And with Smithy in the area, this was an heir who was very fortunate to be born in a bed.) Feeling good. Feeling strong. Did he need to land in the big paddock, a small distance from the homestead? He did not. For he was Smithy.

Far better, and more fun, to land on the sweeping driveway, and take his passengers right up to the door, which he did with aplomb — bar the fact that one of the tyres blew on impact. Not to worry.

One thing led to another, which led to him forgetting about the blown tyre. Country hospitality being what it was, Smithy was invited to join the celebrations and over the next couple of hours held court, telling war stories, drinking champagne, flirting with the women, laughing and charming everyone. In that part of the world, decorated war pilots were a great rarity, and the locals hung off his every word.

When the time came to go, just as the sun was sinking low into the western hills, the burst tyre really had been forgotten. With a last 'cheerio', Smithy and his two passengers climbed into the cockpit before the admiring onlookers, then, without further ado, Smithy gunned it down the driveway. Too late he realised his colossal error, as the plane swerved, then swerved again and again, as he desperately tried to keep it straight. In this instance, however, his masterly pilot skills didn't register as he was less a pilot of a plane than a drunken driver of a vehicle with a busted tyre, and he ended up losing control. The Avro left the driveway and veered right, then one of the wheels suddenly bit into a large rabbit hole, causing the plane to tip forward and have its nose smash into the ground. From the wreckage, the two passengers emerged, bleeding from facial cuts, while Smithy himself suffered two broken ribs and a near broken heart.

'It isn't hurting that much,' he said, 'but there goes my job.'[38]

There was, nevertheless, a saving grace, thought the intrepid pilot, as he explained in the course of a letter to his parents:

> *We had a spill in Cowra, and I was a bit bruised in consequence. However I am okay today and except for being a trifle stiff, have nothing to complain of. Rather bad luck tho', with the new machine, but she was fully insured, and except for the delay the company won't lose. Struck a rabbit burrow at great speed and of course went a thud.*[39]

That thud, as it turned out, was nearly, but not quite as great a thud as the Diggers Co-operative Aviation Company was about to receive. No matter that the insurance assessor, Paddy Lee Murray, was an old mate of Kingsford Smith's, as he had been a fellow wartime pilot with the Royal Flying Corps. It was perhaps because he knew Smithy so well that he suspected the kind of behaviour that might have led to the wreck, and was soon able to produce testimony from people who had witnessed him drinking heavily. Paddy Murray liked Smithy a great deal, and didn't mind a drink himself, but in this instance his duty, his job, was to serve the interests of the insurance company, and so he was instrumental in that company exercising its legal and moral rights in refusing to pay up. When put together with the £600 legal settlement that the Diggers Co-operative Aviation Company had to make with the farmer and his wife, the crash of the Avro meant the company had received an all but mortal wound to its finances. And, for Kingsford Smith, his instant reckoning that the crash would cost him his job proved to be correct. The managers of Diggers Aviation liked him a great deal and were happy to write him a glowing reference, but the bottom line was that as gifted a pilot as Smithy was, they simply could no longer afford to have him in their employ.[40] Good luck. Goodbye.

Smithy left Diggers Aviation and returned to Sydney with little more to show for his time there than a badly broken nose he had received one night in Coonamble, courtesy of a drunken fight with a mechanic. Not to worry. Flying for Diggers Aviation had been fine, but it hadn't altered a jot his dream of flying the Pacific, the very expedition he referred to, in a letter from the New South Wales country town of Wellington to his parents on 4 August 1921, as 'still my ultimate ambition'.[41]

•

In terms of what to do in the meantime, however, Kingsford Smith was fortunate that in the early 1920s, as one aviation company began to falter so would another one or two start up. Such was the case with Major Norman Brearley — he too had received his commission by flying for the Royal Flying Corps in the Great War — who, in mid-August 1921, began to advertise for airline pilots to work for him on his nascent Western Australian Airways Ltd, which was going to provide the first regular airmail service in the west of the country, flying vast distances. The service would go from Geraldton, where the railway line from Perth finished, to Derby, 1200 miles to the north.

Brearley had come a long way since shooting down the German observation balloon and shortly thereafter taking a bullet through both lungs. He had returned to Australia, recovered, married Violet Stubbs, a prominent politician's daughter, received the first commercial pilot's licence from the newly established Civil Aviation Branch and had now got the go-ahead from the government to start up the country's first regular scheduled passenger and airmail service airline. Under the terms of the contract, the Federal government would pay Brearley four shillings for every mile that his planes flew, and in return, space on the aircraft would be reserved for 100 pounds of government mail — while the rest of the space could be used by Brearley for passengers and freight.[42] Western Australian Airways also had to ensure that all its pilots were members of the Air Force Reserve, and therefore available to fly for the government in the event of a national emergency.[43]

•

One dark day, back in Sydney licking his wounds, Smithy spotted an advertisement in one of the local newspapers, inviting pilots to apply for positions with the soon to start Western Australian Airways.[44] He immediately wrote away presenting his credentials. Brearley quickly replied, inviting him to come down to Laverton, just outside Melbourne, where he would shortly be conducting interviews and giving prospective pilots practical tests. Kingsford Smith was overjoyed.[45] The chance of a job flying with a serious aviation company! Certainly he had to borrow the railway fare from Diggers Aviation to get down to Laverton to meet Brearley, but the whole thing went well.

Brearley was extremely impressed with the way Kingsford Smith handled the Avro 504K when he gave him the practical test in the skies above Laverton. After the Sydneysider had passed the practical with flying colours, Brearley gave him the formal interview, beginning by asking his full name and service background.

'Charles Edward Kingsford Smith.'

'And how did you win your Military Cross?'

'For various acts of foolishness.'[46]

Brearley liked his style, and soon afterwards offered him the job. Again Smithy had to borrow the ship fare from his father to get to Western Australia, topped up with another couple of loans from two of his brothers, Eric and Wilf, who happened to have a little spare cash at the time. But the main thing was, he once again had a job, and a quite respectable one it was, too, for a nice change, with Smithy contracting to fly for Brearley's WAA for the relatively handsome salary of £500 per annum — well over double the average annual wage for a male, which was just on £200.

As to Major Brearley, it was clear from the start — in the way Kingsford Smith carried himself and spoke, in his military bearing — that he was not the sort of man who would cop any shenanigans and, given Smithy's near disastrous experience with Diggers Aviation, the younger man was happy enough to knuckle down, at least after a fashion. The next weeks in Perth were filled with getting to know Brearley and his fellow pilots — Val Abbott, Arthur Blake, Bob Fawcett and Len Taplin — as they all worked together with the WAA's mechanics to get the six three-seater, 250-horsepower Armstrong Siddeley Puma-engined Bristol Type 28 Tourer Coupé biplanes ready.

Brearley had shipped these latest models from England and, after uncrating the beauties, the men began to carefully assemble them, before firing them up and taking them to the skies for testing. All the pilots were issued rather smart khaki uniforms with the words *Western Australian Airways* embroidered on their left pocket beneath a freshly designed emblem which showed a large pair of wings sprouting from a globe.

The company's stated intent was to establish a regular route from Geraldton in the south to Derby in the north, with stops at Carnarvon, Onslow, Roebourne, Port Hedland and Broome. To go the whole way from Geraldton to Derby across the vast sprawling region of pearling, mining and farming concerns would take an amazingly quick two and a half days, with overnight stops in pubs at Carnarvon and Port Hedland. In the morning passengers would set off with a fresh pilot and usually in a fresh plane. Western Australia had some of the most isolated towns in the world, and boasted *the* most isolated city on the planet — Perth — but now these towns would be effectively joined up to each other and a major blow struck at the prevailing tyranny of distance. An expensive blow it would be, however, with the price of a ticket calculated at the rough rate of a shilling a mile. This meant that a Geraldton–Derby flight cost around £60![47] And so, too, would 'airmail' be more expensive — 5 pence for a half-ounce letter from Perth to Derby by air, instead of the usual twopence — but given that whereas previously to get a reply to a letter sent between those cities had taken two months and it could now be accomplished in a matter of days, few people were quibbling.

As to the pilots, they would essentially be on an eternal relay around the circuit, handing on passengers and post to each other, before resting and taking the fresh lot on to the next town. Hopefully there would be enough passengers and post to make a healthy profit, but if there wasn't, the government subsidy meant they were assured of survival in the short term.

•

In those last months of 1921, Qantas was seriously struggling. What was already obvious was that without a government subsidy the company would go under. Their one hope was in convincing Prime Minister Billy Hughes of the virtue of subsidising their service in western Queensland — the same way the Federal government had done with Brearley's Western Australian Airways in the great north-west. Matters came to a head on the night of 10 November 1921 in Hughes's private office, located in the basement of Parliament House in Melbourne, the Federal government's then seat of power. Fergus McMaster led a delegation of all the Queensland members of the House of Representatives and Senate in an attempt to convince the prime minister of the justness of their cause.

Given that the Queenslanders were members of the very same Country Party that had been making Hughes's life hell in recent months by voting with the Labor Party and against the Hughes government on matters of expenditure, things were tense from the beginning. For now they wanted *what*? More money so Queenslanders could fly around at the government's expense?

Like a bristling battleship, Hughes began the meeting by raking the Country Party from stem to stern on every issue he could think of, steaming back and forth to fire broadside after ever more devastating broadside.

Twenty minutes into this tirade, however, Hughes suddenly stopped — whether because he was finished or was merely reloading, the delegation wasn't sure. When he reached for an enormous listening device that lay on his desk and put it to his ear, it seemed that it was now McMaster's time to make his presentation.

Which McMaster tried to do, but after only a few minutes Hughes laid down his listening device, as if he were refusing to listen further. And maybe he was, for after McMaster had finished and then other parliamentarians began to make their supporting speeches, Billy Hughes interrupted them, turned to McMaster and said: 'When are you going back to Queensland?'

McMaster: 'As soon as we secure your reply.'

Hughes: 'You have it now. The government has no money. My reply is no!'[48]

•

The launch of Western Australian Airways in Perth went well enough, and Kingsford Smith was pleasantly amazed with all the carry-on during the official opening on 3 December 1921. No less than the Governor of Western Australia, Sir Francis Newdigate, turned up at Perth Town Hall, together with the mayor, and there were speeches and brass bands galore. Later, there was a demonstration of flying from Major Brearley's base in Langley Park, using the foreshore of the Swan River as a runway. Chilla happily informed his parents that evening after the opening was over:

> *The major and myself did all the flying in the new planes as the foreshore is rather small and we are both more experienced with small fields than the others. Our salaries are paid monthly, and I have arranged to have the £5 paid regularly into Leof's account weekly, or else £20 monthly. The fare will be refunded at the end of the month, so that I will be able to pay some of Eric's and all of Wilf's loans back.*
>
> *The major and two pilots leave tomorrow morning to do the first mail …*[49]

And so they did. Amid much fanfare and good wishes on that bright, sunny morning, Len Taplin took off in one Bristol, followed by Bob Fawcett and his mechanic, Ted Broad, in another, while Major Brearley took off last, taking two passengers with him. Flying in rough formation, 100 yards separating them, they made an impressive sight on their way to begin a new era in Australian aviation.

After a brief stopover at Geraldton, they were about 80 miles north of that coastal town and flying over the massive Murchison House station, when Len Taplin's engine began playing up like the devil, so much so that he was obliged to make a forced landing. And yet there was worse, much worse to follow. When Bob Fawcett — a very softly spoken and gentle young man — throttled back and started circling low over Taplin to make sure he was fine, something went wrong and his plane stalled, sending him and his mechanic plummeting earthwards. Both men were killed instantly, and the wife of the station manager later said the only time she ever saw a man cry was when Major Brearley landed a minute later and found out what had happened.[50] Fawcett and Broad were buried in the station's cemetery, with the station manager presiding over proceedings.

It was a catastrophic beginning to the life of the airline, but tradition was observed. Within as short a time as possible, *flying resumed as normal.*

•

Finally, it was 'Ginty' McGinness who effectively refused to take no for an answer from Billy Hughes. Knowing that without the subsidies Qantas was as good as dead, McGinness took extreme measures. Learning that the prime minister would be on the night train returning from parliament in Melbourne to his home in Sydney, Ginty boarded the train with one thing in mind. 'Prime Minister Hughes?' he said, thrusting out his hand. 'Paul McGinness — from Qantas.'

Billy Hughes, his head like a warped walnut with two piercing eyes that missed nothing, sat there looking at him silently and menacingly, and there was nothing for it but for McGinness to quickly state his business.

'Look, is there no way that I can convince you how important it is for us to have that mail contract?'

The fact that Hughes didn't yell at him that he wished to be left in peace McGinness took as a positive sign, and indeed it wasn't long before Hughes even delicately pointed the way towards a deal.

'It's a sad fact,' the prime minister began carefully, 'that these days you have to give something to get something ...'[51]

They continued to talk as the Australian countryside thundered past in the night and, in the early hours of Saturday morning, McMaster was woken in his Brisbane home by an excited Ginty speaking from a railway station somewhere north of Albury.[52] His message was simple. If the Country Party would stop backing Labor in the Senate estimates — the method whereby senators could closely question the government's public servants, to the point of inquisition, about all matters to do with Budget expenditure — and start backing the Hughes government, then it would be quite likely that the government would find the money needed to subsidise a service between Charleville and Cloncurry.

The following morning, McMaster began to make his own calls, and within days, the Country Party had indeed started backing Hughes in parliament. Things began to move, and within three months the news was formally announced. The Hughes government would back Qantas with a subsidy scheme for a one-year trial period similar to the one Western Australian Airways enjoyed, to the tune of four shillings a mile flown, equal to about £30,000 per annum ...[53]

•

Thursday, 13 April 1922.

Just near the Vickers Aircraft factory at Weybridge, England, Sir Ross Smith and Jimmy Bennett, one of the mechanics who had been with him on the flight from London to Darwin, had taken one of the new Vickers Type 54 Viking IVs skywards in preparation for a flight around the *world* that they were planning. The plane was an enormous amphibian, almost like a boat with wings, powered by a 350-horsepower engine and capable of landing *on* the ocean.[54] That day, Sir Keith was meant to have been with them but he had been caught up in London, so Sir Ross and Jimmy had taken off without him to go for a quick spin to test the plane out a little and see what it could do. So it was that Sir Keith arrived just in time to see the plane fall out of the sky from a height of perhaps 1000 feet, and come to earth with a screaming wrench of metal behind nearby fir trees. Sir Keith was at the scene within minutes, and it was immediately obvious that the crash was every bit as bad as he had feared. In the twisted wreckage Jimmy seemed to already be dead, while Sir Ross was showing just the barest glimmer of life, though with a deep gash down the right-hand side of his face. When a man identifying himself as a doctor skidded to a halt, Sir Keith composed himself and said: 'Please look at my brother and see if there is any chance of saving him.'[55]

He then wandered off a little way from the horror of it all, only to see the doctor approaching him less than a minute later.

Sir Keith steeled himself and said to the medical man: 'I see by your face, all is over.'

The doctor nodded, and Sir Keith broke down and wept, and was soon kneeling over his brother's remains.

•

Via the wonders of modern communications, Catherine Kingsford Smith was shocked to read of Sir Ross's death in the following day's edition of the *Sydney Morning Herald* under the headline: 'ROSS SMITH KILLED WHILE TESTING MACHINE.'[56]

The paper went on to editorialise next day: 'With his death Australia has lost the star airman of her flying service, built up during the late war, and the Empire has lost an airman whose heart was in the pioneering of air routes which should link up the dominions with the old country.'[57]

Devouring the account, Catherine wasted no time in writing to her son in Western Australia to voice her concerns. And her youngest son was equally quick in trying to allay her fears. He wrote:

> *Mum, You remark re Ross Smith — 'the air, like the sea, can be pretty treacherous' I would like to correct that impression, Mum. Apart from an actual breakage of a vital part (almost an unheard-of occurrence, thank goodness) the air is never, in my opinion, treacherous to a careful pilot. From what details have come to hand, Ross Smith evidently killed himself through taking a strange (to him) machine up after nearly two years away from the controls, and attempting an evolution that I don't think has been done on that type before ... Poor chap, it is a sad ending to a brilliant career. I wish some*

> *philanthropist would finance me to step into his shoes, and continue the flight. My dream of a trans-Pacific flight is not yet ended, and some day I'll do it.*[58]

At least, in the meantime, Kingsford Smith was gaining enormous experience in an entirely different form of flying. Until this point, in all of England, France, America and eastern Australia he had never had to fly much more than 50 or 60 miles at one time. Now, he would do 300 miles in a single hop and nary turn a hair, finding his way across the terrain by virtue of his compass and recognising known landmarks — such things as the contour of the coast, hills, rivers, various townships and scattered missions. It was a stark landscape, but Kingsford Smith came to love it bit by bit, and was earning a steady wage for the first time since the war.

By mid-1922, the company was in such good shape that Major Brearley decided to replace the two men who had been so tragically killed six months earlier. The new pilot with the jutting jaw was a tall, notably good-looking, quietly spoken fellow by the name of Keith Anderson, another former fighter pilot in France — with five kills to his credit — and he and Kingsford Smith hit it off from the first, each recognising that the other was that greatest of all Australian male things, a 'good bloke'. On their meeting at the aerodrome in Carnarvon, he and Kingsford Smith firmly clasped hands, and Anderson was soon on the back of Smithy's pride and joy — the motorbike he had just bought for £75 — as they hightailed towards the Gascoyne Hotel, where they could slake their thirst and begin to talk.

In character they were entirely different. Charles Kingsford Smith was almost universally 'Smithy' to everyone who knew him, which really *was* just about everyone. Keith Anderson, a year younger, was either 'Keith Anderson' or 'Anderson' to the limited circle of his acquaintances, and 'Keith' or 'Andy' to a precious few. Smithy was loud, while Anderson was quiet; Smithy was gregarious, while Anderson was content with his own company; Smithy could light up a room all on his own and did so at every pub along that north-west Australian coast whenever he was in town, while Anderson was happy to hide his light under a bushel. And yet, the brotherhood of both being war veterans immediately got them off to a strong start, as did the fact that they both had dreams of doing some serious long-distance flying.

Not for a minute had Kingsford Smith abandoned his plans of flying the Pacific, and he had nurtured the dream from the first day it had come to him. As to Anderson, his huge ambition was to fly across the entire Indian Ocean and he had also put a lot of thought into how his ambition might be accomplished.

Naturally enough, the two began to consider each other's dream and before long, Anderson's had folded into Kingsford Smith's. They began to talk about how they might be able to fly the Pacific together. What route should they take? What kind of plane would be best? And once they got the said plane, just where would they be able to put all the petrol tanks that they would need, and how much they would be able to fit in and still take off. Blériot had done his calculations and drawings on the tablecloth, they did theirs more often than not on the back of whatever scrap of paper they might have handy.

Whenever they met, up and down the great north-west coast of Australia — and usually in whichever town's main pub — it became a constant subject of conversation between them, the default topic they would return to. Yes, flying was heaven, but both men felt that heaven needed to have its boundaries extended.

As it was, on a bad day Smithy's experiences could look a lot like hell. At one point, he was flying over Roebuck Bay, just south of Broome, when the engine on his plane ran out of oil and it was all he could do to keep the plane aloft long enough to *just* reach the mangroves on the north side of the bay, where he was able to land on the beach. He and his passengers were stranded there for several days and by the time they were rescued most of them were so badly sunburnt they had to be put to bed for a week.[59]

On other occasions Kingsford Smith or other Western Australian Airways pilots were obliged to land on beaches in moonlight, or make forced landings in rough country, where the general plan was to bring the plane down as close as possible to the Overland Telegraph Line — so they could shinny up the pole and cut the wire — and then sit in the shade under a wing until the wire repair team inevitably arrived a day or two later.

Twice, when Keith Anderson went down in the desert, well away from the Telegraph Line, it was Smithy who managed to find him by scouring the countryside back and forth along the rough path until he located him — and on one of those occasions Anderson had been in particularly desperate straits, being lost for just under three weeks.[60] Though to that point the two had been close, the fact that Anderson felt that Smithy had saved his life drew them closer still.

Smithy learnt better than ever how to fly through heavy rain and shrieking wind, and became more confident flying in the dark, though it was still something to be avoided if possible. So too was his knowledge of the mechanics of aircraft increasing as, in the time that he wasn't actually flying the planes, he was usually busy fixing and maintaining them, and in that manner was able to qualify as a ground engineer Category D.[61]

For all that, it remained aviation on the wild side as Western Australian Airways continued to ply and fly its trade up and down the far north-west coast. Always the emphasis was on getting paying customers into the plane and if there wasn't quite enough room for them, as in when another pilot had to be transported up the coast to do a different leg, then something else would have to be worked out.

On one occasion, thus, when two paying passengers were on offer, Smithy flew while the other pilot sat outside on the lower wing, hugging the strut as the hot air rushed all around him. For Smithy, it was nothing compared to what he and his mates had got up to in America wing-walking, barnstorming and so forth, so what was the problem? He took the same attitude to sometimes strapping his motorbike to the undercarriage of his plane so he could have transport at the next destination.[62]

Of course the Civil Air Regulations strictly forbade such dangerous activities, but who cared? The same government that had sent him to Gallipoli and the Western Front, and facilitated him flying against the Germans with a mortality rate of 25 per cent a week, was now going to threaten blue murder if he took a couple of short cuts here and there, short cuts that he was better qualified than anyone to judge the safety of? He didn't think so.

Besides, even though on one or two occasions they had carried the new Controller of Civil Aviation, Lieutenant Colonel Horace C. Brinsmead, MC, OBE — a distinguished veteran of both Gallipoli and the Australian Flying Corps — Western Australian Airways was generally so far removed from aviation officialdom that the pilots were able to do more or less what they liked.

The bottom line was that, one way or another, both Charles Kingsford Smith and the airline were doing fairly well. In late 1922, Norman Brearley, a good man and canny operator, even formally wrote to him, recording how impressed he was:

> I have had excellent reports about you from all and sundry and am very pleased indeed with the way you are carrying on. I know now that you are all you appear to be, and that is saying a lot. I only hope that my treatment of you meets with your approval too, as I want to keep the show one of the very best.[63]

Not that his star pilot was without blemish. As good as he was in the air, he could still be a wild man on the ground and, although two decades earlier it had been Bishop Wright's avowed hope that his sons' invention of the aeroplane would help to spread the word of Christianity ... it was fair to say that Smithy was not the patron saint of that movement. This was irrespective of the fact that he was flying further than almost any other pilot in the world. A girl in every port? No, but Smithy had a girl in most of the towns they flew to; did enough drinking for two men and at least his fair share of fighting — he remained a good man to have on your side in a bar-room brawl, displaying surprising strength and ferocity — and all up, his days of hymn singing were long gone. Rather, at his best and most comfortable, he would be drunk, at the pub piano and surrounded by cheering chanting punters as he belted out another classic from the Great War, the likes of:

I don't want to join the army …
I don't want to go to war …
I'd rather hang around Piccadilly Underground
Living off the earnings of a well-born lady …

Monday I touched 'er on the ankle
Tuesday I touched 'er on the knee
On Wednesday I confess I lifted up 'er dress
On Thursday I saw it (cor blimey)
Friday I put my hand upon it
Saturday she gave my balls a twist …
But on Sunday after supper … I rammed the bastard UP 'ER
And now I'm paying seven and six a week (cor blimey)

One can't help wondering if on one such occasion a local sage might have quietly pointed Smithy out and said, 'Look, yers wouldn't believe it, but that bloke will have a knighthood within ten years …' Perhaps not.

In the meantime, life in that remote part of Australia was changing courtesy of Western Australian Airways. The well-heeled people of Derby could now get to Perth in as little as three days! And they could have weekly post and newspapers delivered from Perth. Why, the women could get the latest issue of the *Western Mail*, engage in mail-order shopping and have a new dress in their hands in under a week! Similarly, business and legal matters that used to take months to complete could now be expedited in a little more than nothing flat, and the wheels of commerce began to spin in the area as never before.[64]

•

Bloody Chilla!

Once returned from the war, it had become apparent to the rest of the family just how hopeless the youngest of the clan was in managing his money, so Catherine had decided that Leofric, a responsible forty-year-old accountant, should effectively manage the wayward one's money for him. This would entail Leofric having control of a bank account that Chilla would contribute a portion of his weekly wage to, which was fine, on principle. The problem was that Chilla *still* had no idea of saving, and thought that account was something he could raid whenever he needed to. One particular letter, sent on New Year's Eve 1922, demonstrated just how hopeless the task Leofric had been set was.

'Many thanks for the book, Mum, dear,' Chilla wrote warmly, before adding grandly, 'I want you to take a few pounds of my dough, and buy yourself and Dad a little treat of some variety, and will write the Old Dragon re same.'

The 'Old Dragon' in question, Leofric, was then stunned to read several paragraphs later, when his mother had passed it on to him:

> *I'm still plunged in impecuniosity through said motorcycle, but am getting lots of fun with it. By the way, my income tax for the last two years will soon come to hand and as it will be at least £30 I'll have to get assistance from over there, so tell Leofric to make ready in a few weeks.*

Nor was he averse to getting Leofric to do some running around for him, re said motorbike, asking in another letter.

> *If Leofric has time, can he get a kick-starter pedal complete with gear quadrant for a 4¼ Premier (1918 model). Tell the Dragon that I have no dough to spare over here to pay for it, and mainly there are no Premier agencies in this state anyway. Also tell him that I now consider Scrooge an archangel of charity. Also that he won't get the £25 back, as it's gone into the other bike. If he still lives after that it ought to be in a chastened state of mind. I can't bear to think of his poor little daughter going ragged and starving,*

> *a footsore waif, from house to house, begging pennies so that her father can hoard and gloat over them in his avarice ...*[65]

Impossible! On matters of money, it was Leofric's strong view that his brother was simply impossible to keep on the straight and narrow!

Eight
THELMA

I don't know how Taplin's little accident got into the papers. These little spills are only to be expected on a difficult service like this, and the publicity merely unfortunate. Papers, 'blooming ghouls', always mention the accidents. But you never hear that we have already flown about 18,000 miles of the most difficult, loneliest and longest aeroplane mail service in the world. But that's the way of things.

KINGSFORD SMITH, IN A LETTER HOME TO HIS PARENTS, 30 MARCH 1922[1]

McGinness, I think, had even less academic education than I had, but he had something else, something great, something born of the young, immature but intensely venturesome Australian returned from the war, groping with gusto for something ahead, something undreamt of but which he must do. It was men like McGinness, Ross Smith, Kingsford Smith, Ulm, Hinkler and other Australians who infused that first great spark of adventure, Columbus-like, into what air transport is today.

HUDSON FYSH, WRITING IN HIS AUTOBIOGRAPHY, *QANTAS RISING*, IN 1965[2]

When Thelma Corboy first laid eyes on Charles Kingsford Smith in late July 1922, he appeared to be a rather curious cove, though full of life. She and her mother had been in a Port Hedland drapery shop buying material for new dresses for the race-week grand ball when she heard a lot of raucous laughter. Looking up, she saw five or six young men walking past the open shop front.

'Who are they?' her mother asked the shopkeeper, a little disapprovingly.

'It's the Kingsford Smith crowd,' that good woman replied, pointing to the smallest of the group, the one laughing the loudest. 'And that's Kingsford Smith himself, the airways pilot — you must have read about him.'[3]

At this point, to Thelma's amazement, the matronly shopkeeper then took her mother aside and began speaking about the pilot in a low voice. It was not clear what she was saying, only that whatever it was, wasn't proper for the ears of a beautiful 21-year-old girl, which Thelma was.

'What was that about?' Thelma asked her mother as they left the shop.

'You don't need to know,' her mother replied rather primly, before quickly changing both the subject and the direction they were walking.

Thelma was, naturally, intrigued.

A few days later, she saw the dashing 25-year-old pilot at the Race Ball, and was able to get a closer look. There was eye contact ... an introduction ... a whiff of excitement in the air. He asked her to dance. Yes, there had been her mother's admonitions about this man, but on the other hand, she wasn't there and didn't need to know.

He moved quite well, she thought, and she rather liked him. Just mind the foot, Thelma, if you would. Small war wound, you see. Nothing to worry about.

As it happened, Smithy rather liked her, too, and was particularly taken with her vivacious, voluptuous looks, not to mention how finely educated she was, courtesy of a Perth boarding school and Sydney finishing school for young ladies. Thel was all *class*, and so very different to most of the women with whom he had been amorous. Thel and Charles parted from each other that evening with some sorrow, but with no declarations made.

•

That was it then. Though he had probably done more than anyone to get Qantas off the ground, in the end Paul McGinness decided to move on. One reason was that it was all getting too serious and something called a 'management structure' had been put in place. What really stuck in his craw was that while Hudson Fysh was the head of flying operations, and Fergus McMaster was chairman, there was no spot for him, even though he was the biggest shareholder in the company! Another thing that got his goat was that both Fysh and McMaster — neither of whom, for some reason, were drinkers — had decided that there would be a blanket ban on drinking for pilots on duty, and that didn't suit McGinness at all. He *liked* a drink here and there and the truth of it was that, if it came to it, he could still fly better drunk than most men could fly sober. But when he was the only one on the board who voted to rescind the rule, there seemed only one option.[4] Pull out.

As described by John Gunn in his book on the history of Qantas, 'To the carefree and venturesome elements of McGinness's temperament, the slog and detail of daily administration and bureaucratic sword-cross were impossibly pedestrian. The dawning truth that his romantic vision of airline operations had at its centre the combined reality of a railway timetable and a cash book, that adventure and risk must subside into routine, repetitive perseverance, was disillusioning.'[5]

Things weren't so bad that McGinness didn't agree to stay on until Qantas could find a replacement pilot — perhaps a few months — but it simply wasn't as much fun as it had been. While he loved to fly, the deadly seriousness and constant routine of business life didn't really suit him.

•

It was late October 1922, and one hot day as the approaching summer was just beginning to bite and *chew*, Thelma Corboy was stunned to see from the cool shadow of the veranda of her family's homestead at Meentheena something slowly begin to emerge from the shimmering heat waves of the far horizon. She stood up from her chair and gazed closer. Slowly, slowly, alternately appearing and disappearing in the molten mirror of heated air, it soon emerged that it was a man, walking their way, leading an exhausted horse. But *who*? There wasn't a homestead between Meentheena and the railhead at Marble Bar, which was 60 miles away as the exhausted crow flew to the north-west, and not even the station's blackfellas walked like that in the midday sun. The figure was perhaps 200 yards away when she recognised him by his bouncing gait … the insouciant can-do way he carried himself, notwithstanding his slight limp, courtesy of his war wound. It was Charles Kingsford Smith, and he had been riding for the last two days from Marble Bar to get there! Madness, sheer *madness*. Sweating, sunburnt, thirsty, he was quickly ushered inside and plied with water and hospitality. Why was he here exactly?

Thelma suspected only too well — and so, frankly, did her mother — but felt obliged for the moment to go along with the explanation he gave: he was there to reconnoitre for landing strips and thought there might be a good one in those parts, maybe somewhere on their property. Of course he was.

For the next two weeks, as it turned out, Smithy continued his investigations into possible airstrips at Meentheena, riding in the early mornings and late afternoons with Thelma to all parts of the vast property and returning between times for wonderful lunches and lavish dinners put on by Thelma's mother — to her surprise she had really warmed to him after getting to know him a little, as he seemed to be quite the gentleman after all — where he was always at his charming best. Afterwards, Smithy might chat with Thelma's Irish-born stepfather Maurice McKenna, and later take his banjo and sing with the Aboriginal workers for a while, before returning to sit with Thel on the veranda in the cool of the night. Sometimes while Charles played the banjo, Thelma would sing, and she sang beautifully — a further bond between them.[6]

True, Thelma's mother had been nonplussed when he had first appeared but Charles Kingsford Smith was nothing if not charismatic and his natural attentiveness to her personally was wondrous, just as was the gentlemanly approach he took to Thelma. No doubt that scuttlebutt she had heard about him back at the drapery shop was just that, and she should take him as she found him. *Charming!*

For his part, Smithy was equally taken with life at Meentheena, and was quick to write to his parents upon his return:

Went out riding in the bush to reconnoitre possible landing grounds at the stations. Met a nice girl at 'Meentheena' ...

The station is amongst the hills, and except for being hard to get into, is a bonzer place. It is only 900,000 acres in extent. Mrs McKenna and Thelma gave me a splendid time, and I enjoyed the break immensely.[7]

Such a letter from their slightly chaotic son caused mother Catherine, for one, to sit up and take notice. Though Chilla had always been popular with the girls, in all his many letters to the family from all parts of the world he had never noted a particular one who he was keen on.

•

Shit! The bloody goats had been eating the plane again. Qantas mechanic Jack Hazlitt — himself a Gallipoli veteran — had been working hard to get one of the company's old Armstrong Whitworth FK8s it had bought into shape, and yet when he had come back from lunch it was to find several of Charleville's goat scourge munching on the plane's tail. And tomorrow was the big day! It took Jack a while, but after shooing the endlessly munching, farting goats away, he got to work and finally the hole was fixed, so that all was in readiness the following morning ...[8]

One could not quite say that Qantas was prospering, but at least it was surviving, which was a triumph in itself, given the number of other nascent aviation companies around the country going bust. And its breakthrough day did indeed come on 2 November 1922, when the young airline was ready to begin its first regular scheduled service, to carry airmail subsidised by the government *and* a paying passenger. Paul McGinness was to pilot the first leg, in a plane that looked to be in reasonably good shape bar a strange new patch it had in its tail, and before departure he made a speech to the assembled crowd in which he said that one day, 'Qantas will link Australia to Asia, Africa, Europe and Great Britain'. The crowd applauded with enthusiasm. And then Arthur Baird, the Qantas engineer, stepped forward to swing the propeller and the 160-horsepower Beardmore engine burst into deafening life.[9] For this inaugural trip, McGinness delivered 108 letters from Charleville to Longreach, about 300 miles away, in a trip that took just over three hours. And then the following day Hudson Fysh was ready to fly the next leg, with the said passenger aboard.

Though born eighty-seven years earlier, Alexander Kennedy, one of the first investors in the company, was always up for a new experience, and was champing at the bit to get under way and …

And Qantas apologises for this small delay.

After the plane flown the day before failed to generate enough revs in its engine to take off, everything, including Kennedy, had to be transferred into a second plane. Fortunately, Kennedy's baggage was not lost in the process. And in fact, as they took off, half an hour later, Kennedy — resplendent in his aviation cap and goggles and warm coat which he wore despite the hot day, to protect him when they got to the cold awaiting them at 5000 feet — shouted out, 'Be damned to the doubters!'[10]

As a young man, Kennedy had travelled from Longreach to Cloncurry in a bullock wagon, a journey that had taken him eight months. That had been in 1869. This time, over fifty years later, the journey in a Qantas plane took him just four hours and thirty-five minutes, including stops at Winton and McKinlay along the way! McGinness then flew back to Charleville with the company's first female passenger, Miss Ivy McLean. Qantas was now properly launched and the previous estimation that there would be a demand for their services proved correct.

As well as flying passengers on regular flights, Qantas continued to take people up on joyrides, make deliveries of urgent supplies and do anything legal that would turn a pound. This involved everything from delivering fresh fruit and vegies to outlying stations willing to pay for the privilege, to taking doctors on SOS missions, to hunting wild turkeys from the sky. Even, on one famous occasion, tracking down a car thief who had stolen a station owner's vehicle before heading off down the one road in that entire part of the country and thinking he was totally safe from apprehension, as he had a three-hour start on his pursuers.

On another occasion, in a legal case, the judge, the plaintiff, the defendant and two legal counsellors travelled together in a Qantas plane to get to the regional courthouse where the case was to be heard. For two bob a pop, Fysh even ran a little service for lonely and lovelorn blokes, dropping gifts 'neath parachutes with notes attached addressed to the objects of their affection on outback stations! All up, the airline's local renown was growing to the point that when a particular minister was taking a Bible study class at Winton State High School and asked, 'Who was Pontius Pilate?' one of the schoolboys was quick with his answer.

'He's the cove who drives the Qantas mail plane.'[11]

If that was the case, then it was also fair to say that he was very busy. Journalist Norman Ellison documented that Qantas pilots did everything — from making tickets, to handing them out, loading baggage, unloading it, making sandwiches and filling thermos flasks. Fixing planes, arranging accommodation, even selling shares in the company ...[12]

In the hot dusty conditions, it was not always easy to keep the planes in the air, but the company mechanic, and investor, Arthur Baird, was a superb operator who was able to maintain the growing fleet *and* make modifications to improve performance.

•

From Chilla, there continued to be signs that this young woman Thelma was working his spirit, as clearly the relationship was beginning to heat up ... For example, just a month after his first mention of her, at the end of a very chatty letter about this and that and nothing much in particular, Chilla got to the PS, which he wrote down in the margin of the page: 'P.S. Thelma Corboy (Mrs. McKenna's daughter,) heap nice girl. Am very interested ...'[13]

And a month later, again, on the last day of 1922 ... 'Next week I go out to Meentheena again for a few days spell. Guess I'll end up a family man alright. Can't find anyone I fancy better, and I'm tired of pub life. What say you?'[14]

To that question there is no recorded reply though, generally, the Kingsford Smith family was just happy that Chilla sounded as though he might have found someone wonderful to settle down with, after such a prolonged period of rattling around like a spare nut in a jam tin. Too, it was clear he had a good job. One year after Western Australia Airways' disastrous beginning, it had achieved a 97 per cent efficiency rating in terms of keeping to its schedule, and it had actually made such a good profit that it could afford to pay its shareholders a dividend. With his extra responsibilities and greater flying time Kingsford Smith had been granted a £50 increase in his annual salary. Thank heavens he was secure in his employment, and earning a steady and reliable wage for the first time since the war had finished. Not that his wage went far enough for him. It never did. Still, he thought he was closing in on what the problem was, as he wrote to his parents on 7 February 1923 from Geraldton:

> *I have been working out why I can't get ahead of my bank balance. I found out the average weekly bill for hotel and washing comes to just on a fiver, through moving about so much. And as I'm paying off still to Airways for a loan for shares and monthly payment on the motorbike, it doesn't leave me anything to spend at all. I think I'll have to get spliced. Not that I relish losing my erstwhile freedom, but I must have a home at this job, or otherwise I'll have to chuck it. It's a ghastly coast line after one has been up and down it a few dozen times and to finish one's run with one's only prospect of going 'home' to a bush pub — Gawd!*
>
> *Wish I could aviate across the Pacific or do some damn thing, but even that is fading into things impossible, tho' longed for.*[15]

Of the many frustrations that Kingsford Smith had at this time, one particularly gnawed at him. It was that he and his fellow pilots were accomplishing on a daily basis the kind of thing that the press on the east coast were raving about as if it was something world-breaking.

At one point Kingsford Smith was certain that he had broken an Australian record by flying from Broome to Port Hedland — 310 miles in two and three-quarter hours — at an average speed of 113 miles per hour, only to read upon his arrival a breathless account in an east-coast paper about how one Nigel Love — the bloke who had established that new airport at Mascot — had won the second Australian Aerial Derby off Victoria Park racecourse, just ahead of Hudson Fysh, at the colossal speed of 75 miles per hour!

'I'm not too keen on publicity,' he wrote to his parents, for all the world as if he meant it, 'but it seems funny that no-one over there seems to realise that we do quite some flying on this service. About as much in a week, in fact, as the rest of the Commonwealth does in a month altogether! The mileage flown on the mail route alone is now nearly 40,000. Yours truly has done about 19,000 miles of that himself ...'[16]

The answer, of course, was to do something that would make the east-coast press sit up and take notice, and Smithy knew just the thing — a flight around Australia using one of WAA's planes, to bring both the airline and himself favourable attention. His idea had been that such a feat would garner him valuable experience in flying truly long distances against the clock, day after day, and also get for him the publicity and thus, credibility, he needed to attract sponsors. He wanted to fly from Perth, via Derby and Darwin, across to Queensland and down the coast to Sydney, Melbourne and then across to Perth again.

And yet, even though Major Brearley had expressed initial interest, in the end he and the board of the company decided against allowing it on the grounds that they couldn't spare either a plane, or their best pilot, for the time it would take to complete the flight. Too, Brearley noted in a formal letter to Kingsford Smith that even the Controller of Civil Aviation, Horace Brinsmead, was against him making such a flight ...[17]

Still, the Pacific dream burned on, and despite Kingsford Smith's occasional pessimism that it could ever happen, he and Keith Anderson continued talking about it. For the time being, though, all they could do was to continue flying in the hope that something would turn up to bring the possibility of that flight closer ...

•

The British are coming!

In the autumn of 1923, an imposing British naval squadron, including the most powerful battle cruiser afloat, the mighty *Hood*, and four attendant cruisers, was en route to the harbour city of Sydney, and day by day, the newspapers were trying to outdo each other with features, columns, snippets of gossip and endless speculation as to when exactly the squadron would arrive. All put together, such expectation sold papers in enormous numbers and this was good.

In his office at the *Sun* — on Flinders Street in the suburb of Darlinghurst — on the afternoon of Monday, 7 April 1923, the veteran newsman Herbert Campbell-Jones was doing what he did most days. That is, he was trying to work out just how to get a jump on his many rivals in the bitter newspaper war that was then under way, hoping for inspiration on how to get the story or the photo that none of his competitors had. He was in just such a mood, when through the fog of cigarette smoke, stench of printer's ink and endless clatter of typewriters going nineteen to the dozen, emerged a visitor with a very interesting proposal.

His name was Charles Ulm, he was another veteran of the Great War, and more importantly still, he had an aviation company which he wanted to place at the service of the *Sun*, for the right price of course. Why not, he asked, send one of his planes down the south coast to get photos of the fleet *before* it arrived?

Sold!

So quickly in fact did the editor agree to Ulm's requested fee of £500 that the young aviation entrepreneur felt certain that he might have been able to squeeze him for double that amount, if only he had been a little more greedy. It was a mistake he was determined not to make again. Never mind, the object, to establish a deal with a major newspaper and demonstrate the power of planes to lift circulation when the right story was on offer, was on track. For when Ulm did exactly what he had promised to do, and the *Sun* was able to sell every copy by providing photos of the fleet at a time when they hadn't even reached Sydney Harbour, a firm relationship was established between Ulm and Herbert Campbell-Jones.

This timely injection of money allowed Ulm to keep alive what had become his dream — apart from that one he shared with many other pilots of flying the Pacific of course. Surveying the fledging Australian aviation industry, he had become convinced that the best and most profitable way forward was to establish a fleet of planes capable of flying between the major cities, and carrying everything from people to cargo to, particularly, post, which he viewed as the key component of a successful airline. In England, others had reached the same conclusion, and the noted aviation commentator Lieutenant Colonel Felton Vesey Holt, who had been one of the first recruits to the Royal Flying Corps, had written: 'Private aviation having come to nought, there is only one other way to keep a large civil aviation organisation in being, and that is to establish an airmail service in England.'[18]

Exactly! Once 'airmail' took hold in Australia, Ulm was convinced, with a letter being delivered from Perth to Sydney in just a little over a day — instead of the ten days it took currently by ship — the public would refuse to send it any other way, and would be happy to pay the extra cost. The key was to get the tender from the government to carry that post, and Ulm set about proving to the Federal government that he was just the man, with just the airline to do it.

From the beginning, he was up against it. Only a couple of years earlier, Postmaster-General William Webster had been quoted extensively deriding the whole concept: 'The whole question of aerial mails is absolutely impracticable as far as this country is concerned. They may be of some value in densely-populated countries, where short journeys are entailed, but here in Australia, with our sparse population and long distances between big mailing centres, the whole position is as different as night is from day. You just said now that Australia will be the last country to encourage aerial mail services. Let me tell you that, unless I'm very much mistaken, Australia will be the last county in the world to require them.'[19]

Unperturbed by such negativity, and there was plenty of it around, Charles Ulm pushed on. He sent his proposals to the Federal government, who acknowledged receipt, and filed them away in the 'circular filing cabinet'. Forever ...

•

Broke again. Always bloody broke. This could *not* go on. On 2 June 1923, in the middle of a letter to his parents, Kingsford Smith noted, 'I feel bad at not having sent any more over recently, but I have been slugged with £73.18.6 income tax, and have been at my wits end to find it ...' Before that letter had reached home, however, a cable arrived on 6 June 1923 that came as quite a shock.

> Married five minutes ago. Thelma and self send fond love – Chilla.[20]

He'd done *what*? Married a girl they hadn't even met, and without inviting anyone from the family to be there? What had he been *thinking*?

A follow-up letter from their son a few days later, however, explained how it had all happened.

He had gone out to Meentheena to bring Thel in for the Marble Bar Ball — a really big do in those parts, held annually — and one thing had led to another. They were having a bit of a drink in the pub, talking about their plans for the future when the thought hit them — why wait? Why not marry right away, as in, *today*? They were, after all, in the prime of their lives, and every month they weren't married was a month of each other they were missing. If they were married they wouldn't have to keep making these infernal trips to and from Meentheena, and could be *together*. True, Smithy's capacity to be a provider for them in the long term was a little unsure, but Thel proved to be a brick on this subject.

'When,' Smithy wrote to his parents, 'I told Thel that it might prove unfair to her to take on a partner whose future might prove somewhat uncertain, she said that if she didn't face the downs of life as cheerily as the ups with me we shouldn't get married at all.'[21]

So that was good enough for Smithy! By lunchtime they had made up their minds that they would do it, and by 3 pm they were married in the Marble Bar Registrar's Office by special licence with the Marble Bar postmaster presiding.[22] True to form, Smithy had no wedding ring handy, and had to borrow one from a local friend, a Mrs Airey, who only just managed to get it off her own finger for the occasion.[23]

That afternoon and into the evening, the happy couple gloried in one of the biggest, most spontaneous celebrations in the Ironclad Hotel that 'The Bar' had seen in many a long year, as the word spread all over the Pilbara. It's Smithy! He's gorn and married the Corboy girl, Thelma! You know, from Meentheena! Come quick! Local kids would long remember how in the middle of all the festivities, Smithy remembered them and came outside to give them the most unheard of things they'd ever heard of — a case of apples and a case oranges![24]

For their honeymoon, Smithy took his new bride back to Port Hedland on an open railway hand trolley, pumping up and down all of the 124 miles![25] On arrival, he installed her at the place where he and all the airline's crowd stayed when stopping in that town, Mrs Mousher's boarding house, before he had to resume his flying schedule just a couple of days later. No doubt it came as something of a shock to the system for Thelma … ah … *Kingsford Smith*, to find herself no longer with the run of Meentheena but instead put up in the bare room of a boarding house. And it must also have been hard waiting for her, um, *husband* to return to Port Hedland, which he did for two days a week. But she coped. Just.

There was a brief interlude when Smithy took her 'back east' to meet his family, but from the beginning it did not quite go as planned, even though the clan turned out in force to meet them at Sydney's Central Station. The Kingsford Smiths wanted to love Thelma from the beginning, and she, no doubt, wanted to love them.

But she was nothing less than a *lady*, in the slightly elite sense of the word, and they were a boisterous, loud, loving family who were not overly particular about the finer points of etiquette. Making things even more difficult was the fact that only shortly after the newly married couple was installed at Kuranda, Chilla was dashing around like a mad thing, trying to meet up with a fellow by the name of Lebbeus Hordern. This man, himself a veteran of the Royal Flying Corps was a member of the famous retailing family and Charles wanted to see if he could buy one of Hordern's seaplanes to get that infernal Pacific flight going — he was always talking about it! — leaving Thel alone with a group of people she didn't know, even if they were now nominally 'family'.[26] A kiss, a 'bye-bye' and a 'see-you-soon!' Then, when Charles finally returned late in the day, he would only be there for a short time before he would be off to bars all over Sydney catching up with old mates.

Well, hell, Thel.

Most days and many evenings, Thelma found herself high and dry at Kuranda in Longueville, left with Charles's elderly parents, who were old enough to be her grandparents. It was only a very short time before they ran out of things to talk about. After just two weeks, Thelma had had enough, and *insisted* to Charles that they return to their life in the west. And yet he wouldn't hear of it. Thelma was beside herself. It seemed to her that Charles was so absorbed by his own needs that things might be just as bad when they got back west.[27]

As it turned out, they sort of were, and nothing was easier once they had settled back into Mrs Mousher's boarding house again. Sometimes Thelma's mother would come to visit her, and she at least knew quite a few locals at Port Hedland, and generally the Airways people who came through. Mostly, however, Thelma was spending a lot of time waiting for her prince of the air to return to her small part of the earth.

Things got a little better for the newlyweds when in the last months of 1923 they moved up to Carnarvon, by the mouth of the Gascoyne River, and rented a better furnished house than they could quite afford, but Smithy's long absences remained a problem. At this point, he was not only flying 1000 miles a week, but also filling the role of managing director of Western Australian Airways whenever Major Brearley was absent, which was frequently. And then, when her husband did return to

Carnarvon, it turned out that what he most liked to do, after spending the briefest of times with her — fifteen minutes should do it — was catch up with friends at the pub, sing riotous songs till all hours, and laugh and drink the night away. Had she made a *mistake*?

•

Had he made a mistake? At the time, in late 1923, Smithy had seized on the suggestion of Thelma's stepfather, Maurice McKenna, that he take over a pastoral lease of 63,000 acres, right next to Meentheena. It would get Thel closer to her mother and the life she had known, it would provide him with a more settled life to be with her and, most importantly of all, it would give him a chance of making the really big money he needed to reach his goal of the Pacific flight. And he really did like the *idea* of being the lord or laird, or whatever that word was, of such a vast spread of land. His broad vision was to open some of the land up to returned servicemen and between them they could establish a kind of pastoral syndicate.[28] But in the end, after he had committed to it and signed the papers, he decided that the time was not yet right to go through with it, and so he persuaded his sister Elsie and her husband Bert Pike to come over, with his cousin, Phil Kingsford, to run the property for him.

On the trip north from Perth to get there, Elsie could not quite believe how many people knew her little brother. Kingsford Smith, did you say? Kingsford Smith? You're Smithy's sister?! Smithy is a great mate of mine! Jacko, this is Smithy's sister, can you believe it? Come to help him on that property he bought! Good ol' Smithy.

We drink together often at the Gascoyne Hotel.

He helped me out once.

He was seeing my sister for a little while, but we haven't seen him since.

I was on a steamer once when he flew so low over it he nearly blew the bloody boilers off!

I was there the day he dinkum touched the corrugated-iron roof of the Port Hotel in Port Hedland with the wheels of his mail plane![29]

Good ol' Smithy.

Wherever she went, Elsie seemed to be having conversations of that order with just about every second person she met, and it was apparent that whatever else, her little brother was a hugely popular man in these parts.

•

Though generally a happy soul, George Wilkins was as profoundly depressed as ever he had been in his life. At the behest of the British Museum, he had accepted a commission to go on a 2500-mile journey, over two and a half years through the Top End of Australia to collect specimens of fauna and flora to place in the venerable museum's collection — with a particular focus on native mammals. With three companions, and occasional Aboriginal guides in various regions, Wilkins was engaged in doing exactly that, and yet the more he trekked the more he realised just how devastating the effect of European colonisation had been on his homeland. As he travelled he documented the massacres of Aborigines, the wholesale slaughter of wildlife to the point of extinction, the infestation of pests such as rabbits and foxes, and the catastrophic clearing of the natural environment for the purposes of providing grazing lands making the likelihood that dozens of more native mammals would be wiped out a near certainty.

'There is no doubt,' he wrote, 'that we are witnessing the passing of these mammals, and that as far as indigenous life is concerned, Australia is in the death-throes.'[30] Typically, he kept on going, through some of the most forbidding country in Australia, sometimes pondering just how long a man would be able to survive without supplies or native expertise.

•

In the first two years of its existence, Western Australian Airways had done well, in part because of Norman Brearley's astute management and in part because of the dedication of his pilots — none more so than Kingsford Smith, whose log showed he had flown nigh on 100,000 miles of the firm's total of 300,000 miles to date.[31] Not unreasonably, the pilots took the view that their dedication should be rewarded with a pay rise. It was equally evident that Smithy, both their natural leader and official leader as chief pilot, should be the one to represent them in what they were pleased to think of as 'negotiations'.

'Cept the negotiations didn't really get very far — only as long as it took for Smithy to formally threaten on behalf of the pilots that if their demands were not met then 'like Arabs, we will fold our tents and silently steal away',[32] and Brearley to say no to each and every one of those demands. Smithy tried charm, he tried reason, he tried anger, threats of them all walking away and an appeal to Brearley's sense of generosity.

No. No. No. No. *No.* NO.

In the end, such was the stand-off there were only two possibilities. Either Smithy and his fellow pilots would have to back down, or some of them would have to follow through on their threats and leave the company.

Smithy chose the latter. He liked Brearley and he felt he owed him because of the chance Brearley had given him two years earlier when he had been very much down on his luck. But on the other hand, it was also his reckoning that after his faithful service of the last two years, and the money that Western Australian Airways had made, that debt had been paid, and the pilots' demands were not unreasonable. Therefore, in the face of Brearley's refusal to buckle, he would take his hat, his coat and his umbrage and walk out the door, and in this exit was followed by all the other pilots bar two.

Brearley was sorry to see Smithy, particularly, go. 'He was a really first class pilot of the type needed for overcoming the hazards that faced us in the 1921 and '22 period,' he later reminisced. 'Of course, he had to be "tamed" for our course and he submitted when he realised this. His improvement in general behaviour was a gradual process and this development came slowly but surely.'[33]

At the time, however, Smithy had few warm thoughts for Brearley, and was upset about how the negotiations had failed. Not that there weren't some upsides …

'Thelma is very philosophical about it all,' Chilla wrote to his parents on 15 February 1924, perhaps gilding the lily a little about his wife's true feelings. 'She is a great little kid, God bless her and stands behind me in everything.'[34]

Keith Anderson, of course, went with Smithy. Inseparable by now, the two had a plan, beyond the flying of the Pacific, which they talked about interminably, a plan they hoped might deliver them the money they needed to fulfil that dream. Over the past couple of years of flying around the north-west of Australia, they had seen first-hand both how rich some of the station owners were, and at the same time how poor were the facilities they used to move their product to market. It was all very well for the planes to take the station owners to Perth and back in a couple of days, but what about their clips of wool? How did they get to market? And how did the supplies they needed on their stations get to them?

The answer was by such primitive means as camel trains, and as a matter of fact Carnarvon had been built with a main street wide enough for a camel train to turn around. So it was that Kingsford Smith and Anderson decided to buy into an existing garage owned by a Carnarvon local, Tom Carlin, and expand the whole thing. They had formed the view that what was most needed in the north-west of Australia at that time was trucks. *Big* trucks, and lots of them. The idea was that Kingsford Smith and Anderson would personally buy and operate them, and use the contacts they had developed with station owners over the past two years to build the business from there — a business that they co-owned, not merely took a salary from.

If they got it right, they might even be able to make enough money from the business to fly the Pacific! For the funds to get started, they took out a loan with Keith Anderson's mother, Constance, which allowed for their first truck to be bought. Smithy's part of that loan was £150, interest free, for six months, for which he was immensely grateful.[35] Typically, he also borrowed money from his family back east, including his sister Winifred and his brother Eric. (In some ways his financial relationship with his family was a twist on the Marxian model: from each according to their means, to Chilla according to his needs.)

And so the Gascoyne Transport Company was born …

The headquarters was established at Carnarvon, and the initial truck was an enormous American-built 3-ton Republic bought on hire-purchase. This was used to bring the wool from every station within cooee — and sometimes as far away as two or three cooees — and deliver it to the Carnarvon wharves. Certainly, it went against the grain to give up flying, but both men felt it was a means to an end.

And the preliminary signs were good. After just one month's operation, Chilla was very proud to report to his even prouder parents that so far the business was 'a great success', and that their gross takings were 'around £380'.[36] Now, just how much of that was profit, he wasn't quite sure, as figures had never been his forte and he generally found the actual running of a business really dull work, as opposed to the actual fun of doing stuff, but the venture certainly seemed promising. It wasn't long before he and Anderson were able to afford to buy Carlin out and run the show on their own.

And yet, while his trucking business had been growing, his parents-in-law on Meentheena had gone bust with so many debts after the devastating drought they had just been through, that the bank had foreclosed on them. Thelma was deeply upset to see her stepfather reduced to going gold prospecting again, while for his part Smithy was a little stunned to find himself the chief provider for a family he had never heard of two years previously. And, clearly, in such tough times, and without his father-in-law to supervise things, his own hopes of establishing a successful pastoral syndicate were also over — his only hope of salvation lay with his trucking business. (His father-in-law clearly tried other things to stay afloat, as within six months he was convicted in Perth Supreme Court for rustling and received two years' hard labour in Fremantle Gaol, together with twelve strokes of the cat-o'-nine-tails.)[37]

•

Penned in 1906, they were among the most famous lines by an Australian, about Australia:

I love a sunburnt country,
A land of sweeping plains,
Of ragged mountain ranges,
Of drought and flooding rains,
I love her far horizons,
I love her jewel sea,
Her beauty and her terror —
The wide brown land for me.

Which was fine. The truth of it, however, was that Dorothea Mackellar would have been unlikely to have written those immortal lines had she been a long-distance truck driver trying to move along those plains, over those mountains, through those floods and towards those endlessly receding far horizons, ever and always on a track winding back to nowhere in particular.

Kingsford Smith and Anderson's essential idea was a good one, and indeed potentially lucrative. But, bugger them dead, it was *hard* work. To transport tons and tons of wool across a terrain strongly opposed to and willing to fight against *any* movement that wasn't the languid wave of a hand to remove flies, or perhaps the dying twitches of an exhausted animal, was something that would sap any man, and in this case it sapped two men. At any given moment either or both of them could be anywhere from Geraldton to Carnarvon to the Black Stump to out the back of Woop Woop.

How did Thelma cope with Smithy's now even longer absences? Only … just. Still, she might have coped, *just*, if when he finally returned home Smithy had stayed with her exclusively, but he didn't. Once returned from the backblocks, her husband invariably had a thirst that could have drained the Indian Ocean and was wont to spend his evenings at the local pub, downing beer after beer between singing raucous songs and engaging in his favourite party trick, which was to do both of the aforementioned while standing on his head. Thelma had been amused the first time she had seen him do it, irritated a little on the second occasion and completely disgusted the fiftieth time.

And then, complete with a horrible hangover, he would be gone again.

No woman could put up with that kind of treatment for long, least of all a very beautiful and strong-willed one who had other options.

Smithy, meanwhile, remained focused on getting the job done when he was in the scrub and was amazing in his resourcefulness, whatever the circumstances — by simple dint of the fact that he had little choice in those parts. For what else could he do but be resourceful when travelling through such country?

On one occasion, right out in the middle of nowhere, over 60 miles from anywhere, the former war pilot's truck had ground to a horrible, shuddering halt. Upon investigation Kingsford Smith discovered that the oil cock had been knocked off the crankcase, probably by hitting a jutting rock, and all the oil had drained away, causing one of the big-end bearings on the crankshaft to be chewed to pieces for want of lubrication.

The heat beat down, and he faced three days' march in any direction to get help. But not to worry.

Reasoning his way through the many technical problems, Smithy concluded that he could fashion a solution. In his load he had an enormous box of soap, bound for one of the outlying stations. By grinding it down and mixing it with a very small amount of water, he felt he had a rough approximation of oil. Now for the molten and gouged bearing. Cutting down a bit of hardwood gum with an axe, and using his pocket-knife thereafter, he was able to whittle a wooden bearing shell to do the job. After he sealed off the damaged drain valve he poured in the thick mixture of soapy liquid. Then he started the engine for the first time in two days and gingerly moved forward. It worked! It really worked!

Who was his uncle? Bob was his uncle, that's who! In such a fashion did Charles Kingsford Smith and his wounded truck limp forward for the next 60 miles until he was able to get to a town where more sophisticated help was available.[38]

On another occasion, when Smithy found his big truck blocked by the raging Murchison River while he was trying to get to Perth on time for a certain social engagement, he refused to be beaten. It took a while, but after scouting around for enough of the abandoned empty oil drums that abounded in that area, he lashed them together into a rough kind of raft, and *floated* the bastard across![39] As the months went by and the Gascoyne Transport Company became better known — and the station managers could see for themselves what an improvement it was to get their wool straight to Carnarvon and on the first steamer out — the two partners became even busier. If Smithy got word of a record wool consignment that needed to be moved, he immediately insisted on doing it, and always tried to do it in record time.[40]

Smithy liked records.

As to Keith Anderson, he did the best he could, but he did not remotely enjoy the reputation of Kingsford Smith for self-sufficiency and derring-do. Apart from his strong friendship with Smithy, he was essentially a loner and did not mix easily, but he could be counted on to do long hauls, so long as nothing went wrong.

•

And who was minding the office during these adventures and the many prolonged absences they entailed? The more successful the business became — as more trucks were purchased and more drivers put on — the greater the demands of office work, and the less inclined was either Kingsford Smith or Keith Anderson to do it. Again, Chilla called on his sister Elsie, and her ever-reliable husband, Bert Pike, to come and run the business side of things, which they were free to do, given that the pastoral lease had come to nothing. Neither she nor Bert was in any doubt that Chilla needed them, once they had a look at how things were running.

For in ordinary business routine he was clearly hopeless. His office methods were haphazard in the extreme, and he was hopelessly unpunctual and harassed and bewildered by the usual financial adjustments and worries connected with running one's own business. 'A funny thing about Charlie,' Elsie later wrote, 'was that he just could not bear to ask for an account to be paid. He would go out to collect, and usually come back empty handed. When he did collect, he would almost apologise!'[41]

On those rare occasions when Kingsford Smith and Anderson were together and not out 'on the track', as they called it, business was almost the last thing they discussed. The first thing they talked about was flying the Pacific. They continued to examine all aspects of its many possibilities. In terms of finance there was no doubt that it would be extremely expensive, but between them they were not without contacts, or credibility for that matter.

After all, in the entire world there probably weren't two pilots more experienced in long-distance flying, given how long they had been in the air, and their work with Western Australian Airways. And while building the Gascoyne Transport Company, Smithy had kept his hand in flying by doing the odd job for Major Brearley — with whom he had substantially repaired his relationship — sometimes ferrying planes back and forth to Perth. So when the two men talked about flying the Pacific there were people who listened, and some of them were wealthy. Finally, they had a breakthrough.

Through the course of his travels in the north-west, Smithy became very friendly with a wealthy young man from Mundabullangana station, by the name of Keith Mackay, who promised to back them for as much as £2300,[42] so long as he could come with them.

Done!

Keith was a good bloke, very capable, and for the several thousand pounds he was offering, they would be delighted to have him. They could even, at last, maybe be able to afford to buy one of Lebbeus Hordern's seaplanes …

Just when the whole thing was warming up, however, Keith hired a plane from Western Australian Airways to drop him back at his station. Tragically, however, in the course of the trip, which took place on Wednesday, 16 July 1924, the pilot — Smithy's old mate, Len Taplin — lost control of the plane and crashed into the sea, just off the coast. Taplin and the mechanic swam to shore but Keith Mackay didn't make it.

'I'm afraid that's my last hope gone west,' Smithy wrote forlornly to his parents.[43] Still, that thing inside him, that burning desire to fly across the Pacific, come what may, no matter the obstacles, was not long in re-establishing itself.

Keith Anderson felt the same. Early in 1925 Keith wrote to his rich uncle in Toorak, setting out their plans, and their possible financial needs. True, that uncle, after looking at it all said no, but he hadn't said so instantly! And they had also got a positive response from one of the oil companies they had contacted, offering them free fuel if they could actually get a plane into the air. Smithy continued to be keen on buying one of Lebbeus Hordern's seaplanes, berthed in Sydney. And yet, alas … Smithy wrote to his parents:

> *I haven't had any reply from Hordern or his secretary, but am hoping for favourable news. Damn it all, one must have a last flutter at the flying game before one quits if one must. You ought to have seen the things that were said about me when I left flying: 'An irreplaceable master of the air, whose wonderful ability was only equalled by his courtesy and consideration to his confident passengers, etc.' My Gawd, I'm some lad it seems.*[44]

Which seemed, genuinely, to be the widespread view of Kingsford Smith and his flying abilities. But no more firm backers appeared, despite all the talk, which didn't mean that he and Anderson were remotely tempted to give up.

'As a last resort,' Smithy wrote, 'we will work this show at maximum capacity for two years when we will be able to afford to buy a machine ourselves and tell them all to go to hell.'[45]

•

There comes a time in every adventurer's life when he must either embrace a long nurtured dream and try to make it happen or give it up … and know that he will simply die wondering. The times since his air crash in Crete had been particularly busy for George Wilkins, and they had included being second in command of the British Imperial Antarctic Expedition, returning to the same parts the following season with the Sir Ernest Shackleton *Quest* Antarctic Expedition, travelling widely through Russia and also the deeply depressing trek through northern Australia to collect the specimens for the British Museum. But through it all, he, too, had been nurturing a dream — to explore from the air the vast tracts of the Arctic Circle that had never been seen by human eyes. He also felt that once that exploration had been accomplished by fanning out on many trips northwards, he could then make one big hop from the north of Alaska, right over the top of the world and land in Norway!

True, there were many worthy experts who said it couldn't be done and, of these, the great Norwegian explorer Roald Amundsen was foremost, telling Wilkins firmly: 'What you are trying to do, is beyond the possibility of human endeavour.'[46]

And yet by mid-1925 Wilkins was convinced his critics were wrong, and set out to prove it. With the support of a deal with the North American Newspaper Alliance, in return for exclusive news and pictures, and help from the Detroit Aviation Society and the *Detroit News*, he was able to come up with the funding he needed. Courtesy of his old friend and great supporter Anthony Fokker — now a well-established American businessman, adored for his *bon vivant* ways — he was able to buy two Fokker planes. Such was Fokker's personal regard for Wilkins in turn, that the Dutchman personally ensured that they were constructed to the highest standards and precision. The wings and fuselages of the planes were constructed in Holland before being shipped to New York in December 1925, where the engines, the engine mounts, fabric covering and controls were added at the Fokker factory at Hasbrouck Heights, in New Jersey.[47] Once complete, they were disassembled and shipped in crates to Fairbanks in Alaska.

•

Thelma had had a gutful. None of Smithy's grand plans meant anything to her, and she had really had enough of the whole thing. He was almost never at home and she had reached the point where she was just as glad when he wasn't. When he did return, and he wasn't at the pub, all they did was argue and it was becoming clear to both of them that what they had shared together was less a long-lasting love and more a passing passion — a passion that had now passed out of sight. It seemed to Thelma, the only thing her husband was passionate about now was his damned Pacific flight — it was all he talked about, thought about, dreamt about. As hard a worker as he was on his business, it seemed to her that even that was only because he wanted to make enough money so he could make the Pacific flight, the Pacific flight, the Pacific flight … always the Pacific flight!

Well, she wanted no part of it, or him, and one day when he returned home from another long haul, he found that, like an Arab, she had folded her tent and silently stolen away. No-one who knew them both well was particularly surprised.

Though upset at the time, a letter Smithy wrote to his mother a short while after Thelma left showed that it wasn't long before things had returned to normal. A quick mention of the separation and then back to the Pacific flight and ongoing money worries:

> *26th July, 1925*
> *Dearest Mum,*
> *Thanks muchly for your understanding of my troubles. They are pretty heavy on me and I will take some getting over. But all will be ok some day.*
>
> *I hope that there really is a good chance for this Pacific flight as I want to come over next month but cannot risk being away unless it is justified. I need the change tremendously.*
>
> *Unfortunately my income tax has just hit me with a bang (£30) Lord knows how they can possibly reckon I owe that much, but anyway, I'm used to being in debt. I will be amazed if I am ever out of it …*
>
> *Your loving son,*
> *Chilla*[48]

Not long afterwards — leaving Bert Pike and Elsie in charge of running the trucking company — Kingsford Smith and Anderson returned to the east coast on a brief trip to see family and friends, and to do the rounds of possible sponsors, including government bodies, to raise the money they needed to make the flight.

Seeing their nearest and dearest was wonderful. Trying to find sponsors, however, was nigh on impossible.

Their first port of call was the seat of the Federal government, Parliament House in Melbourne, where they were generally flat out getting to the third secretary from the left, let alone any of the relevant ministers. A letter to Prime Minister Stanley Bruce produced only a terse response acknowledging receipt. The Defence Minister was not that interested. The Vacuum Oil Company advised that it wished them well, really well, but was in no position to bankroll the trip, because … *blah, blah, blah, blah, blah* … but it really did wish them well. The only genuine interest came from the editor of the *Sun*, Herbert Campbell-Jones, but the mere £500 that he promised wasn't remotely enough to turn their dream into a reality.

•

All was in readiness.

George Wilkins had now selected a co-pilot for his planned trip across the roof of the world — a phlegmatic Alaskan resident by the name of Ben Eielson — and with him intended to make many trips 500 miles to Point Barrow on Alaska's far north coast and ferry enough petrol there to establish the base from which they would launch on Norway.

That was the plan, anyway. But from the beginning, things did not go as he envisaged.

It was minus 52 degrees Fahrenheit (20 degrees below zero) in Fairbanks when they began to unpack the crates on the morning of 8 March 1926, though that in itself wasn't too much of a problem. There were many goldminers around Fairbanks who warmly remembered how many times Ben Eielson had flown through storms to get medical help to injured miners, and they flocked to assist the aviators. In no time at all they were hauling the two still wingless planes through cheering crowds to the hangar of Ben Eielson's Fairbanks Aeroplane Corporation, where the reassembly process began.

No, the first of the real problems came a few days later, when Palmer Hutchinson, the young correspondent for the newspaper alliance that was helping to finance them, insisted that a 'christening' of the newly assembled planes would make for great copy and photographs. Generally, Wilkins didn't go in for that kind of malarkey but Hutchinson was such a nice bloke and his organisation was such a loyal sponsor that he felt obliged to co-operate. On the morning of 11 March 1926, the two planes were pushed out of their hangars as variously the mayor of Fairbanks, some local dignitaries and a few men of the cloth did the honours. The climax came when the wife of the mayor and another lady stepped forward and, by cracking a bottle of petrol over a propeller of each plane, christened firstly the single-engined Fokker, the *Alaskan*, and then the three-engine machine, the *Detroiter*, as everyone clapped vigorously in the sub-freezing air.

Palmer Hutchinson was appreciative and was about to go back and write his story, when Wilkins had a quiet word with him. Hang around, he told the enthusiastic and likeable young reporter. In a couple of hours, once everyone including the local press has gone, we're going to take the planes up for a test flight and you can have another 'scoop'.

The *Detroiter*, when they at last wheeled it out to the runway proper, was an extraordinary sight. With the wings spanning 71 feet 2 inches, it was the prototype F.VIIb.3m, the biggest Fokker ever constructed, as Wilkins's good friend Anthony Fokker himself had proudly informed him. And now it was time to see how she would fly. With all three Wright Whirlwind radial engines at full throttle, the massive plane lurched forward towards the starting point on the runway ... before getting stuck in a snowdrift.

No problem. There were many willing hands ready to push her out again, including the enthusiastic Palmer Hutchinson. And yet while all the others knew that when pushing a plane with propellers whirring the only proper way was to push from behind, no-one had ever told Palmer. He had been pushing from behind when he decided he could get a better grip by pulling on the wheel stuck in the ice. This placed him between the wheel and the whirring, invisible, propeller of the starboard engine, just inches behind him. George Wilkins was in the cockpit with his co-pilot, and knew nothing of what was going on below.

Straining, *heaving*, to get the plane moving, the other workers spotted Palmer's danger just as the plane broke free and once again lurched forward. To get out of the way of the oncoming wheel, the 28-year-old journalist had to quickly step back …

George Wilkins and his deputy, US Army Major Tom Lanphier suddenly felt a sickening *clunk*. Worse, the instant they turned off the engines, they could hear screams and howls from outside, getting progressively louder as the engine noise lessened. They emerged from the plane to see Palmer Hutchinson decapitated.[49] A newsreel man who had captured the whole thing on his camera was, then and there, pulling open the back of his apparatus and exposing the film to the light, certain that he never wanted to see it again, and nor should anyone. Beyond the obvious tragedy to Palmer Hutchinson and his family, it was a brutal beginning for the whole venture.

Wilkins began to feel that there was a hex on that machine from the beginning. And maybe, in fact, a hex on the whole expedition …

With a man dead before the *Detroiter* had even left the ground, Wilkins decided — after poor Palmer had been removed from the scene — to leave the plane on the ground and take the shorter winged Packard Liberty-engined Fokker F.VIIa *Alaskan* on a trial flight. In the grand tradition, *flying was to resume as normal.*

And yet, after the *Alaskan* had circled satisfactorily for twenty minutes, its sole engine suddenly lost power and the 'heavier-than-air-machine' was suddenly indeed a *lot* heavier than air and obeyed all the laws of physics to the letter as it plummeted earthwards. Though both Wilkins and Eielson survived the crash unscathed, the *Alaskan* was a wreck, with the ski-undercarriage smashed clean off, and the 'propeller twisted like a ram's horn, and engine a total loss'.[50] The next day Wilkins and Lanphier finally took the jinxed *Detroiter* up, only to have it violently swerve on landing and crumple into a snowbank 'within a few feet of the spot where the *Alaskan* had crashed the day before'.[51]

At this point, with US$100,000 worth of planes smashed within a day of each other, and a man already killed, a lesser explorer than George Wilkins would have abandoned the project in tears. But Wilkins was not such a man. He continued to believe that it was possible to do what he had set out to do, and so methodically set about repairing both planes. Though there was no way he would be able to fly over the top of the world that season, he was at least determined to get both planes up in the air long enough before the flying season closed that he would be able to ferry supplies of petrol to Point Barrow, using its frozen lagoon for a runway.

When Wilkins and Eielson first succeeded in getting the *Alaskan* on the ground at Point Barrow, 500 miles north, it created a sensation among the local Eskimo population. The Eskimo lads, mystified, looked it over and asked: 'How can it fly? It has no feathers.' Others said it looked 'like a duck when overhead, but on the ground it looked like a whale with wings'.[52] That notwithstanding, one female Eskimo elder seemed to be not nearly as impressed as the others and, after poking the fabric of the plane with her finger, announced that she was certain that with the right sealskins she would be able to sew one for herself. Which was as may be …

Wilkins and Eielson kept ferrying supplies until one day, loaded down with tins full of petrol, the two pilots were hurtling down the airstrip at Fairbanks in the *Alaskan*, when it was clear that something was wrong, as the plane simply refused to lift.

Crash positions! (Basically, tense up and pray.) While stopping a fast-moving and heavy plane was problematic at the best of times, on snow and ice it was a nightmare. Certainly it was little problem to get the brakes to stop the wheels, but getting the tyres to stop on the ice was something else again … and now the single-engined Fokker began to slide from side to side, careering towards disaster. Finally it came to a crunching rest against the brush and stumps, and the main thing, as ever, was that neither Wilkins nor Eielson was hurt. The mystery remained, however: why had they crashed? They had loaded the plane and done this take-off many times. There had never been a problem. They knew the plane was capable of taking that load. This time, however, the plane had simply refused to leave the ground, as if it were too heavy. But how could that be?

Well, for the moment there was nothing for it but to unload the plane to lighten it enough that they could drag it free and begin repairs. It was while doing exactly that, however, that Eielson suddenly saw something move in the cargo hold. What the devil ...?

Reaching a hand into the semi-darkness he grabbed at a shape, to pull it out into the light, not knowing what to expect and ...

And he was suddenly confronted with a very beautiful young woman, flashing angry eyes at him as she tried to wrench her arm free. Stowaway! George Wilkins recognised her immediately. She was a gypsy, a rather modern independent one who, instead of moving around in a band of other gypsies, was moving around on her own, exploring the world. As a matter of fact he had danced with her just the night before, during which time she had told him she was a bit of everything, a musician, artist, writer and explorer — and wanted to know whether she could accompany him on this flight? It was with some reluctance that he had declined — for fear that her weight would make them crash — but it now turned out she had taken matters into her own hands.

Mindful of his own past, where stowing away had started him off on world adventure, Wilkins was not too angry, despite the wrecked plane and the fact that she was now swearing at them in a manner that would have made an Australian wharfie blush. He understood her compulsion, and besides, she was too beautiful to be angry with for long anyway. Wilkins ignored the damage to the plane and arranged for the girl to be slipped away from the plane into a friend's car, so she would not be embarrassed in the Fairbanks community.

He and Eielson and their mechanic then did the best they could to repair the plane, but something wasn't working, for on their next attempt to take off they crashed again, this time shearing off a wing and further injuring Wilkins's previously broken arm. And that was the end of the *Alaskan*.

One more trip to Point Barrow in the *Detroiter*, and then the fog closed over the Arctic Circle, to the point that their flying season was over. Wilkins would have to return to Detroit, try to find more money, and then return the following season to finish the job, fulfil his dream and fly over the top of the world, all the way from Alaska's Point Barrow to Spitzbergen, Norway — a place that had first come to wider attention when no less than Hans Christian Andersen had written a story saying it was where the 'Snow Queen' lived.

One more time, thus, he left the freezing wastelands behind, to return to rather more modern civilisation.

•

The heat, the flies, the sheer gut-wrenching monotony of it all! Running a trucking business in this part of the world just had a way of getting to a man. Though Kingsford Smith returned to Carnarvon in April 1926 and resumed with the Gascoyne Transport Company, it was not the same as it had been. When he and Keith Anderson had started it up, they had been proving themselves, doing something that hadn't been done before and it had been exciting to build the business up. Too, it was something they pretty much *had* to do, because to fail would be to end up penniless. But now? Now it had turned into hard work without passion, even though the business continued to grow. The more he worked, the more Kingsford Smith became convinced that in his heart of hearts, in the very soul of his soul, that he was a pilot and not a truck driver. When you had known what it was like to zip from one cloud to the next, to dive, to zoom, to fly like a bird and go wherever you wanted, how long could you remain happily earthbound, so often stuck in heavy mud, or chasing bloody prize rams that had got out of the bloody truck and were running bloody wild all over the bloody country until you rounded up every last one of the bloody beasts and got them back in the bloody truck? The short answer, it seemed to Kingsford Smith, was about two and a half bloody years, *tops.* Which, funny he should say that, was right about bloody *now.* Always the dominant partner in both his friendship and his business relationship with the stoical Keith Anderson, Kingsford Smith began to talk to him more seriously about finding a buyer for the business and using the money to have a go at fulfilling their dream to fly across the Pacific.

•

Late September 1926. Flying across the Illinois landscape late one night, delivering the post from St Louis, Missouri, to Chicago, Illinois, the young pilot got to thinking in the moonlight. How much he loved the purity of flying. How much he hated returning to earth, with all its petty worries and hassles. How he wished he could just keep flying and flying and flying … forever, or as near as he could get to it.

'Why submerge myself in brick-walled human problems,' he asked himself, 'when all the crystal universe is mine?'[53]

Why, if he had just a bit more petrol, instead of flying to Chicago as he was now, he could turn right and fly to New York. And if he had the right plane — say, a Bellanca with a Wright engine — *and* more petrol tanks, he could fly through the whole night, like the moon, fly to … fly to …

Suddenly the thought struck him, settled, and didn't move thereafter. He focused on it with wonder, startled at his own audacity. From out of nowhere, a certainty came upon him. If he had the right plane, the right engines and specially designed petrol tanks, he felt that he could fly all the way to *Paris*.

Yes, he could fly from New York to Paris! No matter that he was just a junior mail pilot, with only five years' flying experience. He knew himself to be good enough, and after the idea came to him he couldn't shake the feeling that he had to make the attempt. After all, he had always accepted the fact that risk was a great part of flying, and had long ago decided that, 'if I could fly for ten years before I was killed in a crash, it would be a worthwhile trade for an ordinary lifetime'.[54]

Beyond all that, the truth of it was that as much as he loved flying, he was sick of the mail run, going back and forth between fixed horizons. In his early days of flying he had gone barnstorming and kept body and soul together by doing anything and everything his passengers paid him for, including when one man had wanted to relieve himself while flying above his home town. Certainly, he didn't want to return to that craziness, but he *did* want to try something new. Not long before, he had applied to join the Australian explorer, George Wilkins, on his planned trip across the roof of the world, but that had come to nothing.[55]

Now, within a few days the clean-cut young man with the seeming innocence and sometime demeanour of an enthusiastic schoolboy had begun making calls to the St Louis business community to see if he could get them interested in providing him with the money he needed ...[56]

Oh, Mr Thompson? It's time for your meeting, sir. Mr Charles Lindbergh has arrived to see you ...

•

Hudson Fysh was away and so it was his wife Nell who answered the phone. It was a Qantas pilot getting ready to take off from Cloncurry, who wanted to know what kind of shape Longreach aerodrome was in. When Nell told him that she didn't know, the pilot requested that she go out to the aerodrome wearing her high-heeled shoes, and then call him back. When she did so and duly reported that the high heels did not sink into the runway, the pilot took that as an all-clear and set off for Longreach.[57]

Generally, Qantas was going well, growing in both the number of flights it was offering and the number of passengers it was carrying, as the idea began to take hold with the public that aeroplanes were not just scientific wonders but a genuine alternative means of transport, and a safe one at that, for travelling vast distances. In the early days, something that had helped the company's overall standard had been the insistence by Hudson Fysh that each plane receive a regularly scheduled maintenance overhaul, whether it seemed to be running correctly or not, and that each pilot go through a check list *before and after every flight* to ensure that everything was as it should be. All the logbooks had a notice pasted on the front: The correct carrying out of routine means the difference between the success or failure of our organisation.[58] True, there had been resistance to this order, with one pilot nearly crying when pushed, saying it was 'impossible to remember', but bit by bit over the months and then years this approach became standard, and bush pilots on the books either changed their ways to become serious commercial pilots or were moved on.

And yet Hudson Fysh was convinced Qantas could go a whole lot better still, if the Federal government would institute its own sensible policies. It was for this very reason that Fysh was bending the ear of the Controller of Civil Aviation, Colonel Horace Brinsmead, in the early spring of 1926, as the two men sat side by side on a train from Charleville to Brisbane.

It was crazy, Fysh told the powerful public servant respectfully, that they, not to mention everyone living around Charleville, should be condemned to this long, tedious rail ride to get to Brisbane, when Qantas wanted to provide a Charleville–Brisbane service to fly them there in a tenth of the time, but were prevented from doing so!

In response, Brinsmead would not be moved.

'Fysh, you're just wasting your time. You won't get it, and it's the wrong scheme.[59] Why waste your time trying to expand airways along railway routes. That's ridiculous. The aeroplane cannot compete with the train, and that's the policy of the Federal government, and therefore of my department. In eastern Australia, airlines will remain complementary to the railways.'[60]

Fysh continued to argue hotly against it, with the *clickety-clack* of the infernal earthbound journey adding emphasis to every word. It wasn't fair to the people around western Queensland, particularly, where there were only poor roads and no railways. Why should they be prevented from travelling quickly, like everyone else?

Brinsmead held his ground, maintaining that it was government policy for the railways to be the backbone of the nation's transport infrastructure, and for airlines to provide only the missing link, as it were, between railheads, but …

But it was a hot day, the trip was tedious when a Qantas plane could have got them to Brisbane in no time at all, and the argument put up by Hudson Fysh did make a certain amount of sense. It was at least worth thinking about it, and perhaps talking to some people within the government.

•

By late 1926, the time had come. Both Charles Kingsford Smith and Keith Anderson were so fed up with driving trucks — as witness the rare bickering they now embarked on whenever there was a reason for one of them to go to Perth, say, to pick up a new truck — that they began to actively look around for a buyer for the business. What they had to sell was a thriving driving concern with six trucks and trailers, with no debt attached, together with a fully equipped garage to keep the fleet on the road. What they wanted to buy were a couple of planes, to get them back into the air.

As it turned out, it required only one advertisement placed in a Perth newspaper to find a buyer for their business — their main trucking competitor from Carnarvon did the honours, for the princely sum of £2300, cash.

Henry 'Bob' Hitchcock, one of their mechanics from the old days at Western Australian Airways turned up, filled with enthusiasm for a particular plan. He told them how, up in New Guinea, gold had been discovered in the Highlands, but there were no roads to get into or out of the diggings, see? Bob had been one of thirteen children born and bred in Kalgoorlie and not only knew about the whole goldmining game, but still knew a lot of miners, and there was a fortune, an absolute fortune to be made in New Guinea!

Now, this was interesting news. Like them, Bobby was a veteran of Gallipoli, had in fact been badly wounded there, and though he was a great mechanic and a decent man, he was not one given to easy enthusiasms, being of a rather more lugubrious nature. So if Bobby was fired up about something, it was definitely worth listening to.

Why not, he said, buy a couple of the Bristol Tourer 28s that Brearley wanted to sell — as he was getting some new planes — and head up there? They could start an aviation company based in Port Moresby, flying miners and supplies in and the gold out! And with no competitors to speak of, no-one would worry about what they charged. Bobby would join them as their mechanic, and then, if all worked out well, hopefully make a claim on some of the diggings himself.

Gold, for everyone, in them thar hills, one way or another!

Well, it was a plan, and it seemed like a solid one. With the sale of the truck company they had a start on the money they needed for the Pacific flight, but it wasn't nearly enough. If there was a quick fortune to be made in New Guinea, they were up for it.

One approach to Brearley, and it was done. The two pilots, turned truckers, turned pilots again, bought a couple of the Bristols that they were already so familiar with from the lately renamed West Australian Airways — for £500 a pop — and started working on them immediately to get them into tiptop condition.

•

Now, while getting the planes over to Sydney, before heading north to New Guinea, why not drum up some publicity on the way, in the hope that they could attract some sponsorship for the Pacific flight? With that in mind, Kingsford Smith and Anderson decided to make an attempt at breaking the cross-continental record between Perth and Sydney, which, set by a Lieutenant F.S. Briggs in 1920, then stood at five days, encompassing twenty-one and a half hours actual flying time.

In terms of attracting that publicity, it certainly didn't hurt that Smithy took a reporter from the *Guardian* newspaper, John Marshall, and his wife, Gloria, along as passengers, while Keith Anderson would fly the other plane with Bobby Hitchcock and a third passenger by the name of John Howard. True, the fact that Smithy's two guests were a little nervy — each of them signed a final will and testament just before leaving, using the wing of one of the Bristol as a prop[61] — wasn't perhaps ideal. But Smithy's view was that so long as they sat still it wouldn't matter. Four days and thirty flying hours later, the great and glorious harbour city of Sydney slowly rose like the shining sun out of the eastern horizon, and she had never looked so good. (Certainly not to the rather shaken Mr and Mrs Marshall, who had spent the last four deafening days *willing* the whole journey to end, though Mrs Marshall, at least, had been charmed by the pilot, later recalling 'Kingsford Smith was always so cheerful, with a beautiful smile and lovely teeth'.[62])

And there were press there to meet them! And interviews and stories in the following day's paper! No, they hadn't finally broken the record, but they *had* carried the first female passenger across the country, and that proved a good enough 'hook' to hang the story on. The *Sydney Morning Herald* carried the story on page twelve ... 'LONG FLIGHT. PERTH TO SYDNEY'.

'The aviators, Messrs, Kingsforth Smith and Keith Manderson ...' it began. Fame! Misspelt fame, perhaps, but fame nevertheless. And how sweet it was ...

For days and then weeks, Smithy and Anderson were engaged in a round of festive parties, celebrating their flight, their return to Sydney, and their success in the west. Did they really want to leave all that fun and head off to New Guinea straightaway on another, probably even more gruelling, venture than the Gascoyne Transport Company had turned out to be?

They did not. The initial plan had been for Bert Pike and Bobby Hitchcock to go up to New Guinea by boat soon after they returned to Sydney to scout out landing grounds, but to Bobby Hitchcock's dismay, Smithy decided he could do that job himself, simply by going along to the Burns Philp offices in Sydney and having a look at some of their photos. And he didn't like what he saw, he told Bobby.[63] The landing grounds weren't big enough to cope with the kind of space the Bristols needed to take off and land and look, well ... they had pretty much just lost enthusiasm for the plan, and that's the way things go.

Bottom line?

After nearly a decade in far-flung parts of the world, the idea of living in Sydney for a good spell was extremely attractive. It was just a matter of finding a way to keep flying and getting the money they needed to make that Pacific flight, which was now more of an obsession than ever.

If there was a complication in the relationship between Smithy and Keith Anderson at this point — and there was — it was over a woman. Her name was Bon Hilliard and she was as strong-willed as she was vivacious, the daughter of the well-known and highly respected Sydney solicitor, Arthur Hilliard. Smithy was smitten with her blue-eyed beauty from the moment of first meeting her, while on a trip to Sydney between the time of selling Gascoyne Transport Company and buying and flying the Bristols to Sydney. And Bon, too, was seemingly very taken with him. And yet, something happened in the weeks immediately after Smithy and Anderson returned to

Sydney together, as they were constantly on the social circuit, with Bon as a big part of it. Somehow, in that mad whirl of lunches, dinners, singalong parties, cocktail parties and party-party-parties, Bon changed personal orbits. While she *had* loved gliding around Smithy's bright sun, there was something even more attractive about Keith Anderson's silent, stoical solidity and his gentlemanly attentiveness to her — perhaps even his willingness to have his life revolve around *hers*. A scone, Bon? A cigarette? Your chair pulled out? Keith was there for her, while Smithy was more than likely to be laughing or singing or playing the piano or telling riotous stories in the next room, if not standing on his head while drinking a beer.

In the space of just a few weeks, thus, Kingsford Smith was stunned to see his best girl, Bon, suddenly become Keith's best girl, and then Keith's officially announced fiancée!

Precisely what effect this had on Smithy's friendship and business relationship with Keith is not clear, though the least that can be said is that Smithy was well qualified to conclude that Bon, much as he had been taken with her, was not the only woman in the world with whom he could have fun, and all together they blithely partied on, entirely unaware of just what was to come.

Nine
Pioneers Away ...

Meanwhile, the years were passing. This was 1927, and it was nearly ten years since the war had ended. I was no forrader. I had absolutely nothing to show for those ten years which the locusts had eaten. It was time to be up and doing. One had to do something to attract notice ...

Charles Kingsford Smith in his autobiography, *My Flying Life*[1]

February 1927. Fairbanks, Alaska.

George Wilkins was back. This time he had two new Stinson Detroiter SB-1 planes with him, which he and Ben Eielson thought would be better than the Fokkers for Arctic conditions. True, George still didn't have a pilot's licence, but in these parts there was no-one to bother about that. Ben would be doing most of the flying in any case. Also, as a backup to their Stinsons, they decided to join the small body of the *Alaskan* together with the longer wing and landing gear of the larger Fokker, the *Detroiter*, to make a whole new plane! Alas, *the best laid schemes of mice and men often go awry*, and when the composite Fokker crashed upon their first attempt to take off in it, they left it in the Fairbanks hangar and continued with the Stinsons.

By late March, all was in readiness and the two pilots took off in one of the fully fuelled Stinsons from Point Barrow (where the local Eskimos had come around to calling Wilkins 'Anataka' — as in 'strong wise man') and headed north, in airspace previously unconquered.

At this point there were two pertinent theories about the Arctic that Wilkins felt he could disprove, based on his long explorations while sailing and trekking in the area over a decade earlier. The first was that there was a large landmass to the north of the Alaskan coast. The second was that it would be impossible to land on the frozen Arctic Ocean, because the ice would be far too rough. No less than 650 miles north of Point Barrow, with no land to see, the first theory seemed to be disproved. And now that the plane's sole engine was stuttering in that white frozen world, they were going to have put the second theory to the test, as Wilkins told Eielson to take 'er down.

'There, that's right,' he gestured in defiance of the engine's ragged but shattering staccato, pointing to a dimly perceived spot ahead on the ice. 'Keep her on that course! This ice is thick ... enough to hold a hundred tons.'[2]

In fact, Wilkins had no idea what the ice was like, or if the famous Arctic explorers Roald Amundsen and Richard E. Byrd were right and it really would be impossible to land in these parts, but with no other option, it seemed like the right thing to say to give young Ben confidence as they descended. In that most forsaken part of the planet, with not another human within 650 miles in any direction, the plane touched down to a shuddering, skidding halt. And they were alive! And their plane was intact! Wilkins was exultant, Eielson slightly less so as he contemplated their situation.

Then each got busy with his own work in temperatures that jarred and jangled at about 15 to 20 degrees Fahrenheit below zero. In a few minutes Eielson was deeply relieved to have the engine going again, while Wilkins was just delighted to have cut a hole through the ice in preparation for exploding some dynamite to take a depth sounding. Ah, but one thing, Ben. You'll have to turn off the engine so we can be sure of hearing the echo of the dynamite explosion once it has bounced off the ocean floor and come back to us ...

The strong, silent type was Ben Eielson. For, at this point, he looked at the half-mad, albeit very likeable, Australian and thought, 'All right, go ahead and take your sounding. But if I stop this engine I may never get it going again, and then nobody but us and God will ever know what the sounding is.'[3] And then he turned the engine off. The only sounds now were the whistling of the wind, the chattering of their teeth and the curious humming that Wilkins made as he went about his work. A short time later the dynamite exploded, and it was a long seven and a half seconds before the echo returned. This meant, according to Wilkins's instant calculations, that the ocean floor was 18,000 feet below them, well over three miles! This in turn made the existence of any large landmass anywhere near them most unlikely, and Wilkins had now all but definitively disproved the first theory.

Yes, that's great, thank you, but would anyone else bar them and the Almighty ever know? Fortunately, blessedly, Eielson did get the motor to bark and they were soon airborne again and heading back to Point Barrow, but after only two minutes the engine gave up the ghost once more and they had to land. This time the two men worked for several hours to get the engine going, during which Eielson suffered bad frostbite to his fingers, but once more they got aloft and made it to within 70 miles of Point Barrow before running out of petrol and coming in to land in a howling blizzard ...

Midnight in the Garden of Eden ... Life ... or *death*?

Life! Somehow, impossibly, they survived this third landing, despite the presence of cruel snowdrifts all around. The relief was such that both men burst into hysterical laughter. Life! They had done it again!

Too, it occurred to Wilkins that 'we were the first men ever to land on the sea, with an opportunity to walk home'.[4] Eighteen days later, of which five had been spent waiting in the plane for the blizzard to blow itself out, they managed to do exactly that — walking, walking and walking some more and with frosty feet and fingers, they returned to a Point Barrow overjoyed to see the presumed dead walk again. And that was the end of George Wilkins's second attempt to fly across the top of the world.

•

Things had moved relatively quickly for Charles Lindbergh after he began considering the possibility of flying from New York to Paris. The first thing he had discovered was that he was not the only one who had conceived the idea. In fact, a French-born American by the name of Raymond Orteig, an extremely rich New York hotelier, had put forward a prize of $25,000 back in 1919 for the 'first aviator of any Allied country crossing the Atlantic in one flight, from Paris to New York or New York to Paris',[5] and there had been several attempts since to traverse the 3600 miles. (This, of course, was a far more formidable task than the 1900-mile Newfoundland to Ireland hop across the Atlantic, which had been first accomplished by Captain John Alcock and Lieutenant Arthur Brown only shortly after Harry Hawker and Kenneth Mackenzie Grieve had failed, and several others thereafter.)

As a matter of fact, at much the same time as Lindbergh had felt that he might have a go at getting to Paris himself, the famous French fighting ace René Fonck had lined up a Sikorsky S-35, powered by three Gnome-Rhône Jupiter nine-cylinder radial engines, with a three-man crew, at one end of Roosevelt Field on Long Island and opened the throttle. The massive crowd gathered for the occasion held its breath. Faster and faster the plane tore down towards the far end and … and … steadfastly refused to leave the ground. Terribly overloaded with too much fuel, a wooden bed, red-leather upholstery, two flotation bags and many other accoutrements — not to mention the heated compartments in which specially prepared meals of Long Island duckling and roast turkey could be kept warm and the crew could eat in style all the way to France — the plane had simply refused to lift,[6] crashing instead in a gully at the end of the runway. Fonck and one of the crewmen escaped with their lives, but the two others were burned to death when the 2380 gallons of petrol onboard exploded.

And still there were more pilots coming forward, as advances in aviation permitted longer flights. As many as six other crews besides Fonck's were trying to fly the Atlantic but, not at all put out, Lindbergh kept going. After raising sufficient money from St Louis businessmen, he organised for a Ryan monoplane to be custom-made for him in California, pursuing his model of 'one set of wings, one engine, and one pilot', which he felt was the best way to proceed. There was no doubt that a single-engined monoplane was the most fuel-efficient option and, by swapping the weight of a co-pilot for fuel, and doing all the flying and navigation himself, he calculated he could squeeze 50 gallons more on board and another 300 miles of range. He wrote to his mother, Evangeline, in Detroit:

> *It is probable that two attempts at the NY–Paris flight will be made before I am ready to go. Either or both may succeed, although in both cases, there are reasons to throw doubt on the successful completion of the flight.*
>
> *We are not taking off before everything is ready, and if someone makes the NY–Paris hop, we will probably try a trans-Pacific flight via Honolulu to Australia, which would be a still greater accomplishment ...*[7]

For her part, while his mother was extremely proud of what he was setting out to achieve, she was also very worried for her only son. 'For the first time in my life,' the humble high school teacher wrote back to her son, 'I realise that Columbus also had a mother ...'[8]

•

So it was that in those early months of 1927, the just turned thirty years old Charles Kingsford Smith and Keith Anderson opened the rather grandiosely titled Interstate Flying Services in the very smart premises of Eldon Chambers at 92 Pitt Street, Sydney, just down the hill from where Smithy had attended St Andrew's Cathedral School fifteen years earlier. And look at him now! Nominally, as their letterhead stated, they were engaged in ...

INTERSTATE FLYING SERVICES

AEROPLANE FLIGHTS ARRANGED TO ANY PART OF THE WORLD

AERIAL ADVERTISING

SPECIALISTS IN AERIAL PHOTOGRAPHY

Unfortunately, they were in fact doing very little bar sitting around the office, chatting, waiting for the phone to ring and watching their capital draining away on overheads, all but entirely unleavened by serious paying jobs. The Bristols were parked out at Mascot airport being tended by Bobby Hitchcock — who was still dismayed about the New Guinea venture being abandoned — while Bert Pike had been appointed again as 'business manager', in the hope that some might actually eventuate.

Truth was, they were simply one more flying company among many at this time trying to get off the ground, and there was no real reason why such little work as there was would come to them particularly. They may have been called Interstate but not once in those early months of that year did they actually fly to another state, or indeed beyond the metropolitan confines of Sydney.

And then one day in early April 1927 came a letter which changed everything. It was from a Sydney solicitor by the name of Willis. He had a client, Charles Ulm, who had a proposal he would like to put to them. Was a meeting possible?[9]

Anderson and Kingsford Smith consulted their calendar. A meeting? Yes, they were free for a meeting on ... well, pretty much on any day ... at any time ... for at least the next couple of months. Still, if for nothing more than form's sake, Bert went and met the solicitor and it was all soon arranged.

The meeting took place in the offices of Interstate Flying Services. Tall, dark, dapper Charles Ulm, when he arrived, proved to be a Mosman man, much the same age as Kingsford Smith and Anderson, and just like them, was a war veteran who had been trying to make a go of it by launching various aviation companies, with only mixed success. One or two ventures had worked, and lots hadn't. As a matter of fact, though Charles Ulm wasn't a man much given to witticisms, his experience in recent times justified him uttering one of the defining and oft-repeated lines of those difficult times: 'The greatest risk to life in modern aviation is starvation.'[10]

Nevertheless, Ulm felt that by joining forces, he and Interstate Flying Services could make a serious go of winning the tender for the Adelaide–Perth postal route, which was shortly going to be on offer. Certainly, one Norman Brearley, with his West Australian Airways, would have the inside running on it, but Ulm was confident they could beat him.

Kingsford Smith was keen from the first, as he liked both Ulm's upfront way of going about things and the possibility of getting one up on Major Brearley. Keith Anderson was less so. He simply wasn't sure whether he liked the cut of Ulm's jib in the first place, and it seemed to him unlikely that Interstate Flying Services really would be able to beat their old employer for such a big tender. Still, it was obvious to both partners that Ulm had what they both lacked, which was a keen commercial brain. While Kingsford Smith was happy to be in the 'aviation business', the business part of it interested him only insofar as it allowed him to continue his true passion, which was aviation. Keith Anderson felt much the same.

Maybe under this new arrangement Ulm could take care of all the numbers, making them black rather than red, and Kingsford Smith and Anderson could get on with the flying. And if they could win the tender to fly between Adelaide and Perth, they would have it made. Have it *made*!

Therefore on the following morning, when Ulm returned to hear their answer, they did the deal, shook hands and all started to steer by the same star.

A small parenthesis here. One other key thing Ulm and the two partners of Interstate Flying Services had in common, though none of them knew it, was that they were all broke. Smithy had been quite impressed with Ulm's suit and briefcase, but was unaware that that was basically all Ulm owned, and that in recent times he had been reduced to working by the hour in a billiard saloon, playing against people who needed an opponent. For his part, Ulm was impressed with the salubrious offices of Interstate Flying Services but was unaware that the company had only £49 in the bank and was over £700 in the red. Close parenthesis.

•

In the northern hemisphere at this time, great attention was focusing on the continuing attempts to win the Orteig Prize for being the first to fly the distance between New York and Paris in either direction. On 8 May 1927, none other than Captain Charles Nungesser made ready to leave Paris's Le Bourget airfield, with his navigator, Captain François Coli, and fly to New York. 'I am attempting the flight,' Nungesser had announced grandly, 'to bring honour to French aviation.'[11]

The greatest French hero to beat them all, Nungesser had finished the war with forty-five confirmed kills, and had more or less prospered since, being celebrated everywhere he went and showered with decorations, money and whatever else took his fine fancy. His marriage to an American in 1923 had only temporarily slowed his nocturnal conquests of some of the most beautiful women in France, before divorce had allowed him totally free rein once more. But could he achieve something in peacetime that was the equivalent of his wartime feats, and actually fly all the way from Paris to New York? He was convinced he could, as was much of the French press, who turned up, in the company of thousands of Parisians, to record his departure.

Nungesser's plane carried no radio and no life rafts. When Coli had complained about this to Nungesser, the famous pilot gave him short shrift. 'The idea, *mon cher* Coli, is to reach America by flying over the water, not swimming to New York. You've been in the navy too long, *mon pauvre*.'[12]

And there he was! The crowd swooned as Nungesser himself came out onto the tarmac in a garish yellow flying suit, trailed by a rather hangdog-looking Coli. Nungesser paused to kiss two beautiful women, share a couple of jokes with his great friends the singer Maurice Chevalier and the boxer Georges Carpentier, and then, with a cheery wave to the adoring spectators, climbed up into his cockpit.

And with that the plane, a Levasseur PL-8 biplane named *L'oiseau blanc* — painted with Nungesser's Great War insignia of a black heart, two burning candles, a coffin and skull and crossbones — staggered down the runway and, after *just* managing to take off, headed out towards the Atlantic Ocean. Tragically, after being briefly spotted over Ireland some six hours later, Nungesser and Coli were never seen again.

•

Things had been nearly as grim on the American side of the Atlantic. All the crews attempting to cross from New York had failed to achieve their objectives through a variety of crashes, equipment malfunction and simple failure to leave the ground. Six men had been killed in the process. Some of the surviving crews had repaired and reconfigured their aircraft, and were now readying to take off once more, but there remained one lone entrant, still readying for his first attempt — Charles Augustus Lindbergh — in his plane, the *Spirit of St Louis*. When this unknown, with his tiny single-engined plane, had first announced his intention to fly solo, the papers had dubbed him the 'Flying Fool'.[13]

This, in spite of the fact that another aviator, a Russian by the name of Ivan Federov, announced an even grander intention. A member of the All Inventors Vegetarian Club of Interplanetary Cosmopolitans, Federov announced that in the coming September he was going to fly all the way to the *moon*. He would be going in a 30-metre-long rocket that was half aeroplane and half giant projectile. His co-pilot would be a man by the name of Max Valier, whom he described as a 'German moon fan'.[14]

But back to Lindbergh, the *real* Flying Fool …

It had been a long haul just to get to this point, but Lindbergh did not lack confidence. Indeed, that quiet, unassuming confidence that things would work out come what may — mixed with a very strong work ethic to do everything possible to make sure that they really did — was his most defining characteristic.

He woke on the morning of 19 May 1927 and worked with his team on his plane out at Roosevelt Field, just as he had been doing for the previous few days, and waited for a report that would tell him the weather over the Atlantic was all clear. This did not seem likely, as reports had been uniformly bad, and during the day drizzle over New York did not cease. That evening he was relaxed enough to go and see a performance of the hit Broadway musical *Rio Rita*, and it was while he was returning from that that his world suddenly changed …

On a whim, one of his companions, the chief engineer for Wright Aeronautical, which manufactured the Whirlwind engine his plane was using, decided it would be a good idea to check the latest weather reports for over the Atlantic. They pulled over on 42nd Street so that another Wright man, Dick Blythe, could make the call from an office he had access to. And suddenly he came running back with the news — the weather over the Atlantic had unexpectedly cleared![15] Ask not *for whom the bell tolls, it tolls for thee* ... Lindbergh knew immediately that his hour had come.

Returning to the Garden City Hotel where he was staying to snatch a few hours' sleep, Lindbergh first had to fight off the journalists waiting in the foyer, each of whom wanted just one more quote — something, *anything*, please! — before at last getting back to his room. Outside his door he was pleased to see George Stumpf, a burly National Guardsman from St Louis who had been sent there by Lindbergh's backers as something of a security guard. Stumpf's sole job was to keep the corridor quiet and intruders away from his door. Lindbergh uttered a quick goodnight to Stumpf, told him he would soon be on his way to Paris, and within minutes was in his bed right on the edge of blessed sleep when ... *tap-tap-tap* ... when ... *tap-tap-tap* ... when ... **tap-tap-tap** ... it seemed someone was knocking on his door.

It was the security guard. 'Slim,' Stumpf said, using Lindbergh's St Louis nickname. 'What am I going to do when you're gone?'[16]

Lindbergh, a moderate man by nature, did not at this point leap out of his bed and strangle Stumpf dead. Though aggrieved, he merely said, 'I don't know. There are plenty of other problems to solve before we have to think about that one.'

And then he tried to get back to sleep. Alas, he soon knew it was hopeless. So what else could he do? He decided to head straight to the airport to make his preparations. The plane itself was already packed, and he knew down to the last tiny item what was on board and where. In terms of keeping the weight to a bare minimum, Lindbergh had been *so* disciplined that he had declined to accept $1000 from a rich New York stamp-collector businessman who had simply wanted him to carry a pound of mail to a friend in Paris. He also declined to take a parachute, on the grounds it weighed too much. No sextant — a simple compass would suffice — and beyond that he would steer by dead reckoning alone. After all, although he had minutely tracked his route and intended to stay exactly on it, the large landmass to his east meant that even allowing for catastrophic miscalculation he was bound to cross a coast somewhere between Northern Europe to the west coast of Africa! A radio? Why bother, when by leaving its weight behind he could get another 25 gallons of fuel on the plane? Lindbergh's intense focus on weight extended to cutting the corners off his maps, making his own boots out of the lightest material he could find and ripping unnecessary pages from his notebook.

As to supplies, if he succeeded he would be flying for two days, but he took supplies enough for just one — two ham sandwiches, two roast beef sandwiches, a hard-boiled egg sandwich and a quart of water. 'If I get to Paris I won't need anymore,' Lindbergh smilingly replied when asked, 'and if I don't get to Paris I won't need anymore either.'[17]

(This central idea of stripping down to all bar the *bare* essentials had a long and noble history in aviation. It is a matter of recorded fact that on 7 January 1785 two intrepid adventurers, Jean-Pierre Blanchard and Dr John Jeffries, set off from Dover to cross the English Channel in a hot air balloon. When they got into trouble, they began ditching everything not nailed down, including their clothes, in an effort to stay aloft. When that *still* wouldn't do it, both men performed their ablutions over the side of the basket and did indeed make the French coast!)

At 7.51 am on the morning of 20 May 1927 Lindbergh sat in his Ryan monoplane, put on his goggles, adjusted his flight helmet, and poked his head out the cockpit window to talk to his two mechanics on the ground: 'What do you say — let's try it.'[18]

They nodded and removed the chocks from in front of the wheels. As Lindbergh began to gun the engine, the purple-blue violets that so flourished on the airstrip that they threatened to engulf it, now leaned back in horror at the shattering noise. A mangled propeller in a large blackened circle in that field of flowers — right beside where the *Spirit of St Louis* stood —

marked the spot where René Fonck's last attempt to fly the Atlantic had ended.[19] Lindbergh resolutely refused to look at it, but kept staring straight forward to where *his* destiny lay.

And now …

As the *Spirit of St Louis* cleaved the misty morning and hurtled drunkenly down the muddy runway, heading in the direction of Paris if it got off the ground and a carefully positioned ambulance from the Nassau County Hospital if it didn't, the 500-strong crowd gathered for the occasion leaned forward in nervous anticipation. Many in that crowd were simply neighbours to the field who had been attracted by the early morning noise and excitement, and were stunned that such a tiny plane was really going to attempt to fly such a vast ocean. Others, like Anthony Fokker — one of the most respected figures in aviation manufacturing, and one of the last people to chat with the pilot before take-off — were of the aviation community and knew only too well the risk Lindbergh was taking.

It was known that this was Lindbergh's first attempt to take off with the plane completely full, loaded with 451 gallons of fuel — 145 gallons more than it had ever held before[20] — meaning that it now weighed two and a half tons. Would he …? Could he …?

He could! He did! Nearing the end of the runway's allotted 5000 feet the plane lifted off, cleared the telephone wires at the end of the field by just 20 feet, and brought a great cry of exultation from the crowd — as nearby trees swayed and shook

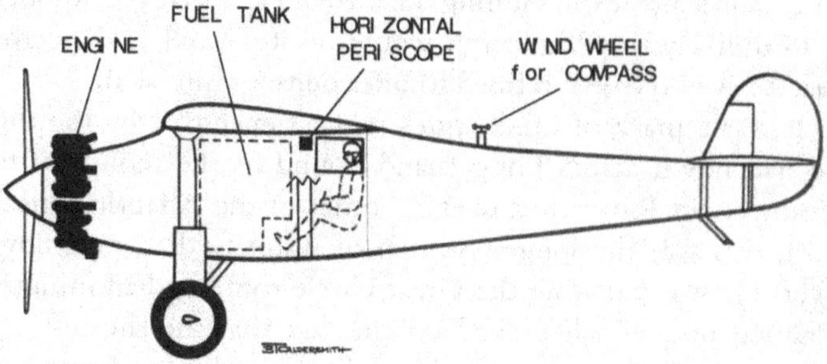

Spirit of St Louis.

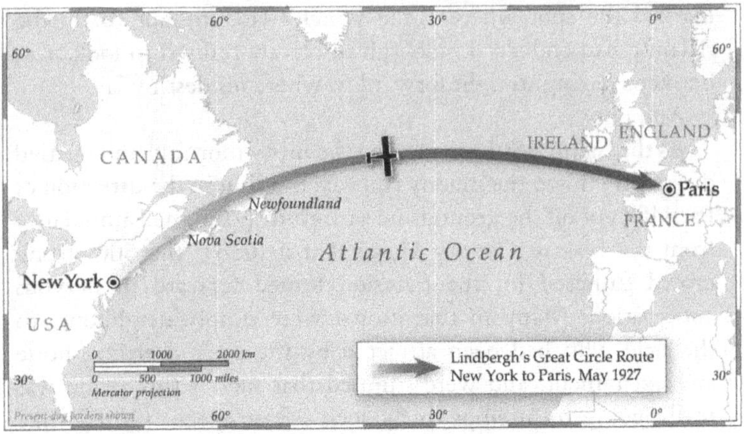

in the trailing air swirls. Lindbergh quickly disappeared into the low-lying haze. Just like that, he was gone! On his way!

Myriad reporters ran for their telephones to get the words to their newspapers, and shortly it was the people of America and France, and indeed much of the world, who held their breath. In Lindbergh's home town of Little Falls, Minnesota, the phone lines were soon buzzing with the news, rousing the good burghers from their slumber: 'The "kid", Lindbergh, is on his way, can you believe it?'[21]

It was admirable to have set off, but could this young fella *possibly* make it all the way to Paris, when so many others had failed? Lloyd's of London, which had initially posted odds of 10 to 1 against any team winning the Orteig Prize that year, thought it so unlikely that Lindbergh would do it — and so dangerous that he even try — it refused to offer odds for him at all.

It was a mark of Lindbergh's *in*experience that by the time he had flown across Long Island Sound to the mouth of the Connecticut River, just over 35 miles of the Atlantic beneath him, this was the longest stretch of water he had ever flown over. He was pursuing the Great Circle route he had minutely planned out, which turned on the fact that the shortest way between two points on the planet, just as a piece of string goes around a globe of the world, proceeds in what appears to be a curve on a flat map. This required him changing compass direction every hour, which was exacting but necessary. Thus, after Connecticut, Rhode Island and Massachusetts fell away behind him, he set off for the lovely green mass of Nova Scotia and the white tips of Newfoundland before embarking on the truly big leap, 2300 miles to hopefully the southern tip of Ireland, then England, then France.

Just before night fell he came around a granite peak and down to buzz low across the harbour township of St John's, Newfoundland — and let the world know he was still going. The citizens of that tiny town stared skywards, open-mouthed at this vision. Onwards Lindbergh flew and shortly thereafter was stunned to see icebergs. Around them stretched a green, rough, *cold*-looking sea that somehow seemed both intimidating and hungry. And then the long night descended. If all went well, it would be many hours before he would again see the light. If it went badly, eternal blackness would be his lot.

As he flew, he had no idea, of course, of the reaction of the world as it followed his path. That night in Manhattan, at the Hotel Commodore, 1200 powerful industrialists were gathered for a black-tie dinner. Before proceedings began, one of them stood up and offered an impromptu benediction: 'I am proud to live under that flag,' he said, pointing to a small star-spangled banner on the table. 'I am thinking of a young American boy who left this morning for Paris with a sandwich in his pocket. May God deliver him there safely.'[22] These words were cheered to the echo.

Across America, people huddled around their radios waiting for news, or prayed for his safety, even as print journalists churned out millions of words in paeans of praise. One of them was Will Rogers, the syndicated columnist, most renowned for his humour. But on this occasion he began his column: 'No attempt at jokes today. A slim, tall, bashful, smiling American boy is somewhere over the middle of the Atlantic Ocean, where no lone human being has ever ventured before. He is being prayed for to every kind of Supreme Being that has a following. If he is lost, it will be the most universally regretted loss we ever had.'[23]

•

Charles Lindbergh was lost. Or at least he momentarily thought he was, as he glanced at his compass and seemed to be 30 degrees off course. Then he remembered. A particularity of many places in high Arctic latitudes is that 'magnetic variation' — the difference between 'true north' and the direction in which the compass needle indicates is north — can vary from nil to 90 degrees, as the compass needle aligns itself with the Earth's lines of magnetic force and other influences such as large iron ore deposits. The magnetic variation at St John's, Newfoundland, was at that time 20 degrees west, but could change by as much as one degree per six-tenths of a mile, meaning the American pilot had to be extremely vigilant in consulting his charts and changing his heading to keep properly on his Great Circle route.

Another challenge was making allowance constantly for the strength and the direction of the wind that was hitting him. It was for this reason he generally kept to a low altitude so he could see the waves beneath and judge from the way the foam blew off the top of them that strength and direction.

Here and there he was spotted. Five hundred miles west of Ireland, the steamer *Hilversum* saw the *Spirit of St Louis*, and promptly reported its position. So too, the steam collier *Nogi* spotted him and gave a fresh position. He was still out there. Still going! Stock exchanges in Amsterdam and Berlin gave updates together with changing stock prices. In Tokyo the latest news on Lindbergh was posted on bulletin boards situated in the main street.

Far over the Atlantic, the *Spirit of St Louis* never missed a beat and kept arrowing eastwards. With generally good weather and only one or two squalls here and there, Lindbergh's greatest enemy was sleepiness. Forty hours without sleep. Forty-two … forty-four … it would be so easy, so wonderfully easy … just to close his eyes and let go … let go … and **NO!** With a start he would come to, put his head out the window into the icy slipstream and for as long as two minutes at a time, he wouldn't feel sleepy anymore. And then it would return … the drowsiness … the heavy lids … the mild hallucinations of phantoms filling the cockpit with him. Time and again, he had to slap himself hard to return to full consciousness, to try and banish the demons from his mind.

'Alone?' an editorial of the New York *Sun* asked on his second day of flight. 'Is he alone at whose right side rides Courage, with Skill within the cockpit and Faith upon the left? Does solitude surround the brave, when Adventure leads the way, and Ambition reads the dials? Is there no company for him for whom the air is cleft by Daring and the darkness is made light by Emprise?

'True, the fragile bodies of his fellows do not weigh down his plane; true, the fretful minds of weaker men are lacking from his crowded cabin; but as his airship keeps her course he holds communion with those rarer spirits that inspire to intrepidity and by their sustaining potency give strength to arm, resource to mind, content to soul.

'Alone? With what other companions would that man fly to whom the choice were given?'[24]

All talk of the 'Flying Fool' had long ago vanished, and Lindbergh was now nothing less than the 'Lone Eagle'.

•

Perhaps nowhere in Australia was news of Lindbergh's progress followed so ravenously as in the offices of Interstate Flying Services. For Lindbergh was doing to the Atlantic Ocean what Smithy and Keith Anderson had long dreamed of doing to the Pacific Ocean. Conquering it. And to Kingsford Smith's delight, Charles Ulm shared much the same dream!

At this time Ulm, who had not long before divorced his wife, Isabel, was boarding with a woman by the name of Mary Josephine Callaghan at her home in Lavender Bay, and often after work Smithy would drop him there on his way home to Kuranda, sometimes popping in for a drink. Since Ulm had joined their aviation company, things were looking up a little, even though they hadn't, in fact, beaten Major Brearley for the Adelaide–Perth mail tender. This upturn was in part courtesy of their new partner having organised a week of taking joyriders aloft during festivities for the opening of the new Parliament

House in Canberra, during the first week of May. And so, of course, as the beer flowed free, Lindbergh's attempt to cross the Atlantic Ocean prompted Kingsford Smith to share with Ulm his own ambitions. Ulm confessed he would love to do the same thing — not least because completing such a challenge would automatically put their aviation business into the big time.

What they needed, they decided, was to do some 'Big Feat' which should bring them what they wanted: fame, money, status. Something like ... flying around Australia in a record time! This was the very plan that Smithy had tried to push with West Australian Airways, to no avail, four years earlier, but now there was no boss to stop him. If they could pull it off, it would give them the credibility they craved, and the experience at long-distance flying they needed to make an attempt at crossing the Pacific.

At the time, the record for the round-Australia journey was held by E.J. Jones of the Department of Civil Aviation, who, back in August 1924, had — together with Lieutenant Colonel Brinsmead as his passenger — flown the 7500 miles in twenty-two days and two hours. This had neatly halved the previous record of forty-four days, which had been set a few months before.

Now, Smithy and Ulm reckoned it was time to halve it again. They began to make plans, even while Lindbergh was still in the air and had just emerged from his first dark night.

•

An island? *Land?* No, fog. Fogginess of mind, fog over the sea — the thing is that it faded as he approached. And then so did another island. And many more. And then one of the islands didn't fade. It really was *land*. 'It is like rain after a drought,' he wrote, 'spring after a northern winter. This is earth again, the earth where I've lived and now will live once more ... I've been to eternity and back. I know how the dead would feel to live again.'[25]

Checking on his maps, he worked out — as the people below ran out of their houses and waved joyously up at him, *it was Lindbergh and he was alive!* — that after crossing an entire ocean in twenty-six hours of flight, he was less than 3 miles off course to the south, and above the Three Sisters near Dingle Bay on the south-western coast of Ireland, three small but easily identifiable peaks. Originally, Lindbergh had hoped to get within 50 miles of it.[26] The American swooped down lower to get a closer look.

Now, this village was in an extremely isolated part of the world, a place where aeroplanes were little more than a rumour and an unlikely one at that, t'be sure, t'be sure. That very day, as a matter of fact, a young lad by the name of Hugh Curran was walking along a road near his house in the tiny hamlet of Baile an Fheirtéaraigh, thinking about a scary story his teacher had told him the day before at school. Apparently in ancient Gaelic times, a giant eagle would swoop down from out of the skies and pluck young kids who had behaved naughtily. And then it would take them away and *eat* them. It was at just that moment that Hugh heard a sound he had never heard before — a roar coming from above. He turned around and saw that very eagle swooping down from the sky, *screaming*, and coming straight for him! If only he had not been naughty!

Oh, young Hughie.

Screaming himself, Hughie ran as fast as his little legs could carry him and dived into a ditch filled with water, crying, hoping against hope that the eagle wouldn't spot him. And amazingly, it worked! For within just a few seconds the giant bird of prey had flown on, and when a minute later he carefully lifted his head from the ditch, he saw only a disappearing speck in the distance.[27]

A few phone calls from the people of Dingle Bay, and the news flashed around the world — Lindbergh was still going! Now, Lloyd's of London relented a little and offered odds, but still quoted his chances as 10 to 3 *against* his getting there.[28] In Paris, those sitting at Café de la Paix, on one of the corners of the Place de l'Opéra, were stunned to notice that the revolving electric sign at the top of the Selfridge building, which sat across the street, was reporting in letters 6 feet high that *l'Américain* Lindbergh, had been spotted off the Irish coast and was heading their way! The word began to spread ...

Lindberrr! Il vient! Il vient! (Lindbergh is coming!)

•

Up in the *Spirit of St Louis*, Lindbergh knew that the promised land, France, and its capital, Paris, were just six hours away and he felt a sudden surge of energy as his fatigue faded. Two hours after leaving the Irish coast, England appeared and almost as quickly disappeared beneath his wings.

Nigh on two decades earlier, Louis Blériot had tootled across the English Channel coming from France, at roughly 30 miles per hour. This time, going the other way, Lindbergh and the *Spirit of St Louis* streaked over at a little more than three times that speed, and he was soon soaring over a France falling dark. Even in the midst of his euphoria at having arrived above the land of his destination, he began to worry that he hadn't had time to get a French visa, didn't speak a word of the French language, and had no French money. Perhaps he could borrow some. He would have to find someone to help when he landed.

Soon enough, far ahead, the famed 'City of Lights', Paris itself appeared, looming larger with every minute, rising over the horizon in much the same way the sun came up, and shining almost as brightly. And there was the Eiffel Tower! Charles Lindbergh took the *Spirit of St Louis* around it a couple of times in celebration. And then it was time to land.

But where was Le Bourget aerodrome, which he had been told was just a few miles to the north-east of the Eiffel Tower? He could see a black spot about where Le Bourget should be, a black spot surrounded by swarming bright lights, but it didn't look like an aerodrome, which always had perimeter lights evenly spaced. Still, he went closer for a look. And then he realised. Those lights were not the lights of a factory or some such as he had first thought, but headlights, the lights of *tens* of *thousands* of Parisians who now surrounded the aerodrome and were there to greet him. Rivers of lights leading to the airfield showed how many Parisians were eager to get there. Stunned, Lindbergh brought his majestic aeroplane down from the heavens, touched, bounced and then came back to mother earth solidly, rolling to a halt at exactly 10.24 pm — thirty-three hours, thirty minutes and thirty seconds since he had left New York.

There was a pause at the moment he shut the engine down, and then, out of the darkness, came an unnerving, almost unearthly, roar. It was the roar of people frantically running to him out of the night, like the phantoms that had so recently been with him in the cockpit, except that these people were all too real and soon had their hands upon him ...[29]

Never in his life, Lindbergh later wrote, had he ever seen anything like the mass of humanity waiting there for him, reaching for him, practically wanting to devour him. 'Dozens of hands took hold of me, my legs, my arms, my body. I found myself on top of the crowd, in the centre of an ocean of heads that extended as far out into the darkness as I could see ... It was like drowning in a human sea.'[30]

As he was carried away, some people in the crowd started snatching at the plane, tearing off strips as souvenirs of this momentous event, this part of history, before the gendarmes succeeded in fighting them off.[31] This was no ordinary crowd with an ordinary purpose — simply to greet a man who had achieved something tremendous. As many writers and commentators have noted, there was something in the air that night, something extraordinary, something that the world had never experienced before. It was instant international fame on a scale never approached before, the transformation of a flesh-and-blood person into a legendary persona whom the public felt it owned and almost had a right to devour.

Six minutes after the Lone Eagle had landed, the *New York Times* received the cabled news and, after the editor had posted a bulletin of it in the front window of its offices on West 43rd Street, the word spread. Upstairs, journalists, editors and copy-editors were focusing on filling the first six pages of the following day's edition with pure Lindbergh. Other papers around America were doing much the same, to the point that 25,000 more tons of newsprint than usual were used up.[32]

Within minutes of that first posting in the window, the ferries on New York Harbour were tooting their whistles, ships were blowing their horns and fire-engines were letting off their sirens, even as people were spilling onto the streets, laughing, crying and exulting all at once. Lindy! Lindy!

'Lucky Lindy', the 'Lone Eagle', has done it! Can you believe it!?!?

•

What Lindbergh had achieved — linking two nations and continents with one flight and suddenly making the world a much smaller place — so resonated with that world that he became almost instantly an international celebrity more famous than any person who had ever lived, at least while still alive. President Calvin Coolidge sent warmest congratulations on behalf of the nation, and noted that after the celebrations in Europe he would like Lindbergh to come home with his marvellous plane. Oh, and he was sending a boat to pick them both up — the light cruiser USS *Memphis*, with the commander of the Atlantic fleet, Vice-Admiral Guy Hamilton Burrage, as his host.

In the meantime, a whirl of receptions and honours in Paris proceeded whereby Lindbergh was paraded before huge crowds of cheering Parisians — even as 100,000 telegrams and cables, 14,000 packages and three and a half million letters poured into the American Embassy.[33]

Amidst the craziness of it all, Lindbergh made time to visit Charles Nungesser's bereaved mother in her humble Parisian apartment. Crying, she kissed him on both cheeks and told him, 'You are a very brave young man. I congratulate you from the bottom of my heart. I too, have a brave son, who I have never ceased to believe is still fighting his way back to civilisation.'[34]

Softly, quietly, Lindbergh kept holding her hand as he told her she must never give up hope, that all things were possible.

And then it was back to the craziness, with 10,000 Parisians having congregated outside Madame Nungesser's apartment once the word got out that Lindbergh — '*Lindberrr! Lindberrr! Lindberrr!*' they chanted — was there.

If there was one man in all Paris who could understand what it was like to be in the eye of a cyclone of such sudden and stunning celebrity, overwhelmed at what was happening, it was Louis Blériot. When Lindbergh was asked if there was any Frenchman he would particularly like to meet, the American had no hesitation in naming Blériot — and a grand lunch was duly arranged in Louis and Alicia Blériot's gracious Parisian apartment in the Avenue Kléber.

Yes, there were ministers of the French cabinet there, and leading figures in the French aviation industry, thirty powerful guests altogether, but the bond between the two men was immediate and personal. At the height of the lunch, the distinguished French aviator and successful aeroplane manufacturer — now a silvery-haired 55-year-old — stood up and made a speech in honour of France's guest: 'So that you may not forget me, I present you with an ordinary piece of wood, of no value to anyone, but which is very dear to me, a fragment of the victorious propeller of the Channel. Kindly accept it as a souvenir of this day that you have so affectionately devoted to me. Monsieur Lindbergh, I raise my glass to you, to your country, and to all who are dear to you.'[35]

Warm applause all round, and Lindbergh was greatly touched by the gift. A short time later, the two aviators adjourned to the balcony to have a quick private chat, with only Blériot's daughter Simone along, *s'il te plait*, to translate for them, and to remember this exchange.

Blériot: '*J'admire votre courage* in this marvellous *exploit* because you risked your life for thirty-six hours, while, *moi*, I risked mine for only thirty-seven minutes.'

Lindbergh: 'No, Monsieur Blériot, I don't accept what you say, for I wouldn't go up in your aeroplane for even one minute.'[36]

Touché!

A whirlwind tour through Europe followed, during which the reluctant but still gracious Lindbergh was fêted by presidents, prime ministers, princes and kings, including King George V himself, the keenest royal aviator of them all, who wasted no time in coming to the point once they met in Buckingham Palace.

'Now tell me, Captain Lindbergh,' said King George V, by the Grace of God, of Great Britain, Ireland, and the British Dominions beyond the Seas, King, Defender of the Faith, Emperor of India. 'There is one thing I long to know. How did you pee?'[37]

A short time later, the King introduced him to his family, including his infant granddaughter, Elizabeth.

Finally, it was time to head home on the USS *Memphis*, which had come for him and the *Spirit of St Louis*, and, if it were possible, the celebration of his feat now ascended to a higher level still.

On the day that Lindbergh left Europe, back in New York one of his previous rivals, Clarence Chamberlin, left New York in *Columbia*, a Wright-Bellanca WB-2, bound for Europe. On board he had Charles A. Levine, his principal sponsor for the trip. A day later they landed in Germany. Well done, but no-one cared particularly. The world had its hero and it was Lindbergh.

For when, after passing through the Virginia Capes at five o'clock on the afternoon of 10 June 1927, the *Memphis* steamed up Chesapeake Bay, to arrive at the mouth of the Potomac River on the following morning, where President Coolidge and tens of thousands of adoring citizens were awaiting Lindbergh before the Washington Monument, he was not alone, even on the water. For this time, not only did he have his usual companions of Courage, Skill, Faith, Adventure, Ambition, Daring and Emprise along for the ride, but the cruiser was being escorted by eighty-eight planes and the US Navy dirigible *Los Angeles* above, and four destroyers all around her. Church bells rang out, fire sirens wailed in ecstasy and people on the shore cheered and screamed.

Did any man, ever, anywhere, make such an entrance? Standing on the bridge of the cruiser beside Vice-Admiral Burrage, Lindbergh could no longer hold it in. 'It is a great and wonderful sight, and I wonder if I really deserve all this.'[38]

Maybe, maybe not. But when President Coolidge — after pausing to bow low in welcome to Lindbergh's mother, who had joined the festivities and was with them on the elevated stage[39] — pinned the Distinguished Flying Cross on his lapel before the largest crowd ever assembled in Washington, and Lindbergh made a brief speech of 106 words in reply, the assembled press and radio reporters immediately compared it to the Gettysburg Address.[40] About thirty-five million Americans had listened in around the country.

•

As part of the general madness that ensued — four and a half million New Yorkers turned out for Lindbergh's ticker-tape parade up Fifth Avenue — it became all the rage to offer large cash prizes to encourage flyers to travel long distances between two fixed points over natural obstacles. One such prize was for the first pilot to fly from San Francisco to Honolulu, a distance of 2387 miles. The offer was put up by a pineapple magnate from Hawaii by the name of James D. Dole, and he offered no less than US$35,000, consisting of US$25,000 for the first one there and US$10,000 for the second. The response was immediate, and with so many pilots announcing their intention to go for the prize, it soon became apparent that the only fair way to do it was to start them all off from the one place at the one time. And so the 'Dole Race' was born ...

•

News of Lindbergh's stunning feat was published around Australia, with coverage in the *Argus* being typical: an account of the flight, and the overwhelming reception in Paris, and a map showing the flight path. Too, there were stunning details on just how much money was being offered to Lindbergh since his success: US$200,000 for acting roles; $250,000 from Vaudeville; $100,000 for miscellaneous writing; $50,000 for book royalties; $30,000 to $100,000 for testimonials and endorsements from manufacturers; and a film offer of $500,000 had already been cabled to Lindbergh in France.[41] Particularly interesting to many, however, was an accompanying article entitled 'AMERICA TO AUSTRALIA: LINDBERGH'S NEXT PLAN', which quoted one of Lindbergh's financial backers, Harry Knight, saying that the next goal of the Lone Eagle was to be the first man to fly across the Pacific, and that he would go via the Hawaiian Islands to land just north of Sydney.[42] The *Sydney Morning Herald* editorial gave details that he would try to do it in two hops, with Hawaii being his first landing spot.[43]

•

Lindbergh now crossing the Pacific? But that was *Smithy's* plan! *Smithy's* dream, dammit! He'd been wrestling with that pretty much since the Great War was over, and now Lindbergh was going to beat him to it? He thought not. Keith Anderson felt much the same. As did Charles Ulm. What was obvious to all of them was that time was now of the essence. If not Lindbergh himself, then someone would soon be crossing the Pacific, and they felt it was morally right it be them. Clearly, they had to fast-track plans to achieve it, and a big part of that really would be breaking the record for flying around Australia.

By late May, Ulm had succeeded in doing a deal with the editor of the *Sun*, Herbert Campbell-Jones, who agreed to back them — in no small part on the strength of how many extra newspapers his group had sold a few years before when Ulm had provided the paper with exclusive pictures of the approaching British naval squadron. Too, there was the fact that in the newspaper war the *Sun* was the young, thrusting upstart taking on the likes of the conservative *Sydney Morning Herald*, Perth's *Guardian*, Melbourne's *Age*, and the Brisbane *Courier*, and it cared little for traditional ways. Aviation, itself young and thrusting, and filled with colourful characters, was the perfect subject for the *Sun* to 'own', and Herbert Campbell-Jones intended doing just that, whatever the cost — and if the conservative rags didn't like it, then all to the good. The *Sun* would get exclusive reports from the flyers, who would be handsomely paid for their efforts.

With the *Sun* on board, Ulm was soon able to stitch up the support of the Vacuum Oil Company as well, as it was clear that the whole venture would be receiving good publicity.

And yet who should make the attempt with Smithy? This proved to be a serious point of contention. The Bristol Tourer could comfortably carry all three of them, but carrying any more than two pilots was unnecessary, considering that it would be better if the weight of the third man was carried in petrol, allowing for longer hops.

Keith Anderson, who was a man as slow to anger as he was to calm down, rose to a boiling fury when he realised that Ulm and Kingsford Smith had agreed that he would be the one left behind — reduced to following them in the company's other Bristol, a few days behind, carrying one of the other sponsors whom Ulm had lined up. And this, despite the fact that Ulm didn't have a pilot's licence, nor did he have the first clue about the mechanics of an aircraft! Anderson simply couldn't believe that Smithy, his great friend, had done it to him ...

But in fact, Kingsford Smith was in a very difficult position. The first thing was, given Keith Anderson's engagement to Bon Hilliard, his ex-girlfriend, Keith was hardly in a position to lecture *him* about what was and wasn't acceptable under the Old Mates Act. And secondly, well, there was one incontrovertible fact that he couldn't get around. For five years, he and Keith had talked endlessly about their dream to fly across the Pacific, and nothing had actually happened. Charles Ulm had been on the ground for only weeks, and already things were starting to fall into place, in terms of contacts, plans, sponsorship monies ... the lot. If Smithy was really going to do this, really going to fly across the Pacific, then he felt he had to give Ulm a fair go in organising the whole thing and if Ulm wanted to go in the first plane with him, then that was the way it was going to have to be. Sorry, Keith.

So it was that when on the morning of 18 June 1927 Charles Kingsford Smith and Charles Ulm set off from Mascot airport to go round Australia in one of their Bristol Tourers, a fuming Keith Anderson was there to see them go.

In the open cockpit, Ulm and Kingsford Smith wore thick World War I-issue flying suits, as necessary protection against the cold air and rain they would be experiencing, but which made them sweat like the Dickens as they kept busy feeding 5-gallon tins of petrol into their main tank via a funnel. A false start shortly after take-off necessitated their return to Mascot to use the other plane, but they were soon on their way again and before their out-stretched wings, the sometimes lush, sometimes stark, always endless landscape of Australia rolled out before them and gradually ceded to their assault.

It was a gruelling exercise to fly for as much as twelve hours a day, only to land and become frantically busy getting the petrol supplies they had organised into the tanks and on board, and then work late into the night on the plane and the recalcitrant old engine to ensure everything would be ready for take-off at dawn the following day. Too, Ulm would have to find time to file his 'EXCLUSIVE!' reports to the *Sun* in Sydney, the *Age* in Melbourne and the *Courier* in Brisbane (and at least they would get the name right, whereas the *Sydney Morning Herald* had reported the departure of Mr C.T.P. Ulm and Mr Hungerford Smith!).[44] Broadly, while Smithy's key responsibility was to fly and look after the plane, Ulm did everything else; from helping to navigate, to cooking, organising, writing and assisting Smithy with the engine maintenance. One way or another, despite their disparate personalities — Smithy extroverted, and Ulm intense — they were, as they discovered, a very good team.

So it was that much of Australia followed their journey, as city after city, state after state after territory, fell behind them and interest built as to just how much they would slash the record by. The hairiest part was crossing some of the godforsaken Kimberley in Western Australia, over a region previously unseen by white men, which Smithy described 'as bristling with buttes of rocks and roughly timbered slopes', before traversing 'an endless ocean of bronze green bush'.[45] If they had been forced to crash-land down there, Kingsford Smith knew, 'our chances of getting back to civilisation would have been slender'.[46] Still, they survived the Kimberley to then knock over Perth, Adelaide and Melbourne, and both pilots were stunned when, ten days and five and a half hours after they left — a record! — they landed once again at Mascot to find no fewer than 50,000 people had turned out to greet them. And one of them was none other than Nellie Stewart, the wonderful Australian actress whose photo Smithy had now carried with him all over the world — a photo which he refused to fly without — and she was as gracious and gorgeous as ever. That good woman kissed the aviators on both cheeks, placed laurels around their necks and said a few wonderful words to them. *Bliss!*

In the midst of the applause and the sheer exuberance of the crowd, Ulm turned to Kingsford Smith and spoke loudly over the tumult: 'If we could fly the Pacific from California to Australia, we'd be made!'

'Ye-e-s,' Smithy replied dryly. 'And if it would only rain pound notes we might be able to try it.'

'It won't rain pound notes,' was the reply from Ulm, 'but I reckon I can fix it up.'[47]

And maybe he could. A bare beginning, right then and there, was to get into the ear of the Premier of New South Wales, Jack Lang, who had turned out to greet them and make a speech of welcome where he warmed to the theme that they had, in his words, 'accomplished something as hazardous as Lindbergh's flight across the Atlantic Ocean'.[48]

As the Premier was a massive man — who towered over the two relatively diminutive aviators by a good 6 inches — getting into his ear wasn't necessarily easy, but he certainly listened to their hurried exhortations as to how this round-Australia trip was only a prelude to what they really wanted to do, which was cross the Pacific, and if only his government could give them some financial backing, they were sure it could be done.

He promised he would come back to them.

•

What on *earth* was going on!? Down in Melbourne, four days behind Kingsford Smith and Ulm, Keith Anderson and Bobby Hitchcock were stunned to read a newspaper report saying that the next challenge for the two men who now had the round-Australia record was to cross the Pacific, and that they had already booked their passage on the RMS *Tahiti* to take them to San Francisco, from where they were going to fly! And there was *no* mention of Anderson or Hitchcock accompanying them! As a matter of fact, it looked to them as though Ulm and Kingsford Smith would be gone even before Anderson and Hitchcock got back to Sydney ...

•

'And so, ladies and gentlemen, would you please put your hands together and welcome to the podium, Charles Kingsford Smith!'

The gathering at the Hotel Australia — where George A. Taylor had formed the Aerial League of Australia seventeen years earlier — for a glittering luncheon the day after they had landed at Mascot had been given by the directors of Sun Newspapers Ltd. The miniature plane of shimmering orange silk, with violets and wattle blossom crusting the wings, dangling above this gathering of the *crème de la crème* of Sydney's business and political classes set exactly the right tone.[49] It was an audience that included none other than Billy Hughes, looking more like a gnarled walnut than ever and now no longer prime minister, but still a very strong supporter of Australian aviation.

'We are met here to welcome back to Sydney two most gallant Australians,' began the Chairman of Directors, Mr H.A. Russell. 'They have blazed afresh the trail that leads to a larger success in commercial aviation. Men from the earliest times have had ideas of flying. They probably came from some subconscious memories of the days when men were angels. If that is so, we seem to be rapidly getting back to an angelic state. The war forced upon us and upon the men who took the risks, the necessity for the full development of aviation. These two men have carried on that development ...'[50]

Hear, hear! Hear, *hear*!

Before such an esteemed group, Kingsford Smith, with Charles Ulm looking on approvingly, made reply in due course. Ever the showman, Smithy told something of their adventures over the previous fortnight — the highs, the lows, the things they had learnt.

'We passed over country we have never seen before,' he said, 'and probably no white man has ever seen. Between Darwin and Wyndham, and Wyndham and Broome, there are tracts that have never been explored. The people at Darwin told us we were mad to fly over the Kimberleys because of the fierceness of the Aborigines, the absolute impossibility of landing, and because, even if by some miracle we did land safely, we could never be located by relief parties.'[51]

Smithy then made the case for the potential of a Pacific flight. It would not be easy, he acknowledged, but it was going to be done, and it might as well be Australians who did it. And not just any Australians. Them. They had proved, they hoped, by their record-breaking trip around Australia that they were at the forefront of long-distance flying, and now they wanted to do it on a bigger stage. The biggest stage in the world: the Pacific Ocean. But it would take money, quite a lot of money, and that is where they hoped that the esteemed patrons of this lunch might come in ...

And so it went. Within days, Premier Lang had indeed made the public announcement that his government would guarantee such a flight to the tune of £3500! Other promises of tentative support started to emerge from some of the men at the lunch, and suddenly what had been just a distant dream actually started to materialise. Maybe they could really do this!

•

The following fortnight was simply a blur. With the money just about assured, Kingsford Smith, Ulm and Anderson were quick to book tickets on the next ship heading across the Pacific to the west coast of America and a seemingly endless round of farewells, drinks, speeches and parties followed, together with an enormous dinner at Kuranda, hosted by Kingsford Smith's parents, to send their boy and his friends away in proper style. Not that all of it was pure joy.

At one point the intrepid trio had to tell their faithful mechanic Bobby Hitchcock that despite their previous plans — and the fact that he had resigned his job on the strength of their promise that he would accompany them to America — there simply wasn't going to be room for him to come with them. The money they had could only go so far, and it wouldn't extend to a party of four. As a matter of fact, they had had an enormously hard time making it stretch to three, with another bitter dispute between Anderson and Ulm occurring as to who should accompany Kingsford Smith on the Pacific attempt.

In various meetings shortly after Keith had returned from his own round-Australia flight behind Kingsford Smith and Ulm, the physically imposing man pointed out the outrageousness of the situation to his old friend, while the usurper Ulm, who had led Smithy astray, listened. It had bloody well been the money of the Anderson family that had got them started in both the trucking and aviation business, *and* got them to this point, where they could now fulfil their dream. And what had Ulm contributed? Nothing! Not a brass bloody razoo!

Actually, Keith, no, Kingsford Smith continued to point out as calmly as he could. In fact, if it hadn't been for Ulm organising the round-Australia flight, the deal with the *Sun*, the sponsorship with the Vacuum Oil Company and others, they simply wouldn't have been able to pull it off. It was only reasonable to ask him to be a part of it, when he had done so much.

Finally, the dispute had been resolved with the mutually reluctant agreement that both of them would go. With that scenario, taking Bobby Hitchcock as well was simply out of the question. Besides, Bobby, the simple fact was that they would be flying an American plane that he wouldn't be familiar with. But not to worry, Bobby. If they succeeded, there would be a thousand quid in it for him.

'Yes,' Charles Ulm told him on the morning of their departure. 'You'll hear a knock on the door, and I'll say, "Sir Charles, Robert awaits outside about his thousand".'

'And I'll say,' Smithy said, though perhaps a little drunkenly, because they had had a big night of it until the wee hours, '"Show the boy in."'

Bobby Hitchcock left their offices, devastated.

A few hours later, on the afternoon of 14 July 1927 the three men stood before the gangplank of the SS *Tahiti*, ready to board. Bon Hilliard was there to see Keith off, and she also farewelled Kingsford Smith in a manner that was somewhere between rather restrained and seriously strained. Ulm was farewelled by his second wife, his former landlady Jo Callaghan, now Jo Ulm, whom he had married on the very afternoon that he had returned from their round-Australia trip. And Charles Kingsford Smith was, as ever, sent off to glory by the Kingsford Smith clan, who turned out in force.

The *Tahiti* passed through Sydney Heads in the early afternoon of a sparkling day. Destination: the United States of America. A one-way ticket, if you please, as they intended *flying* back. And, of course, they travelled first class. After all, with the sort of money that was being bandied around, it seemed crazy to try to save just £30 per man on the difference between first class and steerage.

•

'*Second star on the right, and straight on till morning …*'

So, famously, had run Peter Pan's instructions to Wendy on how to get to Neverland. And yet, as the author J.M. Barrie also noted, those navigational directions were insufficient, as 'even birds, carrying maps and consulting them at windy corners, could not have sighted it with these instructions. For, Peter, you see, just said anything that came into his head.'

In the real world, although navigating their way across the Pacific in an aeroplane was going to be difficult, there really was something in focusing on the 'second star on the right', or the like, just as mariners had done for centuries. And as the Australians were going to be on a ship for the next three weeks, why not learn it from some mariners directly?

So it was that for most of the trip the three aviators studied celestial navigation courtesy of a bloke by the name of Bill Todd, the *Tahiti*'s enormous second officer, aided by the ship's third officer, Hal Litchfield …

Now, the thing you have to understand is that if you knew how to read it all properly, then the sun, the moon and the stars could be nothing less than signposts in the sky. By using a sextant — an instrument for measuring the angle that an object lies up from the horizon — and noting the time of day adjusted to Greenwich Mean Time, you could — by consulting tables minutely designed for the purpose — work out either your approximate or exact position on the earth's surface, depending on whether the sun or the moon was king of the sky. In daytime, you could get your longitude position, but alas not latitude, as you only had the sun to read off, and couldn't cross-reference with any other heavenly bodies. But at night-time, the sky was *filled* with reference points, and once you knew how to read them, you could be remarkably accurate in working out your position. By virtue of knowing the fixed points in the heavens, you could be freed from needing to see fixed recognisable points on earth!

That is, so long as clouds didn't prevent you from getting a fix on the object, *and* you hadn't made even the tiniest error in all of the complex calculations, *and* all your prayers had been heard and answered …

Familiarity with the heavens was half of it. Take the constellation of the Southern Cross, for example, which is always visible in the southern hemisphere. As the earth rotates on its axis over a twenty-four-hour period, so too does the Southern Cross appear to rotate around a fixed point in the night sky known as the south celestial pole — which is, in turn, that spot in the sky pierced by an imaginary line going from the earth's north pole to its south pole and continuing on up towards the Southern Cross's stars.

It was not at all easy to understand, let alone master, and yet, although foremost among them as a pilot pure, Kingsford Smith concentrated every bit as much as the other two. True, in Western Australia you flew 'by guess and by God' and by recognising the landmarks beneath you, while in the Great War, navigation hadn't been that important because the main thing you needed to find was Germans, and even if you couldn't find them, it generally didn't take them long to find you … but this was different. If the aviators were to succeed in their venture to cross the Pacific, they would be landing on islands in the vast blue swirl of the Pacific Ocean that would be no more than needles in the world's biggest haystack, and failure to find them would result in the all but certain deaths of the flyers. So let's try it again. And again and again. And again.

After several days of intense instruction, the three men had achieved some proficiency with the sextant, while remaining aware that it would be far more difficult to operate such an instrument when hurtling above the earth's surface at 100 miles an hour. And they also became more proficient at doing all the calculations, comparing their estimations as to where they were at that moment, against where Todd or Litchfield told them they *actually* were. In the course of the trip and their lessons, the aviators became very close to Todd and Litchfield, strengthened in part by the fact that the massive Todd — he was all of 19 stone — was such a big drinker. He and Smithy, particularly, frequently liked to imbibe late into the night, as the Pacific Ocean slipped by beneath them.

In between such lessons and carousing there was, of course, time for other things, which included discussing in more detail how they were going to do the flight.

On the strength of Lindbergh's achievement, the obvious thing was to purchase a bigger version of the Ryan monoplane, one that would be capable of holding all three of them. As to the route they would take, their plans changed by the day.

At first it seemed as though the best plan would be to have the plane as a land plane and fly it from 'Frisco to Honolulu, at which point they could have it quickly converted to a seaplane, and proceed from there via a series of Pacific islands, such as Fanning Island, the Phoenix Islands and so forth. Perhaps Samoa? Fiji? New Caledonia? There was a lot to discuss and they kept tossing ideas around as America drew closer.

Ten

THE TOUGH GET GOING

Smithy was happily irresponsible on the ground. But as soon as he stepped into a cockpit he became a changed man. His very features altered. He looked like a hawk — a creature of the air with wings to fly, for it is no more than the truth that the plane was part of the man. No matter how friendly he was with his crew — and he was always that — he commanded their respect. Not one of those who worked for him would have refused to follow him anywhere he wanted to go. He had that precious gift of all born leaders of men — an infinite capacity to inspire confidence.

RADIO OPERATOR JOHN STANNAGE, WHO FLEW EXTENSIVELY WITH KINGSFORD SMITH AND WAS ONE OF HIS EARLY BIOGRAPHERS.[1]

On 5 August 1927, the three Australians — Charles Kingsford Smith, Charles Ulm and Keith Anderson — headed down the gangplank of the *Tahiti* onto the San Francisco docks, with their kitbags over their shoulders and a dream in their hearts to fly the Pacific.

How exactly?

Yes, well.

As Kingsford Smith would later write, 'We landed with but vague notions how such a flight was to be successfully carried out; we had some promises from Australia of financial support and I had considerable experience of flying in all types of planes in England, America and Australia. But our determination to make the flight was our principal and indeed our only asset when we set foot in the United States.'[2]

Their first priority after landing was settling into a rather salubrious hotel in downtown San Francisco, where they began to get down to brass tacks. And at least Harold Kingsford Smith, who had met them at the ship, had pledged himself to give them a good start by introducing the adventurers to some of his more well-heeled business contacts.

What was obvious from the first was that there would be no problem getting people interested in crossing at least part of the Pacific Ocean, as they had arrived in San Francisco just when the Dole Air Race was about to take off, and it seemed that all of America was *crazy* for these amazing aviators about to race each other from newly established Oakland airport to Honolulu. Day after day, the papers were filled with breathless accounts of the flyers gathering, the rules of the race, what would be required, who was likely to win and so forth. In the midst of such excitement not a lot of play was given to a comment by Charles Lindbergh to the effect that the race was 'sheer suicide ...'

The Australians came to share that view, after being given cause to look at the project closely. Shortly after their arrival they were offered a plane to fly in the race by a representative of the Vacuum Oil Company — which organisation was acting as the New South Wales government's agent in the matter of the Pacific flight — by extending them up to £3500 capital, as required.

But after looking at the aircraft — an International F-18 air coach biplane, fitted with a Wright Whirlwind engine and named *Miss Hollydale* — and speaking with competing pilots, it became clear that neither the planes nor the personnel were remotely ready to embark on such a venture.

And indeed, there was no doubt that things did not go smoothly for the race from the first. Just five days after the Australians arrived in San Francisco, two US Navy pilots, George D. Covell and Richard S. Waggener, were on their way from San Diego flying to the starting point of Oakland when they completely lost their way in fog and ended up crashing straight into an ocean cliff face and being killed outright, as their flaming plane hit the beach 75 feet below. Less than twenty-four hours later, another intended contestant, Arthur Rogers, took his plane up for a test flight above Montebello,

California, and lost control and crashed, killing himself — in full view of his young wife holding their infant daughter. And even then the race preliminaries were not done with disaster, with two more crashes occurring, although mercifully these were not fatal.

Yet that shocking lead-up did not dampen the enthusiasm of the 85,000 people who turned up at Oakland airport on the foggy morning of Tuesday, 16 August 1927, to see the Dole Air Race formally begin.[3] Eight impossibly tiny aircraft, each one single-engined, lined up in a semicircle at one end of the dusty runway. Around the planes, moving back and forth, were the aviators themselves — fifteen men and a young woman — together with assorted mechanics covered in three-parts grease to two-parts oil, making last-minute preparations for take-off.

And there they go! Ah, how the crowd near burst with excitement, pressing against the wooden fence that kept onlookers at a safe distance, as just before noon the first plane in the queue, *Oklahoma*, responded to the dropped chequered flag and accelerated, lifted off, waggled its wings, and headed out over San Francisco Bay, before heading west-south-west to Hawaii …

But look there! Before their very eyes, the second plane away, *El Encanto* — one of the pre-race favourites — clearly totally overloaded, lost control a couple of seconds after take-off and collapsed down onto its left wing in a shrieking metal groan of agony. At least its two flyers survived and were seen to crawl away from the wreckage as quickly as their knees could carry them, fearful that the huge quantity of petrol they had on board would ignite and explode. The next plane, *Pabco Flyer*, also momentarily got off the ground, before it too gave up the unequal struggle with gravity and returned to earth, becoming bogged in the marsh at the end of the runway. And so it went …

Golden Eagle, *Aloha* and *Woolaroc* got away okay, but though *Miss Doran* — carrying the sole woman in the race, 'the prettiest little pigeon on wings',[4] Mildred Doran, as part of its three-person crew — managed to take off, it returned ten minutes later before taking off again. *Pabco Flyer* was now freed from the marsh, but crashed more seriously on its second attempt.

Another plane, *Dallas Spirit*, also had to return shortly after take-off with engine trouble.

A little over twenty-six hours later, *Woolaroc* did indeed land safely in Honolulu to win the race, followed a couple of hours later by *Aloha*. But that was *it*. Though the people waited, and waited, and waited, with their leis at the ready to drape around the necks of the arriving pilots, no more planes arrived. In fact, no traces of *Golden Eagle* or *Miss Doran* were ever found. Equally tragically, when *Dallas Spirit* went to look for them, it too — with its pilot and navigator, William P. Erwin and Alvin Eichwaldt, both veterans of the Great War — simply vanished into the Pacific's gaping blue maw.

All up, ten lives were lost in the course of just that one race and …

•

And these Australian pilots wanted to do *what*?!?! To go *three* times as far as Hawaii, across the entire Pacific?! Three times further than Lindbergh had gone! They must be insane.

It was no exaggeration to say that in the history of aviation — as young as it was — there could have been no worse time to be asking aeroplane manufacturers, fuel companies and business people to provide planes, fuel or cash for such a venture. In most cases the Australians didn't even get through the front door of their target companies. Yes, Lindbergh had accomplished something phenomenal the year before, but he was an *American* and that was probably a one-off. The Dole Air Race had conclusively proved that flying over the Pacific Ocean in a heavily laden single-engine machine was an extremely dangerous exercise and it would be sheer lunacy to encourage and finance more pilots to needlessly risk their lives.

Against all that, however, what the Dole Air Race gave the Australians was some very clear lessons in how *not* to go about a long ocean flight. The more they looked at it, the more it became obvious that they needed the best equipment available across the board, and that started with the best plane. And that best plane was made by the very same man who had been the bane of Kingsford Smith and other Allied flyers in the Great War — Anthony Fokker.

By now Fokker was well established in the United States, to the point of being the most respected manufacturer in the business, and something worthy of note was that the first plane to make it from San Francisco to Hawaii had been a Fokker tri-motor. Too, the key to a successful journey was to have a robust plane capable of carrying an enormous load of fuel, and at the time the record for the largest load of fuel lifted in a plane was held by two Americans who had crossed the country from coast to coast in a Fokker.

As to engines, what also made a huge impression on Kingsford Smith, Ulm and Anderson was that the only two planes in the Dole Air Race that had made it safely to Hawaii had been powered by Wright Whirlwind engines, just as Lindbergh's Ryan monoplane had been blessed with one. When Richard Byrd had successfully flown to the North Pole and back the previous year, he too had been flying a Fokker powered by three Wright Whirlwind J-4 engines, made by a company of which Orville Wright had a significant share. The key thing about the engine was that it was air-cooled rather than liquid cooled, which meant that it was a lot lighter, required less maintenance and was less vulnerable to malfunction.

Bit by bit, the Australians came to the conclusion that their ideal machine would be a Fokker powered by three Wright Whirlwind engines and thus capable of carrying a crew of four, including a radio man and navigator to accompany the two pilots. This was a far more expensive option than their original plan of a single-engined Ryan monoplane, but what was expense when they were dealing with their own lives? They felt they would somehow find the money.

•

George Wilkins had so many problems he could barely keep track, though there was no problem working out what the key one was. He needed *money*. Badly. Money to keep his project going, to get back to Point Barrow and the 500 gallons of fuel he had cached there and complete the job he had started — to fly across the roof of the world all the way to Spitzbergen in Norway. The two wrecked Fokkers of the last two seasons' attempts were in storage in Seattle, and now he had no money to finance the plane he truly wanted — a Lockheed Vega, with a 225-horsepower engine capable of propelling it at 135 miles per hour. The Vega was an ideal plane because, unlike the Fokkers, it was very fast and fuel efficient, yet not so big that it needed five or six men to handle. When he and the redoubtable Ben Eielson would make the next attempt the following year, they were determined to have a more streamlined, cheaper operation, and the Lockheed would be just perfect for that. Now without the support of the Detroit Aviation Society and the *Detroit News*, as they had effectively given up on him, what he had to do was to sell his Fokkers for whatever he could get for them, and use that money to buy the Lockheed.

And then, while in Seattle, he read it — a bloke called Kingsford Smith was in San Francisco with a couple of other Australian pilots, and they were looking for a plane to fly across the Pacific with.

Wilkins immediately dispatched a cable to Kingsford Smith:

> Have Fokker I can sell you, without engines or instruments.[5]

Who immediately wired back:

> Re Your wire. Come down to 'Frisco and talk it over.

George Wilkins did exactly that, meeting Kingsford Smith, Ulm and Anderson a few days later in their hotel. The older man was not long in coming to the point. As a matter of fact, the first words he spoke to his fellow Australians simply followed up his telegram. 'I think I have the machine you require for your Pacific flight,' he said flatly. 'It is a tri-motored Fokker. No engines or instruments, but the wings and airframe are in excellent condition.'[6]

One didn't achieve as much as George Wilkins had in his life by wasting one's time on small talk. And Charles Kingsford Smith was at least his equal in wanting to get on with the task at hand. 'Well, George, I'd very much like to see the machine. Where is it?'[7]

There was an easy affinity between the pair. Australians in America, they were both pursuing a dream, both adventurers, and both war veterans with a slight limp.

The sticking point was the price. Although £3000 was a more than fair sum for Wilkins to be asking — as it was only about a third of what he had paid for his plane[8] — the simple reality was that Kingsford Smith, Ulm and Anderson just didn't have that kind of money for a Fokker without engines or instruments.

To this point they were living on the money they had from their own capital in Australia, while the money promised from the New South Wales government was held in escrow, to be released if and when they made their start — a government, they noted, which had just changed hands in the October 1927 elections. Their supporter, Premier Jack Lang, had been obliged to hand over the reins to his conservative opponent, Thomas Bavin. They presumed that Bavin would honour the commitments of Lang, but when that money did arrive it would not be enough to pay for the Fokker and fit it out with everything. Where could the rest of their required funds come from? None of their submissions to companies in the United States had produced the tiniest scrap of interest. The answer was not apparent on the instant, but as Wilkins took his leave Kingsford Smith made the promise that they would get back to him as soon as possible, once they had organised their finances. The first step was to cable the New South Wales government and request an extension of funds by another £1000.

Request denied. Back to square one.

Where to now?

•

Where to now? Sometimes, it was hard to keep track. For Charles Lindbergh, the craziness surrounding him simply didn't dissipate with the passage of the weeks and then months. 'I was astonished at the effect my successful landing in France had on the nations of the world,' he later wrote. 'To me, it was like a match lighting a bonfire ...'[9]

With the flying ability of a 'Lone Eagle', and the courage and strength of a grizzly bear, Lindbergh also had the stated morals and apparent manner of a good, God-fearing Sunday school teacher, and America obsessively loved him for it. Everyone wanted a piece of him, and some were prepared to pay for it — with the formerly humble pilot receiving five million dollars worth of commercial offers within a week of landing. Many a man facing one-hundredth of that level of adulation would have been destroyed by the temptations and trappings of fame. Lindbergh, however, remained humble. He didn't drink, didn't smoke, and eschewed casual sexual relationships — he was *precisely* the kind of man fit to be put on an American pedestal. 'The important thing,' Lindbergh later reminisced of this time, 'was to meet and marry a girl you would stay in love with. I intended to pay particular attention to that. It meant not falling in love with one of the first women you met — a question of time, patience and intelligent selection.'[10]

He registered his extreme distaste for the promiscuous approach, and told stories of some of the appalling things he had seen in the aviation world, how *some* pilots would have one-night stands, night after night after night, and others would even use prostitutes. Well, that was not for him. 'My experience in breeding animals on our farm had taught me the importance of good heredity …'[11]

Wherever he went he was photographed, had questions shouted at him, had women faint at his very sight. In St Louis there was even a fight between some women over a corncob he had just gnawed on. In Dayton, Ohio, he not only met Orville Wright, but spent the night in the great man's residence. Back in his home town of Little Falls, souvenir hunters had stolen the doorknobs off his childhood home.[12]

And yet he kept moving, embarking on what was essentially an aviation missionary tour in the *Spirit of St Louis*, across America, visiting eighty-two cities in forty-eight states, as no less than 25 per cent of the entire population turned out to see him in person. At one point, though, he took pause. Passing west over the Rocky Mountains in South Wyoming, he spied desert ahead. With no-one in it! Not a soul. No matter that there were thousands of people and many journalists waiting for him at the next town, he simply had to have some respite, and he brought the *Spirit of St Louis* in for an expert landing.

Silence. Blessed silence. The peace was so overwhelming, he decided he needed to spend the night there, a night that would set the course of the rest of his life, as he took some hard decisions. 'I would reduce my obligations, give away some of my possessions, concentrate my business and social interests. I would take advantage of the civilisation to which I had been born without losing the basic qualities of life from which all works of men must emanate.'[13]

•

Enter Sidney Myer.

It was at this time that, through the loose network of well-heeled Australians living in California — of whom Harold Kingsford Smith was a notable — Kingsford Smith, Ulm and Anderson met the Melbourne retailing magnate and got on well with him from the first. Myer was an interesting man of no little ability. Having arrived in Australia from Poland in 1899, speaking practically no English, he had started a store in Bendigo that went bust, then sold various goods door-to-door to rebuild. With his capital re-established, he opened another store in Ballarat that so prospered he was able to open another one and then another one and another one after that, until the beginnings of a whole Myer chain was developing around the country. He had done so well out of the business personally that he and his wife had decided to buy a mansion in Burlingame, just outside San Francisco, and when not in Melbourne — which was most of the time — it was the place they regularly took their holidays.

One way or another, Myer was a man who had the capacity to back himself against enormous odds and, most importantly, felt a duty to help those who were trying to do the same thing. But really, gentlemen, do you actually think it is possible to fly a plane across the entire Pacific Ocean? They assured him it was feasible, and they had found the very plane to do it in, if only they could get the money together to buy it.

Well, Mr Myer would like to help. But the thing was, boys, he simply didn't feel right having any part in a venture of which he was convinced the best-case outcome was that they would only break their necks, and the worst was their being killed outright. Their counter to his concern was that with or without his financial support they would find a way to do it, and he was therefore absolved of any guilt should the worst case indeed happen.

Finally, Sidney Myer came to a decision. He would simply *give* them £1500, no strings attached, and it was theirs to do with what they would. If they chose to spend the money on their venture that was their business, and no concern of his. He wished them well.

•

Eureka! And a double eureka when, shortly afterwards, the New South Wales government came good after all, with a £1000 extension on the original £3500 guarantee.

Wilkins agreed to turn the machine over to them on the first condition that he receive a down payment of £1500 immediately, with the rest to be paid once they had left for Australia and their money from the New South Wales government was thus released from escrow. The second condition was that the machine be test-flown and prepared by a pilot chosen by Wilkins, who could also instruct Kingsford Smith on how to handle such a large, multi-engined machine.[14]

Done!

It wasn't that the flyers were flush with cash, because the process of getting the plane they had bought from George Wilkins back into the air was going to be an expensive one, but they at least had enough to make a down payment of £1500 to Wilkins and use the rest to get the work done.

Kingsford Smith cabled Wilkins to that effect, and the deal was formalised. The three aviators in San Francisco were now feeling so confident that things were on track that they decided to engage the services of their old mate Bill Todd from the *Tahiti* to be their navigator. Yes, they had all learnt the rudiments of navigation under his tutelage, but none of them wanted to trust their lives to his own calculations when they could get an expert like Todd to take a leave of absence from his maritime service and join them.

Todd soon moved into the Roosevelt Hotel with them, on the promise that it would not be long before they were ready to go. He was happy to have a break from shipboard life and, the laws of Prohibition notwithstanding, had soon ferreted out every speakeasy within staggering distance of the hotel. On excursions to such places as Izzy Gomez's, Monk Young's, Coffee Dan's, the House of Shields or Cafe Du Nord, to which you could gain access if you knew the password of the day, Todd was frequently joined by Smithy, who continued to have an enviable capacity to drink a great deal by night, before performing well the next day, before doing it all again the next night and then the next day. (For ones so disposed, California was probably the best place to be during Prohibition. San Franciscans had voted overwhelmingly — 83 per cent — against the introduction of the Prohibition laws, and more or less ignored them when they were brought in. Although there were raids, no-one particularly cared. It was, for example, the stuff of legend that the speakeasy in the Hotel D'Oloron on Columbus Street had been raided so many times that when the courts would shut one address down, 'the owner simply cut a new door in the wall, slapped on a new address and continued pouring drinks'.[15])

•

Christ! It turned out that every other aspiring aviator in the country had come to the same conclusion about the virtues of the Wright Whirlwind engine as the Australians, who were now informed that they were at the back of a very long queue — ninety orders long in fact — to get their hands on three such engines. It would be a wait of *six months*, minimum. What to do?

It was all very well to be in America — land of the free, home of the brave — but they had been there long enough to know that a good lot of the grease on which the wheels of the country turned was *who knew who*, and how much influence could thus be brought to bear on key decision makers. So it was that via a man who was to become a great friend, Locke T. Harper — a leading executive of the powerful Vacuum Oil Company — they were able to arrange an introduction to Rear Admiral Christian Peables, the US Navy's second-highest ranking man on the West Coast.

This good man, an officer and a gentleman, was initially dead against the whole idea of a flight over the Pacific. 'I do not want to be interested in this thing in any way,' he told them, his moustache bristling as he pounded the table. 'I don't want to be connected with it — you're crazy. Flying to Australia! I want to keep right outside of it. Look at what happened to the Dole flyers!'[16]

These proved to be merely his opening remarks. From that point the rear admiral, supported by his aide-de-camp, expanded on the hideous dangers the flyers faced — the storms, the distance, the winds, the hundreds of thousands of dollars the navy had already spent in trying to retrieve foolish fallen airmen, and so forth. At last, however, there was a small lull in the barrage — much as there used to be occasionally in Gallipoli and on the Western Front — and, seizing the opportunity, Smithy was able to quickly fire his own shot: 'We're going to use a three-engined Fokker.'[17]

On the instant, both the rear admiral and his aide-de-camp calmed down. Using a three-engined Fokker showed the flyers were serious, not mere fly-by-nighters who invariably crashed by night *and* day. The US Navy man was further impressed to be informed by the Australians that they intended to have a four-man crew, including a radio man and professional navigator, the latter of whom they had already hired.

If they used a machine like that, with personnel and specialised equipment, then perhaps it *was* possible to traverse the Pacific. A long discussion ensued, and both the rear admiral and his aide-de-camp agreed that Wright Whirlwind engines were the right choice. By the end of the meeting the rear admiral had pledged the full co-operation of the US Navy in their project, and most crucially, affirmed that the Australians could take the navy's position at the front of the queue for three Whirlwind engines! With this commitment, the men were at last able to engage expert mechanics and get the refitting process under way at the Boeing Aircraft Company, just outside Seattle, where the fuselage and the wing of the *Detroiter* — the bigger plane — were reunited once more, turning the plane back into the Fokker F.VIIb.3m. After that, the engineers began to install the engines and instruments.

Meanwhile, Keith Anderson was sent by ship to Hawaii to reconnoitre the main island for the best place for landing and take-off. He was not long in returning to say that Wheeler Field would be fine for landing, but Barking Sands on the nearby island of Kauai would be much better for taking off as it would provide a longer flat space to get off the ground. As to where they would go from Hawaii, their ideas had evolved in just the few weeks they had been in America.

At the same time their plans had switched from a Ryan monoplane to a Fokker, so too had they decided that converting to a seaplane was impractical. Keeping it a land plane, they explored the possibilities of flying from Honolulu all the way to Lae on the north coast of New Guinea, before hopping down to Brisbane from there. But the problem with that was the massive distance from Honolulu to Lae, a long leap of over 4200 miles. Surely it would be better to fly directly to Fiji — only a bit more than 3100 miles — and then on to Brisbane? After much discussion, the Hawaii–Fiji–Brisbane plan was the one they settled on.

For his part, Bill Todd, their navigator, certainly seemed to think that was the best plan, both when he was drunk *and* when he was sober.

•

The great day came at last, late in September 1927. Their plane, with three big, beautiful, new 200-horsepower Whirlwind J-5-A engines attached — with the consecutive serial numbers 7416, 7417 and 7418 — was ready for testing. In terms of a long-range flyer, it certainly looked the part, with its enormous spruce and plywood wing, so typical of the Fokker, balanced above a slimmed-down fuselage of welded steel tubes covered by fabric. In the small cockpit, the two pilots sat side by side, each with his own control column wheel which, on larger planes, had replaced the once ubiquitous joystick.

To do the initial testing, Wilkins had insisted on hiring a navy pilot of great experience with US Army tri-motor Fokkers, a fellow by the name of Commander George Pond — all to the great chagrin of Keith Anderson, who once again found himself outvoted. After Pond did indeed do the honours, Smithy was able to fly the plane down to San Francisco, where the others were to greet him upon arrival at Mills Field, the San Franciscan airstrip that was to be their base. The original nickname for the *Detroiter* at Fairbanks had been *Big Fokker* — even though an Irishman would probably call it exactly that, and then some — but that would not do here. This plane was their creation, and needed its own name.

Why not, Anderson suggested, call it *Southern Cross*?

The others looked at him. Paused. Thought about it for a moment …

It was Australian. It was aerial. It was somehow upbeat and sparkling in one. It was perfect!

Southern Cross it was, then — soon painted in big white letters on the fuselage, itself painted very close to the colour True Blue, which was then in use by the US Navy — and all seemed right with the world.

•

The enthusiasm the crew of the *Southern Cross* felt, however, was in no way matched by others. The flyers became aware that at home in Australia something of a press campaign had been mounted to get them to stop before they killed themselves. Paradoxically, now that their dream had gone from mere fantasy flight to a real and roaring plane, getting ready to go, the resistance was able to focus intensely.

You see, the critics pointed out, Hawaii and Fiji were no more than a couple of tiny dots in a vast ocean of otherwise near-nothingness, and if the men missed them and ran out of fuel then they were all as good as dead, *precisely* as had happened to those dozen or so other flyers in the Dole Air Race. What made these men think they could succeed in a flight three times as long, when so many others had failed with such disastrous results? It was insane!

'To attempt a flight from Honolulu to Australia in a land machine is an impossible task,' stated Geoffrey Hughes, the co-founder and President of the New South Wales Aero Club, and he should bloody well know, shouldn't he?[18]

And anyway, what were they doing flying a *Fokker*?

Most vociferous in his attacks on the latter point was RAAF Squadron Leader Lawrence Wackett, DFC, AFC, BSc, FRAeS, a highly regarded Australian aircraft designer and former contemporary of the likes of Paul McGinness, Hudson Fysh and Keith Smith in the Australian Flying Corps' prestigious No. 1 Squadron, who just the previous year had become the founding chairman of the inaugural Australasian branch of the Royal Aeronautical Society. 'What they're doing,' he told the press, 'is offering an insult to every returned Australian soldier, sailor and airman. Fokkers were used by the German Air Force to fight us, and many a good Australian died from bullets spewed from them ...'[19]

When Kingsford Smith was told of Wackett's views by an American reporter, he was under the *Southern Cross*. Enraged, he put down his tools, emerged from under the fuselage and told the reporter straight: 'That's crap. No-one loves Australia more than I do. I'm dealing with a plane, not with personalities or nationality. I'm dealing with a fine piece of machinery and engineering. You can quote me as telling Wackett to go to hell.'[20]

Mere criticism, however, he and Ulm and Anderson could have coped with fairly easily. The real blow, however, landed when a cable arrived from the New South Wales government, gravely informing them that their promised extension of funding would not be arriving after all, and it was the government's wish that they pull out immediately. It had taken some time for the full significance of the Dole Air Race disaster to be appreciated at home, but now that it had been, the government wanted no part in helping to bankroll a new aviation disaster, this one involving famous Australians.

Even Sidney Myer seemed to doubt them when — while making it clear that he was not asking for his money back —

he implored them to put the whole thing on hold. Kingsford Smith, Ulm and Anderson were not remotely interested, however. They had come too far and dreamed too long to simply pull up stumps because the nay-sayers were multiplying like rabbits.

Yet while their stoicism and determination to keep going was unwavering, continuing to pay the bills required something beyond mere determination. The *Southern Cross* could fly beautifully, but they still had to fit it out with extra fuel tanks, state-of-the-art radios and the best navigational equipment they could get their hands on. They also had to continue to accommodate and feed themselves, and pay for aviation fuel to keep putting their plane through its paces.

The only answer, as ever, was to get money from people far wealthier than they, and while that precondition described pretty much everyone bar California's hobos, none of the people they approached seemed interested in helping.

For the three Australians, to keep going under such circumstances — to keep knocking, keep ringing, keep asking for a meeting on the off-chance that it would actually take place and then lead to something solid — took a particular fortitude, and neither Charles Kingsford Smith nor Keith Anderson had it. Each brought talents to the project, but neither man would claim organising finance was among them. Instead, after just a few weeks of useless traipsing around, it was Charles Ulm who came into his own, who continued to believe that they would make a breakthrough and find the money they needed … even as the bills they owed just for staying alive and under a roof continued to pile up.

Mostly, thus, it was Ulm who went 'tramping from interview to interview, from oil company to aircraft builder, from Jew to Gentile, seeking monetary backing for a project which nobody in the world, apparently, thought was tenable. For month after month it went on.'[21]

And yet, despite the grimness of the situation, work on the *Southern Cross* progressed, and they kept George Pond on as a test pilot and adviser, benefiting from his enormous experience. It was in this field, of preparing the aircraft, that Kingsford

Smith was at his strongest, rigorously pursuing 'a fixed policy of trusting for the best flying conditions, and preparing for the very worst'.[22]

If Smithy wasn't flying the plane, he was working on it, or supervising work on it, or doing calculations as to just what kind of work should be done on it to make it as safe as possible and as capable as possible of completing the journey. He might have been catch-as-catch-can in much of the rest of his life, but when it came to flying and preparing to fulfil his dream, he was deadly serious.

Let's start with the three Whirlwind J-5-A motors, each one producing 200 horsepower. Each of those engines would consume 6 gallons of fuel an hour when at full throttle, and a little more than 3½ gallons when cruising at optimum speed, or 11 gallons an hour in total. Previous testing had confirmed that the optimum speed for getting the greatest mileage per gallon was 95 miles per hour, with the engines at 1600 revolutions per minute.

On their longest hop, from Hawaii's Honolulu to Suva in Fiji, they would need to cover a distance of 3128 miles, if they were not blown off-course, which meant that the standard tanks they had would be totally insufficient. The answer, as Smithy established in consultation with experts, was to fit four separate tanks, each holding 96 gallons, inside the wings, while in the cockpit, the two co-pilots would be sitting on another tank of 107 gallons. The major tank, however, would be the one directly behind the pilots, between them and the navigator and wireless operator, with 807 gallons, making a total of — *dot three, carry one, subtract two* — 1298 gallons, weighing nearly 3½ tons.

All else being equal, that should give them a very conservative range of 3800 miles, which should be plenty enough, and it also fitted in perfectly with Smithy's firm view that the only time a plane had too much petrol on board was when it was on fire. Other than that, keep pouring …

Which was to the good. But could the *Southern Cross* possibly carry the extra weight that came with the extra petrol, now that that weight had gone up by two *tons*, from five to seven?

More calculations. From tip to tip the wings of the *Southern Cross* stretched 71 feet, 8½ inches, with 12 feet, 6 inches of 'chord', being the average distance of the wing from its leading edge to its trailing edge. All put together, it meant that every square foot of wing surface, which had been designed to lift 11 pounds, would now have to carry 23 pounds 2 ounces.

Could it be done? They thought so. But it would need testing, filling the tanks progressively more — from 40 per cent, to 60 per cent to 80 per cent to, hopefully, 100 per cent — to see whether their maths worked. (If the plan didn't work they would crash either on or shortly after take-off, something which helped Smithy to focus rather fiercely on his sums.)

•

This was the last straw. It was Bill Todd. Pissed out of his mind, he had crashed the car they had been using. Charles Ulm — effectively the boss of all things that happened on the ground, while Smithy was the captain of the air — sent him packing. Out! Out! Out!

Todd was furious. Yes, he had been drunk, and yes, he had crashed the car. But why wouldn't he be drunk? What else did he have to *do*? He had joined them in good faith that the historic flight would take place in a very short time, and here it was, weeks, *months* later, and they were still a long way from taking off. So of course he had had a few drinks. Ulm wasn't moved. Todd was a liability whose actions jeopardised the entire project. This was a serious endeavour for serious people and he had to go. Todd finally left, outraged beyond all measure at his treatment.

It was not long after this that Kingsford Smith met Anthony Fokker for the first time — a rather strange thing, given Smithy's experiences in the war both being shot at by Fokkers as well as shooting them down. Still, Fokker was so personable, such a good man to have a drink with and the war so long ago that they were soon getting on famously. At one point, Smithy asked him straight out about their trans-Pacific project.

'Do you think we can do it — in a Fokker plane?'

'Of course you can do it in a Fokker plane,' the manufacturer replied easily. 'If you can fly.'[23]

In that case, no worries.

•

One day late in 1927, while Smithy was working away on the *Southern Cross* at San Francisco's Mills Field, which had become their base, he looked up to see a young man gazing admiringly back at him. That man, John Stannage, was a Kiwi radio operator with the SS *Makura*, which took passengers on the Sydney to San Francisco run, and he later wrote an account of this meeting. 'I shall never forget my first glimpse of the *Southern Cross*, nor my first handshake with the man who from then on became my hero. His face smudged with oil, and his unruly hair wind-blown in the slip-stream of one of the motors, he gripped my hand as if he really were glad to meet me.

'What do you think of her?

'I still see his infectiously boyish grin as he cast a proud eye over the great machine. Even then I could see that his pride in the big blue Fokker was something more than just the joy of an engineer in a perfect piece of mechanism. Smithy had already endowed the Cross with a soul. For here was no ordinary aircraft, and indeed no ordinary man. Smithy's personality was likeably dynamic, his grin friendly, spontaneous and sincere. I recall that it occurred to me as I studied the man that there were too many lines on his thin, keen face for one so young. It was sun-tanned and healthy, but it was the face of a sentimentalist who had been hurt; a man keenly alive, a man indeed with a heart as large as the sun …

'I watched Smithy and Pond climb up into the cockpit, warm up the three 200-horsepower Wright Whirlwind motors and then taxi to the far end of the long runway. The *Cross* was loaded with 80 per cent of her full tankage. This was to be one of a series of test-flights, in which petrol load was to be gradually increased, so that both men could become acquainted with the behaviour of the aircraft on take-off under all load conditions.'[24]

Stannage watched, mesmerised, as the great plane rumbled down the runway before finally lifting to the skies. He liked this man an enormous amount. (That affection, however, didn't extend to wanting to join Smith and Ulm on their trip, when they later approached him to be their navigator. An adventure was one thing, a suicide mission quite another).[25]

Based on their test flights, the Australians were able to gather more and more information on how their plane needed to be modified, and bit by bit they improved it. Their modifications included redesigning the rudder to make it capable of holding the plane straight if one of the now more powerful side engines failed, then strengthening the fuselage to enable it to carry the modified rudder, and fitting the plane with stronger axles and wheels so they were less likely to collapse under the strain of such a heavy load while still on the ground …

•

It was hopeless. No matter how hard Ulm tried, *facing the round eternal of the cash-book and the journal* — sustained only by passionate drive, and constant loving and encouraging letters from his wife, Jo, at home — he simply couldn't make headway in getting money out of anyone, and things were now getting urgent. It wasn't simply that they lacked the money to make the flight; it was that they didn't have enough money to pay their daily bills.

Things were so grim that they could not afford to even buy a half-decent meal. As for paying their hotel bill, the worst of it wasn't that they couldn't — because that point had been reached several weeks before — but that they were running out of ruses to convince the hotelier that payment was just around the corner. There was a real risk that they would shortly be thrown onto the street.

Clearly, they needed a breakthrough in securing finance, and a quick one. In the short term, all they could cobble together to stay afloat was a series of loans. Keith Anderson's mother sent them £400. His uncle extended them £600, though on the strict and written proviso that when the flight took place, his nephew would be on board. Most importantly, their great friend Locke T. Harper extended them an enormous personal loan, and arranged for the *San Francisco Chronicle* to take out a mortgage on the *Southern Cross* itself — and the name 'Chronicle' soon appeared under both wings, by way of aerial advertisement. Smithy, meantime, cabled his brother Leofric in Australia, asking him to sell the remaining Bristol Tourer and to use the proceeds to hopefully pay some debts they had left behind at home. These, however, were only interim measures, until they could get what they needed, which was serious business backing.

To attract that backing, they needed credibility and, just as had happened six months earlier, it was decided they needed to do something to get their names into the headlines, make everyone sit up and take notice as to just what a fine plane they had and what good aviators they were. Why not set about breaking the world record for the longest time aloft, which then stood at fifty-five hours, twenty-two minutes, thirty-one seconds and was held by two Germans, Cornelius Edzard and Johann Risticz, who achieved it on 5 August 1927.[26] *That* should impress a few folk. At least, just the idea of it impressed the Associated Oil Company, which promised, at Ulm's behest, to pay off their American debts if they did indeed break that record.

If successful, the flight would have three outcomes. Firstly, and most importantly, the aviation manager of the Associated Oil Company promised to clear all their debts.[27] Secondly, it would allow them to test all their theories about long-distance flying during an actual flight and modify their plans accordingly from what they'd learned. And finally, Kingsford Smith could put himself to the personal test, to find how he would perform under such conditions.[28]

•

10 January 1928. It had come to a coin toss.

Three Kiwi men had started out with the dream of being the first to fly from Australia to New Zealand across the Tasman Sea, and yet, after all was said and done the only plane they could afford to buy to make the attempt — a single-engined Ryan B.1 Brougham monoplane by the name of *Aotearoa*, G-AUNZ — could only hold two of them.

So what else could they do? Captain Ivan Kight was devastated to lose the toss. So it would be Lieutenant John Moncrieff and Captain George Hood who would do the honours.

In high excitement, Hood and Moncrieff took off from Richmond air base at 2.44 am on Tuesday, 10 January 1928. Before them lay a journey of 1450 miles to Wellington. With

ABOVE Lawrence Hargrave and James Swaine fly Hargrave's 'cellular' kites at Stanwell Park, New South Wales, 1894.

E.A. Crome Collection, National Library of Australia, vn3723545

LEFT A young Charles Kingsford Smith and his sister Elsie, around the turn of the century.

E.A. Crome Collection, National Library of Australia, vn3722926

ABOVE First flight of the Wright brothers' Flyer I, 17 December 1903. Orville is piloting, with Wilbur at the wingtip. The photograph was taken, using Orville's tripod-mounted camera, by John T. Daniels of Kill Devil Hills Life Saving Station.
Bettman/CORBIS BE060649

LEFT TOP Louis Blériot before taking off on his successful attempt to fly across the English Channel on 25 July 1909.
Bettman/CORBIS U110424ACME

LEFT BOTTOM Harry Houdini flying in Australia in 1910.
State Library of Victoria, mp015781

RIGHT Roland Garros, who rose to fame first as a pioneer aviator and then as a pilot in World War I, and invented a machine gun that could be fired through a plane's propellers.
Getty Images 2665729

LEFT Baron Manfred von Richthofen – the Red Baron. *Courtesy Peter FitzSimons*

BELOW No. 3 Squadron lays to rest with full military honours an old adversary – the Red Baron – at Bertangles cemetery, France, 22 April 1918.
Getty Images 78972517

ABOVE LEFT Harry Hawker in May 1919, about the time of his attempt to fly across the Atlantic.
Photolibrary 17240549

ABOVE RIGHT Charles Kingsford Smith performing stunts in Hollywood.
E.A. Crome Collection, National Library of Australia, vn3723531

ABOVE The first crew to complete a flight from England to Australia in 1919. From left: Sir Keith Smith, Sir Ross Smith, Sergeant Jim Bennett, Sergeant Wally Shiers.
Australian War Memorial, 106074

ABOVE George Gorham, Paul McFinnes and Hudson Fysh at the start of their epic survey trip from Longreach to Darwin, in search of ground suitable for aerodomes and landing strips, in 1919.

Qantas Heritage Collection

ABOVE The Qantas office, next door to the Longreach Club, 1921. *Qantas Heritage Collection*

ABOVE Smartly liveried pilots at Langley Park, Perth, on 4 December 1921, prior to the Bristol 28 Tourers departing for Geraldton in preparation for the first service of West Australian Airways the next day. From left: Charles Kingsford Smith, Bob Fawcett (killed that same day), Norman Brearley, Len Taplin and Val Abbott.
State Library of Western Australia 000616D

BELOW Anthony Fokker aboard a glider for the 1922 Fokker Glider Competition.
Hulton Archive, Getty Images 3421286

ABOVE Welcome to Honolulu. The crew of the Southern Cross garlanded in leis on their arrival in Hawaii after flying more than 2000 miles across the Pacific, 1 June 1928.

Charles T.P. Ulm Aviation Collection, National Library of Australia, vn3930683

BELOW From Hawaii to Fiji. The *Southern Cross* in Suva, after the longest leg of the record-breaking San Francisco to Sydney flight.

Charles T.P. Ulm Aviation Collection, National Library of Australia, vn3930966

ABOVE People lining up along a Brisbane street to welcome the heroes of the Pacific crossing, 9 June 1928.

John Oxley Library, State Library of Queensland, 135100

ABOVE Autographed photo of Charles Kingsford Smith and Charles Ulm, taken after the trans-Pacific flight.

Hood Collection, State Library of New South Wales, a928351

ABOVE Australian National Airways hangar at Mascot aerodrome. Completed in 1929, it was built to house five Avro Ten aircraft for passenger and mail services between Sydney, Melbourne and Brisbane.

John Oxley Library, State Library of Queensland, 135100

RIGHT Keith Anderson bids a passionate farewell to his fiancée, Bon Hilliard.

ABOVE The *Kookaburra* in the Tanami Desert circa 1929, at the site where Keith Anderson and Bobby Hitchcock died while searching for the *Southern Cross* in north-western Australia.

John M.W. Haslett Collection, Northern Territory Library, PHO229/0014

LEFT Kingsford Smith and Ulm chair their saviour, Bertie Heath, with McWilliams (left), and Litchfield (right), in 1929. Heath landed at Coffee Royal, bringing petrol to refuel the *Southern Cross*.

Charles T.P. Ulm Collection, State Library of New South Wales, a1269021

ABOVE The *Kookaburra* in the Tanami Desert circa 1929, at the site where Keith Anderson and Bobby Hitchcock died while searching for the *Southern Cross* in north-western Australia.

John M.W. Haslett Collection, Northern Territory Library, PHO229/0014

BELOW Charles Kingsford Smith and Charles (C.W.A) Scott, who in 1931 broke Smithy's England to Australia record.

Hood Collection, State Library of New Wouth Wales, A169123

ABOVE One of the largest crowds ever seen in Melbourne thronged to witness Sir Charles Kingsford Smith at Essendon aerodrome on Sunday, 15 October 1933.

State Library of Victoria, b52554s

LEFT Charles and Mary with their only child, Charles Jnr, circa 1934.

Courtesy Charles Kingsford Smith Jnr.

RIGHT Mixing with the stars. Smithy flanked by Cary Grant and Myrna Loy in Hollywood during his trip to collect his new Lockheed Altair in 1934. John Stannage stands back left, alongside Sydney radio identity Rus Garling. Two studio executives stand to the right.

Courtesy Ken Garling

RIGHT Poster for the 1934 Centenary Air Race between London and Melbourne, sponsored by Sir Macpherson Robertson, a chocolate manufacturer.

Trompf Collection, State Library of New South Wales, A928613

ABOVE The ANZAC – later rechristened the *Lady Southern Cross* – with Tommy Pethybridge perched on top, is winched from the deck of the *Mariposa* onto a waiting barge in Sydney Harbour.

Hood Collection, State Library of New South Wales, HA_04301

BELOW The strut Taylor made his way along to reach the port engine. Note the proximity of the wind-driven generator and the open cockpit side through which Taylor climbed, past the elevator control wires.

Charles T.P. Ulm Collection, National Library of Australia, vn3930741

LEFT Charles Kingsford Smith with his co-pilot Charles Ulm's son, John, on the day they handed the Southern Cross over to the Australian government.

Hood Collection, State Library of New South Wales, a169043

ABOVE Tommy Pethybridge, P.G. Taylor, Charles Kingsford Smith, John Stannage, Terry White, Stan Neilson and Jack Percival in front of the fuselage of *Southern Cross* VH-USU.

E.A. Crome Collection, National Library of Australia, vn37722944

ABOVE Smithy and co-pilot Tommy Pethybridge beside the Lockhead Altair *Lady Southern Cross*, in which they were to disappear of the Burma coast in 1935.

Newspix

RIGHT Nellie Stewart. Smithy kept his signed picture of the actress as a good luck charm throughout World War I and the rest of his flying career.

David Elliott Theatrical Postcard Collection, National Library of Australia, an22966453 an estimated flying time of between fourteen and seventeen hours, this should see them landing to a heroes' welcome late the following afternoon, New Zealand time.

And New Zealand was ready for them, all right. For the previous few days the New Zealand papers had been in a fever of anticipation about the attempt, and an enormous crowd of spectators and journalists built up at Trentham racetrack when the likely time of arrival approached. As they waited for the plane, the centre of attention was the attractive wives of the two men, Dorothy Moncrieff and Laura Hood. They were alternately laughing with each other and gazing to the west, whence their husbands were due to appear, and the atmosphere was gay and celebratory. This really would be an achievement, and it was to the good that the record of a trans-Tasman flight would be set by New Zealanders and not Australians.

At six o'clock at Trentham racecourse the mood was fever pitch as all eyes strained to the west, everyone wanting to be the first to spot them. At 7 pm there was still no sign, but nor was there undue alarm. Who knew what kind of headwinds they had met over the middle of the Tasman Sea? Why, they could be anything up to a couple of hours later than planned, or maybe even three.

And yet when nine o'clock came and went and there was still no sign, there was no more giggling from the wives, just an earnest, unbroken gaze to the skies, *willing* their husbands to appear. The large crowd didn't like to keep glancing at their watches, as it sort of seemed disloyal, but they couldn't help themselves.

9.20 … 9.30 … 9.45 … still nothing. And so the evening dragged on like a sad leper.

By 10.30 pm, a pall of gloom hung over the racecourse. No-one wanted to say it, but everyone feared the worst.

Finally, at 1 am, Dorothy Moncrieff looked at her watch and said slowly, 'Their petrol has now given out.'[29] She went home.

•

San Francisco, 17 January 1928. After four aborted attempts on the world endurance record, they were ready once again.[30]

The runway at Mills Field extended for just less than 5000 feet and, now that the *Southern Cross* was fully loaded with fuel equalling the weight of sixty-eight men, the reckoning was that the aviators would need every drop of it. True, there was a downside in that a levee had been built around the western end of the field to keep high tides out — meaning that at the end of the runway there was effectively a wall facing them — but they would just have to live with that. At least they *hoped* they could live with that, because it simply didn't bear thinking about what would happen if, so heavily laden down with fuel, they were to hit that wall. (Though the likelihood was that all that would be left to put in their coffins would be their molten tooth fillings.)

In the normal course of things, at the moment that the pilot opened the throttles at one end of the runway, the plane would buck forward rather in the manner of a frisky horse that had just felt the touch of a spur ... but not on this occasion. The *Southern Cross* was so heavily laden that at first there was only barely perceptible movement along the runway, and then for the next 100 feet or so, the plane sort of waddled forward at walking pace. Finally, though, her speed built up enough that she really was rushing down the runway, and at the 2000 feet mark had achieved 90 miles per hour. But still no lift. Three thousand feet ... 4000 feet ...

And then to the moment.

In Kingsford Smith's own words: 'We charged on. Some instinct peculiar to airmen told us that the old bus would make it. The gallant plan was now "all out". When we were still about 300 yards off the wheels left the ground for a few inches. Then they settled again.'

The last hundred yards!

'We deliberately pushed forward the controls. The effect was to drive the machine downwards. At that speed the contact with the ground developed into a bump. We had bounced the now flying machine over the levee.'[31]

Even then, however, danger was stalking close, with death riding shotgun as the *Southern Cross* flew on, only bare feet above the water, which would suck them down in an instant if they just touched it. It was a desperate mile later before they had burnt enough fuel to rise even a small height above the ocean.

From this point, the key, as Smithy saw it, was to 'maintain a nice balance between the maximum speed for safety and the minimum speed for consumption. This meant holding the plane at stalling point all the time — a highly risky proceeding with an overloaded machine. Nevertheless we had to save fuel in every possible way.'[32]

How to stay aloft in such circumstances?

By *concentrating*, fiercely. For hour after hour after freezing, mind-numbing hour, as the sun fell and rose and fell again, they kept flying circles above San Francisco. In the cramped cockpit Kingsford Smith and Pond were pretty much hating every moment of it, but were equally determined to claim the record if it could possibly be done.

•

Back at their hotel, Keith Anderson was writing a long letter to his fiancée, Bon Hilliard, venting his extreme frustration. He and Smithy had pretty much conceived the dream of flying the Pacific together, had planned it over years, worked their way through all the problems together and it had been *his* uncle who had provided the crucial cash to keep them afloat on the specific condition that his nephew be one of the pilots, and yet ...

And yet here Anderson was, six months in America, three months with the *Southern Cross*, and he had still never been allowed to pilot it! Well, he had just about had enough of the whole damn thing and certainly didn't mind telling Bon all about it. He missed her desperately and it was only worth being away from her if the Pacific flight was actually going to take place with him as the co-pilot, which at this time seemed like a real long-shot, as far, faaaar above him, the *Southern Cross* kept going round in circles ...

•

Circle after circle. Smithy and Pond kept flying and flying. On and on and on, closely monitoring their petrol consumption and getting progressively more depressed as it became obvious that they were unlikely to break the record.

At 7.30 am on the second morning, Kingsford Smith sent a message over the wireless to the ground:

> Southern Cross will be compelled to land at 9.30, running out of fuel. She cannot lift enough fuel for more than 50 hours. It is just liveable up here. That is all.[33]

They landed at 10.13 am, 19 January, after fifty hours and four minutes in the air.

The absurdity, of course, was the difference in press coverage that staying aloft for a few more hours would have made. Their achievement had been considerable to stay aloft for so long, but there were no prizes for second. They had not beaten the German record, so no-one particularly cared …

•

Least of all the New South Wales government. Even while Smithy and Pond had been in the air attempting to beat the record, the newly installed government of Premier Thomas Bavin had sent a strongly worded cable to the effect that the flyers' time was up. The money had been guaranteed if they could make the flight within six months, and that six months was now gone. Therefore the offer was withdrawn. The government insisted that they sell the *Southern Cross* for whatever they could get for it, and return home on the next steamer.

It looked like they were finished. Their own money was so long gone that they were feeling genuine hunger pains, and so broke that they couldn't even afford to smoke a cigarette they hadn't cadged. Their one bit of relief was when the *Tahiti* was in port and they could sneak aboard to get some free meals from their old friend Hal Litchfield. And then it was back to real life again.[34]

Affording accommodation at the Roosevelt Hotel was now out of the question, and they moved to a series of progressively cheaper and nastier hotels, interspersed with nights spent sleeping on couches at the hangar.

Those guys? Just some crazy Australians who have this idea that they can fly the Pacific. Been trying for months. Look, if you can spare a dime, buddy, give them a sandwich. They'll appreciate it, and they're not bad guys.

If there was an upside, it was that they were all losing so much weight they would be able to load up even more petrol, should they ever be able to get off the ground and head south-west.

•

For his part, Bert Hinkler's conception of long-distance flight — in his case, all the way from England to Australia — was close to that of Charles Lindbergh's. Instead of a multi-engined plane with a large crew, Hinkler believed that the best way to go was in a single-engined plane bearing just one crew member. Him. He had been flying a long time now, with a resumé that included a Distinguished Service Medal, an Air Force Cross for his efforts as a gunner/observer with the Royal Naval Air Service, flying a Sopwith Camel fighter with the RFC in Italy during the Great War, and five years spent after the war as a test pilot for Avro. He was a man who had justifiable faith in his own abilities, and given that his long-time plan had been to break Ross and Keith Smith's aviation record from England to Australia, he was now trying to make it happen.

So it was that at dawn on Tuesday, 7 February 1928, Hinkler made ready to take off from Croydon aerodrome in his tiny silver Avro Avian 581 prototype biplane G-EBOV. Just 24 feet 3 inches from stem to stern, with a 28-foot wingspan and an 85-horsepower ADC Cirrus Hermes engine, this particular Avro was regarded by most in the aviation world as little more than a toy plane — so small that Hinkler could well have been a 'Lone Sparrow' to Lindbergh's 'Lone Eagle', in his relatively enormous Ryan monoplane.

Now, as the mechanic swung the propeller and the engine burst into life — and the rush of air from the hurtling blades flattened the wet grass all around — the aviator stepped back

The indefatigable Herbert Hinkler. (Ed Coates Collection)

from the plane so he and his beloved, the softly-spoken and beautiful Nancy, whom he had met during the war when she was a hospital sister, could have a few last words together. There were no crowds, because Bert had told only his nearest and dearest that he was going. That morning when he had woken at 4.30 am, to look out on the damp misty morning, so unpromising for flying, he had had a sudden crisis of confidence, but that was all gone now, and he felt much stronger.

'I hope you'll have good weather and safety, Bert,' Nancy said as she held both his hands in hers. 'I'll be thinking of you.'

'Thank you, Nance,' the quiet pilot replied. 'Don't worry.'[35]

At which point he kissed her and then climbed into the cockpit. Always, this was the worst part — leaving Nancy. Chocks away, a wave, and the tiny plane tore down the airstrip, through the last wisps of mist, and was soon a disappearing speck in the eastern skies.

Navigation?

On his lap he had the London *Times Atlas*, and if, a couple of dusks and dawns and several stops later, that little town below him on the North African coast was Tobruk, as he thought, then it must have a small airstrip where he could land and replenish his fuel supply, before snatching a quick sleep and resuming his journey the next day. Somewhere up ahead, he knew, he would see Cairo and pyramids out to his starboard side and about 95 miles after that, according to his atlas, he would spot the Suez Canal. No matter that the scorched desert kept sending up harsh thermal currents to buffet his tiny plane, his trusty compass told him in which direction he needed to steer to cross the canal at the right point and he flew on with as much pluck as confidence, to Jericho, the sands of Syria, the Euphrates River and so on …

Flying in this manner, hopping his way across the world nearly twice as fast as Keith and Ross Smith had done it — they had taken twenty-seven days and twenty hours — Bert Hinkler landed in Darwin on 22 February 1928, less than sixteen days after departure.

Australia went wild, in the now familiar fashion, and the country followed his progress as he continued to fly on to Sydney airport, marvelling that the whole thing had only cost him £55 in the amount he paid for petrol from one side of the planet to another, otherwise stated as a halfpenny a mile![36]

At their home in England, a nervous Nancy was told the news by a journalist just after nine o'clock on a cold Wednesday morning.

'I knew he could do it,' she said. 'But I must admit I've been lying awake almost every night, flying each hop with him. Now that he's there, I'll be able to sleep easily again.'[37]

In London, *The Times* exulted at his breathtaking feat, and even pondered the possibilities of there one day being an airmail service between Great Britain and Australia.[38]

As to Bert, when he approached Bundaberg on a hot afternoon four days after his first Australian landfall in Darwin, it was to find the entire town — and in fact the people of every township within a dozen cooees — gathered around the North Bundaberg recreation reserve, awaiting his arrival. On the ground, his mother had at last been prevailed upon to speak, and was thanking everyone 'for the wonderful reception you are giving my son, and for the thousands of messages received …' when she suddenly broke off with, 'I see my son coming! Goodbye!'[39]

And hello, Bert!

In the bigger cities, the welcome was even greater. At Mascot, an enormous crowd, estimated at 80,000, began singing, '*Hinkler, Hinkler little star, Sixteen days and here you are*,' a line taken from a *Punch* cartoon. So many people wanted to shake his hand everywhere he went that for a time he was reduced to the subterfuge of wearing a bandage around his right hand, but it was no use, as people simply grabbed his left.[40]

I shook his hand, I shook his hand!

He made headlines across the country, poems were penned in his honour, and 'Hustling Hinkler' as he instantly was nicknamed — *sixteen days!* — inspired seven popular songs. At dancehalls, couples began doing the Hinkler Quickstep, while fashionable women began to wear the 'Hinkler Hat', in two-tone felt, with their ears securely covered just as Bert had appeared in so many of those front-page photos. It was London's *Sunday Express*, however, that best captured exactly why he was being so hailed: 'These Antipodean giants help us to look even a Lindbergh in the eye … They enable us to see our prodigies as others see them. Hinkler is a true antidote to our poison of self-humiliation. He provides history a hundred years hence with an excuse for saying that there were giants in those days. A race which breeds a Hinkler is not altogether degenerate …'[41]

Hinkler, it was agreed, was the 'unquestioned monarch of the air'.[42]

•

On the day that Bert Hinkler landed in Australia, Keith Anderson left San Francisco and headed to the same destination. Anderson had had it, for good. Just three days before — while holding a cable from home, from Bon — he had told Smithy he wanted to have a quiet word. He had thought about it, he said, and he was going to go. There was only so long a man could wait by the shore for his ship to come in, or for his plane to go out, and Anderson felt strongly that that time had passed. It was obvious to him, as it must be obvious to Smithy, that their Pacific flight was simply not going to get off the ground and it was time for them all to get on with their lives.

In the end there was nothing that either Kingsford Smith or Ulm could say to dissuade him, though both men tried strongly. Ulm, particularly, was furious at Anderson's decision and felt terribly let down — perhaps because his withdrawal was going to make the finances of their venture all the more precarious as Anderson's mother and uncle would inevitably be insisting on getting their money back. Which was money they didn't have ...

•

At home in Australia, the celebrations went on. All up, in these late days of February 1928, Australia had its aviation hero, and it certainly wasn't Charles Kingsford Smith or — *what's the other guy's name again?* — Charles Ulm. In San Francisco the two aviators read of Hinkler's triumph and, while happy for him, had rarely felt so desolate.

At their lowest ebb, they decided to go to Los Angeles to see if they could sell the *Southern Cross* to the Union Oil Company of California and then ... maybe ... fly it to Australia as employees of the company? It seemed like a good idea, making the best of an exceedingly bad lot.

Some idea of the extent of their penury was that while they were still talking big about flying the entire Pacific Ocean, at this point their biggest problem wasn't that they didn't have the money to buy the petrol to fly to LA. They couldn't even afford the *train fare*.

Somehow, however, they managed to scrounge enough petrol to fly down and arrived with 18 cents between them, half a bottle of bourbon remaining to make them feel better about things and, as if it mattered, a letter of introduction Ulm was carrying that had a vague chance of facilitating access to a supposedly rich banker.[43]

And yet, just as it is known the world over among adventurers from all ages that the 'darkest hour is right before the dawn', so was it proven on this occasion. Not long after the Union Oil Company gave them and their proposal short shrift — and their bourbon and 18 cents were also gone — it so happened that one day in mid-March they were standing rather disconsolately at Rogers airport talking to the president of the Californian Bank of Los Angeles, Andrew Chaffey. And he was *listening* to them! Taking them *seriously*!

Chaffey proved to be an exceedingly friendly American who had once lived in Australia as a lad, courtesy of the fact that his father had worked as an irrigation engineer in Mildura for many years, and he knew just the bloke he would like to introduce them to, one Captain G. Allan Hancock.[44]

Just what the good captain's calling was was not immediately apparent, though he seemed like a nice man, and they didn't mind telling him of their plans for the *Southern Cross* and the terrible troubles they had had in getting it off the ground. The frustrating thing, they told him, was that they knew they had the right plane, and had learnt enough of the lessons from both the Dole Air Race and their own experience over previous months to know that they really could fly the Pacific. It was just that they lacked the last bit of money to make it all happen, and were in fact so deeply in debt that they were on the point of losing everything.

Captain Hancock, on this day, listened, and went for a cruise with them in the *Southern Cross* in the skies above Los Angeles,[45] but said very little. A few days of cadging later, however, came some amazing news from their friendly bank manager, Andrew Chaffey.

He was extending an invitation on behalf of Captain Hancock, who was wondering whether the two Australians would, perhaps, like to accompany him on a cruise in a few days' time, on his steam yacht *Oaxaca* — in reality a small ship — down the Pacific coast to the Mexican port of Mazatlán.

Would they ever! If nothing else, such a trip would provide free accommodation for the Australians and, even more importantly, *free meals.* And speaking of their poverty, both men became suddenly aware that they couldn't possibly go on such a cruise in their current wardrobe, which was so threadbare and patched that on a bad day they could be mistaken for hobos. With some more cadged dollars — because buying new clothes was out of the question — they managed to hire some clothes at a very good rate. (Turns out it was a good rate for a good reason. Neither set of clothes fitted either airman. One set of pants had to be reefed up for Kingsford Smith and the other down for Ulm.)

It was a fairly humbling thing to board such a luxuriously appointed yacht of a millionaire while wearing another man's trousers, but neither aviator focused too heavily on it. It was just a pleasure to be there, and for ten days at least to *pack up their troubles in their old kit bag, and smile, smile, smile boys, that's the style.*

•

An interesting man, Captain Hancock. From very humble beginnings, this child of dirt-poor farmers on the edge of Los Angeles might have remained exactly that if it had not been discovered that the said dirt was in fact afloat on a veritable ocean of oil. First his widowed mother leased 1000 acres of the farm to an oil company, and when that proved fruitful, Hancock decided to put wells on the land that remained. Out of seventy-one wells sunk around the family homestead — right near where the Beverly Wilshire Hotel would later be built at the end of Rodeo Drive — all seventy-one came up gushers!

And yet, far from just sitting back and counting his millions, Hancock continued to invest over the years in everything from banks to railroads to shipping to cinemas; to engage his passions, including helping to fund and occasionally play for the Los Angeles Symphony Orchestra, taking boats and ships on long voyages — hence his 'Captain' honorific by virtue of his master mariner's licence — and to give a lot of his money away to worthy causes.

He was a man of means, matched only by his generosity and charm … and yet both Australians also sensed a certain sadness to him in off-moments, and that story, too, soon emerged as they got to know him on the yacht. A couple of years before, Hancock and his beloved only son, Bertram, then twenty-two years old, had checked into Santa Barbara's luxurious Arlington Hotel just before … an earthquake hit. The hotel had collapsed like a house of cards, and even as Captain Hancock was falling two floors, he was able to catch a 'vivid, never-to-be forgotten glimpse of my son's bed plunging downward in the roaring mass and twisted steel'. The steel rod that impaled Captain Hancock gave him a speech impediment that would be with him for the rest of his life, but Bertram's life had ended instantaneously that night.

Whether Captain Hancock saw in the young Australians all the youthful vigour and dream-pursuit that Bertram had had, he didn't say, but he was certainly paternal in his care for them, and nothing was too good for his guests on the yacht. They rose late for breakfast, sunbathed, chatted, drank, had lunch, played cards, went on jaunts on the motorboat, fished, chatted some more, dressed for dinner, dined like kings, and talked late into the night about anything and everything, including aviation.

And then came the moment.

One night over dinner — *a little more claret, please steward* — as the cruise was nearing its end, Captain Hancock raised the subject himself. Their plane. Their planned trip …

'You're satisfied the *Southern Cross* is the right type of machine for the job?' he asked bluntly.

'Quite,' Smithy replied.

'Why do you want to do this flight?'

'I don't know. I've never asked myself why. I've always known that the Pacific must be flown and I am going to fly it. For glory? For money? For that least of all … I can't see where there would be any money in the job. I guess the real answer is that I can see a future in aerial transport across the oceans.'

Charles Ulm butted in.

'Smithy, you've got the pioneer spirit in you. So have I. We both know that when the trail is broken, others will follow. We want the honour of doing the job first. We want that honour for our countrymen.'

'Yes, Charles, you're right. There are so many reasons why. All of them good reasons. But the flight itself will be child's play to the difficulties of getting started …'[46]

'How much will it cost for you to get into the air?' the captain asked.

Smith looked at Ulm. Ulm looked at Smith.

They knew the exact figure of how much they needed, just as well as they knew how to spell their own names, for it was a figure they had been wrestling with day and night for months, trying vainly to beat it into submission and make it more manageable to no avail. The question was, should they tell Captain Hancock the full amount and likely scare him off doing anything to help, or should they tell him a lower figure in the hope that he would give them enough to at least keep them going until such times as they could get the rest of the money from elsewhere?

It was Charles Ulm who spoke first. Taking a gulp of the white wine and reasoning that they might as well go for the lot because if the captain came across and indeed gave them the money then all their problems — bar actually crossing the Pacific — would be over.

'We need about $16,000,' he said quietly.[47]

There was silence for a moment, leavened only by the sound of the *Oaxaca*'s engines and the lapping of the waters of the Gulf of Mexico. And then Captain Hancock spoke. 'OK,' he said, 'I'll put you into the air. I'll buy the machine from you, boys. I'll see my solicitors and decide the best way to do it.'[48]

For an instant Ulm wanted to leap to his feet and begin dancing around the room, while screaming for joy at the top of his lungs, but just managed to hold it in. As did Kingsford Smith. Just. Instead, they warmly thanked their new benefactor for his munificence and soon retired for the evening.

Kingsford Smith and Ulm went to bed in an attempt to get a good night's sleep, but for both of them it was an all but impossible task. Suddenly, just at a time when it seemed that all was lost, everything had come good with a rush and it … really seemed … as if … they could fly the Pacific!

•

When they were leaving the boat a couple of days later, on the morning of 2 April 1928, Captain Hancock firmly shook them both by the hand and said, 'Boys, you are on your way.'

Ecstatic at their change of fortune, both Australians were back at Mills Field within hours of landing to immediately get to work on the … the …

Where was it? In the spot where they left the *Southern Cross* while they had gone on their cruise there was now just an empty space. What the hell was going on!?!?

Oh. Oh, dear. While they had been on the cruise, their creditors had foreclosed on them and the *Southern Cross* had been taken away by the bailiffs to be sold to the highest bidder. In the end, however, not to worry. This was America. There was generally no problem so great that a big enough cheque couldn't fix it, at least in the short term, and Captain Hancock was indeed as good as his word. Within a couple of days the Australians had the mighty *Southern Cross* restored to them and busily set to work to get her in shape for the journey.

And where as Keith Anderson in all this?

Ulm and Kingsford Smith immediately cabled him in Australia to the effect that they were getting ready to go, but relations quickly became problematic thereafter. For one thing, in no communication with him did they make it clear that they had effectively won the lottery and now had the money they needed. And for another, Anderson cabled that he would only return if they sent him a first-class fare.

One way or another it soon became apparent that they had reached an impasse, and that although Anderson and Kingsford Smith had shared the dream to cross the Pacific for a fair chunk of the previous decade, Anderson was *not* going to come back to be a part of it as Smithy — with Ulm — edged closer to making that dream a reality.

Ulm himself, though, for one, was not sorry. He and Anderson had never got on, and with the positions of pilot and co-pilot already taken by him and Smithy, it wasn't obvious just what position Anderson would fill. He was neither a professional navigator nor radio man, so where would he go? The fact that he didn't return made things much easier.

As to who would be the navigator and radio man, that was quickly solved.

In the course of getting their compasses tested by the best in the business in the US Navy, they asked around for a good navigator and were given a remarkably precise bearing towards a bloke by the name of Captain Harry Lyon, who was in the naval reserve and had served extensively in both the navy and merchant service as a navigator, and had also had a spell captaining his own small ship.

A big drinker and former rum-runner — with the curious predilection of enjoying both brawling and wearing bow ties whatever the circumstances — the rather worn 43-year-old was a first-class navigator.[49] In large part he had learnt at the knee of his father, a rear admiral with the US Navy. Smithy and Ulm met Lyon where they were staying at the Bellevue Hotel, liked him, and were happy when he agreed to join them. For his part, Lyon was impressed with, as he later wrote, 'their extreme earnestness and confidence, not only in the feasibility but of the absolute success of the flight. Then, too, the uncanny thoroughness with which they had been preparing for the flight.'[50]

A few days later, a former navy radio man and now pants salesman from Kansas by the name of Jim Warner was in the shop where he worked in San Francisco, when an old navy mate by the name of 'Packy' rang him up.

'Who,' said Packy, 'do you suppose I ran into the other day?'

'I'll bite.'

'Harry Lyon.'

'Not the old Harry Lyon who was on the old *St Louis*?'

'That's him,' said Packy, 'and he's tangled up with two Australians who are going to fly to Australia. He's going to go as navigator.'

'He's crazy.'

Why, only the year before, in one of his last jobs with the US Navy, Warner had been on one of the ships fruitlessly searching for survivors of the Dole Air Race. Fly to *Australia*? That really was crazy. And yet … selling trousers was kinda dull. And what was that Packy was saying now?

'No, they mean business,' Packy said. 'They need a wireless operator and I thought you might want to go.'

'Say, Packy. I'm a pants salesman. Furthermore, I've never lost anything in Australia. On top of that, I've never been any nearer an airplane than necessary — but tell me, where can I find Harry Lyon?'

'Yah,' yodelled Packy. 'I knew you'd want to go.'

'Nothing doing. I just want to keep Lyon from risking his neck ...'[51]

Within days, Kingsford Smith and Ulm had themselves a first-class radio man, too. Though he had never flown in an aeroplane, the main thing was that there was nothing about radios that Warner didn't know. And while he came across as rather less a knockabout bloke than a rather lugubrious one who had been knocked about through hard living, the Australians were happy to have him on board.

It was now Jim Warner who fine-tuned all the radio equipment similar to the gear that had been installed in the *Dallas Spirit*, piloted by Bill Erwin and Alvin Eichwaldt[52] and which had flown looking for survivors of the Dole Air Race. They had three radios, one of which had been placed in the wing for emergency use if they ditched and were able to saw off the wing for a life raft. One of the two main radios was valved for short-wavelength frequencies for use over vast distances to advise their position and to receive messages in Morse code. The other was in medium wavelength to be used to communicate with ships as they flew over them.

The power for those radios would come from two wind-driven generators, installed on either side of the cockpit exterior, and the 200-foot long-range and 400-foot short-range antennae for each would trail from beneath the plane, from opposite sides of the fuselage.

As to Harry Lyon, he saw to the installation of his navigational table in the rear — complete with a massive map pinned down on each corner, and covered with all his paraphernalia of navigation, including sextants, rulers, pens, dividers and a metal compass. All of these were attached by lengths of string to one central point so they wouldn't go flying off in rough weather.

Certainly the navigational table made it cramped in the back, most particularly for Warner and his radios, but there was no other way. And in fact, the two Americans would be working more closely on this trip than ever before. As an added boon to navigation, it had been arranged that a radio beam would be sent out from Wheeler Field in Hawaii to the US Army's Crissy Field in San Francisco.

If all went well, this would mean that when the *Southern Cross* was on course, Warner would hear a constant reassuring *bzzzz* in his headphones. If they drifted to the north of the correct course, the signal from the beacon would be a series of dots, and to the south a series of dashes. If he heard nothing at all, it would be because the radio had stopped working, they were too far from the beam for it to reach them or they were so hopelessly off course that nothing could save them anyway!

As a further aid to navigation, the *Southern Cross* was blessed with an earth inductor compass, which had only been invented three years earlier to counter the fact that the unavoidable movement and vibration of planes in the air, together with stray electrical currents associated with ferrous metals and radio equipment in close quarters made traditional magnetic compasses less than reliable. The earth inductor compass was designed to align more accurately with the earth's magnetic field, and configured so that Lyon could set the desired course from his position in the back of the plane, and all Smithy and Ulm had to do in the front was to keep the indicator pointing straight upwards to zero. When Lyon changed course to port or starboard, the needle would move away from zero in the appropriate direction and the pilots would have to change direction until it again pointed straight up.

Although Lyon had used sextants many times, he had never used the aviator's 'bubble sextant'. (About this same time the first Australian version of this instrument was being improved for use in aircraft by Patrick Gordon 'Bill' Taylor, a veteran of the Royal Flying Corps, who had continued flying after the war and become interested in solving the problems of aerial navigation. With the help of a Sydney instrument-maker and an aircraft engineer, Taylor took a standard marine sextant and altered the spirit level to create a stable, flat artificial horizon in place of the real one, which was frequently obscured by clouds when you were in the air.[53]) Lyon resolved to get as much practice as possible with the unimproved marine bubble sextant before they took off and initially he was able to sort of simulate a bucking aircraft by having a friend drive fast over a bumpy road while he took readings. Then, when he was competent at that Smithy took him up in a biplane to do it for real.[54]

One way or another, with so many different methods of navigation, it was hoped that Lyon would always be able to determine where they were, and thus what course they needed to set to find the tiny dots in the ocean that were their destination.

To build their fitness for the trip, Kingsford Smith and Ulm embarked on a program where they would frequently go driving for fifteen hours, head back to the airfield to fly for four hours, go running for two hours, then more flying and driving until they had gone for forty hours straight.[55] Bit by bit, they managed it a little more easily as their endurance levels lifted.[56]

As they furiously worked to get themselves and the *Southern Cross* in shape, there was no doubt who the leader was — Kingsford Smith. Now that the project had moved from the realms of business organisation, where Ulm excelled, and into the actual details of the flight, it was the senior pilot who took over and drove his team hard. Certainly there had been many times in his life when he had been scatterbrained and unreliable, when he had been loose in an environment that demanded tightness, when he had been irresponsible in a culture that demanded discipline, but this time it was different. This time, Kingsford Smith was acutely aware both that he was on the edge of fulfilling his long-time dream and that the likely alternative to not fulfilling it was *death*. There was to be no second chances on this, and experience had taught him that just one mistake, just one nut left untightened, one detail left unattended, could spell their d … o … o … m. So let's check, check again, and recheck. Are all the fuel lines cleaned out and their connections tightened? All spare parts for the radio locked away? Carburettors cleaned to within an inch of their lives? Harry, are you positive that you have everything needed for navigation, together with backup systems?

Yes, Harry was damn sure, and now and again, didn't really like Kingsford Smith's attitude. He respected his ability, and his focus, just wasn't used to this kind of intensity, and in fact recorded his impressions of the pilot: 'He is a hellish stickler for perfection. He delegates but is right on top of it. I wouldn't want to fly too often with him. Tough boss. Short tempered. Real individualist.'[57]

The work went on. Courtesy of Captain Hancock's money, Kingsford Smith was able to arrange for a new fabric to be put over the entire fuselage in the Douglas Aircraft facility in Santa Monica in which he frequently slept the night, as well as entirely rebuilding the wings to make them strong enough to hopefully survive the worst Pacific storms.

Safety provisions?

Yes, well ...

They were minimal at best. The key installation was a dump valve on the main petrol tank, which, if activated, would drain the petrol in fifty seconds and then re-seal, hopefully allowing the *Southern Cross* to stay afloat for a lot longer than she otherwise would have if they had to ditch her in the ocean. They also had steel and wood saws on board so that if they were afloat, they would theoretically be able to sever a wing from the plane, and they would stay floating even after the plane itself had sunk. (At least they hoped so.) The *Southern Cross* also carried a small transmitter, encased in a watertight container, with four balloons to carry the aerial aloft if they needed to call for help. Completing their preparations in this field, they also had emergency rations and a small distilling plant to get fresh water from sea water. Still, to save weight they decided not to carry a life raft, life jackets or parachutes. And they also decided as the *Southern Cross* could do without brakes on the ground that they just weren't worth the weight. As Harry Lyon later noted of Kingsford Smith, 'I think he even begrudged the weight of my sextant.'[58]

When asked about the lack of safety provisions, Kingsford Smith was to the point. 'No use cluttering up the machine with that junk,'[59] he laughed lightly.

Supervising closely all the mechanical work on the plane was the legendary Cecil C. 'Doc' Maidment, the most experienced and skilled aviation engineer in America, who specialised in Wright Whirlwind engines. His nickname of 'Doc' was borne of the fact that it was said he could diagnose an engine's ills simply by listening to it for a few moments, before he set about curing those ills in record time. He had worked on Lindbergh's engine, and now he was working on the installation of theirs, and not for nothing would Smithy say of him that he was 'the man who put the whirl in our Whirlwind engines'.[60] When it was done, all the crew required was a happy conjunction of good weather and a full moon and they would be away!

•

This business of building a path across the waters was an extraordinary one. Every day now, from the veranda of his Sydney home, William Kingsford Smith gazed out upon the construction of the massive Sydney Harbour Bridge, as two approaching spans were bit by bit connected to massive pylons that had been built on both sides of the harbour. Soon, according to the diagrams that he pored over in the paper, two massive arches would begin to reach out towards each other across the water.

Retired now, the 76-year-old spent a good many of his days pottering around the garden, solving crossword puzzles and doing the odd handyman thing around the house. His had not been an easy life, and he had never really recovered from his financial misfortune of three decades earlier, the one bad decision that had cost him so dearly.

Against that, he took great comfort from his wider family and a special joy in the achievements of his youngest son, Charles. It was an interesting thing that just as his father had been a distinguished captain of the sea, his son had become a distinguished captain of the air. Yes, perhaps he would have liked to have been a distinguished captain of some kind himself, instead of what he sometimes felt like — a failed bank manager — but still, it was no little thing to be the son and father of such men.

Certainly, William worried about Chilla, but equally had no doubts about his boy's capabilities. From Chilla's teenaged years on he had put himself in danger, and yet had always managed to survive, and also generally to prosper.

This time, though? This time, to attempt to cross the Pacific Ocean with only two tiny stop-off points in between which, if they failed to find, would result in their deaths? The venture seemed incredible. Despite the overwhelming risks his son was taking, however, and his frantic busyness to get everything ready, neither William Kingsford Smith nor his wife Catherine were surprised to receive a cable from him to mark their golden wedding anniversary.[61] Through everything, Chilla had always remained a wonderfully devoted son. And that really was something ...

•

It was the culmination of two years of hard work, and a good day's backbreaking hard yakka. After toiling like navvies with the local Eskimo community to clear a path a mile long and 14 feet wide through the snow on Point Barrow's frozen lagoon, at last, on the afternoon of 15 April 1928, George Wilkins and Ben Eielson took off in their tiny orange Vega and headed for the roof of the world. At that point, their plane weighed in at 4500 pounds, the bulk of which was petrol.

Not in it for the bragging rights so much as for scientific discovery, Wilkins did not head for the North Pole — which Amundsen had already flown over by zeppelin airship and Byrd had reached in another Fokker — but a point 200 miles south that was previously unexplored. When they saw no land there, as had been thought to exist, just endless polar sea, Wilkins had once again added hundreds of thousands of square miles to mankind's knowledge of the planet's geography.

Just over twenty hours and 2200 miles after leaving Point Barrow, they were on their approach to Spitzbergen, Norway, when appalling weather began to force them down. Running low on fuel and at last spotting some land — any land would do under the circumstances — they came back to earth on a desolate island known as Dead Man's Island. For five days and nights they slept in the plane as the blizzard raged all around, and on the sixth day, took off, and completed their journey to Spitzbergen. The world was agog at the feat, and Wilkins and Eielson proceeded on a triumphal tour throughout Europe, which included an audience with King George V, where George Hubert Wilkins was knighted and thereafter became known as Sir Hubert Wilkins.

•

And finally, on the last day of May 1928, they were ready. The *Southern Cross* was ready, the moon was full, and the weather report good. There remained just one more thing to do, in Charles Ulm's view. That was to have Harry Lyon and Jim Warner sign a formal contract which, among other things, prohibited them from making any commercial endorsements; telling or selling their story without the express permission of Kingsford Smith and Ulm; to waive all claims to indemnity in case of injury or death; and to leave the plane at Fiji, by which time the need for a navigator and radio man would be diminished, because Australia was such a big target to aim for. In return, they were promised $500 upon arrival in Fiji, a first-class return berth on a ship back to San Francisco, and another $500 within a month. Both Warner and Lyon were stunned at the terms — clearly, they were being locked out of the spoils of victory if Kingsford Smith and Ulm made it — but were left with little choice but to sign. To refuse would be to make it appear as if they had cold feet, which was unimaginable.[62]

For his part, Charles Ulm was entirely unapologetic. His view was that it was he and Kingsford Smith who had nurtured this dream, taken the risks, got them to this point, and the contract did no more than ensure that Lyon and Warner remain what they were — well-paid hired guns, there to provide a service.

Eleven

ACROSS THE PACIFIC ...

We can't fail, the stars are with us — the stars for which our ship is named — the Southern Cross.

CHARLES KINGSFORD SMITH TO A JOURNALIST FROM THE *NEW YORK TIMES*, BEFORE THE ATTEMPT TO CROSS THE PACIFIC[1]

Kingsford Smith looked like an airman. There was something bird-like about his dapper, short figure, his clean-cut features, his quick movements, his alert air. He spoke rapidly, shortly, tersely. His face was lined by the many anxious hours he had spent in the air, but this rather fine-drawn, care-worn appearance was offset by a bright and sparkling manner.

CHARLES KINGSFORD SMITH'S GREAT FRIEND GEOFFREY RAWSON IN HIS PREFACE TO *MY FLYING LIFE*, BY SIR CHARLES KINGSFORD SMITH

On the misty morning of 31 May 1928, at exactly 8.48 am, the *Southern Cross* made ready to move off down the runway at Oakland airport to take flight, bound for freedom, bound for glory ... bound for Australia. There to watch them go was a pulsing crowd of around a thousand well-wishers, including Captain G. Allan Hancock, incognito, and Smithy's oldest brother, Harold, still rather stunned at his youngest sibling's courage, but glad he had given him a letter to take to the folks at home, which stood a good chance of being the first trans-Pacific bit of airmail ever delivered.[2] Well-wishers had also given the crew good luck charms to go with Smithy's much-loved photo of Nellie Stewart and a Felix the Cat badge on his helmet: a bouquet of flowers, a horseshoe and, most poignantly, the silver ring which had belonged to Alvin Eichwaldt who had perished in a search for survivors of the ill-fated Dole Air Race to Hawaii, given to them by the dead pilot's mother, just before they boarded. They also had with them in the cockpit a silken Australian flag.

In that cockpit, as Smithy ran up each of the engines in turn to a satisfyingly shattering crescendo, he knew there were two possible impediments to a successful take-off. The first was weight. He and Ulm had just managed to get off the ground with the petrol tanks at capacity, but never with the two extra people in the back, and it was always going to be touch and go, as everyone knew. (Not for nothing had the US Army Air Corps parked a fully manned emergency vehicle halfway down the runway.)

And the second possible impediment was a deputy sheriff with an attachment order he wanted to serve on them over the non-payment of some debts.[3] Though Captain Hancock's money had enabled them to pay back nearly everything they owed, there were still a couple of bills outstanding, and the creditors, most particularly one by the name of Tom Catton,[4] had turned nasty. Which made it all the more imperative they get *moving* now. Mercifully, the deputy sheriff was being held back by the same dedicated policemen who were holding the pressing crowd back, officers who were not aware that there was an issue …

It was with extra satisfaction, then, that Smithy gunned it, only to have the centre motor cut out 300 yards down the runway, when they were still at a fat waddle. Bringing the plane to a halt, they found that the problem was an 'altitude control' knob affecting the fuel mixture, which was fixed within a matter of minutes.[5] Harry Lyon, for one, was delighted, as he believed in the mariner's tradition that 'a poor start, is a good ending'.[6] Now, the obvious thing for most people would have been to start again at the beginning of the runway, but the obvious wasn't the best choice when you knew that the deputy sheriff was waiting there.

Upon consideration, Smithy decided it would be better to just start from where they were and chance it. So, with all three engines on full throttle again, the *Southern Cross* began to move off once more …

Another waddle … a jog now … a run … a *sprint* … the machine was hurtling down the runway and seeming to just lift a little, as the watching crowd held its breath. Inside the cockpit, his eyes focused, his lips set, Smithy held her true with the throttles wide open, even as an overflow valve from the central tank gushed petrol upon his shoulders. A mile down the runway the plane lifted a little off the ground … then came back down … then up a little again … and then down … and then up …[7]

Up … *up* … UP, *you beauty.* Staying up! Just a few feet, but getting perceptibly higher with every passing second as the crowd had no sooner let out its breath and everyone was cheering!

In the cockpit of the *Southern Cross*, whatever else, it was a spectacular beginning to the nigh on 7400-mile journey.

At much the same time as the prisoners of Alcatraz heard the sound of screaming engines above them, Kingsford Smith and Ulm could see, out to the right from their cockpit, the bustling rail and car ferry terminus of Sausalito, and beyond that the picturesque fishing village of Tiburon. And now, as they headed straight for the Golden Gate, the channel that connected the bay to the Pacific Ocean, they could glory in the view of San Francisco proper to their left. With the base of it shrouded in fog, it was only the tops of the tall buildings that poked through, giving the metropolis the appearance of being a magical city in the clouds.

Not all of the crew were exuberant, however. Noting the several planes accompanying them for the first few miles, most of which had newspaper photographers on board, Jim Warner couldn't help himself. 'If we do go down,' he told Lyon, 'those photos will make some nice mementos for our friends.'[8]

As Charles Kingsford Smith at last turned away and focused solely on the flight ahead, strong emotions flooded through him. Finally, all the worries, all the problems, the fierce squabbling, the desperation and disappointments were behind them. They were on their way!

Charles Ulm felt much the same and was truly exultant that they were actually setting out on fulfilling a dream they had been separately and jointly nurturing for years. Ulm, though, would acknowledge at a later point that he felt a rather strange presentiment a couple of hours after leaving 'Frisco. From the cheery farewell, and the first lot of sunny skies above and sparkling blue below, they had to climb up over a mountain of slightly forbidding cloud. Looking down upon that formation, into its amazing valleys and ridges from 2000 feet on high, Ulm was suddenly struck by a haunting sense of their complete isolation.

And isolated they truly were. Every second was taking them further away from land and they were still about a dozen hours from the halfway mark, when they would at last be heading *towards* land and their first stop-off point. Strangely, beneath them on the ocean there had so far been no sign of any vessels even though they were flying above what were meant to be fairly busy shipping lanes. Were they indeed on the right course? In the cabin, Harry Lyon checked and rechecked his calculations. Allowing 3 degrees for the southerly drift of wind, he had them on a course of 242 degrees, at the beginning of their Great Circle route to Honolulu. (A curiosity of Harry's style was that he did not keep those calculations in a leather-bound book, like other navigators, but, once done, would scrunch them up and throw them out the window!)[9]

Might this trip be easier than they thought, after all their hard work to get in the air? Might it simply be a matter of pointing the plane in the right direction and letting her rip, giving lie to the local Californian betting agency that had offered odds of 11 to 1 against their even reaching Hawaii?[10] After all, they had passed soon enough through the slightly threatening cloud, and if anything, things were now almost *too* perfect. In a very odd kind of way, the monotony of the blue sea below them, the blue vault above, and the ear-splitting bark of the engines, almost began to *oppress* them.[11]

Now back down to some 1000 feet above the Pacific Ocean, their mighty aeroplane flew on. Both Kingsford Smith and Charles Ulm were generally delighted with how she was performing. (And a 'she' the *Southern Cross* definitely was. A beautiful, protective creation that was going to see them through on this life's journey, and look after them whatever hard times might be coming.)

Meanwhile, Lyon was also giving them updates as to his estimation of how far they had travelled and at one o'clock San Francisco time, told them they had already covered 350 miles of their first hop. They had just over 2000 miles left to go to Hawaii ...

And thar she blew. Seemingly from out of nowhere, they flew into a storm that reduced visibility to nearly nothing and rocked the craft from side to side and up and down, almost as if they were zooming along a terrible aerial road filled with shocking potholes, sudden gullies and sharp corners. With all four of them perched atop wicker chairs that were not attached to the fuselage, with no seat belts, bad bumps could see them airborne in their own right and many curses ensued. Happily, they were soon through it and beneath them a sunny sea quickly appeared again, a shimmering, vivid turquoise so calm that 'not a single fleck of foam marred the endless mirror'.[12]

By now it was 4.30 pm San Francisco time and they had been flying for just over seven and a half hours. *Still* there was no sign of any shipping, which remained a cause of slight concern, but it wasn't as if there was anything they could do about it. Lyon continued to assure them that they were on course, and they were still connected to the rest of the world by the gossamer thread that was the radio beam coming at them from ol' 'Frisco, some 620 miles behind. (Funny, was it *really* only that morning that they had left that magic city in California? Somehow, it seemed extremely difficult to comprehend that that world and this world of aerial wonder could be connected, just by them and eight hours' flight.)

At 6.40 pm Honolulu picked up a Morse message from the *Southern Cross*: 'It's getting dark now. One notices a steady flame pouring out of the exhaust. Engines doing their duty royally, making one feel safe as the pyramids of Egypt.'[13] (This message clearly had not come from Smithy, as he had been inside those pyramids and had not felt safe at all.)

As the twilight began to descend, the 'dream rays lit up a dream city of snowy battlements on the far horizon. The dying sun painted a path of gold across the ocean ...'[14] At this point, Smithy would have loved nothing more than to suck on a cigarette — inevitably someone else's, because though a heavy smoker he was never known to buy his own[15] — but, of course, having a naked flame anywhere near so much petrol was out of the question, and he had to ignore the craving.[16]

Finally, after a long and arduous day, the sun, chased by the *Southern Cross* for the last half of its journey across the skies, at last made its escape and sank into the Pacific for some merciful rest, but not before giving out a last golden burst of blazing light that Smithy would record as, 'a spectacular and glorious sunset as I had seldom seen before'.[17] It seemed to him, in a philosophical moment, to be 'a background of beauty greater by far than anything conceived by the world's masters of painting'.[18]

At 8 pm they had been aloft for just over eleven hours. Like the lights of a Christmas tree being suddenly turned on, the stars burst forth from the velvet sky, gladdening the heart of Harry Lyon, who now had a smorgasbord of twinkling signposts from which to get his bearings. Though it had not been previously planned, Kingsford Smith decided to take the plane up to 4000 feet in the hope of flying over and above whatever storm the night might bring on their course to Hawaii — a course now illumined a little by the silvery full moon, which had wonderfully risen a short time after the sun had gone down.

In the back, Jim Warner felt his spirits — which had been highly troubled by the thought he was on the exact path taken by all the Dole flyers who had died — lift markedly at the sight of the moon. To his mind, it was just like meeting an old friend after a long separation.[19] He gazed for a moment at the lovely moon shadow the *Southern Cross* was making on the cloudy landscape below, and then got back to his work. At least he and Lyon were nothing if not busy.

While Lyon was endlessly taking readings with his sextant, consulting his compasses, scribbling out calculations on his notepad and plotting their position on the map tacked to the table, Warner had his headphones on and was listening to weather reports, receiving messages or tapping them out, all the while listening carefully to make sure that they were 'on beam' — directly on line with the radio signal from Crissy Field. Though it was not easy for 'the boys in the back room' to communicate with the pilots up front — as the passageway between the cockpit and back cabin was almost entirely filled with a petrol tank — after some experimentation they had developed a simple method. With the circular tank fitted into the otherwise rectangular fuselage, there was just space enough for a long stick to be fitted. Thus, when Warner wanted to send a message forward he would scribble it on a piece of paper and attach it to a clip on the end of the stick. Then, by poking the stick through the gap he could prod Kingsford Smith's shoulder to get his attention.

When, in turn, Smithy wanted to get a message to the men in the back he would attach his own scribbled piece of paper to the stick and shake it, at which point they would pull it back into their little cave to devour.

A fair measure of these messages were bright banter. None was Smithy's private fears and anxieties. Yet the truth was that as night fell, so did his spirits. Was everything all right? What effect was the terrific vibration of the three thundering engines having on the rest of the *Southern Cross*? How much of the lifeblood of the plane, the oil, were those engines soaking up? And then there was the petrol, always the petrol. Wild, coursing numbers jumbled, tumbled, rumbled through his head — of distance to travel, fuel consumed, fuel still on hand and time remaining — and sometimes it seemed to him they wouldn't even get close to Hawaii. In bad moments he wished he was thousands of miles away from any aeroplane engine, instead of huddled under three of them. His legs were cramped, and his bad foot hurt. And he was *dying* for a cigarette.

The *Southern Cross* droned on ...[20]

•

Long-distance flying at night was an entirely different art from flying during the day. At 10 pm, Lyon lay down on the floor and jammed opened the door at a 45-degree angle and dropped out a floating flare. This flare was so designed that the moment it hit the water a white phosphorous blaze appeared and remained visible for at least twenty minutes. By keeping his eyes set upon it through his drift meter, long after they had passed over, it was a relatively easy matter to estimate how much the wind was pushing them off course, and therefore what their 'rate of drift' was. On this occasion, Lyon was able to tell his pilots that the wind was pushing them just a little to the south, and so they altered course a couple of degrees to the north. Ideally, that would neutralise the wind drift and they would again be flying exactly on course.

Just before midnight came their first genuinely heavy weather, as their relentless bird suddenly charged into heavy rain clouds and they were buffeted from side to side in complete blackness. To get clear of it, Smithy 'took 'er up', climbing even higher, to 4800 feet, to escape the whole mess and …

And always it was the same thing when you surfaced from a storm like that. Just lovely! After being pummelled from all sides, with lashing rain and wind, all of it in evil and threatening darkness, suddenly you burst through … and all was calm … with the most active thing happening being the winking of the stars above, saying 'welcome back'.

Which was greatly cheering, to a point … It wasn't long, however, before Kingsford Smith and Ulm's previous sense of total isolation, of being in a small craft alone on a vast planet, returned. They were nothing less than downright lonely.

Just before two o'clock in the morning, though, at last, they saw exactly what their eyes had been straining to see: a light, a light in the darkness! It could only belong to a ship. Someone must be alive down there!

And so they were. As the *Southern Cross* flew closer, what had appeared to be one small light turned quickly into many lights, grouped tightly together, the outline of which framed the rough shape of a steamer. Yes! The vision of that craft in the night was like a friendly hand stretched out to them in the wilderness.[21]

Excitedly, Kingsford Smith signalled for Ulm to take the controls, and circle the craft, while he manned the specially installed searchlight fitted with a Morse key, designed to flash pulses of light when he pressed a button in the cockpit. Using the skills he had learned in the Signal Corps all those years ago, he bumped out the letters in Morse code — *dah dah dah, dah dit dah, dit dit dit, dah dit dah dit* — as in O K S C, which in turn stood for *OK Southern Cross.*[22] The ship, ploughing through the waves below, flashed back in return its own name, SS *Maliko.* While the flashing lights between them were essentially fun in the darkness, the serious work was done by the two 'brass pounders', the radio men of the two craft, with Warner soon telling them that he had received an exact fix from the *Maliko* on where they were and the news was fairly good. They were only a few miles to the north of their appointed course and the adjustment was easily made.

It felt strange to the men on the *Southern Cross* how instantaneously they had established such a strong sense of communion with the men below in the middle of the ocean, men whom they had never seen, were not seeing now, and would never see in the future. But for the flying crew, who for hours had been feeling like an insignificant speck all alone in the universe, the bond they felt was powerful.

And yet in only thirty seconds their ship in the night slipped backwards and they were alone again, although immeasurably cheered by the brief encounter. Yet, less than half an hour later James Warner poked a note forward saying that he had been in radio contact with another ship, the SS *Manoa*, and that they should shortly see it up ahead, and sure enough …

Once more, a similar scene played out, with messages winking back and forth in the blackness, and then they were on their way again, at three o'clock in the morning. (This time Warner had the presence of mind to find out from the *Manoa* radio operator just who had won the big baseball game the previous afternoon, and he was joyous to hear that the wonderful New York Yankees had done it again, and beaten the Washington Senators 4–0![23])

•

In Longueville, Mr and Mrs Kingsford Smith sat through the night, with family and friends, glued to the wireless, anxiously waiting to hear the latest information. And, of course, they were not the only ones. All across the western seaboard of Canada and the United States, together with Hawaii and aboard many ships that were within range of the *Southern Cross*'s transmitters, radio professionals and hundreds of amateur radio 'hams' were listening in to the Morse code transmissions from the plane and even marking out on maps where they reckoned it to be. Those messages were also picked up by the La Perouse Receiving Centre near Sydney, where they were decoded and relayed to local radio stations.

•

Shortly after the dawn of 1 June 1928 seeped over the horizon, Lyon informed the pilots via the message stick that they were just 375 miles from Honolulu. They had made it through the dark night, and their optimism began to rise that they were in fact, maybe, going to make it! As the sun continued to rise a splendid vista of the marvellous world of the cloudlands they were traversing revealed itself, complete with canyons, cliffs, foothills, mountains and vast shimmering plains stretching away to never-never land.

Just a few hours later, not long after 8 am, from a height of 1250 feet, they saw it. Way off on their port bow, in a slightly surprising direction — but who were they to argue? — there were cliffs rising from the sea and disappearing into cloud.

You bloody beauty! In the cockpit of the *Southern Cross*, a broadly grinning Kingsford Smith and Ulm shared a triumphal handshake, before Smithy nosed the plane over towards the cliffs. In the rear, however, Harry Lyon was not nearly so exuberant. Having spent four years trading in these parts, he knew the islands well, and was troubled that he didn't recognise this landfall at all. Sure enough, as they drew closer the cliffs suddenly popped up further out of the sea and drifted away …

With a sinking feeling in the pit of their stomachs, the men realised that the whole thing had been a mirage! What they had been seeing was merely what they wanted to see in the cloud formations, instead of what was actually there. It was deeply disappointing, and a lot worrying, but there was nothing they could do but proceed on their original course based on the setting that Lyon gave them, with their eyes scanning the horizon all the while, willing land to appear and trying to work out what was real and what was not. In the back, Jim Warner was becoming more than a little skittish, as his wandering mind kept returning to the Dole flyers. In the hope of easing his concerns, he passed a note to Lyon asking whether they were lost.

YES, Lyon scrawled back.[24] Of the radio beam that had meant to be coming to them from Wheeler Field in Hawaii, there was nothing — because of a problem with the batteries in their receiver. Christ Almighty.

At this point Warner sent out a lugubrious radio message to the world at large:

> I guess we really are lost. Radio 'A' battery down. Please get ship with receiver to get our bearings on my 740 wave. Will keep going so that they can track us.[25]

And then, mercifully, they really did see it: land. *Real* land. There!

Just before 10 am local time, Kingsford Smith knew that he had the island of Molokai off his port bow and steered towards it ... only to have it disappear on them again! What had appeared to be an island again was in fact no more than the shadow thrown by a wayward cloud. Despite everything, they were still out there in the middle of the ocean, totally alone, totally dependent on finding land. Soon.

Though they continued to sight mirages here and there, generally they kept to their course and, just before eleven o'clock, were rewarded with a vision of high land that didn't recede when they approached it, but simply grew bigger and more impressive. What they were staring at was a mountain, a high peak, poking above the clouds. This time there really was no doubt.

A note came forwards from Lyon: *How high is that lump of land?*

About 12,000 feet, Ulm replied with his pencil.

It was, obviously, Hawaii's highest point, the mountain of Mauna Kea — two words which, in the local language meant 'white mountain', courtesy of the fact that its summit was so high it was regularly snowcapped, even in such tropical climes. Now being able to determine exactly where they were, in no time at all — just a little over thirty minutes — they were able to have Maui on the port beam and Molokai on the port bow. Hawaii was at their mercy!

And this time there was no mistake. A bevy of planes had come out to greet them and escort them above the beautiful, fresh greenery of the island — where a patchwork of sugarcane plantations looked like massive garden lawns, amid which the waving people were happy ants — to the landing ground of their dreams. At last, at 12.17 pm, the *Southern Cross* touched down at Wheeler Field, a spot situated 22 miles from Honolulu, and, far more importantly, 2408 miles from San Francisco! They had been in the air for twenty-seven hours and twenty-five minutes, and were on course to do exactly what they had set out to do — conquer the previously unconquerable Pacific Ocean.

When Smithy had brought the plane to a stop and turned all three engines off, the strangest thing happened — a sudden sense of unreality for all of them. For while those roaring engines had indeed been halted, the roaring engine in their heads just wouldn't quit. As they clambered out of the plane, people were talking to them, excitedly crowding around the bleary-eyed and unshaven new arrivals from the heavens like hot children round cold ice-cream, and throwing traditional leis around their necks,[26] but for the life of them none of the crew could hear what they were saying.

Yes … no … what? Delighted. To Jim Warner, everyone sounded like a whole lot of quacking ducks.[27] In the end all they could do was to keep nodding their heads, read their hosts' faces the best they could, keep smiling and try to catch a word here and there in the hope that the shattering noise in their heads would soon stop.

For all that, the warmth of their reception was astounding. The next day was filled with both receiving overwhelming hospitality and expending considerable effort to get away from it, so that they could as quickly as possible be on their way once more. Women fluttered flirtatiously around them while complete strangers clapped them on the back like long-lost brothers and begged to buy them a drink, and they practically needed a social secretary to sort out all the invitations they received. Most invitations had to be refused, as the pressing thing was to get the *Southern Cross* in shape so they could take off again. And yet, the morning after arriving, Kingsford Smith and Ulm happily agreed to make time for the local press to have their photos taken in bathing suits on a sunny Hawaiian beach, while Warner and Lyon looked on in their hot suits, the latter swearing darkly under his breath. Were the pilots the *only* ones who had flown to Hawaii, excuse me, or had he and Jim been on the same flaming plane?[28]

But back to the work of getting away. While it was one thing to land on the relatively short Wheeler Field with tanks that were nearly empty, it was always going to be out of the question to leave from there because with full tanks a much longer runway would be required. For the moment, though, while they rested at the Royal Hawaiian Hotel right on Waikiki Beach, army mechanics worked on the *Southern Cross* and put just 700 gallons back into the tanks, which was just a little over half of its capacity. This allowed them to easily take off the next day and fly 90 miles to that part of the Hawaiian archipelago that Keith Anderson had reconnoitred for them the previous year, Kauai Island, where more fuel awaited them.

•

In Australia, meantime, there was a veritable bushfire of coverage for the journey of the *Southern Cross* as blow-by-blow front-page accounts covered nigh on every paper in the land, and no detail was too obscure or minute to include as a ravenous public devoured it all. Maps showed the plane's route, feature articles focused its technological aspects such as fuel tanks, wireless sets and generator, and every message the airmen had sent over the radio was faithfully recorded, as was every utterance they had said in the public domain since landing.[29] In Arabella Street, it wasn't worth Catherine's while closing the door as the stream of journalists and friends and relatives was so constant it was close to an unbroken chain and ...

Elsie, can you get some more tea at the corner store, because we have run out again!

The coverage in places like America and Europe for the flight was, while not as extensive, certainly comprehensive. The *New York Times*, which rather fancied itself as at the centre of the aviation world, was particularly focused on the flight.

•

That night the crew slept in the grand home of one of the Kauai residents, and in the wee hours of the morning were roused and taken to their plane, at one end of Barking Sands beach. The moon was still bright, the air languidly muggy and, most importantly of all, the weather was clear.

After Smithy had warmed up the engines — enough to heat the oil so it would flow more freely and lubricate the engines for the stresses of take-off and to produce full power, but not so much that more fuel than necessary was consumed in the process — they were ready. At Smithy's instigation, one man stood 3500 feet down the 4000-foot long beach, to give him a good indication of just how much distance he had to play with for take-off.

Ready?

Ready.

And *now*. With all three engines at full and terrible throttle the *Southern Cross* started slowly lurching down the beach in the moonlight, as all those who had helped them stood back and covered their ears.

Barking Sands was so named because of the curious sound made by the sands when stepped upon — *Arf! Arf! Arf!* — but never in all its existence had it borne the kind of weight it did then. At first, it seemed that this time the men really had overloaded the *Southern Cross*, as the plane and the beach simply refused to part company for anything more than a little hop, and the take-off had to be aborted. Finally, however, at 5.22 am on Sunday, 3 June 1928, the *Southern Cross*, laden down with just under 1300 gallons of fuel, started whizzing along the beach with sufficient speed — *Aaaaaaaaaaaarf!* — that some 3400 feet along[30] she was airborne. *Just*. The nearly full moon, preparing for a partial eclipse on the next night, lay low on the western horizon and surveyed benignly this newcomer to the skies.[31]

The *Southern Cross* remained perilously close to the water for all that, and they were 25 miles out to sea before they could rise high enough that in the back Jim Warner could safely reel out his radio antennae, which hung from small weights from both sides of the plane. For the life of him he couldn't work out how Smithy had got her aloft and, as he later recorded: 'I think Smith "wished" her into the air for those first few miles. There's a Pilot!'[32]

But they were not out of danger. Smithy had no sooner got her up to 300 feet than the plane suddenly went through a series of huge bumps, as thought it were a brick bouncing down steep and irregular stairs. Smithy's arms ached in his sockets as he tried to hold her aloft, and he fully expected one or both wings to crumple under the massive strain they were enduring.[33] By the time the turbulence settled down five minutes later, and they had climbed to 600 feet, he was wringing wet with sweat and white as a sheet, his lips pursed and bloodless. That had been close.

But, at least they were still going. Next stop, Suva, some 3150 miles away! This was to be the longest hop on their trip, and certainly it was always going to be the most challenging. They had even added smelling salts to their usual provisions, on the reckoning that staying awake for such a long journey was likely to be one of their many enormous challenges.[34] The day before, the *Honolulu Advertiser* had characterised it as 'a flight to stagger the imagination'. Just this leg alone, after all, was the rough equivalent of the distance of Lindbergh's flight of the year before, except in this instance there would be no broad barn door of the coasts of Europe and Africa to hit if their direction was off — just the tiny dots of Fiji.

Heading 213.75 degrees south-west by south from Hawaii, Kingsford Smith found his thoughts turning to the grandiloquent. While others before them had forged the aerial passage between the mainland of America and Hawaii, the same could not be said for the passage to Fiji.

'Balbao,' he later wrote, firmly identifying with the captain and not the crew, 'had been the first white man to set eyes on the Pacific; Magellan had been the first to furrow its water with his keel; Bligh had navigated its unknown water for 3000 miles in an open boat. I felt that we were following in the footsteps of these great predecessors, and that we could claim kinship with them. They had traversed virgin waters; we were about to traverse virgin air.'[35]

And he also momentarily had time to let his mind drift to other things. Like his old mate Keith Anderson. As well as everything was going with Charles Ulm, he allowed himself a moment of quiet yearning that things had been able to work out so that Keith could have been with them. What, he wondered idly, would Keith be doing now? And how would he be taking all the publicity that their attempt seemed to be generating? Still, it was just a passing thought, and before long the demands of the flight completely absorbed him once more. From the moment the last wisp of vision of the mountain of Mauna Kea disappeared behind them and all that appeared ahead was a vast vault of blue — with the sky and sea merging with no discernible line of horizon between them — both Kingsford Smith and Ulm felt once more a sense of lonely vulnerability wash over them. Could this really be done?

At least for the moment it seemed so — the weather was benign, the motors of the *Southern Cross* were rumbling away and sounded as sweet to Smithy's ears as the choir of St Andrew's had to his mother so many years ago, as their path across the now slightly less mighty Pacific Ocean stretched before them.

And yet … harbingers of doom do not, of course, announce themselves like thunder. Sometimes it is the tiniest of tiny things that can signal the certainty of oncoming disaster. So it was, just a few hours into the trip to Fiji, when Kingsford Smith's roaring reverie of engine noise was interrupted by a nudge in his ribs from Charles Ulm. His co-pilot was pointing with alarm at a tiny trickle of liquid which looked to be seeping from the bottom of the petrol tank situated in their port wing and running back along that wing towards them.

If that was indeed petrol, they were as good as dead, as there were only two possibilities: if they were lucky in their catastrophe, the petrol would ignite and they would be dead in an instant; if they were unlucky, they would run out of petrol and would have to ditch in the ocean, where the likelihood was that a slow and agonising death would await them.

It was with great trepidation thus, that Kingsford Smith removed his flying gloves and put a finger on the rivulet beneath the wing. He then put his finger in his mouth to taste it. Kingsford Smith looked at Ulm and laughed.

It was *water*!

The heavily humid air they were travelling through was condensing when in contact with the cold petrol pipe. They were safe for the moment. But while the possibility of one major catastrophe had faded, it was not long before another potentially all too real disaster arrived.

A prod in Smithy's shoulder was his first warning. It was from Warner. He had lost the buzz from Wheeler Field. The radio had packed it in. He didn't know quite what the problem was, and he was going to try and fix it, but that was the situation as it stood. It was the kind of news that could almost make the fiery conflagration they had just been contemplating look momentarily appealing — for nothing could be worse than getting lost over this endless Pacific and being condemned to continue looking for Fiji until their petrol ran out — but there was no panic. While the radio had been their surest method of checking that they were on track, Smithy was confident that either Warner would be able to fix it or they would still be able to continue to navigate by the other methods of sextant, compass bearings and dead reckoning. The fact that they were no longer in contact with the world markedly increased their sense of isolation, and yet there was little time to contemplate that.

For they were soon heading into a heavy storm, and obliged to climb hard to get out of the driving rain and tearing, ripping gusts as the *Southern Cross* once again bounced upon the bumpy air road in near darkness.

As near as Lyon could work out, by 12.45 pm Honolulu time — some seven and a half hours after they had taken off — the *Southern Cross* had flown 630 miles, with just over 2500 miles still to go to reach Fiji, meaning they were nearly one-fifth of the way through what would be the longest trans-oceanic flight to date.

If they made it …

Some hours later, just after 3.30 pm … *What was that?* A seeming cough from the starboard motor. Pilots listen to engines with the seat of their pants, taking in vibrations every bit as much as with their ears soaking up sounds — hence the expression 'flying by the seat of your pants'[36] — and there was no mistake.

For there it was again. A cough, then a splutter. Bound as one, the ears of all four men on the *Southern Cross* focused on that cough, *willing* it to stop, to right itself, to return to normal … for that engine to continue to carry them across the seas, towards land and safety. And, eight exceedingly long minutes later, maybe it worked. Just as suddenly as it had begun, the coughing stopped and the starboard motor resumed its sweet symphony of pounding pistons, as if being conducted by God Himself.

What had caused the coughing they knew not, nor whether it might return, though in all likelihood it was a speck of dirt stuck in the carburettor that had at last been blown through. The important thing was that it had stopped and they weren't going to be obliged to ditch in the angry sea without even the wherewithal to tell the world where they were.

From the back shortly afterwards came some good news. After long labour in difficult conditions Warner had managed to get the radio to work again.

By five o'clock Lyon's reckoning was that Hawaii was 1000 miles behind them and Fiji just a bit over 2000 miles ahead.

Now, as darkness began to fall, it wasn't immediately apparent if the clouds ahead were blackening in solidarity or of their own accord, as the sun sank, but the crew of the *Southern Cross* was not left wondering for long. In short order the four men in their tiny airborne capsule were in the middle of a major storm from which there seemed to be no respite. Smithy tried to fly above it … but after going all the way up to 5000 feet there was still no break in the deluge. The question was whether to go back down, or use more precious petrol on the chance that there would be relief higher up?

After consideration he decided on the latter and powered higher, in still very heavy going. At last, at 8000 feet, they burst up out of the storm, to see the Southern Cross constellation itself!

•

Courtesy of Warner, an almost blow-by-blow account of their adventures was being picked up by the many radio listeners in Hawaii and on ships dotted throughout the Pacific. At 6.10 pm, Honolulu time, for example, the following message came through:

> We are hitting something. Made a short, sharp turn amid heavy banks of clouds. Altitude 6,000 feet. Smithy still banking for altitude. It's a bit bumpy here now. The air currents are changing.

And then the messages continued:

> 6.12 p.m. A little spitting from the left motor now.
>
> 6.20 p.m. It's going to be a bad night. Motors are doing heavy pulling. Getting dark. Motors straining.
>
> 7.48 p.m. Still trying to gain altitude to avoid storm clouds. Our old friend the moon peeping over a bank of clouds.
>
> 10.43 p.m. That man Smithy deserves credit. He is a good pilot.

And indeed he was, having guided them through a heavy storm over the preceding few hours, without a break, as the *Southern Cross* continued on its appointed course. It was rising midnight when Lyon passed forward a note in his scrawling hand: *Just crossed the equator.*[37]

It was as good a sign as any that they were on the homeward run.

•

In Sydney there was enormous excitement in the ABC's 2BL radio studios at William Street. They were picking up the radio signals from the *Southern Cross*, clear enough that they could translate the Morse code! They immediately did so and broadcast the news, and continued to thereafter, giving their listeners regular updates as soon as possible. And soon, listeners around the country were huddled around their sets. The first message put to air just before midnight on that evening of 4 June recorded the position of the *Southern Cross*: latitude 3 degrees south, longitude 171 degrees west.[38]

•

By the time the sun was about to catch up with the *Southern Cross* again, as dawn approached, they were again flying through heavy storms and into a howling headwind which sapped their precious petrol reserves for little progress. The gnawing fear began to grow that they simply wouldn't have enough to make it, and they began to do tense calculations to ascertain just how much juice remained.

Smithy worked it out to be just five hours' fuel left, which would be not nearly enough, while Ulm reckoned there might be as much as nine hours' worth in the tanks, which meant they *might* make it. Still, as the headwind continued and Smithy tried in vain to get above or below it, it was obvious that however much fuel there was, it was being drained quickly.

At ten o'clock in the morning, after thirty-two hours in the air, Smithy ordered Lyon and Warner to regularly report their position over the airwaves, while he flew on and Ulm checked the petrol that remained. The only way to do this was by hand pumping it from the main tank to the gravity tank and counting how many full pumps it took.

Now, as Ulm took long, precise strokes with the pump, Smithy watched nervously and began counting. Each full stroke meant about another 4 miles that they would be able to fly. As Ulm got to 100 strokes, it meant that there was at least the five hours left that Smithy had calculated, and 400 miles, and every stroke thereafter was a joy and a bonus.

And so it went ... 112 ... 116 ... 120 ... and *still* he was going![39] Finally the pump gurgled in protest that there was nothing left on the 136th stroke, and this meant that they had just over seven hours' flying left in the tanks. Neither Smithy's nor Ulm's cheers made any impact against the shriek of the engines, but they cheered just the same. It was going to be close, but they were still in with a chance of flying all the way to Suva.

In the back, Jim Warner, feeling much more positive, decided to take a look out the window, and was momentarily disconcerted to find himself wet. *Warm rain*, he scribbled in a note to his mate, Lyon, once he had ducked his head back in.

Lyon, however, who could see a little into the cockpit — and noted that after Ulm had relieved Smithy at the controls, Smithy had in fact relieved *himself* into a bottle, which he then emptied out the window — was highly amused.

NO. SMITHY! Lyon replied.[40]

Warner was not so amused and yet things were about to get a whole lot worse. Relieving himself in a manner that required something more than a bottle, he was squatting over a bit of spread newspaper when the *Southern Cross* hit bad turbulence, causing him to fall back into his own waste. What could he do? It was all over him. Him, a trouser salesman. Wiping himself down with the parts of his trousers and underpants that were not already soiled, he threw the lot out the window, and he sat back down to his radio, naked from the waist down.[41]

A few droning hours more, and then for Kingsford Smith it was time for a rest and he handed control of the *Southern Cross* over to Ulm, just as he had throughout the whole journey whenever he needed a short snooze in the pilot's chair. In the back, in the absence of real land appearing, Harry Lyon and Jim Warner consoled themselves by gazing longingly at the chart, where they could see the tiny dots representing the Fiji group.[42]

In those conditions — being buffeted from side to side beneath three shatteringly loud engines, as the rain continued to leak into the cockpit — it was not possible for Kingsford Smith to really sleep. Rather, it was not much more than a light doze where, while one part of his brain shut down, another part hovered on the surface of consciousness, ready to leap into action at the tiniest change in conditions. Three hours after he closed his eyes, Smithy was suddenly alert and swearing loudly at Ulm as soon as he became aware that the direction of their bird had changed. Convinced that Ulm himself had fallen asleep at the wheel, it took Kingsford Smith a few seconds and a sharp nudge in the ribs from his co-pilot before he realised that there had been a very good reason for the altered course.

And yet, far from apologising as Smithy might have expected him to, Ulm was — extremely rarely for him — smiling broadly at him and pointing to the far horizon. Land ho!

Fiji!

Or at least one of the Fijian islands, sitting 'like a brown bulge on a floor of blue'.[43] But which one? To allow Harry Lyon to get a solid sighting with his sextant, Ulm took the *Southern Cross* down to as close to sea level as was safe ... whereupon an amazing thing happened. Right before their eyes, the island simply disappeared, as if Harry Houdini himself had been on the job. Had this just been *another* mirage? Were they, in fact, still on their own in the middle of the deep blue sea, with no sign of land in any direction?

Harry took his sights regardless, while Ulm took the *Southern Cross* higher again. Equally magically — hey, presto! — the island reappeared! How could that be?

They realised: whereas at 10,000 feet on a clear day they could see over 100 miles to the horizon, at sea-level they could only see 3 miles. Thus, when they had descended, Fiji, then some 70 miles away, had disappeared, before slipping back into their vision once they rose.

All to the good then. The main thing was that Harry Lyon, from his calculations, had established that the land they were looking at was Exploring Island — the *easternmost* island of the whole Fiji group. Despite nearly missing it, they had indeed found it, which was the good news ...

The bad news was that, a few minutes later, they crossed the international dateline, and, just like that, even though the time didn't change, they went from Monday to Tuesday. Still, not to worry, as they flew like an arrow towards their destination ...

And then they saw it: Fiji ahoy! Gazing out, they could see frothing white surf and backwash around lots of small islands, swaying palm trees and thatched roofs jutting gently through the thick green foliage that seemed to cover just about everything. They could also see villagers running out into the road, looking up gobsmacked at something they had never seen in their lives before — a 'bird-ship'!

And yet, were they saved after all? As they came in over the spot in downtown Suva that the Fijian authorities had selected for them to land on, an extended sports field called Albert Park, their hearts sank ...

It was big for a football field, certainly, but less than tiny for a landing space, with no more than 400 yards to pull up on. And here they were, flying the biggest and heaviest Fokker that had ever been constructed, a plane which usually needed at least 500 yards to come to a halt. With one glance it was obvious that this was a landing that could only be attempted by one of the best pilots in the world. Fortunately, they had such a one on board, in the person of Charles Kingsford Smith ...

Smithy took the plane around the field to get the lie of the land — even as the citizens of Suva streamed from all directions to the field, all of them gazing skywards at the *Southern Cross*, its wings glistening in the sunlight — and then came around on one last loop to begin his landing run.

Oh ... *shiiiiit.*

It was only when they were lining up on the approach, at 3.50 pm on that sultry tropical afternoon, that Smithy noticed there was an enormous 12-foot drop from the roadway at the southern end of Albert Park. This meant he couldn't get a clear path to touch down at the beginning of the field as he had anticipated and could only hope to land about one-third of the way in; approaching from the south-west to increase the distance available, marginally, by angling diagonally across the field. So it was that the mighty *Southern Cross* — oddly enough surrounded by a flock of enormous white seabirds which seemed to be guiding her in, as a matter of professional respect[44] — touched down at a speed of 65 miles per hour, and with no brakes, only 270 yards to play with, a hill lined with trees and thick undergrowth right in front barring a second chance, and thousands of people all around, many of them watching in horror.

They didn't know much about planes, but couldn't for the life of them see how this speeding monster could possibly slow in time. On the balcony of the nearby Grand Pacific Hotel, many members of the ruling aristocracy who had decided not to face the discomfort of being in the pressing muskiness of the crowd below, now, almost as one, stopped sipping their gins and tonic. How could this chap *possibly* make it?

To try to slow the plane, Smithy began to swerve it as much as possible from side to side, to take a few miles an hour off each time. Two hundred yards ... 150 yards ... 100 yards ... the plane was still hurtling forward at such pace it was a certainty there was going to be grief.

Fifty yards ... 25 yards and still going fast ... *It's going to hit the trees!*

And so it would have if, at the last possible instant, Kingsford Smith hadn't pulled his control wheel down hard to the left and given the rudder a boot while opening up the taps on the starboard motor to violently alter the entire direction of the plane. For an instant, as the left wing dipped and the wheels skidded, it looked as if the plane would topple, but then after a screaming, teetering 'ground-loop', as aviators called it, the plane settled and stopped, facing directly back towards the way it had come. Kingsford Smith had done it!

Pandemonium broke out. In an instant the capacity of the crowd to control itself was shattered and people rushed forward through the overwhelmed police cordon to greet the first plane to visit Fiji, and the one which had just made the longest aerial hop on record — 3138 miles, non-stop, in thirty-four hours and thirty minutes.[45]

In the *Southern Cross* the feeling was overwhelmingly joyous as Charles Kingsford Smith, Charles Ulm, Harry Lyon and Jim War ... hang on ... *Where was Jim Warner?*

Oh.

Oh dear.

Jammed right into the back of the plane for safety's sake, at Smithy's request, the still naked-from-the-waist-down Warner had had the misfortune, in all the shocks and bumps of the difficult landing, to have fallen through the fuselage's thin fabric covering and, as later revealed by author Ian Mackersey, had been knocked out cold once he hit the turf. Fortunately for him, a nurse rushed forward from the madding crowd, covered him with her cape and slowly brought him around.[46]

In the meantime, Kingsford Smith, ever the showman, had emerged from the plane — which was later found to have just 30 gallons of fuel left in its tanks[47] — and was smiling and waving at the throng. As he later recalled: 'As I stepped out to face the crowd I had a feeling of exaltation, a sense of accomplishment.'[48]

In all the hullaballoo, a well-dressed gentleman stepped forward and addressed Kingsford Smith.

'I congratulate you,' he said. 'Will you all lunch with me tomorrow?'

'Yes. Isn't it?' Kingsford Smith replied, taking, as he was now getting used to, a wild stab in the dark as to what the gentleman had just said.

Whereupon the man put his mouth closer to the aviator's ear and said something much louder, but equally incomprehensible.

'Excuse me,' Kingsford Smith replied. 'I didn't catch your name.'

It was Sir Eyre Hutson, British High Commissioner of the Western Pacific and Governor of Fiji, and he was inviting them to lunch at Government House the following day.

The cheering continued, even as the aviators were at last able to make their way to the nearby Grand Pacific Hotel — with its gorgeous deep-shaded verandas perfect for catching the cooling sea breezes — for some precious rest. Behind them, as the Governor had declared a day of national holiday to celebrate this momentous event, most of the population of Suva was either gathering around or filing past this bizarre thing that had appeared from the skies, this *Southern Cross*. Among them, one particularly grizzle-haired Fijian, an older man with many tribal scars, who just a few minutes before had been running around and shouting with the best of them in the carnival air of great excitement, had now calmed, and was overheard to ask in his own language: 'But what are they all doing this for?'[49]

•

Back in Australia, it was the Attorney-General, the Right Honourable John Latham who, in the temporary absence of Prime Minister Stanley Bruce, rose to break the wonderful news, his voice ringing proudly through the august chamber: 'It is with pride and pleasure that I announce to the House that Captain Kingsford Smith and his companions [have] arrived safely at Suva ...'[50]

In response, the House broke into applause, and there were so many resounding cheers and cries of 'Bravo!' 'Bravo!' 'Bravo!' and 'Hear, Hear! Hear, Hear!' that it was a few moments before the Attorney-General could continue.

'On behalf of the government and the members of this House and of the people of Australia, I take this opportunity to congratulate them upon their wonderful and gallant exploit ... It has been decided by the government to make a grant of £5,000 to Captain Kingsford Smith and his associates, as a recognition of a feat of aviation of which Australians are proud ...'

'Hear, Hear! Hear, Hear!'

An indication of the general mood of bipartisan celebration was that his words were promptly seconded by the newly installed Opposition leader, James Scullin. 'On behalf of those honourable members who sit on this side of the House, I desire to endorse most cordially the congratulatory statements of the Attorney-General, Mr Latham. I agree with the honourable gentleman that the flight of Captain Kingsford Smith and his gallant companions has many wonderful features. It is a performance by Australians of which Australia ought to, and does, feel proud. I read recently the statement of an American writer that the six leading flight men of the world all hail from this country. That is a distinction of which we have every reason to feel proud ...'[51]

(Exactly. And who was Charles Lindbergh when he was at home, anyway?)

In short order, this same Australian government, which had all but totally ignored Kingsford Smith and Ulm over the previous twelve months, now deployed the destroyer *Anzac* to leave Port Stephens, north of Newcastle, and head into the Pacific, positioning itself along the route between Brisbane and Suva. As Prime Minister Bruce, now present once more, told the parliament, 'It is anticipated that at the moment when the flyers pass, the destroyer will be about 700 miles off the coast of Australia, and will be able to keep in wireless communication with Captain Kingsford Smith throughout his trip and render him a great deal of assistance.'[52]

Bravo! *Bravo!*

In Arabella Street, most of the neighbourhood — cheering, laughing and crying — seemed to have gathered in the Kingsford Smith living room, treating the beaming Catherine and William as what they were — parents of the most celebrated man in Australia.

In Mosman, meanwhile, Charles Ulm's aged mother was taking it a lot more quietly. She had been on the point of emotional collapse, right up to the point when she heard that her boy was safe, and now it was all she could do to quietly sip some tea.[53] On the streets outside her door, as on streets all over Australia, newsboys were bellowing the wonderful news, and selling out of specially printed extra editions of their papers.

•

There is sleep, deep sleep, the sleep of the dead, the sleep of the damned, and then there is the sleep of an aviator who has flown nearly 6000 miles in just a few days, so far, so fast, that despite his extreme fatigue his natural body clock awakes him at midnight, local time.

So it was for Charles Kingsford Smith on that first night in Fiji. Ulm awoke at much the same time and after the two of them had spent an hour or so opening and reading the hundreds of congratulatory cablegrams that had been flooding in from all parts of the world — including one from Australian Prime Minister Stanley Bruce saying, 'Australia looks forward to welcoming you on the termination of your long and daring achievement'[54] — they decided to go and have a look at the *Southern Cross*. Was it being looked after, as promised by the local authorities? It was too important a question to be left until morning. They needed to know *now* and, wrapped in sarongs, they walked the short distance from the hotel to where they had left the plane, at one end of Albert Park.

At least they tried to. In fact, when they got to within 50 yards of the plane, which was looking rather ghostly in the soft tropical moonlight, four uniformed Fijian men with rifles appeared. Though these men spoke no English, they were able to use international sign language to indicate that if the two white men cared to keep coming on and get anywhere near the plane, there was every chance they would have their heads blown off.

Ulm and Kingsford Smith could not have been more delighted, and returned to their hotel to get some more sleep, mightily relieved.

•

Even beyond Australian shores, the news of the *Southern Cross*'s landing was creating major headlines, particularly in America and Britain, as it seemed as if another of the world's major natural barriers was now on the edge of being conquered.

But just who would be credited with the conquering? Under the original terms of the contract that Warner and Lyon had signed at Charles Ulm's behest on the evening before departure, their services were not required beyond Fiji, and they were to be given the money to simply disappear on a ship back to America. After all, from Suva onwards, the east coast of Australia would be a hard target to miss, so there was a lot less need for a navigator and radio man. And yet, once both the Australian and American press got wind of the plan, the pressure built for the Americans to remain included to the end, something that Lyon and Warner were keen on themselves.

Having broken the back of the journey, it seemed to the Americans that it would be a great pity to be let go now, and both of them said so at a meeting they held on their second night in Fiji. Ulm tried a compromise, offering the Americans a trip by ship to Australia, so they could arrive in time for some of the receptions and so on. Unfortunately, he put this proposal at a time when all of them had just returned from nearly a full day's round of celebrations, including a lunch, civic reception, two cocktail parties and a mayoral ball, all of which had involved the consumption of a great deal of alcohol. This meant that, at midnight, Harry Lyon's natural restraint — never the *particular* feature of his character that he would hang his hat on — was at a rather lowish point.

So Ulm wanted them to sneak to Australia, did he, and arrive after all the hoopla had died down? What kind of damned chumps did he think they were?!?! Something snapped. Grabbing Ulm, Lyon pushed him against the wall and was about to follow this up with the knockout blow, when Kingsford Smith stepped in.[55]

'Harry!'

Smithy, asserting his authority, told Lyon to get a grip and Ulm that he wanted the Americans to come on to Australia. And that was that. An uneasy peace descended, as both men bowed to Kingsford Smith's wishes and Ulm agreed that a fresh contract would be drawn up.[56]

The following morning, Ulm organised that contract and then cabled reports of his adventures to his newspaper contacts in Australia. (And to judge by a newspaper report appearing the following day, Ulm had rather changed his view of Lyon. 'If we were given all the navigators in the world for the next flight,' he told the *New York Times*, 'we would look for Lieutenant Lyon.'[57]) Meanwhile, Smithy flew the *Southern Cross*, with only a small amount of fuel on board, out of the tiny Albert Park to a beach on Naselai Island in the Rewa River Delta, about 20 miles to the north-east, where he was joined by Ulm, Warner and Lyon in the afternoon.

This beach was essentially the Fijian equivalent of Barking Sands — a long, firm, flattish stretch that would allow the *Southern Cross* to gain sufficient speed to take off even when fully loaded. Alas, when the Fijian government steamer *Pioneer* attempted to land twenty-five drums holding some 900 gallons of petrol on that same beach, the sea proved too rough for the steamer to get close to the shore, and it was reluctantly decided to leave it to the many willing locals to individually wrestle and roll the drums ashore with their wooden canoes as the frothy waves burst around them.[58]

In the meantime, the aviators were offered the chance to spend a comfortable night sleeping on the steamer, just with one little ... ah ... rider: one of them should stay ashore with the plane, which was a rather less comfortable prospect.

'My election to this post,' Jim Warner later recorded drolly, 'was practically unanimous. I won by the majority of something like seventy-five per cent.'[59]

That night, Warner was initiated into the Nakelo village and drank of the sacred yangonna ceremonial drink, also known as kava.[60] They proved to be a very gracious people.

We are the people of the Nakelo village, who live on the island of Naselai. Our sacred ancestors came here 40,000 years ago. Our legends tell of magic and powerful things, but never anything as magic or as powerful as this *Wanga Vuk*, bird-ship, this thing that can even stay up in the night, suspended from the top part of the moon and putting a shadow on the rest.[61] As near as we can see, the man with the big smile, who is laughing all the time, is the chief who controls this bird-ship. His name is 'Smizzy' and he is a good man who comes in peace. All the white men seem to look to him. We like him. Our chief Ratu

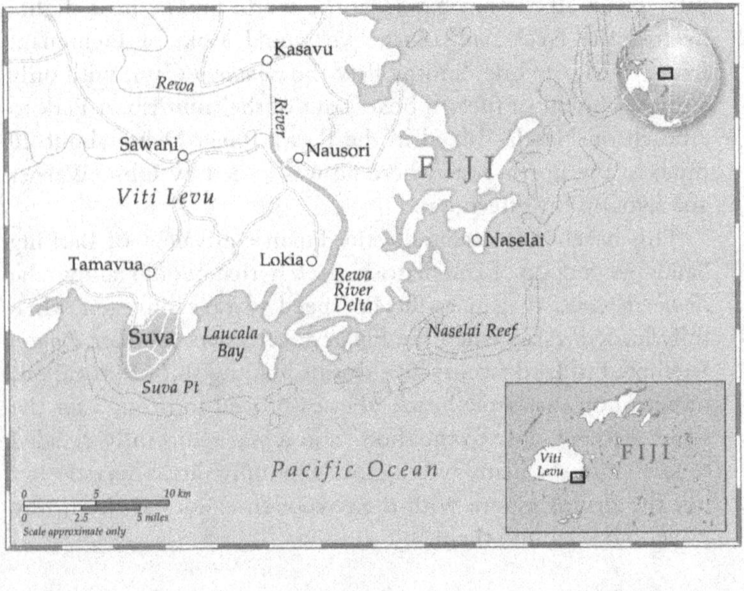

Avakuki, is very proud because this Smizzy has accepted a gift of a walking stick from him.[62] And now it is for us to farewell him and his men, as they depart in their bird-ship across the seas …

•

Finally, on mid-afternoon of Friday, 8 June 1928, at a time when the tide was low and their beach airstrip was near its widest, all was in readiness, with the only quibble being that as a long-time mariner, Harry Lyon was of the view that leaving on a Friday was bad luck.[63] He was ignored. Before the flyers left, however, a ceremony of farewell took place. With the crew making ready to get into the *Southern Cross*, the crowd suddenly made way.

Coming through the grouped natives appeared a vision of loveliness — four comely and bare-breasted young Fijian women, with hibiscus and frangipani flowers in their hair, each bearing a wooden bowl of the local drink of yangonna, which — despite the fact that it looked like brownish, muddy water — the flyers were invited to drink. As was explained to them by chief Ratu Avakuki, this was part of a ceremony dating back centuries, and was designed to ensure their safe passage to their destination. It was only given to visiting chiefs. (What he didn't explain was that as part of the process of preparing this drink from the root of the yangonna plant, those same young maidens would have chewed upon pieces of it, then removed them from their mouths and placed them a ceremonial bowl, before water was added.)

Deeply moved by the offering, the four Western men drank the yangonna — it made their tongues and lips feel numb — and then, through an interpreter, Kingsford Smith thanked the locals for their kindness and assured them they would never forget them.[64]

'Thanks for your hospitality and enthusiastic welcome,' Kingsford Smith called out to them, even after boarding the plane and preparing to depart. After the engines were started, making a thunderous noise the gathered locals had never heard before — like three storms all at once — they could see 'Smizzy' listen intently before he nodded his head to the other one sitting beside him.[65] All was good.

And then, this time with plasticine stuffed into their ears to try to deaden the noise,[66] they were off! The *Southern Cross* lifted off Naselai Beach on the button of 2.52 pm, leaving behind the magical green isles of athletic and friendly men, stunning women, palm trees, endless beautiful beaches and timeless hospitality. On that beach, the locals stayed staring, unspeaking, until the last speck of the plane disappeared in the distance.[67]

Next stop — the Australian mainland!

Though this was undoubtedly the least challenging part of their journey in terms of navigation — as instead of seeking out a dot in the ocean as previously, this time they *were* the dot in the ocean, heading to a massive target that they simply couldn't miss so long as they kept heading broadly west — there remained a huge distance to travel in a plane that had already received a fair old workout in the previous five days. By Lyon's calculations, Brisbane was on a bearing of south-west by west 236.25 degrees, 1756 miles away, but after what they had already been through, this seemed only about half as daunting as the Honolulu to Suva trip had been. As Smithy wrote in a note to his co-pilot Ulm, 'It is really remarkable how one's air mind expands. A few years ago a seventeen hundred mile flight over water was enormous. Now it is the shortest of our three hops.'[68] Practically nothing!

Little did they know, however, just what kind of a workout remained …

For even as they started out from Fiji, the Pacific was conspiring to have one last shot at bringing the *Southern Cross* to heel. On the path ahead of them, the sun had been belting down all day on the ocean, causing a lot of hot moisture to rise into the air. As that vapour rose into the higher realms, and began to condense, the heat from that moisture was released, causing a hot updraft and a heavy in-rush of cooler air below, as a low-pressure cell was formed. The winds rushing over the hot ocean surface now increased the rate of evaporation, causing a greater hot updraft, a lower air pressure, and even greater winds, which then released more heat … and so on. A vicious cycle was created, and was soon not far off from turning into a full-blown cyclone.

Gloriously unaware, the *Southern Cross* flew on towards Brisbane. Not that everything was going perfectly, for all that. Just a couple of hours after they took off, a note came forward from Lyon: E.I.C. *out of action*.

Bastard of a thing! And the worst of it, they realised, was that they had no-one to blame but themselves. While in Suva, they had received a long cable from the makers of the compass giving precise instructions on how their earth inductor compass should be serviced but ... well ... what with the speeches and their fatigue ... and accepting the hospitality of the locals ... they had clean forgotten about the whole thing. It was the only mistake they felt they had made on the trip so far, which was galling, but it was far better that it had happened at this stage rather than earlier on. For the moment, all they could do was to rely on their regular steering compass, though Lyon, for one, had little confidence that it would steer true given the inherent inconsistencies of using a magnetic compass for accurate headings for long distances over featureless water at night in turbulent air. Still, they could only keep going and hope that either Lyon could fix the compass, or their other methods of navigation would suffice.

As darkness fell, Kingsford Smith and Ulm managed, in the cramped cockpit, to get changed into their fur-lined flying suits as it started to get a bit nippy in the open-sided cockpit, before taking the *Southern Cross* up to above 4000 feet, which got them above the low-lying cloud and up into the starlit heavens.

At least for a while it did ... for after only a short time at that height the stars began to disappear and the temperature to drop radically. The plane began to be buffeted from side to side and up and down as gust after gust of dirty wind hit them. Dead ahead, flashes of lightning whiplashed across the sky and illuminated what, to Kingsford Smith, looked perilously close to being the thunderclouds of doom. Those big clouds looked, in the vernacular of the times, 'blacker than a crow's arsehole', and gave off a menace the likes of which Kingsford Smith had rarely seen before ... and he had seen a few storms in his day. In no time at all, the plane was into the storm, being smashed by the screaming angry wind as sheets of rain pounded their rickety craft.

For Kingsford Smith the only way out was *up*, and the plane began to climb again the best it could. He was hoping, as ever, to break through to above the storm where the stars would once again twinkle merrily. This time, however, it was not to be, and all that was achieved was to make them all numb with cold. Certainly, the storm they were going through had a top, but it was a top that the *Southern Cross* was incapable of climbing above, meaning that the only way was to go through. 'It was far worse than flying through the ordinary darkness of the night,' he later recalled. 'We were tearing through a black chaos of rain and cloud at 85 knots, and our very speed increased the latent fury of the storm until it became an active and violent enemy which seemed to rush on us in an endeavour utterly to devour us. This was a tropical deluge such as we had never experienced in our lives.'[69]

Despite the viciousness of the storm, however, and the pressing, crushing blackness, the saving grace was that the mighty Whirlwind engines never missed a beat, and the craft stayed intact! 'Those three engines tore through calm and storm, through rushing walls of tropic storm, through tumbled clouds piled like mountain peaks, through a howling headwind and through a hushed night sown with stars.'[70]

Those engines alone, however, would not have been enough to keep the plane aloft ... In the cockpit, concentrating with an intensity that was almost otherworldly, Kingsford Smith was fighting and riding the storm the way he used to see jackaroos in the Northern Territory and Western Australia fight and ride wild bucking horses in an effort to tame them. While in the back of the *Southern Cross* both Lyon and Warner had abandoned all attempts to navigate and work the radio and simply tried to ride it out for the duration, and Ulm was so cold he could make only occasional entries in his logbook, every fibre of Smithy's being was concentrated on his instruments.

For Smithy was doing what was called in the trade 'blind flying'. In the middle of the turbulent blackness, the only thing he could see by peering out was the endless lashing rain cascading towards them, and the reflected light from their cockpit being flashed back to them from the whirring propellers.

There was no horizon visible to give him any capacity to make the slight correcting movements to maintain stability, just as one does when riding a bike. Without that visible horizon, it was impossible to get any reckoning from their senses alone as to whether they were horizontal, descending, ascending, tilting, pitching or rolling — the only thing Kingsford Smith could do was to rely on reading his instruments. Without those instruments it would have been the rough equivalent of riding a bike blindfolded along a narrow plank.[71]

'Until a man can fly in a black void for hours,' Kingsford Smith would later write, 'seeing those instruments and nothing else, he is not a safe pilot to fly a plane over long stretches of water. A pilot flying blind must have immense faith in his instruments. He must train himself to realise that if the barometer of his senses disagrees with his instruments, then they are right and his senses are wrong ...'[72] And elsewhere: 'Blind flying comes to this — that of the five senses, only one is of any use and that is the ability to see the instruments on the board.'[73]

Broadly speaking, his bank-and-turn indicator told a pilot if he was turning, the rate-of-climb meter indicated whether he was climbing or falling, the earth-inductor compass told him his course and the air speed indicator told him exactly that. In the cabin behind the pilots, with no such array of instruments, no seat belts or secure seats, Lyon and Warner were never certain at any moment if they were flying or falling, and all they could do was give silent thanks for Kingsford Smith's ability to keep them aloft, for even this long.[74] Neither man had any doubt that if anyone could get them through, then Smithy could.

In such circumstances it was nearly impossible to keep up his radio reports, but Warner tried. At the height of the storm, however, Warner found that the transmitter wouldn't work. In looking for the trouble, he put his hand on the long antenna reel that trailed out the window, only to get a strong electric shock! Turning the transmitter off, he reeled in the antenna, and found that it had become tangled with the other.[75] This was going to take some time to sort out ...

•

Silence. Dead air.

Panic around the world. Suddenly, the *Southern Cross* had gone off the air. Had she crashed? Disappeared into the Pacific Ocean? Warner had told them they were in the grip of a powerful storm, and now … *nothing*! Minute, after minute, after minute. NOTHING.

In Arabella Street, Smithy's family, who had been listening to 2BL as if their lives depended on it, tried to fight a rising panic. What could be the explanation? Surely Chilla was all right, wasn't he? They put more coal on the fire, made fresh tea, and stared alternately at the silent radio and the ticking clock: 9 pm … 9.07 … 9.08 … a quarter past nine … a quarter to ten … and then at last, just before ten o'clock, they heard it. The radio sparked into life and they could again hear the *tap-tap-tappety-tap* of the Morse key, with the decoded message shortly thereafter. The *Southern Cross* was all right!

•

On the plane, Warner had untangled the antennae and was again in business. If, somehow, one of the new-fangled Movietone newsreel cameras that were just about to start filming the world in flickering black-and-white images could have been positioned 10 yards out and 5 yards up from the nose of the *Southern Cross*, it would have revealed the fragile craft pitching and yawing, smashed to its left and right, as every fresh hammer of howling wind hit it. And there, through the windscreen being lashed by the torrents of rain, would be just visible the grim and furrowed face of Kingsford Smith, lit up by two small electric bulbs shining on his instruments.

His eyes are bloodshot, his body is shaking with cold as he sits in his sodden flying suit, his muscles aching with cramp and his feet numb, but somehow — just barely, but *somehow* — his frozen but expert hands are on the controls and he keeps the *Southern Cross* airborne and heading home, home to Australia.

•

Rising midnight at last, the flyers seemed to have come through the most extreme of the conditions as the wind abated by perhaps half a dozen banshees, but there remained a dreadful night to get through. Essaying to feel his way through the lesser storm now, Kingsford Smith tried to find the path of least resistance, taking the *Southern Cross* as high as 9000 feet and as low as 500 feet. Sometimes rough vision would return where they could momentarily see stars or distant clouds, but mostly they were flying blind or in near blackness.

The dawn, the dawn, the dawn ... where was it? At last, at around 6.45 am local time, the sky lightened perceptibly and shortly thereafter there was no doubt. They had made it through the night. Almost as if acknowledging defeat, the Pacific now tried to live up to its name and granted much calmer weather, enabling Ulm, Warner and Lyon to come to life. For just as there is a lull before the storm, so too is there a blessed lull after it. Now, in the back, Warner was fiddling with the knobs on his radio, attempting to pick up a bearing for Brisbane, while Lyon was once again busy on his charts, attempting to work out exactly where they were.

An indication of their appreciation for the pilot who had got them through the stormy night had come an hour earlier when Smithy took receipt of a note from Lyon saying that when they landed, he and Warner wanted to nominate him to be the next president of the United States. Both men were in awe of Smithy's skill, with Warner later noting, 'I'd go up with him in a tomato-crate with cracker-box wings, if he said it would fly.'[76]

By half-past eight, the storm was completely left behind and the sun was not only fully up but also shining down benevolently upon them to the point that for the first time in fourteen hours a tiny wisp of warmth penetrated their soaked suits and began to evaporate some of the wetness. Kingsford Smith and Ulm were feeling so confident by now they even instructed Jim Warner to send out the following message:

> Now that we are sure of success, we wish to announce to the world that we could never have made the flight without the generosity and wonderful help given us by Captain G. Allan Hancock. For months

> we had fought against giving up all hope, but we were practically counted out when we met Captain Hancock, who in a most unselfish manner saw us through.[77]

Then to the moment ...

Just before ten o'clock on 9 June 1928 they saw the tiniest of dark lines on the far western horizon, a line that didn't change shape but became only more defined with every passing minute. Within four minutes there could be no denying it. It was the finish line — Australia! Before their very eyes, 'the Australian continent slipped like a purple shadow over the steel-blue rim of the sea'.[78]

Did Captain Cook feel so good after his own long voyage to see the Australian coast? Christopher Columbus to see the Americas? Cortez to see Mexico? Anyone, to see *anything*!?

After seven gruelling nights and eight gruelling days, with eighty-three hours and fifteen minutes of ocean flying, they had crossed the Pacific, with landfall just up ahead! Now, which part of the Australian coast they were going to cross, they weren't yet quite sure — they couldn't help but notice that Moreton Island wasn't where it should be, protecting the mouth of the Brisbane River, if that was indeed what they were heading to — but on the other hand it didn't *really* matter. After flying around 7500 miles over water — around twice the distance flown by Lindbergh — *any* type of land looked good to them, and wild elation continued to surge through them as features of the oncoming coast became ever more apparent.

In fact, as they soon worked out, they were crossing the coast near the town of Ballina, just 110 miles south of Brisbane, making it a simple matter to wheel to starboard and head on up the coast to the Eagle Farm racecourse. As they made their approaches to Brisbane over Moreton Bay, all the steamships on the Brisbane River gave them a siren salute, to which Smithy joyously waggled his wings in reply.[79] Australia! Home! A posse of planes flew out from Brisbane to joyously escort them to their landing ground, where an estimated 15,000 strong crowd (including Bert Hinkler's mother) waited expectantly.

And there was Eagle Farm. As they looked down, the entire field, it seemed, was outlined by a pressing, surging crowd. Brisbane had turned out in force to welcome them. On the ground on this wonderfully sunny yet surprisingly cold winter's day, the ABC radio broadcaster J.W. Robinson was describing in his clipped and cultured tones the wonderful historic scene to much of Australia — to just about anyone who had a radio, and most of their neighbours.

'The *Southern Cross* is now coming very clearly into view. She is flying over the top of the small escorting planes. The sun is glistening on her wingspan. It is impossible to distinguish anyone in her from here. She looks very fine. They are getting closer and closer. The *Southern Cross* dwarfs the escorting planes, being almost three times as large. She is now almost over the top of the aerodrome — is getting quite close up. Listen to the whirr of the propellers. Everybody waving wildly. Is coming now. Coming down and down!'[80]

Fifteen thousand people in the 5000 cars surrounding the field sounded their horns in a glorious cacophony by way of greeting.

At last, the *Southern Cross* landed beside the spot where the crowd was thickest, then rolled to the end of the airfield where there was practically no-one, before turning around to come back. It was at that point of the turn that an eagle-eyed aviation journalist, Norman Ellison, from Sydney's *Daily Guardian*, noticed what seemed to be two figures jump out of the back of the plane, and begin to sneak away from the tumultuous reception that was awaiting …

As the *Southern Cross* started to taxi back, however, it seemed no-one else had noticed, and the entire throng surged forward to the point that police on hand began to fear for both the plane *and* the crowd, should the twain meet.

'Get back! Get back!' the policeman yelled, before uttering what would be an oft-repeated line: 'This is no ordinary plane.'[81]

It was no good. The joyous crowd surged forward and surrounded the plane. And there he was! Smithy himself climbing out of the open side of the cockpit, waving, beaming and now speaking his first words: 'Hello, Aussies!' he said. 'My kingdom for a smoke!'[82]

Hurrah! Again the people crushed in, trying to get to him first, to give him a ciggie, a light, a handshake, a hug, a card, a flower or ... *at least touch him*. There were so many people that the only way out was up, and in no time at all a laughing Smithy, with smoke in hand, was carried around the field on the shoulders of the crowd, with the grinning Ulm, equally aloft, not far behind.

Meanwhile, back at the other end of the field, Ellison had caught up with the two mysterious figures, both of whom were wearing ties and suits, while Kingsford Smith and Ulm had been in overalls. After Ellison had identified himself as a journalist, the chunkier of the two momentarily fumbled with his handkerchief, took out a denture before popping it in his mouth and then said in a broad American accent: 'I'm Harry Lyon, and this is Jim Warner.'[83]

'Why did you leave the plane? And where are you going?'

Both men seemed a little sheepish at being caught out, but responded diplomatically enough that they were sure that the reception was an Australian welcome for Australian flyers, and not the likes of them, so he and Warner had felt it was the best thing to hightail it out of there.

Ellison, when he spoke, felt he was speaking on behalf of the Australian populace, and the upshot of what he said was strong. Not on your Nelly. You have flown *with* the Australians to get here, they clearly couldn't have got here without you, and you will be warmly welcomed at the reception. But you must come to it.

And so they did. And were welcomed accordingly, with Charles Kingsford Smith and Charles Ulm ... as garlands of roses were put around their necks, and both the governor and premier of Queensland made exuberant welcoming speeches. At one point Lyon was heard to joke with Warner, 'Wa-al Jim, we travelled seven thousand miles to get a drink ...' and people fell about with wonder and amusement. What an hilarious accent the Yanks had![84]

From there, the four aviators were placed in an open car — with six burly policemen standing on the running boards as added protection — and as 40,000 Queenslanders lined both sides of the road and cheered them to the echo, were driven to Brisbane Town Hall, where yet another reception awaited.[85] At that function, a telegram was read out from the Prime Minister, announcing a pledge of £5000 to Kingsford Smith and Ulm which resulted, accorded to the *Argus*, in a 'near riot' of acclaim.[86] ('This is a wonderful grant,' Smithy would later quip, 'as it is well known we flew on an overdraft!'[87])

In the absence of the mayor, Vice-Mayor Watson set the tone: 'We meet to do honour to four very gallant men. Captain Kingsford Smith and his daring companions have bridged the mighty Pacific, in their unprecedented hop, step and jump. It is given to few men to write their names on the scroll of fame, but Kingsford Smith has by covering 7,000 miles of ocean, written his name with imperishable glory in the pages of the world's history.'[88]

In the course of all the speech-making, Smithy managed to slip in, 'I am not an orator, but if Sydney is listening on the air, I would like to give a message to the old folk. It is this, "I'll be with you very soon".'[89] Resounding cheers greeted these words.

That evening, when the now world-famous aviators were finally ensconced in their hotel, Colonel Horace Brinsmead, the long-time Controller of Civil Aviation was ushered into their presence. 'Congratulations,' he said warmly, 'on having achieved the end of your flight.'

'No, not the end of the flight,' Smithy corrected him with a smile. 'It's only the end of the first stage of an aerial circumnavigation of the world.'[90]

Then and there, having achieved his ambition of flying the Pacific, Smithy had set his own sights on the ultimate, which was to be the first person to circumnavigate the globe in the one plane, while crossing the equator in the process, and achieve what Sir Ross Smith had died trying to do. Wonderfully, there was now no doubt that the *Southern Cross* would be available for him to make the attempt.

For, that very evening, they had received a cable from Captain Hancock. After congratulating them on their stunning achievement he told them this:

> I am delivering to the California Bank at Los Angeles for transmission to the Commercial Banking Company of Sydney, Bill of Sale transferring to Kingsford Smith and Ulm the Southern Cross together with release and discharge of all your indebtedness to me. I beg you to accept this gift as a token of our mutual friendship, and as my tribute to you and the Southern Cross …[91]

There were hundreds, and then *thousands* of cables, which just kept coming, including one from the President of the United States, Calvin Coolidge:

> Hearty congratulations to you and your companions on successful flight Oakland to Australia. Your brilliant and courageous pioneering has advanced the cause of aviation and strengthened bonds between your Commonwealth and our country.[92]

One other message that particularly stood out for Smithy came from the owner of Mount Philip station, one of the biggest sheep runs that he had served in his days with the Gascoyne Transport Company:

> Heartiest congratulations. How 'bout the contract for this season's loading? It's yours![93]

It was wonderful, absolutely wonderful to have clearly given so much pleasure to so many people they had known through the years, together with the broad mass of their fellow Australians.

•

And yet as frenzied as their reception in Brisbane had been, it was as nothing to what happened in Sydney on the following day. For when they emerged out of a clear blue sky on their approach to Mascot airport, in the mid-afternoon of Sunday, 10 June 1928, they were greeted by forty planes, including one flown by none other than Keith Anderson.

At his home at picturesque Pittwater on the northern outskirts of Sydney, Bill Taylor, the former pilot with the Royal Flying Corps, looked up to see the resplendent *Southern Cross* pass overhead, and was instantly inspired. *That* was what he wanted to do. He wanted to get into some pioneer flying himself. As the mighty plane flew in over the city, factory sirens wailed, ships and ferries sounded their horns and people crowded onto the roofs of city buildings as Smithy circled first over Hyde Park and then dipped low over the Cenotaph in his own tribute to fallen comrades of the Great War. If he was surprised at the lack of people in the streets, then there was an impressive explanation.[94]

For there at Mascot aerodrome when the *Southern Cross* touched down at 3.08 pm was the greatest gathering of Sydneysiders in the one place at the one time that had ever been.[95] Whether it was 200,000, 300,000 or 400,000, all of which estimates were subsequently reported, it was not possible to say. All that everyone knew was that there were more people than anyone had thought possible. *Everyone* was there! And they were all cheering, just as cars were tooting and ships in Botany Bay sounding their horns, with the overall effect so strong that, according to one writer, 'it made Gabriel's trumpet sound like a tin whistle competing with a barrage'.[96]

Once again, amid such a large crowd, it was no small matter to actually get the plane down safely before everyone was rushing towards them in the now familiar fashion. As they alighted and waved, people threw their hats and handkerchiefs in the air and cheered themselves hoarse, the more so when all four airmen were put on the back of a truck and taken for a quick spin around the tarmac so everyone could see them up close.[97]

A rather disconsolate figure standing by the hangars as all the cheers rang out, all but entirely unnoticed except by one observant reporter, Keith Anderson looked rather lost and lonely.[98] He was in an impossible situation, and yet was at least able to rouse himself enough to push through the crowd to rather solemnly shake Smithy's hand and give a curt nod to Ulm, all without saying a word.[99]

On a special dais set up for the occasion, Smithy's parents and family awaited the crew, as did Charles Ulm's new bride, together with many distinguished dignitaries, including the Governor-General of Australia, Lord Stonehaven, and the Governor of New South Wales, Sir Dudley de Chair. The Premier of New South Wales, Thomas Bavin, had the decency to stay away, which was to the good, all things considered. When Ulm placed a full-lipped kiss on his new bride, Josephine, the crowd roared appreciatively.[100]

There was something different about that day, something that felt *Australian* in a way it never had before. It was an effect rather heightened when there was a sudden 'trampling of toppers' and a 'mangling of monocles'[101] as the proud descendants of convicts and other unwanted folk of the Old World surged forward, eager to be part of a new, world achievement.

As to Smithy, he was clearly overcome when embracing his own parents — truly safe at last — even as Catherine Kingsford Smith kissed her beloved boy on his notably tanned cheeks and said with a smile, 'Go and wash your face, you dirty little boy.'[102]

He was home.

Twelve

The Urge to Elsewhere ...

The black chaotic void, punctuated every few seconds by great jagged rents of lightning which, like vivid green snakes, seemed to leap at us from every direction.

Charles Kingsford Smith, on the *Southern Cross*'s trip across the Tasman[1]

An aviator's life may be full of ups and downs, but the only hard thing about flying is the ground.

Charles Kingsford Smith frequently signed autographs in this manner[2]

For Kingsford Smith and Ulm home would never be the same again, in the way that it treated them. They had left Australian shores as no more than a couple of well-known pilots who had a couple of creditable feats to their name, particularly the round-Australia trip. But in a nation starved for heroes — the Great War had been over for ten years, and the national cricket team only middling in recent times — they had returned as the brightest stars in the firmament.

Awards and riches were showered upon them. His Majesty bestowed upon the 31-year-old Kingsford Smith the Air Force Cross, while the Australian government made him an honorary squadron leader in the RAAF — for which he had never flown. Ulm meanwhile became an honorary RAAF flight lieutenant. And they were not even in the air force, a fact which did not escape the attention of officers who were. *Harrumph!*

A rare note of criticism was also penned by one E.J. Hart, the acerbic editor of *Aircraft* magazine:

> With the crossing of the Pacific by a Dutch monoplane, American-engined, fuelled and lubricated by the products of the US, another fatal temptation is finally removed from venturesome spirits who had long aspired to the distinction of being the first to fly a land machine across the water from America to Australia. Now that the goal is reached ... it is fervently to be hoped that land machines will be permitted to resume their proper place in the sphere of practical, commercial utilities — and that there will be no more staking of life and property against that wily old monarch with the loaded dice, King Neptune.[3]

Such churlishness, however, was very much the exception, as almost everyone else seemed to exult at their achievement and the name 'Kingsford Smith', particularly, now resonated to the point where all of the rest of his family were now practically *defined* by the fact that they were related to the great man.

The government's initial cheque of £5000, as a sign of its appreciation, had been promptly matched by Lebbeus Hordern, as he handed over a cheque for the same amount.[4] Those two handsome cheques, though, were just bare beginnings to the riches now coming their way, as the Sydney *Sun* and Melbourne *Herald* made an appeal to their readers to make what was effectively a donation to the 'boys', which brought the total to over £20,000. The cast of the hit musical *Rio Rita*, then playing in Sydney's St James Theatre, invited all the crew of the *Southern Cross* to a performance, and the proceeds of the evening were given to them at the end — at least to Smithy and Ulm, while Lyon and Warner tried not to let their fuming show.[5]

Now, *now* as money continued to pour in, Smithy could at last return to his family much of the generosity he had received from them over the years, and one of the first things he did was to buy Kuranda for his parents, and put it in their names — something he had wanted to do since at least 1922, when he had first started to earn a decent regular wage. He also established a trust fund from which his parents would be able to draw £4 a week for the rest of their lives.

In all the excitement after this triumph of Australian aviation, Lawrence Hargrave was not forgotten. Almost in the manner of paying homage, Kingsford Smith and Ulm paid a visit to Sydney's Technological Museum to inspect the first box-kites and monoplane models constructed by Hargrave, some three decades earlier. Their guide from the museum, a Mr T.C. Roughley, also showed them one of Hargrave's early rotary engines and explained how Henri Farman would not have won the Reims distance competition in 1909 without it.

Afterwards, a singularly thoughtful Kingsford Smith noted to the waiting press how intensely interested he was, and also expressed the view that he was 'convinced that Australia does not yet realise all that the world's aviators owe to the experiments of Lawrence Hargrave'.[6]

The next day Hargrave was also remembered when the two pilots attended a special church service at St Mark's, Darling Point, to mark their safe arrival. From behind his pulpit, the Reverend Canon Howard Lea referred to Lawrence Hargrave as the 'pioneer of aviation', and quoted one Professor Threlfall from 1894, who had written, 'Sydney will someday be noted, not so much for its beautiful harbour, as for the residence of the inventor of the flying machine.'[7]

And amen to that!

Lyon and Warner? Understandably anxious to get back to their families, they had taken the first steamer home after the initial round of celebrations was over, and the two pilots had come aboard the SS *Sonoma* to see them off.

'We did enjoy ourselves,' Harry Lyon told the *Sydney Morning Herald* just before boarding the ship. 'You folks made us feel at home. When our Australian friends come to America, they will get a reception just as big.'[8]

Which was saying something, because for wherever Kingsford Smith and Ulm went — and that was just about everywhere, including major trips to Canberra, Melbourne and Perth — they were greeted with the sight of their fellow citizens lining the streets and cheering them to the echo as they made their way to parliaments, civic receptions, lunches and dinners.

On their way from Laverton, a little west of Melbourne, to Maylands in Perth — which just happened to be the first non-stop flight across the continent, landing on the morning of 9 August 1928 — they slashed the cross-Australia record to twenty-three and a half hours, and managed to buzz Adelaide on the way through. As the *Southern Cross* was now an Australian plane, and as Australia was part of the British Commonwealth, it acquired British registration, with the letters 'G-AUSU', the 'AU' standing for Australia and 'SU' for Smith and Ulm.

Three cheers for Smithy! And for Ulm! And definitely in that order!

There was something about Smithy, that larrikin charm, that twinkle in his eye, that dazzling smile, the wonderfully *Australian* nonchalance he displayed about what he had achieved, that way he had of speaking so that even if you were one of a crowd of 30,000 it felt as though he was talking to just you, that meant that everyone adored him. In a nation sometimes resembling 'little England', ruled by pork-pie hats and three-piece suits, he was an Australian original, a man of the people, with goggles, leather jacket, ciggie and a ready grin that would warm the cockles of your soul.

From being 'Smithy' to just his nearest and dearest, he was now 'Smithy' Australia-wide. Ulm was respected — after all, he had flown with Smithy — but he was not outright loved the way Kingsford Smith was.

Smithy! Smithyy! *Smithyyyyy!* Over here! Over *here*!

•

He was over there. Sitting at the top table at a welcome home lunch in Sydney Town Hall on the Tuesday after they landed, surrounded by some of the city's finest dignitaries, Smithy wasn't exactly hard to find. And Bobby Hitchcock had no hesitation in walking up to him and handing him a writ. He then turned on his heel and walked off. Bobby was suing them, claiming that he had been promised £1000 if they succeeded in their trans-Pacific flight, and he now wanted it, too right he did. Bobby had a wife and three kids to support, and he needed that money, which he felt was rightfully his.

As if that suit wasn't shocking enough, it soon transpired that Keith Anderson was suing them too, with Bon's solicitor father, Arthur Hilliard, calling the shots. And whereas Bobby was suing them for lost salary, Keith wanted a share of the profits! He had taken an action before the New South Wales Supreme Court to recover monies spent to organise the flight and to provide their living expenses while they were in San Francisco.

In response, Smithy was stung and Ulm was stoical. They would fight the writs tooth and nail, and hire King's Counsels to tear their erstwhile friends apart.

•

In the meantime, nothing could be allowed to interfere with their program. A large part of that would be forming their own airline, to be called, grandly, Australian National Airways which they felt could do in New South Wales and Victoria what Qantas did in Queensland and West Australian Airways did in the west. In terms of historic flights, though, one beckoned immediately: the honour of being the first flyers to traverse the Tasman Sea. Of course, now without Lyon and Warner, they would need replacements to man the radio and navigation table but that proved to be no problem. For a navigator they were able to secure their old friend, Australian Hal Litchfield. With Bill Todd, the softly spoken Hal had given them instruction in navigation, and they were delighted to take him on board their craft. For a radio man, both Ulm and Kingsford Smith thought it would be a good gesture to engage a New Zealander to be part of the crew with the honour of crossing the Tasman first, and Tom McWilliams was perfect: he was a first-class wireless operator then teaching at the radio school of the Union Steamship Company in Wellington, a friendly, easygoing veteran of the Great War and, most importantly of all, he was provided by the New Zealand government, free of charge!

In a sign of the changing times, the first that most of the Australian public knew about the trip was when a full-page advertisement appeared in the *Sydney Morning Herald*:

Kingsford Smith To Fly the Tasman

These are the Bonds Woollen Athletic Singlets and Pure Wool Fancy Half Hose that will accompany Capt. Kingsford Smith on his flight to New Zealand.

I shall be delighted to wear them on my flight to New Zealand. I know their worth.

C. Kingsford Smith.

With these Garments Australia's Air Hero will be protected against the Chill and Cold in his effort to bring still greater honour to Australia.

1239 Miles from Sydney to Wellington.

Estimated Flying Time 14½ Hours.

In fact, their destination soon changed to Christchurch chiefly on the grounds that that fair city had a serious airfield, while Wellington didn't. And although Christchurch was only a relatively paltry 1400 miles away — nearly nothing, in comparison to their Honolulu to Suva hop — they had before them the tragic example of Hood and Moncrieff to show that the exercise was not a doddle. As a matter of fact, Kingsford Smith was personally convinced that it represented 'one of the most dangerous and difficult sea-crossings in the world', as it was one of the 'wildest and stormiest seas on the globe',[9] and also comparatively deserted.

Still, it was a sea that was clearly going to be crossed sooner or later, and both Kingsford Smith and Ulm took the view that they might as well be the ones to do it. As Smithy told the press, 'This isn't just a flight across 1,425 miles of stormy sea. This flight's important to us. It'll publicise the feasibility of such a flight, and make people realise that if this trip is possible, our own Australian National Airways Limited is a safe, quick way of getting from point to point in Australia. If we can fly the Tasman safely, we can certainly fly people from Sydney to Melbourne without any trouble. Anyway, however stormy it is, the "Old Bus" can handle it.'[10]

Once committed to the flight, they sent for 'Doc' Maidment to come across from America to recondition the engines once more, and he was assisted in this task by a young RAAF mechanic by the name of Tommy Pethybridge, a tousle-haired young man, who was simply beside himself with joy that he was able to work on the plane of Kingsford Smith, whom he hero-worshipped.

Now, though their every interaction with New Zealand to this point had been positive and welcoming, a sudden glitch occurred when they announced that their likely landing in Christchurch would be on Sunday, 9 September 1928. A *Sunday*? The Lord's day? On a trip sponsored by a commercial enterprise, a brand of petrol? The more conservative elements of wider New Zealand, and Christchurch in particular, took a very dim view of such sacrilege, and a very stern message soon came from the mayor of Christchurch, addressed to Charles Kingsford Smith:

> Christchurch churchmen strongly protest against plans involving arrival on a Sunday. I support the protest. Cannot departure be delayed?[11]

Smithy laughed. It was amazing the things that could upset some fellows. Fortunately he was spared the difficult decision about whether to bow to the Lord or to his instincts to leave as soon as he was ready by the even greater need to bow to the weather bureau. When the boffins reported that it was blowing a powerful gale along the New Zealand coast on the day Kingsford Smith and Ulm wanted to leave, they had no hesitation in delaying the flight.[12]

This reluctance to go when there was a poor forecast made Smithy's predicament all the more surprising, therefore, when just a couple of days later they were flying in a storm as they had never experienced before, an even worse storm than the one that had nearly brought them down off the coast of Fiji.

For *never* had they been in wind and lightning like this. When they had left Richmond in the gathering dusk of 10 September, only a few hours earlier — carrying just 700 gallons of petrol — both the Australian and New Zealand weather bureaus were reporting fine weather in their own parts of the world, and yet neither had the capacity to know what it was like over the heart of the Tasman, as there were no ships out in the middle of it. Well, Kingsford Smith could tell them what the weather was like in the middle, when he arrived. *If* he arrived ...

At the controls, Smithy took the *Southern Cross* as high as she would go, but at 10,000 feet there was not the slightest sign that they were getting above the weather, and the plane refused to go any higher. Regrettably, at that height, the air was so thin that the *Southern Cross* was almost impossible to handle so he took her back down, bouncing off air pockets as they went.

Alas, at 8500 feet, serious danger presented itself, as ice started to form on the plane's wings and all exterior surfaces, changing the craft's contours and adding as much as half a ton weight, slowing it and making it even more unstable. Smithy had calculated that they were covering distance over the water at better than 100 miles per hour, with a spanking tailwind adding 7 miles per hour or so to the plane's usual ground speed of 95 miles per hour. And yet he was stunned to see that the air speed indicator was registering *zero*.

His highly trained instinct was to believe the dials and, on the reckoning that they must now be stalling, he began a steep dive and watched as the altimeter indicated they had gone from 8000 feet to 2500 feet in under a minute, and still the speed showed zero!

Too late, for all the hard-won altitude lost, he realised that the air speed indicator, too, must have become choked with ice, and they were now hurtling down at enormous speed and at a very steep angle. Smithy braced himself and pulled back hard on the control column's wheel as slowly, oh so slowly, the ice-encrusted mass that was the *Southern Cross* yielded to his command. But was there still time? Smithy was suddenly gripped by the appalling feeling that they were going to go 'straight into the angry sea like an ice-sheathed arrow'.[13]

At last, the plane levelled just above the ocean. They were still alive, but not yet out of trouble ...

As they continued on their perilous flight, they soon found themselves in a 'black chaotic void, punctuated every few seconds by great jagged rents of lightning which, like vivid green snakes, seemed to leap at us from every direction'.[14] Precisely what happened when lightning struck a flying petrol tank like the one they were in, they simply didn't know. And yet they were not long in finding out.

When a bolt of lightning *did* strike the plane shortly afterwards, it didn't turn them into a flaming ball as they feared but it did knock out both radio sets. Soon the entire *Southern Cross* sizzled, from its own electrical charge, with a phenomenon called 'St Elmo's Fire' — a frightening effect caused by massive voltages exciting the gases in the air to glow. Amazed, Smithy and Ulm saw the propellers flickering in the lightning bolts, while the leading edges of the wings of the plane seemed to throb with the eerie, electrical brilliance — just as Smithy's grandfather, the roving sea-captain from Kent, may have seen the top of his ship's mast in an electrical storm glow with the same effect.

This time, the theoretical Movietone News cameras would have captured a veritable glowing ghost plane crackling its way through the thunderous heavens. Just one spark in the wrong spot — anywhere near the fumes from the fuel tanks — and everything would have been all over in an instant.[15] True, every metal part of the plane had been carefully joined together by an earthing wire to prevent that spark discharging, but it had never been tested like this before.

As Smithy would later write: 'I was never so frightened in my life before — as also were my three companions.'[16]

Trying not to panic, he took stock of their situation. They were alone in the middle of the deserted Tasman Sea. Above and around them was the worst storm he'd ever seen. Beneath them was a savage hungry sea that would destroy them in seconds if they were forced down.

The *Southern Cross* was encrusted in ice. The radio wasn't working. It was pitch black. They could see nothing, hear nothing but the storm and did not know where they were.

Yes, all things considered, he thought he could up the ante, and not only was he the most frightened he'd ever been, but he was in fact, 'touching the extreme of human fear'.[17]

Shoulda worn the brown underpants.

Still trying to fight off panic, Smithy nearly lost his head and momentarily felt a 'desire to pull her round, dive — climb — do anything, to escape'.[18] With no respite, 'we were like rats in a trap, dazed with fear'.[19]

At least the three wonderful Wright Whirlwind radial engines never missed a beat, though it wasn't long before the propellers were struggling as flying ice tore chunks out of two of them, causing the plane to vibrate terribly.

In the course of that horrifying night, Kingsford Smith made a promise to himself that *never again* would he cross an ocean at night if there was any alternative.[20] Sometimes the going was so tough that it took both Smithy and Ulm together, pulling on the controls, to guide their ship through.[21]

Never had any of the flyers been so glad to see a dawn as that one, on Tuesday, 11 September 1928. Gazing earnestly for a sign of land, it was Hal Litchfield who spotted it first, then passed forward a note using their stick system: *Watch bank of cloud on starboard bow.*[22]

They looked ... and he was right! As opposed to the other clouds all around, this particular bank didn't change form, or position. There could be only one conclusion: it wasn't a cloud. And that high up there was only one other thing that it could be: the far distant snowy peaks of the Southern Alps.

New Zealand. They had made it. At least, they had seen land and, turning to the maps, Litchfield soon worked out exactly where they were, near the entrance to Cook Strait, which separates the North Island from the South Island. The main thing was that the crisis had passed, and before heading to Christchurch they decided to swoop down upon Wellington on the southern end of the North Island, bringing the citizens of that fair city out of their houses to wave them a furious welcome with pyjama tops, tea towels and anything else that came to hand, before heading down to Christchurch. (Two people no doubt excused from expressing such transparent joy — though they certainly would have known of the safe arrival of the *Southern Cross* in New Zealand — were the widows of Lieutenant John Moncrieff and Captain George Hood. All these months later and there had still not been a substantiated clue as to the fate of their husbands. *Home is the sailor, home from the sea, And the hunter, home from the hill* ...[23] but of the aviators nary a sign.)

The *Southern Cross* flew on, triumphant. About 50 miles out of Christchurch they were greeted by four Bristol F.2B fighter machines from the New Zealand Permanent Air Force and escorted to Wigram aerodrome.

Just after 9.30 am, Kingsford Smith, Ulm, Litchfield and McWilliams landed in Christchurch to what Smithy later described as 'the deafening cheers of the most enthusiastic crowd I have ever seen',[24] a gathering of some 30,000 people only narrowly held in check by police and troops. As the smiling airmen disembarked the band struck up 'For He's a Jolly Good Fellow', and the crowd joined in heartily. In many ways, that flight to New Zealand marked the last air link being forged to bind the developed world together.

Despite the fierce storm, they had made it and were still alive! A bath, breakfast and blessed sleep beckoned ...

That evening, while enjoying what they thought was going to be a quiet drink of celebration at the Universal Hotel, Kingsford Smith and Ulm heard shouting. Apparently many of the good burghers of Christchurch had gathered outside and wanted to congratulate them. There were far too many people to greet personally, shake hands with and so forth, but would the Australians mind coming out onto the hotel balcony and giving the crowd a wave?

But of course not ...

There were thousands of people outside, and they cheered as one at the appearance of the Aussies. By way of greeting, Kingsford Smith cupped his hands around his mouth and yelled cheerfully, 'I didn't know there were so many people in Christchurch. We are glad to be here, but by Jove we had a bad time last night and coming through this morning. My hostess is sorry that she can't invite you all in for a drink. We tried to land here on Sunday but couldn't make it.'[25]

'Did you get the cable from the mayor?' someone shouted equally cheerfully.

'Oh yes, we got it all right,' Smithy called back, with laughs all round. They got it all right! Did you hear him? He said they got it all right! That Smithy!

An exceedingly pleasant few weeks in New Zealand ensued, with the two pilots staying on as guests of the national government, and flying from function to function, event to event, at the government's behest in the New Zealand Air Force's Bristols. When they arrived, the waiting crowd was never in any doubt as to which plane boasted Smithy — it was always the one doing loops, chandelles and dives before landing.

That Smithy!

What they were doing was essentially promoting the cause of aviation in the Shaky Isles, as well as talking extensively with the government about the possibility of establishing a regular trans-Tasman postal service. As a matter of fact, Smithy had brought with him a letter from Australian Prime Minister Stanley Bruce to the Prime Minister of New Zealand, Mr Joseph Coates, and was delighted to formally hand it over.

The letter read: 'Through the courtesy of the two intrepid Australian airmen, Squadron-Leader Kingsford Smith and Flight Lieutenant Ulm, I desire to extend to you and, through you, to the people of New Zealand, our warmest felicitations on the linking of our sister Dominions by air. This achievement marks a new epoch in our history and our relations. Its accomplishment alone will tend to draw our peoples closer together. But its deep significance lies in the fact that it points towards a future in which, by regular aerial communication, our two countries will be more firmly united, deriving strength in peace and war from their mutual association.'[26]

There really seemed to be an enormous amount of enthusiasm for the project, and the widespread view was that Kingsford Smith and Ulm were the obvious men to do it. The New Zealand government also honoured them by making them temporary officers in the New Zealand Permanent Air Force, Smithy a major and Ulm a lieutenant. Oddly enough, despite all of his fame as an aviator, Charles Ulm to this point had never been officially certified as a pilot, and so after receiving formal flight training by the NZAF in an Avro 504K, he was awarded his wings, with the temporary rank of lieutenant.[27] Beyond that, the two Australians were warmly greeted by most of the populace, though there were one or two exceptions.

On one occasion, the farmer whose pastures encompassed Christchurch's main airstrip of Wigram Field — whose cows had to be shooed off whenever there was to be a landing — noticed a large crowd had formed to greet the famous pilots, who'd gone to check on the *Southern Cross*, and saw an opportunity. The farmer sent his twelve-year-old son to the airstrip with a gallon of fresh milk, and a cup with which he could dole it out to anyone who had sixpence. This lad wormed his way to the front of the admiring crowd, at which point Smithy spotted him and said, 'Hey sonny, if you will clean down my plane I will give you a joy flight over the city this afternoon.'

The proud and plucky young New Zealander drew himself up to his full 5 feet nothing, stuck out his chest and said, 'I ain't cleaning no cow shit from no plane tyres for no Aussie.'

True, his chance of a flight in the *Southern Cross* evaporated at that moment, but national honour had been served.[28]

When passing through Wellington, Kingsford Smith and Ulm made a brief visit to the home of the mother of Lieutenant John Moncrieff.[29] That good woman still maintained hope that by some miracle her boy would be found alive.

Finally, after new propellers shipped over from Sydney had been fitted to the *Southern Cross*, it was time for them to head home, and Kingsford Smith and Ulm, with Litchfield and McWilliams again as crew, took off at 4.54 in the morning of 13 October 1928 from the Marlborough Aero Club at Blenheim, at the top of the South Island, and proceeded west by north. As they did so, a fearful wind hit them and they flew straight into the teeth of it, all day long. The wind took off so much of their speed that they were only able to make progress at an average ground speed of 65 miles per hour. At that rate, it would be touch and go whether they would make it home.

That rising anxiety, however, was as nothing to what happened at around three in the afternoon, when, shortly after

Charles Ulm had stood up to stretch his cramped legs, the starboard engine cut out. There was no flutter, no splutter, no stutter — it just went *dead*.

With great urgency, but remaining calm, Kingsford Smith drew on his vast experience and immediately went through his mental check list of vital actions to determine what possibly could be the cause of the engine failure, even as the *Southern Cross* started to lose altitude.

Known as FMS: 'F' stood for 'fuel cocks', and they were on, while 'M' was for 'mixture', which had been set at 'full rich'. Too, when the cause of an engine problem was lack of petrol, the engine usually had the decency to cough a few times in protest. Which left 'S' for 'switches'. Could it be an electrical fault, a wire that had come off, magnetos that had died together, a switch that ...?

Then he saw it. The magneto ignition switch for the starboard engine, instead of being in the 'on' position was now in the 'off' position. In the confined cockpit, Ulm must have knocked it accidentally, perhaps as he put out his hand to steady himself.

Smithy reached over, snapped the switch back to 'on', and an instant later the still windmilling propeller on the starboard engine burst into life. Though that was definitely good news, they were still not safe. By the time it became dark at about 7 pm, they remained a long way from the Australian coast, with a third of their journey still to go, and even when they eventually saw the coded flashes of a lighthouse in the distance, it turned out to be Newcastle, a bit over an hour's flying time north of Sydney, meaning the wind had blown them a long way off their correct course. Could they make Richmond air base, on the amount of petrol left in their tanks? The answer was ... maybe.

At last, coming in over the muted lights of Sydney, the crew of the *Southern Cross* were momentarily confused as to just where Richmond air base lay, until, out to the west they saw what was effectively an arrow of light, pointing straight at a dark blob that just *had* to be the field. So many Sydneysiders had followed the drama of the flight on the radio and were now heading out to Richmond to greet them, that a traffic jam had ensued, which meant the *Southern Cross* could follow the cars' headlights all the way to the field, where an arc light, together with a dozen flares — lit kerosene-soaked rags in large tins that had been cut in two — had been set up to guide them in.

Finally, the plane came over the gathered crowd at the airfield 'like a great bat in the darkness',[30] and touched down at 2.15 am. When they mercifully turned their faithful engines off, only 3 gallons of petrol remained in the tanks.[31] That would have been enough to keep them in the air for another ten minutes — at best. The flight had taken just less than twenty-four hours, but the main thing was that they were safe and sound, and those listening on their radios across Australia could now breathe out.

As ever, the Kingsford Smith clan turned out in force to welcome their boy home.

Before Kingsford Smith left the airbase with his family for home, he was handed a telegram addressed to him from the Prime Minister of New Zealand, Joseph Coates:

> Hearty congratulations on successful re-crossing. Now we can all go to bed.[32]

•

The usual slew of glorious headlines followed their achievement, though one headline out of the ordinary that was of particular significance to Smithy's personal life was 'KINGSFORD SMITH DECREE NISI GRANTED'. The article appeared in late October 1928, and noted that his divorce from Thelma had gone through.

Two letters were tabled during the proceedings. One was from him formally asking her to return to him, and the other was her reply:

> *I have no intention whatever of returning to you, and absolutely refuse to live with you again. I am content at home and am capable of supporting myself as I have done for the last four or five months since you went to Sydney. Do not trouble to write again, as this is definite. Thelma.*[33]

Well, that seemed rather final then.

In the final judgment, Smithy was able to give Thelma £250 — now only a tiny percentage of the riches he was amassing — and she was able to give him a wide berth as long as they both would live. All to the good ...

•

What now? After all, they had flown around Australia, crossed the Pacific Ocean and crossed the Tasman. Hinkler had flown from England to Australia in under sixteen days. Blériot had long done the Channel, Lindbergh the Atlantic Ocean from New York to Paris in one hop and Richard Byrd claimed to have flown over the North Pole. And, in 1924, the US Army had flown a fleet of aircraft right around the world in the northern hemisphere. Pioneer aviators had effectively run out of oceans to cross, heroic deeds to do. So what would they do? In Smithy's words, the only answer was for them to focus on 'the exploitation of commercial flying in our own country, where there was much scope for aviation enterprise'.[34]

And so Australian National Airways Limited was formally born. The central idea was for Kingsford Smith and Ulm, together with financial backing from some leading Sydney businessmen who Ulm had rustled up, to buy five tri-motor Avro Ten (licence-built Fokker F.VIIb.3m) aircraft — similar to the *Southern Cross* — and establish regular passenger and postal services between Sydney, Brisbane, Melbourne and Hobart. As a railway line ran between Brisbane, Sydney and Melbourne, this meant that under government policy there was no question of them receiving subsidies — competing as they would be with the government for travel and freight custom — but they still felt the time had come for such a service, and they were just the men to do it.

The only place to buy the five Avro planes they needed was England, as Australia's nascent aircraft manufacturing industry did not have suitable products available, and both Ulm and Kingsford Smith — now 'joint managing directors', if you please — felt strongly that the Australian public would be happy only in planes that were British built.

True, their last attempt at an aviation company, Interstate Flying Services, had been no great success, but this was different. Back then no-one had known anything about them, now they were famous. Now, they had clout. Now, surely, there would be plenty of people who would want to fly with them, just as governments would also be more disposed to listen to their needs. They hoped so, anyway. And yet, there would be some difficult things they would have to get through before making that a reality.

•

It was a minor breakthrough in the midst of a singularly fraught time. In February 1929, soon after the *Anderson v. Ulm & Kingsford Smith* case began, Ulm and Kingsford Smith approached Anderson requesting that he withdraw the action in return for the promise of £1000. Keith and his solicitors considered their offer. It was true that at one point in the protracted negotiations between the three partners when they were in San Francisco, Ulm had ensured that all three of them signed a contract whereby if for any reason a partner pulled out, he would have no further claim either on the assets, or profits, generated by a successful flight. And there was also no dispute that Anderson had left San Francisco of his own free will, and had not returned, even though invited to. In remarks the judge made, it was clear that he took the view that the partnership was thereby dissolved. The chances of legal victory were so small, there was very little likelihood that Kingsford Smith and Ulm would have to share the £50,000 that had come to them. And now they were offering £1000 if he would drop the whole thing? Keith decided to take the money and run. Or more particularly, fly ...

After paying off his legal fees, he put the rest of the money towards buying his own plane — a Westland Widgeon III, G-AUKA — a sporty type of aeroplane, with folding wings, made for speed above all else, including safety. (Among other things, the Cirrus engine the plane used was notoriously only as reliable as a two-bob watch.) And when it turned out that he didn't have quite enough for that, Smithy fronted him another £300. The purchase was completed on 22 February 1929, and

Anderson almost immediately announced plans to make an attempt on the world endurance record for a light aircraft. He decided to call his plane *Kookaburra*.

•

As to Bobby Hitchcock, who brought his own lawsuit a month later, a similar scenario followed. Richard Windeyer, KC, was completely merciless in his cross-examination.

Windeyer: 'You were merely a mechanic, were you not?'

Hitchcock: 'Yes.'

Windeyer: 'You knew nothing about navigation?'

Hitchcock: 'No.'

Windeyer: 'You could not have done any wireless work?'

Hitchcock: 'No.'

Windeyer: 'You were not a pilot?'

Hitchcock: 'No.'

Windeyer: 'Do you realise you would have been only dead weight, absolutely useless while they were in the air?'

Hitchcock: 'While they were in the air.'

Windeyer: 'I suppose you realise, or you won't deny, will you, that at every place where these people would stop it would be possible to find good mechanics?'

Hitchcock: 'No.'[35]

When Kingsford Smith was cross-examined extensively by Hitchcock's own counsel, the aviator denied all knowledge of any promise to pay Hitchcock £1000 if the Pacific flight was successful. In the end, the judge ruled that Kingsford Smith and Ulm had no case to answer. His interpretation was that Hitchcock had been engaged as a mechanic when the project had included the Ryan monoplane, but that engagement had ceased when that project had been abandoned in favour of taking a Fokker.[36]

Hitchcock left the courtroom a shattered man. Kingsford Smith left it troubled. He had hated the whole process from first to last. As for Ulm, he was much as he had always been: stoical. He hadn't liked the case either, but among other talents, he was a hard businessman and accepted that occasional legal action simply went with that territory.

•

With everything now on track with Australian National Airways to get off the ground once they had secured the planes they needed from England, Kingsford Smith and Ulm decided they might as well fly there in the *Southern Cross* and become the first Australians and New Zealanders to do so in that direction. Alan Cobham was the first to fly from Australia to England in his de Havilland DH.50 float-and-land plane, in a magnificent out and back flight between June and October 1926. A knighthood that year was one of his just rewards. While they were at it they could attempt to beat Hinkler's 1928 outward bound flight record. It would surely be a mere trifle to accomplish compared with the overwater trans-Tasman flights.

With the *Southern Cross*, their first intended refuelling point was on the dried mud flat surrounded by long grass that served as the airstrip of the tiny town of Wyndham, high up in the reaches of Australia's vast north-west, near the place on the Australian coast that was the closest to England. Through the good graces of the Atlantic Union Oil Company, they were able to ensure that there would be 750 gallons of petrol waiting for them after their 2000-mile overland hop from Sydney. The oil company also kindly put their local agent, Captain Clive Chateau, at the service of the crew of the *Southern Cross*, so he would be able to advise them when the weather was clear. (There would be few things worse than arriving at Wyndham only to discover that they couldn't find the landing spot in bad weather.) Coming to the party also was the *Sun* newspaper, which agreed to pay them £500 for exclusive coverage, with a £250 bonus if they beat Bert Hinkler's England to Australia record time of fifteen and a half days.

At 10.30 am on Holy Saturday, 30 March 1929, the heavily laden *Southern Cross* made ready to take off from Richmond air base, ready to complete the first leg of a pioneering flight to England, before a crowd some 50,000 strong of cheering well-wishers and attendant press. Many people in the crowd were there for the sheer sake of being around such celebrity, others came with a sense of history and still more were there perhaps in the hope of seeing a spectacular crash. The press was there for *all* of the above. Planes provided wonderful photographs, great copy and moved papers in huge numbers.

Rising to the occasion, Smithy addressed the crowd and told them that it was his most earnest desire to prove that the British Empire need not be a collection of distant outposts but rather, one empire entirely linked by aerial communication.

Hurrah for Smithy!

They hadn't received a cabled 'all-clear' at Wyndham from Captain Chateau, but not to worry. A meteorological map published in the *Sydney Morning Herald* that morning seemed to indicate that the weather would be okay to make a landing.[37] At least okay-ish. They could have waited longer, perhaps, but the agreement they had with the Australian National Airways board stated that they were to be away by 30 March at the latest.

Usually at the moment of take-off on such a trip, the atmosphere on the plane would have been a joyous but tense type of excitement, men born to fly, who were now doing exactly that. And yet, unlike them, Kingsford Smith and Charles Ulm were in rather bad humour on this particular morning. In RAAF parlance, they had S.o.L. (shit on the liver).

It was the Federal government that was troubling them. A few weeks previously the two aviators had written to the government suggesting that perhaps Australia might care to buy the *Southern Cross* from them, on the reckoning that it could be put in a museum or some such. Both had been underwhelmed to receive a very lukewarm response acknowledging receipt of the letter, but also noting that the government would have to think about the offer as it was worried about the high costs of maintaining so large a plane. This, despite the fact that Kingsford Smith and Ulm were only asking for the nominal fee of £3000, a bare fraction of what it was truly worth!

At the same time another department of the government had been pursuing them for rental on the hangar space they had been using to house the *Southern Cross* at Richmond *and* for the work done on it by RAAF mechanics *and* for work done on its propellers. As if that wasn't enough, the government had been insistent that all those bills be paid *before* the men left for England, presumably on the grounds that by doing it in that fashion, the government wouldn't be out of pocket should they crash and burn. Bloody ghouls. Not that they were going to crash and burn, of course. Old hands at this long-distance flying caper by now, both aviators felt confident that all would go well, as Sydney slipped behind them and western New South Wales lay at their mercy.

•

It was the nature of flying, however, that at the very moment when they least expected it, something did in fact go wrong.

In the tightly cramped back of the plane, Hal Litchfield had just got up to move to the port-side window to take a sighting through the drift indicator, when he inadvertently leaned on the catch that released the spool for the radio antenna trailing beneath them. (Such was the technology of the time, that the long-wave antenna connected to their transmitter was in fact nothing more than a couple of hundred feet of copper wire, with a lead weight at the end, trailing down and behind the plane. There was also twice as much again wire tightly wound around the spool.) The instant Litchfield released the spool, the lead was given its head and, caught by the wind, went racing away. Before either Litchfield or McWilliams could do anything to stop it, the line had reached the end of its tether with such velocity that the whole thing snapped off and went ribboning away down to the countryside below!

Oh Christ.

This was a real problem, because, while they could transmit messages on the radio that still had its aerial, they were incapable of receiving any. The first that Smithy and Ulm knew of it in the cockpit was when McWilliams passed a note forward: *Long-wave aerial gone. Shall we return?*[238]

Yes, well. After the fanfare of departure, it was ever and always a difficult thing to meekly return just a short time later to say, '*Ummm*, things didn't quite work out', but that was not what was stopping Ulm and Kingsford Smith from returning now. It was not simply a matter of returning and landing. It was one thing to just manage to take off with the heavy load that they had, but quite another to be able to safely land with that amount, less the ninety minutes of fuel that they would have burned. Certainly they could dump that fuel before landing, but that was an extremely expensive option. And then they would have to face another risky take-off in a heavily laden plane. On the other hand, if they pressed on, and all went well, they would be able to get a fresh reel of copper wire at Wyndham.

After all, what was the lack of a bit of copper wire to men flying in good weather over land, when those same men had traversed the *entire* Pacific Ocean in far worse conditions? They were adventurers and it was in their very nature, once embarked, not to worry too much about unexpected things happening. Had they possessed the 'fretful minds of weaker men' as the *New York Times* had phrased it the year before when lauding the fact that Charles Lindbergh did not have a radio, and had they been the kind of blokes who always turned back from an adventure the first time something went wrong, they would never have been the kind of men to embark on flying the Pacific, or flying to England from Australia, in the first place. So that was the answer. Press on. Bearing 306 degrees, just a bit north of north by west, all the way to Wyndham!

•

Meanwhile, in that very settlement, Clive Chateau had woken to the gobsmacking news that the *Southern Cross* was on its way, without his having sent a telegram that the weather was clear![39] What was worse, far worse, was that not only wasn't the weather at Wyndham clear, it was positively *bad* — windy and stormy, with rain lashing down — and it was getting more frightening by the hour. In general, Chateau was an affable, easygoing, hail-fellow-well-met kind of man, not prone to panic. But under such circumstances he was instantly highly agitated and had no hesitation in immediately cabling Sydney:

> Cannot believe Southern Cross would leave without definite OK from me. If they have left they must be recalled. Conditions are unfavourable and unsafe and will be unsuitable for some time.[40]

And in Sydney, at the La Perouse receiving station of Amalgamated Wireless Australasia Ltd, the radio operators did indeed try very hard to recall the *Southern Cross*. For the life of them they tried. But for some reason they couldn't understand — they had no way of knowing what had happened to the antenna — no-one on the *Southern Cross* replied. How could this be?

•

Trouble ahead. Big, black, billowing bundles of bloody big trouble.

It was obviously a storm as high as it was wide, as black as it was crackling with shafts of catastrophe called lightning, preceded by swirling, red dust. The *Southern Cross* was heading straight into the maelstrom, with visibility almost non-existent through the mud-caked windows, as the sun started to fall away at the end of that first day of flying. Only a short time after crossing the Overland Telegraph Line, they were right in the thick of the storm, and being buffeted from side to side as well as up and down. As the wind howled at them like a thousand banshees and the rain pelted in, Kingsford Smith tried everything to ease the pressure on the craft. Flying in total darkness, with the clouds around them being illuminated by progressively more intense flashes of lightning, Smithy tried first to climb above the storm, but it seemed to have no top — or at least no top that they could get above. Nor could they get around it, so the only thing they could do was keep going on and on through the night, and hope that at dawn they would have left the storm behind and at least be able to see where they were.

•

As the *Southern Cross* smashed her way through the belting, pelting night, Clive Chateau passed the worst night of his life at Wyndham as the rain continued to bucket down from the swarming, low clouds and the wind kept howling. He knew this wasn't just a local storm, as it in fact covered the best portion of north-western Australia. How could the *Southern Cross* ever find one small town in this tempest? That is, if she was still aloft. How had this happened? What had gone wrong? Why had they left, when he hadn't given them the okay? He had no answers.

The storm continued, unabated, with the rain pounding down on the tin roof like an angry devil on drums. A few of the older locals told him it was the worst weather they had experienced in thirty years, while others said it was the worst in their lifetime![41]

•

But the much-awaited dawn, when it finally came, only served further to horrify the flyers. When Smithy carefully tried to bring the *Southern Cross* low enough to get a look at the ground, the only glimpses they could see were of a landscape as uninviting to aircraft as it was possible. Through the swirling clouds and heavy winds they could see thick forests, gullies, hills — just about everything bar any clear space in which to land, should they need to. And the further they flew, the more obvious it was that a forced landing was a real possibility, if not yet a probability.

It wasn't just that there was no sign of Wyndham; it was that there was not the tiniest sign of where *any* bit of civilisation might be. Not a road, or a telegraph line, or a fence, nor the slightest indication that humans had ever even crossed the forbidding landscape below, let alone left their mark on it.

What to do? The one thing they could, which was to keep going and keep looking for some kind of sign.

Finally, they saw what appeared to be a small river and, reasoning that the river must lead to the coast, where they would find Wyndham, they followed it, as scudding dark daylight slowly broke through. When they reached the coast, however, there was no Wyndham, just an angry-looking sea.

Keeping his calm, Smithy reasoned that they must have overshot Wyndham, and were therefore now on the west coast of the Kimberley district, which would mean he had to turn … let's see … north-west.

With lack of fuel not yet a problem, they flew on, expecting at any moment to spot the familiar shape of Cape Londonderry, which Smithy had seen many times in his days with Western Australian Airways.

•

Glory be to God. Another day, another round of reciting prayers and doing the Almighty's work — either shouldering the white man's burden, or being it. Drysdale River Mission was an isolated spot, situated near the coast, about 140 miles north-west of Wyndham. Settled by Benedictine fathers in the early 1900s, it cared for the local indigenous population and had such little contact with the outside world that it was September 1920 before word came to them that the Great War had ended nearly two years earlier and that the Allies had won. From one month to the next, from year to year, it was a life of work and prayer, work and prayer, while tending to their flocks, both real and spiritual.

But on the late morning of Easter Sunday, 31 March 1929, something happened. They heard engines! From the heavens! Both the fathers and the small group of Aborigines living at the mission rushed outside, and were stunned to see an enormous plane circling above them. A plane! They had heard stories of such a thing, and now, here was one. It really existed, praise the Lord. And yet why was it circling? Was the crew on board in trouble? Did they want something from the men on the ground?

Aboard the *Southern Cross*, it was a great relief to see human habitation in the wilderness. No, they didn't have a landing strip but it was something. People were now gathered in a courtyard, looking up at them and waving. Most importantly, they would know something of the geography of the land in which they lived.

While Kingsford Smith circled low, Ulm wrote a message in pencil on a piece of paper in big black letters, wrapped it around a torch, tied it with a piece of string and dropped it out of the window, being sure to drop it far enough away so that it wouldn't hit anyone. On the paper was written: *Please point direction of Wyndham.*

As the plane continued circling around, Smithy and Ulm waited expectantly for the signal to come, expecting the direction to be to the south-east, where, by their reckoning, Wyndham must lie …

To their great consternation, however, the people immediately started pointing to the south-west! But how could that be? Still, there was nothing for it but to take them at their word and head off in that direction, though feeling more desperate and confused with every passing minute.

At the mission they watched the plane disappear over the south-western horizon, and stayed watching long after the last tiny buzz of its faraway engines could no longer be heard. What was that all about? Why had they been circled in such a fashion, and why, when they had clearly indicated where the only bit of flat ground in cooee lay just a few hundred yards away in the south-westerly direction, had the people on the plane so totally ignored it? It was something that would occasion a lot of discussion among them for many days to come. Ulm's message, meanwhile, still lay wrapped around its torch, lost in the landscape near the mission, and remained undiscovered …

•

Flying. Flying. Flying. *Still* flying. And flying on. Beneath them, little in the landscape changed. It remained as inhospitable as ever, and impenetrable for any aircraft that wanted to remain intact after coming to earth. The only thing that did change was the falling amount of precious petrol left in their tanks, and the rising amount of concern they felt. And then they saw another settlement, also a mission to judge by the crosses dotted around at the top of every building.

Now more desperate than ever, Ulm dropped out another message: *Please place white sheets pointing direction of Wyndham, and mark in larger figures number of miles.*[42]

This time the message resulted in an instant burst of activity below with people darting indoors before reappearing bearing sheets. While they sorted themselves out, Ulm and Kingsford Smith checked their petrol gauges and did some calculations. By their best reckoning they had just two hours of flying time left if all went well.

If that was bad, still worse was the arrow and number below them. For a lot of sheets and towels laid out on the ground clearly made an arrow pointing due east — yes, *east*, there could be no doubt about it — and the number that went with it clearly said: 250.

But how could that be? This new information was so confusing because there was no way that the two directions they had been given could both be right. And yet there could be little doubt that these last directions were correct, so clear and precise were they. With little choice but to give it a go, Smithy turned the *Southern Cross* due east and concentrated on throttling down to get as much distance out of the petrol they had remaining as they could possibly manage.

•

Clive Chateau knew it, he just knew it. Something was terribly, terribly wrong. It had to be. All day long at Wyndham he had been hoping against hope — even as the rain had continued to belt down beneath a low cloud cover — to hear the distant throb of approaching engines. All through that grim morning and into the early afternoon, despite hoping against hope, he was not surprised to hear nothing. For how could Kingsford Smith possibly find the small town of Wyndham in such conditions — an even smaller dot in the western wilderness than Fiji was in the Pacific Ocean? Clive was not the only one who was worried. Through all the trials and tribulations of the *Southern Cross*, McWilliams had been sending out an account of their situation, which meant that radio operators throughout Australia, and through them the press and then the flyers' families were aware that the men were lost, low on fuel, and running out of possible solutions to potential disaster.

•

It was clear that the situation was hopeless. The *Southern Cross* was battling a headwind and fuel had fallen so low that it was obvious they were not going to be able to get remotely close to Wyndham. The only sensible thing to do, it seemed, was to head back to the last mission they had seen and bring the *Southern Cross* down as near to it as they could get. That way at least they would have help ... and yet it soon became devastatingly clear that even that was a forlorn hope as the engines were clearly running on fumes alone. With just minutes remaining, at best, until the engines cut out on them, Smithy's eyes roved such landscape as they could see through the storm looking for a spot to land where they would not be killed on impact. Nothing looked remotely promising, with boulders, ravines, termite mounds, gum trees and the distinctive boab trees all conspiring to deny the *Southern Cross* a single flat, open stretch.

And then he saw it. Up ahead about a mile, and a short distance to the right was a small patch of flat ground. It was far too small to land safely on if it was dry, but it was clearly muddy and that meant he would be able to slow down all the more quickly by bogging the wheels, if he could just touch down on the right spot.

The easiest decisions in all the world to make are, of course, those when there is really no other choice, and this was just such an occasion. With the engines threatening to cut at any second there would not even be time to fly around the intended landing spot to reconnoitre, and he would have to nail the landing first time.

For McWilliams in the back, there was just enough time to get out a quick message on the radio to the waiting world:

> Have become hopelessly lost in dense bush.
> Now faced with forced landing at place
> we believe to be 150 miles from Wyndham
> in rotten country. Wish us luck. We will
> communicate again as soon as possible.[43]

Staggering along at just above stalling speed, Kingsford Smith dragged the *Southern Cross* in, nose-high, hanging on the screaming propellers, aiming to touch down on the first yard of mud. Suddenly the windscreen was filled with the vision of boulders and trees whipping past on either side. Triple throttles chopped, and the *Southern Cross* dropped like a shot bird. Contact! The wheels dug into the soft ground and instantly all four of the crew were hurled forward as the spent bird went from flying through air to slushing through wet mud. Smithy stayed wrestling the wheel and dancing a hot jig on the rudder pedals, desperately trying to bring the plane to a controlled stop.

Somehow, extraordinarily, after just 100 squelching yards he managed it, switched off the engines and …

And it was always like this.

After a forced landing, or a crash, there was the sudden cessation of that monotonous blare of the motors, replaced by searing silence, save for the tinkling of the exhaust manifolds cooling, and the wonderful realisation that you were still alive! And substantially unhurt!

It felt like a miracle.

Thirteen
COFFEE ROYAL

A nation's hero may become a nation's whipping boy overnight …
CHARLES KINGSFORD SMITH, 1929

Somehow, somehow, *somehow*, in that godforsaken part of the world, Smithy, against all odds, had got the plane down intact, and his crew with it.

'Smithy,' Hal Litchfield said, after he had picked himself up from the bulkhead where he had landed, 'you're a marvel.'

'Pure luck,' Kingsford Smith smiled in reply.

'No, not luck, Smithy,' Charles Ulm said, and he meant it. 'Nobody else could have put her down in this mud without tipping her on her nose. Look, she didn't run an inch over a hundred yards!'[1]

McWilliams jumped down from the fuselage and pointed out to the others how close a spindly 12-foot gum tree had come to the propeller on the starboard engine. Just another foot forward and the propeller would have shattered against it. As it was, it looked like if they had petrol and a rough flat strip to work with, they could take off again!

But where exactly were they?

Apart from lost-lost in the never-never, that is? That would be something they would have to work out in the hours to come, though it was at least clear that they had landed on a swamp with many tidal inlets. For now, the most important thing was to take stock of just how they were going to survive until help could get to them.

The stocktake of available food did not take long, as the base of it was seven sad sandwiches. Inconceivably, the emergency rations that were meant to be in the plane had been removed by persons unknown before the flight, and the only thing approaching provisions that they had on board was 8 pounds of Allenbury's Baby Food intended for the postmaster's baby at Wyndham. Completing their raggedy roundup was a couple of pounds of coffee, a box of matches, a flask of brandy and a packet of biscuits. The one necessity they didn't lack was fresh water, as they found a waterhole nearby.

Well, there was no other option but make the best of it. To get as good an understanding as they could about the place they had landed, Smithy and Ulm tramped through the muddy swampland — while dodging crocodiles! — to reach and climb to the top of the only hill in the area. Once there they looked in every direction, hoping against hope to see any sign of the mission, or perhaps a column of smoke that would indicate some human habitation nearby, but all they could see was mile after mile of swampland, just as they had seen from the air. At least from that height the wings and body of the *Southern Cross* stood out as a massive silver and blue cross against the landscape, and they had some hope that it would be easy to spot from above.

By the time they got back to the plane, McWilliams had succeeded in doing what he could never have done while the plane was flying, which was to rig up a long-wave aerial, by wrapping copper wire as high around the tree in front of the propeller as he could get it, and already he had news! Despite the roaring of the engines which he could still hear in his ears if not in actuality, he had picked up signals, and had already heard Perth tell Darwin that the *Southern Cross* was missing. That was promising, as surely it couldn't be long before planes came looking for them, and they would be saved.

And so, after getting a desultory fire going, and nibbling sparingly on half a sandwich each, followed by a little bit of baby food — the Ritz, it wasn't — they decided to follow up with a chaser of coffee mixed with brandy.

'Well, mates, we may be lost, but at least we've got coffee royal to drink!'[2] Smithy mocked, as he took his first sip.

A short time later they settled down for the night. Or at least tried to … Only minutes after it became dark, they had visitors. First in ones and twos. Then in their dozens. Then in their hundreds. Then in their *thousands*! Mosquitoes! Swarms of them! On their faces. Their arms. Their legs. Everywhere! Stinging little mongrels. Noisy little bastards that sounded, yes, like three-engined Fokkers. In the ensuing hours each man cursed, slapped and cursed some more, trying to snatch a few minutes' sleep here and there until the weight of the combined pain of all the stings outweighed their extreme fatigue, after a twenty-eight and a half hour flight which had finished in a semi-controlled crash-landing. *Mongrels.*

•

It was no April Fool's joke — not bloody likely it wasn't. On the morning of Easter Monday, 1 April 1929, Australia awoke to the news — emblazoned across every front page in the land — that the *Southern Cross* was missing, and had very likely crash-landed in extremely rough country.

Six-column bold-face headlines in subsequent editions told much of the story.

SOUTHERN CROSS FORCED DOWN IN BAD COUNTRY[3]

SILENCE UNBROKEN

SEARCH FOR THE SOUTHERN CROSS[4]

VEIL OF SILENCE

NO NEWS OF SOUTHERN CROSS[5]

OMINOUS SILENCE: WHERE IS 'VETERAN' SOUTHERN CROSS?[6]

GRAVEST FEARS FOR SAFETY OF SOUTHERN CROSS CREW[7]

It was Sydney's *Sun* that went biggest with the story announcing, with huge headlines across the entire page, that at dawn of that very day, a rescue plane, sponsored by the *Sun* in conjunction with the Melbourne *Herald*, would be on its way to find Smithy and the boys.

Which was to the good, because it seemed unlikely that the Federal government would be sending any search planes. That much had been made clear by Prime Minister Stanley Bruce who, when accosted at his front door while wearing a bathrobe and slippers by a *Daily Telegraph* journalist, and asked why the government wasn't doing anything about finding the *Southern Cross*, had shrugged his shoulders and replied that it was not for the government to 'interfere in private ventures ...'

His response was not good enough for many people in Sydney, particularly. For it was there that a friend of Smithy's by the name of John Garlick, who was also Sydney's Chief Civic Commissioner — effectively a State government-imposed lord mayor, after Sydney Council had been accused of graft — started up a Citizens Southern Cross Rescue Committee and held a mass meeting at Sydney Town Hall to raise money to launch a serious search.

'Australia's national heroes are in danger,' he cried. 'They are in dire distress. It is the duty of the Australian people to hurry to their rescue.'[8]

And so said all of them. And so said all of their wallets.

No less than £2000 was promised in the first twenty minutes of the meeting. Just two days after that, with thousands of Sydneysiders contributing everything from a shilling to several pounds, they had gathered £7000. With that money, they were able to hire the *Canberra*, a de Havilland DH.61 Giant Moth six-passenger, single-engined biplane, boasting at the controls a distinguished former Australian Flying Corps pilot by the name of Les Holden (of the Holden's Motor Body Builders family) and his crew, to begin the search. For his part, Smithy's old boss at West Australian Airways, Major Norman Brearley, was quick to send his three best pilots out in three of his planes — half of his fleet — to search the Kimberley. Within a day, pilots Jim Woods, Bertie Heath and Eric Chater — all former colleagues and good friends of Smithy from his days of flying with West Australian Airways — were on their way, each searching his allotted part of the map, before returning to refuel and going out again to the next part. (The flight of Woods was the one sponsored by the Sydney *Sun* and Melbourne *Herald*.) Time was of the essence. After all, the natives in those parts were said to be cannibals![9]

At Arabella Street, the wider Kingsford Smith family had gathered at the homestead. This was a crisis, and a time for them all to come together. Such was their confidence in Chilla, they felt certain he would have found a way to come down all right, and it was just a question of finding him. They were all conscious that he had been ill with the flu for the week before departure.

'I do hope he has not suffered a relapse,' William had told the *Daily Guardian* the day before. Then, pointing out his newly renovated house, all of which had been done at Chilla's direction and expense, he proudly added, 'Not many of the outside public know this side of Charlie's nature. They know him only as a hero of the air.'[10]

Between them, the Kingsford Smith clan decided that Leofric would be the one liaising with the authorities to ensure that everything that could be done, was done. In the meantime, Catherine stayed glued to the radio, hoping for news, while William manned the phone, fielding no fewer than fifty calls from family, friends and journalists in the first day. The board of Australian National Airways had equally come together at their offices in Martin Place and were meeting with radio and flying experts to try to narrow down just where the *Southern Cross* could be.

•

Meanwhile, watching all the developments extremely closely was Keith Anderson, who of course knew the country around where Smithy and that prick Ulm had disappeared very well, courtesy of his time with West Australian Airlines. A regular at Sydney's Customs House Hotel, situated close to Circular Quay, Anderson told anyone who would listen that he was convinced that the *Southern Cross* would be found somewhere in the Port George area, because he had analysed all the communications from the plane, and it was obvious what had happened. They had overshot Wyndham in the storm, hit the coast, and then bounced back and forth looking for it, until they ran out of petrol.

'I would give anything to be able to go and look for the boys,' Anderson said in the presence of the hotelier, John Cantor.

'Right,' Cantor immediately replied. 'I will back you.'[11]

And indeed, Anderson had been convincing enough in his analysis that it wasn't long before Cantor raised some funds from friends and acquaintances who also believed it made sense to send Anderson in his new Widgeon to start looking. And no matter that the plane was yet to receive its official certificate of registration. There was no time to worry about paperwork.

Anderson began immediate preparations, engaging — surprisingly, although he was in desperate need of any work he could get — Bobby Hitchcock to go with him as his mechanic. They were going to find Smithy!

And then, in response to the general outcry, the government relented and the prime minister at last ordered the seaplane carrier HMAS *Albatross*, which was then berthed in Sydney, to head to the other side of the massive continent with six RAAF No. 101 Fleet Co-operation Flight Supermarine Seagull III amphibians on board to begin searching the area where the *Southern Cross* was thought to have disappeared. In the meantime, luggers had left the rich pearling grounds off the West Australian coast and begun searching the coast for any sign of wreckage that might have washed ashore.

Now, Australia watched, and waited. Anxiously …

SOUTHERN CROSS MEN HAVE NOW BEEN MISSING OVER 40 HOURS:

NATION'S ANXIETY
GRIM SILENCE STILL BROODS OVER LOST PLANE
DESPERATE SEARCH FOR MISSING AVIATORS —
ANOTHER DISAPPOINTING DAY[12]

What no-one could work out was why there had been no contact from the *Southern Cross*. After all, it had both a wireless and wireless operator on board. What on earth were they doing out there? Were they alive? Were they dead, or horribly injured, perhaps? What on earth were they *doing*?!

•

Basically, they were starving, even as the mosquitoes feasted. Slowly and surely. The sandwiches were gone after just the first couple of days, and the baby food had to be divided into tiny portions and mixed with water to make it last longer. After an attempt by 'Mac' to hunt for game with his revolver came to nothing, they decided to go after rather smaller game. Specifically, well, there were … snails. No, they didn't provide as much meat as the birds or kangaroos Mac had been hoping for, but by God they were a whole lot easier to catch and could be found low down on the mangrove trees. Though they tasted godawful, and were gritty with sand, once boiled up and with their shells cracked off with stones, they at least provided a tiny bit of sustenance to fuel the many activities the *Southern Cross* crew embarked upon.

The first chore was to get a fire going on the hill, and then keep wood up to it thereafter, ensuring that in the daylight hours there was always a plume of white smoke heading skywards that search planes would be able to see.

Meantime, on the first full day at 'Coffee Royal', as they decided to call their place, Smithy, Ulm, McWilliams and Litchfield hunkered down, accompanied by perhaps ten thousand flies that seemed keen on swarming around and crawling all over them as if they were massive dog turds on legs. Key among the men's frustrations was that they had been unable to communicate with the outside world, even though Mac had rigged up an aerial that had allowed them to receive transmissions, on battery power alone. Hal Litchfield, meanwhile, once the storm had cleared, had been able to take their bearings from the stars, and they knew exactly where they were — latitude 15° 35' South, longitude 124° 45' East — about 150 miles from Derby and 300 miles due west of Wyndham. They also knew they were somewhere in the area of the Port George Mission, but had no idea where that mission lay — most frustratingly, no-one gave its position over the radio, and it was not marked on the maps they had. A brief point of discussion was whether they should go on an exploratory march to look for the mission, but lost in the wilderness as they were, 'the dear old *Southern Cross*', as Smithy thought of her, 'seemed at least a home, where we should be wise to remain'.[13] At least, the massive wingspan of the plane would surely be easily spotted from the air when the rescuers came their way, whereas if they had been alone on the ground, they would be near invisible.

What they most needed, of course, was to solve the radio problem. There had been no trouble transmitting when the *Southern Cross* had been in the air, as the Aladdin wind-powered generators on the sides of the cockpit had provided plenty of current to the radios. But now that they were on the ground, they had to find a way to get one of the generators to turn equally fast, as the transmitter could not operate without the A/C current they provided. Smithy, a man of no little ingenuity and energy in such matters, just as he had displayed when running the Gascoyne Transport Company, took the lead in trying to solve the problem. First they detached one of the generators from its bracket on the fuselage, and then chocked up one side of the undercarriage on a log resting on rocks, before digging out beneath one of the 4-foot-diameter landing wheels. Smithy also began to carve a wooden roller to attach to the end of the generator. The theory was once they had the wheel spinning furiously, they could hold the roller against it, and that would generate enough electricity to transmit a message to the outside world. It was exhausting, back-breaking work, but they kept at it. They needed to turn the generator at about its normal speed of 2000 revolutions per minute, so they would have had to turn the big wheel about 100 times a minute. Not easy in the heat and the flies and the mud …

At least, in the meantime, they were able to listen to how the search was proceeding, and learnt that the first of the rescue planes would be leaving Derby the following day to look for them, while a launch was going to head up the Drysdale River.

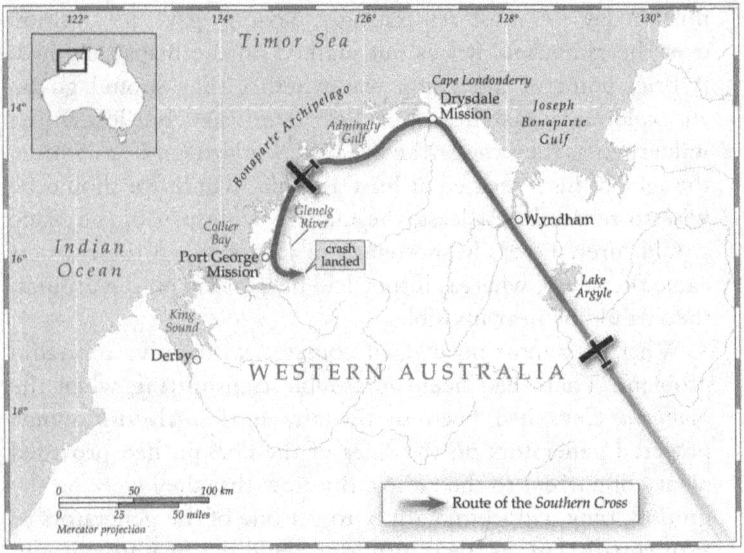

There was some hope that the morrow would bring succour, although no hope that the night would be anything but hell on earth as the mosquitoes now seemed to have organised themselves well enough to come at them in waves.

And then things got *really* bad: Tom McWilliams tried to cheer them all up by playing his mouth organ. At least he did so until, with their last reserves of energy for the day, the others prevailed upon him to stop.

'A major horror of the episode,' recorded Charles Ulm.[14]

Good God, what a *place*.

•

Another *plane*!

On Wednesday, 3 April 1929, at Drysdale Mission, 150 miles north-west of Wyndham, the residents were almost positive that the mysterious plane that had come and gone so quickly must now have returned and they rushed out in the midday sun expecting to see it.[15] But no, this was another, much smaller, single-engined plane and, after circling low, something dropped from it and landed nearby. It was a message from the pilot:

We are looking for another plane, missing since Sunday. Answer these questions in the following manner. Wave sheet to mean Yes. Place sheet flat on the ground to mean no. First question, did plane pass here? Second question, did it throw out a letter? Third question, which way did it go?[16]

Up in the West Australian Airways plane, pilot Jim Woods, with none other than the still deeply worried Clive Chateau as an observer, watched carefully the response.

To the first question there was a violent waving of the sheet, meaning they had definitely seen the *Southern Cross* …

To the second question, one native placed a sheet on the ground, while another waved a sheet … meaning, Woods supposed, that the answer was indeterminate.

And finally, the crucial third question. Which way were they heading? Now, a squad of eleven natives formed up and, evenly spaced out, resolutely marched in the south-westerly direction.

Now, *now*, they were getting somewhere!

•

That evening, their fourth at Coffee Royal, Ulm was so weak he could manage only a bare scrawl in his diary.

I feel gone in the arms and legs. The flies are unbearable, the mosquitoes damnable. We had gruel for lunch.

•

There remained an enormous amount of interest in where the *Southern Cross* was, and sympathy for the crew's plight was as widespread as it was deep, though the *Sydney Morning Herald* on that very day had been intemperate enough to question why on earth Kingsford Smith and Ulm had been so impetuous as to head to the remote Wyndham instead of taking the established route to Darwin, and take off without having received a positive weather report from their desired landing ground. Steering from there 'by God and by guess',[17] surely they had been practically asking for trouble?

In a blistering editorial, the *Sun* weighed in, in reply: 'Judging by the very many mistakes in fact on the subject of the flight and in its theories and criticisms, there is some ground for believing that the "Herald" this morning came out rather "by God and by guess" ...'[18]

•

Friday, 5 April.

The wretched time passed exceedingly slowly for the men. Only a few days before, an hour's worth of fuel had exhausted itself in what seemed like just a few minutes. Now, in this sweltering heat, a few minutes seemed to pass as slowly as whole hours. Listening on the radio, they were at least pleased to hear that the *Canberra* would likely soon be on its way to search for them.

•

Saturday, 6 April.

What's that?

What?

That! That sound? It sounds like ... *it is* ... a plane! A plane in the distance! About four miles off! Like mad things, suddenly re-energised in this hot and hazy mid-afternoon, the four men staggered to the hill and lit the fire again, managing to send billowing plumes of white smoke into the air that the crew on the plane couldn't fail to see ...

But somehow they did.

The plane droned off into the distance and *disappeared* ...

Smithy, for one, felt angry with his own impotence. Here he was, a man *born* to fly, capable of flying most planes the way an expert violinist might play a Stradivarius, and yet he was hopelessly earthbound and powerless to alter the course of the plane of their salvation by even one degree. And why wasn't the bloody pilot looking for smoke, the way he would have been had he been up there?! They so wanted that plane to come their way and save them, but nothing worked — not smoke, not prayers, not anything!

A few hours later, another plane appeared and then it too disappeared, after getting their hopes up. Shattered, desperately lonely and feeling as if the world had forsaken them, they returned to camp. *Christ Almighty.* If the sight of those two planes had done one thing, however, it seemed to have re-energised Smithy, almost as if he had come to the conclusion that if they were ever going to get out of there, it would have to be by virtue of their own endeavour.

Working like a madman, he completed his system to get the generator working.

That evening, at roughly the same time as the day shift of flies reluctantly handed over duties to the night shift of mosquitoes, they tried their luck. Smithy and Litchfield spun the wheel, while Ulm held the generator to it, and they kept spinning till they could spin no more — about thirty seconds, before they fell to the ground exhausted[19] — as Mac tapped furiously away.

'… --- … … --- … … --- …'

'SOS … SOS … SOS … we are at 15" 35' S, longitude 124" 45' E.'

There was no way of knowing, of course, whether the message got through, but as they slumped, exhausted, to the ground, the grim countenance of Mac was a fair indication that it probably hadn't. God Help All Of Us, indeed.

The last of their precious tobacco was gone and they were reduced to trying to smoke the leaves of the gum trees and mangroves. It was a close call, but on balance they decided that they would probably rather die, or at least go without, than smoke them again.

On a more serious matter, another decision had to be taken about whether Mac should try to convert the radio from being a receiver to being a transmitter. A method of doing precisely that had been broadcast from Sydney in the hope that the crew of the *Southern Cross* would hear it — and they did — but, after long discussion, they decided not to risk destroying the radio altogether. For them, the radio was a lifeline and by following closely reports of the rescue operation, they sensed — prayed — it could only be a matter of time before they were found, so long as they could actually survive that long.

In the meantime, they tried a new system with the generator, whereby they joined up the belts from their pants to make a kind of belt-and-pulley drive to turn the wooden roller faster than before, once they got the wheel spinning. In faraway Adelaide, a ham radio operator, Lance Coombe, was surprised to suddenly pick up very faint wireless signals in Morse code and could pick up the letters V … K … but then it faded just as quickly …[20]

•

In Sydney, Bon Hilliard was beside herself with fury. Keith was her fiancé, they were about to build a life together, and she had some say in this matter. And she insisted, stamping her foot, that Keith not risk his life in this foolish manner. It was crazy! She didn't know a lot about aviation, but she knew enough to know that you couldn't prepare a plane for a long flight like that in just a couple of days, and that the Widgeon wasn't designed for long-distance travel. Besides, how could he possibly go looking for Smithy and Ulm after the way those two had treated him over the Pacific flight? Keith had to understand that if he was intent on doing this, then the marriage was off — *off*, do you hear?

Keith, in his manner, listened quietly, but told Bon that it was just something he had to do. He loved her, he hoped she would reconsider, but he could hardly leave them out there when he reckoned he had a fair idea where they were, could he? Besides, years before, Smithy had twice plucked him from the West Australian wilderness — once when he had been lost for three weeks![21] — so this would be a payback.

He was going, and that was that. And quickly. So rushed was he to leave, in fact, that there was no time to install a working radio, or check that such a basic thing as a compass was fitted — Hitchcock had a pocket compass[22] — that the tool kit was complete, that the engine was in as good a shape as it possibly could be.

At dawn the following day, he and Bobby Hitchcock were at Richmond air base, and getting ready to fire up the *Kookaburra*. As they took off, on their way to find the *Southern Cross* and her crew, they left behind on the tarmac a weeping Bon Hilliard, who had relented at least enough to come to see them off.

Not far behind Anderson and Hitchcock in taking to the air was the Giant Moth, *Canberra*, with pilot Les Holden at the controls, though the latter plane, with its much stronger Bristol Jupiter nine-cylinder radial, 435-horsepower engine, quickly overtook the *Kookaburra* and moved well ahead.

•

Tuesday, 9 April.

Another plane in the distance. It passed by once. It passed by again. It didn't see them. If they had more energy they might have despaired at this point. But such a strong emotion was beyond them, so weak did they feel on the tenth day of being lost in the wilderness. Should they, perhaps, try another tack, and build a raft, which they could drift down the river on, and get all the way to the coast? No. The idea might have held merit for stronger men, but for blokes in their condition the only idea that gained unanimity of opinion was to lie like sick dogs in the shade under the wing of the *Southern Cross*, and hope that their rescue would come.

Ulm wrote in his diary:

> Mac and I are much weaker today. Hunger pains are most distressing. Smithy and Litch are failing too. To be passed three times by a plane is just heart-breaking. If only La Perouse radio station would send out the exact position of Port George Mission we would try to walk to it. But we don't know where it is. Matches are giving out: only 22 left. And the water hole is drying up.

On the upside, Ulm and Kingsford Smith were both elated, but also stunned, to hear that Keith Anderson and Bobby Hitchcock had taken off in the *Kookaburra*, and were coming to look for them.

•

Two cables were waiting for Keith Anderson when he finally made it into Alice Springs on the late afternoon of 9 April. One was from Lieutenant Colonel Horace Brinsmead, the Controller of Civil Aviation in Australia, who had been shocked to hear that Anderson and Hitchcock had left. After all, it was a *major* flight across the entire country, and the usual way of doing things would have been to put several weeks' preparation into it beforehand to make sure that any risks were reduced as much as possible. Certain that Anderson and Hitchcock were putting themselves at risk, Brinsmead formally insisted that they abandon their flight — even though they were already halfway there — until their plane could be better prepared. But Anderson would not be dissuaded.

'This has nothing to do with my search. I am flying under private arrangements, and intend going on,' he told one newspaper.[23]

The other cable, though, was a beauty. It was from Bon, sending Keith all her love and telling him that she really did still want to marry him. Hurrah! This was a piece of wonderful news.

For the truth of it was, when it came to the Widgeon, he and Bobby really were having their troubles. There was something wrong with the compass, which meant that at some angles it was pointing as much as 45 degrees off the correct direction — making it worse than useless — and they couldn't find a way to fix it. And someone had stolen their tool set while they were in Broken Hill. Most worryingly of all, they'd had serious engine trouble south of Oodnadatta. Sitting in the forward seat of the plane, directly behind the troublesome Cirrus engine, Hitchcock had seen a locknut coming loose on one of the exposed pushrods to the valve on one cylinder, making the whole engine vibrate badly. Anderson had made an emergency landing, and Hitchcock had fixed it the best he could, using a chisel instead of spanners, but it was a real worry. Still, they decided to press on, and early on the morning of 10 April, they were at Alice Springs airstrip, again preparing to leave.

Before take-off, a mechanic who was loading the last can of petrol pleaded that it would be more prudent to substitute a can of water for the can of petrol. Slightly amused, Anderson demurred.

'No thanks, petrol is worth more to me than water.'[24]

And with that, away they went, lifting off at 7.35 am.

For 100 miles flying north of the Alice, Anderson simply followed the Overland Telegraph Line, which headed through Katherine and all the way up to Darwin. About halfway up that line, they could then follow another line that would take them all the way to Wyndham. It was the surest way to navigate in that part of the world, as they basically couldn't get lost so long as they kept it in sight. And even if they did have to land they could always shinny up the pole, tap into it — or at worst, cut it — and help would soon be at hand.

Still, Anderson was in a hurry. At a place called Woodford Crossing, well before the offshoot telegraph line, he decided to turn west, and duck across the Tanami Desert to get to Halls Creek on the southern edge of the Kimberley, which should save them several hours on their way to Wyndham. It was a risk, but a calculated one.

•

Oh … *mother.*

Five hours after they had headed across the desert on the short cut, Bobby Hitchcock felt, through the seat of his pants, the engine of the *Kookaburra* making the strange vibration again. He looked ahead, and sure enough, the locknut on the jiggling pushrod was working loose. Before his horrified eyes, it loosened further and the vibration increased; then the engine lost power and their plane lost altitude. The plane was heavily laden with petrol, and three cylinders just weren't enough to keep it in the air.

They were going to have to take it down in some of the harshest, hottest country in Australia. Below them stretched an endless expanse of turpentine scrub and loose, dry sand. But they had no choice. Keith Anderson throttled back, and made ready to bring the *Kookaburra* in for a landing …

•

And away they went.

Over at Carnarvon, Major Brearley had at last received permission to suspend the normal postal services that he had contracted to supply, which meant that he could now put another three planes in the air to search for the *Southern Cross*. He watched them take off with some satisfaction, and relief, as the situation had become desperate, with ten days having passed since the *Southern Cross* had disappeared. Where on *earth* could they be?

•

That evening at Coffee Royal, Charles Ulm wrote in his diary:

> Smithy is failing fast. He reels as he walks. Hunger pains are nearly driving Mac and me insane. We discovered a thin, long bean weed today and cooked and ate some. We don't like them but there is some nourishment in them.

•

Keith Anderson and Bobby Hitchcock were in trouble. Even though Keith had brought them in for a perfect landing the day before, and Bobby had quickly been able to fix the engine, the problem was trying to take off. Best as they could, they had hacked away at the turpentine scrub in the terrible heat of the day to clear an airstrip — using just a penknife, their bare hands and a rising sense of desperation — but when they tried to take off, the soft sand had so sucked at the wheels that they couldn't get the speed they needed, and then the stump of a turpentine shrub had punctured one of the tyres, bringing the plane to a sickening, juddering halt. Compounding everything, their water was gone, their supplies were dwindling, and the heat was belting down. They were not far from the kind of country that even the hugely experienced and well-equipped George Wilkins had beaten a hasty retreat from when he had passed through four years earlier. It felt like they were the only two living things in the hostile environment and if they stayed much longer they would not be able to survive.

What could they do?

Only the best they could. After starting a fire to try to clear more of the turpentine shrub, and provide a smoke signal to anyone who might miraculously be looking for them — even though no-one would expect them to be in this spot, because of the short cut they had taken — they put the one spare tube they had in the flat tyre. On this morning, they tried again. And again and again. And now, one more time …

Engine at full throttle, Keith Anderson gunned it across the sand as Bobby Hitchcock held on, and prayed while being bounced furiously as the wheels jumped and bumped from one turpentine stump to the next … getting faster … *nearly* lifting …

PHHHT!

With a sickening finality, the tyre blew again, and the *Kookaburra* came to a shuddering halt in the oppressive silence of the desert.

The sun beat down, sapping them.

They did not have a puncture repair kit.

Were they going to *die* out here?

Not without a very big fight they weren't. In desperation to stay alive long enough for help to arrive, after thirty-six hours of maddening thirst they tried drinking their own urine, with variations of oil, petrol, and methylated spirits from the wretched compass mixed in. (Which was the only bloody thing the compass turned out to be good for.) And when that was gone, they played their last card.

Though exhausted and desperate, they were still thinking straight enough to reason that their one hope of salvation was to dig down far enough to get to the water table below them. And so, slowly, laboriously, they began to dig. There *had* to be a chance they would find water if they could just keep going.

•

Charles Ulm's diary:

> *Heat, flies, mosquitoes, light fires, pull down trees, pull up grass for smoke, walk for water, eat a few snails, drink water and a very thin cup of gruel, listen to radio, turn generator until every ounce of energy is gone; then lie down to be eaten alive by mosquitoes — that is our day! When will it end?*

•

It was just a small article, and it appeared in the Friday, 12 April 1929 edition of the *Sydney Morning Herald*:

> **KEITH ANDERSON OVERDUE**
>
> When this edition went to press, there was no news of the *Kookaburra*, which was being flown by Lieutenant Keith Anderson to Wyndham …

For most of the newspaper's readership, the report no doubt warranted little attention, lost as it was in the huge coverage devoted to the continuing search for the *Southern Cross*. But for Bon Hilliard, already worried sick because there had been no cable from Keith the evening before to say he had arrived safely, it was like a stab to the heart. Seeing it written there in black and white, made it all too real — Keith and Bobby Hitchcock were really missing, themselves lost in the wilderness.

•

It had taken a while, but at last they were on their way. In Sydney, HMAS *Albatross*, with its six RAAF amphibian craft on board, now went steaming through Sydney Heads, on its way to Western Australia to join the search. Yes, it had taken just under a fortnight to get the ship and her crew organised, but these things couldn't be rushed. And at least the Federal government was seen to be doing something …

•

At Coffee Royal, it was obvious that the dreadful weather that had made them miss Wyndham, and land in this godforsaken place was the last burst of the wet season, and they were now at the beginning of the dry season because since that time it had barely rained with intent. All they were left with was this dreadful sweltering, dripping *heat*. It was intolerable, appalling, debilitating and …

And what was that? Another plane? Yes, over there, to the south-east. And of course, just as the search planes had ever done, just as they would always do, the plane veered away to the east. Kingsford Smith and Litchfield were at the top of the hill, keeping a desultory fire going.

'For God's sake,' the pilot urgently told the exhausted navigator, 'let's stick everything green on the fire. This bird may possibly see us.'[25]

And so, with their last gasping reserves of energy, they managed to get the fire roaring once more, with thick, billowing white smoke resulting.

And then, as they watched — Smithy boring holes through his binoculars — the plane changed course and came straight towards them. It had seen them! It was coming lower! G-AUHW it said in big letters under the wings. It was the *Canberra*! They were saved! Kingsford Smith, for one, burst into tears.[26]

•

There they were! In the cockpit of the *Canberra*, flying at 2000 feet, there was wild rejoicing, even as John Stannage — who had met Kingsford Smith eighteen months before in San Francisco — was sending out the message that a few blinks of the eye later was picked up in Darwin before being relayed to the Amalgamated Wireless radio station at La Perouse in Sydney, and soon thereafter was reverberating around Australia: *Found! Found! Found!*[27]

Even more wondrous, as the *Canberra* descended and began to circle, they could see two raggedy figures staggering down a hill from which a thin line of smoke was ascending, and two more figures coming out from under the shade of the plane's wing.[28] That made four, so they were all all right! Twelve days lost, but all right!

On the ground, compounding their joy at finally being found, was the fact that from the window of the *Canberra*'s cockpit soon came a few basic supplies and the four members of the crew fell upon the cans of corned beef like ravenous dogs, tearing off the tops and pushing the food into their mouths. The relief! The sheer gut-filling *pleasure* of it!

From the plane now dropped a message: *Back tomorrow*. With which, the *Canberra* flew away, though only after Holden had taken it up to 5000 feet to get an absolutely certain fix on where they were in this wilderness, so he could be sure of making his way back to it.

•

At home in Arabella Street, the mood was so grim as they sat around waiting for the glad tidings that didn't come that Catherine told her daughter to switch off the radio they had been glued to for the last week. Elsie was rising to do just that, when an excited announcer broke into the shipping news, with the newsflash.

'I have some wonderful news for you ...' he began.[29]

They had found the *Southern Cross* and all four men appeared to be without injury! Chilla was okay!

Ferries tooted their whistles as the news spread; motorists beeped their horns, and such was the joy that at the Sydney Stock Exchange where things had been quite troubled of late, business briefly ceased.[30]

'This is a great day for Mother and Father,'[31] Leofric told a *Sydney Morning Herald* journalist a short time later, even as at Longueville his father had hung a Union Jack from the window of the family home, and put an Australian flag on a bamboo pole in the garden.

For it was in fact nothing less than a great day for Australia! The boys had been found and would soon be on their way home! In the eastern Sydney suburb of Dover Heights, Charles Ulm's wife, Jo, was equally thrilled, telling a journalist that at half-past five that morning she had had such a vivid dream — of Charles holding a map and pointing to a spot just north of Derby, telling her they were safe — that she had immediately rung her sister to tell her.[32] For his part, Charles Ulm's father took the opportunity to deride those people he'd heard of lately who'd been saying the whole disappearance had been a stunt to generate publicity. This was extraordinarily 'ungenerous' of them, he said.[33] All that mattered now was that they were safe.

And now here they were!

In Sydney, it was the *Evening News* that led the way, with front page banner headlines:

SOUTHERN CROSS FOUND: ALL SAFE
Captain Holden the Finder.
Near Port George.
All Well. HURRAH![34]

From the moment of the discovery of the *Southern Cross*, things moved quickly. The *Canberra* returned to Wyndham to a hero's welcome, and started to gather more serious supplies to be dropped the following day. Returning on the morrow without problem, they were to see a much more cheery crew waving at them this time, and they were delighted to be able to drop four carefully prepared packages, which included mosquito nets, cans of food, hats, soap and even towels. But had they forgotten something? As they watched carefully, one of the crew on the ground was clearly gouging a message into the mud. Going down closer they tried to make it out — a 'C', an 'I', a 'G' … and an 'S' made CIGS!

A quick whip-round and a minute later, the *Canberra* swooped low and rained cigarettes upon the men on the ground. Another package that tumbled down contained the eighty-five telegrams that had been received at Wyndham overnight, offering salutations, celebrations and congratulations. Australia was cheering, with only one discordant note.

Keith Anderson and Bob Hitchcock had still not turned up, and had been missing for three days. Where were they and why wasn't there a greater effort to find them?

As John Cantor of the Customs House Hotel told the *Herald*, 'Their lives are just as valuable to the State as any other lives and, in the circumstances in which they went out, an effort should be made to find them.'

Cantor was supported in this, the *Herald* reported, by Mr Arthur V. Hilliard, Anderson's legal representative. Mr Hilliard said that he could not understand why there was an apparent apathy in the Citizens Rescue Committee concerning plans for the search for the crew of the *Kookaburra*. 'Lieutenant Anderson left at short notice to search for his former pals in the *Southern Cross*. He never for a moment considered his own safety in the search. It may be that he had a misadventure and no time should be lost in organising a search for him.'[35]

As concern about Anderson and Hitchcock rose, so too, bit by bit, did details begin to emerge of their trip, each one more worrying than the last. They'd had a faulty compass when they had landed at Broken Hill from Sydney. Apparently, when they left Alice Springs to fly over the hottest, most arid part of Australia, they had been carrying only two bottles of water and a few sandwiches. They had no radio with them. Bobby Hitchcock had been so ill with a case of blood poisoning that he'd had to receive treatment at Alice Springs hospital. They had left no kind of flight plan as to what route they intended to take. Wherever they were, if still alive, it seemed unlikely that they would be able to last long.

The urgency to find them began to grow. Bowing to growing pressure, the Citizens Rescue Committee contacted Les Holden and asked him to take the *Canberra* and go to look for the *Kookaburra*. Meanwhile, two worn-out RAAF de Havilland DH.9A planes left Melbourne bound for Alice Springs so they, too, could join the search.

At Coffee Royal, still monitoring the radio as they waited for the mud to dry enough that a light plane bringing petrol could land — and they could hopefully fly themselves out — the crew of the *Southern Cross* was deeply worried by the news that Anderson and Hitchcock were missing. Smithy's first desperate hope was that they had landed near water, as he knew only too well how forbidding the country to the west of the Overland Telegraph Line was.[36]

At last, five days after the *Southern Cross* had been found, one of Norman Brearley's pilots by the name of 'Bertie' Heath — an old friend of Anderson and Kingsford Smith — managed to land right beside Coffee Royal in a small de Havilland DH.50. It *was* possible. Before Bertie left, Charles Ulm handed over his logbook with instructions that its contents be cabled to Sydney for exclusive publication in the *Sun*.[37] Heath agreed, took off, and the next day returned with another plane, carrying petrol and oil supplies.

In the meantime, the mood of several newspapers vis-à-vis the *Southern Cross* was beginning to harden, with the *Daily Guardian* leading the way, questioning whether the crew's situation had really been so dire after all.

ULM'S TALE: THEY LIVED ON SNAILS AND GRASS ONLY 25 MILES AWAY FROM MISSION!
TOO WEAK TO MAKE SMOKE SIGNALS, THOUGH PLANES PASSING OVERHEAD
SIMPLY WAITED FOR 12 DAYS
HEARD EVERYTHING ON WIRELESS; MADE SMITHY GRIN

'For a fortnight,' it stated archly, the four men 'have been within easy walking distance of Port George Mission. In fact, the true sensation has been the fever of apprehension of the public, not the actual plight of the flyers. A startling, but happily not tragic, jest has been played on public emotion by circumstance and by the failure or inability of the four missing men to show signals to searching planes which passed and re-passed the locality where the *Southern Cross* lay unseen ... The [searching pilots] are reported as being amazed that at no time were they given any smoke signals from Kingsford Smith and his party.'[38]

The truth was, not all the journalists in the *Guardian*'s Philip Street offices felt happy about the slant the paper was taking on the story, as it was practically accusing Smithy and Ulm and the others of fabricating the whole thing, but on the other hand they understood.[39] The *Sun* had prospered mightily in recent times with the exclusive deal it had with Kingsford Smith and Ulm as the principal engine that had sold millions of extra papers, and this was the *Guardian*'s perfect opportunity to turn things around. Certainly, it was tough on Smithy and Ulm, but all was fair in love and newspaper wars.

And certainly, the *Sun*, in many ways, redressed the balance by now publishing the airmen's 'exclusive reports' on their front page, with Ulm's account of such things as how, when the *Canberra* arrived overhead, 'we tore open packages of food like wild beasts'.[40] The *Sun* presented none of the queries and doubts that were being posed by other papers, and simply milked the story for all it was worth — which was plenty, as circulation continued to soar. The *Sun* focused very little on the fact that Anderson and Hitchcock were still missing. For the *Guardian*, it was front-page news, the main story of the day.

•

There is a visitor for you, Mr Garlick, and here is her card.

John Garlick, the Chief Civic Commissioner of Sydney and the head of the Citizens Southern Cross Rescue Committee, looked at it and recognised the name immediately. It was Bon Hilliard, the fiancée of Keith Anderson. For all that, he still kept her waiting in an anteroom in the town hall for an hour before receiving her, but finally she could be put off no longer. She was slim, pretty, blue-eyed and furious.

'Was the *Canberra* out looking for Keith and Bobby Hitchcock yesterday?' she wanted to know.

The commissioner had to confess that he wasn't certain.

'*Why* aren't you certain? Aren't *you* the one who should be certain, above all?'

The commissioner, staggered at her anger and upset, tried to detail what he had done to find the missing plane.

'And you should do it, too!' Bon told him, before leaving.[41] The *Guardian* delighted in reporting the conversation the following day. The *Sun* ignored it.

•

And finally, at Coffee Royal, this was what heaven felt like: *sleep* under a mosquito net that kept the beggars out, *food* in their bellies, and the knowledge that they were found and would soon be on their way home. Further lifting their spirits was the knowledge that, after everything the *Southern Cross* had been through, she was still in good shape. With petrol restored to her, she once again came to life and, with one of her side engines at full throttle, Kingsford Smith was able to turn her round from the spot she had been stuck in for the previous two weeks, and point her in the opposite direction whence she came. When they had landed, Smithy had had no more than 100 yards of free space to work with. Now, courtesy of the work the men had put in over the previous days with the axes and shovels that had also been dropped — and their new-found strength from the food — he had a little over 200 yards of serviceable runway.

After eighteen days in that godforsaken part of the planet, they were away! In no more than a minute, the mud, the mosquitoes and the monotony of their swampy prison had been left behind, and an hour and a half later, they were in Derby. The joy of landing back in civilisation, however, was tempered by the news that there was *still* no sign of Anderson and Hitchcock. What was more, there was a telegram waiting for them, from John Cantor, which hit them like a hard punch to the solar plexus:

> The boys sent Keith to look for you. For God's sake look for him and Bob.[42]

And they learned for the first time about the scurrilous attacks that had been made on them by the *Guardian*. They were appalled and outraged in equal measure — and Kingsford Smith and Ulm quickly cabled instructions to their solicitor in Sydney, Eric Campbell, to institute legal proceedings against the paper, as well as its printer, Clyde Packer. They sought a total of £20,000 in damages.[43]

At least, they learned, the pride of the Qantas fleet, the de Havilland DH.50J *Atalanta* G-AUHE, was about to leave Brisbane to join the search for Anderson and Hitchcock, and another five decrepit RAAF DH.9A planes had left Laverton. And they wanted to join them immediately.

Wiser heads prevailed, however, and they were persuaded to get at least a couple of days' medical attention with proper sleep and rest, while the *Southern Cross* had work done on her, before they would be in shape to do anything at all.

•

Success, at last ...

On the morning of 17 April 1929, Pilot Percy 'Skipper' Moody — none other than Smithy's old flying companion from Royal Flying Corps days, with whom he had taken the salute from the Life Guard in Whitehall — took off from Brisbane in a brand new de Havilland DH.61 Giant Moth, named *Apollo*, on the inaugural Qantas service from Brisbane to Charleville.

They were bearing just one passenger, 91-year-old Alexander Kennedy, who had been Qantas's first passenger seven years before, and 1004 postal items, in its first link to the coast. On that first flight of the new service, the speed averaged 97 miles per hour, which was a 50 per cent increase on the speed registered on the inaugural Qantas flight in 1922.[44] Still, of the many hold-the-phone things about this plane, the most blessed was that it was the first one in Australia to have, if you can believe it, an internal lavatory! No more would the company's passengers after long flights be seen to frequently burst forth and sprint towards old tin sheds.[45] Broadly, Qantas customers had gone from being fellow aviators, as they had been in the early years of operation, to being genuine passive passengers, who could begin to relax.

Qantas had taken a step up again.

•

Four days after that first launch, however, on the morning of 21 April, Lester Brain, with a two-man crew, was flying the *Atalanta* — which had been chartered by the Sydney Citizens Rescue Committee to join the search for the *Kookaburra*, as well as sponsored by the *Guardian* — over a particularly barren part of the Tanami Desert about halfway between Alice Springs and Wyndham. Brain was a new breed of pilot — the first man hired by Qantas to fly their planes *not* to have flown in the war — and he was a careful, considered type of man far removed from the hard-drinking larrikin type.[46] Before taking off, he had been sure there was plenty of water and supplies on board, should the worst come to the worst. For over a week he had reckoned that the *Kookaburra* would be located in this part of the country and he was keeping an eagle-eye out for any sign that his theory might be correct.

And now, from a distance of about 60 miles, he really did spot something odd. It was a smudge of smoke rising slowly from the south-west. He knew this was a region of Australia where there were no habitations and no blacks as there was no available water, so the smoke was definitely worth investigating. In the cabin, advised of the smoke they were going to investigate, the

Atalanta's mechanic, P.H. Compston, was immediately reminded of a conversation he'd had that morning with an old Aboriginal man at Wave Hill station, where they were flying from.

'You been hunting dead fella,' the old man said. 'Where you fly?'

Compston pointed south, to which the elder replied, 'I see big smoke out that way, but dunno.'[47]

Altering course, it was not long before they saw burnt and still smouldering bushes and something else, Lester Brain thought — something that obviously didn't belong in the desert.

Could it be ...?

It was!

A plane! Surely, it was the *Kookaburra*. Exultant, Brain nosed his plane down, hoping to see a couple of ragged men — both of whom were close friends of his[48] — excitedly waving their arms in the air, when he saw it. Under the starboard wing of the plane, at least in the rough shade, lay a body, belly-down.

Perhaps sleeping?

Alas ... no. As the pilot flew back and forth at a height of just 15 feet above the stricken aircraft, there was not the tiniest sign of movement from whoever it was — though Brain was almost certain it was Anderson. What he was in no doubt about now was that the person was dead. His face was burnt black, his head resting on his right arm, while his left arm appeared to be beneath his body. But where was the other man? From the air he could see the crisscrossing tracks back and forth where the plane had clearly tried, but failed, to take off. It was as obvious what had happened, as it was apparent that to land his own plane on that wasteland would be suicide — the *Atalanta* would be unlikely to ever get off the ground again.

The most important thing was to get a land party in there and, after dropping by parachute water and food on the off chance that the missing man was still alive, Brain quickly headed towards Wave Hill station, 80 miles to the north.

•

It was Arthur Hilliard who quietly told his daughter Bon the news at their Cremorne home that evening. It was hard, darling, he knew, but they must face reality. Bon wept — of all the hard things, one of the hardest was the thought that Keith might have died without getting her telegram telling him that she still loved him and did want to marry him — but then rallied.

'We must tell Keith's mother how we feel,' she said. And in short order they sent a telegram to that devastated lonely woman in Perth, now confined to her room under medical care. It read:

> Do not grieve. We must be brave. Keith is magnificent.[49]

Charles Kingsford Smith and the rest of the *Southern Cross* crew were at the Wyndham airstrip, about to take off to join the search, when they were quietly told the news. The *Kookaburra* had been found in the Tanami Desert. One body located. One still missing, though, after ten days in the desert, almost certainly dead. The plane was at a point 22 degrees to the right of where Anderson had intended to go, and they had gone down 115 miles to the north-east of where anyone might have expected to find them. In the exact middle of nowhere …

It was one of the low points of Smithy's life. For Keith and Bobby to have died was bad enough. To have died while searching for them, however, was excruciating. And there would be a lot more pain to come.

•

For its part, the *Guardian* was now in full cry against both Kingsford Smith and Ulm, and their key newspaper competitors. 'Only one advantage has appeared from the tragic incidents of the Smith-Ulm venture,' it thundered, 'namely an increase in certain newspaper circulations. The Sydney *Sun*, the Sydney *Daily Telegraph* and the *Melbourne Herald*, have financially interested themselves in 'exclusive world rights', to anything written or spoken by the crew of the *Southern Cross* … and gleefully proclaim they have sold more papers.'[50]

What was to be done?

The *Guardian* had no doubt. It was nothing less than the 'imperative duty' of Prime Minister Bruce to *immediately* launch a public inquiry to get to the bottom of how the whole disaster occurred, and how it could be prevented from occurring again.

So great had the public outcry become, and the accusations that were flying back and forth, that the following day Stanley Bruce did indeed announce that an official Air Inquiry Committee would be formed to investigate the affair. The committee's terms of reference included, crucially, 'to investigate all aspects of the flight from its start to the landing at Coffee Royal', and to 'search out thoroughly all facts concerning the deaths of Anderson and Hitchcock'. (On the subject of those dead airmen, Prime Minister Bruce announced a short time afterwards that a fresh expedition would be sent into the nation's interior to retrieve their bodies.)

The members of the board of the inquiry were also subsequently announced as Brigadier General Lachlan C. Wilson, Captain Geoffrey Hughes and Cecil Newton McKay. Wilson was a no-nonsense lawyer, just as he had been a no-nonsense army man who had fought at Gallipoli and in Palestine, before commanding the 3rd Light Horse Brigade in serious battles in Jordan. Hughes was a distinguished and decorated war veteran, having flown with the Royal Flying Corps and been twice mentioned in dispatches before co-founding the New South Wales Aero Club. Although Hughes enjoyed great respect from his peers, his impartiality in this affair may not have been total, as he had been one of the earliest and most strident critics of the trans-Pacific venture, saying that it was 'impossible' to fly from Honolulu to Australia. Cecil McKay ran a successful engineering business and was also chairman of the Victorian branch of the Royal Aero Club, with a long background in flying.

Both Kingsford Smith and Ulm expressed satisfaction at the announcement of the inquiry. 'We wholeheartedly welcome the fullest possible inquiry,' Ulm was shortly thereafter quoted. 'We have nothing to hide. On behalf of all of us in the *Southern Cross*, I would like to say how terribly distressed we feel about the fate of poor Keith Anderson and Bob Hitchcock. I became a close personal friend of Andy in America, and it is not possible for me to find words to tell how awfully upset I am about it.'[51]

•

While the land party from Wave Hill — under the command of Flight Lieutenant Charles Eaton of the RAAF — was still struggling to get to the *Kookaburra* in a group that included three white men in a 1927 Buick tourer and three Aboriginal stockmen with twenty-six horses, the *Southern Cross* departed Wyndham and headed back to Sydney, abandoning the London trip for the moment. At Smithy's insistence they took a detour across the desert and found the *Kookaburra*, exactly as Brain had described it. The fire was still burning across a 5-mile front, and there lay the plane that had been heading towards their salvation, but now marked the spot where two good men had died. They could see one of them, clad only in singlet and underpants, still lying under one wing, face down. On the *Southern Cross*, no-one spoke. They, too, dropped some food and water in the vain hope that someone was alive, but — after taking aerial photographs — flew on to Newcastle Waters all but certain that it was hopeless.

•

On 25 April the *Guardian* published a startling headline across the top of its front page:

INFAMOUS ATTACK BY 'SUN' ON ANDERSON[52]

It was in response to an editorial in the *Sun* the day before, where its editors had appeared to exculpate Kingsford Smith and Ulm and blame Anderson and Hitchcock, by noting that the latter had gone out there 'of their own free will' in an attempt that was 'suddenly conceived and hastily equipped … less carefully organised than the flight of the *Southern Cross*'.[53]

'Everybody knows,' the *Guardian* responded, 'that the *Sun* and *Telegraph* were financially interested in Smith and Ulm's flight. The *Sun*'s shameless attempt to promote condemnation against Anderson (who is dead) and to arouse approbation for Smith and Ulm (who are living) was a vile debasement of a newspaper's opportunities. The mean and caddish endeavour to escape the due inquiry was beneath all public decency.'[54]

In fact, however, none of the papers, or the aircrews they were sponsoring, could have been said to be above commercial considerations in the face of Anderson and Hitchcock's tragic deaths. At Newcastle Waters, Lester Brain and his crew had come face to face with Kingsford Smith, Ulm, Litchfield and McWilliams. It wasn't long before both parties realised that they were in possession of photos of the *Kookaburra* and the prone body beneath the wing, which their respective papers were screaming for. A veritable race would ensue to see who could get their photos to their papers first, with the two planes setting off early the following morning.[55]

•

In Longreach, meanwhile, Hudson Fysh was still exulting over the success of Lester Brain in the *Atalanta*, when he reported to the Qantas board: 'Owing to the nature of the trip the publicity which we received amounted to a tremendous boost for Mr Brain and for Qantas. The helpful publicity which we have received through the success of the two search trips could probably not have been bought for any money.'[56]

•

On the morning of Saturday, 27 April 1929, the journal *Smith's Weekly* covered its entire front page with an attack on Kingsford Smith and Ulm, while simultaneously lionising Keith Anderson and Bob Hitchcock:

THE SACRIFICE!
Why Was It Necessary For Anderson
to Have Crashed as He Did?
SOUTHERN CROSS FIASCO.

> Dead … dead … dead … that lonely body under the plane wing with the smouldering bush around him as a majestic funeral pyre …[57]

The most scathing article was penned by Sir Joynton Smith, the proprietor of the newspaper, and it charged Sun Newspapers with obscuring the Anderson affair in order to glorify the *Southern Cross* crew.

'For the sake of that sun-blackened body in the northern wilderness,' the knight of the realm thundered, 'all Australia will make enquiry, and will demand answers ... Australia's eyes are dim with sorrow; but Australia's eyes are heavy with a dim regret. We must find out why this chapter of accidents came to be written, with so dread an ending. It is S.M. Bruce's business to discover the answers to which all Australia is asking.'[58]

Into just such a storm did the *Southern Cross* land, when on that very morning — the day after the *Guardian* had published its exclusive photos of the stricken *Kookaburra* — it arrived at Richmond before a tiny crowd of just a few hundred people, including a large pack of pressmen. So gravely had the public mood changed since the four men had left a month earlier, that some in the crowd even hissed and booed at the airmen after they emerged, yelling out such things as 'Liar!' 'Cheat!' 'Hoaxer!'[59] — something that, again, stunned them.

Ordinarily, whenever on a tarmac of any description, going to or coming from anywhere, Smithy was a cyclone of charismatic energy, waving to all and sundry, kissing pretty women, shaking hands with anyone who proffered theirs and dropping one-liners. Not on this occasion, however. He was devastated by the accusations and outraged by them.

'I have nothing to say,' he told the reporters. 'As all the papers seem to misinterpret what we say, I will say nothing in future.'[60] That notwithstanding, he and Ulm did then give an exclusive interview to a reporter from the *Sun*, where they were able to get their own side of the story across.

Not that this quelled the public attack in any way. The most outrageously slanderous one came from a publication called *Plain Talk*, which stated outright, 'It has been asserted that Smith and Ulm should lose themselves where they did and that Keith Anderson should find them; the idea being that Keith Anderson should be given public reward.'[61]

And people believed this nonsense! They actually thought that while on a journey to buy planes to set up an airline, he and Ulm had thought it might be a good idea to crash-land their uninsured plane on a West Australian swamp, on the reckoning that, if they survived, the resultant publicity might be advantageous to them.

At Kuranda, Smithy started to receive hate mail, as did his brothers and sisters at their own homes. Hissing editorials continued to spit at him, and some people shouted insults at him in the street.

In response, Kingsford Smith was devastated. Already shattered by the tragic deaths of Anderson and Hitchcock, he was now confronted full on by the fickle nature of the Australian public. Less than a year before, he had been cheered to the echo wherever he went, hailed as a hero — the man who'd flown across the Pacific Ocean! And now he was a pariah, a coward, a cur, practically a *murderer*! Within days the influential journal *Aircraft* recorded its view that 'the attempted flight to England was a publicity stunt, and an ill-advised one at that'.[62] And this was a widely held view!

'I cannot forget,' he later recorded, 'how certain of my countrymen turned from adulants to defaments almost overnight … The public which had been 100 per cent "Smithy" when we took off now began tossing mud and rocking the pedestal upon which they had placed me.'[63]

He came to the realisation that by some strange dynamic he had previously been unaware of, there were only a few short steps between the position of being the nation's hero and being its whipping boy.[64]

•

Good God Almighty. It was not that the search party that finally reached the *Kookaburra* on the mid-afternoon of Monday, 29 April 1929, was holding out much hope of finding Anderson or Hitchcock still alive. The aviators had, after all, been missing for nigh on a fortnight in some of the most inhospitable country on the planet. It was that when they got to the *Kookaburra*, the scene was so appalling.

The man under the wing, putrescent and stinking, maggots crawling into one eye socket and out the other, was Bobby Hitchcock. They could only tell it was him from the bandage wrapped around his right arm that they knew he'd had on when the plane left Alice Springs. He was lying beside a thinly scratched hole, bone dry, which had clearly been begun in the hope of finding water. While the three white men buried him where he lay, saying the Lord's Prayer by way of religious observation, the two Aboriginal men, Sambo and Daylight, went in search of Anderson.[65] An hour later, they found him — dead, bloated and burnt from the sun — lying a tragically short distance of just half a mile away, as if he had decided to walk to salvation and collapsed shortly after departure. In fact, Daylight, who was an expert tracker, was able to explain to the white men in some detail what had happened.

This fella had left the *Kookaburra* carrying two empty water bottles and a cushion, and after walking 500 yards in a south-westerly direction had sat down under some scrub. At this point, Daylight said, 'the white fella was very sick',[66] as the tracks showed that from this point, when the white man started off again, he had kept going through the scrub instead of around it, as previously. And then he had begun to crawl in circles. The white fella then threw off his coat, hat, goggles, water bottle and cushion, and kept crawling, soon abandoning his shirt, aircraft log, watch and scarf. Just 50 yards after he dropped his scarf, the crawling stopped, and here he was.

Dead before them.

Listening to the story, told over his body, all of them were humbled by the courage that Anderson had shown, how he had clearly fought his fate right to the bitter end. As Sergeant Douglas later described it, 'it was clear that he kept his mind to the last, and fought against the odds, and died fighting. His courage and determination must have been unlimited'.[67]

With few words, they buried Keith Anderson, too.

Though all the men were keen to leave this place of death as soon as possible, lest they suffer the same fate — a genuine possibility as their own supplies were low and the heat was sapping them — there remained some work to be done. Examining the plane, they found the petrol tank contained well over 20 gallons and Sergeant Douglas had no trouble in starting the engine up. Searching the interior of the plane, they were amazed to find there was still some food there; suggesting that the lack of water was so severe the flyers couldn't get any food down. And so, pausing only long enough to cut from the rudder of the plane a small piece of fabric upon which Anderson had left a rough account of their experience, they began their sombre journey back to Wave Hill.

As the ground party left, Lieutenant Eaton noted when they looked back, 'high up, right above the *Kookaburra*, in an otherwise clear sky, a perfect cross formed by a cirrus cloud. We did not say much to each other, but I think we all thought a lot as we made our weary journey home.'[68]

Fourteen

Trials and Tribulations

Don't ever think you will reap the reward of your pioneering efforts. You'll be acclaimed a hero, people will fawn upon you; but you will always be thought a visionary. The things that you want to do will be done after your death ...

Sir Hubert Wilkins, formerly George Wilkins, to Smithy, circa 1930[1]

The hearing proper for the Air Accident Investigation Committee Inquiry started on the morning of 16 May 1929 in Darlinghurst Courthouse, which was as packed with people as it was thick with tension. Not surprisingly, the first man in the dock — and make no mistake that was exactly where he was — was Charles Kingsford Smith. He had been the captain of the ill-fated flight, and it was for him to explain himself and to answer the very serious allegations that had been made to the effect that the whole episode had been a publicity sham gone wrong, and that as a result two good men were lying dead in their desert graves.

As he swore to tell the truth, the whole truth, and nothing but the truth, the famous pilot looked rumpled, tense and jumpy ... and still not quite recovered from his experience at Coffee Royal, to judge from his rather haunted gauntness, although whether that was from physical or emotional trauma was not clear.

There was no doubt, however, that he could still scarcely fathom that it had all come to this, that Keith and Bobby were dead and he was being asked to defend his role in their deaths. Around the court, the press and the spectators, including devastated and angry family members of the two dead men —

most of whom blamed Smithy for their loss — leaned forward so as not to miss a word as the proceedings proper began. Foremost among them was the clearly grieving Bon Hilliard, staring at her former boyfriend through the puffy eyes of one who had spent a lot of time crying.

Mr J.H. Hammond, KC, the barrister assisting the Crown, was at first relatively gentle, taking Kingsford Smith through the background of the flight before starting to get to the core of the matter.

The food taken on the flight, for example, was that really sufficient for a trip that always had the potential to land in extreme conditions?

Pretty much, came the reply. It was true they hadn't foreseen what subsequently happened to them — who would? — but it was more than enough for a trip 50 per cent longer than the 'hop' they thought they were going to take.

'When we landed,' said Kingsford Smith sombrely, 'we had seven sandwiches and about a flask and a half of coffee.'

'And where were the emergency rations?' asked the barrister.

They had definitely been stowed in the *Southern Cross*, the pilot explained patiently, but unfortunately someone had removed them before departure. Neither he, nor Ulm, nor any one member of the crew had any idea of that before they had taken off.

It wasn't that the barrister snorted derisively at this response — he was far too sophisticated for that — but an eyebrow raised quizzically throughout left no-one in any doubt what he thought. But moving right along. The next line of questioning focused on the charts the men had taken on the flight, and whether those, too, were sufficient for the task at hand.

Nothing that the aviator replied to this made the eyebrow drop, but at least the barrister was not long in getting to the next, rather more serious matter. It was about the decision to leave Richmond air base when they did, even without the favourable weather report they needed.

Yes … well.

On this subject Kingsford Smith seemed a lot less sure of his ground and it wasn't necessarily easy for the furiously scribbling journalists in the court to follow the trail of telegrams back and forth, but it at least seemed established that the *Southern Cross* had, in fact, departed without having received the favourable weather report that would have been expected.

And then the counsel ratcheted up the tension even further.

Why, when the aerial had broken, had they continued on their transcontinental flight?

'We regarded the risk of another take-off as not worth turning back,'[2] he replied.

Over the next several days, Kingsford Smith was led to give his account of the rest of the journey: how they hit terrible weather, couldn't find Wyndham, came across the two missions, had to make an emergency landing on the mangrove flats at the place they had come to call 'Coffee Royal' and so forth. With the barrister questioning him all the while, Kingsford Smith then took the court through the efforts they made to get themselves rescued, including lighting the fire, fixing a makeshift generator and trying to send a signal out on the radio.

Why had they only burnt wood on their signal fires, when if they'd burned some of their remaining engine oil, they could have made black smoke?

'Because,' Kingsford Smith explained patiently, 'we were in a green environment, and the white smoke from wood fires shows up better against that, than the black smoke would have.'

This time the barrister not only raised a quizzical eyebrow, but followed up with a lengthy question as to how that could *possibly* be. Billowing black smoke less visible than tepid white smoke? What nonsense!

No sir, not nonsense. That was just the way it was.

It was when the question was put as to why they had not tried to transform the receiver into a transmitter, however, that things became tense again.

Smithy replied: 'We wanted to hear if anybody would have the sense to send out the latitude and longitude of Port George Mission Station, which had seen us pass over.'

So none of this was contrived to be a publicity stunt?

A stir in the courtroom ... Now they were really getting to the heart of the matter, as the examining counsel produced and tabled a copy of the contract that had been signed by Ulm and Kingsford Smith with Sun Newspapers together with the Melbourne *Herald and Weekly Times*. It stipulated that the sum of £500 be paid to the pilots for the exclusive account of their flight to England, and a further £500 if they beat Bert Hinkler's record time of sixteen days — and only £250 if they made it to England but failed to beat Hinkler's time. In return, the pilots undertook that the only information they would provide would be to the aforementioned newspapers, and they would be in breach of the said contract if they talked to anyone else in the press.

Thus definitively establishing the strength of the bond between the pilots and these newspapers, and the kind of money on offer, the first day's proceedings ended as the myriad journalists rushed to file their copy. Kingsford Smith could read the largest account, in the *Sydney Morning Herald* the following morning — 'DRAMATIC FLIGHT STORY: KINGSFORD SMITH'S EVIDENCE' — as he made his way back to the court for another day of testimony.

And on this morning, Mr Hammond was not long in causing the journalists to start furiously scribbling once again. In precise, clipped, emotionless tones, he read to Kingsford Smith the article from *Aircraft*, which stated flat-out that the whole thing was nothing but a 'publicity stunt', implying that the airmen had deliberately got themselves lost. And then, rather theatrically, the barrister laid the clipping on the table, before suddenly turning savagely towards Kingsford Smith and thrusting his head forward the better to spit out his words.

'Was there any premeditation?' he snapped. The members of the Air Investigation Committee leaned forwards, as did everyone else in the courtroom, evincing the ancient human instinct that bringing your ear just a tiny bit closer could make all the difference. No-one wanted to miss the response.

'It is an absolute deliberate and malicious lie,' Kingsford Smith answered with no little force, 'and I am very glad to have been given the opportunity to publicly say so.'

The barrister shuffled his papers, with the same definite action that a man might use to reload a rifle, and came up with a second clipping from *Plain Talk*, the purport of which was that Keith Anderson had been in on the whole ruse, and had gone out after the *Southern Cross* so he could reap a public reward, while Ulm and Kingsford Smith's part of the deal was the massive publicity that was generated.

This time Kingsford Smith was *really* angry, barely able to get his words out such had the fury taken hold of him. His hands gripped the dock.

'Another deliberate malicious lie, that affects a dead man's reputation, and which I consider disgusting,' Smith replied. 'I think it is disgraceful.'

Mr Hammond: 'It has been said that a certain newspaper was party to this supposed stunt. What do you say to that?'

'There was no stunt at all, and there was no arrangement with any newspapers or person other than the perfectly fair contract mentioned yesterday.'[3]

Fred Myers, who was representing the Anderson and Hitchcock families, stood up and addressed the wearying pilot.

'You have heard the extract from the publication stating that it was suggested that Anderson was to find you. There has been also a suggestion that you endorsed a promissory note for £300 on Anderson's plane and that that was part of the same arrangement. Is that so?'

'That is a *deliberate lie*!' Kingsford Smith burst in.

'It was merely a personal friendship?'

'Yes.'

The journalists kept scribbling. This was providing terrific copy for their newspapers and no-one wanted to miss a word.

A moment of rare relief from the tension in the courtroom came when Smithy was closely questioned about his health prior to take-off. He told the inquiry that although he had the flu in the days leading up to the flight, his doctor had told him he would be right to fly.

'Did you get a certificate to this effect?' asked one of the members of the investigation committee.

'I could get one,' Smithy replied deadpan. 'All I have at present is a bill.'[4]

Muted laughter swept the courtroom.

Perhaps the most exciting moment of the first few days' proceedings began when, from the bench, Geoffrey Hughes asked Kingsford Smith if he would again attempt the flight to England.

'Probably, yes,' was his answer, 'with even more adequate provisions.'

'Although you considered the preparations for this flight were perfect?'

Kingsford Smith controlled himself.

'We are not supermen,' he said quietly.

'Don't think that I am suggesting you are not a superman,' Hughes replied. 'Why did you take risks on this flight?'

'We are in the position of pioneers,' was the quiet answer, in the manner of one explaining something patiently to another who just can't grasp the concept. 'And pioneers always take risks.'

'But it was not necessary to pioneer difficult routes when there were other routes?' Hughes suggested.

'I do not see why,' Smithy replied firmly, 'that in the future, direct long-distance routes should not be used, and why we should not help to eliminate the risks on those routes.'

As in, yes, they could have got to Wyndham by making lots of short hops between aerodromes, but that was not what the trip had been about. They were *pioneers* of getting from one spot to another, in the most direct manner possible, and by forging forward in that manner they would be making the way easier for those who would follow, who would inevitably include passengers.

At least there was some positive testimony from Captain Leslie Herbert Holden on how only a pilot of consummate skill could *ever* have put the *Southern Cross* down in the spot that Smithy had.

And then it was the turn of Charles Thomas Phillipe Ulm.

What of the assertions that the whole thing was a 'publicity stunt'?

'It is a deliberate lie; too despicable to talk about!' Ulm snapped, glaring angrily at both Mr Hammond and the journalists who had penned these slurs. 'I'd like to get some of those newspaper men out there for a while.'

'In a publication called *Aircraft*,' said Mr Hammond, 'the word "stunt" is used in connection with the flight.'

'I have read that article,' the grim answer came, 'and I know the man named Hart who wrote it. We did not sue him for libel because we know he has no money and never will have any. The paper is not published in Sydney. He brings it out wherever he can find some poor stupid printer to print it. The writer is a deliberate liar.'

'It is said that it was a "stunt" and a "newspaper stunt" at that,' persisted counsel.

'An absolute lie!' Ulm retorted.

Counsel went on reading from the article, which included the statement that 'Mr C.E. Kingsford Smith's attempted stunt flight to England has resulted in the death of Commercial Pilot Keith Anderson.' Ulm broke in on the reading with a protest to the chairman: 'I think this is most unfair!'

Brigadier General Wilson turned to Ulm.

'You are getting the opportunity of answering them,' he said.

'Well, I deny it!' Ulm was getting very angry.

'Don't deny it until you hear it read.'

'I know who wrote it, sir,' protested the outraged airman.

'Do I understand from your attitude that you would rather I did not ask these questions?'

'No, go on, go on! I'm glad you are asking them.'

'Do you think I am asking them in anybody's interest but your own?'

'No,' Ulm answered, 'I am sorry. I got heated for a moment.'

'Do you think steps should be taken to prevent people going off on harebrained flights?' Hughes asked.

'If they are harebrained, yes. But I would not like to say what form the control should take,' answered Ulm.

Dozens of other witnesses were then heard — seventy-four in all, with the hearing also being held in Melbourne and Adelaide — including Captain Clive Chateau, who told of his angst when he heard that the *Southern Cross* had left without receiving his favourable weather report, and that the plane also couldn't be contacted. He nevertheless was most forceful in dismissing any suggestion that Ulm and Kingsford Smith had set the whole thing up so as to generate publicity as 'absurd'.

Harold Arthur Litchfield, who had of course lived through it all, was equally forceful in rejecting the insinuations as 'malicious lies'.

One who received a particularly hard time was Tom McWilliams, who seemed to be attacked from all sides for having failed to even *attempt* to turn their receiver into a transmitter. In response, McWilliams steadfastly stuck to what he had said all along — they as a group had decided against it, because the chance of ending up without a transmitter or a receiver was too risky — the receiver was their lifeline.

Though the inquiry was declared closed on 7 June, suddenly on 13 June 1929 the whole thing was resumed to enable the Crown to call a surprise witness … a man by the name of William Angus Todd.

And wasn't that a turn-up for the books!

Both Kingsford Smith and Ulm knew this man as Bill Todd, the second mate of the *Tahiti*, who had first taught them the principles of navigation, and was then going to accompany them on their flight across the Pacific, until he had been asked to leave after too much boozing. For the purposes of this exercise, however, he was no longer 'Bill' from the *Tahiti*, but a witness who was out to do them damage.

But, oh, what a story he told, his red-visaged countenance of the heavy drinker getting even redder as he progressed.

'In October 1927 at the Hotel Roosevelt in San Francisco,' he recounted to the hushed courtroom, 'we were talking about finance. Finances were extremely low. We were discussing some method of getting enough money to get the flight started. During that conversation Ulm said that had his plan for getting lost in central Australia for four or five days been followed, sufficient money would be available and public sympathy and support would enable them to have no cause to worry. Keith Anderson and myself were present. Anderson's only comment was that it would not work …'

Pandemonium broke out in the courtroom. Here was a first-hand witness, claiming the whole thing was a long-planned scam! Ulm, for one, looked thunderstruck and beside himself with rage at Todd's claims.

Why, counsel now wanted to know, had he not come forward earlier?

He had been in New Zealand, he said, ill in a Wellington hospital, and it was only on reading press reports of Ulm's denials when a previous witness had claimed to have heard Ulm say the best way to get publicity would be to get lost in the middle of Australia, that he realised the significance of this conversation he had had with him.

Whatever the sensation Todd's claims in the courtroom made, however high the tension had climbed as a result, and however much the journalists were furiously scribbling down every word, none of it seemed to have had any effect whatsoever on Jack Cassidy, who was the counsel for Kingsford Smith and Charles Ulm. M'learned friend was nothing less than acidly amused with Todd's fantastic claims when he tiredly and rather theatrically took the trouble to cross-examine this clearly completely unreliable witness.

'So we may take it,' he suggested of Todd's impulse to suddenly come and give evidence to the inquiry, 'that you did it out of a sense of public duty?'

'I did so,' declared Todd defensively, 'because I saw the statement that he had denied saying it. I *heard* him say it.'

Cassidy, no longer acidly amused but outright angry, got straight to the nub of it: 'You have got your knife into Ulm, have you not?'

'I won't admit that at all.'

Cassidy took Todd through some of the details of his problematic relationship with Ulm, pointing out that a contract between him and Ulm and Kingsford Smith had never been formally signed.

Cassidy: 'Were you pressing that they should sign it?'

Todd: 'I did, on several occasions.'

'They were in serious financial straits?'

'Yes, they were.'

'And you had the right to go back to your job if you wanted to go?'

'Yes ...'

'Have you anything against Litchfield?'

'Not at all ...'

'Did you say to Litchfield that if you ever got a chance to do Ulm a bad turn, you would do it?'

Mr Todd was sure that there must be a mistake, because he was quite sure he had said no such thing.

With another theatrical pause, Cassidy steadied for a moment, almost as if he wanted to make Todd think that the worst was over ... before he bored in hard again.

'You understand I am suggesting that you are a man whose word cannot be relied upon?'

Yes, Mr Todd understood that.

'You understand I am suggesting that you did this from spite?'

'Yes, I can see that quite clearly ...'

As it turned out, Cassidy almost seemed better informed about Todd's background than he was himself. Step by step, the barrister walked him through it, from the fact that he had no previous flying experience to the fact that he had feared that his nerves might 'crack' under the strain of the proposed flight. He also highlighted the fact that Todd was claiming Ulm had made this statement on the same day that Todd had crashed the car while drunk — a day when it would be surprising if Todd could remember *anything.*

•

Hail Mary, Full of Grace, the Lord is with thee. Blessed art thou among women, and blessed is the fruit of thy womb, Jesus. Holy Mary, Mother of God, pray for us sinners now, and at the hour of death ...

If it had been a horrifying, gut-turning job to bury Anderson and Hitchcock, it was probably a worse one to exhume them. And yet, by prime ministerial command, it was a job that had to be done and, after a tough journey overland from Alice Springs lasting a mere two weeks, courtesy of a new-fangled, twin rear axle, four-wheel-drive truck, an A3 Thornycroft, the men assigned to the task were now in position to do exactly that. Under the command of Constable George Murray of Alice

Springs, the eight-man party, which included four Aboriginal guides, had arrived at the haunting scene late on the afternoon of Wednesday, 13 June 1929; just hours after Todd had given his devastating testimony. The plane stood forlornly facing the east, tilted to one side by the punctured tyre, and somehow the members of the party were all immediately struck by the pathos of this 'man-made machine ... marooned in the pitiless waste of primeval nature'.[5] They shook off the feeling and immediately got to work on exhuming poor Bobby Hitchcock.

Under the command of Constable Murray, they dug a trench parallel to the grave until they reached the level of his body. Then, after they carefully laid matting at the bottom of the trench, they were able to roll the body onto it, before lifting it up and delicately placing the remains in the pine coffin they had brought for that purpose, and then painstakingly sealing the lead lid.[6]

If it was a process troubling to the white men in the party, it was deeply disturbing to the Aboriginal stockmen who had again accompanied them. At night it had been their practice to sleep a small distance from the white fellas, but on this night they camped beside the white men, between two large fires which they had placed almost in a manner to ward off evil spirits.[7] Of such spirits there was no sign, but a very strong wind blew up overnight, rocking the *Kookaburra* to an extent that two of the white men folded back its wings for fear that it would tip over.

At the first light of dawn, Constable Murray and another white man arose and exhumed Anderson's body, repeating the same grisly process. It was weird, and seemed almost supernatural, how the glow of the rising sun cast a strange bluish light over the country around them, while the burnt and blackened area in which they were digging seemed to remain dark and sombre.[8]

By mid-morning, Keith's body, too, was sealed in a pine coffin, and with both dead bodies secured atop the Thornycroft, the party set off for the long journey back to what passed for civilisation in the Northern Territory. They took with them the small blackened penknife they had found in the cockpit, the one that Anderson and Hitchcock had used to try to clear an air strip with, all of its blades pathetically broken.[9]

•

Charles Ulm was recalled to the stand to refute Todd's devastatingly damaging testimony.

'What do you say to Todd's statements [about the virtue of staging crash-landings to generate publicity]?'

'I say that Todd is a deliberate liar of the lowest order, and that the statement was malice.'

'Is there any reason for his being malicious?'

'He thinks,' answered Ulm firmly, 'that with Anderson dead there is nobody to refute his statement. He is an excellent navigator, but he is a big chap with a frightful temper. There were times in America when the crew had to go without meals. On these occasions Todd would abuse me. As you see, he is a big lump of a fellow, and you can't do anything with him. I would have knocked him down otherwise …'

Ulm was followed in the dock by one Harold William Lilja, a sales manager, who — fortunately for Ulm and Kingsford Smith — gave devastating testimony against Todd.

Lilja told the court that he had met Todd just after he had left the *Southern Cross* expedition and was returning from San Francisco on the *Makura*, upon which he was working as a navigator.

'On the ship,' Lilja said in a confident, no-nonsense, this-is-precisely-what-happened voice, 'Todd told me he had his knife into Ulm because Ulm had been the cause of his leaving the expedition.'

•

At last, after a week and a half of deliberations, on the morning of 24 June the Air Investigation Committee assembled in Sydney to announce its findings and Kingsford Smith and Ulm were able to find out if their reputations had been ruined or repaired.

It took Brigadier General Wilson only seven minutes to read the report in front of the packed courtroom. There were several key points. Firstly, and most importantly, the committee found that the crash-landing of the *Southern Cross* was *not* premeditated, which thus dealt with the most heinous allegation of all. Against that, the committee recorded its suspicions that Ulm had exaggerated his diary entries with a view to publication, and that he probably had talked about the virtues of getting lost even if he hadn't meant them. McWilliams was strongly criticised for his failure to convert the wireless into a transmitter, as the committee recorded that it was 'surprised at Mr McWilliams' lack of knowledge. It attributes the failure to communicate by wireless to ignorance or lack of initiative on the part of Mr McWilliams.'[10] The report also reserved some rather trenchant criticism about the lack of emergency rations, the inadequate equipment that the *Southern Cross* carried and the failure to make a bigger signal fire by using available oil but …

But the bottom line remained the same: their forced landing had been genuine, and not some put-up con job on the public sympathy.[11]

Although Kingsford Smith and Ulm were immensely relieved that they had been found innocent of the most devastating accusation that had been levelled against them, there was little time to focus on it. For after all had been said and done, and written, it was time to resume the trip to England that they had been on three months earlier, when they had crash-landed at Coffee Royal. They still had to go, and for the same reason as before — to buy the planes they needed to get Australian National Airways off the ground.

On the very day after the findings by the Air Investigation Committee had been released, at 2.25 pm on 25 June 1929, the *Southern Cross* took off from Richmond air base bound for England once more — this time extremely well stocked with thirty fresh sandwiches, a dozen apples, lots of chewing gum, spare antennae, tools and water — departing before a bare handful of family and friends as the big crowds had simply vanished.

On board were Kingsford Smith, Ulm, Litchfield and McWilliams, exactly the same crew as before, too bloody right they were.

When, the day before, a reporter from *Smith's Weekly* had intimated that Kingsford Smith and Ulm were taking a risk in including the maligned McWilliams once more as their radio operator, Smithy very quickly turned savage: 'Why don't you stop mouthing such nonsense ... go and find a large toilet and pull the damned chain on yourself?'[12]

A relatively uneventful trip followed through Derby, Singapore, Rangoon, Allahabad, Karachi and Baghdad, with the crew's spirits rising as they made good time and seemingly left their troubles in Australia behind. There was something about being in the air that just *cleansed* them. The first real glitch they had came in Athens when, after refuelling and a good night's sleep in a hotel near the airport, they tried to leave.

Where was their permit, an official in gold braid asked them.

'What permit?'

'The permit which says you can leave,' the official said.

'We don't have one, and didn't know we needed one.'

'Well, you can't leave.'

'But we're not bothering anyone. Why can't we go?'

'Sorry, no permit.'

'Okay, we'll wait. But can we give the engines a whirr to keep them loose?'

'Whirr? What you mean — whirr?' asked the official.

'Just give the plane a dry run ... take her to the end of the runway and bring her back — just to make sure the engines are okay.'

'Just a run, no flying?'

'No flying.'[13]

In fact, of course, Smithy gunned the engines and the crew in the *Southern Cross* — '#!?*#! Those sons of bitches!' — were soon winging their way to Rome, and from there to London, where they arrived in the record time of twelve days and eighteen hours.[14]

•

A few days before their arrival, at a time when the *Southern Cross* had just been leaving the hot winds of Karachi behind, the body of Keith Anderson had at last arrived in Sydney, after a long journey by rail. At Central Station, his flag-draped coffin had been met by his mother, Mrs Constance Anderson, Bon Hilliard and her parents, a party of RAAF officers who acted as pall-bearers and a large crowd of sympathisers.[15] From there his coffin had lain 'in state', at St Stephen's Church in Phillip Street, where thousands of Sydneysiders could file past and pay their respects. Many women, particularly, fell to their knees and sobbed before the casket.[16]

And on the cold morning of Saturday, 6 July 1929, after the funeral service at the Presbyterian Church on Belmont Road in the harbourside suburb of Mosman, 6000 mourners filed behind the horse-drawn gun carriage upon which Keith's coffin lay, as it made its way to his final, final resting place in nearby beautiful Rawson Park, with views stretching far out through Sydney Heads into the Pacific Ocean over which he had long dreamed of flying. It was the day of his thirty-eighth birthday. Overhead, five Gipsy Moths flew in the formation of a cross, followed by eight No. 3 Squadron RAAF Westland Wapiti biplanes that swooped down low to drop wreaths on the burial site.[17] As Keith's coffin was lowered into the grave, a high-winged monoplane broke away, a Westland Widgeon III and, swooping low, managed to drop a wreath of red roses and green leaves nearly right on top.

An honour guard of soldiers fired their rifles in the air as a last salute — rather as had been done at the Red Baron's funeral at Bertangles a decade earlier — as Bon Hilliard quietly wept, supported by her family. A lone bugler played the 'Last Post' as the coffin was laid beneath the sod.

'He died there in the course of duty, out there in the waste places of Australia,' the Reverend D.P. MacDonald intoned, 'but he will live forever in the hearts of the Australian people.'[18]

Vale, Keith.

Bobby Hitchcock, meanwhile, at his wife's insistence, had been buried a couple of days earlier in Perth's Karrakatta cemetery after a relatively quiet funeral. For this farewell, Smithy and the crew of the *Southern Cross* had sent messages of condolence and flowers.

•

Although the purpose of the trip to London had been to buy planes for the Australian domestic route, already the thoughts of Kingsford Smith and Ulm were turning to opening up international commercial routes — in particular, expanding Imperial Airways' current London to Karachi route, all the way to Australia.

'I anticipate an efficient Sydney to Melbourne air service,' Smithy told waiting pressmen on the ground in England, 'and am also interested in the inauguration of the Karachi to Australia service.'

'I hope,' Ulm added, 'the Commonwealth and Imperial governments will subsidise the proposed services. This is a very important subject in the closer linking of the Empire.'[19]

Once again the *Southern Cross* had performed so well on the flight that if all else had been equal, Kingsford Smith and Ulm would have liked to have purchased six Fokkers to establish their airline, and yet that would not have been a good look with their future passengers who had been raised on the notion, as had they, that 'British is best'. The solution was to buy four Avro 618 Ten monoplanes from A.V. Roe and Company, which had purchased the rights to manufacture Fokker's F.VIIb.3m machines in Britain — and the two pilots cum businessmen, soon journeyed to the company's headquarters in Manchester to begin negotiations.[20] They decided to buy five planes and have them fitted with 225-horsepower Armstrong Siddeley Lynx seven-cylinder engines instead of the Wright Whirlwinds, which would make them 5 miles per hour faster.

It was at this point that Anthony Fokker sent Smithy and Ulm a cable to the effect that if they could get the *Southern Cross* back to where it was first built, in Amsterdam, he would see that the whole plane was entirely reconditioned, from wing tip to wing tip, tail to propellers, at his own expense — an extremely generous offer. When the negotiations were completed with the Avro people, they flew their champion plane to Amsterdam and were thrilled to be greeted by a veritable honour guard of Fokker fighter planes sent up by the Dutch government's LVA *Luchtvaartafdeling* (aviation department) to escort them to Schiphol aerodrome. There, an enormous crowd awaited them

— an indication of the pride all of Holland had taken in the achievements of the *Southern Cross*.[21]

The four aviators were hailed as such great heroes that it was hard to imagine only two months previously they had been vilified as liars and cheats by a significant portion of their own public at home. Within a fortnight, however, it was time to head back to London, and they left the *Southern Cross* in the wonderfully skilled hands of the Fokker engineers. The board of Australian National Airways had made it clear that it wanted Ulm to return immediately to help get their new airline set up, while it had very reluctantly agreed to allow Kingsford Smith to head to America by ship, to explore the possibilities of fulfilling his dream of being the first man to fly around the world.[22] (At least, while crossing the equator. In 1924, a US Army team using massive resources had managed to get two planes around the world while staying wholly within the northern hemisphere.)

Having done the San Francisco to Sydney leg, and then the Sydney to London leg, all he needed now was to cross the Atlantic from Europe to the American mainland, and then proceed to San Francisco, and it would be done! If it worked out, Smithy could also claim to have made the first *successful* crossing east to west, as although two Germans, Günther von Hünefeld and Hermann Köhl, together with Irishman Captain James C. Fitzmaurice, DFC, had partially done it a couple of years earlier, they had crash-landed on an island off Labrador and then been stranded for several weeks, so that hardly counted!

When Smithy landed in New York on this preliminary trip, he was delighted to meet his old friend Anthony Fokker once more who, hail-fellow-well-met, showed his eagerness to help Smithy be the first man to fly the Atlantic from the other direction by immediately pulling out his pen and chequebook and handing over a cheque for £1000.[23]

Now *that* was Smithy's kind of encouragement!

•

October 1929. Vancouver.

What was going on? On her regular course back and forth across the Pacific, the RMS *Aorangi* had been due to leave the docks of Vancouver at high noon, and yet here it was, two o'clock in the afternoon, and there was still no sign of movement. Finally, the word went round. There was to be a slight delay, because one of the passengers to come was the famous Australian aviator Charles Kingsford Smith, who was then and there addressing Vancouver's almost equally prestigious Canadian Club. He should be boarding very shortly, apparently, and then they would be full steam ahead across the Pacific. Which was all right for *some.*

Many passengers were thrilled at the news that for the next three weeks they would have Australia's most famous man among them. Others, however, were furious — *furious*, do you hear — that an entire ship and all her passengers were being held up for just *one* man, and none was angrier than one Mary Powell, the eighteen-year-old daughter of the rich Melbourne horse breeder Arthur Powell and his wife, Floss. Mary and her parents had been on a grand tour of the world for the last nine months, and were now about to leave on the last leg home, and would have already left, if not for this wretched pilot chappie. Bother. Bother. *Bother.*

At last, near three o'clock, there was a flurry of activity on the docks. A car pulled up and out of it got a man with a young woman, both of whom were soon hurrying up the gangplank, with the porters carrying their luggage scurrying behind.

'Here's Kingsford Smith at last,' Arthur Powell said to his daughter.

Mary looked. *That* was Kingsford Smith? She was stunned.

'It was a bit like saying,' Mary later recounted, '"Here's the King." I remember my absolute amazement that in the flesh, he was such a little man. I said, "How insignificant he looks to have done all those things."'[24]

Well, her parents didn't think him insignificant. When he had touched down at Essendon aerodrome the previous year, they, like some 80,000 fellow citizens of Melbourne, had been there to greet him — while Mary had had a tennis party — and they were now delighted to be seeing him up close …

And yet, if Mary Powell was not impressed with the aviator, Kingsford Smith felt quite the opposite that evening at dinner when he cast his eye over the assembled company and picked her out as the most attractive young lady present. Small and gorgeous, elegant and poised, impeccably groomed, with high cheekbones and full lips, this ravishing brunette had piercing blue eyes that simply mesmerised him.

On that first night on the high seas, only a few minutes after spotting Mary, Kingsford Smith breathed quietly to his 25-year-old niece, Beris — Harold's daughter, to whom he was shouting a trip to Australia, after he had spent a couple of weeks catching up with the American branch of the family in their Californian home — that he had made his choice.

'The one in red will do me,' he said. 'I wouldn't mind practising on her.'[25]

And he was as good as his word.

From that moment on, as the Pacific Ocean opened up before them, the rising 33-year-old pilot turned the full force of his charm on both the young woman and her parents. As he was quickly installed on the captain's table, it didn't take long for him to organise for the Powell family to be invited, too, and it was not long until they were *all* in his thrall.

No matter what the subject, Smithy usually had a well-turned, self-deprecating story to go with it. When it came up that, on their recent tour, Mary had been presented at court to King George V, the war veteran was able to tell his own story of meeting the King when he had, can you believe it, tripped over his own feet and gone to ground! Laughter all round.

When Arthur Powell mentioned that he and his wife had been there at Melbourne airport the previous year after the trans-Pacific flight, Smithy was able to relate to the family anecdotes about that splendid afternoon, what the Governor and Premier had said, and so forth.

And what of India, where the Powell family had lived for many years, as Arthur bred his horses? Smithy had been there many times on his cross-global travels, and was a wonderful mimic of the Indian accent, complete with imitation of the curiously sideways nodding Indian head. Ah, how he could make the family laugh, just as he could reduce many of Mary's friends, who were also on board the ship and all eager to meet him via her, to tears of mirth.

And yet, despite the breadth and grandeur of Kingsford Smith's experiences, somehow he managed to present it all in such a down-to-earth and humble fashion that he didn't seem to have an ounce of arrogance about him. Nothing could make him tell a story about one of his adventures where he was made to come across as heroic. Rather than talk about himself, he seemed every bit as interested in them, as they were in him. He was a good listener too. And while everyone on the ship seemed to be competing for his attention, it was clear that the Powells were at the top of his list.

Dance, Mary?

Yes, Charles, she would like to dance, and did so beautifully, around the floor as he held her close. Mind the foot, dear. Small war wound, nothing to worry about …

The hit of the era, because it was both romantic and also captured so wonderfully the enduring prosperous spirit of the times was Irving Berlin's 'Blue Skies':

Blue skies
Smiling at me
Nothing but blue skies
Do I see

Bluebirds
Singing a song
Nothing but bluebirds
All day long

Never saw the sun shining so bright
Never saw things going so right
Noticing the days hurrying by
When you're in love, my how they fly …

•

In America, as Charles and Mary danced on, night after night, a curious thing was happening at the New York Stock Exchange, the world's largest and most powerful exchange. On the morning of Thursday, 24 October 1929, turmoil had set in as the price of shares started to tumble, and then continued to fall at an ever-increasing rate. Panic begat panic. By virtue of the fact that every 'buy' order was on a black pad and every 'sell' order was on a red pad, this panic was soon represented by a sea of fluttering red papers being furiously waved on the floor by desperate stockbrokers trying to unload shares and save their clients.

Something had to be done, and it was. By noon of that day the most influential of the Wall Street bankers had a meeting in the House of Morgan, directly opposite the exchange, in an effort to find a solution and turn the market back around. On the spot, they put together an effective fighting fund to support the market, and an hour later Dick Whitney, the vice-president of the exchange, made what was to become a famous walk across the floor. Speaking in a firm voice and holding a black order form, he called out in a loud voice, calculated for effect, 'I give $205 for 10,000 US Steel.' This was ten dollars up on the asking price!

Then he moved to the next post and standing on a chair, called out: 'I give $45 for 50,000 Standard Oil.' Another huge, high order!

On the instant, the stockbrokers began to applaud, and kept applauding as Whitney moved from post to post, pouring millions into the market. And his strategy seemed to work. The stampede of the stockbrokers to keep selling at any price stopped, and even turned a little. Some began to buy again. If Morgan was putting their money in, then maybe the crash was over!

By the end of the day the market had indeed risen slightly and wobbled its way forward on the Friday, not losing too much. But over the weekend, the mood changed once more. Huge numbers of speculators decided that, to be on the safe side, it would be best to get their money out.

The market fell sharply on the Monday and then, on the day that would forevermore be known as 'Black Tuesday', 29 October 1929, it was all over. The market lost $14 billion in a day — 12 per cent of its value — to go with the $16 billion of the previous four trading days. People walking along Wall Street were seen to be nervously looking skywards as rumours spread that stockbrokers and investors were queuing up to leap to their deaths. A savage worldwide economic downturn had just begun, a downturn that the aspiring American presidential candidate Franklin Delano Roosevelt would soon refer to as 'this depression'. It was terrible news for everyone, but most particularly those who had gone deep into debt to launch new business ventures.

•

And so what he was going to do, Charles Kingsford Smith explained to the charming Mary, as they continued to glide oh so sweetly over the Pacific Ocean, was to start up his own aviation company with Charles Ulm. They now had the reputation they needed together with the experience, and had already bought the planes they required to get started. It would be a long haul, no doubt, but Smithy had made his reputation through bringing off long hauls, and he was confident he could do so with this one, too. The future looked bright.

So bright, in fact, that one night, not long after they had crossed the equator — in a far more pleasurable manner than the last time he had crossed it heading towards Australia — Smithy asked Mary to marry him. Less than three weeks since she'd first laid eyes on him — she was completely stunned.

Though they had exchanged some rather chaste kisses outside under the stars, she had no idea that his thoughts were turning towards a lifetime commitment. She hadn't been planning on getting married for years. And yet, he was so nice, so charming, and while he could have had just about any single woman in Australia, he had chosen her!

Realising what an important decision it was, she managed to hold him off for a couple of days, until agreeing that yes, she would marry him so long as it was all right with her parents. In fact, she was near certain that it wouldn't be.

'We'll see about that,' Smithy replied, before marching straight off to find her father and present his case.

A hard man, Arthur Powell — a man of the world who knew which way was up. While he admired Kingsford Smith and all he had achieved, he was far more concerned about his beautiful daughter and her future. So, after the first shock of Kingsford Smith's words had passed, as had a moment's heavy silence, he chose his words carefully and spoke, hard man to hard man: 'You've got a damned cheek. You're much too old for her.'[26]

What, a mere fourteen years difference? Not at all, not at all.

In the end, a compromise was reached. So long as the young couple delayed announcing their engagement for twelve months then they could see.

'If, after you'd done the Atlantic flight, you and Mary still feel the same way, I suppose you can go ahead,' he said gruffly. 'Not before.'

Done!

Dockside in Sydney, as ever, the Kingsford Smith family had turned out in force on this sunny morning of 9 November 1929 to greet the prodigal pilot, and he immediately introduced Mary as 'the girl I want to marry'.[27]

From which point, everything went swimmingly. Whereas Thelma had not gelled with the Kingsford Smith clan, it was entirely different with Mary. Whisked out to Kuranda, she was quickly embraced to the family's bosom, and embraced them in turn, loving their life, their laughter.

'It was so full of fun,' she later recalled of Kuranda. 'A relaxed happy-go-lucky place, with such a good feeling about it.'[28]

•

And so to work …

Mary returned home to Melbourne, while Kingsford Smith headed to the Australian National Airways office newly established in Challis House in Sydney's Martin Place, opposite the GPO. Just a few days before he'd arrived in Sydney, the first three Avro 618 Ten planes he and Ulm had bought in England had also arrived at the Sydney docks, on the SS *Huntingdon*, and it was time to assemble them in the company's hangar at Mascot, get them into the air, and test them.

Initially, the pride aircraft of their fleet were to be the *Southern Cloud*, the *Southern Sky* and the *Southern Sun*. The next planes to arrive were called the *Southern Star* and *Southern Moon*. All were decked out with royal blue fuselages and silver wings to capitalise on the fame of the similarly fashioned *Southern Cross*.

Prospective pilots also had to be interviewed and hired, and good ones they were, too. They included Eric Chaseling, Scotty Allan, James Mollison, Jerry Pentland (second only to the great Captain Arthur Cobby with the number of Huns he had shot down during the war[29]), Travis Shortridge, Paddy Shepherd and P.W. Lynch-Blosse, with the man who had virtually invented the Australian version of the bubble sextant, Bill Taylor, joining a short time later. An envious Hudson Fysh would label the group later, as 'the finest group of pilots ever to be gathered together in Australia'.[30]

The inaugural flights of Australian National Airways took place simultaneously on New Year's Day 1930. Smithy himself flying the mighty *Southern Cloud* with Scotty Allan as co-pilot, took off at 8 am from Mascot with seven of the eight seats filled — each of the passengers paying £9 13s for the privilege of flying one way, plus an excess fee for all baggage weighing over 10 pounds.[31] A large gathering of the press watched them depart and they landed at Eagle Farm aerodrome in Brisbane at 1.30 pm.

At the same time, Charles Ulm and Paddy Shepherd in the *Southern Sky* took off southwards from Brisbane.[32] As it happened, however, bad weather forced Ulm's plane down onto a ploughed paddock at Old Bonalbo in northern New South Wales, and it was a little over a fortnight before it could take off again. Although it was an inauspicious beginning, ANA was soon able to recover its equilibrium.

Every morning, an ANA aircraft took off from Sydney airport and headed to Brisbane, while its counterpart left Brisbane heading to Sydney. Following the model established for cruise liners, each day the major newspapers published passenger lists, more often than not including the names of the good and great of the day. Yet Smithy was more than a little restless.

A decade and a half earlier, at the conclusion of the Great War, he had written to his parents that 'I am going to continue flying if possible, so long as it doesn't come down to the level of being a chauffeur'.[33] Yes, he had done his fair share of precisely that kind of flying when working for West Australian Airways, but that had been before he had inhaled deeply the intoxicating vapours of record-breaking flights around the planet.

Once he knew what it was like to be greeted by 300,000 of his fellow citizens at Sydney airport after crossing the Pacific, or break records left, right and across central Australia, it did not sit easily on him to do the regular Sydney to Brisbane service and fly other tiny hops back and forth. And nor did office life suit Smithy's temperament. All those damn numbers and papers! That stultifying *routine*. It was only by endlessly playing his ukulele in the ANA offices at Martin Place that helped to make his time there a little more tolerable, and even then it was only just. The truth of it was, he was made for neither flying aircraft back and forth on regular runs nor administering the business that organised those flights.

To those who knew him well, it was no surprise when in early March 1930 Smithy announced that he was going to head back to Europe to collect the *Southern Cross* and finally reach his goal of circumnavigating the globe. After long, agonised discussions, Mary had finally agreed to give her blessing for him to make the attempt, chiefly on the grounds that it was the only big thing left for him to do in aviation, and that if he didn't do it, the likelihood was that it would nag him forever.

So go, darling.

Smithy, in turn, faithfully promised that once the Atlantic flight was done, he would not undertake any more big flights.[34]

True, crossing the Atlantic Ocean from east to west was a fraught affair, as for most of the trip he would be buffeted by strong headwinds, and the North Atlantic coast of the American continent was notoriously foggy — making navigation and landing difficult — but Smithy felt he was just the man for the job.

Though Ulm had wanted to accompany him, the board of the ANA — consisting of such leading Sydney businessmen as Frederick Stewart, Mark Reid and Arthur Vickery — had made it absolutely clear that that was out of the question. They had personally put up serious money to get this company — capitalised at £200,000 — off the ground, and wanted to be absolutely certain that it was going to work. Ulm would have to stay in Australia, supervising the firm's forty staff, and keeping the operations going, which were now running from 7 am to 7 pm. Truth be told, the board didn't want Kingsford Smith to go either, but knew that ultimately, they could not hold him back.

With Smithy thus forced to go it alone, he and Ulm came to a deal whereby, in return for Smithy handing over a portion of his shares in ANA, Ulm would hand over his half-share of the *Southern Cross* to Smithy — the deal to be confirmed the instant that the trans-Atlantic attempt was under way.

•

But a moment before you go, Smithy. It was around this time that the same Lester Brain who had discovered the *Kookaburra* in the Tanami Desert, and first seen the body of Bobby Hitchcock lying beneath the wing, requested a meeting with Kingsford Smith and Ulm in their office in Martin Place. He was concerned, he told them frankly, by reports that they were going to expand the Australian National Airways route to include a daily Sydney–Melbourne/Melbourne–Sydney shuttle.

They had to realise, he told them, the difficulties of the weather on that route, taking them above the highest mountains in Australia — how the cloud was frequently impenetrable, the wind vicious, and ice would form on the plane's wings. It was not feasible to mount a regular service with safety, he said.

Smithy, by Brain's later account, looked him right in the eye and said: 'We're going to fly through a brick wall if necessary. We're going to run on schedule whatever the weather is and I'm going to be a millionaire or go bust.'[35]

•

Of course Mary went to see him off, as he sailed on the *Sonoma*, departing from Sydney on 15 March 1930, to head first to San Francisco, and then catch a train to New York before crossing the Atlantic on the *Statendam* for Holland, where he would reclaim the reconditioned *Southern Cross.*

•

While Kingsford Smith was off on yet another adventure, to no doubt break more records, make more headlines, and be fawned over once again before flying off to various far-flung parts of the world, at Qantas Hudson Fysh and Fergus McMaster were quietly going about the business of business. They were not making a public splash like Smithy, but they were making money, developing contacts, consolidating relationships and maximising the ability to run a major airline, mastering everything from how to ensure that the planes were regularly and meticulously serviced to a requisite degree of excellence, to the financial complexities of operating their expensive aircraft in the tightening regulatory environment.

Just a few weeks after Smithy had gone overseas once more, in fact, it was a big day in the life of the Fysh family in Longreach. As one, they piled into a Qantas de Havilland DH.61, and took off, bound for Brisbane, where the new headquarters of Qantas had been set up. After nine years of struggle in the nation's interior — carrying 10,400 passengers just over one million miles — Hudson Fysh had, together with the Qantas board, decided it was time to move to the Big Smoke, to try their luck in the capital city. He and the rest of the Qantas management left the rustically charming Longreach with heavy hearts, but the opportunities that beckoned were enormous.

The chairman of Qantas, Fergus McMaster, put it grandiloquently in his official farewell speech at the Longreach premises: 'Is it not a high honour to participate in man's last and final accomplishment in the development of a rapid convenient mode of transportation which eventually will give each individual in ANY part of the World a common economic interest in every part of the World?'[36]

Aeroplane travel was changing the way commerce between nations was conducted and both Hudson Fysh and McMaster were determined that Qantas would lay claim to a big part of Australian aviation's next frontier — international routes leading to and from Australia. In the view of many, it was nothing less than a matter of national urgency that this frontier be conquered. The South Australian Governor, Sir Alexander Hore-Ruthven, had put it well: 'Every hour by which we can shorten the journey between the Old Country and the New, will further the progress and prosperity of the Empire.'[37]

Already, that remoteness was diminishing, thanks to aviation companies following the paths now blazed by the pioneers to set up commercial routes. The previous year, in 1929, the Dutch airline, *Koninklijke Luchtvaart Maatschappij* — or KLM as it was known — had begun a fortnightly service between Amsterdam and Batavia (as Jakarta was then named), while Britain's Imperial Airways had inaugurated a weekly service between London and Delhi. The obvious thing, therefore, was for an Australian airline to begin a service to either Batavia or Delhi — preferably the latter, on the grounds of loyalty to the Empire — and be part of a lucrative route that would take passengers and post around the entire planet! Who would get it? Qantas felt it was a strong contender, as did ANA, as did Norman Brearley's West Australian Airways.

•

In the meantime, Kingsford Smith and Ulm were expanding Australian National Airways, even while Kingsford Smith was overseas, and on 1 June 1930 the airline inaugurated its daily Sydney to Melbourne service. From a standing start only a year before, ANA had now established the first regular service between the major cities of the eastern states, all of it without a penny of subsidy from the government.

Getting the passengers to their destination on time was important, but so too was facilitating their journey, with ANA having a bus service in Sydney that delivered passengers straight from the GPO in Martin Place, to the steps of the aeroplane. Each of the eight passenger seats — a wicker chair with a cushion, though without a seat-belt — had a side-pocket containing the daily newspaper, and they were also provided with a map showing the route and the times they should be above certain landmarks. And, oh yes, a sick bag.[38] The tightening effect of the Depression notwithstanding, generally the numbers were good and the planes were full.

Though interested in ANA's expansion, and certainly impressed by Ulm's business acumen, Hudson Fysh did not feel that the airline threatened their own pre-eminence in the Australian aviation market. He later recorded: 'It was rather felt that the service was run on the experience and ideals of the pioneer record-breakers, who braved all elements, and in this respect we felt ANA had operated ahead of the supporting ground organisation. The tenet "the mails must fly", over which I used to argue with Charles Ulm, was ahead of time for passenger carriage.'[39]

In broad brushstrokes, ANA pilot Bill Taylor was also of the view that the airline was particular in its approach to commercial services, always leaning towards the we-can-do-it! approach, above all else.

'Right from the start,' he later noted, 'the spirit of this airline was the spirit of the Pacific flight.'[40] That is, no flying task was impossible, no weather too bad to overcome, if you just had the right pilots. Smithy's view was that 'contact navigation', otherwise known as 'track crawling', as every other airline in the country did it — steering by visual contact with the ground — was primitive, and that ANA would lead the way with modern navigation by instrument flying in and above clouds. Just as they had done it to cross the Pacific and the Tasman.[41]

Fifteen

NEW FRONTIERS

My heart is in adventure and the last frontier is the air.
CHARLES KINGSFORD SMITH TO AMERICAN JOURNALIST EDWIN C. PARSONS[1]

Kingsford Smith I regard as the greatest flyer in the world today. Balchen is perhaps comparable to him, but only in the cockpit.[2] Kingsford Smith has the advantage of being a great commander as well as flyer. He is the best organiser for success I know, and has the most courage of any airman I have met. Slight, he is like an animate copper wire, surging with electrical energy, a man not to be downed no matter what the odds pitted against him.
ANTHONY FOKKER WRITING IN HIS AUTOBIOGRAPHY, IN 1931[3]

Smithy was now devoted to making his long dreamed of trans-Atlantic hop a reality. At Anthony Fokker's suggestion, Smithy engaged a Dutch co-pilot by the name of Evert van Dijk, who normally flew with KLM.

But who should be his radio man?

He was pondering that very question in London's Royal Air Force Club one afternoon, when he heard a familiar voice behind him. It was that of John Stannage, whom he had first met at Mills Field in 1927 and who had been the radio man aboard the *Canberra* when it had found them at Coffee Royal. Now, after much furious handshaking and back-slapping, Smithy was delighted to hear Stannage report that he was trying to get back to Australia by the quickest possible means. As a matter of fact …

'You don't happen,' Stannage asked, 'to be looking for a radio operator to fly the Atlantic, do you?'[4]

Smithy signed him on the spot. Not only was he a very good radio operator, but he was tiny in stature, and that meant they could load more petrol on.

As to the final member of the crew, upon inquiry, Smithy was able to sign a Celtic navigator, the genial and ebullient Paddy Saul, who was an ex-mariner, just as all the best navigators were. Part of the bond formed between Smithy and Paddy was that the Irishman had married an Australian woman — alas, who had recently died tragically, leaving him with an eight-year-old daughter to raise on his own — and in the course of his many travels had even served with the AIF at Gallipoli. This made him Smithy's kind of bloke.[5]

Retrieving the *Southern Cross* from Amsterdam — with van Dijk, Stannage and Doc Maidment — Smithy found his beautiful bird had been so superbly reconditioned that he dared do a loop-de-loop soon after taking off from the Fokker headquarters![6] After a few days in Croydon, about 10 miles out of London, they then flew to Baldonnel in the Irish Free State to pick up Paddy Saul, and by the early hours of Tuesday, 24 June 1930, everything was in readiness.

The *Southern Cross* was in position on Ireland's magnificently long Portmarnock Beach — at low tide as wide and flat as a billiard table — with the summery dawn still a couple of hours away. Even at that absurdly early hour of 4 am, around 1000 Irish locals and a few enthusiasts from Dublin, which lay just a little to the south, had turned up to see the historic flight begin, and flares placed around the plane and along the beach threw an ethereal, dancing light upon their expectant faces.[7]

For just under twenty-five minutes, Smithy kept the engines of the *Southern Cross* turning over, on the reckoning that they would have to be thoroughly warm to be able to give maximum power when the time came. No matter the shattering sound, Paddy Saul's dog, Kips, who had accompanied his master on many plane trips, now sensed that he was being very rudely left behind and steadfastly refused to move from beneath the fuselage in front of the plane's wheels. It was some time before he could be forcibly removed.[8] They were less insistent about stopping the pretty Irish colleens who continued to break through and kiss the fuselage of the plane to bring it good luck.[9] At last, at 4.25 am GMT the moment arrived, and Smithy gave the *Southern Cross* full throttle, its shattering roar rolling for miles across the Emerald Isle as, in John Stannage's words, 'a thin, blue stiletto flame showed at each of the stub exhausts and stabbed the dark fabric of the pre-dawn gloom'.[10]

Before the entranced eyes of the Irish spectators, the plane first waddled, then trotted, then sprinted, then *hurtled* down the beach at 80 miles per hour and took off after just 1000 yards. The *Southern Cross* then took a long sweeping circle out to sea, and winged its way back over the beach, dipping one wing a little as a farewell salute to the crowd, before beginning the journey proper, across the Atlantic. Back in Ireland, a friend of Smithy's sent a prearranged cable to Mary, now that the *Southern Cross* was safely off the ground: `Safely on our way – home.`[11]

•

They were away!

Ahead lay America. They hoped.

For Smithy, this time, at first, was just like it had been when he had left San Francisco bound for Australia. For the first few hours the skies sparkled, the engines hummed along and beyond everything feeling easy, it almost seemed *too* easy. Nary a problem in the world! True, before departure they had been warned by the chief of the US Weather Bureau that the American coast was fogbound, and they would be getting such strong winds against them he felt they should delay their start. But, Smithy being Smithy, he decided, just as he had in the lead-up to the Coffee Royal affair, to ignore that advice and deal with the problems as he found them.[12] He was confident they would find a way through.

Besides, this time — together with his trusty talismanic photo of Nellie Stewart which, all these years later, he still flew with tucked under his seat — he had another good luck charm: a gold plaque in the form of a four-leaf shamrock on which was inscribed a Gaelic motto, '*God Speed Thee, West.*' This was the gift of Mrs James McNeil, the wife of the Governor of the Free State.[13]

She, and much of the world — including Charles Lindbergh, who in his Hopewell, New Jersey, mansion was following the flight closely — was hungry for every detail that could be garnered about this trans-Atlantic attempt. Under an exclusive and lucrative arrangement with the *New York Times*, the *Southern Cross* was to keep up a steady stream of messages in Morse code, which the paper subsequently published.

> Getting darker now. The outboard motors are shrouded in a blue haze. Each exhaust port has a faint, pink flame feathering from it. It is very uncanny. The lettering on the starboard wing is embossed in gold as the last faint radiance from the western sky touches it.[14]

And then, of course, as ever, things began to change. Mid-Atlantic, they were suddenly confronted by cloud castles of an unknown but evil aerial kingdom, and soon thereafter were entirely engulfed by fog so thick that in every direction — up, down, left, right and forward — everything looked exactly the same. *Blank.* When Smithy took the *Southern Cross* up to try to get out of it, he found headwinds so strong that they could make no more than 50 miles per hour against them, which meant the fuel would be exhausted before they even got close to America, so he was obliged to go back down into the fog. Calling it 'pea soup' didn't begin to do it justice. In the back of the plane it was out of the question for Paddy Saul to get any bearings on where they were, but fortunately John Stannage was able to maintain contact with many ships below — who relayed their own positions and the direction they were getting the signals from the *Southern Cross* on, so that he was able to cross-reference them — that they were able to retain a fair idea of where they were at any given time.[15] And that was, despite the lack of vision, flying like an arrow to New York!

```
1.29 New York Time. O.K. Old boy. Have
been messing about trying to get a
bearing. It is very dark, and we are flying
blind. The motors are ringed with flames.
Still 160 miles from Cape Race. Dickens of
a struggle to keep awake now. The drone
makes you tired.[16]
```

Of course, sleep was not an option. In the cockpit, Smithy was obliged to engage in the longest period of 'blind flying' he had ever done, well over twelve hours and counting, which was exhausting and unnerving.

Mijn God, van Dijk wrote in his journal, *how long is this going to last? If he and I don't make it, then no one will ever make it.*[17]

All they could do was keep going, and hope for a break in the fog. In fact, the break in the monotony of it all came in a rather upsetting fashion. Smithy had taken the *Southern Cross* a little lower, in the hope of at least sighting the ocean, when a shocked Stannage — whose radio signals had suddenly gone dead — sent through a frantically scribbled note: *UP, UP! Aerial dragged water twice!*[18]

Horrified, Smithy did exactly that, not realising that their altitude had dropped to such a low level, for his altimeter clearly showed them at 600 feet, and the antenna was only 200 feet long. In the cabin, John Stannage removed his helmet and wiped his brow, knowing how close they had just come to a catastrophe.[19] And yet in short order it was Paddy Saul who had his own complaint, which was at least as troubling, and also quickly passed forward to Smithy: *My compass shows up to ninety degrees divergence from course, and Stannage has two radio bearings which I find inexplicable.*[20]

Dumbfounded, Kingsford Smith showed the message to van Dijk, who was equally stunned. What on *earth* was going on? According to their compass they had been flying on course for the whole time, and they soon advised that to Saul in a note.

In the middle of the Atlantic Ocean, 400 miles south of the coast of Newfoundland, their compasses, quivering with indecision, had gone haywire, and not even uniformly haywire, which would have given them a chance of working out exactly on which course they were heading. It was one thing to know where they were, but quite another to know what course to fix on to get to where they wanted to go. The problem was compounded when Paddy Saul informed them that in the last two hours, by his calculations, they had made no progress to the west *at all*.[21] The only explanation was that in the fog they had been flying in a series of massive arcs. Was this what had happened to Nungesser and Coli on their journey, not to mention the many others who had tried, and failed, to cross the Atlantic from east to west?[22] Was there something about this part of the world that sent compasses crazy? Was everyone who attempted it doomed to fly around in useless circles until the ocean claimed them?

Smithy knew what he needed at this point. He needed a drink. Taking up his pen, he wrote a note to Stannage and Saul in the cabin behind, and sent it back: *I'd give anything for a toot. Do either of you birds happen to have one back there?*[23]

Almost immediately, a tiny bottle of whisky that John Stannage had been hiding from the skipper came forward. Smithy took a long swig.

Calling on all his experience, Smithy tried to think the problem through. Considering his options, it became clear that really only one gave the men any chance of salvation. He would have to ignore the vicious headwinds and take the plane up again, in the hope that being in clear air would sort things out.

At last, just when the situation was getting absolutely desperate, the *Southern Cross* got to an altitude of 3500 feet and emerged from the fog of both the skies and the crew's panic.[24] Stars twinkled above. Everything seemed bathed in an odd kind of ethereal blue light, while away on their starboard horizon the sky showed a streak of peculiar red that was possibly an effect of the aurora borealis phenomenon.[25] It was a moment in time none of them would ever forget …

And, almost as one, after a hurried committee meeting it seemed, all their compasses at last agreed and started pointing in exactly the same direction again! A direction that made sense and aligned precisely with where the moon was. Setting a confident course, it was not long before they had moved beyond the worst of the fog and the waves of the Atlantic were, in patches, visible below them in the moonlight.

Which was the good news. The bad news was that they had burnt up so much fuel flying in circles in the fog it was now out of the question they would make it all the way to New York, and it was even going to be a close-run thing to make it to Newfoundland. Smithy throttled well back, at a speed designed to gain maximum mileage and John Stannage managed to raise the Cape Race radio station on the coast of Newfoundland. Unfortunately, Stannage was told that Newfoundland's principal airstrip, at St John's — from where Hawker and Grieve had taken off over a decade before on their own Atlantic attempt, heading east — was entirely fogged in, and that most of Newfoundland was in exactly the same state. The only place not entirely lost in the fog was a remote fishing village called Harbour Grace, about 25 miles beyond St John's.

It was their only hope. To give themselves every chance, as the dirty dawn began to break, they radioed ahead to Harbour Grace with the desperate appeal for a local plane to be sent up above the fog, which they might be able to follow closely to the landing ground.[26] And even when they reached the point where they knew land must be beneath them, there was no respite. The cloud cover went so low that it was the exact conditions where Australian pilots used the expression, 'even the bloody birds are walking today', on the reckoning that the birds were sensible enough never to fly when they couldn't see.[27]

Of that plane, alas, there was no sign, and yet, just when it seemed as if all was lost, at a time that they knew they were practically flying on fumes alone and were expecting the engines to cough dead at any second, a brief break in the fog revealed the landing strip they were looking for, with people waving white sheets near a fire lit to signal the field's position!

Smithy brought the mighty *Southern Cross* down from out of the clouds where it had been for the last thirty-one and a half hours, and executed a perfect landing at 7.53 am local time. The Atlantic had been conquered from the east, by a plane with just one last gasp left in it. It had been a close-run thing, as it so often was with Smithy, pushing everything to its limits, but they had done it. They had flown 1900 miles by the chart, but considerably more in actual fact.

•

Early the next morning, refreshed from a wonderful sleep in a local hostelry, and still more than a little amazed that they had survived the terrible ordeal of the day before, they took off again for New York.

Compared to the first leg of their trip, this was relatively clear flying — so clear that looking down upon the rugged country of Nova Scotia, they could clearly see enormous brown bears running away from the sound of the plane's engines. From there they traversed the Bay of Fundy, where they could gaze upon a massive shark basking on the ocean's surface, and shortly afterwards they saw the United States Atlantic Fleet on manoeuvres — whose sailors all waved their caps at them and cheered as they buzzed low — before they continued over Boston, New Haven and then Long Island Sound.[28] As they were nearing New York, Smithy penned a message and had John Stannage send it to the world:

> All going fine. Have just climbed through fog to clear air at 2,500 ft. Stop. Everyone happy, and I expect my girl in Australia is glad that my last ocean is flown ...

And this time he meant it. He was getting too old for this caper. He had done it for too long, taken too many risks, and now he needed to find something easier to do. Build up Australian National Airways, for a start. He knew that Mary worried about him terribly when he was away, and he simply wanted to spend more time with her.

This time there really were twenty welcoming planes coming out from New York to guide them towards their destination. Following them, the legendary *Southern Cross*, the most travelled aeroplane in the world, well on its way to completing the first circumnavigation of the entire planet while crossing the equator, briefly deviated from its appointed path along the Hudson River and circled around the New York skyscrapers — much as Lindbergh had circled the Eiffel Tower in Paris four years earlier. Those roofs were crowded with New Yorkers waving an enthusiastic welcome. And then, after 'performing several side slips that tilted its wings at almost right angles to the ground in triumphant salute to the delighted, cheering crowd',[29] came in to land on the spot where Lindbergh had himself started, Roosevelt Field, with a glorious setting sun appropriately marking the completion of the circle. Some 5000 New Yorkers had gathered to witness the occasion. For a moment after Smithy switched the engines off, he took pause before the madness began, as a wave of complete exhaustion washed over him. The long hours of darkness, the flying blind, the dark ocean reaching up at them through the mist, all passed kaleidoscopically before his eyes.[30] They dinkum had done it.

It was 7.30 pm on 26 June 1930 and Charles Kingsford Smith was second only to Lindbergh in terms of his world celebrity as an aviator. Among the cognoscenti of aviation he may have even moved beyond Lindbergh, and that was certainly the view of the American himself. Via his father-in-law, the famed diplomat Dwight Morrow, Lindbergh expressed his considered and expert opinion to the press that the two greatest achievements in aviation both had Kingsford Smith's signature on them — the first crossing of the Pacific, and the crossing of the Atlantic from the east to the west, against the prevailing winds.[31] Kingsford Smith was, in Lindbergh's view, 'the greatest of long distance pilots'.[32]

That also seemed to be the view of the crowd, who were so enthusiastic that the aviators were for a short while effective prisoners in their plane, as it took the 150 Nassau County Police officers and sixteen motorcycle cops nearly fifteen minutes to herd the crowd under control and allow them a safe exit.[33]

This latest of Kingsford Smith's feats made front-page headlines all over the world, particularly in France — where the ill-fated trip of Nungesser and Coli was remembered — and in Holland, where there was great pride that a Fokker had once again set a major aviation record.

One particular line from the press conference that occurred immediately after landing was widely quoted. Kingsford Smith heaped praise on the machine that he loved so deeply, almost like a woman, and said with feeling: 'That plane has carried me, with the same motors, close to 80,000 miles since we left Oakland a year ago. It has flown all the oceans but the Polar oceans, carried me safely over the deserts of Australia and America, the jungles of India and Burma, and the towns and cities of Europe, and she still has a lot of flying left.'[34]

As to the real woman he loved, Mary, there was a wonderfully warm and loving telegram that he had received from her, even before leaving the field. She had been waiting up through the night for news that he was safe, that he had done it, and hopefully got these long-distance trips out of his system once and for all.

'Isn't it wonderful?' she told the press in Melbourne. 'My mother insisted that I spend last evening playing bridge to keep me from worrying. Oh, but the terrible things I did at bridge!'[35]

In Australia, it was the Controller of Civil Aviation, Lieutenant Colonel Horace Brinsmead, who perhaps best spoke for the proud nation. 'In my opinion,' he was quoted as saying, 'Squadron Leader Kingsford Smith must be classed as No.1 in the list of the world's best pilots.'[36] For his part, a thrilled Charles Ulm exulted: 'Kingsford Smith undoubtedly is the world's premier pilot. And surely the authorities will confer some signal honour upon him. I would suggest an entirely new title, K.M.A., Knight Master of the Air.'[37]

As ever for Smithy, the next few days were a blur, beginning with a hair-raising trip into New York's Roosevelt Hotel, behind four motorcycle cops with sirens blaring through streets lined with masses of cheering New Yorkers. Though they politely declined the offer of a ticker-tape parade down New York's Broadway,[38] thinking that was too much for such as them, they did agree to a welcome on the steps of City Hall where, in front of a massive crowd, Mayor Jimmy Walker, after making a robust welcoming speech, presented them all with the city's Medal of Honor. There were so many photographers there to record the event that the stand upon which they were perched collapsed, fortunately with no major injuries.

When, shortly afterwards, Smithy was able to speak to Mary in Melbourne via a special radio hook-up, the *New York Times* was there to record his end of the conversation: 'Hello — yes, hello darling. I'm speaking from New York. I am thrilled myself. How are you? I'm here for only two or three days. Then I am going to San Francisco. No, I am not going to fly back across the Atlantic. Not a chance! Ah, I told you I'd make it old dear, and not to fear about it …'[39]

In a subsequent radio hook-up with his mother in Sydney, Smithy was equally firm when Catherine began by saying, 'No more ocean flying, I hope.'

'I told you I had to do the last one,' her son retorted, for all the world to hear. 'There are no more oceans left to fly.'[40]

Then Anthony Fokker himself flew them down to Washington in a — can you believe it? — *four*-engined, thirty-two-seat Fokker F.32, where nothing less than an official lunch at the White House awaited. At the height of the proceedings, President Herbert Hoover told them: 'Your feat of flying across the Atlantic is remarkable enough, even though it has been done before, but Kingsford Smith's achievement in becoming the first flyer to completely circumnavigate the world by aeroplane is enough to take one's breath away.'[41]

Thunderous applause all round.

And yet, when Smithy rose to graciously reply, he couldn't help but make a small correction. 'I thank you on behalf of my crew and myself for this wonderful reception, sir. But you are premature in crediting me with complete circumnavigation of the world. I have to fly my "Old Bus" to Oakland, California, before I can claim that distinction … And I wouldn't be here with you now, if I hadn't had the help of Evert van Dijk, Paddy Saul and John Stannage, my New Zealand friend.'[42]

Two days later, Kingsford Smith was back in his suite at New York's Hotel Roosevelt, when he looked up to see a familiar figure framed in the doorway, come to pay a visit. It was Colonel Charles A. Lindbergh himself. Smithy jumped to his feet and eagerly grasped his hand: 'Why, hello, old fellow!'[43] Though the two had never met, there was an instant warmth between them as they exchanged congratulations — on Smithy's coming marriage and the birth of Lindbergh's first child, Charles Jnr — before moving on to the obvious subject of how each man had managed to cross the Atlantic, going in opposite directions. Upon leaving, Lindbergh was gracious enough to repeat to journalists in the foyer that in his view, 'Kingsford Smith's feat of crossing the Pacific remains the greatest of all trans-oceanic flights.'[44]

For Smithy, John Stannage, Evert van Dijk and Paddy Saul, a glorious three weeks in New York as Anthony Fokker's guests followed, and Stannage, for one, was stunned at the Dutchman's generosity, which included taking them out on New York Harbor with a bevy of the most beautiful women he had ever seen.

By early July, though, it was time to move on once more and the *Southern Cross* crew took a relatively leisurely flight across the American continent. Over Illinois, they paid a flying cheerio call on the *City of Chicago* plane which had just passed its 500th hour of continuous flight, courtesy of refuelling in the air.[45] Was it really only two and a half years ago that Smithy had tried to break the German record of fifty-five hours? The world of aviation was changing so rapidly it was dizzying. Two nights in Chicago featured a visit to one of Al Capone's nightclubs, with its free-flowing grog and raw entertainment.

On, then, to Salt Lake City in fifteen hours, flying over Des Moines, Omaha, Cheyenne and the Rocky Mountains, before they approached Oakland airport, where Smithy — actually now *Wing Commander* Kingsford Smith, courtesy of a decision taken by the Australian government to honour his Atlantic achievement — had taken off from some two years earlier.

It was an emotional moment. Smithy later wrote: 'As I sighted once again the hangars of Oakland Municipal Airport, I felt a thrill of satisfaction that I had been able to bring the dear old bus safely around the world. She had now returned to the port whence she had set out across the Pacific. On that occasion her bows had been turned West. Now she came from the East. She had completed the circuit of the Globe around its greatest circumference. She had crossed and re-crossed the Equator, and to me, who had been her pilot in all her long journeys, there came a sense of quiet pride in our achievements. This was our Journey's End.'[46]

And now it was time for the successful team to break up, as Evert van Dijk took a ship back to Holland to resume his flying duties with KLM.

After the hoopla in San Francisco had died down, Smithy, Stannage and Saul made one last, small hop with the *Southern Cross* down to Santa Maria, to thank his key benefactor, Captain Allan Hancock. Again, the fatted calf was killed, again the champagne flowed, and again the hospitality extended to the aviators was overwhelming.

Under the circumstances, Smithy felt honour-bound to offer Hancock his plane back but, as the Australian later recorded of the American, 'with his wonderful tact, he realised that I could ill afford such a sacrifice and insisted that the plane should remain mine'.[47]

In fact, Kingsford Smith could have been released of all financial worries had he accepted an offer to stay on in California and make a series of flights for the state, at a salary equivalent to £10,000 a year. But, given that one condition of the deal was that he became an American citizen, and the fact that he actually loved his life in Australia, he declined.[48] So too to other lucrative offers he received to stay in America. Thank you, but no. He wanted to live a life in Australia, with Mary.[49]

•

What could possibly top piloting the first flight west across the Atlantic? Nothing, of course. But at least Smithy decided that on his way home he may as well go back to London — by ship this time — pick up a new Avro Avian that the company had bought, *Southern Cross Junior*, and set a new *solo* record for getting it back to Australia. Compared to flying over massive oceans, flying across continents was not nearly so challenging, and Smithy felt that he may as well have a go at picking up the record on the way home, while trying the new experience of flying without a co-pilot, radio operator and navigator. Smithy and Stannage sailed to Bremerhaven in the liner *Europa*, while Paddy Saul sailed independently to Ireland after enjoying his rewards on the west coast of the United States.

After arriving in Germany with that in mind — strange to be landing in the country of his former enemies — Smithy nevertheless made time to go on a brief sojourn in Holland as Anthony Fokker's guest, where 'scenes of indescribable enthusiasm' awaited.[50] In the course of his visit the Australian pilot, together with Evert van Dijk and John Stannage, were given a ticker-tape parade, before the munificent Fokker accompanied them on a triumphal trip to Berlin, where they were greeted by an estimated 160,000 Germans.[51]

Finally, though, Smithy felt that he was ready to give it a shake.

Or was he? For some time he had not been quite right physically and after a quick medical examination, he was put straight into a Dutch hospital for surgery to have his appendix and then his tonsils removed (the latter without anaesthetic).

'Dis vill hurt a liddle,' the old be-whiskered Dutch doctor had told him beforehand, and he was not wrong.[52]

And yet while those operations put him back in reasonably good shape physically, it was not just his throat that was troubling Smithy. He was somehow … flat. And nervy at the same time …

Once back in London what little energy he could muster was spent engaged in such a debilitating anxiety that he was struck down for days at a time. He stayed in bed, with the blinds closed, drifting in and out of sleep, remembering dead Germans, fallen friends both in the Great War and since, and feeling such a boiling angst that he was incapable of functioning. Nerve specialists he consulted advised him to give up flying, but in response, Kingsford Smith was dismissive.

'Hell to my nerves,' he said. 'If I were dead I should still fly an aeroplane.'[53]

Another worry was that he felt he had no time to go by ship. He was desperate to get home to marry Mary, in a wedding ceremony that had already been pushed back from September to December, and he had also been advised that his beloved father had been taken ill. It was time to get back to home and hearth. He was an aviator. He would *fly* home, and that was that.

At last, and despite all of the doctors' tut-tutting, Smithy was set to make the attempt by early October 1930. Press interest had particularly grown at this time, as in this perfect flying season there were no fewer than *four* flyers who were intending to make separate attempts to beat the England to Australia record, which turned their departures into a kind of an informal race. By the time Smithy was ready to go, Captain George 'Skip' Matthews was long gone, but had broken down at Rangoon, while a couple of flyers by the names of Pickthorne and Chabot were already across the Persian Gulf, and seemingly going well. Kingsford Smith was not particularly concerned about them, as he was after Bert Hinkler's solo record. No, the fellow who truly interested both Smithy and the press was Australian Flight Lieutenant Cedric Hill, who had got away four days earlier, and was apparently going well.

When Smithy was asked by a journalist how he felt he would go, the aviator was quick with his reply.

'I'll do all right,' he said firmly. 'I'll soon be blowing hot air down Hill's neck. The others don't worry me. Hill's the bloke I have to beat.'[54]

At dawn on 9 October 1930, Smithy took off from Heston aerodrome, to the west of London, in his unique *Southern Cross Junior*, G-ABCF, a modified, one-off, long-range Avro 616 Avian IVA sports-model biplane with a 120-horsepower de Havilland Gipsy II engine capable of generating a cruising speed of 90 miles per hour, at 1900 revolutions per minute. With a capacity of 113 gallons of petrol — including a good-sized tank inside the passenger's cockpit — she could go as far as 1700 miles, which was not bad for such a small plane. Painted blue with silver wings, she had the silver stars of the Southern Cross constellation painted on both sides of the fuselage.

•

Long-distance flying, of course, has good days and bad days. Rarely, however, had Smithy had a better day than that first one out of London. Everything went perfectly from first to last, and late that afternoon he had his highest moment. 'There are few more beautiful scenes for the airman than the blue waters of the Mediterranean. To fly serenely down the Italian coast in the late afternoon is one of those pleasures not experienced by many; but to catch one's first glimpse of Rome, at sunset, from a height of 3,000 feet, is a unique experience. For the moment I forgot the urgent nature of the mission upon which I was engaged … the ever-present underlying thought that I was engaged in a race, for once in a while vanished. I could only marvel at the grandeur and the glory that met my gaze as a thousand facets threw back the rays of the westering sun, and the full majesty of the City of Rome burst upon my sight. There are indeed moments, even in the life of a twentieth century airman, when he forgets his plane, his engine and himself.'[55]

With Rome thus conquered in a day — and a shorter day than usual it was, too, as he was flying east towards the sun — he was off to a wonderful start. And so it continued for most of the rest of the journey.

Crossing Italy's perilous Apennine Ranges the following day at a height of 8000 feet, he continued keeping up a good speed through to glorious Athens — where he still made time to zip away from the airstrip to visit the Acropolis by moonlight[56] — and then to Aleppo in Syria, a place that had had human habitation for 13,000 years! From there, leaving at dawn on 12 October, he kept in sight the grand Euphrates River all the way until he could spy the towering mosques of Baghdad and then turned down the valley of the Tigris, the heartland of the former Babylonian and Assyrian empires … which now had a new king. *Him!*

At least that was the way he felt, soaring over those ancient lands, as both physically and spiritually he continued to feel stronger the longer the journey went on, like a fish that was back in water. At the endlessly sprawling, teeming city of Karachi — which had twice as many people in its city confines as Australia had in a whole continent — he met up with Pickthorne and Chabot, who had crash-landed and were now out of the race. They advised, among other things, that the redoubtable Hill had passed through Karachi just two days before, and was flagging fast.

Onward Christian soldiers.

Leaving an hour before dawn the following day, Kingsford Smith was indeed now breathing down Hill's neck, as he set off for the mosques and minarets of Allahabad. Arriving in the late afternoon, exhausted, he announced to the local press, 'No more long-distance flights for me. There is nothing left for me to do, and besides, I am getting married when I arrive in Australia.'[57]

Winging his way south-east, he was soon over the teeming lands crisscrossed by canals and rice paddies that led to Rangoon. Over Burma, it stunned him to see peasants wading knee-deep behind ploughs drawn by buffalo, just as they had done for centuries, though he was probably not as stunned as they were to see him, essentially a soaring visitor from the future. When he landed on Rangoon racecourse, he was promptly told that Hill was now less than *one day* ahead of him, having left Rangoon the previous midnight.[58]

The next day's long flying took him to Singapore without serious incident, and the day after that, his ninth day in the air, he was in Sourabaya in East Java. Every report he received of Hill was that the Australian was exhausted beyond measure, but, conversely, Smithy continued to feel stronger than ever, as he fair *ate up* the route: 'I swept over the dense jungle of the east coast of Sumatra; down past the sunlit sea immortalised by Conrad; over rivers and waterfalls, past villages, islands, and so on, over the ocean again to the Java coast ...'[59]

Had to catch Hill. *Had* to catch Hill. Of course Smithy knew he was going to beat Hill's time, as he had closed the gap on him by nearly four days already, but it had become a point of honour to beat him outright.

Finally, when Smithy landed at Atamboea, in Timor, just as the sun was setting on that gorgeous green island, it was to see a lone and rather forlorn figure waiting for him at the end of the airfield. Dr Livingstone, he presumed? It was Smithy's quarry of the last week, a very sunburned Flight Lieutenant Cedric Hill, who just that morning had crashed into a fence while attempting to take off for Darwin, and smashed his plane beyond any hope of repair. A string bean of a man, given to easy laughter, Hill offered Smithy both a rueful smile and congratulatory handshake.

The two passed a pleasant evening together in Atamboea's lone guesthouse, comparing notes over several ales, and at dawn the following morning Hill was there to see Smithy go. A mark of the instant camaraderie between the airmen was that the Queenslander, upon hearing that Smithy did not have a small collapsible rubber boat as a backup should the *Southern Cross Junior* come down while crossing the 450-mile stretch of the Timor Sea that awaited, insisted that he take his own. Which Smithy did, with great appreciation.

He flew off and, a little over eight hours later, after crossing the bulk of the extraordinarily calm, glassy Timor Sea, the magic moment came. Sighting the Australian shoreline, Smithy let out a spontaneous yell of joy that was just as soon swallowed by the shriek of the engine,[60] and then said quietly to himself: 'Good old Aussie.'[61]

Sweeping in from the Clarence Strait and over the sunbaked roofs of Darwin a short time later, he landed to an extravagant welcome similar to the one accorded Ross and Keith Smith when they landed at the same spot a decade earlier. Back then, the Smith brothers had taken twenty-seven days to complete the journey, while Hinkler had taken just under sixteen days. And now, Charles Kingsford Smith, landing at 1.50 pm on 19 October 1930, had done the 10,070 miles in a total of nine days, twenty-one hours and forty minutes, lopping roughly one-third from the Hinkler record that had so amazed the aviation world only two years previously.[62] Hurrah! As it happened, the first telegram he opened on arrival was from Hinkler himself, congratulating him on his feat.[63] Another cable shortly afterwards offered the congratulations of His Majesty King George V himself, and there was even talk that he might receive a knighthood in the not too distant future — an extraordinary honour for one who had been divorced! As to the Australian government, it was not long in announcing that Smithy had been promoted to air commodore in the Royal Australian Air Force.

A triumphal tour across the continent and down the east coast of Australia followed, as Smithy graciously accepted all the laurels heaped upon him. In the words of Horace Brinsmead, Smithy was now 'as pre-eminent, when compared with any other international pilot, as Bradman is, when compared with any other international cricketer'.[64]

It had been one thing to have been greeted as an all-conquering hero in London, Amsterdam and Berlin, but very satisfying to now receive a similar demonstration in his own country. True, he could have done without the endless receptions in every town he visited, where usually the mayor or other high dignitaries made endless speeches welcoming the '*Honorary Hair* Commodore',[65] but it was touching for all that.

The Coffee Royal affair now seemed all but forgotten, and he was a bigger hero than he had ever been. In a radio interview conducted in the studios of 4QG Brisbane — relayed to other stations around the country — he announced that as much as he had loved it, his days of long-distance flying were over.

'The only long distance of flying I am thinking of at the moment,' he said, 'is a matrimonial one, which is a kind of dual control affair.'[66]

A triple hurrah for Smithy!

The following day, at Mascot aerodrome, there were the now almost familiar scenes of wild jubilation — which went up three notches as the famous aviator was given a kiss and a hug on the podium from his gorgeous fiancée, Mary, whom he had not seen for seven months — punctuated by the main speeches of official welcome. Representing the Federal government, the Assistant Minister for Industry, Mr Jack Beasley, noted that every Australian was extremely proud of Air Commodore Kingsford Smith's achievement, and it was a pleasure to welcome him back to his native country.

'I feel,' the Assistant Minister added, 'that he can be rightly acclaimed today as "King of the Air". It is exploits of this character that build nations, and Australia owes more than it can ever pay to Kingsford Smith.'[67]

Strong applause greeted these words from all and sundry, including Smithy's family, who had turned out in force. And yet, as a group, they were all far less joyous than usual.

It was about Dad, his brother Leofric told him quietly a short time later. He was ailing, and going downhill fast, so ill with bowel cancer that he had not been able to make it to Mascot to greet his youngest son, something that nearly killed him in itself. So, after Smithy and Mary had been driven through the streets of Sydney in a kind of ticker-tape parade without the ticker-tape, he was not long in making his way home to Kuranda, to see his father and effectively begin to say his goodbyes. Within a few days, William's condition had deteriorated to the point that he was admitted to nearby Longueville Hospital, where he could receive professional care around the clock.

•

One thing the 78-year-old patriarch of the family was able to express over the last few days of his life was that when he died, he wanted his ashes to be scattered upon the Pacific Ocean.[68]

Just nine days after Smithy had arrived in Sydney, on the morning of Sunday, 2 November 1930, with his sons Chilla, Leofric and Eric by his side, William Kingsford Smith died. Grief-stricken, Smithy was able to honour his father's wishes by taking up the *Southern Moon* a few days later with a very special cargo. Once well out and high over the Pacific Ocean, Smithy shut off the engines to let her glide gracefully downwards, and allowed Charles Ulm to take the controls while he moved back into the main cabin where his brothers, sisters, niece and nephew awaited him. There as well were two clergymen, Bishop Wilton and Reverend G. Morris Fielding, who conducted a quick final service for William Kingsford, before Smithy leaned out the cabin window and scattered his father's ashes from a silver urn, followed by a bunch of rosemary and three roses, his father's favourite flower.[69]

Of the many regrets the youngest Kingsford Smith offspring had about William's death, one of the biggest was that his father would not be present for his wedding to Mary, the following month in Melbourne, which proved to be a grand occasion.

•

On the sparkling afternoon of Wednesday, 10 December 1930, the gorgeous Mary Powell in a flowing white wedding dress, escorted by her proud father Arthur and attended by four bridesmaids, including Beris Kingsford Smith, walked down the aisle of Melbourne's grand Scots Church in Russell Street. Waiting there, beaming back, and decked out in full ceremonial dress was Air Commodore Charles Kingsford Smith, with Wing Commander Charles Ulm beside him as his best man, and other RAAF officers beside him. It was a 'fairytale wedding' indeed, between the stunning twenty-year-old from one of the richest families in Melbourne and the 'World's Greatest Airman', as he was frequently described. The bride, as recorded by the *Sydney Morning Herald*, 'wore a frock of ivory georgette, interwoven with gleaming velvet thread in a closely set lace pattern. A pink foundation gave a delicate glow to the graceful draperies which fell from the waist-line at the back with a long train. Her full veil of pale pink tulle enveloped her like a sunset cloud.'[70]

On the streets around the church no fewer than 10,000 people were standing tightly together or had climbed nearby trees in the hope of catching a glimpse of the happy couple. Upon the couple's exit from the church these spectators were so enthusiastic that the wooden barriers which had been set up to keep them back toppled and it was only with the help of the police that the newlyweds were able to get away.

A blissful honeymoon in Tasmania ensued, which Mary would remember ever after as one of the rare times she could have her husband all to herself. And in many ways, she was still getting to know him, as in their whirlwind romance to date, extending just over a year — during which he had been overseas for seven months in total, and living in Sydney for the rest, while she had remained in Melbourne — the actual time they had spent together was limited. 'He was a very physical but gentle and endlessly patient person,' she later told Kingsford Smith's biographer Ian Mackersey. 'He taught me to smoke, to drink and introduced me to highly risqué stories. "A dirty mind is a perpetual solace," he would often say. And he loved to announce outrageously: "My greatest ambition is to be hanged for rape when I'm ninety-two!" He had this deep need to be surrounded by people. He hardly ever read and had very few books.'[71]

Among other things, Mary was amused by Smithy's capacity to stand on his head while drinking a beer.

As it happened, Kingsford Smith was back in Tasmania just a few weeks later in the company of ANA pilot James Mollison, as the two took the *Southern Cloud* on their company's inaugural trip to Launceston. A couple of happy days of being bathed in glory by the good burghers of that town ensued, but on the night before leaving Smithy decided it was time to take Jimmy in hand.

'Jim,' he said firmly, 'we must impress the Tasmanians with our steadiness and sobriety. In the company's interest we'll spend a quiet evening and be early in bed, say about eleven o'clock.'

Aye-aye, Cap'n sir. No matter that Jimmy was himself a big drinker who characterised himself as the 'flying playboy',[72] by his own account he duly went to bed in the room he was sharing with Smithy, mildly surprised that his skipper wasn't there, only to be awoken in the wee hours by a very noisy '*Shhhh* ...'

'Staggering slightly and wild of eye,' Mollison later recounted, 'Smithy tip-toed towards the twin beds, noiseless as a battery of horse-artillery at the canter, finger to his lips. A slightly rumpled blonde behind him made shaky efforts to bolt the door on the inside. Between them they made clatter enough to bring the ceiling down. We all drank and made merry together until the smallest hours.'[73]

Meanwhile, Smithy had arranged for the *Southern Cross* to be shipped to Sydney from San Francisco on the steamer *Golden Bear.* As it left, the San Francisco *Examiner* editorialised: 'It will take 26 days to cover what those roaring Whirlwind motors accomplished in 88 hours. There will be no gallant conquest of the darkness now; no tempestuous storm to encounter, no lashing gales and no cheering throngs — just a crowded place in the hold of a crawling tramp steamer. The dauntless path-finder that kings and presidents acclaimed — now a lonely old crate — follows its master home.'[74]

•

All up, 1930 for Charles Kingsford Smith had been an amazing year, one in which he had married the woman of his dreams and dominated headlines around the world for his derring-do and pioneering spirit. Australian National Airways could be confident that in Smithy they had one of the most famous and accomplished aviators as their public face — with only Charles Lindbergh able to argue the toss. Most importantly, the name 'Kingsford Smith' and travel to and from England by air were practically synonymous, meaning that ANA was now extremely well positioned should there be a breakthrough in opening a commercial England to Australia run.

And yet, while there was no pilot flying for Qantas who had achieved remotely as much, that company could also take some quiet satisfaction in how it had been able to consolidate its early growth, and how well the move to Brisbane had gone. At the end of the financial year, Qantas was able to pay its third dividend to its shareholders, distributing the £5770 profit it had made for the year, which was 14.6 per cent of its capital.

•

When it came to money, somehow Smithy never seemed to have enough, and for a marital home all he and Mary could afford was a relatively modest apartment in Sydney's Bellevue Hill that his mother Catherine had scouted out for them while they had been on their honeymoon.[75] Something that perturbed him was being endlessly pursued by the British Air Ministry for £96 10s expenses, incurred in sending cables to the countries where he had landed during his latest record-breaking flight. In an aggrieved letter to the secretary of that air ministry the famed pilot made his position clear:

> As a British subject, it seems most peculiar that I have had nothing but the most helpful attitude from Foreign countries towards my flights, whereas in my dealings with Great Britain a reply to the slightest request is always accompanied by an account for payment.

After all, I am a loyal British subject, and my flights have, I claim, done a little to increase the prestige of the Empire in the air.

Yours very truly,

C.E. Kingsford Smith.[76]

•

At last, the international breakthrough. After long correspondence between Australia and Great Britain's civil aviation authorities, and their respective General Post Offices, it had been decided in the early months of 1931 that two test round-trip airmail services would take place between London and Sydney, with two lots of post leaving London, on 4 April and 25 April. Imperial Airways would expand their London to Delhi services for the occasion and get the mail all the way to Darwin, where it would be sent on to Sydney via … Qantas.[77]

Bugger! How on earth could that be?! What had Qantas ever done to open international routes? Where, now, were the government's statements that Australia owed Smithy *more than it could ever repay*? Was there to be nothing for those who had blazed the path of Australia's international air-routes more than any other flyers in the country? Just a month earlier the Australian Post Office had deeply honoured Kingsford Smith by releasing a range of postage stamps bearing his image — to celebrate his achievement in circumnavigating the globe — and yet he was now adjudged as not good enough to even *carry* the mail on which his image was frequently plastered.

It took some time to get over missing out on such a plum, but there was little ANA could do. For the moment the airline decided to focus on building up its domestic routes between the major eastern cities, which a few months previously had expanded to Launceston. All the company could do was keep going and hope that it would continue to prosper without mishap. Something the board thought would help with the matter of safety would be to erect a series of ground radio stations along its principal routes, so company management could always be in touch with its planes, but the Federal authorities had refused permission on the basis that it intended to build its own stations, which facilities would be available to all airlines.[78]

•

Saturday, 21 March 1931 dawned in Sydney cold, blustery and wet. Although it was not yet winter, it was the kind of morning where the instinctive human reaction was to stay in bed and snuggle up.

Alas, that morning, as on most mornings, ANA's engine foreman, Dan Macfarlane, had a job to do, which was to get the Avros shipshape and away on their regular runs, come rain, hail or shine. But still, even on *this* morning? He wasn't sure, as he pulled up outside ANA's hangars at Mascot and wind gusts fiercely shook his old Vauxhall. What a bloody day!

Macfarlane's unease grew as the time came to get the *Southern Cloud* away to Melbourne. If the plane was going into a sustained 40-mile per hour headwind, strong enough to blow the chicken out of a chicken sandwich, its ground speed would be cut to 50 miles per hour, making it a nine-hour trip to the Victorian capital. And yet the planes only carried eight hours of fuel in their tanks! Of course, it probably wouldn't be a headwind that strong all the way, but still … Dan personally ensured that all four fuel tanks were topped up right to the brim.

He signed the maintenance release and gave it to the ex-British Army officer and now ANA pilot 'Shorty' Shortridge for countersignature, whereupon Shorty asked, sort of disinterestedly, in his British burr, 'What's the weather report?'

'Nothing in this morning, but last report was a low, east of the mountains, and strong south to south-west winds.'

Shorty grunted in the manner of a man who had seen a few storms in his time — three months earlier he had published a guide to 'Blind and Bad Weather Flying'[79] — and had never been too impressed by them.

'Sounds like bloody blind flying and bumps. Tanks full?'

'Topped them up myself,' Dan replied.

'How many passengers?'

'Only six, so you don't have much of a load.'

'Good job. Might be able to get above some of the dirt anyhow. May have to land at Benalla for fuel if it stays too bad.'[80]

And with that, Shorty climbed into the cockpit of the *Southern Cloud*, where young Charles Dunnell was already in the co-pilot's seat, and only a few minutes later they were taxiing to the northern end of the airstrip. In the cabin the six passengers were themselves a little nervous, as the plane rocked in the buffeting wind. Of them all — theatre producer Clyde Hood, electrical engineer Julian Margules, businessman Hubert Farrall, accountant Bill O'Reilly and holiday-makers Elsie Glasgow and Claire Stokes[81] — one had the most reason to be nervous. Young Claire had never flown before, and this hardly looked like the day to start. And yet, once they were rolling, one didn't really want to make a scene and demand to be let off the plane. She was, after all, in the hands of professionals.

It was just after 8.10 am when Dan Macfarlane watched the plane take off — slower than usual, it seemed to him, struggling against the headwind — still feeling most uneasy. His unease grew when, only an hour after they left, a phone call came in from the weather bureau, with nothing less than a cyclone warning, saying that something close to the worst weather in thirty years was hitting the area south of the new Federal capital of Canberra.

Though there were no means of contacting the *Southern Cloud* to relay this warning, there was no great alarm in the ANA offices. Shorty, with 4000 hours' flying time logged to his credit, would surely find either a way through or around it. Short of Kingsford Smith himself, the plane could barely have been in safer hands.

And later that afternoon, when Charles Ulm took a phone call at the company's offices from ANA's Melbourne manager, to inform him that the plane had not arrived at Melbourne, there was still no panic. All that meant was that Shorty hadn't found a way through, and had no doubt headed west to the vast farming flat-lands around the Riverina that were an aircraft's friend.

At Ulm's behest, Dan Macfarlane sat down and began calling small towns and villages along the *Southern Cloud*'s designated route, asking the operator whether he or she had heard the plane go over, and then collating the results. By 10 pm, he had the answer: the *Southern Cloud* had been sighted everywhere and nowhere. There was no rhyme or reason in the reports, as some claimed to have heard it while others just one town away said they hadn't and then it showed up again two towns on and then again it was clear that for all the reports to be correct, the *Southern Cloud* would have had to have been in several places at once.

Smithy, informed at home by Ulm that evening of the situation, felt sure that in the morning they would receive a phone call from Shorty, saying he had been forced down by lack of petrol, and could someone come and get him, please? And then, hopefully, they would all have a good laugh and say that that had been a close one — as had happened to Smithy personally, *dozens* of times. They were some of his best stories, in fact.

The families of the passengers and pilots were kept informed, and told not to worry too much. The following morning, however, at the ANA offices with Kingsford Smith and Ulm both present, the hours began to crawl by like sick slugs — 9 am, and no word; 10 am, nothing; 11 am, and though phones were ringing hard, none of them bore good news. *Noon*, and there was still not the smallest clue as to what had happened to the *Southern Cloud*. When dusk had fallen, it was time to pull out all the stops.

'All hands', was the call, and all hands answered, with every one of ANA's employees reporting for work at Mascot and putting enormous efforts in to getting the planes ready to go, fully prepared, as part of a coordinated push to find the lost plane. Everyone's unspoken fear was that the *Southern Cloud* had hit the side of a mountain, and all crew and passengers were either dead or dying. In the case of the latter, urgency was paramount. For once, within the confines of ANA, there was no joking or skylarking, as everyone set to work. In the office canteen, Mrs MacDonald — red-haired, Scottish and motherly — organised the half-dozen office girls as helpers and got to feeding the increasingly hungry twenty men.[82]

Kingsford Smith spent a sleepless night organising a team of observers to accompany him in the *Southern Sun* to leave before dawn the following morning to begin the search in the rugged area that lay south of Albury.[83]

Other planes also joined in the search and the area north of Melbourne was in particular thoroughly scoured. Throughout, Kingsford Smith remained at the forefront of the search, day after day. Searching systematically, with all his team of eight observers on board armed with binoculars, he first scoured the Snowy Mountains, looking closely around Mount Kosciuszko, before working his way south to Cooma and down to Melbourne. Most nights, he would be landing at Essendon airport just on dusk, where weeping family members of the missing passengers and crew would be waiting for him, hoping for good news. But he never had any.

By this time a formal search committee had been formed in Melbourne to coordinate the massive effort, involving no fewer than thirty planes, of which six were provided by the RAAF. And, of course, the whole tragedy was closely followed by the press. In fact, beyond being a tragedy, it was also a great *mystery*. How could such a massive plane just have disappeared like that?

Australia's pubs and dinner tables ran wild with theories — *don't forget the Coffee Royal affair, and how the plane turned up again after a fortnight, well that'll happen again this time, you mark my words* — even as ground parties were sent into some of the most heavily wooded areas, where it was feared that a crashed plane could not be spotted from the air. Alas, all returned with nothing to report bar their own exhaustion. It was as if the *Southern Cloud* had simply been swallowed whole by the wild Australian landscape.

Complicating matters were the many reports that came in from the public, with tips ranging from Bathurst to Bega, to hearing a low-flying plane in the Dandenongs, to spotting a fast-descending plane over Port Phillip Bay.[84] People in the tiny village of Tintaldra in the foothills of the Snowy Mountains were convinced they saw lights flashing in the night from those mountains as if someone was trying to signal them, so they sent out land expeditions to look for them.[85] Even so august a journal as the *Sydney Morning Herald* reported as fact, under a headline of 'FLASHES IN THE HILLS', that residents of Tintaldra had seen a fire in the hills on the afternoon of the disappearance and up to ten o'clock that night, and had seen flashes every fifteen minutes on the Toolong Range.[86] Smithy himself had flown from Melbourne to investigate that one, passing low over the spot where the flashes had been reported.[87] As much as possible, each tip-off had to be investigated, but as the days turned into a week, and then two weeks, hope inevitably faded.

So thorough had been the search that Kingsford Smith became convinced that the *Southern Cloud* must have passed over Melbourne and crashed in the sea. Charles Ulm couldn't help but agree. After spending two days investigating reported smoke and fire signals in the Snowy River district, he returned to tell the *Sydney Morning Herald* that, 'it is a million to one chance of the aeroplane being anywhere else but in the water'.[88] Part of their conviction came from the fact that the great Australian war hero and RAAF Squadron Leader Arthur Cobby reported that he had been in the Melbourne suburb of Elsternwick on the day, at the height of the storm at 2.15 pm, when he had heard a three-engined plane pass over, in a south-eastern direction, heading towards the bay. It was unlikely that a man of his experience could be mistaken.[89]

The truth, of course, was that even if the crew and passengers were on land and had survived the crash, they would have been unlikely to survive in the wilderness for a fortnight, notwithstanding the crew of the *Southern Cross*'s experience at Coffee Royal.

On his own final day of searching, Smithy spent eight hours in the air, traipsing back and forth between Sydney and Canberra. Haunted by the memory of the *Southern Cross* being missed by its own search planes, he did not want to give up, but in the end, he had to. There was simply no further point in continuing and with the ANA now having taken a possibly mortal blow to its reputation, as well as a £10,000 loss from the uninsured crashed plane and subsequent costs of searching, everything had to be done to save the company.

In the end, though, they were wading against a tide that could not be stemmed. In the middle of the Depression, money to fly was already in short supply, and after the loss of the *Southern Cloud*, no-one wanted to fly with ANA. After all, what was wrong with the old way of getting to Melbourne — the overnight train, with a wake-up at dawn at Albury, to change trains and go from there? It was much cheaper than flying, there was almost no chance of the train crashing, and even if it did, they'd at least know where to find you to bring help. A *plane* to Melbourne? No thank you.

•

At least the record-breaking flights went on. Only a few days after the search had been abandoned, an English pilot by the name of Charles William Anderson Scott, oft known as C.W.A. Scott, landed his de Havilland DH.60M Metal Moth, *Kathleen*, at Mascot after breaking Smithy's England to Australia record a few days before, when he had arrived in Darwin, just nine days and five hours after leaving England, on 10 April 1931. Scott had been a burly heavyweight champion of the RAF[90] before becoming a door-to-door mousetrap salesman in Melbourne[91] and then a flying instructor for Qantas at their Brisbane Flying School, and this was his first real taste of fame.

Smithy was on the tarmac at Mascot to greet the Englishman, distracted as he was, as the cameras rolled.

Sixteen

TO AND FRO …

Yes, I am scared out of my seven senses sometimes,
but I don't let on.

CHARLES KINGSFORD SMITH, TO HIS MOTHER, CATHERINE, WHEN SHE ASKED HIM IF HE WAS NOT NERVOUS WHEN HE MADE THOSE LONG AND DANGEROUS FLIGHTS.[1]

Another crash. This time it wasn't an Australian National Airways plane, but an Imperial Airways one, the first of the test airmail flights between England and Australia.

Heavily loaded with 15,000 letters from England, the *City of Cairo* had been approaching Koepang in Timor on 19 April 1931, when it had run out of fuel and crash-landed 10 miles short of the airfield into a rice paddy. It now became a matter of urgency to get another plane there as soon as possible, to ensure that the mail went through. But whose? One from Qantas, which had a plane waiting in Darwin for the post to arrive? Not on your nelly.

In all its expanding fleet, Qantas did not yet have a multi-engined aircraft, considered *de rigueur* for flying over water. The only company that had that kind of aircraft *and* a pilot experienced in flying long distances over water was ANA with — that man again — Smithy!

It was for this reason that on 21 April, Charles Kingsford Smith, on just twenty-four-hours' notice — and at the personal request of Prime Minister James Scullin — was given a welcome respite from the ongoing agony of the disappearance of the *Southern Cloud*, and was, with fellow ANA pilot Scotty Allan and two others, flying towards Koepang with all the speed that the now rather ageing engines of the *Southern Cross* could muster.

'It is a great opportunity,' Smithy had told the press before departure, 'for Australian aviation to show its merits. I earnestly hope that in the near future the airmail authorities will allow Australian aviators to work on the Australian end of the route.'[2]

Once in Koepang, the mail was transferred to the *Southern Cross*, and yet Smithy was no sooner back in Darwin than he had to go again — this time taking 25,000 letters weighing 700 pounds from the Qantas DH.61 *Apollo*, which had brought them from Brisbane in new white canvas bags with bold red stripes, and flying them on to Akyab, in Burma. There, he was able to hand them on to the Imperial Airways plane doing the second of the England to Australia airmail flights, to take back to London, and in turn take that plane's post back to Darwin. All up, it was a confusing blur of comings and goings, take-offs and landings, but the bottom line was that the first test run of England to Australia airmail had taken twenty-four days.

And though originally Kingsford Smith's ANA was meant to have had no part in either of the first two historic test airmail flights, it had soon been proved that the firm was indispensable in making it happen — a wonderful advertisement. Smithy later wrote, 'This experience, at very short notice, of carrying a long-distance mail, convinced me of the practicability of establishing a regular route without further delay, provided that the government assistance — for a limited period only — was available.'[3]

Ulm was equally convinced and while Smithy had been flying, he had been making another approach to the government, to secure a certain contract to carry post on the Australian end of the England to Australia journey. In tough times, such a contract would be a guarantee of survival, and the times had never been tougher since the *Southern Cloud* had been lost. They *had* to get that contract or Ulm feared all would be lost.

•

Hudson Fysh felt equally strongly that Qantas would also take an enormous hit if they didn't get the contract, and sent a telegram to McMaster to that effect:

```
Application made by A.N.A. to operate
permanent route Brisbane-Darwin and to
India. Receiving considerable support.
Position fairly critical to our interest.[4]
```

In short, if Fysh hadn't taken ANA seriously before, he certainly was now, because if the Kingsford Smith crowd won the contract for the route to India, they would be a very serious force indeed. Other contenders for the prize were West Australian Airways, and Imperial Airways flying the whole route alone.

What to do? It was something that McMaster mulled over for some time before coming up with a possible solution. In mid May, he wrote to Fysh suggesting that Qantas form a subsidiary company with Imperial Airways, which could be called Qantas Empire Airways. And he also asked Fysh to push 'the matter of triple-engined machines as much as possible, and to get in touch with Westland Aircraft and Blackburn, as well as the American people'.[5] While Australians felt that it was a matter of national honour to 'buy British', McMaster was not of their number. He just wanted the best planes at the best price.

•

She was a charming, gracious lady, beloved by the people of Australia for her performances on stage and screen over the previous half-century, but by the winter of 1931 her body had had enough. On Monday, 21 June 1931, following a three-day downhill spiral from pleurisy and heart trouble, 72-year-old Nellie Stewart died in her Clifton Gardens home by Sydney Harbour.[6] Typical of this happy soul, she begged that no black be worn at her funeral — a request that was respected by the thousands of people who turned up to farewell her from St James's Anglican Church in Sydney — and as the hearse bearing her coffin moved away on its journey to Rookwood cemetery, many people threw rose petals upon it. Ah, she was loved, not least by Smithy.

There had always been something about her serene, warm beauty and manner that touched his soul and he was devastated at her death. And although some people said it was bad luck to continue to bear her photo in his plane as a good-luck charm,

Smithy didn't agree and insisted on taking it with him. Her photo had got him through Gallipoli, the Western Front, across the Pacific and the Tasman, through countless other adventures in the air and he wasn't going to give it up now.[7]

•

Finally, there was no way out. In the middle of the Depression, with enormous public concern about ANA's safety standards in the wake of the loss of the *Southern Cloud*, the airline simply did not have the custom to keep the planes going — sometimes scheduled flights were leaving *empty* — and on Friday, 26 June 1931, it shut down regular services between Brisbane, Sydney, Melbourne and Launceston, with all the planes returning to Sydney on the Saturday. This did not mean the end of the company, as there was still a chance they would be able to keep it going through charter work and joyriding until such time as it could hopefully secure the contract from the Federal government to carry the post on the international route to link up with Imperial Airways, but in such straitened economic times it was always going to be a close-run thing.

Clearly, the best asset the company had, apart from the planes themselves, was the love the Australian public had for Smithy. And if Smithy was who they wanted, then Smithy was who they would get. This meant that for the next couple of months, he was kept busy going everywhere from Albury, through Corowa, Jerilderie, Wagga, Coolamon, Leeton, Griffith, West Wyalong, Parkes, Forbes, Newcastle and Goulburn. And back again.

•

Everywhere in Australia the times were tough and getting tougher. The economic malaise that had started at the New York Stock Exchange in late October 1929 had spread throughout most of the world, and Australia was hit particularly hard. Unemployment queues continued to grow, as did the numbers of homeless people living in places such as Sydney's Domain, where hundreds of unfortunate people slept outside every night under whatever newspapers they could gather around themselves to try to keep warm. A shantytown grew like topsy in the sand hills at La Perouse, consisting of huts constructed out of whatever spare timber could be found, upon which were tacked old sugar bags and galvanised iron. Any job vacancy advertised would draw hundreds of applications, with fights frequently breaking out to see who could get in the door first. Hit particularly hard were returned soldiers, most of whom were in their mid-thirties, and often unskilled and uneducated, as their careers had taken a five-year pause while they had been serving in places like Gallipoli and the Western Front. Was *this* what they had been fighting for? A world where they didn't have enough money to even feed their kids?

All up, there was enough anger around and enough madness in the air that a strange, paramilitary fascism movement called the New Guard began in New South Wales, with a membership base composed largely of disaffected soldiers and a leadership that was made up of solid returned servicemen. Though difficult to define, the New Guard was broadly composed of extreme loyalists to the Crown who regarded themselves as an auxiliary to the police to prevent there being any possibility of a Bolshevik revolution taking place in Australia — and they cared nought that the police did not want their support.

A particular target of the New Guard was the duly elected New South Wales government of the day, led by Jack Lang, who had returned to power and staked out a remarkable position. That was, that if the government was caught in a choice between paying for such things as food rations for the people of New South Wales and making due interest payments to the British bond-holders from whom it had borrowed money to build such things as the nearly completed Sydney Harbour Bridge, it would be the citizens who came first. Lang would 'repudiate' the debt to Great Britain. Cry treason!

The New Guard's first major rally was held in the Sydney Town Hall on 24 July 1931, where they sang loyalist songs and cheered their leader Eric Campbell — none other than Charles Kingsford Smith and Charles Ulm's long-time solicitor. Whether Smithy attended that meeting or subsequent New Guard meetings is not definitively documented, though Campbell would later describe them both as 'sound New Guard members', as was, by Campbell's account, Sir Frederick Stewart, one of the leading directors with ANA.[8] What is certain is that both the State and Federal governments of the day took the view that they were involved, after police surveillance spotted Kingsford Smith's car outside New Guard meetings. It was *not* something calculated to find favour for him or ANA in high circles of power.

•

Whatever Smithy's involvement with the New Guard, it was certainly tangential, as he had to keep barnstorming to pay the bills. While it wasn't a great existence, at least he was still in the air, still flying. Clearly, it was important to keep his name before the public, to maximise the company's chances of being awarded the contract. And, as ever, the best way to keep his name out there was to break not one but two records in one fell swoop.

It was with this imperative in mind that he set his sights on Jimmy Mollison's Australia to England record of eight days, twenty-one hours, in itself over half a day better than the former Qantas pilot C.W.A. Scott's record. Then he would turn around and sprint back home, to flags waving, in less than nine days — or, even better, eight days. He felt he had just the plane to do it in, the *Southern Cross Minor*, another Avro 616 Avian biplane that he had just purchased with the help of his rich father-in-law, but this time it was the MK.V fitted with long-range fuel tanks.

To get to his starting point of Wyndham, Smithy — after bidding a tearful Mary goodbye — flew first to Alice Springs, where he was obliged to get some running repairs done, just as Keith Anderson and Bobby Hitchcock had done two years earlier when one of the tappets had come loose, causing the engine to vibrate. Smithy's problem was that the vibration had caused an oil-gauge pipe to fracture, though he wasn't particularly concerned. In fact, so little concerned was he with this problem that the next day, when he was following the Overland Telegraph Line north, just as Keith Anderson had done, he decided to take a short cut inland over the Tanami Desert, just as Keith had done …[9]

With Keith, of course, the decision had resulted in his and Bobby Hitchcock's tragic deaths. In Smithy's case, however, he was able to fly on through to Wyndham, no worries.

Such was the luck of the draw for intrepid aviators ...

•

After leaving Wyndham in the *Southern Cross Minor*, at two o'clock on the morning of 24 September 1931, Smithy landed in Cheribon, in Java, just sixteen hours and fifteen minutes later, and left the following morning at dawn, bound for Victoria Point, which was 1390 miles distant on the southernmost coast of Burma. Alas, after circling the RAF aerodrome at Seletar in Singapore, only a short time later he found himself in a monsoonal rainstorm and became disoriented. Effectively flying blind, he had no idea where he was, or whether he could stay aloft long enough to make it to Burma, even if he could navigate his way there in the storm. The only way forward was to fly within 30 feet of the ground and keep the coast in sight. The monsoonal rain kept battering his slender craft, almost as if it was in a conspiracy with the wretched wind to force him to crash. *In extremis* it became obvious that his one hope of salvation was to land on a beach and wait the storm out.

•

Just as the sun was setting that day, a group of villagers on the deep southern coast of Burma were taking shelter from the terrible storm when they heard a sound they had not heard before, at least not up close. It was that of a motor, getting nearer and nearer, until it was screaming loud enough to wake the spirits of the dead and ... then it stopped.

The braver of them ventured out, moving stealthily through the jungle until they could see the beach. And there was an amazing-looking thing, like some kind of giant bird, with its wings stretched out, sitting on the beach! The two bravest of the men ventured forward and peered into the interior of this strange thing, only to find that it had swallowed a white man who was peering back at them!

Two Burmese men, possibly hostile, stared at Smithy from just outside the cockpit, while the raging storm pounded the plane with no sign of cessation. In front, the dark jungle. Behind him: the raging sea, with an incoming tide. And no-one knew where he was.

Just another day in his life …

At last the two men went away, which eased the situation somewhat. The most urgent thing to do was to secure his plane and ensure that the wheels did not sink into the sand. To do that he would have to gather light wood from the jungle and get it beneath the wheels to spread the weight. Cautiously, he ventured into the jungle to retrieve a couple of saplings, when, from perhaps 100 yards away but it felt like 10 yards at the time, he heard the unmistakable roar of a tiger.[10] Now, although Smithy had not necessarily been the fastest sprinter in his school days at St Andrew's, on this occasion he broke all records as he crashed through the brushwood to get back to the plane and bolt the door shut, before lying there trembling for some time — and bugger the tide![11] The water was lapping at the wheels before he tentatively re-emerged — positive that the tiger must be right on the edge of the jungle and about to charge — to at last secure the plane. In record time.

A dreadful night followed where every sound from the jungle was clearly the hungry tiger coming for him, getting angrier and hungrier by the minute. Could it be that Mary was right, and his proper place in the world when the sun went down was at home with her and not dashing around all over the world?

By dawn the following morning the storm had passed and he was able to take off again and fly for an hour to Victoria Point on his scant fuel reserves. Having refuelled he flew on to the Burmese capital of Rangoon, now behind Mollison's time. Yet that was not all. He began to suffer dizzy spells that stayed with him, following the thirty-eight hours and fifty-five minutes he had spent in the air over the previous three days. After a quick bit of shut-eye, he was on his way again at three o'clock in the morning, but if anything he now felt worse. What was wrong with him?

While well out over the Bay of Bengal his condition suddenly deteriorated. What had started as a headache and a kind of fuzzy feeling — like he was not all there — descended from that point with no relief. As he flew on, the headache worsened, feeling almost as though someone was taking a drill to his head and he began to feel ... faint ... becoming *dimly aware that he had been hit in the left foot and that a fog of blackness was filling his cockpit ... no ... maybe just his head. Must ... turn ... and get back to ... have another ... go ... at the bastard ... who had got him.*

No! Coming back to himself from a state where he didn't know who he was or what he was doing, he found that he had put the plane into a frantic spin and now he was just a few hundred feet above the water and heading down fast. Getting the plane back under control, he vomited twice in quick succession — not an easy thing in an open cockpit with the wind rushing by — as dizziness continued to engulf him, 'like a warm, soft cloud'. He had the sensation that not only was he about to die, but, curiously, that he didn't particularly care: 'And you know, it didn't bother me much, either'.[12] Fortunately, the worst of it passed and he was able to recover enough to fly on, and even note in his log:

> Feel awful! Just suffered a fit of vomiting. It must be sunstroke, should have worn a suitable hat ... no protection in this helmet.

And then:

> All that vast wilderness below. I feel very lonely.

•

And he was not the only one. In Sydney, waiting for news, Mary often felt very lonely. It had been no easy thing to adjust from her relatively gay, carefree life in Melbourne, surrounded by her family, young friends and things familiar to her, to forge a new life as the wife of a frequently absent national icon, but she had coped. Her most earnest hope was that her husband would get the pioneering, record-breaking bug out of his system, that he would accomplish what he wanted to accomplish and then settle down, as he *promised* that he would. In the meantime she had great support from the rest of the Kingsford Smith family and was a frequent guest at Kuranda, as well as at the homes of her brothers- and sisters-in-law. Still, when he was making dangerous flights like the one at present, the time dribbled by at best, and all she could do was pray that he was safe.

For Smithy, the next couple of days proceeded in a blur, as he kept going — and despite his illness he was now ahead of Mollison's time — through Calcutta, Jhansi, Karachi, Bushire and Aleppo. He *had* to get to London within eight days and nineteen hours. At last, though, it became clear that something was going to have to give:

> *What am I doing here? Why am I here? Only desert below ... must be off my head. I know I can't keep this up much longer.*[13]

Finally, on 30 September 1931, on his seventh day of flight — and a full day ahead of record time — he found himself flying over the Gulf of Alexandretta, an inlet of the eastern Mediterranean Sea, and only just remaining conscious, as he approached land and flew along the coast of Asia Minor.

> *I feel as though I might die before this flight is over. Must find a place to land. If I don't I'll crash for sure.*

Not long afterwards he spied a small village and just managed to get his plane down near it, taking out a barbed-wire fence as he did so, before collapsing. He awoke to find himself surrounded by villagers and then, shortly afterwards, soldiers with guns arrived, all looking down at him and talking gibberish.[14] Actually, Turkish. He had landed near an impoverished settlement by the name of Milas.

For their part, the villagers looked down upon the fallen flyer, wondering what this strange word he kept gurgling — 'Cognac, *cognac*, cognac!' — meant in their own language. Whatever it was, he seemed insistent about it. Minutes later, Smithy was under arrest, for having landed without a permit. (In fact, he had previously landed in Turkey without a permit, at Gallipoli in 1915, but that was another story and one that he probably shouldn't cite right now.)

Too sick to care — there was no hope of getting the record now, so what did it matter? — it was four days before Kingsford Smith was free to go, courtesy of an American businessman living locally who recognised the Australian and was able to pull strings with the local authorities. And yet, even when he was back in the air after four days' comparative rest, the illness soon returned. Was it sunstroke? Carbon monoxide poisoning, perhaps? Or, at thirty-six, was he just getting too old?

A clue was provided by the fact that after landing in Athens and divulging his distress to English expats, he was persuaded to see an American nerve specialist who told him in no uncertain terms that he must stop his flight immediately and get some rest.[15]

Smithy, typically, ignored this professional advice and finally dribbled into London on 7 October 1931, where the chief aviation news of the day was not that he had arrived, but that one RAF Flight Lieutenant G.H. Stainforth, AFC, had just set a new speed record in his Vickers Supermarine S6B seaplane of 408.8 miles per hour![16] Was there no *end* to how fast these modern planes could go?

As to the ailing Smithy, he was deeply upset over what had happened. 'The machine did not let me down,' he told journalists. 'This is the first time I have ever let my machine down.'[17]

A round of medical professionals confirmed the opinion that one way or another he was too sick to fly, and should stop immediately and return to Australia by ship. As to exactly what the Australian was suffering from, that was not clear. The theories put forward ranged from sunstroke in the open cockpit to carbon monoxide poisoning from the shortened exhaust pipe on the *Southern Cross Minor*, to some kind of nervous breakdown that became acute when he was flying long distances, most particularly over water — the acute reaction perhaps stemming back all the way to his near-drowning at Bondi Beach in 1907.

At the least, doubt was intruding on him, perhaps for the first time.

'It was not the sunstroke alone which cruelled me,' he said openly to one journalist. 'It was the climax of a series of nervous troubles.'

Asked if he would be attending a planned meeting of trans-oceanic fliers the following year in Rome, an uncharacteristically diffident Kingsford Smith replied: 'It will depend on whether my wife allows me to make the journey again.'[18]

Smithy took the first ship for home.

•

At one point during the Great War, the German Army had been able to crash through the forces of France's highest ranking military man, Marshal Ferdinand Foch, causing great celebrations on the part of the Germans. In the face of the disaster, Foch sent what would be a famous cable to his headquarters:

> My centre gives way, my right recedes; the situation is excellent. I shall attack.

In that case, Foch had gone on to engineer a great and unexpected victory.

Now, taking a leaf out of Foch's book, Charles Ulm, Kingsford Smith and the board of the Australian National Airways decided to do much the same thing. Their regular service along the eastern seaboard had been shut down for lack of custom. They had lost a plane, with no subsequent trace of it being found. The Federal government had not given them a cracker for any domestic subsidies, had denied their requests for financial assistance of any kind and had shut them out of the international route that could have guaranteed their survival. They had no capital left and the company was heading into deeper debt.

In short, their centre had given way. Their right flank had receded. The situation was excellent. They *attacked*.

On 23 October 1931, the company announced that one of their planes would leave Melbourne on 20 November with Christmas post for England. That post would arrive in London on 2 December, and the plane would return to Australia with English post, just in time for Christmas. Too, it was something of a coup when Lieutenant Colonel Horace Brinsmead, the Controller of Civil Aviation and the most influential and powerful man in the field of Australian aviation, agreed to go on the 20 November flight as a paying passenger, all the way to London. Given that he was travelling to Old Blighty to conclude negotiations on establishing a permanent aerial passenger and mail service between England and Australia, what better time was there to show what they could do? If they could pull this off, they really might be in with a chance of surviving, and even prospering!

With Kingsford Smith having only just arrived home in Australia, and still of uncertain health, it was decided that Scotty Allan would take the pride of the fleet, the *Southern Sun*, to do the job, and he left on schedule with many bulging sacks on board containing 45,288 letters from enthusiastic Australians to loved ones in Britain. Though each individual letter was feather-light — paid at a shilling for every 14 grams, added on to the normal sea-mail postage rate[19] — together they weighed well over half a ton.

All went well right up until the plane arrived in Alor Star in Malaya. Then disaster struck when Allan tried to take off from the rain-drenched field with the heavy load. He crashed into a ditch at the end of the runway, and though the precious cargo of mail was retrieved and there was no significant injury to the crew or Horace Brinsmead, the *Southern Sun* had been damaged beyond repair.

•

At Kuranda, Catherine got the call shortly afterwards. Her son was off again. There had been a crash in Malaya and Chilla had been sent for in the *Southern Star* to go and finish the job. Of course he had been. He was *always* being sent for, or heading off somewhere. Yes, he always survived, and eventually returned home, but it did worry her. The papers were filled with news of aeroplane crashes in Australia and various parts of the world, and she knew only too well the risks her boy took. Like Mary, though, all she could do was wait, and pray that he would be all right on this trip, too.

As it turned out, Smithy very nearly wasn't all right — in extremely heavy weather he crashed while landing in Darwin.

Fortunately he was not hurt, but it did cause a three-day delay while repairs were done. An impatient Horace Brinsmead decided not to wait, and instead get to England via Amsterdam, by catching one of the regular KLM flights from Bangkok. This time, true disaster struck, as the KLM Fokker F.VIIb.3m *Ooivaar* crashed while attempting to take off on 6 December from Bangkok, with the centre engine coming into the cabin and killing three of the four-man crew, two passengers and critically injuring Brinsmead.[20] He was immediately admitted to hospital with broken ribs, a damaged lung, a contusion of the brain and one side of his body paralysed — a bitterly ironic fate for one whose professional life since the Great War had been almost exclusively devoted to lifting aviation safety standards.

Arriving in Bangkok just five hours after the tragedy, Kingsford Smith was particularly devastated as he had such an enormous regard for Colonel Brinsmead. And yet, advised there was nothing he could do to help the Controller of Civil Aviation, Smithy — with both the mail and Scotty Allan on board, as he had picked up both in Alor Star — flew on.[21]

Apart from a brief return of Smithy's illness, when he was again taken ill while over the Bay of Bengal and had to excuse himself while Allan took over the controls, so he could stagger back to lie on the mailbags to recover, the flight went well.[22] After proceeding via Bangkok, Karachi, Aleppo, Le Touquet and Lyons, they landed at Croydon, 10 miles out of London, on 16 December 1931, twelve days, twenty-one hours and eighteen minutes after leaving Australia, to hand the mail to the representatives of the General Post Office.[23]

'I am very proud to bring the first direct air mail to England,' Smithy told waiting pressmen. 'I hope it will be the forerunner of a regular service. The Australian public has shown that it wants an air mail. If I get a similar load on the homeward trip, it will show that England also appreciates the service.'[24]

Mail from Australia in less than thirteen days! Hinkler's sixteen-day record cut to pieces! The achievement caught the popular imagination, and for a day or two Smithy's feat was the talk, if not the toast, of London.

•

Even as Kingsford Smith was approaching London, however, another famous Australian aviator had already reached the end of his even more amazing journey to that destination from afar. In the annals of long-distance aviation, Bert Hinkler's trip would always be a standout. In his tiny single-engined 120-horsepower de Havilland DH.80A Puss Moth monoplane, travelling solo, as ever — with no radio and just a compass and *Times Atlas* for guidance — in late November he hopped first from Toronto to New York and then down to Jamaica, before crossing over 700 miles of open sea to Venezuela. After that, a little jaunt to Trinidad before popping across the Gulf of Mexico to the land of Alberto Santos-Dumont, Brazil, where the 39-year-old from Bundaberg was stunned to see enormous flocks of brightly coloured birds rising from the jungle to greet him.[25]

After a short rest, he made ready for the *big* leap, across the South Atlantic. On the morning of 25 November, Hinkler flew above the enormous jungle beside the mighty Amazon River and was reflecting that it looked like a motionless green sea, when he saw it: the *real* sea, the Atlantic Ocean up ahead. At its sight he experienced a momentary quavering of confidence and then came the familiar surge of steel.

'Now or never,'[26] he breathed to himself, and flew on.

Using, among other things, his uncanny ability to judge wind direction by the shape of the clouds he was heading into, and making allowance accordingly, Hinkler was able to stay on course.[27] After flying for twenty-two hours and forty minutes across the storm-tossed ocean he arrived at Bathurst in British Gambia, where he sent his wife, Nancy, a typical cable: `Landed at Bathurst, Gambia. OK. Bert.` (At that point Nancy would not have been surprised if he had popped up in Patagonia.)[28]

'I am thrilled at his great success,' Nancy told the *Evening Standard*, 'for only one other man, Colonel Lindbergh, has succeeded in flying across the Atlantic alone ... I think he has done wonderfully, but then he is a wonderful husband.'[29] A few more hops and he was touching down in Casablanca, in Morocco, before heading off to Madrid, the town of Tours in France, and finally ... England! And there was his Nancy, waiting for him, and throwing her arms around him joyfully the moment he emerged from the plane.

'I must admit,' Bert said quietly at the formal welcome that awaited him at Hanworth Air Park in Middlesex, 'that on a certain night my hopes of dying as a respectable old man with long white whiskers appeared as if they would not be realised.'[30]

In honour of his achievement, the Royal Aero Club announced that Bert Hinkler would receive their gold medal at a dinner on the night of Wednesday, 16 December 1931. On the following evening, Hinkler was invited to attend a Guild of Air Pilots and Navigators dinner in the Florence Restaurant in London. And perhaps the just-landed Kingsford Smith would like to come too? Indeed he would. It was an odd circumstance that despite having both flown in the Great War and then crisscrossed the skies over and by each other through the 1920s in various parts of the world, the two aviators had never actually met. Both were delighted to do so, just as they were delighted that Amy Johnson, a young Englishwoman of extraordinary pluck — who had stunningly risen to fame the year before when she had become the first woman to fly solo to Australia, in nineteen days — was also at the dinner.

The wine flowed, the conversation warmed up and there was no doubt in the mind of anyone that the future of the splendid aviators at that dinner was a bright one, just as was the future of aviation itself. For in this game the sky wasn't the limit — there *were* no limits!

As the Royal Aero Club chairman, His Grace the Duke of Atholl, exulted in his toast that very evening: 'I foresee the time when women can fly from England to Australia with their hair newly Eton-cropped and return in a week's time, with their hair in the same smart condition.'[31]

As a matter of fact, this fitted in rather well with Hinkler's own views of where aviation was heading, as he was firmly of the belief that in the future most long-distance flying would be done at night, while the days would be reserved for seeing things. He thought that a whole industry might grow up around this, with masses of people flying around the world to different places, to sightsee by day, before climbing back into the plane to sleep at night and travel somewhere else, before seeing another thing![32]

Invited to say a few words, Kingsford Smith made an elegant speech saying he was proud to claim Bert Hinkler as 'a brother Aussie'. He did, however, jestingly reprimand Hinkler for the risks he took in flying the South Atlantic in such a slender craft, and would Bert mind telling everyone if there was a big flight that he *wasn't* going to do, as Smithy himself would like to have a crack at it.

Laughter all around, as the drinks continued to flow into the merry evening.[33] Pass the port …

•

'*Hello Mary, darling. Chilla here. I'm in London …*'

It was her husband, Charles, on the phone, sounding very distant, which, of course, he was. Though they had been married for a year, the way things had worked out, Mary — just like so many wives of pioneering aviators — had spent much of her time on her own in their Bellevue Hill home, waiting for him to return, and in fact had even spent their first wedding anniversary, Christmas Day and New Year's Eve without him. This time she had hoped he would be soon on his way back, bringing New Year's post from England to Australia, but now he had bad news.

There had been *another* accident, and again it was with Scotty Allan at the controls. Scotty had been moving the *Southern Star* from the Hamble aerodrome over to nearby Croydon in preparation for departure, when a smothering fog had closed in and he had lost his bearings. With little petrol on board Scotty had brought the plane down on a flat bit of ground in Kent, which would have been perfect except an orchard was planted on it, and he had smashed the undercarriage, knocked the wing off its pegs and finished with one of the engines half-buried in the soft ground. Charles was very sorry, Mary, but it looked like at least a week's worth of repairs before they could again be under way.

Never mind, darling, the main thing is that you're all right, and Scotty wasn't hurt either.

Mary finally hung up, feeling lonely. Being the wife of a famous aviator had many upsides, but on other occasions it wasn't easy at all.

•

In fact, the penalties of being part of the family of a famous aviator were never so graphically illustrated as when, late on the evening of 1 March 1932, it was discovered that not only was the first-born child of Charles and Anne Lindbergh missing from his bed in the family mansion in East Amwell, New Jersey, but a ransom note had been left on the windowsill. It read:

> *Dear Sir, Have 50,000 $ redy $25,000 in 20 $ bills 15,000 $ in 10$ bills and 10,000 $ in 5 $ bills. After 2–4 days we will inform you were to deliver the Mony.*
>
> *We warn you for making anyding public or for notify the Police the child is in gut care.*
>
> *Indication for all letters are singnature and 3 holes.*

The greatest search in American history was immediately launched, ending a few weeks later when a truck driver pulled over to allow his assistant, William Allen, to relieve himself beneath a grove of trees 5 miles from the Lindbergh home, only to discover the badly decomposed remains of the child, with a caved-in skull that had almost certainly occurred on the night. Even amid such tragedy the press did not respect the Lindbergh family's privacy, with photographers trying to break into the mortuary to get a photo of their dead son.

Smithy was devastated by the news, and constantly thought back to his meeting with Lindbergh two years earlier in New York's Roosevelt Hotel, when the American pilot had been so thrilled at Charles Jnr's recent birth and had shown him photos of his baby son.

•

Smithy! *Smithy!* It's Smithy! Come quick!

And come quickly they did, first in Sydney — where the discovery of a nudist colony in the thick bush around Kingsgrove which could be viewed from the air helped boost business no end[34] — before heading off through the likes of Tamworth, Newcastle, Bendigo, Echuca, Deniliquin, Kyabram, Melbourne, Colac, Terang, Warrnambool, Maryborough, Ballarat and Geelong. In the first months of 1932, Smithy earned his living by taking enormous numbers of endless joyrides charged at 10 shillings a pop, which might have been steep for some, but a small price to pay to say you were one of the select few who had been 'up in an aeroplane!' and 'with Smithy!' to boot. All those who purchased a ride were given a ticket embossed with the words 'Souvenir Flight in *Southern Cross* Piloted by C. E. Kingsford Smith', and for many people it was the experience of a lifetime, something they would remember fondly and talk about for *decades* afterwards. Often local councils would be so excited about the impending visit of Australia's most famous man that school children would be given a half-day holiday, which helped business no end.

Ideally, of course, Smithy would have been able to put another pilot in charge of the *Southern Cross*, but over the years they had learnt that that simply didn't work. The person everyone wanted to fly with was Smithy himself, one of the most celebrated men in Australia — with only Donald Bradman able to argue the toss (*heads*), and perhaps Phar Lap to snort derisively. True, it was a pity he didn't have more serious flying work to do, as the Christmas postal venture had actually turned a profit despite all the misadventure, but for the moment nothing beckoned.

Except Sydney and its newly minted Harbour Bridge. And so in March he returned in time to take part in the celebrations that marked its opening, leading a fly-past in the *Southern Cross* and then taking people for joyrides.

That evening he took a party of celebrants, all in evening wear, including his mother-in-law, for a spin over Sydney. Was he 'flying blind', in a different sense of the word? Perhaps. At the very least, there was a lot of alcohol around on that momentous day and evening.

In any case, with an undetected tailwind he landed way too hard, collapsing the undercarriage and sliding along the airstrip. Holding the plane straight the best he could, even as the *Southern*

Cross slithered and squirmed in agonised protest, Smithy mentally calculated the cost — £500 … £800 … £1000 … £2000 — before it finally came to a merciful halt. Fortunately no-one was injured, the chief casualty being what was left of Smithy's bank balance.[35] In fact, six weeks and £1500 later he had no choice but to head back out again, through Wellington, Warren, Narromine, Dubbo, Forbes, Young, Grenfell, Temora, Canberra, Cowra, Bathurst, Canowindra and Orange.

As it happened, Smithy was in Grenfell on the early morning of 3 June 1932, when young Tommy Pethybridge — whom Smithy had first met as an RAAF mechanic, but who had recently left that service so he could work for his hero — burst into his boss's hotel room, beside himself with some stunning news he had just heard on the radio. The King's birthday honours had been announced and, wait for it, King George V had knighted Smithy! He was now Air Commodore *Sir* Charles Kingsford Smith. In an instant, Smithy's world changed, as phone calls were made, telegrams began to arrive, everyone was giving him three cheers together with newly respectful slaps on the back, and he immediately had to make plans to fly Mary to Canberra that very afternoon in preparation for the investiture.[36] (It was the second bit of wonderful news for the couple in recent times, after confirmation that Mary was pregnant, when he had been back in Sydney for the opening of the Sydney Harbour Bridge celebrations.) For his part, Tommy Pethybridge was thrilled that he was the one who got to tell *Sir* Charles the news.

True, not everyone was pleased, as there was a strong view in certain sections of conservative society that a divorced man should never get a knighthood, and indeed Smithy was the first divorced man to ever be so honoured.

Never mind. That evening Sir Charles and *Lady* Kingsford Smith, if you please, dined with His Excellency the Governor-General Sir Isaac Isaacs, at a banquet at Government House given in honour of the King's birthday. Asked the following day how her husband felt about the honour, Lady Kingsford Smith said her husband was very pleased, as 'it was at least some tangible proof that Australia felt about him the way he felt about Australia'.[37]

Smithy himself was quoted: 'In view of this new honour, I am more determined than ever to remain in Australia. I was born here. I have lived here and I like Australia better than any other country I have visited. While it is true that I should by now have been a comparatively wealthy man had I become a naturalised American or had some of the lucrative offers from abroad been accepted, I am content to remain here and to earn my own living in my own way.'[38]

Though many of his supporters were public in their view that the government should 'look after' Smithy and give him the job of the unfortunate and still hospitalised Horace Brinsmead as Controller of Civil Aviation, nothing had come of that. Kingsford Smith didn't ask for the position, and the government didn't offer it. This meant that giving joy flights was the way he had left to make a living, and even if there were many people who took a dim view of a knight of the realm engaging in such common commerce, Smithy himself had no such compunction.

'While there is a living to be made in the *Southern Cross*,' he told a packed house at Brisbane City Hall on the evening of 1 August 1932, during one of his paid public lectures, 'I do not think it is any disgrace for one on whom His Majesty has conferred the honour of knighthood to remain in his own country and earn his living in an honest way.'[39] The response was warm applause. Thus, 'Smithy' — and that is what he insisted he be addressed as, and never Sir Charles — kept on flying, much as he had ever done, with his one concession to his new status being to acquiesce to Mary's insistence that he get a couple of tailored suits to wear on formal occasions.

Which was as well, because there were even more of them to get through, as mayors positively *outdid* themselves to welcome the '*Honorary Hair* Commodore *Sir* Charles Kingsford Smith', though on one occasion a particular mayor decided to go the whole hog.

'And we are honoured to have here today,' he said, '*Lord* Smith ... who 'as conquered the Hatlantic Hocean, the Pacific Hocean, and heven the great [Mediterr-hanean Hocean ...]'[40]

Only just was the aviator able to prevent himself from bursting out laughing. But enough of all that. It wouldn't be long before there was a particularly strong reason to stay closer to home. On 22 December 1932, not long after his flying for the year was done, Mary gave birth to a fine son, whom they christened Charles Arthur Kingsford Smith.

•

Late on the evening of 6 January 1933, at about eleven o'clock at night, Bert Hinkler called two of his closest friends. He asked if they would meet him at Harmondsworth aerodrome in a couple of hours' time to help him get away on his planned trip to Australia, in which he hoped to break C.W.A. Scott's latest record from England to Australia of eight days, twenty hours and forty-seven minutes, which the Englishman had set eight months previously.

Hinkler's friends agreed, and at one o'clock on that Saturday morning met him in fog so thick it was like being in a coalmine at midnight with a blindfold on. Bert had intended to get away at 2 am, but it was 3.10 am before — between them — they managed to get the Puss Moth into position, with its engine warmed up and ready to go, lit by the headlights of the cars the friends had driven there. Bert now opened 'er up and the tiny plane was quickly lost in the fog. His two friends, chilled to the bone and desperately rubbing their gloved hands together to try to get circulation back in them, returned hastily to the warmth of their homes, while Bert flew to the south-east.

He was spotted first over France, and then in Italy to the west of Turin, heading on a straight course to the Italian Riviera. That accomplished, just after eleven o'clock local time on the morning of 7 January, he was spotted over Florence, still heading south-east. His next task was to get over the Apennines, the mountain range that effectively forms the backbone of the Italian peninsula.[41]

And then Bert Hinkler, son of Bundaberg, love of Nancy's life and famous through much of the world, simply disappeared. There was no word of him at either Brindisi or in Athens — his possible landing points that afternoon — and the alarm was slowly raised. The devastating news was passed to Nancy as she was about to return to her ship in Auckland — on her way, she thought, to meet up with her Bert in Bundaberg — as a search operation was launched by the governments of France, Italy and Switzerland.

•

Though very concerned about Hinkler's disappearance, Charles Kingsford Smith had his own worries early in the new year of 1933. On 11 January, he took the *Southern Cross* down to Seven Mile Beach at Gerroa, a thirty-five-minute flight south of Sydney, in preparation for another trans-Tasman crossing. Seven Mile Beach had been chosen because its long, flat and hard surface of slightly curved shoreline and distinctly compact sand — often used for horse, car and motorcycle racing — was perfect to give their plane, heavily burdened with post and fuel, every chance to take off and if necessary to stop safely if that take-off had to be aborted. (Mascot runway was too short with such a heavy load on board, and Richmond too near the Blue Mountains, which represented a potential obstacle should the wind dictate a westerly departure as the most desirable.)

Once positioned at the Berry Surf Club about 2 miles down the beach from the village of Gerroa, in the wee hours of the following morning, by the light of myriad car headlights and the flaming flares strung along the beach and those of the two Fox Movietone newsreel film crews, the *Southern Cross* rumbled along the beach like an ungainly albatross trying to get up enough speed to get off the ground.[42] On board, co-pilot Bill Taylor — who had been a pioneer of aerial navigation and ANA's most outstanding regular pilot — was awestruck at Smithy's skill in keeping the right-hand wheel of the heavy plane on a straight course just above the rising tide, and the left-hand wheel just below the soft sand.[43] Any deviation meant disaster, and yet Kingsford Smith kept the hurtling plane precisely on track. The faithful bird finally left the sand just before 3.00 am, before swinging in a graceful arc back over the surf club, her searchlight glaring balefully in the foggy night, to set course to the east, towards New Zealand.[44]

Never before, on a serious flight, had the *Southern Cross* been carrying so many people. As well as navigator and co-pilot Bill

Taylor, the crew included radio man John Stannage (who had just married Smithy's niece Beris after something of a whirlwind romance), Associated Newspapers journalist Jack Percival and one Stan Nielson, the secretary of the New Plymouth and New Zealand Aero Club, who had not only been instrumental in upgrading the club's airstrip so the *Southern Cross* could use it, but had also parted with a cheque for £100 for the privilege of being the first fare-paying passenger to fly to New Zealand with them.[45]

For once, *for once*, this proved to be a relatively uneventful flight — apart from Bill Taylor at one point fearing they were frightfully lost, and John Stannage getting severe electrical shocks from his radio gear — and no more than fifteen hours later they were able to land at Bell Block aerodrome in New Plymouth, escorted by five de Havilland Gipsy Moths, to be greeted by Smithy's old friend and flying companion from the Coffee Royal days Tom McWilliams, as well as Chilla's brother Wilfrid, who had gone on ahead to make arrangements, in a new managerial role he had just taken over. Also there waiting was Tommy Pethybridge, who was jubilant. He had been extremely worried about whether the *Southern Cross* was going to make it, and at its very sight had leaped into the air, danced around and yelled, 'Those bloody marvellous engines!'[46] They had done it again, pulling Smithy and his crew through mortal danger.

Kingsford Smith's first focused words upon landing, after the preliminary greetings, were to the point: 'By the way, is there any word of my friend Hinkler? He is an extraordinarily resourceful man. I am by no means unduly alarmed. He has probably landed somewhere on one of the various mountain ranges on his route, and is beyond communication.'[47]

That Hinkler was beyond communication was certainly clear, as no further word from him was heard, and the search was finally called off. Though Smithy grieved, he knew, almost better than anyone that the strong possibility of death and disappearance were to him and his fellow pioneer flyers what a bad back was to a bricklayer — it simply went with the job.

For now, at least, he didn't need to engage in any great risks and continued barnstorming in New Zealand for the next three months, punctuated only by a short stint at home when his plane was in need of repair. A sign of his ailing emotional health, however, was his brief hospitalisation in Auckland for 'nervous exhaustion', before he returned once more to the air to take as many people as possible on joyrides.[48]

Not that barnstorming *ever* offered much respite from the constant pressure, as wherever he went the well-meaning public always wanted a piece of him. Once, after a very long day, one of Smithy's mechanics, Harold Affleck, was resting on his hotel bed when the door burst open and a wild-eyed Smithy rushed in.

'These two blokes are after me,' he blurted out. 'Tell them I've jumped over the balcony and gone out.' Without another word, he dived under Harold's bed, just before two men came in clutching bottles of champagne.

'Where's Smithy?' they asked.

Gone over the balcony and run off, Harold replied. Deeply disappointed — why would ol' Smithy do something like that, when they just wanted to have a bit of fun with him? — they left the bottles on the bed and said, 'When you find him, tell him to have a drink on us.'[49]

Heightening the pilot's great celebrity was the publicity being organised for him by a man fast becoming a great friend, one Beau Sheil who was with Vacuum Oil, and had a part in ensuring that both the oil company and Smithy received plenty of column inches in the newspapers. Travelling a town ahead of them, Sheil would make sure that journalists were forewarned of the great man's arrival, where he would be staying, where he would be doing the barnstorming from and so forth.

Such advance publicity meant very good business for joyrides in the *Southern Cross*, and just as it had been in Australia when business was good — and they were able to gross as much as £200 a day[50] — Smithy was so keen not to lose time for so much as a toilet break that he used what was effectively a urinal in the cockpit, a funnel attached to a tube, that led to a container beneath the fuselage.[51] (James Warner could only wish that Smithy had had such a thing back in 1928!)

On 26 March 1933 their sojourn was finally over and, with Bill Taylor, John Stannage, Tommy Pethybridge and a New Zealand businessman by the name of Mackay — who was interested in establishing a commercial air link between New Zealand and Australia — Smithy flew the *Southern Cross* back across the Tasman, leaving from Ninety Mile Beach at Hukatere. This particular flight had the distinction of being the first time that an amazing new technology called 'wireless telephony' was used in an aircraft in the southern hemisphere.[52] Unbelievably, as the *Southern Cross* flew on, radio operators in both Australia and New Zealand could actually hear the crew *speaking*.

What listeners didn't hear, mercifully, was Smithy experiencing another spell of illness halfway across the Tasman. Once again, he had to scrawl a message asking Bill Taylor to take over the controls, then excuse himself and go and lie down on the mailbags for a couple of hours until the nausea passed.

On the upside, however, during the trip back — in a manner that was reminiscent of Louis Blériot flying over Alicia on the *Escopette* going across the Channel two decades earlier — Smithy was able to use the wireless telephony to speak to his wife on the MV *Wanganella*, which had left New Zealand before them and was also heading to Sydney. True, Mary had to reply by Morse code, courtesy of a ship radio man who could do the translations for her, but the technology was simply *stunning*.

Smithy later wrote for public consumption: 'Our flight emphasised the practicability of instituting a regular airmail service between the two Dominions, and it confirmed in me the belief I had long held, that the day was not far distant when the pioneer flights that we were then making would be succeeded by regular commercial flights, made to schedule, on a dividend-earning basis.'[53]

And Smithy was desperate to have a part of that action, as there was only so long he could continue barnstorming and the like, as well as taking the risks he did on long flights. The fact that he was now a married man with a child meant that the game had changed. He was really starting to feel older, and not quite so bulletproof as he had in his wild days.

As it happened, his bank account was also feeling a little weary. While Smithy had been in New Zealand, ANA had gone into voluntary liquidation — with nary even a final gurgled 'kaput' to mark its passing. It was really only the formalisation of a situation that had existed for most of the previous year, as all work had evaporated. All the company's planes were put up for sale, the proceeds of which would go towards paying back some £79,440 to its creditors, although less than £17,000 would be retrieved by selling the planes. (And while Smithy kept the *Southern Cross* because he owned it independently from ANA, Charles Ulm purchased the *Southern Moon* from the firm's creditors, rebuilt it and renamed it *Faith in Australia*.)

There may well have been recriminations between Kingsford Smith and Ulm about the company's demise, had they been seeing or talking to each other on a regular basis. But their friendship had become extremely strained in recent times, perhaps in part due to Ulm's resentment at having to constantly play tenth fiddle to Smithy's whole orchestra of acclaim, at least in the public domain. What had particularly got Ulm's goat — and he took legal action to rectify it — was that, in his view, Smithy had not given him due recognition in a book he had penned the previous year about the flights of the *Southern Cross*, titled *The Old Bus*. At the behest of Ulm's lawyers, the manuscript had to be changed so that Ulm was given equal credit as a co-pilot and chief organiser and, by the time the book hit the bookstores, Smithy had even been obliged to dedicate the book to Ulm, 'Without whose genius for organisation, and courageous spirit, many flights in the *Southern Cross* could never have been achieved.'[54]

•

Early spring is a wonderful time in Europe, most particularly after a bitter winter, as people leave their burrows, take off their heavy clothing and emerge into the fresh and sparkling air once more to enjoy the blossoming of tulips and daffodils. So it was that on the morning of Friday, 27 April 1933, a 25-year-old Italian hiker by the name of Gino Tocchioni, with his knapsack on his back, did cheerily go a-wandering, along the mountain track —

tra-la-leee, tra-la-LAAAA — making his way up the slopes of the Pratomagno Alps, about 25 miles east of Florence, fording the now bursting mountain streams that were carrying away the melting snow. And then his whistling suddenly stopped. What was that? Somewhere above him something was glinting. Approaching, he saw it was the shattered wreckage of an aeroplane. After only a few minutes of looking around he found the pilot, lying on his back and surely staring to the eternity above when he had died. According to the papers he found on the body, the pilot's name was Herbert, and he was born in Bundaberg, Australia, on 8 December 1892. His surname was illegible. The Puss Moth was identified by its Canadian registration, CF-APK.

Two days later, his body had been retrieved by the local *carabinieri* and taken to the village of Strada-in-Casentino.[55] There, 114 days after his disappearance, the remains of Bert Hinkler were placed in a walnut coffin in the Casa del Fascio, the House of the Fascists, and soon covered by a Union Jack, which the local women had painstakingly sewn. Candles were placed at the head and foot of the coffin, and spring wildflowers, picked by the locals, were laid all around it. Armed Italian soldiers stood guard, their heads bowed.

Nancy was having tea on the liner *Strathaird* — then docked in Fremantle and about to sail for England — when she heard the shocking news, by virtue of a radio message from a reporter from the *West Australian* newspaper which was quietly handed to her.[56] She dropped her tea with a resounding clatter, burst into tears and rushed from the room. There was no way she could get to Italy in time for her husband's funeral, but in her absence she certainly could not have asked that her Bert be treated with more respect.

By order of Italy's leader, Benito Mussolini himself — a keen student of aviation who knew exactly who the dead pilot was — Bert Hinkler was given a state funeral of great pomp and ceremony. On the evening of 1 May 1933, his horse-drawn hearse, at the head of a long cortege, passed along the cobbled streets of old Florence, through thick crowds of Florentines, all with their heads bowed and many of them weeping. Past the mediaeval Cathedral of St Maria del Fiore, the procession crossed the ancient stone bridge above the Arno River, and halted at Porta Romana, the gates of the city. Then, following custom, a voice cried out the name of the deceased.

'*Senor Hubert* Hinkler!'

'*Presente!*' responded the many mourners. Bert was here, and here he would remain, as the procession moved into the Protestant section of the *Cimiterio Evangelico degli Allori*, where he was buried.

Seventeen

Troubles

The successful aviator who performs some startling feat will always have the microphones and newspapermen around him. There will always be an excess of publicity that will spread his name to the ends of the world with the speed of radio. But when it all ends and the captains and kings depart, he is left high and dry, stranded in a financial desert from which he must find his own way out.

Charles Kingsford Smith to a journalist, circa 1933[1]

It was time to go it alone. Despite Smithy's financial woes there were still enough men of money who believed in him that, in May 1933, he was able to announce the formation of Kingsford-Smith Air Service Ltd, with its base a massive 80 by 90 foot hangar to be built at Mascot. As ever, the jewel in his flying stock was the old faithful *Southern Cross* — now a venerable seven years old — but he was able to add to this with five other, smaller planes, including three Gipsy Moths.

'To hell with the Depression!' Smithy told those who cautioned him about the expenditure at a time of such terrible economic trouble. 'If people let Depression talk stop them, we'll never be through with it.'[2]

The company would be part flying school, part charter service, part joy-flying base, part air-taxi, part whatever-kind-of-work-came-up-so-long-as-he-could-keep-flying. Two key appointments were John Stannage as manager and the ever-enthusiastic Tommy Pethybridge as chief engineer. They essentially moved just a few hundred yards from their old Australian National Airways hangar, which had been taken over by Charles Ulm, where he was operating his new company, Great Pacific Airways Ltd.

And yet, the fact that Smithy and Ulm were operating in an aviation world that was evolving and advancing with the rapidity of the planes themselves, was evidenced by the arrival in Australia in late June 1933 of a massive Imperial Airways passenger plane, the *Astraea*. Just as West Australian Airways had been at the forefront of regional travel in Australia in the early 1920s, Imperial Airways was now leading the way in international travel, pushing ever outwards from its home base in London to the farthest reaches of the world — a push that was given extra oomph by a British government backing it all the way with generous subsidies.

The *Astraea* was there on what was called a 'survey flight' to effectively do whatever the aerial version of 'testing the waters' was. The Armstrong Whitworth AW.15 high-wing monoplane, with four 340-horsepower engines, could cruise at 110 to 125 miles per hour, go as high at 14,200 feet, as far as 640 miles in one hop and had the capacity to carry between nine and seventeen passengers with luggage and three crew members — and was already extensively used by Imperial Airways on routes from England to both Africa and India. To the question of whether those routes could be extended to Australia, the answer seemed to be a resounding yes, and the issue the Australian aviation world was dealing with at that time was, could and should one of their own companies have a part of it?

For much of the early 1930s there had been discussions between ANA, Qantas and West Australian Airways about whether they should form a combined company to take on the Australian end of the route, perhaps from Singapore on. Ultimately, however, those talks had come to nothing. In the absence of an all-Australian option, thus, Hudson Fysh had pushed hard with his long-time proposal that Qantas and Imperial Airways form a subsidiary company to take on that end of the route, and the presence of the *Astraea* was in fact part of a publicity campaign to promote Imperial Airways to the Australian public.

In fact, many people of influence were outraged about the whole idea of Imperial having anything to do with the Australian end of the route. Thundering in the Senate on the afternoon of 1 September 1933, Senator James Patrick Digger Dunn extolled the virtues of Charles Kingsford Smith and Charles Ulm before thrusting his point home: 'Apparently these men are to be left on the beach, while this profitable contract goes to Imperial Airways, to be run on British capital, manned by British airmen, and paid for with good Australian cash. What chance has Smith or Ulm, or any other Australian without money, to compete with this wealthy monopoly in open tenders? They will be frozen out and the Government, by its encouragement of the propaganda stunt of the *Astraea*, is already preparing the public mind to see them frozen out ...'[3]

That, the government very likely, was. And yet the tender process had to be observed. On 22 September 1933 the Federal government made its announcement calling for aviation companies wishing to bid for the Singapore to Darwin section, and for the Darwin to other parts of Australia section. Those wishing to apply had to have aeroplanes with a cruising speed of not less than 110 miles per hour, and a range of at least 600 miles.

Gentlemen, start your engines ...

•

Ladies, fix them. At least this lady did. Her name was Nancy Bird and, as a seventeen-year-old, the Manly girl had been one of the first pupils at Kingsford Smith's flying school at Mascot. Her first lesson had been with Smithy himself and it had instantly consolidated her view that flying was to be the great passion of her life. So much so, that she announced that she would like to learn something about the engineering side.

'We'll learn her to learn engineering,' Smithy's chief engineer, Tommy Pethybridge, exulted gleefully, 'give her some dirty jobs to do.'[4]

Soon enough, Nancy Bird was up to her elbows in them, soaked in petrol and oil, and more often than not wielding a steel brush on filthy spark plugs — including those of the

Southern Cross — to get the carbon off them, or wriggling under the engine to remove the sump plug and letting the oil flow out. Tommy wasn't necessarily mean in giving her such jobs — even though, like Kingsford Smith, he wasn't sure if there was a place in aviation for females — but he did think it would be a fair test to see if she had what it took.

Up to the task, Nancy kept working away, while she continued to take flying lessons. She eventually became the first woman to fly professionally in Australia.

•

From the first, both Kingsford Smith and Charles Ulm expressed interest in submitting tenders. 'I told Mr Ulm,' Kingsford Smith informed the press, 'that if his company, which will also tender, was successful in getting the contract, I would join his board of directors in an advisory capacity. Meantime, I am preparing ... for my own tender for the aerial mail contract.'[5]

Smithy's view as to how to best present his credentials to win that tender was not to continue to build his aviation company or to bury himself in oh-so-boring paperwork, but rather to have another go at the England to Australia record, on the reckoning that the resultant publicity could only help his cause as it had done so many times before — and to hell with those who thought he was too old to keep going after records. 'At the age of thirty-six, and after seventeen years of flying,' he later recounted, 'I began to recognise that I was fast becoming one of the "veterans", a conviction forced on me by the fact that in the United States I enjoyed the honorific title among airmen there of "Daddy". The years pass, but though "getting on", I felt that I was still not too old to compete on equal terms with the younger generation, and in any case, we "veterans" have the right, and indeed the duty, to show the up-and-coming-young-fellows that there is "life in the old dog yet".'[6]

To some people, the constant quest to break records was both tedious and dangerous, and foremost of these nay-sayers was the co-winner of the 1919 Air Race, Sir Keith Smith. In his own way, echoing the grizzled Fijian who six years earlier in Suva had asked, 'But what are they all doing this for?'[7], Sir

Keith stated firmly his own view that 'records serve no good purpose'.[8]

To this Smithy responded, 'I am an old friend of Sir Keith, but I venture to disagree with him. In my opinion they cannot be done without ... There must be pioneering in everything, and record flights help to establish the worth of human stamina, the worth of machinery, and I am satisfied that if record flights were abandoned the British nation would become decadent, and the pioneering spirit would disappear.'[9]

So there.

•

On 4 October 1933, Sir Charles Kingsford Smith took off from Lympne, in Kent, on yet one more record-breaking attempt on the England to Australia route. This time he was in *Miss Southern Cross*, a powerful, all-wood, fabric-covered, low-wing Percival Gull monoplane with an enclosed cabin, and 130-horsepower de Havilland Gipsy Major engine which had been designed by Edgar Percival, an Australian who had been born in Albury and raised on a farm adjacent to Ham Common, the original name for the cleared fields which were to become Richmond RAAF station. His intentions were avowedly moderate. 'I am allowing time for a good night's rest at each stopping-place,' he said before leaving. 'I am not going to reduce myself to a shadow with successive days of sleeplessness. I am a family man now, and the only record that has really interested me is to be the oldest living airman. That is worth trying for nowadays.'[10]

It was to be a torrid flight, as despite his proclaimed hopes for a healthy flight, Kingsford Smith started to feel nauseous, faint and shaky after his first hop to Brindisi, Italy, on the first day.[11] On top of all that, he was continually beset by terrible anxiety — an overwhelming sense of oncoming disaster which seemed all the worse because it was a panic with no focus on a particular peril that he could take action against. Though he felt a little better after a brief rest, the feeling of great distress was compounded as dawn broke when, off the coast of Greece, he felt the familiar sense of sinking spirits and rising panic. Suddenly, he really did feel, as he wrote in his log, *Too old and worn out for these capers*. But what could he do? He flew on, vowing to master both his physical and spiritual ills.

That evening, when he consulted an English-speaking doctor in Baghdad, the medical man was shocked at the pilot's condition and told him he had to abandon the flight *immediately*.

'You're ill,' he said. 'Keep this up and you'll kill yourself.'[12]

And yet, it was only doctor's orders and not something truly significant, like a faulty engine or a broken wing. After a terrible night, lying practically sleepless as he faced his many demons of the dark hours — tempered only by thoughts of Mary and Charles Jnr waiting patiently for him at home — Kingsford Smith took off at dawn the following day for Gwadar, on the south-western coast of Pakistan, and his log entries tell much of the story for the rest of the troubled trip:

> *In the middle of the Bay of Angels — about 100 miles over water ... Will be glad to reach land again as the water looks very wet ...*
>
> *Another recurrence of nervousness. Nasty feeling, as if I were going to faint. Hope I can get through.*
>
> *Landed by flares at Baghdad last night. Couldn't sleep for nerves and had a bad night. Felt pretty rotten today.*
>
> *Had a very bad turn and had to come down to 200 feet. Thought I was fainting. Will try to make Bandar Abbas.*

Despite it all, with the constitution of *two* mules, Kingsford Smith was able to land in Wyndham at 5.14 pm on 11 October 1933, seven days, four hours and fifty minutes after leaving — the first time the record had entered the public consciousness in minutes — to smash Charles Scott's record by one day, fifteen hours, fifty-four minutes and receive a hero's welcome.

Still, he did acknowledge to the pressing reporters something of the horrors he had endured, noting that 'I'm getting too old for these stunts', and that while traversing the Persian Gulf, 'I went to pieces and had to put in a day in bed. I don't like travelling over the sea with one engine. It has been a pretty constant fight against sleeplessness and that extraordinary sickness and nervousness I get over water. I suppose doctors would call it aquaphobia. At one stage over the Timor Sea I felt I would have to break out of the cabin.'[13]

No matter, Australia celebrated his achievement anyway, and he was soon lost once more in that intoxicating rush of mass adulation that greeted him at his every appearance. Cables came from everywhere, including one from Australia's Kangaroos rugby league team on tour in England, who had heard the joyous news at half-time of a match against Bradford, and cabled their congratulations as soon as the match was over.[14] When arriving in Sydney to the usual tumultuous welcome at Mascot — that blessedly included a beaming Mary and a now *walking* son — his mother Catherine was asked to say a few words.

'I always had confidence that he would break the record,' she said in front of her beaming son. 'I expected him to do it and he has done it. He generally does what he sets out to do.'[15]

Cheers all round!

By the time he got to Melbourne, no fewer than 100,000 people had gathered to greet him. The Commonwealth government, caught up in the general celebration that the record had returned to an Australian, announced that it would make a grant to Smithy of £3000, income-tax free — news that was broken to the airman in a personal phone call from the leader of the nation, Prime Minister Joseph Lyons. More spoils quickly followed. The Vacuum Oil Company offered, and he accepted, a lucrative position as their aviation consultant.[16]

But just what was it that had been ailing him? This never became quite clear, though at least a part of it had to have been the fact that at thirty-six years old, both his body and his mind were showing signs of enormous fatigue, if not outright rebellion, due to the tremendous exertions he had put himself through over the previous two decades.

And it wasn't as if everything was fine again on those occasions when he was home with Mary and young Charles …

•

Tossing. Turning. Sweating. Hot. Diving now. An angel of death in his SPAD, he was swooping down on the tightly bunched German troops below, holding his fire until he was so close he simply couldn't miss … *Now!*[17]

And always, always, always it was the same thing. The instant his finger tightened on the trigger, his two machine guns would start spitting lead and before him, dozens upon *dozens* of German soldiers were simply flung every which way by his bullets. He couldn't miss! And he didn't.

Screaming now — some kind of primeval shriek that came from deep within him — he lived the horror of it once more. His bullets ripped them open like sliced sausages, blew some of their heads off, and left others pitching and heaving and dying in the mud, with their intestines spilling out of their lacerated stomachs — some trying vainly to push them back in, to stay alive … to live … live … live … not die.

And then he would wake up, sweating, sometimes even screaming, with Mary holding him, trying to soothe him, telling him it was just one more bad dream, darling, and it is all right. It was long ago. You were doing what you had to do. It will pass. Gentle, darling. Sleep, darling. Back to sleep. Sleep … sleep … sleep. And when he was lucky, he really would get back to sleep. But most times the horror of the war years would stay with him and he could no longer shake it off. Sometimes he cried. And then, at least he could talk to Mary about it, and tell her, while all the rest of the world was sleeping and the only sound was the growl of a distant car engine taking a late-night reveller home, how unfair it all was that young Germans who loved their parents or their wives as dearly as he loved his family, had had to die. He was less haunted by the pilots he had shot down as that was a case of kill or be killed — and they had an equal chance with him.[18] But those soldiers on the ground who he had slaughtered — *slaughtered*, Mary, do you understand? — those poor devils never had a chance, had just been doing their duty as they saw it, marching to the front, and he had come along and killed them. Do you really understand the horror of it, Mary? She understood, or at least tried to. She soothed him.

If this was an all too common occurrence among veterans of the Great War, to be forced to relive the horrors of what they had seen and done too many times in the silent watch of the night, still there were few, if any, other veterans who put themselves under such constant psychological pressure as Kingsford Smith did in his post-war life. And in these early years of the 1930s, just as it had been in the early 1920s, when Catherine Kingsford Smith had seen it up close and worried about the mental health of her son after what had happened in the Great War, there were signs that he might be on the edge of a complete breakdown. And yet he had to keep going, pushing himself, in the hope, among other things that he could find the financial breakthrough that would allow him the luxury of pulling back entirely.

A sure sign that records alone wouldn't save him was that the new record he had set for his flight from England lasted no longer than a week. After leaving Feltham aerodrome near London on 13 October, none other than Charles Ulm, accompanied by Bill Taylor and Scotty Allan in the newly christened *Faith in Australia*, made it to Derby in the early hours of 20 October, just six days, seventeen hours and fifty-six minutes later. The new record was down to under a week!

For Ulm, however, there would be no government largesse of £3000. That had already gone to Smithy, and besides, Smithy had done it alone. In fact, so highly regarded was Sir Charles by the public that, again, the subject arose of whether the government *owed* him a highly paid position in the Commonwealth Service.

'It is believed,' the *Courier-Mail* reported in late October, that with such a job, Kingsford Smith 'would be able to build up a sound business enterprise, and be able to forsake for all time the barnstorming career which he has had to follow in the last few years. Fear has been expressed in ministerial circles on more than one occasion that the loss of the aviator, while engaged in one of his record breaking solo flights, would be an Australian calamity of the blackest character. It is to prevent the possibility of any such occurrence that immediate attention will be given to the proposal to assist him.'[19]

Alas, after Cabinet met to decide the issue, the answer that came back was a firm 'no'. The grant of £3000 would stand, but there would be no safe government position for the airman. Yes, he was one of the two most revered men in Australia, with Bradman, but Smithy was always an outsider, not an insider, and the government simply did not care to offer him a secure sinecure.

•

In the meantime, the airline tendering process had gone on. In the final wash-up, while Qantas had indeed thrown in their lot with Imperial Airways to submit a joint bid, Charles Ulm had combined with Norman Brearley and the two had submitted a joint tender where they announced their intention to form, if successful, a company called Commonwealth Airways. As to Smithy, the most famous aviator in the land, in the end he advised his position in February 1934 — from New Zealand, where he had gone for another burst of barnstorming — in a personal letter to the new Controller of Civil Aviation, Edgar Johnston, yet another veteran of the Royal Flying Corps. He wanted Johnston to know that 'definitely I am associated with Robinson [of New England Airways] in his tender for the mail subsidy and anything that can be done to help him, will also help me. Naturally, old man, I am not suggesting you do not consider each tender on its merits.'[20]

Perish the thought.

For his part, Qantas chairman Fergus McMaster refused to take either alternative bid seriously, writing to Fysh on 2 March: 'There is no telling what will be done about the tenders, but it could hardly be imagined that the Ulm and Brearley lot would be considered for the Singapore–Brisbane section, or that the loose arrangement between Robinson and Kingsford Smith would be seriously considered – with three old Avro Tens and the even older *Southern Cross*. There is no doubt they were hard pushed, to make use of loose sentiment when they included the *Southern Cross*.'[21]

Smithy stayed on barnstorming in New Zealand, though he had another motive for being there, which he noted publicly: 'To establish my claims to the regular airmail service between the two countries that must come before very much longer.'[22]

Kingsford Smith's reasoning was, as he wrote, 'that we, who had pioneered the Tasman sea route, who had repeatedly crossed it, carried mails to and fro over it, and had by our activities created an air-mindedness in the people of New Zealand, should be entrusted with the organisation and maintenance of this section of the Empire airmail route'.

For Smithy at this time, establishing that route under his own umbrella had become nothing less than 'my life's objective ...'[23]

•

At least he was back in Australia when on 19 April 1934, Prime Minister Joseph Lyons himself announced the news. The winner of the tender for the Singapore–Darwin–Brisbane route was Qantas Empire Airways.[24]

Using the five de Havilland DH.86A aircraft — fitted with Gipsy Six engines and capable of carrying ten passengers and two crew — that it had had especially built, Qantas Empire Airways would receive £228,478 from the government in subsidies over the next five years.[25] As if that wasn't enough of a blow to their competitors, Qantas Empire was also awarded the contract to distribute the post through the bulk of the rest of Australia — with subsidies bringing its total payment to £318,426 — with a couple of tiny sections reserved for a few minor local airlines. For Charles Kingsford Smith, Charles Ulm and Norman Brearley there was nothing.

This, in Kingsford Smith's view, was a major injustice that Australian airmen such as he and Ulm, 'who have been primarily responsible for the development of aviation in Australia, have been overlooked. I feel that the men who brought to Australia a realisation of the value of air transport and have successfully striven against tremendous odds to provide efficient services for Australia have suffered a serious injustice. Apparently my tender was not even considered.'[26]

One pilot who did take the news very well was none other than Paul McGinness, the co-founder of Qantas, who wired Fysh from his farm in Western Australia: `Congratulations on your success in securing the contract. Best wishes future.`[27]

And a wonderful future it looked to be, too, with Qantas having grown from a tiny outback operator in 1921 to a genuine international operator with an assured government income by 1933.

•

Which was all right for some. For Smithy, money was getting progressively tighter, and despite his only half-hearted tender he had been devastated by the government announcement, wandering around his house and telling Mary endlessly, 'Nothing — absolutely nothing — is working for me.'[28]

Inevitably, he began to wonder how he could make his way out of his growing financial difficulties. Before, in bad times, he had been able to live on nothing but fresh air and love. Now, with a wife and baby Charles to support, he needed to have them secure.

At least there was one easy way to earn a lot of money on the near horizon. The previous year, a Scottish-born Melbourne chocolate manufacturer by the name of Sir Macpherson Robertson had announced a £10,000 prize for a Centenary Air Race between London and Melbourne in the coming October, to celebrate 100 years since John Batman had sailed 6 miles up the Yarra River, found the water good and deep, and famously proclaimed 'this will be the place for a village', a village later to be called Melbourne.

There was to be no limit to the size of the aircraft, the nationality of entrants, or how many crew it could have, though when it came to plane and crew, 'I am hoping that both will be Empire products'.[29] Robertson was very insistent, however, that safety was a top priority — there was to be no repeat of the disaster of the 1927 Dole Air Race or the deaths of the 1919 race from England to Australia. The key stipulation, thus, was that all entrants must present a certificate of airworthiness

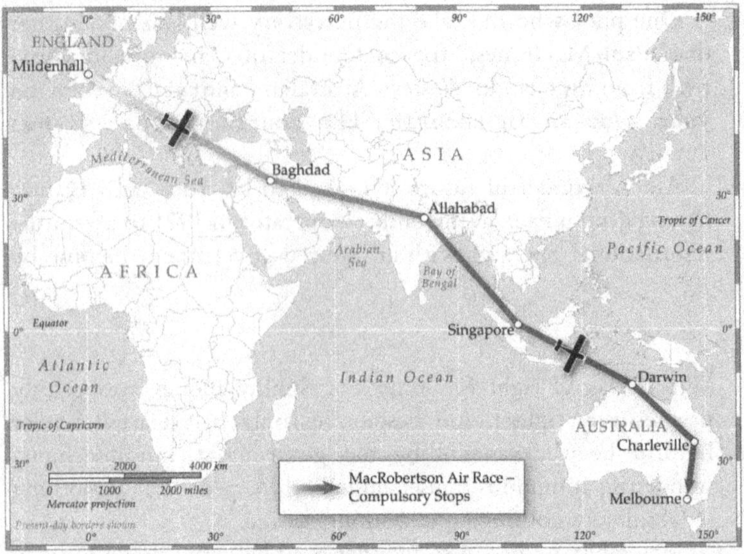

from their country of origin to show that the aeroplane they were flying met the minimum safety requirements of the International Commission on Air Navigation, which had been signed by member countries in Paris in 1919. The idea was that the aircraft were not to be dangerously overloaded flying petrol tanks, but to compete with a fuel capacity that was 'normal' for that design of plane.

This was obviously the greatest air race ever conceived, over a route with which he was more familiar than any other airman, and if Smithy could win it, it would crown his already splendid flying career.[30] To Mary's expressed worries that she no longer wanted him to take the risks of long-distance flying, most particularly when his health had not been good, he laughingly replied, as he always did, with the reassurance that 'Poppa is going to die in his bed, with his socks on'.[31] Too, as he had already announced firmly to the press, 'my last long flight will be the Melbourne Centenary Air Race',[32] so Mary would just have to accept that he needed to do it one last time and then he would be able to settle down.

The truth of it was, he didn't have a lot of choice. He needed that money, and with £10,000 he would be able to see his way clear of most of his financial trouble. The further good news was that not only was Robertson funding the race, he was also keen to help finance Smithy, to the tune of £5000, into buying a British plane that might win it. Smithy was, after all, a national hero and there was no doubt he was such a public favourite that a victory for him would cause the greatest splash of publicity.

The only difference the aviator and businessman had was over the choice of plane. After due consideration, Smithy had decided that the most capable machine for the job would be an American one — as their planes had lately been leading the field in long-range high-speed jobs — and he thought probably a Northrop Gamma would do the trick.[33] It was a single-engine, solo cockpit, all-metal screamer with a long range. Robertson's instant riposte was that he would much prefer that Smithy bought a British plane. Given that Robertson was the principal backer — although Smithy's father-in-law also put in £1000, as did the *Melbourne Herald*, while Sidney Myer once again backed him with £500 — Smithy agreed to look at it, but his investigations didn't last long. The only British plane that would come close would be one of the radical de Havilland DH.88 Comets then under construction, but there was a serious problem. All three machines had been promised to other competitors, including to the two piloting partnerships Smithy already regarded as his principal competitors, Charles Scott and Tom Campbell Black, and Jimmy Mollison with his new wife, the former Amy Johnson. (Jimmy had met Amy four years earlier when she had arrived in Australia, flying solo. So impressed was he that he had proposed to her within eight hours of their meeting.)

Now, while Captain Geoffrey de Havilland, AFC, could supply another Comet for Smithy if he ordered and paid for it, he regretted to say that de Havillands had insufficient resources to also install a crucial Ratier 'variable pitch propeller'. French-made, the company had only three of them and there would be no more available for some time. A recent innovation in sophisticated aircraft, the variable pitch propeller was the rough equivalent of gears in cars, whereby the pilot could alter the 'pitch' at which the propeller blades bit into the air — the 'pitch' being the angle at which the blade was positioned along its axis. Whereas for taking off and climbing, a fine pitch of the propeller was the most efficient way to get a grip on the air, a much coarser pitch was required for economical cruising.

The bottom line was that if Smithy flew without such a propeller, the likes of Scott and Campbell Black would have 400 miles extra range on long hops, meaning that he had no chance of winning. And if he couldn't win, what was the point? So it *had* to be an American plane, where variable pitch propellers were readily available off the shelf. Oddly enough, Smithy was fully supported in this decision by former RAAF Wing Commander Lawrence Wackett, who had so bitterly criticised him and Ulm six years earlier when they had decided to fly a Fokker across the Pacific. Their relationship now repaired and firm, Wackett accompanied Smithy in May 1934 when he went to see Robertson to tell him that the logic of buying an American plane with a variable pitch propeller was unalterable. With some passion — this is *important*, Mr Robertson, as there is simply no other way the race can be won — they explained that even if Smithy didn't get a Northrop Gamma, which was proving to be prohibitively expensive, then he likely could at least get a second-hand Lockheed Altair, which had much the same performance for a fraction of the price.

Robertson finally agreed and Smithy began to make his arrangements. As it was effectively against the law to bring in an American plane because the United States was not a signatory to the International Civil Aviation Organisation, the only way Smithy would be able to secure one would be to go to America, purchase one, and ship it back home to have it certified in Australia.

Done!

Before leaving, however, the Controller of Civil Aviation himself, Captain Edgar Johnston, personally told Smithy to be sure to get a Certificate of Airworthiness from the American Department of Commerce, affirming that the machine conformed substantially to the 'normal' category of the commission's regulations.[34] Although America was one of the few developed countries not to be a signatory to that convention, its Federal Department of Commerce — which governed aviation in the United States — had an equivalent, the Approved-Type Certificate, which Australia recognised. The point, Johnston told Smithy, was that without that certificate his plane would neither be able to fly in Australia, nor able to participate in the Centenary Race, under Rule 16(v) of its conditions of entry: *Each aircraft must bear a certificate from its country of registration that it conforms substantially to the minimum airworthiness requirements of the ICAN normal category.*

Smithy was wryly amused at the warning, recognising that Johnno must have been aware of his reputation in the matter of paperwork. True, he wasn't renowned for crossing his t's and dotting his i's, but he assured Johnno that he would see to it. Blah, blah, blah.

Things were starting to break his way, and he was also pleased to secure as his navigator and co-pilot for the coming race Bill Taylor, with whom he had been working on and off over the last five years, first with ANA and then on his New Zealand trips. It was Smithy's view that the quietly spoken Bill was one of the best in the business, totally professional, entirely unflappable and precisely the kind of man he wanted for backup. As to Taylor, he felt that he and Smithy were a great team, no matter, or perhaps even because of, the difference in their temperaments — Smithy being an extrovert and Bill a very careful, considered, introverted man of quiet habits.[35]

•

After sailing to America with Mary in mid-May — for the first time leaving the eighteen-month-old Charles Jnr behind with the family nanny — Smithy looked around and quickly decided that the best plane for him was indeed a particular Lockheed racer he saw in a hangar in Burbank, which had been previously designed and built as a Lockheed Sirius for an attempt on the New York to Paris record that had never happened. A pioneering airman's *dream*, it was a single-engined, tandem-seater — one behind the other, with dual controls — and variable pitch propeller, powered by a massive 542-horsepower supercharged Pratt & Whitney Wasp engine that was almost as powerful as the three engines of the *Southern Cross* put together. It could fly at over 200 miles per hour and go as high as 15,000 feet, which would be enough to get him above most storms (even if one couldn't stay up there long for lack of oxygen). Now, *now* the Comets in the Centenary Air Race would have some competition!

Smithy loved the Altair from the first moment he saw it and quickly made arrangements to buy it from its previous owner for the equivalent of £6000. This was more than he could raise on the spot, but the retail magnate Sidney Myer had once again offered to help, with another £500, and his father-in-law, Arthur Powell, also contributed. Smithy immediately made plans to make modifications to the plane, starting with putting in extra petrol tanks. Normally, the Altair had capacity for 150 gallons — which was nowhere near enough for him to make the big 2500-mile hops across the world he would need to win the Centenary Race. Smithy wanted to have four more tanks put in, to get it up to 418 gallons, which would give him a cruising range of 2800 miles.

For their part, Lockheed, while thrilled that one of their planes might win such a prestigious race with such a famous pilot, were also more than a little anxious. They pointed out to the Australian that the changes he wished to make were extremely unlikely to get the tick of approval he needed from the US Department of Commerce, an Approved-Type Certificate, which was certification that the plane was airworthy.

Not to worry, said Smithy. He had a lot of influence in Australia, would have the public behind him, and the man who was sponsoring the race, Sir Macpherson Robertson, was also backing him and his plane.

'If I can't get this plane into the race,' Kingsford Smith said to Robert Gross, the president of Lockheed, 'then nobody can.'[36]

So strong was Kingsford Smith in his confidence, so insistent that there would be no problem that couldn't be overcome once he got the plane back in Australia, the executives at Lockheed reluctantly agreed to expand the fuel capacity, and even agreed to do it at next to no cost. They also fitted a single canopy over the dual cockpits, installed a new engine and a new wing with retractable undercarriage and the extra petrol tanks. No problem.

All done, Lockheed's specially licensed test pilot flew it to the facility at the Department of Commerce's aerodrome for certification. Alas, all he came back with was an Experimental License of Airworthiness, which would expire in a matter of weeks, on 30 June 1934. Lockheed was not surprised. The company never believed that its Altair, set up as it was with over-sized fuel tanks, would get the full airworthiness certificate.

Smithy — in a glorious daze as to what a fine machine it was, and what an excellent chance he had of winning the race and the £10,000[37] that was going to fix everything — didn't worry particularly. This, notwithstanding the fact that, from Australia, the Controller of Civil Aviation had again, via John Stannage, repeated his earlier message: 'Make sure you tell your boss, to get that Certificate of Airworthiness.'[38]

For Smithy, paperwork had always been the thing that Charles Ulm and various minions had taken care of while he had concentrated on the glorious flying part of the operation. And yet even beyond Lockheed's warnings, it wasn't as if he wasn't aware that there might be a problem upon his return. A journalist with *The Age* interviewed Smithy while the pilot was in America, and quoted him saying that 'the controversy ... over the Melbourne Centenary race is far from settled ...'[39] And yet, the journalist noted, Smithy 'intended to seek approval of his entry when he returned home and, although he expected considerable opposition, he was confident as to the outcome, because he believed public opinion would support him.'[40]

•

It was one of those perfect July days where, although the calendar says it is winter, Sydney decides to turn on spring weather. In the company of the other planes from Kingsford-Smith Air Services, Bill Taylor swept up the sparkling harbour in the same Percival Gull that Smithy had broken the England to Australia record in the year before, and reckoned that his home city had rarely looked more stunning.

And yet he was about to see something more stunning still. Coming through the heads of Sydney Harbour that late morning of 16 July 1934 was the *Mariposa*, on which Smithy and Mary were returning from the States, and there on the deck he saw it for the first time. 'It was the Lockheed Altair,' he later wrote, 'her tapered wings glistening below her blue streamlined fuselage, a real thoroughbred: no contraption of wires and struts and gadgets hanging everywhere; just a wing, a body, and a tail of perfect form, like a beautiful blue bird poised ready for flight.'[41]

Ah, but the Australian Customs officers certainly didn't think so. No automated bird could fly without the proper papers, so where were they? Smithy handed over the Experimental License of Airworthiness received from the US Commerce Department. It had expired on 30 June.

Did he have a Certificate of Airworthiness?

He did not.

Did he at least have a Certificate of Importation, allowing him to bring into Australia an American aircraft?

No, he did not.

Well, it was impounded then, wasn't it?

He supposed so.

All Smithy could manage in the short term — as the plane couldn't stay aboard the *Mariposa* and had to be moved to Mascot one way or another — was to get permission to fly it there. From where, exactly? He favoured clearing the traffic from Macquarie Street in downtown Sydney and using that as a runway, but not surprisingly permission for that was refused, so he came up with another idea.

•

On the equally shining afternoon of 17 July, hundreds of locals had gathered on the north side of Sydney Harbour at Neutral Bay's Anderson Park. Kids, grannies, mums and dads, dogs, everyone from Blind Freddie to Mrs Cafoops to Johnnie Bloggs ... For the word had spread. Smithy was down at that little green corner by the harbour, with one of his flying machines, and he was going to take off!

And sure enough, it was true. Just a short time earlier, a massive crane had lifted this most extraordinary-looking machine — with Smithy's exultant chief engineer, Tommy Pethybridge, sitting on top — onto a barge, from which it was rolled ashore at the southern end of the park. The *excitement* of seeing Smithy himself! Looking just like he did in the newspapers and on the newsreels, a chiselled man in crumpled cloth, he was standing right there, beaming up at his beauty, as the crowd continued to swell around him. Beside him was Bill Taylor, who was going to be his co-pilot for the Centenary Race.

And there was the name he had given the plane, painted in big white letters on the Consolidated blue fuselage: *ANZAC*. An old Digger, who had parked his lorry on Kurraba Road and wandered over, looked up at the name and then said to the famous airman, 'Yer got a good name for 'er Smithy. The Diggers are behind yer, boy.'[42]

Well, they might have been, but the Customs officers most certainly were *not*. As a matter of fact, that name should not have been visible, as it was the Defence Department that declared that calling the plane *ANZAC* represented a gross commercialisation of the sacred name, notwithstanding that Smithy was an Anzac himself and had risked his life on those shores, nor even that the famed Australian racing driver Norman Leslie 'Wizard' Smith named his car 'Anzac' which he drove to set speed records in Australia and New Zealand.

A condition of this small flight to Mascot was that the name be covered with brown paper before he was allowed to take off.

Speaking of which ... there was only a measly 175 yards to do it in. It was the growing crowd's strong view that it surely couldn't be done.

Then the great man stirred. The wind had at last changed to his satisfaction and, climbing in, with Bill Taylor getting into the back cockpit, he cranked the engine and, as people fell back when mysterious whining noises were heard from the front cowling, the huge radial engine suddenly belched smoke and burst into a shattering cacophony of sound. Smithy then taxied the plane up to the northern end of the tiny park.

To get maximum revs up before letting her loose, Smithy kept his feet stamped down hard on the pedals as he brought the engine up to full throttle and then, with the variable propeller pitch set to 'fine' and the flaps a little extended to get maximum grip on the air, he released the brakes.[43] The snarling monoplane leapt forward like an emu stung by a wasp. But this bird had wings ...

As the crowd held its breath, the tail of the Altair lifted first and it was clear that Smithy and his navigator were going to be smashed to pieces on the wall, when at what seemed like the last possible moment, the nose came up and, as people would tell it ever afterwards, the plane cleared the wall by the hairs of Smithy's chinny-chin-chin.

Past Neutral Bay's Hayes Street Wharf it still seemed to be perilously low, but then it soared high and away. Away to the wild blue and beyond-er. Then, and only then, did the crowd — to that point caught mute between horror and awe — let out a mighty cheer that continued until Smithy was just a will-o'-the-wisp beyond the clouds, on his way to Mascot. That marvellous man, in his flying machine.

People walked home. It was a great day.

•

And it proved to be a great aeroplane — the fastest ever seen in Australia. Though the Altair was impounded the instant it landed at Mascot, had its name painted over, and was even immobilised with the removal of the ignition leads to No. 5 and No. 6 cylinders, Smithy — or for this purpose Air Commodore Sir Charles Kingsford Smith, MC, AFC — was not long in bringing his own weight and that of his adoring public to bear on those who would try to *wilfully* prevent him from flying this beauty. On the firm promise that Smithy would soon produce the missing documentation, the Defence Department allowed the Customs Department to release the plane, and the Civil Aviation Branch of the Department of Defence to give him permission to fly it, on a temporary basis, on condition that it not be flown for profit and to undergo rigorous local testing at Richmond air base. That testing completed satisfactorily, all he needed in the short term was a name to replace 'Anzac'. After considering all of *Aurora Australis*, *Spirit of Phar Lap*, *Hargrave's Hope*, *Star of Gallipoli*, *Shipmates*, *Merino*, *Blue Streak*, *Trade Wind* and *Sunny South*, none of which grabbed him for longer than a few minutes, inspiration struck …[44]

'*Lady Southern Cross!*'

As he explained to the press, 'The name *Southern Cross* has always been a lucky one for me. I have prefixed *Lady* as a compliment to my wife.'[45]

And so, the *Lady Southern Cross*, with Smithy and Taylor pushing the plane hard, started to set new records on nearly every long trip they took through August and September, in times that were previously unimaginable. They included:

Sydney–Melbourne — 2 hours, 23 minutes.

Melbourne–Perth — 10 hours, 22 minutes.

Perth–Sydney — 9 hours, 32 minutes.

Sydney–Brisbane — 2 hours, 35 minutes.

The plane was so fast it made the *Southern Cross* herself almost look like she was going backwards.

For example, on the record-breaking trip to Brisbane, Smithy was able to give the *Southern Cross*, piloted by another, four hours start, and still get into Brisbane first. It was some kind of plane, and Smithy was more confident than ever that it was the machine he needed to win the Centenary Race.

There remained one problem, however, as he contemplated the coming race, which was due to start at 6.30 am on 20 October 1934 — now just weeks away — in England. Under the race rules, all competitors had to report in at the Royal Air Force's newly constructed Mildenhall aerodrome in Suffolk, before 6 am, on 14 October 1934 in preparation for taking off six days later. Mildenhall had been chosen for its superb 1400-yard-long by 110-yard-wide airstrip.

Smithy was yet to receive official approval for his plane to enter the competition, as he did not yet have the certification required to prove that it conformed to the ICAN standard. This, despite a blistering array of correspondence between Kingsford Smith, the Australian Controller of Civil Aviation, the Minister for Defence, the Prime Minister's Department, the air race committees in Melbourne and London, Lockheed and the US Department of Commerce. The broad dilemma was that the modifications Smithy had made to the plane had moved it way beyond the 'normal' range for a plane of that type, meaning that it needed all kinds of stress analyses to determine if it could safely carry such an excessive load as 418 gallons of fuel. Lockheed engineers had estimated that this would result in an overload of almost 2000 pounds. Fresh from the factory, the plane could weigh 5400 pounds, whereas Smithy planned to fly with a load of 7300 pounds.

Further, the US Department of Commerce could not certify as airworthy a plane it hadn't inspected, and Lockheed couldn't affirm it was airworthy when they had made their doubts clear to Kingsford Smith from the beginning. And under Australian law it could not be given a Certificate of Airworthiness without an appropriate certification from its country of construction.

For his part, the Controller of Civil Aviation, Edgar Johnston, was stunned at the way things had turned out. What *could* Smithy have been thinking? How could he possibly have so totally ignored written and verbal advice? What was happening now was precisely what both Johnston, *and* Lockheed, *and* the US Department of Commerce had told him would happen, and yet he was acting as if everyone was out to get him!

When it came to judging the safety of the plane, Smithy — and to an even greater extent, his supporters — took rather the reverse view. After all, this was *Air Commodore Sir Charles Kingsford Smith*, for God's sake! He had landed and fought at Gallipoli, survived the Western Front, flown the cross-Continental route to Europe and back, crossed the Pacific, the Tasman, the Atlantic; been feted as a hero in New York City; dined at the White House and held dozens of aviation records and firsts around the world. Surely, *he* was the best one equipped to judge whether his plane was airworthy or not? Surely some deference should have been paid to the fact that there was no more experienced, or accomplished airman in the entire world?

To which, the short answer was that deference *had* been paid, with people on both sides of the Pacific obliged to engage in a mad scramble to try to find a way around the fact that

Kingsford Smith — despite being warned from all sides, both in written and verbal form, that it would be a disaster if he did so — had imported to Australia a potentially lethal aeroplane that had little more certification than a tomato box. And yes, they knew he was probably capable of flying a tomato box if it came to that, but not without bloody certification he couldn't.

Smithy would not back down.

'I am sick of all the delay,' he thundered to the press, 'and the difficulties which are being placed in my path. Why cannot the Australian Government observe the spirit of the law, rather than the letter?'[46]

The deadline for leaving Australia loomed closer. As to a rash of rumours that Smithy didn't actually want to compete in the race at all, the pilot had a firm answer: 'If my critics think that I am frightened, then they can accompany me on the race ...'[47]

Finally, a compromise of sorts was reached. Australia's Department of Civil Aviation agreed to give him a restricted Certificate of Airworthiness, which would enable him to fly to England at least, but he would be constrained to a maximum gross weight of 6700 pounds, which was to say, 394 American gallons of fuel instead of 510 American gallons.

Smithy, finally brought to ground by rules and officialdom, had no choice but to bow and agree to have the wing tanks of the Lockheed sealed. The bottom line was that with the fuel capacity reduced, he would have to make *nine* stops on his way from Mildenhall to Melbourne, instead of just five — all but eliminating his chances of winning the race. But he had to try.

The remaining question was, would the Royal Aero Club in London accept this as sufficient certification to allow him to enter the race? Smithy phoned the club and stated his position, and the RAC promised it would come back to him with their decision. That decision came via a 2.15 am phone call to Smithy's home on 29 September 1934 — he could enter subject to restricting his fuel capacity to 300 gallons — and he and Taylor took off from Mascot less than four hours later.

Before they knew it, they were all the way to Cloncurry — it was still only 2.30 in the afternoon! This sense that they were flying into the future, in a machine that made their past look impossibly slow and old fashioned was heightened when only a short time after landing they were stunned to see heading towards them from out of the dusty skies nothing other than the *Southern Cross* herself! On assignment to take government geologists on a survey of remote parts of the Northern Territory, the old girl was being piloted by Harry Purvis, a Kingsford-Smith Air Services stalwart, who was also a skilled engineer.

'Would you mind checking the engine for me,' Smithy asked him immediately upon landing, 'and giving the airframe a general run over?'

Frankly Harry would. He was exhausted, but as Smithy was, after all, his boss and a fine fellow he reluctantly agreed.[48] Which was just as well, because in no time at all, Purvis was horrified to note a dozen serious cracks around the cowling of the new plane, the conical metal cover that was effectively a bonnet around the aeroplane's extra powerful engine that Smithy had had specially fitted, perhaps producing stronger vibrations than the cowling was designed for. All the cracks stemmed from the rivet holes.

Cloncurry was without the means to have the plane repaired, so Smithy and Taylor had no choice but to return to their starting point. Frustrated beyond measure, Smithy nursed the plane back to Sydney and immediately employed that city's foremost engineering firm, Holder and Stroud, to try to repair it.

When, in fact, it proved beyond repair, the company set about spinning a new cowling from scratch. There was endless to-ing and fro-ing, putting extra people on and working in late shifts, but when all was said and done, it took — as 30 September, 1 October, 2 October, 4 October dribbled by — too long to make the trip feasible.

By now, to get to Mildenhall by the deadline and be in shape to race back he would have to break the Australia to England record just to reach the starting line, supervise a four-day overhaul of the Altair prior to the race start, obtain final clearances, rehearse and organise his ground crews, and procure petrol and oil supplies.[49]

No matter which way Smithy cut it, and he cut it every which way, there was just *no* way he would be able to get to

England in time for the race either in the *Lady Southern Cross* or an alternative plane from America and then get both himself and the plane in shape to win the race. Finally, he was left with no option, and on the morning of 4 October 1934 he was obliged, with a very heavy heart, to cable the race organisers:

> Deeply regret on account of delays and the difficulties of completing the job, that I am unable to participate in the Centenary Air Race. Please accept this as formal withdrawal, coupled with sincerest best wishes for the winner and the safe carrying out of the most spectacular air race in the history of aviation.
>
> C. Kingsford Smith[50]

•

The criticism began. Coward! Cur! Sell-out! Obviously he was pulling out of the race because he was chicken, because he knew his American plane would be beaten by the good ol' British planes.

They had a cracked cowling did they, and so couldn't fly? Diddums. Good thing all the people in the country with cracks in their car and truck bonnets didn't take the same approach, wasn't it? Or the country would dinkum grind to a halt, wouldn't it? Huh? *Huh?* HUH?

He began to receive vicious letters, one even accompanied by a white feather. When the first lot arrived at his office at Mascot, Smithy's face turned ashen with shock.[51] As Smithy noted one more time, 'A nation's hero may become a nation's whipping boy overnight.'

In the middle of the maelstrom, Smithy was particularly pleased to receive a cable from Charles Ulm, then in America: Tell Kingsford Smith, I will obtain a suitable plane in U.S.A. and fly it to London for him.[52]

It was a singularly kind offer from his old mate, whatever their differences had been, but after looking at it closely Smithy had to decline. Time, which he had so often trounced in his many record-breaking flights, had now defeated him.

Well, the hell with the lot of them. On the afternoon of 5 October, Smithy and Bill Taylor were in Smithy's office at Mascot, both of them feeling lower than a snake's bellybutton when Smithy opened the *Times Atlas* to page 102, laid it before Bill, and looked at him meaningfully. It was a map of the Pacific Ocean.[53] They would bloody well fly *that*, is what they would do, and be the first to fly it from west to east. Bill nodded his head, and it was done. They would fly the *Lady Southern Cross*, and Smithy would sell it on arrival to retrieve the money provided by his backers.

This announcement in no way quelled the many attacks on him, and on 13 October 1934, Smithy made a personal reply in a front-page diatribe he penned for — of all papers (given how bitterly it had attacked him during the Coffee Royal affair) — *Smith's Weekly*, aimed squarely at his critics. Entitled 'HIS CARDS ON THE TABLE', and emblazoned across the top of the front page, Smithy got straight to the point: 'I've done some foolish things in connection with the big air race. I admit them. But I'm no squib. I know there are people who say I am. I know there are others who contend that I'm pleased to be out of the race; and others again say I'm wholly and solely to blame for being out … And about this "squibbing" business. Have a look at the map, you "squib" critics! See whether an England–Australia flight — looks, I say — any worse than a flight across the Pacific …

'Well, I'm putting my cards on the table — I'm saying my piece. I'm out of the race. That's a punch in the solar plexus. But, worse is that squib talk. That's hitting below the belt. Anyway, I'd like anyone who says I'm a squib to say so in my hearing. And don't get the idea I'm thinking of legal action.'[54]

Even then, Kingsford Smith was barely clearing his throat, as over the next two thousand words or so, he acknowledged all his mistakes, even as he took aim and shot down the bulk of other charges made against him. He explained the reasons behind choosing an American plane, and noted that many of his critics probably drove American cars, so where the hell did *they* get off?

The damaged cowling? Glad they mentioned it: 'I know there are critics who assert that a small matter like cracks in the cowling would never have held me up if I didn't want to be held up. I know they've been saying that cracks in the bonnet would not hold up a car. Maybe not. If a bit of bonnet comes adrift, it would not sheer away a rear wheel. But if a bit of cowling breaks off — as it certainly threatened to do so on the Altair – it would be immediately whisked into the slipstream and bashed against the tail. If you've got any imagination you may be able to figure out what a piece of metal travelling at anything up to 280 miles per hour could do to a vital part of a plane. I may be a mug, but there are limits to the risks I take …'[55]

It was a bravura performance from Kingsford Smith, a bit of elegant writing mixed with closed-fist thwacks at his most trenchant critics, and acidic little pats on the heads for those who thought they were critics but simply didn't understand — well, now he hoped they did. He finished: 'It is primarily because of my backers that I am tackling the Pacific flight. They are going to be paid. If I pull this off there will be money for them and for me; and I'll certainly be able to sell the Altair in America. Anyway, I've put my cards on the table. I did my best, but the fates were against me. I'm sorry.'[56]

Bravo! Bravo!

Encore! Encore!

•

Almost on the instant, the public mood towards Kingsford Smith changed, so powerful a case had he made. Because, apart from being a superman, it was now obvious he was just like them. He had made mistakes, and was man enough to acknowledge them, and apologise to those people he had let down. From delivering letters accusing him of cowardice, the postman was for the next week getting a hernia carrying fan-mail to him, as the public poured out their belief in him, and their outrage at his critics.[57]

Now all he needed to do was to become the first man across the Pacific flying eastwards, and make the flight a success.

Eighteen
THE GREAT RACE

Throughout his life, Smithy was completely uninterested in business matters. Flying came first. If business considerations made the advancement of flying difficult, then it was always Smithy's contention that business methods should be altered to fit the circumstances ...

JOHN STANNAGE, ONE OF KINGSFORD SMITH'S GREAT FRIENDS, COLLEAGUES AND EARLY BIOGRAPHERS[1]

At three o'clock on the foggy Saturday morning of 20 October 1934, the gigantic steel doors of the hangars at the brand-new Royal Air Force base at Mildenhall in Suffolk, 62 miles north-east of London, were slowly opened, as young RAF cadets hauled on the chains. Within minutes, no fewer than twenty sleek, resplendent aeroplanes were wheeled outside, and in short order had their motors purring as shadowy mechanics, pilots, press, officials and even beautiful women in evening dresses flitted around on the flood-lit field. The greatest air race the world had ever seen was just hours away from beginning. Mildenhall to Melbourne, 11,000 miles, with a £10,000 prize to the winner![2] Particular among those planes were the three purpose-built de Havilland DH.88 Comets with variable pitch propellers that Smithy had long before identified as the main contenders for the prize. One of those Comets, *Black Magic*, was to be piloted by Jim Mollison and his wife Amy Johnson. Another Comet, *Grosvenor House*, was flown by the burly Flight Lieutenant Charles Scott with the dapper chappie Captain Tom Campbell Black as his co-pilot.

The two biggest planes in the gathering were a couple of passenger liners, entered to demonstrate the feasibility of around-the-world travel in comfort, and speed.[3] One was a Boeing 247-D piloted by a former lion-tamer from Mississippi, Roscoe Turner, famous for always wearing a gaudy gold-and-crimson flying helmet, whipcord breeches, Sam Browne belt, blue tunic and black riding boots — and flying most places with his pet lion cub, who answered to the name of 'Gilmore'. He even had a stick made of a lion's tail, and a coat made of the lion that had been attached to it![4] Of him it had been written in *Aero Digest*: 'A pilot with nerve enough to wear that uniform and kick a half-grown lion in the pants is bound to come in first eventually.'[5] (Turner was also the talk of the town for his delightful, if daring, informality when he had been introduced to King George V when His Majesty and Queen Mary had visited all the flyers the day before. His Majesty had offered his hand, and Roscoe had taken it, saying simply, 'Hallo, King.'[6])

The other big aircraft was a KLM Royal Dutch Airlines Douglas DC-2 all-metal monoplane called *Uiver* — 'stork' in Dutch — with Captain Koene Dirk Parmentier in command and Captain Jan Johannes Moll as co-pilot, and it was flying with two further crew members, three paying passengers and a full load of post, weighing over 400 pounds! A feature of this plane, along with the Orions, the Boeing, the Comets and several other entrants, was its amazing retractable undercarriage which, at the heave of a lever, allowed the wheels to be tucked up into the bottom of the engine housings, reducing drag by a significant degree. It was the *coming thing* in aeroplane efficiency.

As dawn approached the planes were lined up on the airstrip, and all was in readiness, including no fewer than 60,000 spectators — among whom were many lords and ladies and a gaily attired Anthony Fokker — and 700 members of the press. On the stroke of 6.30 am, Sir Alfred Bower, the Acting Lord Mayor of London, gave the starting signal by dropping his flag — a small Union Jack — beside Jim and Amy Mollison's *Black Magic*, and they were the first to take to the skies. Exactly two minutes later his flag dropped again, and they were followed by Roscoe Turner in his Boeing 247-D airliner and, in quick succession, the others, as the sun began its own climb into the sky in admiration. Just a short time before seven o'clock, they were all on their way.

As Sir Macpherson Robertson enthusiastically told the listening audience of ABC Melbourne, 'Never in the history of aviation has there been such a line up of aviators and never in the history of the world has there been such an aerial contest.'[7] And certainly never such international interest in a race of any nature, as newspaper accounts around the world gave breathless updates.

•

On the next day in Australia, Charles Kingsford Smith and Bill Taylor were getting ready to make their own enormous trip. In the old days, when he had been younger and fresher, Smithy had approached each pioneering flight with a mixture of overwhelming enthusiasm and energy. But things had changed. Now he was thirty-seven years old, vastly experienced but also more than a little exhausted, and much of his energy and enthusiasm had dissipated to be replaced by a gritted-teeth determination to do what he had to do. Of joy, there was little. Rather, as he later noted of his approach to this first leg of flying to Fiji, Kingsford Smith's primary feeling was a strong sense of boredom that he would have to sit in the pilot's seat for the next twenty hours.

Not so for Bill Taylor. For him it was still a curious, nay, *amazing*, thing to be driven through the streets of Brisbane in the early hours of this Saturday morning, as an entire city slept cosily, totally unaware that just outside their door were two airmen on their way to risk their lives for … for … for what?

Taylor was never quite sure of the answer to that question. He was glad to be with Kingsford Smith on this venture as he liked and admired the man a great deal, but he was not certain what it was that drove either of them to do it. Instead, at times like this, he felt an overpowering sense of isolation and loneliness. In that instant he didn't want to be going to Archerfield, didn't want to be risking his life, didn't want any of it — he would much rather have been at home, tucked up safely in bed. And yet, of course, the feeling passed as the excitement took hold.

When they reached the aerodrome a crowd of several hundred people had gathered, notwithstanding the fact that the sun had not yet risen. They were there to witness the beginning of what they hoped would be one more historic Smithy flight — across the Pacific from west to east! A cheer rose as the flyers alighted from their car, and it was a cheer that doubled an hour or so later, when after more preparations, Smithy started the engine of the *Lady Southern Cross*, which immediately gave out a throaty growl of appreciation. Just before they started to move off towards the end of the runway at around 4 am, a gorgeous young woman rushed out from the crowd and handed a white rose up to Taylor in the rear cockpit.

'Wear it for luck,' she said.

He put it in the lapel of his coat, and thanked her warmly.[8] Absurdly, he felt that as long as it remained there, the engine would keep running.[9]

In the front cockpit everything seemed in order to Smithy. There were no problems with the new cowling, the tanks had been filled to the brim, and the engine ran sweetly at the lower cruise revolutions per minute calculated to deliver the best fuel economy. As to personal luggage, he checked he had packed everything. A comb in his left pocket. A toothbrush in his right pocket. The photo of Nellie Stewart tucked beneath his seat? Yup. He was done.

Oh, actually, one more thing. He also had his wallet, in which, apart from money and a photo of Mary and Charles Jnr, he had kept the white feather so recently received, perhaps as a reminder of what he was about with this trip. This would show them all!

And then they were off, the Lockheed smoothly winging its way over Moreton Bay and towards the heart of the Pacific Ocean, with Suva as the first stop. It was a measure of how far the 1928 trans-Pacific trip had been ahead of its time that, in the six years since Smithy and Ulm had accomplished it with Lyon and Warner, no-one had duplicated the feat, even though the science of aviation had leapt forward in the interim. In 1928, the *Southern Cross* had averaged 100 miles per hour across the water, whereas on this trip, in the sleek and powerful Altair, that speed was up by over 50 per cent, to an average of 155 miles per hour.

Kingsford Smith and Taylor shared the piloting duties, with Taylor sometimes setting his sights on cirrus clouds, hundreds of miles ahead in the distance, which he found helped to ease the strain and monotony of concentrating on the compass alone. Initially Taylor set a course for New Caledonia, just over 900 miles away, which he intended to use as a checkpoint, and their reward was that late that afternoon, off to their port side, they spotted the joyous white line of breakers which told them they had made it. And what a grand pleasure it was to sweep from out of the skies and buzz above the languid water inside the stunningly colourful coral reefs, see open-mouthed villagers waving at them, and then swoop like an avenging angel down the coast towards the capital Nouméa — once spotted, it would give them an exact pinpoint from which they could set off for the next haul to Suva.

Had they remained with their previous 300-gallon limit on petrol tanks, they would have run out about halfway between New Caledonia and Fiji, but fortunately — with the relevant authorities seeming to turn at least half a blind eye — Smithy had been able to have Lawrence Wackett install three extra petrol tanks before departure, taking the capacity right up to 514 gallons.

Still, as it was just starting to get dark, they were beginning to worry. If they didn't spot Fiji soon, they would have only one alternative. They would have to climb above the clouds, get a definite sextant 'fix' on the stars to navigate from, then go back under the clouds and hope they could spot the lights of Suva. It was far from ideal, but it was their only choice. About twenty minutes before dusk, however, Fiji wondrously hove into view and in no time at all, they were swooping in low over Suva's Albert Park, where Smithy had landed the *Southern Cross* six years earlier. This time in the much smaller plane — with the luxury of brakes — he was able to stop her within 150 yards, to once again be engulfed by an enthusiastic crowd. That thing of legend, the *Wanga Vuk*, the bird-ship, had returned!

In the middle of the welcoming ceremony, Smithy looked out on the sea of black faces gazing up at him and spotted a familiar white one — that of young Tommy Pethybridge, who had come on ahead to Fiji by ship to act as an advance party to arrange their fuel and so forth.

'There you are, Tommy,' Smithy called out to him. 'Come up here, you belong up here with us.'[10]

A delighted Tommy scrambled onto the podium, as Smithy introduced him to the many onlookers as 'an invaluable member of our team'. And that he was. And a good man, besides.

That evening, Smithy and Taylor were able to wash, eat and retire to their rooms in the full knowledge that Tommy would work around the clock on the *Lady Southern Cross*, cleaning and checking everything, and ensuring that the plane was in the best possible shape to take off the following day. Before sleep, however, Bill Taylor decided to take in a little night air, from the balcony of his room.

A small distance away, he could see where they had parked the *Lady Southern Cross*. Tommy had covered it in tarpaulins and the lights dancing behind those tarps, throwing jigging shadows, told him that Tommy was still on the job, going through his endless check list of things to be done. It was gorgeous to be there, if slightly amazing to have so quickly hopped from one entirely different world to another, and Bill could go to sleep with the satisfaction that everything pointed to a good start on the morrow.

Alas, when they awoke at dawn it was to the knowledge that they were in the middle of a severe tropical storm — as the windows clattered, the hallways whistled and a river ran off the roof — and while it was one thing to find themselves in the thick of a storm while in the air, and obliged to battle through, it was quite another to take off in one, and there was no doubt they would not be able to leave on that day.

•

And there they were! Just after 3.35 pm on the afternoon of Tuesday, 23 October 1934, the Comet *Grosvenor House*, flown by Flight Lieutenant Charles Scott and Captain Tom Campbell Black, approached Flemington Racecourse in Melbourne after a higgledy-piggledy, helter-skelter journey that had them crossing three continents, sixteen countries and countless deserts, mountains and jungles. In Scott's later words, 'It was a terrible trip, and that is praising it.'[11]

Throwing caution to the four winds, Scott and Black gingerly opened up the Comet's lame port engine as they dipped and swept for the finishing line 'at a height not exceeding 200 feet'.[12] At full noise, the blood-red racer flashed around the two circuits required by the rules, to the adulation of over 50,000 people cheering themselves hoarse and waving — the men throwing their hats and women their handbags into the air — all in the Melbourne drizzle. The pilots, clamped in their Plexiglas cockpit and barely awake, were only dimly aware, if at all, of their reception, and headed off to land at Laverton RAAF base, 14 miles west.[13] The most amazing thing of all was their time: seventy-one hours, one minute and three seconds — just under three days — completely blowing away the record of six days, seventeen hours and fifty-six minutes, which had been set by Charles Ulm only the year before. (And they had arrived in Darwin in an even more stunning time, as witness the headlines across the country: 'TO AUSTRALIA IN 2 DAYS, 4 HOURS, 38 MINUTES'; 'AIRMEN SET UP AMAZING RECORD!')[14] Their times beggared belief. England to Australia, in little more than a weekend …

This, then, was the surest proof of the rate at which aviation was advancing. Just five years earlier, Australia and much of the world had been agog when Bert Hinkler had winged his way from London to Darwin in sixteen days, and now an even greater distance, from Mildenhall to Melbourne, had been done in one-fifth of the time — in a machine with an enclosed cockpit, powered by twin 225-horsepower Gipsy Six R engines.

(And a sign of how public expectations had changed, in the wake of Scott and Black's time, was the flurry of criticism that now came down on Qantas Empire Airways for their absurdly long schedule to get from London to Brisbane. Twelve days? *Twelve* days? When Scott and Black could do it in three? And a Dutch airliner in just under four, including an emergency landing in a storm that cost it ten hours? 'This achievement,' the *Bulletin* magazine sniped, 'has made the Commonwealth's twelve day schedule look ridiculous, and even the bureaucracy admits that something will have to be done about it.'[15])

In fact, however, it had been a close-run thing. When the two Britons had arrived in Darwin, it had been with the left engine shut down after its oil pressure had dropped alarmingly over the Timor Sea. No matter the potentially lame engine, they were being pressed hard by the Dutch airliner *Uiver,* and all Scott wanted was two beers for himself, some fuel for his plane, the oil filters cleaned and they were on their way again! By comparison, *Uiver,* when it landed several hours later, was in fine fettle, and the crew and passengers all seemingly well rested.

By the time *Grosvenor House* made it to Charleville, its lead over *Uiver* had been further cut, and it was down to the one good engine once more. Again, however, Scott and Campbell Black took off, against all common sense and regard for self-preservation, and the reward for the Britons had been their breathtaking victory.

After landing at Laverton, the two were then flown back to Flemington in a DH.80A Puss Moth, where they were presented to the cheering crowd as they were driven around the course in a motorcar.

In his welcoming speech Melbourne's Lord Mayor Sir Harold Gengoult Smith said rather pointedly, 'You have thrilled the world, and earned the admiration and gratitude of the British Empire. You have won the greatest race in history … It is with intense pride that we remember you flew in a British race and in a British machine.'[16]

Which was, surely, one in the eye for Kingsford Smith, who had wanted to do it in an extremely unpatriotic American plane.

As to the completely exhausted Charles Scott, however, he was beyond caring what nationality of plane he had flown in. As he climbed wearily out of the Comet at Laverton, he was heard to say to Campbell Black, 'I never want to see that red bastard again.'[17]

The next question at Flemington though, was, where was *Uiver*? Some of the crowd at the racecourse waited expectantly on into the night, hoping the plane might soon appear. But 9 pm … 10 pm … 11 pm … and midnight passed … still *nothing.* A pall of black gloom hung over the airfield. No-one wanted to say it, but everyone feared the worst.

Where could she be? It was a dark and stormy night …

With the cracking of lightning as the only thing to pierce the gloom above Albury, on the New South Wales–Victoria border, residents were woken in their beds just after midnight by the sound of a plane rumbling low overhead with a pained, throaty growl. Back and forth, round and around. It sounded like a plane in trouble. Could it be?

A phone call to Melbourne established that the KLM *Uiver* had not yet arrived, and also that for some reason, probably by virtue of a lightning strike, its radio appeared to have been knocked out. Without the radio to help with the navigation, and in the middle of a storm, they must have become lost. So that must be them!

Things moved quickly from there. At 2CO there was movement at the station, as local ABC radio announcer, Arthur Newnham, left his home and rushed like a mad thing to the broadcasting studio, where he broke into regular programming on relay from 3AR Melbourne and made an appeal for everyone who could to head to the racecourse, so that, between all of their car headlights they would be able to illuminate a makeshift runway for the stricken craft.[18] Meanwhile, notwithstanding the terrible weather and flooding rain, Albury electrical engineer Lyle Ferris dashed down to Albury's electrical supply in South Albury, where he got a telegraphist, a bloke he knew as Turner, to pull a master switch to turn the town's lights on and off in a fashion to spell out in Morse code: A … L … B … U … R … Y.

Genius.

Suddenly the quiet streets of Albury became very busy. Phones rang, doors were knocked on, and hundreds of cars were soon on their way to the racecourse. Much of the drama was broadcast not just around Australia on relay from 2CO, where Arthur Newnham and colleagues were giving a blow-by-blow description of events, but also — by the wonders of modern radio technology — all the way to Holland, where it was late afternoon and regular updates from Australia meant that the Dutch people could closely follow the fortunes of some of their own on the other side of the planet.

In the DC-2 *Uiver* meanwhile, Captain Parmentier had been at his wits' end to know quite what to do, other than to momentarily leave the controls in the hands of his co-pilot while he conducted a small religious service for the crew and passengers — though this was more to keep morale up, rather than the genuine expectation that the Lord might get them down on a wing and a prayer. Knowing that their only hope was to stay near civilisation, he had continued to circle the town, when at last he spotted a 'blazing crescent' of headlights at the eastern end of the town.

An airstrip! The wonderful people of Albury had turned a light on for them, and at exactly the right spot. Coming in low for a quick look-see, the Dutch air captain turned and made his approach for a landing from the north-east. It was 1.15 am on the morning of 24 October 1934.

The people, huddled in their cars, watched closely as this visitor arriving from another world, all bellowing big radial engines and twinkling landing lights — a bloody *massive* thing I'm telling you — suddenly filled their windscreens, descended and landed safely on the sodden soil.

Waiter! More tea! And blankets! And pumpkin scones and beds in local hotels for our new friends![19]

And a wonderful night was had by all …

•

The following morning the Alburians turned out in force and with 120 people divided between two ropes, all hauling together — and heave, and *heave*, and *HEAAAVE* — managed to pull the plane out of the mud and get it on its way. Despite the delay, the *Uiver* still managed to finish second overall, and win the handicap section. No, on this occasion the passenger airliner had not surpassed the two-pilot screamers as the King of the Skies, but its finishing position of close second was the surest indication that that era was about to begin — the more so when Roscoe Turner's Boeing landed just two hours behind *Uiver*. Roscoe had himself had a 'helluva trip', seeing things that he had not known previously existed on heaven or earth, chief among which were the beautiful bare-breasted women in sarongs he had spied when passing through Bali. Once all the fussing was over, he declared, he wanted to return to Bali, to 'buy me an acre o' tits, and walk on 'em barefoot!'[20]

A good sport, he was also noted for being quick to congratulate the victors.

'Mr Scott,' he boomed, 'I certainly do congratulate you. It sure was an honour to breathe the fumes from your exhaust …'[21]

As to Jim and Amy Mollison, they had been forced to retire at Allahabad, in India, after having terrible engine trouble. The chief engineer there was amazed to find three empty whisky bottles in Jim Mollison's cockpit.

Overall, of the twenty competitors who began the race, seven finished within the sixteen-day time limit, and another two afterwards.

A few days after the first celebrations had begun to die down, *Uiver*, while on its way back to Europe, again swooped low over Albury racecourse and dropped a package. In it was a cigarette case attached to a Dutch flag on which was written a message: '*To all our good friends in Albury, we salute you and say farewell.*'[22]

Queen Wilhelmina of the Netherlands shortly afterwards awarded to the Mayor of Albury, Alf Waugh, the Order of the Orange Nassau, and sent personal gifts to particular people who had gone out of their way to help those in the plane. For its part, KLM made a handsome donation to Albury District Hospital of 1000 guilders, the equivalent of £180.[23]

Amsterdam's main newspaper, the *Telegraaf*, ran many letters of praise to the editor, including one who waxed particularly lyrical about 'the unknown Australians who gathered in cars at Albury, despite terrible weather, at dead of night. Thanks to you, we walk the streets today with smiling faces. Here's to world comradeship and to the Australians!'[24]

•

Still in Fiji, Kingsford Smith was asked by the *Fiji Times* for his view on the result of the Centenary Race and he did his very best to be gracious … nearly pulling it off.

'It was a stout showing on Scott's part,' he told the journalist. 'I am very glad to see it. I have a shade more horsepower and would probably have bettered his time, but I was handicapped by the petrol loading they allowed me. I am disgruntled. It was stated that with a load, owing to its undercarriage, the Comet was able to get under way very fast, but I myself can get off very fast with a big load of petrol.'[25]

Famous last words?

As it happened, that was not always the way with the Altair. After Tommy Pethybridge had finished repair work on its wings and fitted new spark plugs, and a local weather phenomenon — the *thangi walu*, or eight-day wind, with its low cloud and rain — had abated enough, Smithy and Taylor were able to take off from the sodden Albert Park to re-position at Naselai Beach for departure on the afternoon of 24 October, with full fuel tanks.[26] With the *thangi walu* still strong, it was always going to be a close-run thing …

At two o'clock they commenced their take-off run on the narrow, curving strip of beach, its width reduced by the windblown waves of the rising tide. Alas, a sudden gust gripped the Altair, causing it to swing uncontrollably at 60 miles per hour into the surf, engulfing the wheels. Only Smithy's instant and instinctive airmanship saved the aircraft from certain catastrophe. The motor, now at full bore, drove streams of water from the propeller over the entire plane, while the wheels threatened to sink into the softening sand.

Lady Southern Cross shook herself clear of the rising tide, like a big, angry, wet blue cattle dog; Smithy using judicious bursts of throttle to help pull her above the high watermark. Taylor could only pray and marvel at his skill. Finally, the plane shuddered to a halt and they could assess the damage.

For a further four days the crew luxuriated in Fijian hospitality, staying on board the government's vessel HMCS *Pioneer* in Suva, per courtesy of the genial Captain Mullins, for three nights and then with islanders on the final two evenings. At last the weather cleared with only some scattered cumulus dotting the sky and nary a sign of the high cirrus clouds which portend deteriorating conditions aloft. At 6.08 am, Fiji time, on

29 October, Smithy opened up the Altair's Wasp engine — this time with no dramas — and the take-off was both very fast and flawless, as they tore away to the eastern skies.

At 2.30 pm they spotted the Phoenix group of islands which had so frustratingly escaped Smithy on his previous trip across the Pacific — the sign they were looking for that they were on course. All well and good, and it was a time for quiet reflection. 'As we roared across the placid ocean I could not help reflecting how different were the circumstances on this occasion. Then, I had had three companions; now, only one; then I had three engines; now, only one; then I was flying in triumph to my native land; now, I was flying from it.'[27]

It was not long, however, before there would be no more time for quiet reflection …

About twelve hours out from Fiji, just after evening fell, they hit a wild tropical storm. Smithy tried to get above it, but at 15,000 feet, it was as fierce as ever and the rain was hitting their windscreen like bullets from a machine gun. Once again flying blind, as sudden gusts of wind battered them from every angle, Smithy was himself being hurled around in the cockpit. With his brain feeling foggy at this altitude due to lack of oxygen, he kept turning the landing lights on and off, anxiously checking that the driving rain had not damaged the fabric cover of the leading edge of the Altair's wooden wings, when he saw something that froze his heart. The airspeed indicator had fallen from 130 miles per hour to just 90 miles per hour, and the plane had turned sluggish, like it was suddenly flying through honey. Then the airspeed indicator suddenly snapped to zero and the Altair's left wing dropped. The blind-flying instruments showed a steep bank to the left and *stayed* there, meaning they were in a spin![28]

At other times Smithy might have been tempted to think that it was a problem with the instruments and not the plane. But in an instant there was no doubt that they really were in terrible trouble, as he heard the deathly, familiar *whoosh-whoosh* sound of the wings whirling round and round through the airstream. Two decades earlier he had been in a similar situation after being hit by a Hun in France, but then he had been able to pull out of the wild spinning by pushing forward on the stick, in the method pioneered by Harry Hawker. Now, bracing himself against the seat, he pushed the Altair's stick with everything he had in him, as he jammed both feet onto the right-side rudder-pedal, but still the *Lady Southern Cross* kept plummeting seawards, entirely out of control. He cut the engine, causing the plane's klaxon horn — wired to sound the alarm if the engine's revs fell below a certain level when the undercarriage was not extended — to start wailing its warning of impending peril: *aah ooo gah, aah ooo gah*.

Nothing worked.

Was this, indeed, the end?

Even in the extremity of the situation, however, one thing gave Smithy solace. It was that behind him, Bill Taylor sat quietly, knowing that they were in real trouble and equally that the only person who could get them out of it was Smithy and, therefore, panic on his part would not be helpful. To Smithy's mind, Bill's silence was his way of saying, 'Look mate, you're in charge, and I know you can get us out of this bloody mess'.[29]

And finally, when Bill did speak, it was in a voice of calm, even as they continued hurtling downwards.

'What's wrong?' he asked through the speaking tube.

'I don't know. She won't give any more power, that's all.'

Smithy tried with everything he had in him, ramming hard on the opposite rudder — as in the side of the rudder opposite to the way they were spinning, which in this case was left — and shoving the stick forward. Still nothing.

Hurtling … hurtling … hurtling … and spinning all the way. Smithy continued to try everything he could think of.

'I'm sorry, Bill,' he finally said quietly, 'but I can't get her out.'[30]

In the back, Bill Taylor was amazed at Smithy's calm and his courtesy, even in the extremes of their situation. He was apologising for their coming death, and the fact that he couldn't find the solution to whatever the problem was.

As to Bill Taylor's own equanimity in the face of death, he was in fact so controlled he had time to reflect on it. He felt no horror at his impending departure from life on earth, nor sadness that he would be separated from his loved ones. 'It simply seemed,' he thought, that he and Smithy 'had flown out from the earth and a dawning of real consciousness was near, a consciousness which seemed to bring light on all things, which held some happy revelation to the mystery of life and which seemed the most natural sequence of events.'[31]

Still, he was at least concerned enough to ask Smithy: 'Do you mind if I have a go at her?'[32]

'Yes, go ahead,' Smithy replied calmly, as he felt Bill's inputs on the stick and rudder pedals.

And Bill Taylor really tried. He pushed the stick fully forward and jammed his foot on the opposite rudder to the direction of the spin, but with absolutely no effect. Smithy took over the controls and still the altimeter showed that their altitude continued to fall, now below 6000 feet …

And then, an instant later, just when it seemed as if everything was lost and they would crash into the sea, he heard Smithy say calmly, 'I've got it'.[33] And so he had.

The plane stopped spinning and entered a controllable dive, from which Smithy was able to slowly pull out of to level off and, even though they were still flying through honey, the immediate crisis had been averted. They now probably had as long as twenty minutes to live instead of just a couple, which seemed like sheer bliss at the time. Somehow, by heaving everything every which way, Smithy had managed to pull her out of the spin, but he still had not found the cause of the problem.[34]

As it turned out, however, in just a few minutes everything slowly returned to normal and Smithy explained what had happened. Just as, a couple of years before, Charles Ulm had inadvertently bumped an engine magneto switch that had nearly sent them into the Tasman Sea, on this occasion he had, instead of flicking the landing light switch, mistakenly flipped the switch to the landing flaps!

Once he realised the mistake, he raised the flaps, which eliminated their drag and everything had slowly returned to normal. They flew on through the now smooth night air and at daybreak the following morning began scanning the horizon for a sign of Hawaii.

Just after eight o'clock, Taylor heard Smithy say nonchalantly through his earphones, 'Land ahead', for all the world as if he had expected nothing less. Taylor, whose navigational skills had got them to this pinprick in the Pacific, was not so blasé about it, and felt an enormous surge of pride — the more so when Smithy briefly veered to starboard to show his co-pilot in the second cockpit a view of that wonderful mass of coral, sand and swaying palm trees. Success!

Much as had happened on the previous occasion when Smithy had been there, a formation of US Army Air Corps planes soon came out to greet and guide them first over Pearl Harbor and then onto the green, green grass of Wheeler Field. Upon landing they were engulfed by 5000 wildly cheering people as welcoming speeches were made. If there was a difference this time, it was that Smithy had to sign a series of US Customs forms, as they were the first foreign-registered plane to land there — just as Blériot had been obliged to do in 1909 when he had landed at Dover.

Afterwards Kingsford Smith and Taylor were put in a gigantic motorcar and taken by blaring police escort back to the grand Royal Hawaiian Hotel where Smithy had stayed six years earlier, and he was even given the same room, which he promptly dubbed for the press 'my lucky room'.[35] And indeed, extraordinarily lucky he had been. And not just because he had escaped calamity after the wing flaps had been inadvertently extended mid-flight.

The following day, when Smithy took the officer in charge of maintenance, Major Wright, for a test flight, they hadn't been aloft for more than a few minutes when the engine cut out … for want of petrol![36] In extremis, Smithy was able to glide the *Lady Southern Cross* back to Wheeler Field and disaster was averted, and then the mechanical investigations began. A leak was discovered in the gravity tank in the fuselage, but then the engineers of the US Army Air Corps subsequently found a crack in the oil tank. And then, in getting access to the oil tank they found the most horrifying thing of all: a protruding rivet head had been chafing on the main aluminium fuel tank so badly that the metal was paper thin and had almost broken through. Had the tank been penetrated on the way to Honolulu, or after leaving it, the entire fuselage would have been sloshing with petrol, and the best case would have been the motor simply cutting out.

Although the repair necessitated separating the Altair's fuselage from the one-piece wing, the engineers fixed all the problems and, to Smithy's infinite relief, told him that the work was free. (Either the USAAC were particularly kind, or they sensed that the payment of blood from Smithy's stone wouldn't do them any good anyway.)

After departing four days later, the fifteen-hour trip from Honolulu was without major incident. Passing over what, in 1928 had once been the empty opening to San Francisco Bay but was now the massive Golden Gate Bridge, they arrived at Oakland across the bay on 4 November 1934, at 7.40 am, fourteen days after departure from Brisbane, to a great welcome with swarms of press and people, judged by the *Washington Post* to be 20,000 strong.

And there he is now! After the plane taxied to a halt in front of a specially erected spectator stand, the canopy of the cockpit was rolled back and a grinning Smithy, his face grease-smudged, poked his head out.

'My kingdom for a cigarette, a bath and something to eat,' he laughed, as from the gathered crowd many hands reached up, proffering whole packets. 'I am sorry to be so early, but you will have to blame my navigator Captain Taylor.'[37]

Amid laughter, cheers and wild celebrations, the airmen descended from the plane and the throng rushed forward. In the maelstrom, Smithy heard his name being called urgently and looked across to see a much older-looking Harry Lyon and Jim Warner waving at him, but they were soon lost in the crush.[38]

For his part, Bill Taylor noticed that he still had in his lapel the flower which the beautiful woman in Brisbane had given him. For no good reason, he picked a small boy out of the crowd and gave it to him — special delivery, sonny Jim, all the way from Australia!

The American press, generally, was delighted with their safe arrival, with the *New York Times* opining in a leading article:

'Sir Charles Kingsford Smith has so many firsts to his credit that no poet could ever repeat the mistake of Keats in allowing "Stout Cortez", to stare first upon the Pacific. The name Kingsford Smith will always be first for the Pacific whenever flying records are later made in crossing it …'[39]

From Washington, Senator William Gibbs McAdoo, the President of the United States National Aeronautic Association, released a statement saying, 'Sir Charles Kingsford Smith deserves the title of the greatest of all annihilators of space since time began.'[40]

They also received telegrams of congratulations from, among others, Hitler, Mussolini and Lord Bledisloe, the Governor-General of New Zealand — though, oddly enough, nothing from King George V. Perhaps it was that with the glory of the Centenary Air Race just completed, Smithy's feat was not regarded by either the British or Australian public with quite the fervour that it otherwise would have been. Still, for the moment at least, Smithy was riding high enough again in the public eye that he was able to use his sudden resurgence of celebrity for a good cause.

'The flight will pave the way for transpacific air traffic between the United States and Australia,' he declared to the American press time and again. 'This flight convinces me that a transpacific air service will be a realisation in the not distant future.'[41]

And, of course, he knew just the person to establish it. Him …

It was a familiar song, well sung. And yet for all Smithy's enthusiasm, he remained exhausted, shocked and even depressed over his and Taylor's near death on the Suva to Honolulu leg, and the way things had turned out in general. How long could these near misses go on before disaster really did strike? Was he a madman to continue taking these risks? What about Mary? Didn't she deserve to have a life free of continual worry over whether her husband was going to return home to her and their child? Didn't Charles Arthur deserve to grow up with a father? The doubts gnawed at him from the inside, making him anxious and nervy.

Harold had been shocked at the state of Chilla after his youngest brother landed, and had done what he could to care for him, though no solution beckoned. For some unaccountable reason his brother had left for Los Angeles in the early afternoon on the same day of his arrival, telling his brother he had 'urgent business' to attend to. But what that business was, there was no sign. As Smithy's newly appointed business manager John Stannage soon found out, it was obvious that none of the usual money-making ventures after a pioneering flight — delivering lectures, endorsing products, writing articles — were to be a goer this time, because he could barely get Smithy to leave his Los Angeles hotel room.[42] And though John Stannage tried to keep it out of the press, in the end it was not possible with the United Press Association releasing a story over the wires on 17 November 1934 entitled 'KINGSFORD SMITH HARASSED. DETERMINED TO REST'.

'Sir Charles Kingsford Smith, harassed by autograph hunters and multitudes of admirers since he landed a fortnight ago, today locked himself in his hotel suite and sent out word by his manager, Mr J.S.W. Stannage, that his nerves were ragged and he was determined to get some rest. "Sir Charles must have rest and quiet," said Mr Stannage. "If need be I'll take him away to some remote spot in the hills. He has been pestered no end and he's tired of it all" ...'[43]

What, precisely, was wrong, beyond the minor irritation of autograph hunters?

Again, the answer was unclear. But the symptoms were readily apparent: exhaustion, depression, anxiety over anything and everything, an inability to function as he had.[44] They could only hope that with rest, he would pull out of it and come good.

Something that didn't help was the pressing need to find a buyer for the plane, and the difficulties encountered in doing so. One complication was when, the day after his arrival, the plane was seized by a deputy marshal in Los Angeles on behalf of an irate American businessman by the name of Tom Catton who had had an attachment order served until such times as he was paid US$2750 he claimed he was owed for services and goods he had rendered for Smithy and Ulm's 1928 trans-Pacific venture.[45] Smithy told the press that the claim was 'absurd, preposterous and ridiculous',[46] but ended up paying at least enough of the money that the matter was settled out of court and the plane released. And yet, it was proving very difficult to find a buyer for a plane which was perfect to use if you wanted to attempt a record to cross the Pacific or the Atlantic, but was not necessarily good for much else without major modification.

Tragically, something was about to occur that would perfectly highlight the dangers of Smithy's calling, even in an age when aviation had taken a quantum leap forward from its rustic beginnings ...

•

On the afternoon of Monday, 3 December 1934, Charles Ulm, farewelled by his dear friend and fellow famous aviator, Amelia Earhart, as well as a crowd of about 300 spectators, took off in his British-built Airspeed Envoy *Stella Australis* from Oakland airport in California.[47] He was attempting to repeat his feat with Smithy of six years before and fly across the Pacific Ocean, hoping to demonstrate that, with modern aircraft, his new company Great Pacific Airways — which admittedly existed more on paper than anywhere else — had reduced the hazard of over-water flying to nothing and would be capable of mounting a regular cross-Pacific service.[48] Well, he thought it was modern anyway. Behind him at Oakland airport, the aircraft mechanics had been distinctly underwhelmed — on the reckoning the plane was all wood and fabric, such as they had not worked on for years, instead of all metal, which was the way truly modern aircraft were constructed. They quietly worried for the safety of Ulm and his crew, going on such a journey in such a *crate*.[49] Another man feeling anxious was radio technician Jack Kaufman, who had begged Ulm to take a hand generator with him, so that if they came down they could still get a signal over their radio.

'I don't intend getting my feet wet,' Ulm had laughed lightly in reply, and it was for the same reason there was no life raft or life preservers on board.[50] She'll be right, mate.

At the controls of the plane, Ulm had a wealthy young Australian flying instructor, George Littlejohn, and a man by the name of J. Leon Skilling as both navigator and wireless officer. Initially the *Stella Australis* benefited from singularly good weather, and Skilling sent out a series of cheery messages to the many listeners following the voyage on their radio.

> `6:30 p.m. Engine fine, weather perfect, starting lunch. Don't expect to get wet feet, flew low as [steamer] Lurline displayed searchlights.`[51]

> `8:30 p.m. Everything is OK.`[52]

> `11:45 p.m. All's well, still making one hundred and thirty mph. We are out about eleven hundred miles. Weather clear, radio in constant touch with ships and shore.`[53]

At 2.41 am, however — some eleven hours after leaving — the tone of the messages changed, when Skilling sent out a message advising that they were in the middle of a storm and had gone to 12,000 feet to try to get above it, with no luck. From that point the messages became ever more downbeat, and then desperate as they continued to fire off requests for detailed weather reports to be transmitted to them and, more particularly, for radio beacons to be turned on, because they simply couldn't hear any.

> `3:30 a.m. We have very little gasoline left.`

> `4:00 a.m. Ulm: I don't know whether I am north or south of the islands.`[54]

It was soon clear that *Stella Australis* and her crew were in mortal peril.

> `5 a.m. Lost. We are running short of gas, unable to pick up radio. May be forced to send SOS in a few minutes, unless sight land.`[55]

```
5:03 a.m. SOS.

5:08 a.m. Going down into the sea. Plane
will float for two days.

5:13 a.m. SOS SOS SOS.

5:24 a.m. We are turning into the wind.
Come pick us up. We are turning into the
wind … Come and pick us up. The plane
will float for two days.

5:30 a.m. On water now. SOS.[56]
```

From then, the radio of *Stella Australis* transmitted six minutes solid of the SOS signal, and then there was nothing.[57] All but immediately, the US Navy base at Honolulu — which, on the basis of the previous alarming messages, already had two ships on watch for the flyers — swung into action. The United States Army Air Corps was seconded to put all available planes into the air — some seventeen of them — searching in a 350-mile radius of Honolulu. For its part, the US Navy put everything from patrol boats to destroyers to submarines to sea — twenty-three in all — and all merchant and passenger ships in the area were also requested to join in.

In Hollywood, Kingsford Smith and John Stannage were having lunch at Fox Studios with the actor and famous syndicated newspaper columnist Will Rogers. They had been delighted when, nearing the end of the lunch, the tiny Shirley Temple had rushed up to Will Rogers, saying, 'Take me for another ride on that little pony, Uncle Will.'[58] Introduced, they found this girl, the world's most famous child, to be charming and completely unspoiled, rather like she appeared in the movies. And then one of the Fox executives came and told them the devastating news. Ulm and his crew had gone missing, after sending out distress signals.

An ashen-faced Smithy immediately abandoned the lunch. 'Let's go,' he said to Stannage.[59] The two went straight back to their room at Los Angeles's Roosevelt Hotel and for the next five or six hours worked their contacts to try to learn as much information as they could about the last fixed position of the *Stella Australis* — where it had likely gone down, and precisely what was being done to find them. In the end, Smithy couldn't stand it any longer, and gave Stannage the order: 'Get the plane ready.'[60] They were going to search for Ulm.

Surely Smithy couldn't be serious? Surely he understood that it would be *madness* to simply jump in a plane and head to Honolulu unprepared? (That was, after all, precisely what had led Keith Anderson and Bobby Hitchcock to their deaths, when they had gone looking for the *Southern Cross* four years earlier.)

But no, Smithy was dead set upon it, and no amount of protestations from Stannage or his brother Harold — nor even a teary phone call from Mary in Sydney, begging him not to go — could dissuade him.

All right then, Smithy, what about at least a farewell drink? Smithy agreed, but before he could drink it, Smithy's friend Bud Morriss managed to slip a very powerful sedative into it, which knocked the half-crazed airman out for the next twenty-four hours, by which point some of his rationality had returned.[61] By the time he was properly back on his feet, the *Los Angeles Times* was running a story on its front page with the ominous headline, 'FLYERS DEAD, SAY EXPERTS IN SEA HUNT'. The article detailed how, 'despite the largest rescue force ever pressed into action, forty-eight hours now having passed since they went missing and the chances are probable that Ulm and his companions have perished'.[62]

•

In Sydney meanwhile, and refusing to believe any such thing, Charles Ulm's second wife, Josephine, kept up a teary vigil, supported by family and friends, as she desperately waited for news. Day by day the newspapers delivered ever more grim reports, focusing on the news that there really was no news. *Nothing*.

Despite the massive search with planes and ships combing and re-combing the area where the plane was thought to have disappeared, there was not the tiniest sign. After a week the American authorities were left with no choice but to regretfully call off the search. While appreciating the efforts of the United States, the grief-stricken Mrs Ulm refused to give up hope and clung to the belief that her husband *must* still be alive — just as Harry Hawker's wife Muriel had done a decade and a half earlier when it appeared that Harry had been lost in the Atlantic.

The only way that could be so would be if Ulm and his crew had landed somewhere on the chain of tiny islands which extend for 1200 miles from Honolulu in the south to Midway Island in the far north. So it was that, via the good offices of the British consul in Honolulu, she was able to charter a cutter by the name of *Lanikai* to keep searching along that chain.

Still nothing. Stone cold motherless nothing.

As to thirteen-year-old John Ulm, he found that wherever he went people were suddenly going out of their way to offer their deepest condolences on the tragic death of his father. They would cross the road to embrace him, to mutter their grief, people whom he'd never even met before. He really felt very important.

A cruel juxtaposition to the tragedy — as if marking the final triumph of successful passenger airlines over the pioneers who had blazed the path — was that just six days after Ulm's death, the first Qantas Empire Airways link between England and Australia was successfully inaugurated (albeit with older planes following a terrible accident as one of the new planes was being delivered), after being officially launched in Brisbane by Prime Minister Joseph Lyons and His Royal Highness Prince Henry, Duke of Gloucester. That first regular airmail, carrying precisely 1267 pounds and 4¾ ounces of letters and packages to England, where it arrived just fourteen days later, was the beginning of a new era.[63]

•

Struggling to find a role in this new aviation world that was developing all around him, Smithy remained devastated by Ulm's death — Stannage would later write that he 'cracked up'[64] —

and wrestled with the problem of what could have gone wrong. He wrote to the Controller of Civil Aviation, Edgar Johnston, 'It is impossible, from the scarcity of information available to form any very definite opinion of how it all happened, but it looks as though they were somewhat uncertain of their position throughout the flight, and were relying on picking up the wireless beam at Honolulu. Whether their uncertainty of position was due to bad weather conditions or to laxity or inefficiency in navigation I do not know, but it seems almost inconceivable that with Charles in charge the latter could be the cause.'[65]

It didn't make sense that Charles Ulm would have been anything other than totally assiduous in his preparations and selection of his crew, but against that, Smithy knew better than most just how many things *could* have gone wrong.

As a matter of fact, as he knew only too well, that even safely on the ground things could go wrong. A case in point was that, despite all his plans, he could not sell his Lockheed in America for love nor money, and was eventually obliged to leave it in a hangar at Burbank and return home via ship, leaving San Francisco on the SS *Monterey* on 28 January 1935. Such was his reduced state at this time, that at Smithy's insistence, Mary had to cross the Pacific from Sydney to come and get him to accompany him home.

As to where his energies should be concentrated now, once again the answer was not obvious. While in America he had fielded another offer from Anthony Fokker to join his company as part consultant and part roving ambassador. Though flattered, he had declined. For better or worse, for richer or poorer, he loved his life in Australia and wanted to remain there, as did Mary. Apart from everything else, it was where they wanted to raise their son, now a bonny two-year-old with blond curls, rather like his baby photos showed Chilla to have been at the same age.

Once his strength had partially returned he was able to do a little barnstorming, but the situation was far from satisfactory, and there were many people who thought that a well-paid role should be found for the great man. One who felt like this was Bill Taylor. He wrote that it was a sad situation when 'the world's greatest airman has to live a hand-to-mouth existence by giving people joyrides in *Southern Cross* when, in fact, his achievements were such that they should have been bringing him the rewards of Government sponsorship and other encouragements'.[66]

But there was none.

•

It was a time when aviation companies came and aviation companies went. Within just a few weeks of Smithy arriving home from America in early 1935, Kingsford-Smith Air Services Ltd — *going, going, gone!* — was sold to rival Eastern Air Transport, which was planning to extend air services into rural New South Wales. Throughout his company's brief life span it never achieved great heights, and in fact could often be found rumbling low between the craggy walls of the Valley of Death. It had never made any big money, even at the best of times, and Smithy no longer had the energy or interest to run it. Besides which, selling it would free up some much-needed capital to play the last card he had in his business deck …

Yes, he had had his troubles in Australia and Great Britain and America, but never in New Zealand. There, his welcome had been unwavering. There, they had listened to his proposals. There, he was taken seriously as both an aviator *and* as a businessman. So it was there that he hoped to finally organise, and get up and running, a twice-weekly trans-Tasman air service between Sydney and New Plymouth, backed by the weight of the New Zealand government. With that in mind, Smithy, Bill Taylor and Beau Sheil — who had left Vacuum Oil and practically become Smithy's manager — firmed up plans to form the Trans-Tasman Air Service Development Company Ltd, with the idea of getting a service up and running by early 1936.

The response was lukewarm at best. The Australian government evinced almost no interest, and although Smithy was received by the New Zealand cabinet when he ducked across the Tasman on a quick visit by ship, it was obvious that they, too, felt that as the most far-flung outpost of the British Empire, they were almost obliged to use that Empire's leading air company, Imperial Airways, for such an important leg. Broadly, while Smithy was most certainly the man they wanted to have a drink with, and tell their wives they had met, he wasn't necessarily the one they would choose to run a serious aviation concern.

•

Why, the people of Melbourne wanted to know, was that plane buzzing Flemington racecourse on this afternoon of Wednesday, 13 February 1935? Oh! Oh dear. Why it was none other than … yes it was, Raymond Parer, 'The Reparer'! With his flying partner Godfrey Hemsworth, Parer was arriving in Melbourne rather later than the three days it had taken C.W.A. Scott and Tom Campbell Black when they had won the race. As a matter of fact, it had taken Parer the Reparer no fewer than 116 days. Fuel trouble. Engine trouble. Wing trouble. Propeller trouble. Trouble-trouble. Still fuming, Raymond Parer didn't want to talk about it. But at least he and Hemsworth had finished, which was something …[67]

Nineteen

Out on a Wing and a Prayer

He was always fond of saying 'I don't want to be the world's most famous pilot, I want to be the world's oldest pilot ...'
LADY KINGSFORD SMITH, 1978[1]

Kingsford Smith, his gallant spirit never admitting defeat, gradually had his essential fibre whittled away, leaving effective only his spirit and his body with his unafraid smile.
BILL TAYLOR[2]

To conquer or die — that was life's eternal challenge for this truly great adventurer ...
JOHN STANNAGE[3]

Just before midnight on 14 May 1935, Smithy was sitting in the Officers' Mess at Richmond air base when a rather ominous thought struck him: 'Here I am, thirty-eight, apparently sane and sensible, and yet I'm going out over the ocean again, in the middle of the night.'[4]

In half an hour, he was due to head off in the *Southern Cross* over the treacherous Tasman Sea once more. As May 1935 was the twenty-fifth anniversary of the accession of King George V, Smithy had conceived the idea to take a 'Jubilee Flight' across the Tasman and for the first time carry mail from Australia to New Zealand. He hoped the flight would so capture the imagination of the public of both New Zealand and Australia, that the trip would be the forerunner of a regular service — to be run by him and his partners.

To double the impact, the original plan had been to take the late Charles Ulm's *Faith in Australia*, the former Australian National Airways *Southern Moon*, as well, but this plan fell through at the last moment.

For the trip, Smithy had chosen the redoubtable Bill Taylor as his co-pilot and navigator, and the ever-faithful John Stannage as his radio operator, who would be broadcasting to stations on both sides of the Tasman as this historic flight took place. On board, they had 34,000 letters to be delivered, together with several other items of freight, including wrapped bundles of Sydney newspapers.

So long as they got there, of course ...

Bill Taylor thought it was no sure thing and was also beginning to question his own sanity in going on this trip. Just the day before, he had wandered into Smithy's hangar at Mascot to see John Stannage and the Associated Newspapers aviation correspondent, Jack Percival — neither of whom were even close to being trained mechanics — up to their elbows in what had been the starboard motor, but which they had now stripped down into tiny pieces to replace the cracked crankcase. In Taylor's mind this was not the stuff successful flights were made of and, given a rising presentiment that he was about 'to walk the plank into the Tasman Sea',[5] he considered refusing to go. In the end, however, his loyalty to Smithy was such that he decided he just couldn't pull out. He would go on the flight, walk the plank, and hope for the best. So too, John Stannage, who had his own grave doubts, but simply couldn't say no to Smithy. For Smithy was not a man you let down, and to refuse to go would be to question his judgment, which was *unthinkable*.

At 12.20 am on the morning of 15 May 1935, the *Southern Cross* roared down the Richmond airstrip and headed towards New Plymouth, some 1300 miles away. On the tarmac behind them, they left Smithy's wife, Mary, his aged mother, Catherine, and his niece, Beris, who was, of course, married to John Stannage — all of them heavily rugged up against the cold and sombrely ruminating on the same emotion that always pressed at such moments ... the desperate hope that the aviators would be all right. All else being equal, Smithy should land late the following afternoon New Zealand time.

Racing towards the rising sun, the night would be compressed, meaning that dawn was not so far away, which was comforting to Smithy as, like most airmen, he found night-flying a debilitating exercise.

Well before dawn was due, he saw dead ahead a large black blot in the eastern starry night that could only be a massive storm. 'Johnnie,' Kingsford Smith called over his shoulder to Stannage down the narrow passageway that was again open, now that the large petrol tank previously blocking it had been removed. 'Ask Sydney if there has been a change in the weather. Look at that!'[6]

•

In Arabella Street — as in many homes around Australia and in New Zealand, where families stuck close to the radio — the Kingsford Smith family took the news of the storm with equanimity and gallons of tea. It was the view of the matriarch Catherine, for one, that her Chilla had gone through so many storms that there wasn't one out there that could bring him down. The near-octogenerian had been afraid so many times before, and he had always turned up safely, that she refused to put herself through it again. Otherwise, most people were simply stunned at the wonders of modern radio — they could actually hear John Stannage, with the muted engines in the background, giving reports of the journey, even though the plane was hundreds of miles away, and occasionally they could even hear Sir Charles Kingsford Smith himself!

•

For once, *for once*, this storm didn't prove to be too much of a problem and when the blessed dawn did welcome them back to the land of the living they were above the sort of lovely, white, billowy clouds that are to airmen what daisies are to the earth bound — the loveliest things imaginable to skip your way through. Things were looking up.

Smithy handed the controls over to Bill Taylor, so he could stretch his legs and have a chat to Johnnie — who, in turn, had taken a break from his radio duties to prepare a breakfast for them of hard-boiled eggs, sandwiches and coffee from a black thermos flask. All seemed right with the world as, happily munching and sipping away, they worked out that they had already knocked off at least half of their journey. Then something was suddenly up.

Bill Taylor, his mouth agape beneath his trim moustache, handed over to Smithy and pointed through the windscreen. Just back from the centre motor, which lay before their cockpit, they could see a tiny but angry sliver of flame coming from the point where the exhaust was connected. At first glance the situation didn't look *too* dangerous, as it seemed that just a little bit of welding or some such on the manifold had come unstuck. And yet, as they put their breakfast aside and watched, mesmerised, the flame got bigger and the gap on the exhaust manifold widened. Something had to give … and it did.[7]

While they were travelling at well over 90 miles per hour, at an altitude of 3000 feet, a solid piece of the exhaust manifold broke loose and was hurled by the slipstream straight at the starboard propeller … And where was Roland Garros or Anthony Fokker when they were needed? Two decades earlier, both men had mastered the art of getting small bits of metal through whirring propellers without causing any damage, and it was still possible that this could happen on this occasion. Alas, at speed, the piece of manifold hit and broke off a large chunk of the wooden starboard propeller, instantly causing the *Southern Cross* to vibrate appallingly — almost shaking them out of the sky.[8]

At this point only a master pilot could have kept them in the air, but again, the *Southern Cross* was fortunate to have one on board. Realising on the instant what had happened, Smithy hauled the wheel into his chest to point the nose of the *Southern Cross* up high and bring her to just above the point of a shuddering stall. With a deft flash of his right hand he cut the magneto switch of the starboard engine and it windmilled, reluctantly, to a stop. Now the vibration had mercifully ceased, and with the Old Bus barely flying — her nose so high in the air — they could see the damage. One blade of the propeller had broken off about two-thirds from the tip and was wafting back and forth pathetically. For all that, Bill Taylor, witnessing Smithy's manoeuvre first-hand, was stunned at the instantaneous, precise and intuitive skills displayed and, as he told John Stannage shortly afterwards, Smithy was pretty much the only pilot in the world who could have pulled it off.[9]

The first that any of the many people following the course of the trip in Australia and New Zealand knew of the drama was the urgent voice of Stannage as it crackled through the static:

> Prop gone on starboard motor! Please inform all stations stand by. Please ask all stations stand by. May not be able to hold height.[10]

Which left them where, precisely? Out in the middle of the Tasman Sea, with one engine useless and two engines snarling under the severe strain of having to work so hard to keep them aloft. It was just before seven o'clock in the morning, Australian time, and the immediate question to be answered was whether to keep going or to turn back? Again, Smithy was quick with his decision. To avoid the storms and heavy headwinds that were reported ahead, he immediately turned the plane for home, while Taylor worked out the proper course to get them to the nearest strip of hard sand on Stockton Beach just south of Port Stephens, on the New South Wales coast.

And then they faced the next problem. Their weight was too great to maintain altitude on just two engines and they were already starting to sink towards the Tasman Sea. 'Have to dump some weight!' Taylor shouted to Smithy. 'Shall I go ahead?'

'Anything, except the mail!'[11] Smithy yelled back. It was a decision that, frankly, rather underwhelmed Taylor in their extreme circumstances, but Smithy was the captain, and he didn't argue, simply going back to pass on the order to Stannage.

For Smithy's part, there was never any question: he wanted to do all possible to save that post, the *King's* post, and wouldn't even consider dropping it, unless he had the permission of the Postmaster General.

To further lighten the load, however, Bill Taylor activated the dump valve on the main tank to lose 100 gallons of petrol, then moved to the cabin's navigation table to try to plot exactly just how many miles up Shit Creek they actually were. All the while, John Stannage continued to report to the world both their position and their plight, his voice crackling with tension.

> 7.07 a.m. Have to dump the lot, I think. Blast it. Can't keep height. Hope they have a fast destroyer at Garden Island. What a hard end for the old Cross. Will get position. Stand by a sec. Bill has marked on chart that we are near the figures 166 W. Long.[12]

'Come quick! It's Smithy and he's in real trouble. I've just been listening to the radio, and they've cracked a propeller and lost an engine. They're trying to get back home now, but it looks pretty bad!' Quickly, around Australia and New Zealand, the word spread — a real crisis was at hand.

Aboard the *Southern Cross*, at least, the release of the fuel had lightened the load considerably and, to Smithy's feel, the plane was now behaving less like a rock with wings — but it was clearly not enough to save them as they continued to descend.

> 7.15 a.m. Looks like we are going in. Gee! It's cold. Get that? Get that? Just climbing 100 feet. Get that?[13]

At the La Perouse receiving station of Amalgamated Wireless Australasia Limited, as soon as the *Southern Cross*'s messages were picked up, a general alert went out to government departments with relevant jurisdictions, including the Navigation Department, so that the course of the stricken plane could be plotted and those ships in her vicinity could alter course to try to save them, the same way Harry Hawker had been saved fifteen years earlier, should Smithy have to ditch her in the sea. All news organisations were also soon onto the story, as a desperate scramble began to get the drama into print and onto the streets. New-fangled things called 'news flashes' interrupted regular radio programming as breathless announcers told the troubles of the *Southern Cross*, with Kingsford Smith and his crew teetering on tragedy.

> 7.25 a.m. … Don't let them worry our wives unnecessarily. Thank God, we have this marvellous radio set. My antenna must be nearly in the 'drink' by now.
>
> 7.34 a.m. Wish you could see Smithy clawing the air, he's a world beater; makes a few feet and then tries to save the other two engines.[14]

Despite John Stannage's nose beginning to bleed with fright, he felt certain that if anyone could keep them aloft then it was Smithy, as he watched him 'holding the plane with hands and feet, juggling, fighting, and coaxing her, getting that little bit extra that only he could get from his old machine'.[15] Somehow Smithy managed to hold the plane perpetually in the zone that was just two or three knots above stalling, and a knot or two below the speed that would have the broken propeller turn again and shake the old girl to bloody bits.[16] His injured left foot ached from the constant pressure on the rudder to counter the thrust of the good port Whirlwind against the drag of the mortally wounded starboard engine.

And yet how much did the Old Bus actually have left to give? As the Australian coast edged a little closer, the port engine was clearly starting to show the strain. It began to trail blue smoke, and the gauge in the cockpit showed that it was losing oil pressure — which was beyond serious, as oil was the lifeblood of the motor.

There had been 11 gallons of oil in that engine when they had taken off from Mascot but God only knew how much was left now, as the blue smoke indicated that a lot of it had been burned and she was getting hot. At least, after experimentation, Smithy had found the best altitude to hold the stricken plane, where the denser air helped to keep them aloft and yet still gave them enough height to act in case they lost power.

> `9.27 a.m. Holding 500 feet at just below full revolutions, making very poor headway against this foul head wind, and with only two motors. Hell, that port motor keeps spitting, and every time it does, I feel like she's going to quit, and we'll go straight down.`

There might have been some comfort for them if they'd had a life raft on board the *Southern Cross* or even a few simple life jackets, but they did not. Why? Because — in the words, almost, of the Frenchman Charles Nungesser a decade earlier — 'The idea, *mon cher* Coli, was to reach New Zealand by flying over the water, not swimming there …'

By now every ship in the Tasman had been notified of the drama in the skies above them, and the pilot boat *Captain Cook* was about to leave Sydney Harbour at full speed to try to intercept them, just as a visiting British destroyer, HMS *Sussex*, was also being prevailed upon to come to the aid of one of the Empire's favourite sons. At Mascot, Charles Ulm's modified Avro Ten, *Faith in Australia*, had been loaded with flotation gear and was being urgently prepared for take-off, as a crew was being sought to man it. Ideally, *Faith* could meet the *Southern Cross* and then escort it back, available to circle overhead and mark the position if the plane did have to come down. On city streets all over Australia and New Zealand, newsboys were scurrying hither and thither and blaring the news, with a poster by the Melbourne *Herald* setting the tone:

HERALD

KINGSFORD SMITH IN GREAT DANGER

In London, Australian Prime Minister Joseph Lyons had been told of the situation and had instructed that he be kept informed of developments as they arose.

Back on board the stricken craft, John Stannage continued to be filled with admiration for the *Southern Cross*'s ability to keep going. Even in the extremity of the situation Stannage had time for a few philosophical thoughts: 'Is it fantastic to think that a man-made mechanism can possess a soul — a spirit, a personality, call it what you will? A man may become attached to a car so that it becomes almost part of him. He is the brains and the machine is the body. The dear old Southern Cross always seemed to be something more than the sum of her parts. She had spirit. She had feeling. Certainly she had a sensitivity of response to her skipper.'[17]

In this case, 'a newly made inanimate piece of iron', which did *not* have a soul, 'practically tore the vitals from the stout old bus; yet she still staggered on when her master was forced cruelly to spur her on'.[18]

Not that Stannage was totally in accord with everything that master did. `I wish he would tell us to dump the mail,` he tapped out, a little disloyally. `Then we could climb. I don't like this being right down on the water.`[19]

The tension ebbed and flowed. One thing John Stannage had particularly noticed in his brief flying career was how the ocean itself had moods. On some days it looked as bright, breezy and welcoming as a beautiful girl on a summer's day. On other days it scowled and threatened, angrily. This was such a day. At times he was certain that all was lost —

`9.37 a.m. Going down, I think. Wait!`

— and was aghast to look out the window and see the hungry ocean just 100 feet or so beneath them, but then things would come good for a bit —

`9.38 a.m. No! She's right! Picked up again.`

Shortly afterwards Stannage went forward and was immensely cheered to see that Smithy's familiar broad grin was back. 'Just holding it now, Johnnie,' Smithy shouted above the slightly muted roar of what used to be three motors, but was now just two. 'She'll do it if the motors can stand up to full throttle.'[20]

And in many ways, 'holding it' was exactly what he was doing — holding the plane in the sky. John Stannage didn't know how. Somehow, amazingly, Smithy achieved an aerial equilibrium between stalling and setting the starboard propeller windmilling that enabled them to continue inching their way towards the Australian coast. Smithy's confidence was reassuring too.

But just as Stannage was feeling less worried, their situation deteriorated again. This time, as they slowly began to lose altitude with the wavering and overheated motors, Smithy reluctantly called for him to hurl out the door all their luggage, their spares and the freight — everything except the mail — which Stannage instantly did, as if his life depended on it, because it most certainly did.

As Smithy, with Bill Taylor right beside him, kept nursing the plane onwards the best he could, all of them were now physically and mentally spent. The minutes crawled by and they continued to approach the Australian coast at a rate of about 70 miles per hour, with still around 300 miles to go to reach solid land. John Stannage kept broadcasting:

> 9.49 a.m. Smithy says could you please spare a boat to come out on our course with plenty of smoke. Port engine dropped a cylinder now. Smithy says also to tell them he is frightfully sorry about it all.
>
> 10.05 a.m. Smithy says could you get a message to all of our wives, and tell them not to worry. We are not in the water yet.[21]
>
> 11.16 a.m. Things look much brighter now as the petrol load gets less. She can be throttled back a bit to save the motors. The port motor seems to be hanging on O.K. If we carry on like this, we will probably strike the coast about Port Stephens and, boy, will the coast look good![22]

In fact, a favourable shift in the wind direction meant that they soon altered course and headed straight to Sydney, instead of Stockton Beach. But then things took another bad turn. It became clear that the port motor was in agonised death throes, blowing more and more smoke and screaming its protest at being made to operate so hard without sufficient oil.

In the cabin, John Stannage looked up to see an obviously exhausted Smithy coming back from the tight cockpit for some room to get out of his heavy flying clothes while Bill Taylor took over the flying. Almost as if he thought he would soon be … *swimming*?

Christ. Yes.

Now Smithy held both thumbs down and told him straight: 'Looks like we've collected it this time, Johnnie,' he said surprisingly calmly. 'Port motor can't last another hour. Let's have a spot.'[23] With which the two had a few swigs from a small bottle of whisky Stannage had been given by friends in New Zealand, marked *Radio Operator's Moaning Fluid*. Stannage could only wish that he had Smithy's calm in the face of their perilous situation.[24]

It was Smithy's next words, however, that really hit him hard. 'Now just one cigarette.'[25]

Under normal circumstances in a plane like the *Southern Cross*, ever awash in petrol fumes, lighting a match to start a cigarette was strictly forbidden. It was only something you would contemplate if it looked like it didn't matter any more. As Smithy now said, 'It doesn't really matter if it does blow up, does it?'[26]

With one match, which didn't turn their plane into a flaming hulk, Smithy lit both their cigarettes and they drew the wonderfully consoling smoke back into their lungs.

'When we go in you'll have to get out of there quite smartly,' Smithy now told him calmly. 'Collect all the demolition tools, tie them together and make them fast to a longeron. The tail will finish up high in the air, and you'll have to make your way down the fuselage to try and dig Bill and me out of the cockpit if we get stuck. We might be a good way under too. The weight of the engines will drag the nose well down. Take your boots off, John. Bad luck, isn't it? But we've had fun, haven't we?'[27]

With which, he took a last deep draw on his cigarette, stubbed it out, and went back to take over from Bill in the cockpit.

Have *mercy*! This time, it looked like it really was all over.

> 12.12 p.m. Port motor only last a quarter hour. Please stand by for exact position. Going, going, going …
>
> 12.15 p.m. She's going fast.
>
> 12.16 p.m. Wait a sec. Going down any minute.

Up the front, Bill Taylor had been doing some serious thinking, even as he stared, mesmerised, at the wavering needle on the oil pressure dial, heading inexorably lower. They needed to get oil into the port engine. If they didn't get it there, their deaths would be all but certain, and grisly deaths they would be. And yet they had oil with them! The only problem was, it was in the crippled starboard engine. All he needed to do was to find a way to get the oil from the one engine into the other. Yes, he would have to climb out the small opening on the side of the cockpit, into the slipstream, and get that oil! After all, Smithy — who had just come back and taken over again — couldn't do it as they needed his skills to nurse the plane home, and Johnnie couldn't do it, as it was very important that he maintained contact with the authorities to give them regular updates on their positions. So, it was up to him.

The decision taken, he moved swiftly. Leaving the controls to Smithy, he moved back into the cabin and yelled at John Stannage.

'I'm going to have a crack at getting oil out of the tank of the starboard motor! Got anything to put it in?'

Stannage, delighted to have a plan of action, though barely believing that Taylor could be serious, looked around. The thermos flask that had contained the coffee was an obvious choice. Putting the end of a spanner down its mirrored throat, he broke the internal glass to expand its capacity, and then looked around for something else. In a blessed instant he spied the small leather case which contained some radio spares and other tools. It wasn't much, but it could definitely contain oil.

Bill calmly removed his boots and bound his long leather coat around him as tightly as possible, before moving back into the cockpit. As he went, he kept repeating to himself, almost as a mantra: '*Get the oil from the starboard tank. Go out and get it. Get the oil from the starboard tank. Go out and get it ...*'[28]

And there was Smithy, hunched over the controls, every fibre of his being concentrated on keeping the *Southern Cross* aloft for as long as possible.

Taylor shouted at him: 'Going to have a stab at getting some oil!'[29]

In response Smithy shook his head violently, in the manner of a man wondering whether Taylor had taken leave of his senses, and then stopped. The look in Taylor's eyes said he would not be stopped, even if he *had* taken leave of his senses. Meanwhile Taylor's mental mantra went on ... '*Get the oil from the starboard tank. Go out and get it. Get the oil from the starboard tank. Go out and get it ...*'[30]

One more thing, though. As a safety measure, he tied a thin postal bag cord around his waist and attached it to a strong piece of steel in the cockpit, in the admittedly vain hope that if he fell, this would save him. Absurdly, it made him feel better.

And then he climbed up onto the starboard pilot's seat and agonisingly slipped through the opening straight into the teeth of a 100-mile per hour cyclone from the centre motor! And with every inch more of his body that he got out there, the more the wind clawed at him. For an instant, he was overwhelmed by the sheer *futility* of what he was trying to do, but one look at the sea below was enough to settle him down. If he was going to die, at least let him die while trying to save them. He pressed on, his spirit forcing his body to do something that his mind told him was insane ...

12.24 p.m. Bill is trying to get oil out
of the other engine. Stand by.

In that fierce slipstream, Bill Taylor was fighting for his life, as the rushing wind was a living, killing thing, slapping his face, pulling his hair, tearing at his entire body, billowing into his shirt, up his sleeves, inside his coat, even as the breath was sucked from his lungs and his ears were filled with the roar of a thousand banshees screaming his death song. And all Smithy could do was to keep the *Southern Cross* as steady as possible, just as he had back in the Hollywood days with a madman on his wing.

Despite everything, Bill got a foot onto the horizontal strut that joined the motor to the fuselage, pressed his head and neck hard against the leading edge of the wing and hung on with both hands to the cockpit window for grim death, acutely aware that that was exactly what awaited him if he slipped.

Then with both feet on the crossbar, he risked releasing the death grip of his right hand, and grabbed for an engine-mounting strut. Then both hands. He was still alive! Fighting a strong urge to make a mad rush along the beam and grab the now-cold engine, he inched his way forward … steady … steady … steady … ever so slowly.

Bill Taylor on the horizontal strut.

And all of a sudden he was there! Blasted by the wind still, but securely holding onto the support strut of the starboard engine. With faltering hands he worked to loosen the cowl pins, not an easy task at the best of times, yet somehow he managed it, with bleeding, shaking fingers and torn nails to expose the engine proper and ... and then he realised he'd forgotten something. A spanner with which to loosen the oil plug. He looked back to see that John Stannage was on top of the problem and was leaning out of the cockpit proffering the only adjustable spanner that hadn't been jettisoned with everything else. With both men leaning out to their maximum degree, Taylor was *just* able to get his fingers on the spanner's end and breathlessly secure it.

Now, carefully, oh so carefully, Taylor sat and linked an arm around the engine strut then got the spanner onto the drain plug on the oil tank at the back of the engine and began to loosen it. Then he quickly jammed the vacuum flask beneath it to collect the liquid gold, the sauce of their salvation. It was no easy thing to remove the flask and get the plug back in without spilling the precious oil, but he at last got this part of the job done, and passed the flask to Stannage in the cockpit, who emptied it into the briefcase. Both men repeated the process several times until the briefcase was full, and then the exhausted, frozen Taylor fought his way back inside the *Southern Cross*, away from the blasting wind. The job had been half done.

> 12.54 p.m. Still in the air. Bill the hero, climbed out and got oil for the dud motor.

Now for the port engine. It was at this point that John Stannage himself attempted to finish the job by climbing out the window to the port side, only to find that he was facing certain death if he tried to continue. A much shorter man, when he stood on the strut his head did not come up to the bottom of the wing, meaning he had no capacity to get out to the engine. It would have to be Bill once more or no-one.[31]

Smithy had to change seats to the starboard side, to give Bill room to get out the other cockpit opening. And this time it not only looked impossible, but *was* impossible. For no sooner had Bill begun to force his body out the opening than he was nearly hurled into all eternity, as he was hit with the wash of both the central *and* port propellers. And yet it had to be done, as the oil pressure on the port motor had nearly fallen away to just 15 pounds from its normal level of 63 pounds per square inch, and it could only be a matter of moments before the engine seized solid. The solution?

There is safety in speed and height.

Well, on just two engines, he couldn't get speed, but Smithy could maybe get a little height. By gunning both the healthy centre engine and oil-starved port engine, he managed to climb to an altitude of about 700 feet, at which point he idled the port engine. Yes, on only one engine they would swiftly lose altitude, but with the howling slipstream reduced it might be possible for Bill to climb out to the port engine to pour the precious oil into its reservoir before Smithy would have to power the engines back up to escape the gaping jaws of the grey waves below.

Bill would do it, or die in the attempt.

Once more he disappeared out the window and was soon wrapped around the struts like a koala to a gum tree in a cyclone, at which point Smithy gunned the engine once more, and they began to torturously climb. The instant the engine was up to full throttle Bill was again in the wash of the two propellers and was nearly blown to oblivion.

> 1.03 p.m. Still in the air. Changing oil from the dud motor to the sick one.[32]

Then the blessed moment came, after altitude had been regained, when Smithy cut the throttle once more and Bill was able to get thermos after thermos of precious oil flowing into the engine, each one passed to him by John Stannage from the cockpit. In short order Bill heard shouts against the wind and looked up to see Smithy and Johnnie waving at him and grinning hugely. To their delight, the oil-pressure gauge had started to inch upwards and was soon back to normal!

Bill Taylor, a man not given to great surges of emotion in any direction, nevertheless felt a burst of exhilaration that made him want to stand, laugh, and scream *back* at the screaming wind that had tried to stop him but failed. He had DONE it![33] And all he had to do now was to inch his way back along the strut into the plane and he would live.

> `1.10 p.m. Bill Taylor is the world's greatest hero. Hope to see land now in about ten minutes ...`

Not that they were out of trouble for all that. Though the port engine now had black dinosaur-juice back in it and was able to keep going, it was obvious that damage had been done to it through the terrible hiding it had copped, and it was unable to deliver full power. Finally, Smithy took the decision that he had put off until there really was no other choice.

As John Stannage peered anxiously at him from the open cockpit door, Smithy told him: 'You'll have to dump the mail, Johnnie! We can't keep height.'[34]

John Stannage didn't have to be asked twice. With only 50 feet separating them from the waves below, he took out his knife and slashed the cords that bound the tops of the forty blue mailbags — each one over 20 pounds of dead weight — and hurled them out the door with every ounce of strength he had in him. In fact, the Postmaster General had already radioed permission for this, but it hit Smithy hard all the same, as a trail of sinking blue bags now lay behind them.

Still, there was no doubt that the *Southern Cross* responded well to the decreased burden and he was able to get a little altitude once more, helped by the fact that over the previous hours they had burnt a lot of fuel. Only Smithy could have kept them aloft to this point, and every minute that passed was a good minute, bringing them closer to Mascot, and the help that was now on its way.

The Australian coast was just 100 miles away when off their port bow they sighted a small steamer, a New Zealand vessel, the *Port Waikato*. An important decision had to be made. Should they do what Harry Hawker and Kenneth Mackenzie Grieve had done sixteen years earlier and ditch in front of the steamer, thus probably saving their lives? The downside was that they would lose the *Southern Cross*. Or should they chance it, keep going, and try to save both themselves *and* their legendary plane? Ditching the *Southern Cross*, which had never let him down, would not be easy if it came to it. As absurd as it might sound to an outsider, he loved her like a woman, and almost felt that she loved him. In the end, after Smithy discussed it with the crew, they decided to fly on.

At last, on the horizon they saw a purple streak that didn't alter, a line that proved to be the Australian coast about 30 miles away, but even then there was no lessening of tension. Now that they could see the promised land it looked infinitely far away, as the *Southern Cross* barely seemed to move towards it, or be likely ever to reach it.[35]

Once more the oil pressure on the port engine fell away and it was obvious that either the completely sapped and bloodless Bill Taylor was going to have to risk his life again or they would have to ditch the plane. Smithy told Taylor he didn't want him to do it, but this time it was Taylor who insisted they try to save the *Southern Cross*, and he climbed out the window once more to repeat the whole dramatic process until the port engine again gurgled with some blessed relief.[36]

Six trips in all Bill made. Three to each side. Finally all he could do was sit beside Smithy, covered in oil from head to toe, and hope that the centre engine, also low on oil, could hang in there.

At last, at 4.45 pm, the *Southern Cross* hotly coughed and hacked its way over Cronulla beach and dribbled in to Mascot airport — touching down fifteen hours and thirty-five minutes after taking off.

Such was the drama of the day that a huge crowd of public and press had built up awaiting the return of the plane and they rushed forward en masse, once Smithy had cut the two engines and the propellers had stopped whirring. Observers could see oil dripping from the fuselage, and the shattered starboard propeller. For a moment there was nothing — no triumphant, grinning Smithy bursting forth hailing all and sundry, cracking one-liners. No sign of Stannage or Taylor either. Nothing.

Inside the plane, none of the three men — barely believing they had made it and were still alive — could move.

Finally, the door opened and out they came. Sort of … Were they *ghosts* of the men they had been? Smithy was barely recognisable, his eyes set deep in his skull, his face pale, every wrinkle a crevasse. He was so totally spent that he had to be helped on the arms of friends to make his way through the pressing throng.[37] For his part, John Stannage seemed stooped, weighed down, perhaps by the enormity of the ordeal they had been through.

'God, what a time we have had,' he said, as he fell into the arms of his wife Beris, who had rushed to the airport. And yes, there was Taylor, covered in oil from top to toe, but showing signs of life, his bloodshot eyes sparkling from his blackened visage.

Smithy was able to rouse himself to say, pointing to Bill, 'If it wasn't for him, we wouldn't be here now.'[38]

'Once is enough, that's all I can say,'[39] the navigator and new Australian hero smiled tiredly in reply.

The aviators were led away to a private room in the Mascot hangar where, among others, Mary was waiting for her husband. Smithy embraced his weeping wife and held her long. 'It's all right,' he tried to soothe her, 'they can't kill me.'[40]

That evening, the exhausted Smithy finally made it home at about 10 pm, and promptly excused himself to have a hot bath. A friend of the family who was visiting became worried at his long absence and knocked on the bathroom door. Receiving no answer, and becoming alarmed, he opened the door to find Smithy fast asleep with the water up to his chin.[41]

The following day's newspapers, both in Australia and around the British Empire, were filled with accounts of the extraordinary episode. And yet while much of the focus was on the heroics of Bill Taylor, there was also much comment on the fact that despite 'KINGSFORD SMITH'S MISHAP', as the headline in *The Times* ran,[42] the 'Jubilee' mail had been lost, including a letter from the Governor-General to the King.

For its part, the British aeronautical journal *Aeroplane* had no hesitation in attacking the whole concept of Kingsford Smith's trans-Tasman flight. 'If he were to disappear on a silly stunt such as the New Zealand flight,' it thundered, 'no sensible person could feel any sympathy ... Kingsford Smith has tried his luck too high already on his trans-Pacific and Tasman flights.'[43]

At least the man of the moment, Bill Taylor, was able to use the opportunity to tell the press that the whole point of the flight had been to generate public interest 'so that people of the two Dominions would ensure that the trans-Tasman airmail service would be owned and operated by their own people. Quite frankly, we do not want the English company, Imperial Airways, to operate a service which is our own by right of the pioneering development which has been done.'[44]

But against that, at a time when they had been obliged to dump 28,000 letters and packages, it was hardly the time to press their case that they should be given the privilege of carrying letters in the future.

No doubt aware of the damage that had been done, Smithy was keen on flying to New Zealand as soon as the following day, in Ulm's old machine *Faith in Australia*, to take a few mailbags that had been found in the tail of the *Southern Cross* and so had survived with 1000 letters, but received no support from anyone for such madness.[45] (This proved to be extremely fortunate for Kingsford Smith, as just five flight hours later, one of the *Faith*'s engines blew a cylinder head, and had Smithy been over the Tasman at the time, the far greater weight of that plane would have sent him quickly into the drink.[46]) The mailbags would later make their way safely across the Tasman by steamer.[47] If the whole episode proved anything, said New Zealand Prime Minister George Forbes, it was that the right type of machine had not yet been found to make a regular crossing to New Zealand practical.[48]

In short, while it was wonderful to have survived, there was no escaping the fact that Smithy and his proposed ventures had taken yet one more hit. Compounding the situation was a severe lack of capital both to get his new airline up and running, and to pay for the new family home, which, thanks to hefty financial input from his father-in-law, was nearing completion at 33 Greenoaks Avenue, Darling Point.

Beyond that generosity from Mary's father, Smithy was broke and the only way out was to sell the now clearly past it *Southern Cross* to the Federal government, on the reckoning that it would put her on permanent display for the public. After negotiations, the government upped its offer from £1500 to £3000 — not nearly as much as Smithy wanted but clearly as much as he was going to get — so he accepted, though he was not happy about it.

As a matter of fact, Smithy wasn't happy about much at all these days, as even on a good day he seemed restless, tetchy and demoralised. On a bad day he could swing back and forth between depression and anger. Nothing was going right. Everything was going to hell. This included money and energy he had put the previous year towards the building of a revolutionary chassis-less car with a body of laminated wood, built on much the same principles as the fuselage of an aircraft, to be called the *Southern Cross*. Though six models had been made, it was already apparent that the idea was not going to take off, unlike its namesake.

Another failed venture was a specially designed plane he had commissioned to be ready to fly the commercial trans-Tasman route. At a cost of £3700 to Smithy, the 'Codock' was a one-off twin-engined, high-wing monoplane conceived and built by Lawrence Wackett on Cockatoo Island, and its key characteristic was that, through myriad engine faults, it had a great deal of trouble staying in the air. In its final form it was judged to be worth just £75 ... and the financial pressure continued to build.[49] (Other aviation entrepreneurs were far more careful with their money. At the modest family home of Hudson Fysh, in Brisbane, when the economic times had been at their toughest, they had ceased to buy the afternoon paper and gone to the picture theatre only when the cheapest sessions were on.[50])

But something wasn't right. For the first time Smithy started having rows with Mary, who was at a loss to know quite what was wrong with her husband.[51] What she did know was that he was a long way from the relatively carefree legend of a larrikin she had met six years earlier. And it was equally obvious that he was not yet ready to stay home with her and young Charles Jnr to do the gardening.

•

On 6 June 1935, Smithy formally announced that he and his partners had formed a new company, rather grandly called the Trans-Tasman Air Service Development Company Ltd, with the stated aim of offering a regular air service between Australia and New Zealand. Imperial Airways, of course, was somewhat underwhelmed, as it was *not* of the view that an air service between Australia and New Zealand should be the preserve of those nations' peoples. Rather, as a spokesman told the Melbourne *Argus* on the same day that Smithy made his announcement, that route 'was certain to be included among the trunk lines of the great Imperial system'.[52]

This Kingsford Smith fellow would have to be stopped.

•

Behold, the ancient mariner … Why, it was none other than Captain Phillips, who thirty years earlier had put the fear of God into young Chilla when the youngster had been running amok on the *Aorangi*, when the family had been on its way to Vancouver for the first time. Smithy ran into him on a street in downtown Sydney, and was delighted to do so. The old man had followed the aviator's career since he had first come to fame and was thrilled to meet him again now. Still, he couldn't resist offering some advice.

'You've done enough flying,' he said with a smile. 'I'd like to put those irons on you now and keep you here.'[53]

•

18 July 1935 was a very big day in young John Ulm's life. It was the day when the *Southern Cross* — once again scrubbed clean and repaired enough to safely fly a little way — would be handed over to the Australian government. At Smithy's invitation the fourteen-year-old was going to be sitting in his late father's co-pilot seat, beside Australia's most famous man, as he flew the tri-

motor Fokker from Mascot to Richmond. The 'Old Bus' was to be temporarily housed there until permanent accommodation in a museum-like environment could be found for her.

'This is a great man's seat, John,' Smithy told the young'un, as the cameras rolled. 'A man who took chances with a smile in this dear old bus of mine. A man whose name any boy would be proud to bear ...'[54]

'Gee I wish Dad would [be with me] on this last flight,' John Ulm near whispered in reply.

'Perhaps he is, John ...'

For the occasion, a crowd of several thousand people had gathered at the Mascot hangar where the *Southern Cross* had been prepared for her last flight. Smithy was in the formal dress-uniform of air commodore for the occasion, and looked resplendent in blue, with gold braids. A swagger stick completed the imposing picture.

The *Southern Cross*, with young John in the cockpit — and Lady Mary Kingsford Smith, Bill Taylor, Beau Sheil and John Stannage in the cabin, together with one of Smithy's friends from New Zealand, Reverend Colin Scrimgeour — took off and was escorted towards Richmond by no fewer than six Hawker Demon biplanes from the Royal Australian Air Force.[55] In the course of the journey, Smithy made three brief detours. First he dipped down in sad salute over Keith Anderson's grave at Mosman, before heading over to Longueville where — in the manner of Bert Hinkler several years before — he was able to buzz low over his mother standing in the front yard of her home, waving. Most exciting for young John Ulm, though, was when Smithy also swooped down joyously low over his primary school at Chatswood, with all the kids running into the yard and waving up to them, as John ecstatically waved back. Such fun!

Smithy was kind to the lad, but at the same time the great pilot also seemed a little sad at having to part company with the plane with which his name had become synonymous, a plane that had taken him around the world, across the seven seas, through wind, storm, hail and snow, and had never let him down.

When they landed at Richmond RAAF base, Smithy seemed reluctant to get out of his seat, almost like he was glued to it, or it was a part of him. Finally, though, he stood up and slowly walked down the narrow passage which allowed him to exit via the rear stairs. There, a small crowd had gathered for the occasion, including a glitteringly turned-out Minister for Defence, Archdale Parkhill, who was often known as 'Archduke' for his propensity to overdress.

'I am proud,' the Defence Minister told Smithy in his brief formal speech, 'to take over for the people this most famous aeroplane, from a man whose magnificent airmanship has made history for Australia.'[56]

Everyone applauded, and Smithy then addressed them in a low, sorrowful voice about the plane that he loved: 'She has been a living thing to me. I've spent one hundred and fifty days and twenty whole nights on board. During all her long flights she had never let me down. Even on that last flight across the Tasman, it was not the *Southern Cross* that failed me.

'When the propeller was smashed, I seemed to hear her call out: "It isn't me, boss! It's that new bit of cowling." One day, I want to put a brass plate on the old plane. It will bear an inscription something like this: "To my faithful Old Bus, in grateful memory and regard — from her boss."'[57]

With quavering voice, Smithy then read a poem he had composed.

ODE TO THE OLD BUS

Old faithful friend — a fond adieu,
These are poor words with which to tell
Of all my pride, my joy in you,
True to the end you've served me well.

I pity those who cannot see
That heart and soul are housed within
This thing of steel and wood — to me
You live in every bolt and pin.

And so my staunch and steadfast steed
Your deep and mighty voice must cease
Faithful to death, if God will heed
My prayer, dear pal. You'll rest in peace![58]

Then, with a tear in his eye, he took a single step back, looked at the cockpit and snapped off a formal salute.[59]

•

And then to business … Smithy and Beau Sheil were scheduled to leave for New Zealand that very afternoon on the *Aorangi*, with Smithy being farewelled on the docks by the once again pregnant Mary, two-and-a-half-year-old Charles Jnr, and the woman who had been the rock of his existence since his birth, Catherine.

With a persistence that the *Southern Cross* itself would have been proud of, the famed aviator's intention was to address the New Zealand Cabinet once more before heading across the Pacific to reclaim the *Lady Southern Cross*, which was still sitting in the hangar in Burbank where he had left it.

And from there? Well, he wasn't quite sure. A few years ago there had been neither enough hours in the day, nor days in the week for him to get through all the things he wanted to do, as opportunities abounded, red carpets ribboned before him, and every door he passed opened automatically, even as it rained pound notes. But it was no longer like that.

At the age of thirty-eight, everything was a struggle as he no longer had the energy or strength that once drove him at will; the red carpets had become endless reams of red tape that near strangled a man, and in terms of opportunities the most familiar sound was that of doors shutting in his face. To top it all off, he was just about broke. Despite the government's repeated use of such flowery sentiments in various speeches that 'Australia owes more than it can ever pay to Kingsford Smith', when it came right down to it, the government seemed to do everything in its power to thwart him. None of the routes he and Ulm had pioneered had ever been granted to them to run, not one penny of government subsidy had ever come their way and, while it was obvious that the world of aviation was at the dawn of a new age in terms of commercial travel, his place in that new age was not readily apparent.

Twenty years earlier, when the youthful Smithy had been about to board a ship leaving Sydney Harbour on his way to the Great War, he had been a young man who laughed easily and was possessed by an overwhelming sense of adventure. Now, though, it was a sombre, quiet and exhausted man who held Mary close — with an extra gentle pat for their new baby that was on its way and due just before Christmas, five months hence — hugged Charles Jnr and told him to look after his mother, and kissed his own mother goodbye before marching up the gangplank. The *Aorangi* was the ship he had first gone to Vancouver on as a child and the ship he had met Mary on, when near the height of his fame. Now, who knew to what fate it was taking him?

Catherine, Mary and Charles Jnr watched silently until the ship disappeared from view. It was a cold, windy day. Getting chilly. Winter had set in. Time to head home — Mary and Charles Jnr to their suddenly empty Darling Point house; Catherine to Kuranda, where she was living totally alone since William had died. They hoped that Chilla would be all right.

•

Sitting around a table in the New Zealand parliament in Wellington, on the afternoon of 24 July 1935, was Acting Prime Minister Sir Ethelbert Ransom and the members of the Cabinet. Smithy had been invited to address them on his proposals, and he did so for the next three hours as they questioned him.

He spelled out the estimated cost of the service, the planes his company wanted to use, schedules, their proposed landing grounds — the lot. All that was needed was the New Zealand government's commitment to back them.

At the end of the meeting, the Cabinet had made no commitments, but nor had they said no. Their primary concern, it seemed, was that British aeroplanes be used, not American ones, which was a little problematic as Smithy was of the firm view that the only planes capable of flying the Tasman on a regular basis were the American planes — the Douglas DC-2s, Sikorsky S-42s and Martin M-130 China Clipper flying boats. The amazing thing, as Smithy pointed out to Beau Sheil from atop the steps of the parliament building on their way out, was just how many American cars were in the parliamentary car park, given the lecture he had just received on the importance of buying British.

Still, it was something to go on with at a time when not a whole lot else beckoned, and after another meeting with the New Zealand leader of the Opposition, Michael Savage, which was very positive, Kingsford Smith headed for California. He had a good feeling after his meetings, and was hopeful that things were moving his way at last.

•

Behind him, things were certainly beginning to *move*, anyway … For the aviation industry had been watching Kingsford Smith carefully. 'It is obvious,' Hudson Fysh, Managing Director of Qantas, wrote crisply to George Woods Humphreys, his Imperial Airways counterpart, 'that Taylor and Kingsford Smith are unbusinesslike and incapable when it comes to organising and operating a service like that between Sydney and New Zealand. But they have a certain following in Parliament and among the public which it is not wise to ignore …'[60]

Woods Humphreys didn't ignore it, and wrote to Fysh by return mail: 'On the subject of Kingsford Smith's activities, I have arranged with the Air Ministry and the Dominion's office for them to telegraph the New Zealand Government, asking them not to commit themselves to anything before consulting with the Government here. In the meantime, we are preparing a scheme … to put to the United Kingdom government.'[61]

Soon afterwards, Australia's Controller of Civil Aviation, Edgar Johnston, received a letter from his deputy: 'The New Zealand Government is not taking kindly to Kingsford Smith's proposal.'[62]

Enormously powerful forces were being brought to bear on the Kingsford Smith problem, even as he sailed for San Francisco. For its part, the London *Daily Express* took a dim view rather representative of the Establishment, saying that 'Sir Charles Kingsford Smith is today planning a pirate air route with American aircraft over the 1,200 miles between Australia and New Zealand. It will compete with the general Empire airmail speed-up and extension scheduled to begin in 1937.'

The *Express* even quoted Sir Ethelbert Ransom panning the idea on behalf of his government: 'It would scarcely be keeping faith with Britain and would certainly be an embarrassment were New Zealand at this stage to become prematurely committed to a separate proposal. The Tasman service must be considered part of a comprehensive Empire scheme.'[63]

The Australian government took the same view, with the Defence Minister Archdale Parkhill announcing that Kingsford Smith's scheme 'was both very expensive and unnecessary'.[64]

Shortly after docking in San Francisco, Smithy was apprised of both decisions. Two more doors — big ones — had just been firmly slammed in his face.

Well, bugger the lot of them. He and Sheil would just have to raise the money elsewhere, and launch their airline independently of any government assistance. To get that money, they would go to the financial capital of the world, London. And, once again setting eyes on the *Lady Southern Cross*, where she had been waiting for him in the Burbank hangar, Smithy felt he had unfinished business with her, too — and not just having to pay more precious money to free the plane from the usual attachment imposed by a San Pedro court because of unpaid debts.[65] Perhaps one more, just one more record-breaking flight, to show everyone that he was as good as he had ever been, and could still grab the world's attention, even if the Australian and New Zealand governments had turned their backs on him.

All of this was clearly on his mind when, shortly after arriving in America, he was interviewed by the famous American aviation journalist Edwin C. Parsons, for *Liberty* magazine. 'Despite strict adherence to my creed, "Never take an unnecessary chance",' the Australian told Parsons, 'there has arrived a time on nearly every hop when I've been thoroughly frightened. I've been in so many tough spots when it's been touch and go whether I lived or died that I'm convinced that I shan't wash out for good till my number is up.'[66]

Was it perhaps time to give it away before that number did come up? Not in Smithy's view. 'The flying life of pilots, as of planes, is short compared with other forms of transport. At thirty-eight I recognise that I am a veteran. Well, there is life in the old dog yet! — and I still sigh for uncharted spaces and new worlds to conquer — even though trans-oceanic flights are selling at two cents to the bushel and there is the ever-present problem of financing to worry me. To be sure, I have a nice little air business in Sydney, but my heart is in adventure and the last frontier is the air.'[67]

After flying the *Lady Southern Cross* to New York, Smithy used the absolute last gasp of his financial resources to arrange passage for both himself and his plane on separate ships to England, where he would meet up with Beau Sheil to see if they could rustle up the money they needed.

Alas, when he got to London after a four-day voyage, the problem Smithy came up against was an all too familiar one. That is, while his record as a pilot was without peer, his resumé as a businessman was a lot less illustrious and he was yet to demonstrate his capacity to make an aviation company grow in the long term.

Knock-back followed knock-back and, in many ways, the situation was reminiscent of the one that Smithy had previously known in San Francisco before his first Pacific flight. It was one thing for people to wish you well, slap you on the back and invite you for a drink, and quite another for them to commit to writing a big cheque, most particularly when you had a record of squandering the big cheques others had written. And while it was true that the world of business and the world of aviation were merging in the mid-1930s Depression era, with bankruptcies rife and unemployment continuing to rise the men that the businessmen were putting their money behind were not the hardy pioneer adventurous types but responsible buttoned-down men who put long hours in at the office — a description which Smithy just didn't fit.

Compounding Kingsford Smith's problems was that not only was he not getting the hundreds of thousands of pounds he needed but, well, he didn't actually have the money he needed to live on, to pay his travel expenses, hotel accommodation and so forth. If the Australian government had fully paid for the *Southern Cross* as they had promised to do, he would have been okay, but — because government lawyers had yet to get to the bottom of the documentation to prove that Smithy was the plane's actual legal owner — they had withheld half the payment and an increasingly angry, frustrated and depressed Kingsford Smith was reduced to cabling John Stannage in Australia and asking him to take it up with the government on his behalf.[68] He needed that money, and he needed it immediately.

Despite his claims to journalist Edwin Parsons that he had a 'nice little air business' in Australia, the truth was that that business no longer existed, he had no capital of note as backup, and he was clearly unable to raise the money he needed in London to launch the trans-Tasman venture he just knew would work if given the chance! The walls were closing in, and there seemed precious few ways out.

In difficult times in the past, Smithy had traditionally fallen back on one of two options: taking up barnstorming until things got better, or breaking a record. Although in 1935 breaking records was not the wondrous thing it had been in the past — people didn't seem to care quite as much anymore — it was at least something. The more he thought about it, lying awake late at night, tossing and turning, the more it seemed like he had just one last option, now that the *Lady Southern Cross* had arrived and been offloaded.

'I'll fly her back to Australia,' he told Beau, 'and break Scott and Black's record of seventy-one hours to Melbourne. The publicity will do us a lot of good.'[69]

Beau argued strongly against it. In his passionately held view, 'breaking records and trying to start an international airline are two totally unrelated things ...!'[70] There was no doubt that Smithy was a wonderful pioneer flyer, as he had proved time and time and time again. What he had to prove now was that he was a canny aviation businessman who could be trusted to wisely spend whatever capital they could raise. If anything, breaking another record would work against them. Smithy, don't you see?!??

But Smithy wouldn't hear of it. He was going to break the record; going to show he could have won the Centenary Race if he had been given the chance, and that was that.

Beau was not nearly so sure.

For one thing, it was obvious to him that Smithy wasn't well. To fly a plane from England to Darwin in under fifty-two hours as he intended to do, was a gruelling task and could only be undertaken safely by someone who was physically fit and mentally strong. And Smithy in no way answered that description. Emotionally and physically exhausted, often bedridden, he was not remotely close to the level of fitness required, but nor would he hear of cancelling the flight.

Even beyond Smithy's determination to make the attempt, however, there were many problems, starting with the same one he had had with Australian officials over his plane's fuel capacity. Smithy's plan had been to use the American certification to get British certification, which would then allow him to get Australian certification when he got home. But, as before, the American certification would only allow a capacity of 145 gallons, which was the normal capacity for the Altair. And so the British — in the form of a twenty-year-old air official from the Air Ministry, still in his nappies when Smithy had flown his first plane — informed Kingsford Smith, quite reasonably, that he would only get certification for that amount and, *furthermore, hereto with pursuant, see Paragraph 3, Clause A*, he would have to remove all the extra tanks from the *Lady Southern Cross* that it had arrived in Britain with, or he wouldn't be able to fly it at all.

F—ing officals!

Scarcely believing that it was happening again, Smithy, at the end of his tether, was beside himself with rage. *He* was the one risking his life, not *them*, and *he* should bloody well know how much *his* plane could take! And it could take 514 gallons! How *dare* they impose a limit on him that was way less than a third of the amount he'd had in it when he had flown the bleeding Pacific Ocean! And back then, of course, as the first man in, the bloody bureaucrats hadn't yet had a chance to set up shop to try and strangle him. Back then there had been no certificates, no stamps, no endless paperwork, no officious officials continually trying to stop a man from doing what a man could do when left to his own devices.

Well, Smithy was on to their game, all right, he was. He just knew that all this was part of a British plan to prevent him, in an American plane, breaking Scott and Black's record, which had so magnificently and patriotically been done in a British plane.

In an attempt to break the impasse, the British Air Ministry gave the Australian the option to submit the Altair for stress analysis at the Royal Aircraft Establishment at Farnborough. Smithy declined — perhaps on the reckoning that she wouldn't pass muster when overloaded.

The usual flurry of telegrams, letters and meetings ensued as August turned into September turned into October and the weather began to cool, and finally the Air Ministry relented, at least a little. They agreed to allow him to keep the extra tanks on board, on the *strict* condition that he 'blank off' the extra tanks and take on no more than 145 gallons. Smithy agreed promptly, knowing full well that once he was out of British jurisdiction he could land at Marseilles and fill 'er up Bluey — up to bursting.

To go with him on this record attempt he decided to offer the position to young Tommy Pethybridge whom he had known, liked and worked with for many years, and who had, in fact, accompanied the *Lady Southern Cross* on her journey across the Atlantic. While Smithy would fly most of the way, Tommy's job would be to handle everything at each stop — to fill in the bloody paperwork, oversee the refuelling, attend to any mechanical needs and so forth — enabling Smithy to get at least a little shut-eye.

As to Tommy, he was, of course, delighted to receive the offer. He near worshipped Sir Charles, and to have a chance to fly with him into history and have his own name in the record books was something he could only have dreamed of. True, he also had concerns about the deteriorating health of Sir

Charles — who didn't look good, and seemed very jumpy and perpetually exhausted — but on the other hand, young Tommy was hardly in a position to question the greatest flyer in history as to whether or not he was up to the task. Time and again Smithy had proved himself the veritable Houdini of the air, somehow always managing to escape from situations that would have killed lesser pilots.

In fact, however, Smithy was finally beginning to have his own concerns about whether he was up to it or not, and after confiding in Beau, began to consult London's medical establishment. In the end there didn't seem to be a specific thing that ailed him, so much as an unhappy concurrence of exhaustion, anxiety and a general fug of depression.

Over the crackling phone all the way from Sydney, Mary begged him — positively *begged* him not to fly — and instead come back by sea with the *Lady Southern Cross* strapped on to the deck, as it had first arrived in Australia. So crook did he feel that Smithy was at last mercifully convinced, and after consultations with Beau, decided to do exactly that. There was, however, a problem …

Smithy had no more money than a squirrel. Getting himself and his plane home was an expensive exercise, not to mention keeping up mortgage payments on his new Darling Point home, and he *still* had not received a brass razoo further from the Australian government, which was continuing to quibble over the lack of proven ownership of the *Southern Cross.* An urgent cable was sent to John Stannage in Sydney, asking him to press the government for at least an advance on the money.

Finally, the answer came back from John Stannage. Sir Charles could have a further advance of £500, so long as he signed a document whereby the government would have the right to take, and sell, all of his household furniture if it turned out that the *Southern Cross* wasn't his to sell, and he therefore had no right to the money.[71]

And that, was indeed, the last straw.

TO HELL with the lot of them! He would be *damned* if he would sign any such humiliating document, even if he could have proved he owned the plane three times over. With no money to go back by ship, and no money to stay on, now he really did have no choice. He would *have* to fly home — and if he was going to do that he would make sure he broke the record and that would be the end of it. His whole flying experience to that point had been that no matter how bad he felt going into a flight, once in the air he mostly came good so he triumphed in the end, and he could only hope that would hold true this time as well.

After one false start when he had been beset so badly by a terrible flu that the flight had to be postponed, just after dawn on the morning of Wednesday, 23 October, he began to warm up the engine of the *Lady Southern Cross* and prepare to mount his attempt. There to see him off was Charles Scott, a good sport, whose fifty-two-and-a-half-hour record to Darwin and seventy-one-hour record to Melbourne Smithy was now determined to break. This was it, his last hurrah …

'I am now 38,' he told journalists gathered for the occasion, 'and win or lose, this is my last record attempt. Really, my last.'[72] And this time he really did mean it, acutely aware that this was his fair-dinkum last long flight. A bastard of a one, but one he just had to do.

No matter that he was back within a couple of days, after hitting a violent storm over Greece which did some damage to the wings, and he was obliged to limp back to Croydon via Brindisi, Italy. Of course, he was intent on trying again.

In the interim, Beau Sheil was preparing to leave for America hoping to raise in New York the capital they needed to get the Trans-Tasman Air Service Development Company Ltd established. He made one last attempt to convince Smithy to accompany him, on the grounds that his name and clout was what was needed, but Smithy refused to be dissuaded.[73] Beau, reluctantly, left him to it and sailed west across the Atlantic on 3 November 1935 after failing, at dockside, one last time to convince his friend to abandon the flight.

'I don't feel fit enough for the job,' Smithy told him, 'but I am going to see it through.'[74]

•

Mary pleaded with her husband. *Begged* him, her desperation crackling down the line. *Please* don't make this flight! PLEASE. Alas, the heavily pregnant Mary had no more success in the phone call she made the night before Charles was due to take off this second time around. She promised that if he would just get on a ship, she would meet him halfway in Ceylon, but nothing she said would change his mind. As she later told author Ian Mackersey, 'He admitted he was ill, but I knew that nothing I said would stop him. He just kept saying he wanted very desperately to get home to be with me. There was a sense of panic about the urgency, as if he couldn't hold out much longer.'[75]

That afternoon Smithy and Tommy Pethybridge flew the Altair from Croydon to Lympne on the Kentish coast, from where they reckoned they would have less chance of being fogged in for an early-morning departure. They stayed in Hythe Hotel at the Norman-times Cinque Port town of Hythe, 3½ miles from the airstrip.

At the first flush of dawn on 6 November 1935, they were ready once more. 'There'll be no turning back this time,' Smithy told one journalist, 'I must stick up somehow.'[76]

On top of everything else, Smithy had had a gutful of the cold and fog of England, of the constant sniffles, of wrapping up in heavy clothing and hopping up and down to keep warm, as his teeth chattered. If he could pull this off he would be back into an Australian summer before he knew it.

'I want to see the sunshine again,' he told another journalist, 'but most of all, get back to my family ...'[77]

And with that, they were off, flying away to the south-east at 6.28 am.

At 4.30 pm local time, they were in Athens, having traversed the 1760 miles in just eight hours, at an average speed of some 220 miles per hour. All good, everything going well. Next stop Baghdad, and they were on their way in only a couple of hours, arriving there at dawn the following day. Again their time was good, only ninety minutes behind Scott and Black at that stage, even though the Englishmen with their full tanks, from the beginning, had been able to fly there directly.

In Australia, everyone was waiting for news on his flight, but nowhere more than in Melbourne, where Mary had gone home to her mother's house to await the arrival of her husband in that city, and in Arabella Street, where Catherine was monitoring closely the progress of her last-born.

•

The good news was that at one o'clock on the afternoon of Thursday, 7 November, the *Lady Southern Cross* was spotted by an airport controller using binoculars at Karachi, cruising south-east at an altitude of about 15,000 feet — proven to be the level at which the supercharged Wasp engine worked at optimum efficiency, even if aviators had to breathe heavily to get enough oxygen in their lungs — a tiny speck in the far skies. Due to an infernal headwind, however, when Smithy and Pethybridge arrived at sundown at Allahabad's Bamrauli aerodrome, in Northern India, just over 2300 miles away from Baghdad, their time had fallen back to being nearly three hours behind Scott and Black's mark.[78]

One way of catching up was to simply refuel and keep going, barely taking the time to wolf down some food, let alone anything as indulgent as a rest. In total, they were on the ground for no more than an hour before they were winging their way onwards once again. Next stop, Singapore, which was 2200 miles away. If they could get the wind to go their way, they really might be able to cut into Scott and Black's record.

Just after 9 pm, the *Lady Southern Cross* was spotted in the moonlight over Calcutta's Dum Dum aerodrome, before Smithy took her out over his dreaded Bay of Bengal, the one exceedingly long stretch of water on the trip. Still, they made it, and around midnight, they were spotted above Akyab aerodrome in northern Burma, making good time by the light of a setting full tropical moon. From there, Smithy was heard, but not seen, flying over the Burmese capital of Rangoon at around 1.30 am. At three o'clock that morning of 8 November 1935, another Australian pilot by the name of Jimmy Melrose — endeavouring to break Smithy's solo record of seven days and four hours between England and Australia in his green

Percival Gull Four, *Westley* — was on his way to Singapore from Rangoon. Flying above the Andaman Sea off the coast of Burma, to his great excitement he thought he saw the blue glow from the twin exhaust pipes of Smithy's much faster Altair overtake him at an altitude of about 10,000 feet, a couple of hundred feet above him. An imprecise thing, true, at that time, in that situation, to positively identify another plane, but that was certainly his impression. It *had* to be good ol' Smithy. Still out there, still going strong! It was an honour to be in the same skies as the famous aviator.

When Jimmy landed in Singapore several hours later, a short time after dawn, he looked out for the *Lady Southern Cross* and was surprised it was not visible on the tarmac. Perhaps it was in one of the hangars being worked on or, just maybe, Smithy had already refuelled and taken off again, as his stamina was legendary. Either way, Jimmy's sense of disappointment was keen.

Where was Smithy, he asked cheerfully, upon alighting from his cockpit. Smithy hasn't arrived yet? But that's not possible! Jimmy had been in his much slower Percival Gull, while Smithy had been in his speedy Lockheed Altair, nudging 200 miles per hour at 13,000 feet altitude and he had *personally* seen Smithy overtake him in the wee hours of the morning! How could it be that he hadn't landed?

After talking it over with ground staff, the situation became as clear as it was serious. There were no other airports within cooee of the *Lady Southern Cross*'s fuel range, and the only possible explanation was that Smithy and Tommy Pethybridge had met with misadventure and perhaps … disaster. Within hours a major search operation was under way as squadrons of planes and fleets of ships methodically covered every square mile along his route. The searchers included Jimmy Melrose who announced that, 'I cannot continue while there is a chance of finding my fellow Australian',[79] and so immediately retraced his path to see if he could spot anything.

In Australia, Smithy's family was devastated that he had clearly failed to break the record, but not unduly worried that he hadn't turned up yet. Smithy's brother Wilfrid told the press: 'It is not likely the boys overflew Singapore. It is my theory he took the jungle route to Burma to avoid monsoon storms over the ocean. It is also possible that if forced down he may have landed on one of the emergency airport fields which have been established along the Malay Peninsula on the coast line of the Bay of Bengal, without radio communication. I have no fear for his safety. He has been lost several times before and I feel confident he will come out all right.'[80]

And so said all of them.

As to Mary, in Melbourne with Tommy Pethybridge's wife, she too was very upset that the record would not now be broken, but not unduly alarmed. 'He has been in many difficult situations,' she told the press, 'and his ability has always pulled him through. I have the utmost confidence in him, and I am sure that if he has met trouble he has made a safe landing.'

Strangely, despite all her previous fears about what *might* happen to him, now that he *had* actually disappeared she felt confident that her husband was safe somewhere. There had been other times when he'd gone missing, or had been hideously overdue and always, always he had turned up. That would no doubt be the case this time, too.

The search continued, with two RAF planes based in Penang flying off the coast of Siam, as well as over the Burmese jungle for any sign. Ships in the area were alerted to keep a lookout, as were the Imperial Airways and KLM aircraft travelling the route.[81] From Singapore, none other than Charles Scott himself, who happened to be passing through, took an RAF Singapore III reconnaissance flying boat and, after refuelling at Victoria Point began flying low over the Bay of Bengal, looking for the tiniest sign.[82]

Alas, between them all, after those first few days of frantic searching they turned up with … nothing. Undaunted, they continued to search, and before a week had passed every island on his route had been looked at, sometimes with landing parties. Wireless broadcasts went out to all stations asking people for any information they might have on the aviators, and leaflets were circulated among jungle dwellers in their own language, asking the same.[83] In Sydney, Hudson Fysh of Qantas Airways made plans to get one of their planes from Sydney to join in the search, and this was soon done.[84] All up, the biggest land and sea search operation in history was quickly under way.

Inevitably, in such circumstances there was a lot of focus on Jimmy Melrose's last sighting of the *Lady Southern Cross*, and just where that occurred, though not everyone gave that sighting credence. Qantas pilot George Urquhart 'Scotty' Allan, for one, went public with his view that the light of a ship on the horizon was easily mistaken for the exhaust trail of an aeroplane.[85]

As the days passed there was still no sign. No-one wanted to believe it — no-one *could* believe it — but inevitably hope began to fade. In the House of Representatives five days after the disappearance, Minister of Defence Archie Parkhill gravely informed the honourable members that the only action left was to search the dense jungle. What made it difficult, he noted, was that Kingsford Smith had left little in the way of a flight plan, and after he was certainly spotted above Rangoon, everything else was mere conjecture as to his next destination.

This was not good enough for the Opposition, with the ALP Member for Hunter, Rowland James, boring in, asking whether the government felt they had contributed to Kingsford Smith's death by having considered him too old for a government position. The government did not. The member for Melbourne, Mr William Maloney, asked the minister whether, with all the loss of life in such endeavours, record-breaking flights should be prevented from continuing. No, the government did not.[86]

From Arabella Street, Eric Kingsford Smith, Chilla's next oldest brother, told of how his family had been contacted by many mediums and spiritualists and received conflicting information about where the two men had come down.[87] One of these psychics divulged publicly that the men were no longer alive, their plane had landed in the sea at 8.12 am, floated for three hours and thirty-two seconds before sinking and drowning both aviators. They had sunk — let's see — 68 miles offshore.[88]

And then, just when despair was starting to set in, at last came the breakthrough. On Friday, 22 November, a fortnight after they had disappeared, flares were sighted by the captain of a vessel steaming past Sayer Island just off the coast of Siam — a place that was *right on Smithy's flight path.*[89] That had to be them! They should have known that Smithy would have survived!

Alas, as quickly as hope surged in Mary — now back in Sydney with Charles Jnr — as she took cautiously congratulatory phone calls and visits from her nearest and dearest, it died. A Qantas plane was assigned to buzz low over Sayer Island and did so for a couple of hours, but saw nothing. Had the missing pilots in fact been there, they surely would have managed to make themselves known. Clearly it was a false report.

On that very day, as it happened, the Defence Minister advised that the RAF would no longer be participating in the search, as the situation was now judged to be hopeless.

And then, as is the way of these things, another report came in. On Sunday, 24 November 1935, a report filtered back from a Siamese train-driver that he had heard from a woodcutter living in the area that, on the night Smithy disappeared, he had seen a plane in flames heading towards the Setul Mountains, on the border of Malaya and Siam, in the middle of a fierce storm.[90] Alas, after an RAF plane was dispatched to closely check the area this proved to be another false alarm.

Hope slumped. Mary hugged Charles Jnr all the tighter, and the Kingsford Smith clan held the both of them close to their collective bosom, as they hoped against hope there would be a breakthrough and that the obvious conclusion — that their beloved was dead — was not true.

And then, at last, and this time it really had to be something, came a genuinely credible report.

On Monday, 25 November, a crackly wireless message was received from the remote Siamese village of Kjupun, whereby a villager told how four days earlier he had met someone in another village who told him of how two weeks earlier a plane with a broken wing had landed in the jungle in the Laik Pu area, 85 miles south of Victoria Point. And they had found two airmen! One of them had a broken leg and the other was unhurt!

This time, *this time*, it had to be true. The whole report was too detailed to be conjured out of nothing.[91]

Sure enough, it more or less was true. But alas, when the whole thing was sorted out, it turned out to be two Polish airmen.

Smithy and Tommy Pethybridge remained missing as Christmas came and went. Mary took Charles Jnr down to spend some time with her parents in Melbourne, trying not to weep too often in front of her son, but not always succeeding. Catherine, under no such constraints, wept openly most of the time. Then New Year was upon them all.

Bit by bit the realisation really did sink in. As impossible as it seemed, that wonderful, laughing man — so full of energy, fun, vitality, charisma, derring-do, wisecracks, courage, vigour — had gone the way of Manfred von Richthofen, Harry Hawker, Ross Smith, Ormer Locklear, Charles Nungesser, John Moncrieff, George Hood, Bert Hinkler and so many, many others. How could they have believed it would have ended any other way? Could Smithy have truly believed it could turn out differently?

He was a daring flying man in a daring flying age when, almost without exception, flyers of daring died. Charles Kingsford Smith and those magnificent men all knew the risk, and went on regardless. They all had in common that they had pursued the greatest passion of their lives, and very much the passion of the age — flying — to the point that it had ended their lives.

The widows wept, the masses mourned, but at least these men had lived lives like no others, before or since — something worth remembering, and saluting, nigh on a century later.

Vale.

EPILOGUE

Surely it cannot be that this laughing, sunny-haired baby, eager boy and great-hearted man, who gave so much happiness to all around him, has really left us. Is it not more likely that in some sea-girt isle, carried thither by the drift of reckless ocean currents far from the ebb and flow of our fitful civilisation, he and his companion keep watch, with wistful eyes, for the help that seems so long in coming?

WINIFRED SEALBY, CHARLES KINGSFORD SMITH'S OLDEST SISTER, WRITING WHIMSICALLY IN 1950[1]

We need such performances as Sir Charles Kingsford Smith's, not only to advance the technique of transportation, but to enlarge our conception of our social destiny. The man who thinks nothing of skimming through the air for a distance of 3,000 miles between sunrise and sunset sets us dreaming of a Wellsian future, when the whole atmosphere will become a playground and the barriers to the free intercourse of nations seem ridiculous.

EDITORIAL IN THE *NEW YORK TIMES*, NOVEMBER 1935[2]

As it was, there was no other way for Smithy. To have dragged out his life in some physically secure but drab situation would have been death for him anyhow. He was completely right in setting out upon this flight. It was necessary for the freedom of spirit on which he lived.

BILL TAYLOR, ON SMITHY'S FINAL FLIGHT, AND ITS RESULT[3]

On 16 March 1936, Lady Kingsford Smith appeared in Sydney's Probate Court and swore to the death of her husband. 'From today,' said one press report, 'Sir

Charles Kingsford Smith is legally dead.'[4] Only a few months afterwards, on Friday, 14 August 1936, the Defence Minister, Archie Parkhill, announced that Mascot airport in Sydney would officially become Kingsford Smith Aerodrome to mark his contribution to world aviation.[5]

So what *did* happen to Smithy and Tommy Pethybridge?

To this day, no-one knows. The only trace that ever emerged came in May 1937, when two fishermen were walking along the rocky shore of Aye Island off the south coast of Burma (today's Myanmar), about 145 miles south-east of Rangoon, and came across the inflated wheel of an aircraft still attached to its undercarriage leg. Upon investigation, it was established that this wreckage belonged to the *Lady Southern Cross* — tangible proof, at least, that Smithy had crashed in water.

The most popular theory to have emerged since the disappearance is that, flying late that night, Smithy clipped the 463-foot top of the jungle-covered island, tried to get his plane back under control but ended up crashing into the waters just off the island — hence the wheel floating to the shore eighteen months later, as the action of the incoming and outgoing tides broke one of the wheels loose. That theory has at its base the investigation conducted by Captain Alan Eadon, the Director of Civil Aviation of Burma at the time, who wrote in his report 'if my suppositions are correct, then Aye Island must definitely be the scene of the accident and that the remainder of the wreckage of the aircraft lies covered with the sea around its shores.'[6]

The other theory — which I personally find compelling — is put most cogently by the New Zealand writer Ian Mackersey, who studied the issue from all angles for many years and even managed to obtain a rare permit from the Myanmar's military government in 1996 to visit Myanmar's south coast. There he was able to interview locals, including those of such age that they could remember the events of 1935.

Mackersey's view is that Jimmy Melrose's testimony that he saw the *Lady Southern Cross* can be accepted, and therefore Smithy was sighted at least 100 miles *south* of Aye Island. He contends that the prevailing currents in that area explain why the wheel, once it bobbed to the surface, would have subsequently drifted north.

In an effort to prove the Aye Island theory correct, searches have been mounted in those waters, first by Jack Hodder in 1938, and by Ted Wixted in 1983 with, alas, no trace found of an aircraft lying at the bottom of the sea. Then, in late February 2009, the Australian documentary maker Damien Lay — the man who originally approached me to write this book — mounted a major search with state-of-the-art sonar equipment looking for traces of a plane around Aye Island. In late March, Lay claimed he had been successful, based on sonar images he said matched remains of the plane, with the news first breaking in Sydney's *Daily Telegraph*.

'To me it's 100 per cent proof positive,' Lay was quoted as saying. 'The critical pieces of evidence are three equilateral triangles contained within what I believe is the starboard wing. These structures don't occur in nature and they measure exactly 1.5m × 1.5m × 1.5m. We know those are the dimensions in which these aircraft were manufactured.'[7]

What Lay took as proof-positive, however, others saw only as indeterminate grainy images, and most outspoken in extreme scepticism was Ian Mackersey himself, who called the claims 'nonsense'.

'The two occupants' bodies would have quickly disappeared without trace,' Mackersey told the press, 'and so, in those tropical waters, would all the wooden components — followed eventually by the light alloy sections which would include quite a bit of the engine. All that will remain somewhere, probably spread across 200 yards of the ocean floor, will be the few steel parts of the engine.'

For his part, Dick Smith told the *Sydney Morning Herald* of Lay's claims: 'It could be so but I think it's about a one in 1000 chance.'[8]

Undeterred, Lay has announced a plan to head back to Myanmar later in 2009 and mount a major retrieval operation to bring the plane back to Australia. I wish him well and hope he can prove us all wrong.

Whoever is right, there is no clue as to what catastrophic failure of equipment — or total exhaustion or just possibly terrible judgment of the pilot — led to the crash, wherever it occurred. But what is certain is that there had been a time on nearly every long flight when Kingsford Smith, in his own words, had been in many, many 'tough spots when it's been touch and go whether I lived or died ...'[9] Always, in those situations he had managed to find the solution, often *in extremis*, that had allowed him to live. This time, sick, exhausted, older, slower ... he did not and, again in his own words, it turned out that his 'number was up'.

Rest in peace, Smithy. You were a fascinating, courageous and inspiring man, a mixture of so many talents that for two decades of your adult life you were able to overcome your flaws to accomplish extraordinary things.

•

For her part, Catherine Kingsford Smith was devastated by her youngest son's death, outlived him by only a couple of years, and died at home on 18 March 1938.

•

Smithy's first wife, Thelma Corboy, never talked publicly about her first marriage, though in 1990 Mackersey was astounded to find that she was still alive at the age of eighty-nine and living in Perth. He made his best efforts to interview her, but was firmly rebuffed on the grounds that that part of her life was long gone and she wanted no-one to know that she had once been married to the 'great aviator', as she apparently referred to him. She had since gone on to a much happier second marriage.

Nevertheless, Mackersey persisted and via the intermediary of one of Thelma's cousins, Milton Baxter, was able to get much valuable detail about her time with Smithy, before she died in September of that year.

•

As to Lady Mary Kingsford Smith, in 1937 she married again, this time an Englishman, Alan Tully, who was the Australasian and Far Eastern manager of the Ethyl Corporation. From then on she lived mainly in America and Canada, where she raised her son, Charles Jnr — who was just three years old when his father died — as well as a second child, Belinda, who was born to the couple. (Sadly, the baby with whom she was pregnant to Smithy, was miscarried shortly after he disappeared.) After Alan Tully died in 1975, following thirty-eight years of marriage, Mary married in 1984 for a third time, to a former General Motors executive, Frank Noldin, and they lived in Florida. Mary lived until the middle of 1997 — dying at the age of eighty-seven — and generally remembered her first husband fondly, making herself available to appear at various commemorations over the years, as well as happily talking to most journalists and authors who asked her about him.

•

Charles Jnr is now retired from his career as an electronics engineer and lives in Colorado. Among other passions, he is a pilot and a courageous one. In 1978, to commemorate the fiftieth anniversary of the Pacific Ocean being crossed for the first time, he decided to co-pilot a Cessna 340 II pressurised twin — fitted with extra fuel tanks, of course — on its delivery flight from San Francisco to Sydney. During the preparations for this flight, the young Australian television journalist Ray Martin, then working for the ABC's *This Day Tonight*, turned up with the famed Vietnam War cameraman David Brill, wanting to fly with Charles Jnr from Wichita back to Colorado. And they would have, too, but when a tornado rolled in from Texas, blocking their path, Martin and Brill decided that it would be something close to suicide to take off.

Not Charles Kingsford Smith Jnr, though. Spying on his radar a tiny window of opportunity in the middle of the tornado, he decided to go and at least have a look as to how manageable the weather was, and took off without them … As he discovered, it wasn't remotely manageable and he ended up landing at a nearby airport, where he spent the night on a couch in the pilot's lounge.

No big deal. These things happen. Soon afterwards, Charles Jnr did indeed cross the Pacific in the path of his father, and was fêted upon arrival. For the record, the only memory he retains of his father is being taken on 'an airplane ride and sitting between two big men, one of them my father, I'm quite sure. I can still visualise the propeller turning in front — it must have been idling because I could see the blades. It was noisy and scary, and I was crying, and I think my mother was not too far away trying to comfort me. I don't remember the ride itself, nor coming back. But I definitely was not happy about the whole experience!'[10]

•

Captain Hancock continued his business and philanthropical ventures for another thirty years and passed away, just nudging ninety years old, in 1965, to the end the very personification of his motto 'Keep Moving'.

•

In September 1931, Captain Les Holden who was piloting the *Canberra* when it discovered the *Southern Cross* and its crew at Coffee Royal, flew from Sydney to New Guinea in an historic first, and essentially followed up on Bobby Hitchcock's dream by starting a successful air-freight business in those parts. Alas, the following year, on 18 September 1932, while briefly back in Australia, he was killed when a plane he was travelling in from Sydney to Brisbane crashed near Byron Bay.

•

Jimmy Melrose did not survive Charles Kingsford Smith for long. On Sunday, 5 July 1936, he was killed instantly when, in the middle of a terrible storm over South Melton, Victoria, his wooden Heston Phoenix plane crashed into a field strewn with boulders, one of which connected with his head, splitting it, according to the *Canberra Times*, 'like an overripe rockmelon'.[11]

•

After years of languishing in storage, the *Southern Cross* at last emerged to public view when it was placed in a hangar at Brisbane's Eagle Farm airport on 17 August 1958. High in the air above, a skywriter traced the word 'Smithy' in the clear blue Brisbane sky, while five RAAF Meteor jets flew over the ceremony in a formation representing the celestial Southern Cross.[12] Charles Ulm's son, John — who had gone on to a distinguished career as a journalist and then executive with Qantas — presided at the dedication. Most interestingly, he had been instrumental in getting Harry Lyon, now a rather crotchety 73-year-old, to attend with his wife. Ol' Harry — who had served his country once again in World War II, even commanding a small cargo vessel — said very little at the ceremony, but one thing that he stated into a microphone John Ulm would treasure ever afterwards: 'Without Charlie Ulm, we would never have got into the air.'[13] Thirty years on, and it was at last all even on the cards between Harry and Charles Ulm.

Harry passed away in the Veterans Hospital at Togus, Maine, on 30 May 1963.

•

As to Jim Warner, who also came out to Australia for the dedication with one of the six wives he married in his allotted life span, the one constant in his life was radio. After returning from that first Pacific crossing he opened a radio shop in Fresno, California, before serving in World War II as a radio instructor. He did, nevertheless, complain for the rest of his life — I said, he did, NEVERTHELESS, COMPLAIN for the rest of his life — that the *Southern Cross* journey had permanently damaged his hearing. He died in 1970 at the age of seventy-eight.[14]

•

With Eagle Farm airport closing, the *Southern Cross* was moved again in late 1987 to its present and permanent home at the Sir Charles Kingsford Smith Memorial, on the approaches to Brisbane airport.

•

The fate of the effete Alberto Santos-Dumont, who first came to fame as the flying dandy of Paris and the first man to get an aircraft aloft in Europe, is a curious one. By the early 1930s, he was living in the land of his birth, Brazil, and on 23 July 1932, while in the city of Guarujá, he hanged himself, without leaving a note. It was, however, said that he was depressed over both the fact that he had been diagnosed with multiple sclerosis, and how aircraft, his beloved flying machines, had become devastating weapons of war. (A mercy then, perhaps, that he did not live to see the likes of the London Blitz, or the levelling of Dresden by Allied bombers in World War II.)

•

Of the *14-bis* itself, I can find no trace. The best reckoning seems to be that Santos-Dumont broke up that original to use in subsequent planes. A number of flying replicas have been built and are extant in Brazil. One of the replicas was displayed at the 2005 Le Bourget Paris Airshow. Another replica was unsuccessful in becoming airborne during a test flight at Bagatelle in 2006 when a wing folded.

•

The *Blériot XI* hangs from the ceiling of the *Musée National des Art et Metiers Techniques* in Paris, not quite forgotten but certainly with little fanfare. To look at it up close is to be simply staggered by both its fragility and Blériot's courage in setting off across the English Channel in it. At Les Barraques, from where he set off, the once rolling farmlands are now densely populated and the point of departure is today a school, but at least that school is named after Blériot. Alicia would have been proud.

•

Louis Blériot, with his wife, Alicia, beside him all the way, continued to prosper through the 1920s and early 1930s, as his aviation manufacturing company Blériot-Aéronautique maintained its position as a leader in its field. He remained a highly respected figure in the international aviation community until his death on 1 August 1936, in Paris. He is buried in the Cimetière des Gonards in Versailles.

•

Anthony Fokker also prospered throughout the 1930s, the Depression notwithstanding, with his planes being placed with no fewer than fifty-four airlines around the world. Alas, in 1939 he contracted pneumococcal meningitis — an inflammation of the brain and spinal cord — and, after fighting a losing battle for three weeks, died in New York City. He was forty-nine years old.

•

These days, Roland Garros is famed as the name of the stadium where the French Tennis Open is played in Paris every year, though the man himself, his long-distance aviation feats and the fact that he was the first to turn his plane into a flying machine gun has been substantially forgotten. After he was shot down by the Germans in 1915 and taken prisoner, he was well treated by his captors, being put in a camp for elite prisoners. Desperate to get back to fight in the war, Garros made many attempts to escape and finally succeeded in February 1918, when he crossed the border into Holland. He returned to an air war that was unrecognisable from the one he had left, in which the planes were far faster and more manoeuvrable, and the guns far more lethal than anything he had experienced to that point. On 5 October 1918, just five weeks before Armistice, and the day before his thirtieth birthday, Roland Garros was shot down and killed at Vouziers, in the Ardennes region. There he was buried, and there lie his remains today.

•

And then there was Charles Nungesser. As recounted in Mark Sufrin's book, *The Brave Men*, a lobster fisherman was working his pots in Casco Bay off Maine, on the east coast of the United States, in January 1961 when he was surprised to haul onto his boat a strange catch — a large piece of aluminium with some rivets apparent. He handed it over to police and, after scientific examination, the word came back that it appeared to be part of an aircraft made in the 1920s. What is more, when all the gunk over the metal was cleaned off, it showed a coat of white paint, with an edging of black. Perhaps part of an enormous black heart?[15] If so, Nungesser and Coli really did get extraordinarily close to flying across the Atlantic Ocean, from Paris to New York.

•

Not the slightest trace of the New Zealand aviators Moncrieff and Hood has ever been found, though there have been many false dawns. As to their widows, Dorothy Moncrieff lived at the same address in Wellington for many years afterwards, but a few months after her 31-year-old husband disappeared, the very private Laura Hood returned to her native England to nurse her ill mother and never returned.

•

Wigram Field, where Kingsford Smith and Ulm landed in September 1928 to complete the first trans-Tasman crossing, remained the hub of New Zealand aviation for many decades afterwards. By pure happenstance, I visited Wigram on 27 February 2009, the last day it was to be operational as an airfield. Though houses will soon be marching across it — as part of a new development — the actual spot where the *Southern Cross* landed will be marked for perpetuity by a plaque in a park.

•

Harry Hawker has been substantially forgotten in his native Australia, despite his massive contribution to international aviation. Melbourne's Moorabbin airport is also known as Harry Hawker Airport, and his name lives on in the the famed aero-structure component-manufacturing company Hawker de Havilland, a division of Boeing. This is a direct descendant on the corporate family tree of the company H.G. Hawker Engineering, which Hawker had established in 1920 with Sir Thomas Sopwith and two others, which continued to prosper after his tragic death at the age of thirty-two.

•

Muriel Hawker, aged twenty-six, was left with two toddler daughters when her husband died. Consumed by grief, she could only just function. Spurred on by Mrs Phyllis Sopwith, however, she resolved to set down for posterity the extraordinary events of Harry's life, and in July 1922 her book, *HG Hawker: Airman — His Life and Work*, was published. To provide an income Muriel started a shop in London selling smallgoods, put it on its feet, and in due course, bought another. And then another. And then still another. In 1929 she married again, this time a ship's doctor, whom she had met on a voyage to New York — but sadly, he died only six years later. Bowed but unbroken, Muriel married a third time just before the outbreak of World War II — another doctor — and more or less lived happily ever after, never too far from her daughters or subsequent six grandchildren, and great-grandchild. 'It must have been an odd sort of life,' her grandson, Kenneth Hope-Jones, noted in a letter to me in December 2008. 'The early years with Harry were meat and drink to a girl of Muriel's spirit, and were surely the most entrancing years of her life: and yet she lived for another sixty-two years after Harry's death. But she never lived in the past: she got on with her life and lived it to the full. I, her eldest grandchild, remember her with great affection.'

Muriel died in 1983 at the age of eighty-seven, adored by all of her descendants.

•

Both of Bert Hinkler's most famous aeroplanes — the Avro Baby, G-EACQ, and his Avro Avian, G-EBOV — are at the Queensland Museum in Brisbane and are impressively displayed. As to Nancy, the seeming love of Hinkler's life, there is little trace of her beyond the first few months after his death — and for good reason. In a bizarre tale, it turned out that although they had intended to marry after the Great War, there was a legal impediment caused by her previous marriage being technically still in existence. So they had simply lived together as a married couple to all intents and purposes — and certainly, Nancy was always described in the press as his wife, 'Mrs Hinkler'. But wait, there's more. For Nancy, Bert's family and the Australian authorities were all staggered to find out in the weeks after his death that on Saturday, 21 May 1932, eight months before his death, Hinkler had secretly married in Connecticut an American woman by the name of Katherine Rome, whom he had met seven years previously. As this was, apparently, his only legal marriage, it was Katherine who subsequently inherited his estate. It was a saga worthy of a book, and the late, great, Ted Wixted has written it: *The Last Flight of Bert Hinkler.*

In 1936 Bert's mother, Frances, travelled from her home in Bundaberg, Queensland, all the way to the other side of the world, to Italy, and visited both the monument that had been built at the spot where her Bert had crashed, and his grave in Florence. In 2008, that gravesite was refurbished by the Hinkler House Memorial Museum, situated in his home town of Bundaberg.

•

The good fortune of the DC-2 *Uiver*, which was so wonderfully saved in Albury, did not last long. Only a few months later, it disappeared while on a routine flight between Amsterdam and Batavia in the Dutch East Indies — now Indonesia — flying the Cairo-to-Baghdad leg in the early hours of 20 December 1934. At 2.30 am, a radio message was received in Baghdad reporting that the DC-2 was lost, and then nothing more was heard. Its burnt-out wreckage was found two days later in the Syrian desert, with the loss of all seven lives on board, although many items of its singed cargo of Christmas mail were retrieved and today attract a premium on the philatelic market.[16]

•

Sir Keith Smith, who had first risen to fame as the co-winner of the famous £10,000 race in 1919 between England and Australia, with his brother Sir Ross Smith in their Vickers Vimy plane, long endured as a respected figure in the Australian aviation industry. After that victory, and the subsequent tragic death of his brother, he became the representative of Vickers in Australia, and was a highly regarded director of many airlines and other public companies. He died, aged sixty-five, on 19 December 1955, a wealthy man. In his will, he left a bequest to Wally Shiers, the only surviving crew member of the England to Australia flight. The Vickers Vimy plane G-EAOU is now proudly displayed at Adelaide airport.

•

As to Koene Dirk Parmentier — the *Uiver*'s courageous pilot on that dark and stormy night over Albury — he fared a little better.

By the end of World War II he had risen to the position of the Dutch airline KLM's chief pilot, and then devoted himself to the company's training school, where he was particularly strong on lecturing young pilots on aviation's many dangers and how to avoid them. Especially, the importance of watching out for the power lines on the approaches to Prestwick airport in Scotland, he said, showing slides. Tragically, in 1948, while in command of KLM Lockheed Constellation *Nijmegen* in deteriorating weather, he took the big airliner into those very wires, and all on board were killed. The airport's approach charts were riddled with errors and the pylons for the 132,000-volt main national-grid cables were shown as being 45 feet high. They were really at 450 feet — the height at which Parmentier was circling to an alternative runway which he had forbidden KLM pilots to use at Prestwick in low cloud.[17]

•

In 1977, the multimillionaire electronics entrepreneur and aviation enthusiast Dick Smith set out with a team in well-equipped four-wheel drives and a helicopter to find the *Kookaburra* in the Tanami Desert. It eluded them. Undeterred, and knowing it was there, he and his team returned the following year and, after another six days' search, they found it, on 21 August 1978. The Northern Territory Museum immediately sent out a ground party to recover the wreckage, which is now on permanent display in Alice Springs, a stone's throw from where it took off for its last flight.

•

Bon Hilliard never really got over the death of Keith Anderson. In 1935, she did marry another good man, Major Thomas Tate, though he died just eleven years later, and she never remarried. And yet the wounds caused by the aviator's tragic death remained raw. In 1977, it was Dick Smith who told her personally that the telegram she had sent to Keith in April 1929, advising that she did still want to marry him, had reached him at Broken Hill, as it was found on his corpse. She cried at the news — it was something that had haunted her for decades. Such was her feeling for Anderson that a part of her final will and testament, opened upon her death in 1982 was the request that her ashes be scattered from the air above Keith's grave in Mosman's Rawson Park. Sadly, it was no simple matter in the early 1980s to take a light plane low over a heavily built-up area for such a purpose, and it was not possible to fulfil that request.

•

In the meantime, on 12 May 1981, after much searching, Dick Smith also located the site of Coffee Royal where Smithy had put the *Southern Cross* down in 1929. As a matter of interest, he decided to burn some sump oil to see if it would show up against the green foliage that abounded all around. It didn't show up. And yet burning some branches that they cut down clearly did.

Smithy had been right!

•

From being no more than a remote religious settlement, Drysdale River Mission achieved rather more significant aviation fame in World War II, when it became the site for an air base, and was heavily bombed by the Japanese for its trouble in 1943. It now has the name of Kalumburu and is a closed Aboriginal community.

•

On the fortieth anniversary of the first aerial crossing of the Tasman Sea — 11 September 1968 — Ross McWilliams, a pilot for Air New Zealand, flew one of that airline's DC-8s from Christchurch to Sydney. On board was his father, none other than Tom McWilliams. Greeting them in Sydney was Hal Litchfield — whose career after his flying days were over had encompassed returning to marine navigation on the *Tahiti*, and joining the Royal Australian Navy Reserve — thus reuniting the last two survivors of the first Tasman flight, as well as the Coffee Royal episode.

After those adventures, Tom had forged a successful career as a sales representative with the Shell Oil Company, before being put in charge of the Royal New Zealand Air Force's Air Training Corps during World War II, and then embarking on a successful career in business after the war was over. When the fiftieth anniversary of the first crossing was celebrated, this time with Ross McWilliams flying an Air New Zealand DC-10 from Sydney to Christchurch, alas Tom McWilliams had been in his grave for five months, having died on 28 April 1978. And yet, on board was not only Hal Litchfield, still going strong, but Charles Kingsford Smith Jnr and John Ulm. Hal Litchfield, after a career in the Royal Australian Naval Reserve, died in 1987.

•

On 26 October 1958, a young construction worker on the Snowy Mountains Scheme, by the name of Tom Sonter, momentarily jack of working seven days a week, decided to take Sunday morning off to go for a walk up Mount Blackjack, within a few cooees of the tiny village of Tumbarumba.[18] It was a beautiful day and, wandering from his original destination, he was heading through heavy foliage in Deep Creek Gorge, about 150 yards below the ridge line, when, for no good reason he could think of, he stopped to look around.[19] Then he saw something that looked a little odd. It was a mound of earth that didn't look natural in an environment that was otherwise entirely untouched by man. Going over to investigate, he found a bit of metal, from which tall saplings protruded, and put his hand on it. It looked like some kind of tubular steel. And this, what was this? A moveable horizontal flap on what looked to be the tail of … an aircraft? In an instant, the big lump of indeterminate shape before him formed up into what it was — the remains of a crashed plane from long ago. In the silence, birds twittering nearby suddenly seemed unnaturally loud, and the buzz of the Australian bush almost a little oppressive. Uncertain if this wreck was known or unknown, he walked back to camp with a petrol cap and a stamped engine part. Before long his world went crazy — it turned out he had discovered the *Southern Cloud*.

Among the few human remains that were found — basically fragments of bone — was a gold men's watch that had stopped at 1.15 pm. From Sydney the plane had only made 220 miles, at an average of just 44 miles per hour. For the families of those who had gone missing all those years ago the discovery of the wreckage was a bittersweet relief.

The granddaughter of pilot Travis 'Shorty' Shortridge, Cynthia Balderstone, would ever after remember going with her brother Christopher, as they accompanied their mother, Yvonne — Shorty's daughter — down to Bondi Beach on a moonlit night not long afterwards.[20] All their lives, their mother had never said that their grandfather had 'died', only that he was 'lost'. And now she at last knew the truth. As they stood there by the water's edge in the moonlight, their middle-aged mother used a stick to scrawl in the sand, the words:

Daddy, now I know where you are[21]

And then the three of them stood alone on the beach in the moonlight, watching that scrawl until a wave came and washed it away. After her death, Yvonne's ashes were scattered at the crash site.

•

Bill Taylor was awarded an MBE for his bravery in saving the *Southern Cross* in 1934 as it staggered back across the Tasman, and this was later changed to a George Cross, when the awards system was altered. He went on to a sterling aviation career which included being the first man to cross the Indian Ocean by air. In 1954, Taylor was knighted for his services to aviation and, as one of the most respected aviators in the world, died of a heart attack in Honolulu on 16 December 1966, aged seventy.

•

As to the other notable Taylor of Australian aviation, George A. Taylor, who founded the Aerial League of Australia and was at the forefront of the need for the Australian government to get behind Australian aviation — he died in his bath in his Sydney home on 20 January 1928, after an epileptic seizure.

•

Harry Houdini, of course, continued to build his extraordinary fame as a magician, long after his visit to Australia in 1910, though there is no record of him ever flying again after his efforts at Rosehill Racecourse in April of that year. In 1926 he was in Montreal and was asked by an aggressive McGill University theology student, J. Gordon Whitehead, what the magician's opinion was 'of the miracles mentioned in the Bible'? Houdini was instantly cautious. He had run a long and public campaign against so-called spiritualists, mediums and the like, exposing them as frauds and charlatans, but had learnt to draw the line before attacking religion, as many people were easily offended.

'I prefer,' he therefore said in reply, 'not to discuss or to comment on matters of this nature.'[22]

But then, uncharacteristically deciding to go a bit further, Houdini continued. 'I would make one observation however — what would succeeding generations have said of Houdini's feats had he performed them in Biblical times? Would they have been referred to as "miracles"?'

Whitehead was indeed offended, perhaps outraged, and followed up with another, aggressive question. 'Is it true, Mr. Houdini that you can resist the hardest blow struck to the abdomen?'[23]

On safer ground, Houdini replied that that was true — as he was also a physical fitness fanatic and sometimes gave demonstrations of his physical strength — and yet, before he was properly ready to take any blows, Whitehead then hit Houdini four or five hard blows to the stomach before the 52-year-old protested. Although Houdini didn't know it, his appendix had burst and peritonitis soon set in. Two nights later at the Garrick Theater in Detroit, Michigan, on 24 October 1926, Harry collapsed on stage with a raging fever. He was revived and — a trouper to the end — finished the show, and was hospitalised at Detroit's Grace Hospital the next day where his appendix was immediately removed. It was there that he died, at 1.26 pm on 31 October (Halloween) 1926, in room 401.[24]

For his funeral — held at the Machpelah Cemetery in Queens, New York, before 2000 mourners — Houdini was laid in the very coffin that he had long used in his magic shows, and atop it was placed a broken wooden wand to symbolise that without its master, the wand no longer had the magic and so was broken. Inside the coffin the magician's head rested, as he had instructed, on a packet of letters from his mother. As it was lowered, his great friend, and pallbearer, Broadway impresario Florenz Ziegfeld, whispered, 'Suppose he isn't in it?'[25]

To this day there is no sign that he has escaped. And yet, deep reverence for him continues. Each year, in November, the Society of American Magicians holds its 'Broken Wand' ceremony at his gravesite, where they gather to remember the greatest magician of them all.

•

Tom Campbell Black, who rose to fame as one-half of the celebrated Scott and Campbell Black team that won the Centenary Air Race died, as did so many pilots of those early times of aviation, in a freak, tragic accident on 19 September 1936. Having just been christened *Miss Liverpool 1* at a ceremony at Speke airport, Tom's Percival Mew Gull was being taxied out to give the large crowd a demonstration of the tiny, sleek racer's grace and pace when an RAF Hawker Hart light-bomber biplane landed and collided head-on with the almost invisible white Gull. The whirling propeller savaged a gash in the cockpit and inflicted fatal injuries to Tom's shoulder and left arm. He died in the ambulance. He was forty-seven years old.

•

And yet, even for those famous pilots who were spared death by tragic crashes, their lives often became problematic. A case in point was Campbell Black's partner, Charles Scott, forever known in aviation circles as C.W.A. Scott.[26] The immediate years after his win were a triumph for Scott as he went from dinner to dinner, to champagne-soaked gala day to aviation gathering of the good and the great, to … all hail Scottie, as we lift a glass once more! One of the most celebrated men of his day — and here's to Scottie one more time for the road — his autobiography was a best-seller. From there he earned a living, among other things, writing elegant aviation pieces for *The Times* and the *Daily Telegraph* and winning air races.

Then World War II changed everything. Aviation again took a quantum leap forward — alas, this time without him on board. For a while all he could do was get work as an ambulance driver; then he joined the Royal Navy Volunteer Reserve as a lieutenant, and took part in the Dakar landing. He also spent a period as an Atlantic ferry pilot. By the time the war was over, the air race that had made him famous, although it had occurred only eleven years earlier, was ancient history. Great Britain had an entirely new crop of heroes and he was not remotely of their number. Of the many fatalities of that war, one of the key ones was the world he had known before it. Marriages came and went, and it was only alcohol that seemed to help, and then just for a short time. On 15 April 1946 he had had enough and shot himself dead.[27] C.W.A. Scott was aged forty-two.

•

Max Valier, the man who first came to the world's attention when he was described by Ivan Federov of the All Inventors Vegetarian Club of Interplanetary Cosmopolitans as a 'German moon fan' who was going to accompany him on a rocket to the moon, actually went on to do some very good work in the field. Educated in physics at the University of Innsbruck, Valier was passionate in his advocacy of the use of rockets for space flights and, in fact, did a lot of experimentation with them in the late 1920s. He wrote a book, *Der Vorstoß in den Weltenraum* (The Advance into Space), which helped to popularise the idea to the wider public, and in 1928 he and two close colleagues were credited with building the world's first rocket-powered automobile. He started to be taken seriously as not just a moon fan but as a rocket scientist. Alas, two years later while he was testing another rocket engine it blew up and killed him.

For all that, many of Valier's strange ideas were entirely vindicated on 20 July 1969, when Neil Armstrong — himself something of a moon fan — took one small step for a man, one giant leap for mankind and so lived aviation's most stunning moment since Orville Wright left the ground in the *Flyer* on the late morning of 17 December 1903. In just sixty-six years, aviation had gone from a few feet off the ground to one foot on the moon.

•

Orville Wright lived in Dayton, Ohio, until 30 January 1948 and died at the age of seventy-six — at a time when planes had not only breached the mythological 'sound barrier' of Mach 1, around 700 miles per hour, but had gone faster than 1000 miles per hour.

•

As to the men who had survived the horrors of the Great War in Passchendaele, Fromelles, Villers-Bretonneux and the like, they and those thousands who had fallen were not forgotten and, in fact, there has been a resurgence of interest in that war in Australia in recent years. Those who survived it took the memory of it to their graves. On 12 July 2007, the last survivor of Passchendaele, a Brit by the name of Harry Patch, was quoted in the London *Daily Telegraph*: 'I fell in a trench. There was a fella there. He must have been about our age. He was ripped shoulder to waist with shrapnel. I held his hand for the last 60 seconds of his life. He only said one word: "Mother". I didn't see her, but she was there. No doubt about it. He passed from this life into the next, and it felt as if I was in God's presence. I've never got over it. You never forget it. Never.'[28]

Harry himself is, at the time of writing in April 2009, 110 years old, making him the second oldest man living in the United Kingdom and believed to be the ninth oldest man in the world. Old soldiers never die …

•

Fergus McMaster remained chairman of Qantas until he was obliged to retire in 1947 because of ill-health. He was knighted in 1941 for his contribution to Australian aviation and died on 8 August 1950, aged seventy-one.

•

After leaving Qantas in 1922, Paul 'Ginty' McGinness worked first as a stockbroker and eked out a rough living on his Morawa property in Western Australia — going through two marriages along the way — before suffering a heart condition and losing his land. When World War II broke out, he volunteered once more and served with the RAAF, training young recruits to fly. When the war ended he returned to farming, trying his luck growing tobacco, but both his physical and spiritual health were waning. On 25 January 1952 he died in Perth's Hollywood Hospital, aged just fifty-six, and his body is buried in a humble grave in Perth's Karrakatta Cemetery. The grave was paid for by the government for the fact that McGinness was a war veteran, though long after he died Qantas put a plaque by his grave to honour his founding role in the company.

•

Hudson Fysh remained first the managing director and then the chairman of Qantas, until he retired in 1966, at which time Qantas had nineteen passenger jets. He was knighted in 1953, 'in recognition of outstanding services in pioneering and developing Australian aviation'.[29] The last decision he took as chairman was to encourage the board to ratify buying Boeing 747 jumbo jet aircraft, which they did. He died in 1974, aged seventy-nine. To this day, when Qantas produces an advertisement that involves showing the name of a passenger on a frequent flyer card or boarding pass or some such, the name Hudson Fysh is used. Also, the Qantas Boeing 747-400 fleet have *Longreach* printed on their fuselage, as a doffing of the cap to their rustic beginnings. Qantas currently carries around 30 million passengers a year to eighty-one destinations in forty countries scattered across the globe. It also carries mail for some 114 postal administrations around the world. Airmail subsidies were stopped in 1954.

•

Norman Brearley withdrew from commercial aviation in 1936 after West Australian Airways was purchased by Adelaide Airways for £25,000 to become part the new Australian National Airways. Still not done with flying, however, he went on to serve with the RAAF during World War II. A highly respected figure in the aviation community, he was knighted in 1971, and died in Perth in 1989 at the age of ninety-nine.

•

Lester Brain, who discovered the lost *Kookaburra*, went on to a glittering aviation career and became the first general manager of Trans-Australia Airlines. A book by Neil Cadigan was recently published on him, entitled *A Man Among Mavericks: Lester Brain, Australia's Greatest Aviator.* Lester Brain died on 30 June 1980.

•

Information on John Stannage is, frankly, hard to come by. It is known that by the late 1930s he and his wife Beris had moved back to New Zealand and opened a radio shop called Stannage Wireless in Auckland, and he also seems to have tried his hand briefly at radio broadcasting, on 1XB. In 1944 he wrote and published his reminiscences about his time flying, *High Adventure*, and when this was well received followed it up in 1950 with an affectionate biography of his former boss, *Smithy*. And then he faded from view …

•

Nancy-Bird Walton passed away peacefully in her Neutral Bay home on Tuesday, 13 January 2009.

•

George Hubert Wilkins lived a long and fruitful life — amazing for the number of things he did. In the northern summer of 1931 he was the captain and key mover of an expedition to take a Nautilus submarine under the North Pole. They said it couldn't be done and … and in that particular instance they were right. Nevertheless, Wilkins did much of the work whereby it later was done and he is acknowledged as, effectively, the father of exploration in that region — this, despite a litany of spectacular aeroplane crashes.

A measure of the respect in which he was held by the scientific community is wonderfully recounted by Simon Nasht in his book *Last Explorer.* Nasht tells the story of what happened after Sir Hubert Wilkins died suddenly and unexpectedly, aged seventy, in his Framingham, Massachusetts, hotel room on 30 November 1958, and was subsequently cremated. Four months later, on 17 March 1959, the American submarine USS *Skate* broke through the polar ice cap at a point near the North Pole and scattered Wilkins's ashes in that part of the world that he, more than anyone, had done so much to explore.

•

Ben Eielson, George Wilkins's faithful pilot, was tragically killed in 1929, just a year after his great triumph with Wilkins. Typically, he was flying into the black heart of a raging storm to try to rescue the crew of a whaler stuck in ice off the coast of Alaska. It was three months before a rescue party found the plane and the dead pilot.[30]

•

And Robert Buie, the man many credit as being the one who shot down the Red Baron? Not long after accomplishing that feat he suffered a heart attack and was invalided out of the front line and sent home to Australia. There, he tried to get a war pension, but this was refused by the government on the grounds that his heart condition was not believed to be war related.[31] He subsequently lived a relatively gentle life, fishing and oyster farming on the Hawkesbury River, on the New South Wales central coast, where he had grown up. A certain renown followed him as the man who had shot down the Red Baron and I remember my own mother proudly telling me that the man who had accomplished that feat had lived not far from us, on our farm at Peats Ridge. Alas, on Anzac Day 1964, at the age of seventy, Robert Buie was found dead in his boat, adrift on the Hawkesbury. His headstone in Brooklyn cemetery has the simple epitaph: '*He shot down the Red Baron.*' (And for what it's worth, I reckon he did exactly that.)

•

As to the Red Baron himself, Manfred von Richthofen, his fate after his death at the age of twenty-six was a curious one. Immediately after the war was over, his body was moved from Bertangles to a nearby German military cemetery on the outskirts of the French town of Fricourt. It was from there in 1925 that his brother Bolko claimed it, intending to rebury him in the family plot at Schweidnitz Cemetery — beside their father, who had died of natural causes in 1920, and their 28-year-old brother, Lothar, who had been killed when his plane had crashed in 1922. And yet once the German government became aware that one of the Fatherland's most famous sons was returning to German soil, it managed to persuade Bolko to have him buried in the Invalidenfriedhof Cemetery in Berlin, a place where most of Germany's greatest military heroes and leaders are interred.[32]

On the occasion of his re-interment, on 20 November 1925, none less than the German President, Paul von Hindenburg, attended, together with the German Chancellor Hans Luther, and most of the cabinet and the good and the great of the day. In 1938, Hermann Wilhelm Göring, then Adolf Hitler's Minister for Economic Affairs, and given the responsibility for the German rearmament program, added a massive monument atop the grave.

When the Berlin Wall was built in 1961, it transpired that the Invalidenfriedhof was in the Communist Russian eastern sector, meaning that the von Richthofen family, who substantially lived in the western sector, could only visit the gravesite with special permission. It was because of this that Bolko applied for permission from the East German government to once again reclaim his brother's body and this time do what he had intended to do in 1925, and bury him in the family plot. Though this did not happen before Bolko died in 1971, the reburial did take place in 1976, and that is where Manfred von Richthofen lies to this day, in the family's tomb in Wiesbaden.

•

Charles Lindbergh's life was forever altered by his feat of flying solo over the Atlantic, and although his fame never faltered, his popularity certainly did. In 1941 — by which time the couple had three other children in addition to their deceased oldest child, the kidnapped Charles Jnr — Lindbergh emerged as a leading exponent of the view that America should not enter World War II, just as his father, a Congressman from Minnesota, had been outspoken against America entering World War I. At Des Moines, in 1941, Lindbergh was quoted as saying, 'the three most important groups who have been pressing this country towards war are the Roosevelt administration, the British, and the Jews'.[33] To be fair, he went on to soften that seemingly anti-Semitic slur by saying how he, for one, could understand Jews agitating the way they did. 'The persecutions they suffered in Germany would be sufficient to make bitter enemies of any race. But instead of agitating for war, the Jewish groups in this country should be opposing it in every possible way, for they will be among the first to feel its consequences. A few far-sighted Jewish people realise this. But the majority still does not.'

And then to the line that finished him.

'Their greatest danger to this country lies in their large ownership and influence in our motion pictures, our press, our radio, and our government.'

His reputation never recovered, though after the Japanese attack on Pearl Harbor a few months later he did drop his resistance to the war and surreptitiously flew with the American Army Air Forces, flying fifty combat missions in the Pacific and downing one Japanese plane. After the war he devoted himself, among other things — which we'll get to — to writing his memoirs, and his 1953 autobiography, *The Spirit of St. Louis*, went on to win the Pulitzer Prize.

Lindbergh kept flying, and he was one of the few pioneer aviators of his generation not to have died in a plane crash. And over the years, most particularly from the mid 1950s on, he couldn't help noticing how much the America beneath his wings was changing from what it once had been. The vast tracts of wilderness he had seen from the air were, year by year, and then month by month, disappearing. It turned him into a committed environmentalist.

'Few men,' he said in a rare chat with reporters, while passing through Hawaii in 1971, 'have seen with their own eyes, as I have in the past 50 years, the serious breakdown — catastrophic in some instances — of America's land surface. I have seen the fences pushed westwards, enclosing once-open land. I have seen bird and animal life disappear. I have seen forest land converted to agriculture, farm land in turn become suburban subdivisions, mountains slashed through with superhighways, rivers and lakes fouled by pollution, the skies hazed by smog — all evidence of human thoughtlessness about the environment.'[34]

(Interestingly, the changing face of the land surface can be illustrated by what happened to Roosevelt Field, from where Lindbergh set off to fly to Paris, and where Kingsford Smith landed after his own cross-Atlantic flight. When I visited there in early January 2009, I was fascinated to find that the whole thing is now a wall-to-wall shopping mall.)

From the mid 1960s Lindbergh was an active supporter of the World Wildlife Fund. 'Where civilisation is most advanced, few birds exist,' he wrote in an article for *Readers Digest* in 1971. 'I realised that if I had to choose, I would rather have birds than airplanes.'[35]

Three years later, early on the morning of 26 August 1974, he died in Hawaii, aged seventy-two. A particularity of his funeral was that it was held within three hours of his death, a final blow struck for the privacy that he had so fiercely fought for in his life. And yet that privacy did not last …

In the late 1990s, a German woman, Astrid Bouteil, who had grown up in the small Bavarian town of Geretsried, just south of Munich, came across a magazine article about Lindbergh together with 112 letters he had written to her mother and recognised him immediately as … her father. This was the man who visited them — her mother Brigitte, and her two brothers Dyrk and David — for a few days, twice a year, every year, going by the name of 'Careu Kent'. Astrid confronted her mother, Brigitte Hesshaimer, who cried and acknowledged that their affair had begun in 1957 and continued until just before his death. Astrid waited until both her own mother and Lindbergh's wife, Anne Morrow Lindbergh, had died before revealing the shattering secret. DNA tests in 2003 established beyond doubt that Lindbergh was in fact the father of her and her brothers.

And yet there was more. For, as it subsequently emerged, while having his affair with Brigitte, Lindbergh had also had a simultaneous affair with Brigitte's sister Marietta, who bore him two sons, Vago and Christoph. But wait … it then came to light that Lindbergh had also had a third affair with a close friend of the Hesshaimer sisters, a woman by the name of Valeska, with whom he had a son and a daughter in 1959 and 1961. In the space of nine years, Lindbergh had sired seven children in Europe, in addition to his six children born in America, and had managed to keep the whole thing going by virtue of his wealth and the fact that, as far as his American wife and family knew, 'business' frequently took him to Europe. In 2005 the German author Rudolf Schroeck wrote a book, *Das Doppelleben des Charles A. Lindbergh*, laying everything bare, including the fact that 'ten days before he died in August 1974, Lindbergh wrote three letters from his hospital bed to his three mistresses and requested "utmost secrecy"'. It was not to be.

The *Spirit of St Louis* hangs proudly in the Smithsonian Institution's National Air and Space Museum in Washington DC, just thirty-five paces — by my stride — from the Wright *Flyer I*.

•

The world of aviation, of course, continues to expand. As I write this — from a Qantas Boeing 747-400 jet, as it happens, which will get me into London shortly, about twenty-two hours after leaving Sydney — the big news in commercial aviation is the advent of the Airbus A380 passenger airliner, capable of carrying 450 passengers around the world at a speed of 927 kilometres per hour, which is 576 miles per hour in the old money, or a staggering 85 per cent of the speed of sound at 30,000 feet. Each of those Qantas planes will bear a name from Australian aviation history, and they include Charles Kingsford Smith, Charles Ulm, Lawrence Hargrave, Hudson Fysh, Paul McGinness, Fergus McMaster, Bert Hinkler, Keith Smith, Ross Smith, Lester Brain, Norman Brearley, Scotty Allan, P.G. Taylor and Nancy-Bird Walton (after whom the first airbus was named).

And yet the true glory days of the pilot are substantially gone.

In Australia, in 1989, when the pilots of the domestic carrier Ansett were agitating for more money, Prime Minister Bob Hawke held his ground and refused to back down. He derided their whole profession for good measure, saying that in the modern world, pilots were nothing more than 'glorified bus drivers'. This was a harsh assessment, most particularly when pilots demonstrate their extraordinary importance in times of crisis, as most famously happened recently, when, with both engines of US Airways Airbus A320 failed due to a bird-strike, a wonderfully calm and vastly experienced pilot by the name of Chesley B. 'Sully' Sullenberger III managed to bring his bird down to a beautiful landing on the Hudson River and save all 155 lives on board. In the annals of aviation that pilot's feat will long stand out as a stunning example of cool professionalism at work.

And yet, just as Charles Kingsford Smith said it would, his spirit lives on, even in the strictly regulated corporate aviation age. In January 2008, the *South China Morning Post* reported the story of an Australian pilot, Ian Wilkinson, chief pilot of Hong Kong's Cathay Pacific Airways' Boeing 777 fleet who — with Cathay Pacific chairman Chris Pratt and many VIP passengers on board — was piloting the Boeing 777-300ER when it took off on its maiden flight from the manufacturer's plant in Everett, Washington. Though Wilkinson was a pilot of high standing and excellent record, something got into him on that day. Instead of simply taking 'er up and letting the automatic pilot do the rest, flying them all the way to Hong Kong, Wilkinson suddenly turned her around and performed what was described as a 'Top Gun-like manoeuvre', which included swooping down to within 10 metres of the runway. After a disciplinary hearing, sadly, Wilkinson was sacked, while his co-pilot was suspended from training duties for six months.

Just what got into Wilkinson that day? I don't think there can be any doubt. Surely, the spirit of Smithy …

Endnotes

Pages vii–viii

1 Brogden, Stanley, *The History of Australian Aviation*, Hawthorne Press, Melbourne, 1960, p. 101.
2 Taylor, Captain Sir Gordon, 'Kingsford Smith as I Remember Him', Hudson Fysh Papers, ca. 1817–1974, ML MSS 2413, Box 10, K21829, Mitchell Library, Sydney.
3 Written 3 September 1941, aged seventeen.

Chapter 1: In the Beginning ...

1 Kingsford Smith, Sir Charles, *My Flying Life: An Authentic Biography Prepared under the Personal Supervision of and from the Diaries and Papers of the Late Sir Charles Kingsford-Smith,* Andrew Melrose, London, 1937, p. 15.
2 Wordsworth, William, 'The Prelude', Book XI, 1.108, 1850.
3 Ellison, Norman, *Daredevils of the Skies*, Angus & Robertson, Sydney, 1941, p. 27.
4 Chanute, Octave, letter to Francis Wenham, 13 September 1892, Chanute Letterpress books (1860–1910), Manuscript Division, Library of Congress, Washington.
5 *Flight: The Aircraft Engineer and Airships*, Vol. 67, 12 November 1954, St Martin's Publishing Co., London, p. 703.
6 Chanute, Octave, *Progress in Flying Machines*, Dover Publications, New York, 1997, p. 218.
7 English, Dave, *Slipping the Surly Bonds: Great Quotations on Flight*, poem 'High Flight', J.G. Magee, Jnr, RCAF, McGraw-Hill, New York, 1998, p. 1.
8 Shaw, W. Hudson and Ruhen, Olaf, *Lawrence Hargrave: Aviation Pioneer, Inventor and Explorer*, University of Queensland Press, St Lucia, Queensland, 1988, p. 81.
9 http://www.kitehistory.com/Miscellaneous/Hargrave.htm
10 Adams, Michael, *Wind Beneath his Wing: Lawrence Hargrave at Stanwell Park*, Cultural Exchange International, New South Wales, 2005, p. 129.
11 Hargrave, Lawrence to Octave Chanute, 2 December 1892, Lawrence Hargrave Archive: Flying Machine Vol. 1892–95, pp. 29–30, FM4/1057, Mitchell Library, Sydney.
12 Sealby, Winifred Kingsford, *Recollections: Personal and Scenic; Our Dumb Friends*, (Australian Library Collections, Record ID 5583222), 1951, p. 16.
13 ibid., p. 17.
14 ibid., p. 18.
15 ibid., p. 19.

16 Ellison, Norman, *Flying Matilda: Early Days in Australian Aviation*, Angus & Robertson, Sydney, 1957, p. 197.
17 'Flight to Fiji', *The Times*, 6 June 1928.
18 Sealby, op. cit., p. 17.
19 Adams, op. cit., p. 103.
20 Mackersey, Ian, *The Wright Brothers: A Remarkable Story of the Aviation Pioneers Who Changed the World*, Time Warner, London, 2004, p. 96.
21 ibid., p. 166.
22 ibid.
23 Shaw and Ruhen, op. cit., p. 133.
24 ibid., p. 134.
25 Kingsford Smith, Charles, letter to father in Canada, sent from Greenwich, Sydney, date unknown, Ellison Collection, National Library of Australia, Canberra.
26 Wixted, Edward P., *The Life and Times of Sir Charles Kingsford Smith: An Illustrated Chronology*, private source, Queensland, 1996, p. 7.
27 Burton, Walt and Findsen, Owen, *The Wright Brothers Legacy: Orville and Wilbur Wright and Their Aeroplanes,* Harry N. Abrams Inc., New York, 2003, p. 64.
28 Wallace, Graham, *The Flying Witness*, Putnam, London, 1958, p. 44.
29 ibid., p. 52.
30 ibid., p.57.
31 Shaw and Ruhen, op. cit., p. 115.
32 ibid., p. 144.
33 'Review of Hargrave's Work', *The Technical Gazette of New South Wales*, 1924, p. 46.
34 'Another Sensation at Bondi', *Sydney Morning Herald*, 3 January 1907.
35 Brawley, Sean, *The Bondi Lifesaver: A History of an Australian Icon*, ABC Books, Sydney, 2007, p. 29.
36 Trubuhovich, Ronald V., *History of Mouth-to-Mouth Ventilation, Part 3: The 19th to mid-20th Centuries and 'Rediscovery'*, (Vol. 9), Department of Critical Care Medicine, Auckland, 2007, pp. 62–78.
37 Wixted, op. cit., p. 5.
38 Wohl, Robert, *A Passion for Wings: Aviation and the Western Imagination, 1908–1918*, Yale University Press, New Haven/London, 1994, p. 25.
39 Wallace, op. cit., p. 81.
40 'Wright's Airship in Rapid Flight', *New York Times*, 9 August 1908.
41 Wallace, op. cit., p. 82.
42 ibid., p. 85.
43 Kelly, Fred C. (ed), *Miracle at Kitty Hawk: The Letters of Wilbur and Orville Wright*, Farrar & Straus, New York, 1951.
44 Wallace, op. cit., p. 80.
45 Wixted, op. cit., p. 6.
46 Sprigg, C. St John, *Great Flights*, Thomas Nelson & Sons, London, 1936, p. 15.
47 http://www.nps.gov/history/history/online_books/hh/34/hh34n.htm
48 'M Blériot in London: Great Public Welcome', *Daily Mail*, 27 July 1909.
49 'Aerial League: Flying Machines to Defend Australia', *Sydney Morning Herald*, 29 April 1909.
50 'Aerial League: Inauguration Decided Upon', *Daily Telegraph*, 29 April

1909.
51 ibid.

Chapter 2: Distance

1 Fokker, Anthony, *Flying Dutchman*, Penguin Books, Harmondsworth, 1938, p. 5.
2 Wallace, Graham, *The Flying Witness*, Putnam, London, 1958, p. 54.
3 Wohl, Robert, *A Passion for Wings: Aviation and the Western Imagination, 1908–1918*, Yale University Press, New Haven/London, 1994, p. 112.
4 Elliott, Brian A., *Blériot: Herald of an Age*, Tempus Publishing, Gloucestershire, 2000, p. 60.
5 ibid., p. 102.
6 'The Cross-Channel Flight Accomplished', *The Times*, 26 July 1908.
7 Wallace, op. cit., p. 118.
8 'Cheered at News of Success', *Washington Post*, 26 July 1909.
9 Elliott, op. cit., p. 114.
10 Wallace, op. cit., p. 119.
11 'A Memorable Flight', *Sydney Morning Herald,* 22 October 1930.
12 Wallace, op. cit., p. 121.
13 Elliott op. cit., p. 115.
14 Wallace, op. cit., p. 123.
15 Elliott, op. cit., p. 124.
16 Wallace, op. cit., p. 123.
17 'M Blériot in London: Great Public Welcome', *Daily Mail*, 27 July 1909.
18 'Triomphe de Blériot', *Le Figaro*, 25 July 1909, p. 1.
19 'The Cross-Channel Flight Accomplished', *The Times*, 26 July 1908.
20 'M Blériot in London: Great Public Welcome', *Daily Mail*, 27 July 1909.
21 Pound, Reginald and Harmsworth, Geoffrey, *Northcliffe*, Cassell, London, 1959, p. 375.
22 'M Blériot in London: Great Public Welcome', *Daily Mail*, 27 July 1909.
23 Fontaine, Charles, *Comment Blériot a Traversé la Manche*, Librairie Aéronautique, Paris, 1909, p. 67.
24 Wallace, op. cit., p. 124.
25 Wohl, op. cit., p. 69.
26 Fontaine, op. cit., p. 137.
27 Mattioli, Guido, *Mussolini Aviatore e la Sua Opera per L'Aviazione, Prefazione di Paolo Orano*, Casa Editrice Pinciana, Rome, 1938, p. 25.
28 'The Aerial Defence of Australia' (an Appeal to the Editor), *Daily Telegraph*, 27 July 1909.
29 Sheil, Beau, *Caesar of the Skies: The Life Story of Sir Charles Kingsford Smith*, Cassell, London, 1937, p. 9.
30 Wallace, op. cit., p. 72.
31 Kalush, William and Sloman, Larry, *The Secret Life of Houdini: The Making of America's First Superhero*, Simon & Schuster, London, 2007, p. 245.
32 'Like a Bird: Successful Aerial Flights by Houdini the "Handcuff King".', *Daily Telegraph*, 19 March 1910.
33 ibid.
34 Kalush and Sloman, op. cit., p. 248.
35 ibid.

36 Blackmore, L.K., *Hawker: A Biography of Harry Hawker*, Airlife, Shrewsbury, 1993, p. 43.
37 ibid.
38 'Like a Bird: Successful Aerial Flights by Houdini the "Handcuff King".', *Daily Telegraph*, 19 March 1910.
39 Finlay, Peter, 'Australia's First Aviator', *Aero Australia*, Issue No 14, 2007.
40 As quoted in Kalush and Sloman, op. cit., p. 252.
41 ibid., p. 253.
42 Joy, William, *The Aviators*, Shakespeare Head Press, Sydney, 1971, p. 23.
43 Target, Simon (producer), *Rewind*, ABC Television, Sydney, 2004. See also: Brogden, Stanley, *The History of Australian Aviation*, Hawthorne Press, Melbourne, 1960, p. 17.
44 Ellison, Norman, *Flying Matilda: Early Days in Australian Aviation*, Angus & Robertson, Sydney, 1957, p. 199.
45 'Smithy Among Schoolmates', *Sydney Morning Herald*, 18 June 1928.
46 Wright, Milton, diaries, 30 May 1912, Box 116, Library of Congress, Washington.
47 Blackmore, op. cit., p. 51.
48 Fokker, op. cit., p. 59.
49 Ellison, op. cit., p. 13.
50 Sealby, Winifred Kingsford, *Recollections: Personal and Scenic; Our Dumb Friends*, (Australian Library Collections, Record ID 5583222), 1951, p. 36.
51 Ellison, op. cit., p. 201.

Chapter Three: War!

1 Fysh, Sir Hudson, *Qantas Rising: The Autobiography of the Flying Fysh*, Angus & Robertson, Sydney, 1966, p. 27.
2 http://www.bbc.co.uk/dna/h2g2/A11873900
3 Fokker, Anthony, *Flying Dutchman*, Penguin Books, Harmondsworth, 1938, p. 121.
4 'The Empire's Call', *Argus*, 1 August 1914.
5 *Sydney Morning Herald*, 6 August 1914.
6 Sealby, Winifred Kingsford, letter to Norman Ellison, sent from Ladstock, Saratoga, New South Wales, 20 January 1956, Ellison Collection, National Library of Australia, Canberra.
7 Ellison, Norman, manuscript of *Flying Matilda: Early Days in Australian Aviation* (Angus & Robertson, Sydney, 1957), National Library of Australia, Canberra, p. 19.
8 Thomas, Lowell, *Sir Hubert Wilkins: His World of Adventure*, McGraw-Hill, New York, 1961, p. 86.
9 Grierson, John, *Sir Hubert Wilkins: Enigma of Exploration*, Robert Hale, London, 1960, p. 54.
10 Thomas, op. cit., p. 86.
11 Nasht, Simon, *The Last Explorer: Hubert Wilkins — Australia's Unknown Hero*, Hachette Livre Australia/Hodder, Sydney, 2007, p. 34.
12 Garros, Roland, *Memoires présentés par Jacques Quellennec*, Hachette, Paris, 1966, p. 253f.
13 Schurmacher, Emile C., *Richthofen: The Red Baron*, Paperback Library, New York, 1971, p. 30.

14 Barker, Ralph, *A Brief History of the Royal Flying Corps in World War I*, Constable & Robinson, London, 2002, p. 43.
15 Ellison, *Flying Matilda*, op. cit., p. 204.
16 Schurmacher, op. cit., p. 93.
17 Margetts, Captain I.S., diary, 25 April 1915, 1 DRL/0478, Australian War Memorial, Canberra.
18 Bean, C.E.W., *The Story of Anzac*, Vol. I, Angus & Robertson, Sydney, 1924.
19 Fokker, op. cit., p. 130.
20 *Egyptian Gazette*, 18 December 1914.
21 Kingsford Smith, Charles, letter to parents sent from Egypt, date unknown, ca. July 1915, Ellison Collection National Library of Australia, Canberra.
22 Hawker, Muriel, *H.G. Hawker, Airman: His Life and Work*, Hutchinson & Co., London, 1922, p. 182.
23 Kingsford Smith, Charles, letter to parents, sent from Cairo, 27 July 1915, Ellison Collection, National Library of Australia, Canberra.
24 Kingsford Smith, Charles, letter to parents, sent from Cairo, 8 August 1915, Ellison Collection, National Library of Australia, Canberra. Quoted in Ellison, *Flying Matilda*, op. cit., p. 206.
25 ibid.
26 Omek, Tolga, *Gallipoli*, Ekip Film, Turkey, 2005.

Chapter Four: In the Trenches

1 Young, Margaret and Gammage, Bill (eds), *Hail and Farewell: Letters From Two Brothers Killed in France in 1916*, Kangaroo Press, Sydney, 1995, p. 145.
2 Kingsford Smith, Charles, letter to parents, sent from Cairo, 8 August 1915, Ellison Collection, National Library of Australia, Canberra.
3 Kingsford Smith, Charles, letter to parents, sent from Gallipoli, 6 October 1915, Ellison Collection, National Library of Australia, Canberra.
4 Carlyon, Les, *Gallipoli*, Macmillan, Sydney, 2001 p. 293.
5 Ellison, Norman, *Flying Matilda: Early Days in Australian Aviation*, Angus & Robertson, Sydney, 1957, p. 210.
6 Kingsford Smith, Charles, letter to parents, sent from Cairo, 25 January 1916, Ellison Collection, National Library of Australia, Canberra. Quoted in Ellison, op. cit., p. 211.
7 ibid.
8 Hare, Paul R., *Aeroplanes of the Royal Aircraft Factory*, Crowood Press, Marlborough, 1999, p. 34.
9 Kingsford Smith, Charles, letter to parents, sent from France, 19 July 1916, Ellison Collection, National Library of Australia, Canberra.
10 McMullin, Ross, *Pompey, Elliott*, Scribe Publications, Melbourne, 2002, p. 220.
11 Horne, Donald, *In Search of Billy Hughes*, Macmillan, Melbourne, 1979, p. 70.
12 Kingsford Smith, Charles, letter to parents, sent from France, 11 September 1916, Ellison Collection, National Library of Australia, Canberra.

13 Ellison op. cit., p. 213.
14 Cutlack, F.M., *Official Histories: First World War, Volume VIII, The Australian Flying Corps in the Western and Eastern Theatres of War, 1914–1918*, Angus & Robertson, Sydney, 1941, p. 421.
15 Ellison, Norman, *Daredevils of the Skies*, Angus & Robertson, Sydney, 1941, p. 57.
16 Kingsford Smith, Sir Charles, *My Flying Life: An Authentic Biography Prepared under the Personal Supervision of and from the Diaries and Papers of the Late Sir Charles Kingsford-Smith*, Andrew Melrose, London, 1937, p. 14.
17 Ellison, *Flying Matilda*, op. cit., p. 215.
18 ibid., p. 216.
19 ibid., p. 217.
20 ibid., p. 219.
21 Gammage, Bill, *The Broken Years: Australian Soldiers in the Great War*, Australian National University Press, Canberra, 1974, p. 25.
22 That actual moniker, however, was not applied until after the war was over.
23 Taylor, Sir Gordon, *Sopwith Scout 7309*, Cassell, London, 1968, p. 53.
24 Morton, Fred, *'Smithy': Sir Charles Kingsford Smith — The World's Greatest Aviator*, New Image Publications, Melbourne, 1984, p. 3.
25 Stannage, John, *Smithy*, Oxford University Press, London, 1950, pp. 2–4.
26 Kingsford Smith, Charles, letter to parents, sent from Denham, January 1917, Ellison Collection, National Library of Australia, Canberra. Quoted in Ellison, *Flying Matilda*, op. cit., p. 222.
27 Mackenzie, Roy D., *Solo: The Bert Hinkler Story*, Ure Smith, Sydney, 1979, p. 6.
28 Kilduff, Peter, *Richthofen: Beyond the Legend of the Red Baron*, Arms and Armour Press, London, 1999, p. 69.
29 Lindsay, Alan (director), *Air Australia*, Village Roadshow Entertainment, Sydney, 2007.
30 Morton, op. cit., p. 2.
31 Stannage, John, *High Adventure*, MacDonald, Christchurch, 1944, p. 78f.
32 Schurmacher, Emile C., *Richthofen: The Red Baron*, Paperback Library, New York, 1971, p. 86.

Chapter Five: Aces at Dawn ...

1 Haynes, Jim and Dellit, Jillian, *Great Australian Aviation Stories: Characters, Pioneers, Triumphs, Tragedies and Near Misses*, ABC Books, Sydney, 2006, p. 65.
2 Richthofen, Manfred von, *The Red Fighter Pilot: The Autobiography of the Red Baron*, Red and Black Publishers, Florida, 2007, p. 56.
3 Kingsford Smith, Charles, letter to parents in Sydney, sent from France, 14 July 1917, Ellison Collection, National Library of Australia, Canberra.
4 Thomas, Lowell, *Sir Hubert Wilkins: His World of Adventure*, McGraw-Hill, New York, 1961, p. 94f.
5 ibid., p. 86.
6 Nasht, Simon, *The Last Explorer: Hubert Wilkins — Australia's Unknown*

Hero, Hachette Livre Australia/Hodder, Australia, 2007, p. 57.
7 ibid., p. 61.
8 Sufrin, Mark, *The Brave Men: Twelve Portraits of Courage*, Platt & Munk, New York, 1967, p. 233.
9 ibid., p. 242.
10 Kingsford Smith, Charles, letter to parents in Sydney, sent from France, 10 August 1917, Ellison Collection, National Library of Australia, Canberra.
11 Stannage, John, *High Adventure*, MacDonald, Christchurch, 1944, pp. 79–83.
12 Stannage, John, *Smithy*, Oxford University Press, London, 1950, p. 7.
13 Kingsford Smith's own reckoning, in a letter to parents, was that he had killed a few dozen.
14 Stannage, *High Adventure*, op. cit., p. 83.
15 Elliott, Brian A., *Blériot: Herald of an Age*, Tempus Publishing, Gloucestershire, 2000, p. 208.
16 Pound, Reginald and Harmsworth, Geoffrey, *Northcliffe*, Cassell, London, 1959, p. 467.
17 Interview with John Ulm, Australia, May 2008.
18 Yeates, V.M., *Winged Victory (Echoes of War)*, Buchan & Enright, London, 1985, p. 217.
19 Kingsford Smith, Sir Charles, *My Flying Life: An Authentic Biography Prepared under the Personal Supervision of and from the Diaries and Papers of the Late Sir Charles Kingsford-Smith*, Andrew Melrose, London, 1937, p. 16.
20 Ellison, Norman, *Flying Matilda: Early Days in Australian Aviation*, Angus & Robertson, Sydney, 1957.
21 Mackersey, Ian, *Smithy: The Life of Sir Charles Kingsford Smith*, Little, Brown, London, 1999, p. 34.
22 Guttman, Jon, *Sopwith Camel vs Fokker Dr I: Western Front 1917–18*, Osprey Publishing, Oxford, 2008, p. 17.
23 Ellison, op. cit., p. 237.
24 Davis, Pedr, *Charles Kingsford Smith: Smithy, The World's Greatest Aviator*, Lansdowne Press, Sydney, 1985, p. 26.
25 Mackersey, op. cit., p. 35.
26 FitzSimons, Peter, 'Being Mike Carlton', *Sydney Morning Herald*, 8 January 2000.
27 Wixted, Edward P., *The Life and Times of Sir Charles Kingsford Smith: An Illustrated Chronology*, private source, Queensland, 1996, p. 16.
28 Kilduff, Peter, *Richthofen: Beyond the Legend of the Red Baron*, Arms & Armour Press, London, 1999, p. 174.
29 Wohl, Robert, *A Passion for Wings: Aviation and the Western Imagination, 1908–1918*, Yale University Press, New Haven/London, 1994, p. 228.
30 Ellison, op. cit., p. 239.
31 ibid.
32 *Aviation Magazine*, 12 June 2006.
33 Kilduff, op. cit., p. 239.
34 ibid., p. 203.
35 'Diggers' Red Baron Blue', *Daily Telegraph* (Sydney), 26 March 2007.
36 Day, Mark, 'Unsung No 1 with a Bullet', *Australian*, 11 April 2007.

37 Younger, James (director), *Unsolved History: Death of the Red Baron*, Termite Art Productions, USA, 2002.
38 This anecdote comes from the man I consider Kingsford Smith's principal biographer, Ian Mackersey, who in the 1990s was able to track down one of the last survivors from that whole era — James Cross — who told him that story when he was ninety-three. Mackersey, op. cit., p. 37.
39 ibid.
40 Joy, William, *The Aviators*, Shakespeare Head Press, Sydney, 1971, p. 28.
41 Lawrence, T.E., *Seven Pillars of Wisdom*, Penguin, Harmondsworth, 1979, p. 639.
42 ibid.

Chapter 6: Après la Guerre

1 Wohl, Robert, *A Passion for Wings: Aviation and the Western Imagination, 1908–1918*, Yale University Press, New Haven/London, 1994, p. 1.
2 Kingsford Smith, Sir Charles, *My Flying Life: An Authentic Biography Prepared under the Personal Supervision of and from the Diaries and Papers of the Late Sir Charles Kingsford-Smith*, Andrew Melrose, London, 1937.
3 'Gaiety on the Boulevards', *The Times*, 12 November 1918.
4 'We Want King George', *The Times*, 12 November 1918.
5 Ellison, Norman, *Flying Matilda: Early Days in Australian Aviation*, Angus & Robertson, Sydney, 1957, p. 244.
6 ibid.
7 Kingsford Smith, Charles, letter to parents, sent from the RAF Station in Eastchurch, Kent, 12 January 1919, Ellison Collection, National Library of Australia, Canberra.
8 Hughes, Aneurin, *Billy Hughes: Prime Minister and Controversial Founding Father of the Australian Labor Party*, John Wiley & Sons, Brisbane, 2005, p. 77.
9 Hughes, William, cable to Australian Cabinet, sent from Paris, 18 February 1919, National Library of Australia, Canberra.
10 *New York Times*, 1919.
11 Kingsford Smith, Charles, letter to parents in Sydney, sent from Hitchin, 17 April 1919, Ellison Collection, National Library of Australia, Canberra.
12 Fokker, Anthony, *Flying Dutchman*, George Routledge & Sons, London, 1932, p. 229f.
13 ibid., p. 241.
14 Kingsford Smith, Charles, letter to parents in Sydney, May 1919, Ellison Collection, National Library of Australia, Canberra.
15 Blackmore, L.K., *Hawker: A Biography of Harry Hawker*, Airlife, Shrewsbury, 1993, p. 160.
16 'Hold Thanksgiving Services at Hawker's Old Home', *The Times*, 27 May 1919.
17 'Hawker Saved — A Mid-Atlantic Rescue', *The Times*, 26 May 1919.
18 'Mr Hawker's Own Story — Why the Machine Came Down', *The Times*, 27 May 1919.
19 'Hawker Saved — A Mid-Atlantic Rescue', *The Times*, 26 May 1919.
20 'Mr Hawker's Own Story — Why the Machine Came Down', *The*

Times, 27 May 1919.
21 Blackmore, op. cit., p. 25.
22 'London Gives Airmen an Uproarious Welcome', *New York Times*, 28 May 1919.
23 Hawker, Muriel, *H.G. Hawker, Airman: His Life and Work*, Hutchinson & Co., London, 1922, p. 266.
24 'A Great Welcome to the Airmen, Mobbed by Cheering Crowds, Royal Reception To-Day', *The Times*, 28 May 1919.
25 ibid.
26 ibid.
27 'London Gives Airmen an Uproarious Welcome: Ovation all the Way from the North, Huge Crowds Acclaimed Them, Acclaimed by Australians', *New York Times*, 28 May 1919.
28 Williams, Sir Richard, *These Are Facts: The Autobiography of Air Marshall Sir Richard Williams*, Australian War Memorial and the Australian Government Publishing Service, Canberra, 1977, p. 114f.
29 Gall, Jennifer, *From Bullocks to Boeings: An Illustrated History of Sydney Airport*, Australian Government Publishing Service, Canberra, 1986, p. 9.
30 Ellison, op. cit., p. 25.
31 Gall, op. cit., p. 11.
32 Fysh, Sir Hudson, *Qantas Rising: The Autobiography of the Flying Fysh*, Angus & Robertson, Sydney, 1966, p. 68.
33 ibid., p. 52.
34 'Australian Flight, Captain Wilkins Leaves', *Daily Telegraph*, 24 November 1919.
35 Thomas, Lowell, *Sir Hubert Wilkins: His World of Adventure*, McGraw-Hill, New York, 1961, p. 114.
36 '"Kangaroo" Farewell', *Daily Telegraph*, 25 November 1919.
37 Kingsford Smith, Elsie, letter to her parents, sent from Menlo Park, California, 10 November 1919, Ellison Collection, National Library of Australia, Canberra.
38 http://en.wikipedia.org/wiki/Harry_Hawker
39 Fysh, op. cit., p. 69.
40 Haynes, Jim and Dellit, Jillian, *Great Australian Aviation Stories: Characters, Pioneers, Triumphs, Tragedies and Near Misses*, ABC Books, Sydney, 2006, p. 124.
41 Eustis, Nelson, *Australia's Greatest Air Race: England–Australia 1919*, Rigby, Adelaide, 1977, p. 42.
42 'Douglas and Ross, Details of Crash', *Daily Telegraph*, 17 November 1919.
43 Swinson, Arthur, *The Great Air Race*, Cassell, London, 1968, p. 17.
44 Sheil, Beau, *Caesar of the Skies: The Life Story of Sir Charles Kingsford Smith*, Cassell, London, 1937, p. 31.
45 'Airmen Bushed', *Daily Telegraph*, 15 December 1919.
46 Haynes and Dellit, op. cit., p. 119.
47 ibid., p. 165.
48 'Last Stage, Messages for Ross Smith, Australia's Tribute', *Daily Telegraph*, 10 December 1919.

49 Swinson, *op. cit.*, p. 18.
50 'The Pathfinders', *Daily Telegraph*, 13 December 1919.
51 ibid.
52 Fysh, op. cit., p. 86.
53 ibid., p. 93.
54 Lindsay, Alan (director), *Air Australia*, Village Roadshow Entertainment, Sydney, 2007.
55 ibid., interview with Mary Cottrill, the daughter of Paul McGinness.
56 Love, Nigel B., *The Autobiography of Nigel B. Love (Part One), Aviation in Australia, 1915–1923*, self-published, Sydney, ca. 1968.

Chapter Seven: Homeward Bound

1 Gunn, John, *The Defeat of Distance: Qantas 1919–1939*, University of Queensland Press, St Lucia, Queensland, 1988, p. 85.
2 Kingsford Smith, Elsie, letter to parents, sent from Oakland, California, 15 February 1920, Ellison Collection, National Library of Australia, Canberra.
3 Mackersey, Ian, *Smithy: The Life of Sir Charles Kingsford Smith*, Little, Brown, London, 1999, p. 49.
4 While these numbers do not, in fact add up, that is the way they appear in the Ellison Collection.
5 This figure in the Ellison Collection actually says $22,000, but it is an error.
6 Ellison, Norman, *Flying Matilda: Early Days in Australian Aviation*, Angus & Robertson, Sydney, 1957, p. 258f.
7 Kingsford Smith, Charles, letter to parents, sent from California, 20 September 1920, Ellison Collection, National Library of Australia, Canberra.
8 Kingsford Smith, Sir Charles, *My Flying Life: An Authentic Biography Prepared under the Personal Supervision of and from the Diaries and Papers of the Late Sir Charles Kingsford-Smith,* Andrew Melrose, London, 1937, p. 20.
9 Kingsford Smith, Elsie, letter to parents, sent from San Francisco, 3 November 1920, Ellison Collection, National Library of Australia, Canberra.
10 Sprigg, C. St John, *Great Flights*, Thomas Nelson & Sons, London, 1936, p. 68.
11 Gunn, op. cit., p. 23.
12 ibid., p. 21.
13 Fysh, Sir Hudson, *Qantas Rising: The Autobiography of the Flying Fysh*, Angus & Robertson, Sydney, 1966, p. 97.
14 ibid., p. 99.
15 'Locklear Killed in Flying for Film', *New York Times*, 4 August 1920.
16 Kingsford Smith, Elsie, letter to parents in Sydney, sent from San Francisco, 12 November 1920, Ellison Collection, National Library of Australia, Canberra.
17 Kingsford Smith, Charles, letter to parents, sent from San Francisco, December 1920, Ellison Collection, National Library of Australia, Canberra.
18 Sheil, Beau, *Caesar of the Skies: The Life Story of Sir Charles Kingsford*

Smith, Cassell, London, 1937, p. 36.
19 Pearce, Sir George F., speech, 17 September 1920, Commonwealth Parliamentary Debates, Vol. 93, p. 4717; second reading of the Air Navigation Bill, 4 November 1920; Commonwealth Parliamentary Debates, Vol. 94, pp. 6231–5.
20 Hughes, William M., speech, 9 September 1920, Commonwealth Parliamentary Debates, Vol. 93, p. 4389f.
21 Gregory, H. (MP), letter to the prime minister, 10 August 1920, Congressional Research Service, A2, file 1920/3061.
22 Pearce, Sir George F., letter to the prime minister, 18 April 1921, Congressional Research Service, A2717, Vol. III, Folder 11, file note, CRS A1195.
23 Brearley, Sir Norman, *Australian Aviator*, Rigby, Adelaide, 1971, p. 66.
24 Sheil, op. cit., p. 38.
25 From what Catherine Kingsford Smith told Norman Ellison (Mackersey, op. cit., p. 51).
26 Wixted, Edward P., *The Life and Times of Sir Charles Kingsford Smith: An Illustrated Chronology*, private source, Queensland, 1996, p. 14.
27 Fysh, op. cit., p. 104.
28 Gunn, op. cit., p. 34f.
29 Fysh, op. cit., p. 105.
30 ibid., p. 108.
31 Mackersey, op. cit., p. 53.
32 Wixted, Edward P., *The Last Flight of Bert Hinkler*, Vantage Press, New York, 1992, p. 10.
33 Mackenzie, Roy D., *Solo: The Bert Hinkler Story*, Ure Smith, Sydney, 1979, p. 43.
34 ibid.
35 'Mr Hawker Killed, Crash in Trial Flight', *The Times*, 13 July 1921.
36 'How Mr Hawker Died, Not Strong Enough to Fly', *The Times*, 18 July 1921.
37 Hawker, Muriel, *H.G. Hawker, Airman: His Life and Work*, Hutchinson & Co., London, 1922, p. 318.
38 Ellison, op. cit., p. 283.
39 Kingsford Smith, Charles, letter to parents, sent from Wellington, 20 July 1921, Ellison Collection, National Library of Australia, Canberra.
40 Ellison, op. cit., p. 284.
41 Kingsford Smith, Charles, letter to parents, sent from Wellington, 4 August 1921, Ellison Collection, National Library of Australia, Canberra.
42 'Aerial Service. Geraldton to Derby. Major Brearly Successful', *Western Mail*, 4 August 1921.
43 'Aeroplane Service Between Geraldton and Derby, Western Australia, Conditions of Tender', *Daily News*, 13 June 1925.
44 Kingsford Smith, Elsie, account of her brother's life, Ellison Collection, National Library of Australia, Canberra.
45 http://www.spiritsofansett.com/legends/brealey.htm
46 Brearley, op. cit., p. 81.
47 http://www.spiritsofansett.com/legends/brealey.htm
48 Gunn, op. cit., p. 50.

49 Kingsford Smith, Charles, letter to parents, sent from Perth, 3 December 1921, Ellison Collection, National Library of Australia, Canberra.
50 Lindsay, Alan (director), *Air Australia*, Village Roadshow Entertainment, Sydney, 2007.
51 ibid.
52 Gunn, op. cit., p. 51.
53 Fysh, op. cit., p. 113.
54 'Preparations for the Flight', *Adelaide Advertiser*, 14 April 1922.
55 'A Brother's Grief', *Adelaide Advertiser*, 17 April 1922.
56 'Ross Smith Killed While Testing Machine', *Sydney Morning Herald*, 14 April 1922.
57 'A Great Airman', *Sydney Morning Herald*, 15 April 1922.
58 Kingsford Smith, Charles, letter to parents, sent from Carnarvon, 3 May 1922, Ellison Collection, National Library of Australia, Canberra.
59 Kingsford Smith, Charles, letter to parents, sent from Port Hedland, 1 September 1922. Ellison Collection, National Library of Australia, Canberra.
60 Davis, Pedr, *Kookaburra: The Most Compelling Story in Australia's Aviation History*, Lansdowne Press, Sydney, 1980, p. 98.
61 Ellison, op. cit., p. 291.
62 Edwards, Hugh, *Gold Dust & Iron Mountains: Marble Bar and Beyond*, East Pilbara Shire, Western Australia, 1993, p. 162.
63 Brearley, Norman, letter to Charles Kingsford Smith (Western Australian Airways letterhead), 23 May 1922.
64 'Problems of Defence, Isolation and Development; What Civil Aviation Could Do to Help', *Aviation Historical Society of Australia Newsletter*, Vol. 6 No 3, 1991, pp. 50–55.
65 Kingsford Smith, Charles, letter to parents, sent from Broome, 19 November 1922, Ellison Collection, National Library of Australia, Canberra.

Chapter Eight: Thelma

1 Ellison, Norman, *Flying Matilda: Early Days in Australian Aviation*, Angus & Robertson, Sydney, 1957, p. 287.
2 Fysh, Sir Hudson, *Qantas Rising: The Autobiography of the Flying Fysh*, Angus & Robertson, Sydney, 1966, p. 128.
3 Mackersey, Ian, *Smithy: The Life of Sir Charles Kingsford Smith*, Little, Brown, London, 1999, p. 71.
4 Fysh, op. cit., p. 127.
5 Gunn, John, *The Defeat of Distance: Qantas 1919–1939*, University of Queensland Press, St Lucia, Queensland, 1988, p. 86.
6 Edwards, Hugh, *Gold Dust & Iron Mountains:Marble Bar and Beyond*, East Pilbara Shire, Western Australia, 1993, p. 163.
7 Kingsford Smith, Charles, letter to parents, sent from Port Hedland, 26 October 1922, Ellison Collection, National Library of Australia, Canberra.
8 Hazlitt, Lesley, *Just Call Me Jack*, Lexington Avenue Press, New South Wales, 2004, p. 60.
9 ibid.

10 Byrnes, Paul, *Qantas by George! The Remarkable Story of George Roberts*, Watermark Press, Sydney, 2000, p. 83.
11 Ellison, op. cit., p. 48.
12 ibid., pp. 49–50.
13 Kingsford Smith, Charles, letter to parents, sent from Broome, 19 November 1922, Ellison Collection, National Library of Australia, Canberra.
14 Kingsford Smith, Charles, letter to parents, sent from Broome, 31 December 1922, Ellison Collection, National Library of Australia, Canberra.
15 Kingsford Smith, Charles, letter to parents, sent from Geraldton, 7 February 1923, Ellison Collection, National Library of Australia, Canberra.
16 Kingsford Smith, Charles, letter to parents, sent from Port Hedland, 3 May 1922, Ellison Collection, National Library of Australia, Canberra.
17 Brearley, Norman, letter to Charles Kingsford Smith, sent from TSS *Katoomba*, 12 November 1922.
18 'An Airmail Suggestion', *Aeronautics*, May 1921.
19 Joy, William, *The Aviators*, Shakespeare Head Press, Sydney, 1971, p. 102.
20 Kingsford Smith, Charles, cable to parents, sent from Marble Bar, 9 June 1923, Ellison Collection, National Library of Australia, Canberra.
21 ibid.
22 Edwards, op. cit., p. 164.
23 ibid., p. 163.
24 ibid.
25 ibid., p. 165.
26 Mackersey, op. cit., p. 74.
27 ibid., p. 75.
28 Kingsford Smith, Charles, letter to parents, 21 November 1923, Ellison Collection, National Library of Australia, Canberra.
29 Edwards, op. cit., p. 163.
30 Nasht, Simon, *The Last Explorer: Hubert Wilkins — Australia's Unknown Hero*, Hachette Livre Australia/Hodder, Sydney, 2007, p. 125.
31 Kingsford Smith, Charles, letter to parents, 23 November 1923, Ellison Collection, National Library of Australia, Canberra.
32 Kingsford Smith, Charles, letter to parents, 15 February 1924, Ellison Collection, National Library of Australia, Canberra.
33 Davis, Pedr, *Kookaburra: The Most Compelling Story in Australia's Aviation History*, Lansdowne Press, Sydney, 1980, p. 16.
34 Kingsford Smith, Charles, letter to parents, 15 February 1924, Ellison Collection, National Library of Australia, Canberra.
35 Kingsford Smith, Charles, letter to parents, 27 March 1924, Ellison Collection, National Library of Australia, Canberra.
36 ibid.
37 Edwards, op. cit., p. 165.
38 Stannage, John, *Smithy*, Oxford University Press, London, 1950, pp. 18–19.
39 Kingsford Smith, Elsie, account of her brother's life, Ellison Collection, National Library of Australia, Canberra.

40 ibid.
41 ibid.
42 Kingsford Smith, Charles, letter to parents, sent from Carnarvon, 22 June 1924, Ellison Collection, National Library of Australia, Canberra.
43 Kingsford Smith, Charles, letter to parents, sent from Carnarvon, 23 June 1924, Ellison Collection, National Library of Australia, Canberra.
44 Kingsford Smith, Charles, letter to parents, sent from Carnarvon, 22 June 1924, Ellison Collection, National Library of Australia, Canberra.
45 Kingsford Smith, Charles, letter to parents, sent from Carnarvon, 15 February 1925, Ellison Collection, National Library of Australia, Canberra.
46 Thomas, Lowell, *Sir Hubert Wilkins: His World of Adventure*, McGraw-Hill, New York, 1961, p. 184.
47 Wilkins, Hubert, letter to a Mr Byrne, sent from New York City, 29 October 1936.
48 Kingsford Smith, Charles, letter to parents, 26 July 1925, Ellison Collection, National Library of Australia, Canberra.
49 Thomas, op. cit., p. 159.
50 ibid., p. 160.
51 ibid., p. 161.
52 ibid., p. 164.
53 Lindbergh, Charles Augustus, *The Spirit of St. Louis*, Tandem Publishing, London, 1975, p. 12.
54 Berg, A. Scott, *Lindbergh*, Putnam Adult, New York, 1998, p. 66.
55 Lindbergh, op. cit., p. 124.
56 ibid., p.16
57 Joy, op. cit., p. 50.
58 Lindsay, Alan (director), *Air Australia*, Village Roadshow Entertainment, Sydney, 2007.
59 Fysh, op. cit., p. 177.
60 Ellison, op. cit., p. 52.
61 'A Flight with Smithy, The First Woman to Fly from Perth to Sydney Looks Back on the Epic Journey', *Australian Women's Weekly*, 5 November 1969.
62 ibid.
63 Kingsford Smith, Elsie, op. cit.

Chapter Nine: Pioneers Away ...

1 Kingsford Smith, Sir Charles, *My Flying Life: An Authentic Biography Prepared under the Personal Supervision of and from the Diaries and Papers of the Late Sir Charles Kingsford-Smith*, Andrew Melrose, London, 1937, p. 21.
2 Thomas, Lowell, *Sir Hubert Wilkins: His World of Adventure*, McGraw-Hill, New York, 1961, p. 175.
3 ibid., p. 176.
4 ibid., p. 177.
5 Berg, A. Scott, *Lindbergh*, Putnam Adult, New York, 1998, p. 91.
6 Cross, James Giblin, *Charles A. Lindbergh: A Human Hero*, Clarion Books, New York, 1997, p. 40.
7 Berg, op. cit., p. 104.

8 ibid., p. 101.
9 Kingsford Smith, Elsie, account of her brother's life, Ellison collection, National Library of Australia, Canberra.
10 Rogers, Ellen, *Faith In Australia: Charles Ulm and Australian Aviation*, Book Production Services, Sydney, 1987, p. 14.
11 http://www.homeofheroes.com/wings/part1/7_lindbergh.html
12 Sufrin, Mark, *The Brave Men: Twelve Portraits of Courage*, Platt & Munk, New York, 1967, p. 258.
13 Cross, op. cit., p. 59.
14 Montague, Richard, *Oceans, Poles and Airmen: The First Flights Over Wide Waters and Desolate Ice*, Random House, New York, 1971, p. 53.
15 Berg, op. cit., 110.
16 ibid., p. 113.
17 'Lindbergh Leaves New York at 7:52 A.M.', *New York Times*, 21 May 1927.
18 http://www.charleslindbergh.com/hall/spirit.asp
19 'Lindbergh Leaves New York at 7:52 A.M.', *New York Times*, 21 May 1927.
20 ibid.
21 'Hometown Eager for News as Lindbergh Speeds Over the Sea', *New York Times*, 21 May 1927.
22 Berg, op. cit., p. 122.
23 'Young Pilot Speeds on Towards Paris In the Night', *Los Angeles Times*, 21 May 1927.
24 'Lindbergh Flies Alone', *Sun* (New York), 21 May 1927.
25 Lindbergh, Charles Augustus, *The Spirit of St. Louis*, Tandem Publishing, London, 1975, p. 224.
26 Ross, Walter Sanford, *The Last Hero: Charles A. Lindbergh*, Manor Books, New York, 1974, p. 117.
27 http://www.charleslindbergh.com/mystory/index.asp
28 http://www.time.com/time/magazine/article/0,9171,989136-1,00.html
29 'Welcome to Flyer Puts 10 in Hospital', *Chicago Daily Tribune*, 23 May 1927.
30 Lindbergh, op. cit., p. 247.
31 'New York–Paris Flight, Capt. Lindbergh's Lone Voyage', *The Times*, 23 May 1927.
32 Cross, op. cit., p. 82.
33 Ives, Stephen (director), *The American Experience — Lindbergh*, Insignia Films, USA, 1990.
34 Berg, op. cit., p. 139.
35 Elliott, Brian A., *Blériot: Herald of an Age*, Tempus Publishing, Gloucestershire, 2000, p. 226.
36 ibid.
37 Berg, op. cit., p. 148.
38 Ives, op. cit., 1990.
39 'Lindbergh Crowd Shatters Record', *New York Times*, 12 June 1927.
40 Cross, op. cit., p. 90.
41 'Atlantic Flights, Lindbergh's Achievement', *Argus*, 25 May 1927.
42 'America to Australia, Lindbergh's Next Plan', *Argus*, 23 May 1927.
43 'Lindbergh's Great Flight', *Sydney Morning Herald*, 23 May 1927.

44 'Aviation Round Australia Flight', *Sydney Morning Herald*, 20 June 1927.
45 'No Sign of Keith Anderson: Anxiety Deepens', *Daily Guardian*, 12 April 1929.
46 ibid.
47 Cogger, Percy, Wings and the Man — the Private Papers of Charles Ulm, Aviator, unpublished manuscript, Mitchell Library, Sydney.
48 'Round Australia', *Sydney Morning Herald*, 30 June 1927.
49 'Welcome Back. Sun's Lunch to Airmen', *Sun* (Sydney) 30 June 1927.
50 ibid.
51 'Endurance Epic', *Sun*, 30 June 1927. These are the words used by Kingsford Smith and Ulm to a *Sun* journalist on the same day as the luncheon, and may be assumed to be close to the account that Kingsford Smith gave to the gathering of their adventures.

Chapter Ten: The Tough Get Going
1 Stannage, John, *Smithy*, Oxford University Press, London, 1950, p. 76.
2 Kingsford Smith, Sir Charles, *My Flying Life: An Authentic Biography Prepared under the Personal Supervision of and from the Diaries and Papers of the Late Sir Charles Kingsford-Smith,* Andrew Melrose, London, 1937, p. 25.
3 'Pioneer Pacific Fliers Wrote Tragic Chapter In Air History', *San Francisco Call-Bulletin*, 10 October 1955.
4 Joy, William, *The Aviators*, Shakespeare Head Press, Sydney, 1971, p. 68.
5 Kingsford Smith, Sir Charles, *The Old Bus*, Herald Press, Melbourne, 1932, p. 9.
6 Stannage, op. cit, p. 23.
7 ibid.
8 Wilkins, Hubert, letter to a Mr Byrne, sent from New York City, 29 October 1936.
9 Courtwright, David T., *Sky as Frontier: Adventure, Aviation and Empire* (Centennial of Flight Series), Texas A & M University Press, USA, 2005, p. 80.
10 Lindbergh, Charles A., *Of Flight and Life*, Scribner's Sons, New York, 1948, p. 118.
11 Lindbergh, Charles A., *Charles A. Lindbergh: Autobiography of Values,* Harcourt Brace Jovanovich, New York, 1977, p. 118.
12 Ives, Stephen (director), *The American Experience — Lindbergh*, Insignia Films, USA, 1990.
13 Cross, James Giblin, *Charles A. Lindbergh: A Human Hero,* Clarion Books, New York, 1997, p. 176.
14 Wilkins, op. cit.
15 'Speakeasies Then and Now', *San Francisco Chronicle*, 16 December 2007.
16 Kingsford Smith, Sir Charles E. and Ulm, Charles T.P., *The Great Trans-Pacific Flight: The Story of the 'Southern Cross'*, Hutchinson, London, 1928, p. 48.
17 ibid., p. 49.
18 Sheil, Beau, *Caesar of the Skies: The Life Story of Sir Charles Kingsford Smith*, Cassell, London, 1937, p. 68.
19 McNally, Ward, *The Man on the Twenty Dollar Note: Sir Charles Kingsford-Smith*, A & A Reed, Sydney, 1976, p. 60.

20 ibid.
21 Wixted, Edward P., *The Life and Times of Sir Charles Kingsford Smith: An Illustrated Chronology*, private source, Queensland, 1996, p. 48.
22 'Our Conquest of the Pacific', *National Geographic*, October 1928.
23 Kingsford Smith, *My Flying Life*, op. cit., p. 132.
24 Stannage, op. cit., p. 26.
25 ibid., p. 8.
26 'Californians Face Failure, Fuel Low, but Keep on Flying', *Chicago Daily Tribune*, 19 January 1928.
27 McNally, Ward, *Smithy: The Kingsford-Smith Story*, Robert Hale, London, 1966, p. 51f.
28 Kingsford Smith, *The Old Bus*, op. cit., p. 15.
29 'Vain Vigil at Trentham', *The Evening Post*, 11 January 1928.
30 'Flyers Try Again for New Record', *Los Angeles Times*, 18 January 1928.
31 Kingsford Smith, *The Old Bus*, op. cit., p. 17.
32 Kingsford Smith, *My Flying Life*, op. cit., p. 36.
33 ibid., p. 37.
34 'The Trans-Pacific Flight, Being the Saga of the Southern Cross', *Liberty Magazine*, 19 April 1930.
35 Mackenzie, Roy D., *Solo: The Bert Hinkler Story*, Ure Smith, Sydney, 1979, p. 64.
36 Lex, Rowland via Hinkler House Memorial Museum Bundaberg, quoting an interview Hinkler gave to a Bundaberg newspaper at the conclusion of his flight.
37 Mackenzie, op. cit., p. 79.
38 ibid., p. 78.
39 ibid., p. 83.
40 ibid., p. 94.
41 'Conquerors of the Pacific', *Sydney Mail*, 13 June 1928.
42 Mackenzie, op. cit., p. 78.
43 Kingsford Smith, *The Old Bus*, op. cit., p. 20.
44 Clover, Sam T., *A Pioneer Heritage*, Saturday Night Publishing Co., Los Angeles, 1932, p. 101.
45 ibid., p. 102.
46 Stannage, op. cit., p. 31f.
47 The actual figure is difficult to determine. Kingsford Smith's account in *The Old Bus* (op. cit., p. 21) and *My Flying Life* (op. cit., p. 40) places the figure at £3200.00. In his biography of Kingsford Smith, *Smithy* (op. cit., p. 32), John Stannage has the figure at $20,000. It is, however, in memoirs that Ulm puts it at $16,000, and in terms of their subsequent expenditure, that seems to fit best.
48 Kingsford Smith, *The Old Bus*, op. cit., p. 21.
49 'Harry Lyon and The Southern Cross', *American Aviation Historical Society Journal*, Winter 1979 (Vol. 24, Issue 4).
50 ibid.
51 'The Trans-Pacific Flight, Being the Saga of the Southern Cross', *Liberty Magazine*, 19 April 1930.
52 'Jim Warner Radioman', *American Aviation Historical Society Journal*, Summer 1983 (Vol. 28, Issue 2).
53 Swinton, Stuart, *P.G. Taylor: The Last of the Great Air Pioneers — A*

Personal Tribute From Stuart Swinton, Australian Military History Publications, Loftus, New South Wales, 2006, p. 16.
54 'Harry Lyon and The Southern Cross', *American Aviation Historical Society Journal*, Winter 1979 (Vol. 24, Issue 4).
55 Sprigg, C. St John, *Great Flights*, Thomas Nelson & Sons, London, 1936, p. 140.
56 Davis, Pedr, *Charles Kingsford Smith: Smithy, The World's Greatest Aviator*, Lansdowne Press, Sydney, 1985, p. 50.
57 McNally, *The Man on the Twenty Dollar Note*, op. cit., p. 72.
58 'Harry Lyon and The Southern Cross', *American Aviation Historical Society Journal*, Winter 1979 (Vol. 24, Issue 4).
59 'Plane Ready For Longest Ocean Hop', *San Francisco Chronicle*, 31 May 1928.
60 Kingsford Smith, C.E. and Ulm, C.T.P., *Story of 'Southern Cross' Trans-Pacific Flight 1928*, Penlington & Somerville, Sydney 1928, p. 227.
61 Sealby, Winifred Kingsford, *Recollections: Personal and Scenic; Our Dumb Friends*, (Australian Library Collections, Record ID 5583222), 1951, p. 10.
62 'The Trans-Pacific Flight, Being the Saga of the Southern Cross', *Liberty Magazine*, 19 April 1930.

Chapter Eleven: Across the Pacific ...

1 'Oaklands Take Off: Fliers Hit an Air Pocket Half Way Across Pacific, Escape Disaster and Go On', *New York Times*, 1 June 1928.
2 'Arrival in Sydney', *Argus*, 11 June 1928.
3 'The Trans-Pacific Flight: Being the Saga of the Southern Cross', *Liberty Magazine*, 19 April 1930.
4 'Pacific Airplane Seized for Debt', *New York Times*, 6 November 1934.
5 'Oaklands Take Off: Fliers Hit an Air Pocket Half Way Across Pacific, Escape Disaster and Go On', *New York Times*, 1 June 1928.
6 'Harry Lyon and The Southern Cross', *American Aviation Historical Society Journal*, Winter 1979 (Vol. 24, Issue 4).
7 'Oaklands Take Off: Fliers Hit an Air Pocket Half Way Across Pacific, Escape Disaster and Go On', *New York Times*, 1 June 1928.
8 'Harry Lyon and The Southern Cross', *American Aviation Historical Society Journal*, Winter 1979 (Vol. 24, Issue 4).
9 Taylor, Sir Gordon, 'Kingsford Smith as I Remember Him', Sir Hudson Fysh Papers, Mitchell Library, ML MSS 2413, Box 10, K21829, ca. 1817–1974.
10 http://www.sl.nsw.gov.au/discover_collections/history_nation/aviation/crossing_oceans/smithy.html
11 Kingsford Smith, Sir Charles, *The Old Bus*, Herald Press, Melbourne, 1932, p. 29.
12 'Our Conquest of the Pacific', *National Geographic*, October 1928.
13 'Conquerors of the Pacific', *Sydney Mail*, 13 June 1928.
14 'Our Conquest of the Pacific', *National Geographic*, October 1928.
15 'Life of Thrills: "Smithy" as Pal, The Man in the Air', *Sun*, 10 December 1935.
16 Kingsford Smith, Sir Charles, *My Flying Life: An Authentic Biography Prepared under the Personal Supervision of and from the Diaries and Papers of*

the Late Sir Charles Kingsford-Smith, Andrew Melrose, London, 1937, p. 48.

17 Kingsford Smith, *The Old Bus*, op. cit., p. 29.

18 'Our Conquest of the Pacific', *National Geographic*, October 1928.

19 'The Trans-Pacific Flight, Being the Saga of the Southern Cross', *Liberty Magazine*, 19 April 1930.

20 'My Co-Pilot was Called Death', *Liberty Magazine*, 28 December 1935.

21 ibid.

22 Kingsford Smith, *The Old Bus*, op. cit., 1932, p. 30.

23 'Conquerors of the Pacific', *Sydney Mail*, 13 June 1928.

24 'The Trans-Pacific Flight, Being the Saga of the Southern Cross', *Liberty Magazine*, 19 April 1930.

25 'Arrival at Honolulu', *Argus*, 4 June 1928.

26 'Fliers Cross Pacific in 27 Hours, Reach Hawaii with Fuel Supply Low, Call it a Perfect Trip, No Trouble', *New York Times*, 2 June 1928.

27 'The Trans-Pacific Flight, Being the Saga of the Southern Cross', *Liberty Magazine*, 19 April 1930.

28 ibid.

29 'Southern Cross on the Wing', *Canberra Times*, 2 June 1928.

30 'Four Left Kauai at Dawn', *New York Times*, 4 June 1928.

31 ibid.

32 'The Trans-Pacific Flight, Being the Saga of the Southern Cross', *Liberty Magazine*, 19 April 1930.

33 'My Co-Pilot was Called Death', *Liberty Magazine*, 28 December 1935.

34 'Four left Kauai at Dawn', *New York Times*, 4 June 1928.

35 Kingsford Smith, *The Old Bus*, op. cit., p. 27.

36 Purvis, Harry and Priest, Joan, *Outback Airman*, Rigby, Adelaide, 1979, p. 6.

37 Kingsford Smith, *The Old Bus*, op. cit., p. 40.

38 Wixted, Edward P., *The Life and Times of Sir Charles Kingsford Smith: An Illustrated Chronology*, private source, Queensland, 1996, p. 62.

39 Author's calculations only, based on how many strokes of the pump it would normally have taken to move that many gallons.

40 Mackersey, Ian, *Smithy: The Life of Sir Charles Kingsford Smith*, Little, Brown, London, 1999, p. 152.

41 ibid.

42 'The Trans-Pacific Flight, Being the Saga of the Southern Cross', *Liberty Magazine*, 19 April 1930.

43 'Our Conquest of the Pacific', *National Geographic*, October 1928.

44 'Suva Landing Spectacular', *New York Times*, 6 June 1928.

45 'Airmen Reach Suva', *Argus*, 6 June 1928.

46 Mackersey, op. cit., p. 154f.

47 'Americans Play Quit at Suva', *Washington Post*, 6 June 1928.

48 Kingsford Smith, *The Old Bus*, op. cit., p. 45.

49 'Suva Landing Spectacular', *New York Times*, 6 June 1928.

50 Australian Hansard, National Library of Australia, Canberra, 5 June 1928.

51 ibid.

52 ibid.

53 'A World Record', *Chicago Daily Tribune*, 5 June 1928.

54 'Airmen Reach Suva', *Argus*, 6 June 1928.
55 Mackersey, op. cit., p. 157.
56 ibid.
57 'Pacific Fliers Off for Australia on 1,762 Mile Hop from Fiji Isles', *New York Times*, 7 June 1928.
58 ibid.
59 'The Trans-Pacific Flight, Being the Saga of the Southern Cross', *Liberty Magazine*, 19 April 1930.
60 ibid.
61 ibid.
62 'Fliers Off to Australia after Delay on Fueling', *New York Times*, 8 June 1928.
63 Sheil, Beau, *Caesar of the Skies: The Life Story of Sir Charles Kingsford Smith*, Cassell, Sydney, 1937, p. 79.
64 Kingsford Smith, *The Old Bus*, op. cit., p. 51.
65 'Sea Flyers Battle Storms', *Chicago Daily Tribune*, 8 June 1928.
66 Sheil, op. cit., p. 79.
67 'Fliers Off to Australia after Delay on Fueling', *New York Times*, 8 June 1928.
68 'Story Minute by Minute', *Argus*, 9 June 1928
69 Kingsford Smith, *The Old Bus*, op. cit., p. 54.
70 'Our Conquest of the Pacific', *National Geographic*, October 1928.
71 Sprigg, C. St John, *Great Flights*, Thomas Nelson & Sons, London, 1936, p. 31.
72 'Our Conquest of the Pacific', *National Geographic*, October 1928.
73 Kingsford Smith, *The Old Bus*, op. cit., p. 38.
74 'The Trans-Pacific Flight, Being the Saga of the Southern Cross', *Liberty Magazine*, 19 April 1930.
75 ibid.
76 ibid.
77 'Southern Cross Talks on Way to Brisbane', *The Herald*, 8 June 1928.
78 'Our Conquest of the Pacific', *National Geographic*, October 1928.
79 'Flyers Wildly Cheered on Reaching Australia', *Los Angeles Times*, 9 June 1928.
80 'How our Fliers Won Through', *Herald*, 9 June 1928.
81 Kingsford Smith, *The Old Bus*, op. cit., p. 57.
82 'Arrival Brisbane', *Argus*, 11 June 1928.
83 Ellison, Norman, *Flying Matilda: Early Days in Australian Aviation*, Angus & Robertson, Sydney, 1957, p. 133.
84 'Arrival Brisbane', *Argus*, 11 June 1928.
85 ibid.
86 ibid.
87 'Government Behind Future Flights', *Sydney Morning Herald*, 16 June 1928.
88 'Civic Reception', *Sydney Morning Herald*, 11 June 1928.
89 *Sydney Morning Herald*, 9 June 1928.
90 Ellison, op. cit., p. 297.
91 Clover, Sam T., *A Pioneer Heritage*, Saturday Night Publishing Company, Los Angeles, 1932, p. 103.
92 'Coolidge Praises Fliers for "Courageous Pioneering"', *New York Times*,

9 June 1928.
93 Kingsford Smith, Elsie, account of her brother's life, Ellison Collection, National Library of Australia, Canberra.
94 'Sydney Goes Wild over Ocean Fliers', *New York Times*, 11 June 1928.
95 'Epic Trans Pacific Flight Ended', *Canberra Times*, 11 June 1928.
96 Joy, William, *The Aviators*, Shakespeare Head Press, Sydney, 1971, p. 67.
97 'Sydney Goes Wild over Ocean Fliers', *New York Times*, 11 June 1928.
98 ibid.
99 Davis, Pedr, *Kookaburra: The Most Compelling Story in Australia's Aviation History*, Lansdowne Press, Sydney, 1980, p. 10.
100 'Epic Trans Pacific Flight Ended', *Canberra Times*, 11 June 1928.
101 Joy, op. cit., p. 66.
102 Stannage, John, *Smithy*, Oxford University Press, London, 1950, p. 50.

Chapter Twelve: The Urge to Elsewhere ...

1 Kingsford Smith, Sir Charles, *My Flying Life: An Authentic Biography Prepared under the Personal Supervision of and from the Diaries and Papers of the Late Sir Charles Kingsford-Smith,* Andrew Melrose, London, 1937, p. 82.
2 Davis, Pedr, *Charles Kingsford Smith: Smithy, The World's Greatest Aviator*, Lansdowne Press, Sydney, 1985, p. 11.
3 'The Pacific Flight: A Cosmopolitan Achievement', *Aircraft*, June 1928.
4 'Another 5,000 for Fliers', *New York Times*, 13 June 1928.
5 Wixted, Edward P., *The Life and Times of Sir Charles Kingsford Smith: An Illustrated Chronology*, private source, Queensland, 1996, p. 64.
6 'Hargraves Models Inspected by Airmen', *Sydney Morning Herald*, 20 June 1928.
7 'Lawrence Hargrave', *Sydney Morning Herald*, 25 June 1928.
8 'Pacific Flyers: Americans Depart', *Sydney Morning Herald*, 25 June 1928.
9 Kingsford Smith, op. cit., p. 79.
10 '50th Anniversary Southern Cross', *Wings*, 15 August 1978.
11 Joy, William, *The Aviators*, Shakespeare Head Press, Sydney, 1971, p. 68.
12 'Southern Cross Leaves', *Canberra Times*, 11 September 1928.
13 'My Co-Pilot was Called Death', *Liberty Magazine*, 28 December 1935.
14 Kingsford Smith, op. cit., p. 82.
15 Stannage, John, *Smithy*, Oxford University Press, London, 1950, p. 56.
16 Kingsford Smith, op. cit., p. 82.
17 ibid., p. 83.
18 ibid.
19 'My Co-Pilot was Called Death', *Liberty Magazine*, 28 December 1935.
20 Stannage, op. cit., p. 58.
21 'Tasman Flight Successfully Accomplished', *Sydney Morning Herald*, 12 September 1928.
22 Kingsford Smith, Sir Charles, *The Old Bus*, Herald Press, Melbourne, 1932, p. 74.
23 Robert Lewis Stevenson (Requiem)
24 Kingsford Smith, *The Old Bus*, op. cit., p. 75.
25 'Tasman Flight Successful Ending', *Argus*, 12 September 1928.
26 ibid.
27 Ewing, Ross, and MacPherson, Ross, *The History of New Zealand*

Aviation, Heinemann, Auckland, 1986, p. 81f.
28 Interview with Col Maybury, Kurri Kurri, New South Wales, September 2008.
29 'Southern Cross: Crew Entertained', *Sydney Morning Herald*, 18 September 1928.
30 Joy, op. cit., p. 70.
31 'Only Three Gallons Left', *Sydney Morning Herald*, 15 October 1928.
32 Kingsford Smith, *My Flying Life*, op. cit., p. 90.
33 'Kingsford Smith Married in W.A., Letters from Wife, Decree Nisi Granted', *Sun*, 26 October 1928.
34 Kingsford Smith, *My Flying Life*, op. cit., p. 90.
35 *Hitchcock v. Kingsford Smith & Ulm*, Supreme Court of New South Wales, 21 March 1930.
36 'Hitchcock vs Kingsford Smith and Ulm: Verdict for Defendants', *Aircraft*, 31 March 1929.
37 'Ulm's Tale: Viewed with Some Suspicion', *Daily Guardian*, 25 June 1929.
38 Kingsford Smith, *The Old Bus*, op. cit., p. 82.
39 'Missing Aviators', *Sydney Morning Herald*, 3 April 1929.
40 'With the Aerial Game: Airmen Could Not Be Recalled', *Sun*, 2 April 1929.
41 'Air Inquiry: McWilliams Evidence', *Sydney Morning Herald*, 23 May 1929.
42 Stannage, op. cit., p. 64.
43 Brearley, Sir Norman, *Australian Aviator*, Rigby, Adelaide, 1971, p. 144.

Chapter Thirteen: Coffee Royal

1 Stannage, John, *Smithy*, Oxford University Press, London, 1950, p. 60.
2 McNally, Ward, *Smithy: The Kingsford-Smith Story*, Robert Hale, London, 1966, p. 72.
3 *Daily Guardian*, 1 April 1929.
4 *Sydney Morning Herald*, 4 April 1929.
5 *Sun*, 2 April 1929.
6 *Daily Guardian*, 2 April 1929.
7 *Daily Guardian*, 3 April 1929.
8 Joy, William, *The Aviators*, Shakespeare Head Press, Sydney, 1971, p. 79.
9 'Ominous Silence: Where is "Veteran" Southern Cross?', *Daily Guardian*, 2 April 1929.
10 ibid.
11 '"Andy" To Rescue', *Sun*, 7 April 1929.
12 *Sydney Morning Herald*, 5 April 1929.
13 Kingsford Smith, Sir Charles, *My Flying Life: An Authentic Biography Prepared under the Personal Supervision of and from the Diaries and Papers of the Late Sir Charles Kingsford-Smith*, Andrew Melrose, London, 1937, p. 97.
14 Cogger, Percy, Wings and the Man — the Private Papers of Charles Ulm, Aviator, unpublished manuscript, Mitchell Library, Sydney.
15 'Fruitless Flight. Plane Returns to Base', *Sydney Morning Herald*, 6 April 1929.
16 'Port George Mission News Narrows Radius of Search', *Sun*, 8 April

1929.
17 'The Paramount Aspect', *Sydney Morning Herald*, 3 April 1929.
18 'Risks in Aviation and Journalism', *Sun*, 3 April 1929.
19 Sheil, Beau, *Caesar of the Skies: The Life Story of Sir Charles Kingsford Smith*, Cassell, London, 1937, p. 101.
20 Rogers, Ellen, *Faith In Australia: Charles Ulm And Australian Aviation*, Book Production Services, Sydney, 1987, p. 46f.
21 Davis, Pedr, *Kookaburra: The Most Compelling Story in Australia's Aviation History*, Lansdowne Press, Sydney, 1980, p. 98.
22 Curran, Stan, 'The Kookaburra is Lost', *The Whisperer*, newsletter of the Beaufighter and Boston Association of Queensland, September 2001, p. 4.
23 Joy, op. cit., p. 82.
24 'Gallantry of Keith Anderson', *Daily Guardian*, 28 June 1929.
25 'Day of Joy: Kingsford Smith's Story', *Sun*, 20 April 1929.
26 'Dramatic Flight Story', *Sydney Morning Herald*, 17 May 1929.
27 Stannage, John, *High Adventure*, MacDonald, Christchurch, 1944, p. 16.
28 ibid., p. 14.
29 'Canberra's Success', *Sun*, 12 April 1929.
30 ibid.
31 'Memorable Search Ends', *Sydney Morning Herald*, 13 April 1929.
32 'Canberra's Success', *Sun*, 12 April 1929.
33 'Relatives Hear the News', *Canberra Times*, 13 April 1929.
34 *Evening News*, 12 April 1929.
35 'Memorable Search Ends', *Sydney Morning Herald*, 13 April 1929.
36 Kingsford Smith, op. cit., p. 109.
37 'Dramatic Flight Story', *Sydney Morning Herald*, 17 May 1929.
38 'Ulm's Tale: They Lived on Snails and Grass Only 25 Miles From Mission!', *Daily Guardian*, 16 April 1929.
39 Rogers, op. cit., p. 51.
40 'Death by Starvation Four Days Away', *Sun*, 16 April 1929.
41 'Lt Anderson Still in the Silence', *Daily Guardian*, 16 April 1929.
42 Mackersey, Ian, *Smithy: The Life of Sir Charles Kingsford Smith*, Little, Brown, London, 1999, p. 217.
43 'Two Writs Against "Guardian"', *Sun*, 16 April 1929.
44 Fysh, Sir Hudson, *Qantas Rising: The Autobiography of the Flying Fysh*, Angus & Robertson, Sydney, 1966, p. 244.
45 Gunn, John, *The Defeat of Distance: Qantas 1919–1939*, University of Queensland Press, St Lucia, Queensland, 1988, p. 110.
46 Fysh, op. cit., p. 163.
47 'How Pilot Brain Discovered Kookaburra in Desert', *Daily Guardian*, 26 April 1929.
48 Cadigan, Neil, *A Man Among Mavericks: Lester Brain, Australia's Greatest Aviator*, ABC Books, Sydney, 2008, p. 62.
49 'Infamous Attack by "Sun" on Anderson', *Daily Guardian*, 25 April 1929.
50 'Grim Ending to Search for Keith Anderson', *Daily Guardian*, 22 April 1929.
51 'Off Again', *Sun*, 28 April 1929.
52 *Daily Guardian*, 25 April 1929.

53 'Infamous Attack by "Sun" on Anderson', *Daily Guardian*, 25 April 1929.
54 ibid.
55 '1000 Miles Air Dash: Kookaburra Pictures', *Daily Guardian*, 26 April 1929.
56 Fysh, op. cit., p. 229.
57 'The Sacrifice', *Smith's Weekly*, 27 April 1929.
58 ibid.
59 Davis, Pedr, *Charles Kingsford Smith: Smithy, The World's Greatest Aviator*, Lansdowne Press, Sydney, 1985, p. 73.
60 Mackersey, op. cit., p. 225.
61 'Reputations in the Mud', *Plain Talk*, 27 April 1929.
62 '"Southern Cross" Rumours', *Aircraft*, 30 June 1928.
63 Sheil, op. cit., p. 105.
64 McNally, Ward, *The Man on the Twenty Dollar Note: Sir Charles Kingsford-Smith*, A & A Reed, Sydney, 1976, p. 94.
65 Davis, *Kookaburra*, op. cit., p. 76.
66 ibid., p. 77.
67 ibid., p. 80.
68 ibid., p. 78.

Chapter Fourteen: Trials and Tribulations

1 Stannage, John, *Smithy*, Oxford University Press, London, 1950, p. 101.
2 'Dramatic Flight Story. Kingsford Smith's Evidence.', *Sydney Morning Herald*, 17 May 1929.
3 'Indignant Denials', *Sydney Morning Herald*, 18 May 1929.
4 Davis, Pedr, *Charles Kingsford Smith: Smithy, The World's Greatest Aviator*, Lansdowne Press, Sydney, 1985, p. 23.
5 'Gallantry of Keith Anderson', *Daily Guardian*, 28 June 1929.
6 Davis, Pedr, *Kookaburra: The Most Compelling Story in Australia's Aviation History*, Lansdowne Press, Sydney, 1980, p. 88.
7 'Gallantry of Keith Anderson', *Daily Guardian*, 28 June 1929.
8 ibid.
9 ibid.
10 'Ulm's Tale: Viewed with Some Suspicion', *Daily Guardian*, 25 June 1929.
11 ibid.
12 McNally, Ward, *The Man on the Twenty Dollar Note: Sir Charles Kingsford-Smith*, A & A Reed, Sydney, 1976, p. 97.
13 ibid., p. 100.
14 Stannage, op. cit., p. 74.
15 'Anderson's Body Here Today', *Daily Guardian*, 29 June 1929.
16 'Public Tributes Keith Anderson: Body Lying in State', *Sydney Morning Herald*, 6 July 1929.
17 Davis, *Kookaburra*, op. cit., p. 109.
18 'Last Tribute to Keith Anderson', *Sydney Morning Herald*, 8 July 1929.
19 'Southern Cross at London', *Sydney Morning Herald*, 12 July 1929.
20 Kingsford Smith, Sir Charles, *My Flying Life: An Authentic Biography Prepared under the Personal Supervision of and from the Diaries and Papers of the Late Sir Charles Kingsford-Smith*, Andrew Melrose, London, 1937, p.

130f.
21 ibid., p. 131.
22 ibid., p. 132f.
23 ibid., p. 133.
24 Mackersey, Ian, *Smithy: The Life of Sir Charles Kingsford Smith*, Little, Brown, London, 1999, p. 242.
25 ibid.
26 ibid., p. 244.
27 ibid.
28 ibid., p. 244f.
29 Sheil, Beau, *Caesar of the Skies: The Life Story of Sir Charles Kingsford Smith*, Cassell, London, 1937, p. 131.
30 Fysh, Sir Hudson, *Qantas Rising: The Autobiography of the Flying Fysh*, Angus & Robertson, Sydney, 1966, p. 232.
31 Davis, Pedr, *Charles Kingsford Smith*, op. cit., p. 95.
32 'New Air Service: Forced Landing Made', *Sydney Morning Herald*, 2 January 1930.
33 Ellison, Norman, *Flying Matilda: Early Days in Australian Aviation*, Angus & Robertson, Sydney, 1957, p. 244.
34 'Kingsford-Smith's Fiancée in Australia Elated; Miss Powell Says He Has Won Last Air Laurel', *New York Times*, 26 June 1930.
35 Morton, Fred, *'Smithy': Sir Charles Kingsford Smith — The World's Greatest Aviator*, New Image Publications, Melbourne, 1984, p. 10.
36 Fysh, op. cit., p. 237.
37 'Inaugurating the East–West Service', *Aircraft*, 31 July 1929.
38 Rogers, Ellen, *Faith In Australia: Charles Ulm And Australian Aviation*, Book Production Services, Sydney, 1987, p. 56f.
39 Fysh, op. cit., p. 233.
40 Taylor, Sir Gordon, *The Sky Beyond*, Cassell, Melbourne, 1963, p. 29.
41 Taylor, Sir Gordon, 'Kingsford Smith as I Remember Him', Sir Hudson Fysh Papers, Mitchell Library, ML MSS 2413, Box 10, K21829, ca. 1817–1974.

Chapter Fifteen: New Frontiers

1 'My Co-Pilot was Called Death', *Liberty Magazine*, 28 December 1935.
2 Bernt Balchen, D.F.C., 1899–1973, was a grand Norwegian–American polar aviator who flew Richard E. Byrd on his pioneering Antarctic expedition over the South Pole in 1929. Balchen flew Byrd across the Atlantic from the USA to France in 1927. Anthony Fokker employed Balchen as a test pilot in 1926 where his admiration for the man's abilities were fostered. George Wilkins also employed Balchen's skills as a polar-region pilot.
3 Fokker, Anthony, *Flying Dutchman*, George Routledge & Sons, London, 1932, p. 272.
4 'Kingsford Smith in His Own Story Takes Up Newfoundland Riddle', *New York Times*, 28 June 1930.
5 Mackersey, Ian, *Smithy: The Life of Sir Charles Kingsford Smith*, Little, Brown, London, 1999, p. 250.
6 Purvis, Harry and Priest, Joan, *Outback Airman*, Rigby, Adelaide, 1979, p. 17.

7 'Flying Across the Atlantic', *Sydney Morning Herald*, 25 June 1930.
8 'Fly for U.S. from Ireland', *Chicago Daily Tribune*, 24 June 1930.
9 'Weather Bars Hop', *New York Times*, 8 June 1930.
10 Stannage, John, *Smithy*, Oxford University Press, London, 1950, p. 79.
11 'Kingsford-Smith has Letter From Cosgrove for Hoover', *New York Times*, 25 June 1930.
12 Kingsford Smith, Sir Charles, *My Flying Life: An Authentic Biography Prepared under the Personal Supervision of and from the Diaries and Papers of the Late Sir Charles Kingsford-Smith,* Andrew Melrose, London, 1937, p. 142.
13 'Flying Across the Atlantic', *Sydney Morning Herald*, 25 June 1930.
14 ibid.
15 Stannage, John, *High Adventure*, MacDonald, Christchurch, 1944, p. 47.
16 'Safe Crossing of Atlantic', *Sydney Morning Herald*, 26 June 1930.
17 Mackersey, op. cit., p. 254.
18 Stannage, *Smithy*, op. cit., p. 81.
19 ibid.
20 Kingsford Smith, op. cit., p. 146.
21 Stannage, *High Adventure*, op. cit., p. 53.
22 'My Co-Pilot was Called Death', *Liberty Magazine*, 28 December 1935.
23 'The Real Smithy: Stannage's Tribute', *Sun*, 9 December 1935.
24 'My Co-Pilot was Called Death', *Liberty Magazine*, 28 December 1935.
25 Stannage, *High Adventure*, op. cit., p. 50.
26 'Safe Crossing of Atlantic', *Sydney Morning Herald*, 26 June 1930.
27 Purvis and Priest, op. cit., p. 6f.
28 Stannage, *High Adventure*, op. cit., p. 55.
29 'Flyers at New York', *Los Angeles Times*, 27 June 1930.
30 'Southern Cross Reception at New York', *Sydney Morning Herald*, 28 June 1930.
31 'High Praise in the United States', *Sydney Morning Herald*, 27 June 1930.
32 Sprigg, C. St John, *Great Flights*, Thomas Nelson & Sons, London, 1936, p. 147.
33 'Fighting Mob Greets Atlantic Victors on New York Arrival', *The Washington Post*, 27 June 1930.
34 'Southern Cross Reception at New York', *Sydney Morning Herald*, 28 June 1930.
35 'Kingsford-Smith's Fiancée in Australia Elated: Miss Powell Says He Has Won Last Air Laurel', *New York Times*, 26 June 1930.
36 'Dramatic Story: Perils of the Atlantic Flight', *Sydney Morning Herald*, 27 June 1930.
37 'Fliers Feat Rallies Seriously Ill Father', *New York Times*, 28 June 1930.
38 'Airmen Decline Triumphal Broadway Parade', *New York Times*, 27 June 1930.
39 'Phones Australia to Greet Fiancée', *New York Times*, 28 June 1930.
40 'Nation Hears Flyer Talk to Australia', *New York Times*, 29 June 1930.
41 McNally, Ward, *The Man on the Twenty Dollar Note: Sir Charles Kingsford-Smith*, A & A Reed, Sydney, 1976, p. 105.
42 ibid.
43 'Kingsford Smith Off Today for the Coast', *New York Times*, 2 July 1930.
44 ibid.

45 'Southern Cross Hops to Chicago', *New York Times*, 2 July 1930.
46 Kingsford Smith, op. cit., p. 157.
47 ibid., p. 159.
48 Mackersey, op. cit., p. 258.
49 Stannage, *High Adventure*, op. cit., p. 89.
50 Kingsford Smith, op. cit., p. 159.
51 Wixted, Edward P., *The Life and Times of Sir Charles Kingsford Smith: An Illustrated Chronology*, private source, Queensland, 1996, p. 77.
52 Stannage, *High Adventure*, op. cit., p. 90.
53 Wixted, op. cit., p. 95.
54 McNally, op. cit., p. 106.
55 Kingsford Smith, op. cit., p. 165.
56 Sheil, Beau, *Caesar of the Skies: The Life Story of Sir Charles Kingsford Smith*, Cassell, London, 1937, p. 122.
57 'The Air Race: Smith at Rangoon', *Sydney Morning Herald*, 16 October 1930.
58 Kingsford Smith, op. cit., p. 173.
59 ibid., p. 176.
60 Stannage, *Smithy*, op. cit., p. 90.
61 'Kingsford Smith Relates Incidents of Flight', *Sydney Morning Herald*, 20 October 1930.
62 Kingsford Smith, op. cit., p. 183.
63 'Kingsford Smith Relates Incidents of Flight', *Sydney Morning Herald*, 20 October 1930.
64 'World Fliers Reach Darwin: Smith Breaks the Record', *Sydney Morning Herald*, 20 October 1930.
65 Purvis and Priest, op. cit., p. 12.
66 'Broadcast Address', *Sydney Morning Herald*, 22 October 1930.
67 'Official Welcome Mascot Aerodrome', *Sydney Morning Herald*, 23 October 1930.
68 'Father's Ashes Cast on Pacific by Kingsford Smith from Plane', *New York Times*, 5 November 1930.
69 '"Smithy " Spreads Father's Ashes over Ocean Rollers', *Daily Telegraph*, 5 November 1930.
70 'Kingsford Smith: Scenes at the Wedding', *Sydney Morning Herald*, 11 December 1930.
71 Mackersey, op. cit., p. 263.
72 Mollison, Jim, *Playboy of the Air*, Michael Joseph, London, 1937, p. 23.
73 ibid., p. 58f
74 Kingsford Smith, op. cit., p. 186.
75 Mackersey, op. cit., p. 264.
76 Kingsford Smith, Charles, letter to the Secretary of the British Air Ministry, sent from Sydney, November 1930.
77 Fysh, Sir Hudson, *Qantas Rising: The Autobiography of the Flying Fysh*, Angus & Robertson, Sydney, 1966, p. 257.
78 Davis, Pedr, *Charles Kingsford Smith: Smithy, The World's Greatest Aviator*, Lansdowne Press, Sydney, 1985, p. 94.
79 *Slipstream*, 1 December 1930 (Vol. 2, No. 4).
80 Macfarlane, Dan, previously unpublished reminiscences, 1967, private collection of his daughter, Ashlyn Edwards.

81 'Southern Cloud Laid to Rest', *Friends*, 3 September 2006 (Vol. 17).
82 Edwards, op. cit.
83 Kingsford Smith, *My Flying Life*, op. cit., p. 189.
84 'Desperate Search for the Missing Plane', *Sydney Morning Herald*, 25 March 1931.
85 *Tumut and Adelong Times*, 31 October 1958.
86 'Flashes in the Hills', *Sydney Morning Herald*, 26 March 1931.
87 'The Southern Cloud: Kingsford Smith's Spectacular Flight', *Sydney Morning Herald*, 26 March 1931.
88 'Missing Plane Search Continues', *Sydney Morning Herald*, 30 March 1931.
89 'The Southern Cloud: Hope Practically Abandoned', *Sydney Morning Herald*, 27 March 1931.
90 Scott, C.W.A., *The Life and Mildenhall–Melbourne Flight of C.W.A. Scott*, Hodder & Stoughton, London, 1934, pp. 29, 33f.
91 Swinson, Arthur, *The Great Air Race,* Cassell, London, 1968, p. 137.

Chapter Sixteen: To and Fro ...

1 'Kingsford Smith, Life of Adventure', *Sydney Morning Herald*, 7 June 1928.
2 'Arrival at Brisbane, Kingsford Smith's Plans', *Sydney Morning Herald*, 22 April 1931.
3 Kingsford Smith, Sir Charles, *My Flying Life: An Authentic Biography Prepared under the Personal Supervision of and from the Diaries and Papers of the Late Sir Charles Kingsford-Smith*, Andrew Melrose, London, 1937, p. 198.
4 Qantas Heritage Collection, Kingsford Smith Airport, Sydney.
5 ibid.
6 'Death of Nellie Stewart', *Argus*, 22 June 1931.
7 *Argus*, 24 June 1931.
8 Campbell, Eric, *The Rallying Point: My Story of the New Guard*, Melbourne University Press, Melbourne, 1965, p. 100.
9 Kingsford Smith, op. cit., p. 202.
10 'My Co-Pilot was Called Death', *Liberty Magazine*, 28 December 1935.
11 'Kingsford Smith Reaches England, Story of the Flight', *Sydney Morning Herald*, 9 October 1931.
12 McNally, Ward, *The Man on the Twenty Dollar Note: Sir Charles Kingsford-Smith*, A & A Reed, Sydney, 1976, p. 119.
13 ibid., p. 119.
14 'My Co-Pilot was Called Death', *Liberty Magazine*, 28 December 1935.
15 'Kingsford Smith, Delay at Athens', *Sydney Morning Herald*, 5 October 1931.
16 'Speed Record 408.8 Miles an Hour', *Sydney Morning Herald*, 1 October 1931.
17 'Kingsford Smith, Overdue at Marseilles', *Sydney Morning Herald*, 8 October 1931.
18 ibid.
19 Rogers, Ellen, *Faith In Australia: Charles Ulm And Australian Aviation*, Book Production Services, Sydney, 1987, p. 74.
20 'Air Liner Crashes in Siam, Col. Brinsmead Injured', *Sydney Morning*

Herald, 8 December 1931.
21 ibid.
22 Taylor, Sir Gordon, 'Kingsford Smith as I Remember Him', Sir Hudson Fysh Papers, Mitchell Library, ML MSS 2413, Box-10, K21829, ca. 1817–1974.
23 Rogers, op. cit., p. 52.
24 'Southern Star, Arrival in England', *Sydney Morning Herald*, 17 December 1931.
25 'Hinkler at the Royal Aero Club', *Flight*, December 1931 (Vol. XXIII).
26 'Mr Bert Hinkler, South Atlantic Flight, Most Hazardous of his Career', *Sydney Morning Herald*, 5 December 1931.
27 Sprigg, C. St John, *Great Flights*, London, Thomas Nelson & Sons, 1936, p. 86.
28 'Mr Hinkler Successful Flight', *Sydney Morning Herald*, 30 November 1931.
29 ibid.
30 'Mr Hinkler Story of Flight', *Sydney Morning Herald*, 8 December 1931.
31 Mackenzie, Roy D., *Solo: The Bert Hinkler Story*, Ure Smith, Sydney, 1979, p. 110.
32 ibid., p. 92.
33 'Hinkler at the Royal Aero Club', *Flight*, December 1931 (Vol. XXIII).
34 Purvis, Harry and Priest, Joan, *Outback Airman*, Rigby, Adelaide, 1979, p. 15.
35 ibid., p. 12
36 'Sir "Smithy" Intrepid Airman Here', *Canberra Times*, 4 June 1932.
37 Wixted, Edward P., *The Life and Times of Sir Charles Kingsford Smith: An Illustrated Chronology*, private source, Queensland, 1996, p. 140.
38 'Sir "Smithy" Intrepid Airman Here', *Canberra Times*, 4 June 1932.
39 Wixted, op. cit., p. 140.
40 Purvis and Priest, op. cit., p. 20.
41 Wixted, Edward P., *The Last Flight of Bert Hinkler*, Vantage Press, New York, 1992, p. 10.
42 'Seeing "Smithy" off', *Kiama Independent*, 14 January 1933.
43 Taylor, op. cit.
44 'Seeing "Smithy" off', *Kiama Independent*, 14 January 1933.
45 Priest, Elaine; Bellini, Bruce; Dobson, Peter and Lockstone, Brian (eds), *Bell Block: A Local Aviation History*, New Plymouth Aero Club, New Plymouth, 2003, p. 28.
46 Purvis and Priest, op. cit., p. 25.
47 Wixted, *The Life and Times of Sir Charles Kingsford Smith*, op. cit., p. 153.
48 Mackersey, Ian, *Smithy: The Life of Sir Charles Kingsford Smith*, Little, Brown, London, 1999, p. 292.
49 Davis, Pedr, *Charles Kingsford Smith: Smithy, The World's Greatest Aviator*, Lansdowne Press, Sydney, 1985, p. 17.
50 'Joyriding Flights, Smithy Makes Money', *Northern Territory Times*, 10 June 1932.
51 Purvis and Priest, op. cit., p. 17.
52 Priest, et al., op. cit., p. 18f.
53 Kingsford Smith, op. cit., p. 154.
54 Mackersey, op. cit., p. 279f.

55 Mackenzie, op. cit., p. 119.
56 Wixted, *The Last Flight of Bert Hinkler*, op. cit., p. 49.

Chapter Seventeen: Troubles

1 McNally, Ward, *The Man on the Twenty Dollar Note: Sir Charles Kingsford-Smith*, A & A Reed, Sydney, 1976, p. 156.
2 Purvis, Harry and Priest, Joan, *Outback Airman*, Rigby, Adelaide, 1979, p. 10.
3 Australian Hansard, National Library of Australia, Canberra, 4 July 1933.
4 Bird, Nancy, *My God, It's A Woman!*, Angus & Robertson, Sydney, 1990, p. 31.
5 'Mail in Ten Days, London to Sydney', *Brisbane Courier Mail*, 16 October 1933.
6 Kingsford Smith, Sir Charles, *My Flying Life: An Authentic Biography Prepared under the Personal Supervision of and from the Diaries and Papers of the Late Sir Charles Kingsford-Smith*, Andrew Melrose, London, 1937, p. 236.
7 'Suva Landing Spectacular', *New York Times*, 6 June 1928.
8 Wixted, Edward P., *The Life and Times of Sir Charles Kingsford Smith: An Illustrated Chronology*, private source, Queensland, 1996, p. 141.
9 ibid.
10 'Aviation, Kingsford Smith's Flight', *Sydney Morning Herald*, 5 October 1933.
11 Sheil, Beau, *Caesar of the Skies: The Life Story of Sir Charles Kingsford Smith*, Cassell, London, 1937, p. 138f.
12 McNally, Ward, op. cit., p. 141.
13 'To Australia in 7 Days, Record Broken', *The Times*, 12 October 1933.
14 'League Team's Message', *Sydney Morning Herald*, 13 October 1933.
15 'Kingsford Smith Enthusiast Welcome in Sydney', *Sydney Morning Herald*, 16 October 1933.
16 Kingsford Smith, op. cit., p. 241.
17 Stannage, John, *Smithy*, Oxford University Press, London, 1950, p. 7.
18 McNally, op. cit., p. 25.
19 'Grant of £5,000 or a Job, Kingsford Smith, Federal Cabinet Proposal', *Courier-Mail*, 19 October 1933.
20 Gunn, John, *The Defeat of Distance: Qantas 1919–1939*, University of Queensland Press, St Lucia, Queensland, 1988, p. 195.
21 McMaster, Fergus to Hudson Fysh, 23 April 1934, Hudson Fysh Papers, Mitchell Library, Sydney.
22 McNally, op. cit., p. 143.
23 Kingsford Smith, op. cit., p. 241.
24 'Qantas Australian Air Mail Successful Tenders', *The Times*, 20 April 1934.
25 'Brisbane Is Air Mail Terminal', *Courier-Mail*, 20 April 1934.
26 'Kingsford Smith's Disappointment', *Sydney Morning Herald*, 21 April 1934.
27 McGinness, Paul to Hudson Fysh, 23 April 1934, Hudson Fysh Papers, Mitchell Library, Sydney.
28 Mackersey, Ian, *Smithy: The Life of Sir Charles Kingsford Smith*, Little,

Brown, London, 1999, p. 306.
29 Swinson, Arthur, *The Great Air Race*, Cassell, London, 1968, p. 7.
30 Kingsford Smith, op. cit., p. 242.
31 *This Fabulous Century*, TV series, 1979, Peter Luck.
32 'To Australia in 7 Days, Record Broken', *The Times*, 12 October 1933.
33 'His Cards On the Table', *Smith's Weekly*, 13 October 1934.
34 ibid.
35 Taylor, Sir Gordon, *The Sky Beyond*, Cassell, Melbourne, 1963, p. 48.
36 http://www.adastron.com/lockheed/altair/h1gross.htm A letter written on 28 August 1934 by Robert E. Gross, the president of Lockheed, to one Carter Tiffany, who is believed to have been an east coast representative of Lockheed.
37 'His Cards On the Table', *Smith's Weekly*, 13 October 1934.
38 Sheil, op. cit., p 182.
39 'The Air Race, Kingsford Smith in New York', *Age*, 18 June 1934.
40 ibid.
41 Taylor, P.G., *Pacific Flight: The Story of the Lady Southern Cross*, John Hamilton, London, 1936, p. 5.
42 ibid., p. 7.
43 Purvis and Priest, op. cit., p. 45.
44 For this, and much of the research which follows, I am indebted to Ron Cuskelly's website *The Lockheed File*. Its comprehensive history of the *Lady Southern Cross* draws heavily on the National Archives of Australia Series: MP 113/1 Item: VH/USB. It can be accessed on http://www.adastron.com/lockheed/altair/altair.htm.
45 http://www.adastron.com/lockheed/altair/altair4.htm
46 Swinson, op. cit., p. 74.
47 'Flier Issues A Denial', *New York Times*, 30 August 1934.
48 Purvis and Priest, op. cit., p. 52.
49 'Tremendous Task Faced "Smithy"', *Sydney Morning Herald*, 8 October 1934.
50 Kingsford Smith, op. cit., p. 248.
51 Ellison, Norman, *Flying Matilda: Early Days in Australian Aviation*, Angus & Robertson, Sydney, 1957, p. 317.
52 Kingsford Smith, op. cit., p. 249.
53 Taylor, Sir Gordon, 'Kingsford Smith as I Remember Him', Sir Hudson Fysh Papers, Mitchell Library, ML MSS 2413, Box 10, K21829, ca. 1817–1974.
54 'His Cards On the Table', *Smith's Weekly*, 13 October 1934.
55 ibid.
56 ibid.
57 'Smithy Gets the White Feather', *Smith's Weekly*, 20 October 1934.

Chapter Eighteen: The Great Race

1 Stannage, John, *Smithy*, Oxford University Press, London, 1950, p. 14.
2 'Mildenhall to Melbourne', *Time*, 29 October 1934.
3 Swinson, Arthur, *The Great Air Race*, Cassell, London, 1968, p. 101.
4 ibid., p. 89.
5 'Mildenhall to Melbourne', *Time*, 29 October 1934.
6 Swinson, op. cit., p. 89

7 *This Australia Program*, ABC Radio, Albury, 14 February 1984.
8 Swinton, Stuart, *P.G. Taylor: The Last of the Great Air Pioneers — A Personal Tribute From Stuart Swinton*, Australian Military History Publications, Loftus, New South Wales, 2006, p. 32.
9 Taylor, Sir Gordon, *The Sky Beyond*, Cassell, Melbourne, 1963, p. 50.
10 McNally, Ward, *The Man on the Twenty Dollar Note: Sir Charles Kingsford-Smith*, A & A Reed, Sydney, 1976, p. 152.
11 'The Comet's Amazing Flight', *The Times*, 24 October 1934.
12 Swinson, op. cit., p. 137.
13 'The End of the Race', *Canberra Times*, 24 October 1934.
14 Swinson, op. cit., p. 131.
15 'A Case for Snail Brooms', *Bulletin*, 7 November 1934.
16 'The Centenary Air Race', *Canberra Times*, 25 October 1934.
17 'The Centenary Air Race', *Aviation Heritage, The Journal of the Aviation Historical Society of Australia*, (Vol. 24, No 1/2, special combined issue), p. 43, http://www.ctie.monash.edu.au/hargrave/ahsabackissues301101.doc.
18 http://airsports.fai.org/mar2001/mar200015.html
19 *This Australia Program*, ABC Radio, Albury, 14 February 1984.
20 Purvis, Harry and Priest, Joan, *Outback Airman*, Rigby, Adelaide, 1979, p. 60.
21 Swinson, op. cit., p. 151.
22 *This Australia Program*, ABC Radio, Albury, 14 February 1984.
23 'The Resourceful Australian', *Bulletin*, 7 November 1934.
24 ibid.
25 'Kingsford Smith Has Grudge', *Canberra Times*, 24 October 1934.
26 Taylor, P.G., *Pacific Flight: The Story of the Lady Southern Cross*, John Hamilton, London, 1936, pp. 122, 124.
27 Kingsford Smith, Sir Charles, *My Flying Life: An Authentic Biography Prepared under the Personal Supervision of and from the Diaries and Papers of the Late Sir Charles Kingsford-Smith*, Andrew Melrose, London, 1937, p. 252.
28 'My Co-Pilot was Called Death', *Liberty Magazine*, 28 December 1935.
29 McNally, op. cit., p. 154. See also: Taylor, Sir Gordon, 'Kingsford Smith as I Remember Him', Sir Hudson Fysh Papers, Mitchell Library, ML MSS 2413, Box 10, K21829, ca. 1817–1974
30 Taylor, *The Sky Beyond*, op. cit., p. 53.
31 Swinton, op. cit., p. 40.
32 Taylor, *The Sky Beyond*, op. cit., p. 53.
33 Swinton, op. cit., p. 40.
34 Taylor, 'Kingsford Smith as I Remember Him', op. cit.
35 'At Honolulu Kingsford Smith's Pacific Flight', *Sydney Morning Herald*, 31 October 1934.
36 Taylor, *Pacific Flight*, op. cit., p. 218.
37 'Kingsford Smith Here After Epoch-Making Trans-Pacific Flight, Cheered by 20,000', *Los Angeles Times*, 5 November 1934.
38 ibid.
39 McNally, op. cit., p. 155.
40 'Pacific Fliers Warm Welcome', *Sydney Morning Herald*, 6 November 1934.

41 'At Honolulu Kingsford Smith's Pacific Flight', *Sydney Morning Herald*, 31 October 1934.
42 Stannage, John, *High Adventure*, MacDonald, Christchurch, 1944, p. 154.
43 United Press Association, Telegraph Copyright (Rec. 7.10 p.m.), San Francisco, 17 November 1934.
44 'Kingsford Smith Harassed', *Southland Times*, 19 November 1934.
45 'Pacific Airplane Seized for Debt', *New York Times*, 6 November 1934.
46 ibid.
47 'Ulm Ship Takes Off for Sydney from California', *Chicago Daily Tribune*, 4 December 1934.
48 'Air Service Within Two Years, Honolulu–Sydney, Ulm Plans Weekly "Planes"', *Canberra Times*, 3 December 1934.
49 'Ulm Lost Somewhere at Sea', *Canberra Times*, 6 December 1934.
50 'Ulm's Ill-Fated Dash Held a Blow to Flying', *Washington Post*, 8 December 1934.
51 'Ulm on Trans-Pacific Flight, Good Speed to Honolulu Flying at 150 Miles an Hour, "Plane Makes Excellent Progress"', *Canberra Times*, 5 December 1934.
52 'Ulm Ship Takes Off for Sydney from California', *Chicago Daily Tribune*, 4 December 1934.
53 'Ulm on Trans-Pacific Flight, Good Speed to Honolulu Flying at 150 Miles an Hour, "Plane Makes Excellent Progress"', *Canberra Times*, 5 December 1934.
54 'Ulm, Forced Down at Sea Near Hawaii, Hunted by Surface Craft and Planes', *Los Angeles Times*, 5 December 1934.
55 ibid.
56 ibid.
57 'Ulm Lost Somewhere at Sea', *Canberra Times*, 6 December 1934.
58 Stannage, *High Adventure*, op. cit., p. 156.
59 '"Smithy" in Joy and Sorrow, Loss of Ulm, Flying Pal Grief-Stricken', *Sun*, 11 December 1935.
60 ibid.
61 Taylor, Sir Gordon, lecture, Royal Aeronautical Society, New South Wales, 12 November 1959.
62 'Flyers Dead, Say Experts in the Sea Hunt', *Los Angeles Times*, 7 December 1934.
63 Gunn, John, *The Defeat of Distance: Qantas 1919–1939*, University of Queensland Press, St Lucia, Queensland, 1988, pp. 211–15.
64 '"Smithy" in Joy and Sorrow, Loss of Ulm, Flying Pal Grief-Stricken', *Sun*, 11 December 1935.
65 Gunn, op. cit., p. 213.
66 McNally, op. cit., p. 160.
67 Swinson, op. cit., p. 173.

Chapter Nineteen: Out On a Wing and a Prayer

1 Sprigg, C. St John, *Great Flights*, Thomas Nelson & Sons, London, 1936, p. 148.
2 Taylor, Sir Gordon, *The Sky Beyond*, Cassell, Melbourne, 1963, p. 88.
3 Stannage, John, *Smithy*, Oxford University Press, London, 1950, p. 85.

4 Kingsford Smith, Sir Charles, *My Flying Life: An Authentic Biography Prepared under the Personal Supervision of and from the Diaries and Papers of the Late Sir Charles Kingsford-Smith*, Andrew Melrose, London, 1937, p. 263.
5 Swinton, Stuart, *P.G. Taylor: The Last of the Great Air Pioneers — A Personal Tribute From Stuart Swinton*, Australian Military History Publications, Loftus, New South Wales, 2006, p. 48.
6 Stannage, op. cit., p. 102.
7 Taylor, Sir Gordon, 'Kingsford Smith as I Remember Him', Sir Hudson Fysh Papers, Mitchell Library, ML MSS 2413, Box 10, K21829, ca. 1817–1974.
8 Stannage, op. cit., p. 103.
9 Kingsford Smith, op. cit., p. 269.
10 ibid., p. 266.
11 Taylor, *The Sky Beyond*, op. cit., p. 69.
12 Kingsford Smith, op. cit., p. 267.
13 ibid.
14 ibid.
15 Stannage, op. cit., p. 104.
16 Taylor, 'Kingsford Smith as I Remember Him', op. cit.
17 Stannage, op. cit., p. 104.
18 ibid., p. 105.
19 Davis, Pedr, *Charles Kingsford Smith: Smithy, The World's Greatest Aviator*, Lansdowne Press, Sydney, 1985, p. 63.
20 Stannage, op. cit., p. 105.
21 Kingsford Smith, op. cit., p. 270.
22 ibid.
23 'Life of Thrills: "Smithy" as Pal, The Man in the Air', *Sun*, 10 December 1935.
24 Stannage, op. cit., p. 106.
25 'Life of Thrills: "Smithy" as Pal, The Man in the Air', *Sun*, 10 December 1935.
26 ibid.
27 Stannage, op. cit., p. 107.
28 Taylor, *The Sky Beyond*, op. cit., p. 78.
29 ibid.
30 ibid.
31 Stannage, John, *High Adventure*, MacDonald, Christchurch, 1944, p. 148.
32 Kingsford Smith, op. cit., p. 271.
33 Taylor, *The Sky Beyond*, op. cit., p. 82.
34 Stannage, *Smithy*, op. cit., p. 108.
35 Taylor, *The Sky Beyond*, op. cit., p. 85.
36 Stannage, *Smithy*, op. cit., p. 109.
37 'Defied Death', *Canberra Times*, 16 May 1935.
38 Swinton, op. cit., p. 52.
39 'Heroism Saves Kingsford Smith from Sea', *Chicago Daily Tribune*, 16 May 1935.
40 ibid.
41 Kingsford Smith, op. cit., p. 278.

42 'Kingsford Smith's Mishap', *The Times*, 17 May 1935.
43 'Silly Stunt, Attack on Kingsford Smith, London', *Canberra Times*, 24 May 1935.
44 'Dominions Should Operate Service, Tasman Flight Abandoned', *Canberra Times*, 17 May 1935.
45 'Defied Death', *Canberra Times*, 16 May 1935.
46 Stannage, *High Adventure*, op. cit., p. 151.
47 'Kingsford Smith's Mishap', *The Times*, 17 May 1935.
48 'Dominions Should Operate Service, Tasman Flight Abandoned', *Canberra Times*, 17 May 1935.
49 Wixted, Edward P., *The Life and Times of Sir Charles Kingsford Smith: An Illustrated Chronology*, private source, Queensland, 1996, p. 160.
50 Fysh, Sir Hudson, *Qantas Rising: The Autobiography of the Flying Fysh*, Angus & Robertson, Sydney, 1966, p. 241.
51 Mackersey, op. cit., p. 354.
52 Gunn, John, *The Defeat of Distance: Qantas 1919–1939*, University of Queensland Press, St Lucia, Queensland, 1988, p. 268.
53 Sheil, Beau, *Caesar of the Skies: The Life Story of Sir Charles Kingsford Smith*, Cassell, London, 1937, p. 4.
54 *This Fabulous Century*, TV series, 1979, Peter Luck.
55 'Last Flight, Southern Cross for Richmond, Temporary Home Sydney', *Canberra Times*, 18 July 1935.
56 ibid.
57 Kingsford Smith, op. cit., p. 280.
58 Wixted, op. cit., p. 211.
59 Mackersey, op. cit., p. 356.
60 Fysh, Hudson to G.E. Woods Humphrey, 23 April 1934, Hudson Fysh Papers, Mitchell Library, Sydney.
61 Humphrey, G.E. Woods to Hudson Fysh, 30 July 1935, Hudson Fysh Papers, Mitchell Library, Sydney.
62 Gunn, op. cit., p. 276.
63 ibid., p. 278.
64 Mackersey, op. cit., p. 357.
65 'Kingsford Smith at San Pedro', *New York Times*, 11 August 1935.
66 'My Co-Pilot was Called Death', *Liberty Magazine*, 28 December 1935.
67 ibid.
68 Morton, Fred, *'Smithy': Sir Charles Kingsford Smith — The World's Greatest Aviator*, New Image Publications, Melbourne, 1984, p 38.
69 McNally, Ward, *The Man on the Twenty Dollar Note: Sir Charles Kingsford-Smith*, A & A Reed, Sydney, 1976, p. 177.
70 Morton, op. cit., p 23.
71 Mackersey, op. cit., p. 362.
72 ibid., p. 363.
73 Morton, op. cit., (50th Anniversary Edition), 'Beau Sheil: Smithy's PR Man', p. 21.
74 Sheil, op. cit., p. 187.
75 Mackersey, op. cit., p. 366.
76 'Reported Battling Monsoon', *New York Times*, 9 November 1935.
77 Mackersey, op. cit., p. 367.
78 'Kingsford-Smith Overdue', *New York Times*, 8 November 1935.

79 'Kingsford-Smith still Unreported', *New York Times*, 9 November 1935.
80 'Brother Not Worried', *New York Times*, 9 November 1935.
81 'R.A.F. Searching for Kingsford Smith, Flights Over Land and Sea', *The Times*, 11 November 1935.
82 'Kingsford Smith, Planes Find No Trace', *Sydney Morning Herald*, 11 November 1935.
83 'Search Called Off for Flyers', *Canberra Times*, 19 November 1935.
84 'Qantas Plane for Search', *Canberra Times*, 20 November 1935.
85 'The Search in the Jungle, R.A.F. Commodore's Message', *Sydney Morning Herald*, 2 December 1935.
86 'Hopes Fading for Missing Fliers', *Canberra Times*, 14 November 1935.
87 'Spiritualists Disagree on Airmen's Fate', *Canberra Times*, 21 November 1935.
88 'Medium's Replies Alleges Flyers' Loss at Sea', *Canberra Times*, 20 November 1935.
89 'New Hopes Raised in Sydney', *Canberra Times*, 23 November 1935.
90 'Further Reports of Plane Crash', *Canberra Times*, 26 November 1935.
91 'Kingsford Smith, New Hopes Raised, Reported Crash of Plane in Jungle', *Canberra Times*, 27 November 1935.

Epilogue

1 Sealby, Winifred Kingsford, *Recollections: Personal and Scenic; Our Dumb Friends*, (Australian Library Collections, Record ID 5583222), 1951, p. 22.
2 Davis, Pedr, *Charles Kingsford Smith: Smithy, The World's Greatest Aviator*, Lansdowne Press, Sydney, 1985, p. 91.
3 Taylor, Sir Gordon, *The Sky Beyond*, Cassell, Melbourne, 1963, p. 95.
4 Gunn, John, *The Defeat of Distance: Qantas 1919–1939*, University of Queensland Press, St Lucia, Queensland, 1988, p. 286.
5 'Kingsford Smith Mascot 'Drome to Perpetuate Name', *Canberra Times*, 14 August 1936.
6 Morton, Fred, *'Smithy': Sir Charles Kingsford Smith — The World's Greatest Aviator*, New Image Publications, Melbourne, 1984, p 47.
7 'Has Charles Kingsford Smith's Plane Been Found?', *Daily Telegraph*, 21 March 2009.
8 'Kingsford Smith? Not Likely, Says Dick Smith', *Sydney Morning Herald*, 22 March 2009.
9 'My Co-Pilot was Called Death', *Liberty Magazine*, 28 December 1935.
10 Interview with Charles Kingsford-Smith Jnr, March 2009.
11 'C.J. Melrose, Young Airman Killed, Crash in Storm at Melton, Mining Engineer Killed', *Canberra Times*, 6 July 1936.
12 Wixted, Edward P., *The Life and Times of Sir Charles Kingsford Smith: An Illustrated Chronology*, private source, Queensland, 1996, p. 264.
13 Interview with John Ulm, Australia, May 2008.
14 'Jim Warner Radioman', *American Aviation Historical Society Journal*, Summer 1983 (Vol. 28, Issue 2).
15 Sufrin, Mark, *The Brave Men: Twelve Portraits of Courage*, Platt & Munk, New York, 1967, p. 259.
16 http://www.bcphilatelic.org/images/BCPS_fall_2008_newsletter.pdf Author of the article in question is Bob Ingraham of the British

Columbia Philatelic Society.

17 http://en.wikipedia.org/wiki/1948_KLM_Constellation_air_disaster references to: Barker, Ralph, *Great Mysteries of the Air*, Macmillan, New York, 1967. See also: http://aviation-safety.net/database/record.php?id=19481020-0 and www.aircrashsites-scotland.co.uk/connie_mauchline.htm

18 'Southern Cloud Discoverer Retraces His Steps', *7.30 Report*, ABC TV, 30 October 2008.

19 Interview with Tom Sonter, Sydney, December 2008.

20 Interview with Cynthia Balderstone, Sydney, December 2008.

21 'Southern Cloud Discoverer Retraces His Steps', *7.30 Report*, ABC TV, 30 October 2008.

22 Kalush, William and Sloman, Larry, *The Secret Life of Houdini: The Making of America's First Superhero*, Atria, New York, 2006, p. 509.

23 ibid.

24 ibid., p. 513f.

25 Bouffard, James Charles, *The Magician's Flight! How The Magician Fought for His Art*, Lulu, North Carolina, 2008, p. 48.

26 Swinson, Arthur, *The Great Air Race,* Cassell, London, 1968, p. 188f.

27 ibid.

28 'I've Never Got Over It', *Daily Telegraph*, 12 July 2007.

29 'Coronation Honours List Military Division K.B.E.', *Canberra Times*, 1 June 1953.

30 Page, Dorothy G., *Polar Pilot: The Carl Ben Eielson Story*, Interstate Publishers, Danville, Illinois, 1992, p. 367.

31 'Unsung No 1 with a Bullet', *Australian*, 11 April 2007.

32 Kilduff, Peter, *Richthofen: Beyond the Legend of the Red Baron*, Arms and Armour Press, London, 1999, p. 220.

33 Cross, James Giblin, *Charles A. Lindbergh: A Human Hero*, Clarion Books, New York, 1997, p. 181.

34 Whitman, Alden, 'The Return Of Charles Lindbergh', *New York Times*, 23 May 1971.

35 Cross, op. cit., p. 191.

BIBLIOGRAPHY

Adams, Michael, *Wind Beneath his Wing: Lawrence Hargrave At Stanwell Park*, Cultural Exchange International, New South Wales, 2005.

Aughton, Peter, *Voyages that Changed the World*, Murdoch Books, Sydney, 2007.

Barker, Ralph, *A Brief History of the Royal Flying Corps in World War I*, Constable & Robinson, London, 2002.

Battye, Jas S. (ed), *The History of the North West of Australia: Embracing Kimberley, Gascoyne and Murchison Districts*, Hesperian Press, Victoria Park, Western Australia, 1985.

Bean, C.E.W., *The Story of Anzac*, Vol. I, Sydney, 1924.

Berg, A. Scott, *Lindbergh*, Putnam Adult, New York, USA, 1998.

Blackmore, L.K., *Hawker: A Biography of Harry Hawker*, Airlife, Shrewsbury, 1993.

Bouffard, James Charles, *The Magician's Flight! How the Magician Fought for His Art*, Lulu, North Carolina, 2008.

Braudy, Leo, *The Frenzy of Renown: Fame and Its History*, Oxford University Press, New York, 1987.

Brawley, Sean, *The Bondi Lifesaver: A History of an Australian Icon*, ABC Books, Sydney, 2007.

Brearley, Sir Norman, *Australian Aviator*, Rigby, Adelaide, 1971.

Briggs, F.S. and Harris, S.H., *Joysticks and Fiddlesticks: The Unofficial History of a Flying Kangaroo*, Hutchinson & Co, London, 1936.

Brogden, Stanley, *The History of Australian Aviation*, Hawthorne Press, Melbourne, 1960.

Burton, Walt and Findsen, Owen, *The Wright Brothers Legacy: Orville and Wilbur Wright and Their Aeroplanes*, Harry N. Abrams Inc., New York, 2003.

Byrnes, Paul, *Qantas by George! The Remarkable Story of George Roberts*, The Watermark Press, Sydney, 2000.

Cadigan, Neil, *A Man Among Mavericks: Lester Brain, Australia's Greatest Aviator*, ABC Books, Sydney, 2008.

Campbell, Eric, *The Rallying Point: My Story of the New Guard*, Melbourne University Press, Melbourne, 1965.

Carlyon, Les, *Gallipoli*, Macmillan, Sydney, 2001.

Carroll, Brian, *Australian Aviators: An Illustrated History*, Cassell, Sydney, 1980.

Chanute, Octave, *Progress in Flying Machines*, Dover Publications, New York, 1997.

Clark, Alan, *Aces High, The War in the Air Over the Western Front, 1914–18* (revised edition), Cassell, London, 1999.

Clover, Sam T., *A Pioneer Heritage*, Saturday Night Publishing Company, Los

Angeles, 1932.
Cole, Duane, *Conquest of Lines and Symmetry*, Ken Cook Transnational, Wisconsin, 1970.
Courtwright, David T., *Sky as Frontier: Adventure, Aviation and Empire* (Centennial of Flight Series), Texas A & M University Press, USA, 2005.
Cross, James Giblin, *Charles A. Lindbergh: A Human Hero*, Clarion Books, New York, 1997.
Cutlack, F.M., *Official Histories: First World War Volume VIII, The Australian Flying Corps in the Western and Eastern Theatres of War, 1914–1918*, Angus & Robertson, Sydney, 1941.
Davis, Pedr, *Charles Kingsford Smith: Smithy, The World's Greatest Aviator*, Lansdowne Press, Sydney, 1985.
Davis, Pedr, *Kookaburra: The Most Compelling Story in Australia's Aviation History*, Lansdowne Press, Sydney, 1980.
Edwards, Hugh, *Gold Dust & Iron Mountains: Marble Bar and Beyond*, East Pilbara Shire, Western Australia, 1993.
Elliott, Brian A., *Blériot: Herald of an Age*, Tempus Publishing, Gloucestershire, 2000.
Ellison, Norman, *Daredevils of the Skies*, Angus & Robertson, Sydney, 1941.
Ellison, Norman, *Flying Matilda: Early Days in Australian Aviation*, Angus & Robertson, Sydney, 1957.
Eustis, Nelson, *Australia's Greatest Air Race: England–Australia 1919*, Rigby, Adelaide, 1977.
Ewing, Ross and MacPherson, Ross, *The History of New Zealand Aviation*, Heinemann, Auckland, 1986.
Finlay, Peter, *Australia's First Aviator*, Aero Australia, Issue 14, April 2007.
Fokker, Anthony, *Flying Dutchman*, George Routledge & Sons, London, 1932.
Fontaine, Charles, *Comment Blériot a Traversé la Manche*, Librairie Aéronautique, Paris, 1909.
Fysh, Sir Hudson, *Qantas Rising: The Autobiography of the Flying Fysh*, Angus & Robertson, Sydney, 1966.
Gall, Jennifer, *From Bullocks to Boeings: An Illustrated History of Sydney Airport*, Australian Government Publishing Service, Canberra, 1986.
Gammage, Bill, *The Broken Years: Australian Soldiers in the Great War*, Australian National University Press, Canberra, 1974.
Garland, Thomas Ownsworth, *Artificial Respiration: With Special Emphasis on the Holger Nielsen Method*, Faber, London, 1955.
Garros, Roland, *Memoires présentés par Jacques Quellennec*, Hachette, Paris, 1966.
Godwin, John, *Battling Parer*, Rigby, Adelaide, 1968.
Grahame-White, Claude, *The Story of the Aeroplane*, Small, Maynard & Co., Boston, 1911.
Grierson, John, *Sir Hubert Wilkins: Enigma of Exploration*, Robert Hale, London, 1960.
Gunn, John, *The Defeat of Distance: Qantas 1919–1939*, University of Queensland Press, St Lucia, Queensland, 1988.
Guttman, Jon, *Sopwith Camel vs Fokker Dr I: Western Front 1917–18*, Osprey

Publishing, Oxford, 2008.
Hare, Paul R., *Aeroplanes of the Royal Aircraft Factory*, The Crowood Press, Marlborough, 1999.
Hawker, Muriel, *H.G. Hawker, Airman: His Life and Work*, Hutchinson & Co, London, 1922.
Haynes, Jim and Dellit, Jillian, *Great Australian Aviation Stories: Characters, Pioneers, Triumphs, Tragedies and Near Misses*, ABC Books, Sydney, 2006.
Hazlitt, Lesley, *Just Call Me Jack*, Lexington Avenue Press, New South Wales, 2004.
Hillary, Richard, *The Last Enemy*, Battle of Britain Series, Pan Books, London, 1969.
Holloway, David, *Hooves, Wheels & Tracks: A History of the 4th/19th Prince of Wales's Light Horse Regiment and Its Predecessors*, Regimental Trustees, Melbourne, 1990.
Horne, Donald, *In Search of Billy Hughes*, Macmillan, Melbourne, 1979.
Horvat, William Joseph, *Above the Pacific*, Aero Publishers, Fallbrook, California, 1966.
Howard, Frederick, *Wilbur & Orville*, Knopf, New York, 1987.
Hughes, Aneurin, *Billy Hughes: Prime Minister and Controversial Founding Father of the Australian Labor Party*, John Wiley & Sons, Brisbane, 2005.
Isaacs, Keith, *Military Aircraft of Australia 1909–1918*, Australian War Memorial, Canberra, 1971.
Joy, William, *The Aviators*, Shakespeare Head Press, Sydney, 1971.
Judd, Stephen and Cable, Kenneth, *Sydney Anglicans*, Anglican Information Office, Sydney, 1987.
Kalush, William and Sloman, Larry, *The Secret Life of Houdini: The Making of America's First Superhero*, Atria, New York, 2006.
Kelly, Fred C. (ed), *Miracle at Kitty Hawk: The Letters of Wilbur and Orville Wright*, Farrar & Straus, New York, 1951.
Kilduff, Peter, *Richthofen: Beyond the Legend of the Red Baron*, Arms and Armour Press, London, 1999.
Kingsford Smith, Sir Charles E. and Ulm, Charles T.P., *The Great Trans-Pacific Flight: The Story of the 'Southern Cross'*, Hutchinson, London, 1928.
Kingsford Smith, Sir Charles, *My Flying Life: An Authentic Biography Prepared under the Personal Supervision of and from the Diaries and Papers of the Late Sir Charles Kingsford-Smith*, Andrew Melrose, London, 1937.
Kingsford Smith, Sir Charles, *The Old Bus*, Herald Press, Melbourne, 1932.
Lawrence, T.E., *Seven Pillars of Wisdom*, Penguin, Harmondsworth, 1979.
Lindbergh, Charles A., *Charles A. Lindbergh: Autobiography of Values*, Harcourt Brace Jovanovich, New York, USA, 1977.
Lindbergh, Charles A., *Of Flight and Life*, Scribner's Sons, New York, 1948.
Lindbergh, Charles Augustus, *The Spirit of St. Louis*, Tandem Publishing, London, 1975.
Love, Nigel B., *The Autobiography of Nigel B. Love (Part One), Aviation in Australia, 1915–1923*, self-published, Sydney, ca. 1968.
Lumsden, Alec, *British Piston Engines and Their Aircraft*, Airlife, 2003.
Mackenzie, Roy D., *Solo: The Bert Hinkler Story*, Ure Smith, Sydney, 1979.
Mackersey, Ian, *Smithy: The Life of Sir Charles Kingsford Smith*, Little, Brown,

London, 1999.
Mackersey, Ian, *The Wright Brothers: The Remarkable Story of the Aviation Pioneers Who Changed the World*, Time Warner, 2004.
Mattioli, Guido, *Mussolini Aviatore e la Sua Opera per L'Aviaziane, Prefazione di Paolo Orano*, Casa Editrice Pinciana, Rome, 1938.
McMullin, Ross, *Pompey, Elliott*, Scribe Publications, Melbourne, 2002.
McNally, Ward, *Smithy: The Kingsford-Smith Story*, Robert Hale, London, 1966.
McNally, Ward, *The Man on the Twenty Dollar Note: Sir Charles Kingsford-Smith*, A & A Reed, Sydney, 1976.
Mills, Robert Lockwood, *The Lindbergh Syndrome: Heroes and Celebrities in a New Golden Age*, Fenestra Books, Arizona, 2005.
Mollison, Jim, *Playboy of the Air*, Michael Joseph, London, 1937.
Montague, Richard, *Oceans, Poles and Airmen: The First Flights Over Wide Waters and Desolate Ice*, Random House, New York, 1971.
Morton, Fred, *'Smithy': Sir Charles Kingsford Smith — The World's Greatest Aviator*, New Image Publications, Melbourne, 1984.
Nasht, Simon, *The Last Explorer: Hubert Wilkins — Australia's Unknown Hero*, Hachette Livre Australia/Hodder, Sydney, 2007.
Noonan, Michael, *In the Land of the Talking Trees — A Fantasy*, Angus & Robertson, Sydney, 1946.
Page, Dorothy G., *Polar Pilot: The Carl Ben Eielson Story*, Interstate Publishers, Danville, Illinois, 1992.
Pound, Reginald and Harmsworth, Geoffrey, *Northcliffe*, Cassell, London, 1959.
Priest, Elaine; Bellini, Bruce; Dobson, Peter and Lockstone, Brian (eds), *Bell Block: A Local Aviation History*, New Plymouth Aero Club, New Plymouth, 2003.
Purvis, Harry and Priest, Joan, *Outback Airman*, Rigby, Adelaide, 1979.
Robinson, Anthony (ed), *In the Cockpit: Flying the World's Great Aircraft*, Orbis Pub, London, 1984.
Rogers, Ellen, *Faith In Australia: Charles Ulm and Australian Aviation*, Book Production Services, Sydney, 1987.
Ross, Walter Sanford, *The Last Hero: Charles A. Lindbergh*, Manor Books, New York, 1974.
Rudge, Chris, *Missing!*, Adventure Air, Lyttelton, 2001.
Rukin, Peter, *The Aviators Nest, Richmond, Wings over the Hawkesbury, An Historical Scrapbook*, Peter Rukin, Richmond, New South Wales, 2006.
Schurmacher, Emile C., *Richthofen: The Red Baron*, Paperback Library, New York, 1971.
Scott, C.W.A., *The Life and Mildenhall–Melbourne Flight of C.W.A. Scott*, Hodder & Stoughton, London, 1934.
Sealby, Winifred Kingsford, *Recollections: Personal and Scenic; Our Dumb Friends*, (Australian Library Collections, Record ID 5583222), 1951.
Shaw, W. Hudson and Ruhen, Olaf, *Lawrence Hargrave: Aviation Pioneer, Inventor and Explorer*, University of Queensland Press, St Lucia, Queensland, 1988.
Sheil, Beau, *Caesar of the Skies: The Life Story of Sir Charles Kingsford Smith*, Cassell, London, 1937.

Smith, Neil C., *Men of Beersheba: A History of the 4th Light Horse Regiment, 1914–1919*, Mostly Unsung Military History Research and Publications, Melbourne, 1993.
Sprigg, C. St John, *Great Flights*, Thomas Nelson & Sons, London, 1936.
Stannage, John, *High Adventure*, MacDonald, Christchurch, 1944.
Stannage, John, *Smithy*, Oxford University Press, London, 1950.
Sufrin, Mark, *The Brave Men: Twelve Portraits of Courage*, Platt & Munk, New York, 1967.
Swinson, Arthur, *The Great Air Race*, Cassell, London, 1968.
Swinton, Stuart, *P.G. Taylor: The Last of the Great Air Pioneers — A Personal Tribute From Stuart Swinton*, Australian Military History Publications, Loftus, New South Wales, 2006.
Taylor, P.G., *Pacific Flight: The Story of the Lady Southern Cross*, John Hamilton, London, 1936.
Taylor, Sir Gordon, *Sopwith Scout 7309*, Cassell, London, 1968.
Taylor, Sir Gordon, *The Sky Beyond*, Cassell, Melbourne, 1963.
Thomas, Lowell, *Sir Hubert Wilkins: His World of Adventure*, McGraw-Hill, New York, 1961.
Trubuhovich, Ronald V., *History of Mouth-to-Mouth Ventilation, Part 3: The 19th to mid-20th Centuries and 'Rediscovery'* (Vol. 9), Department of Critical Care Medicine, Auckland, 2007.
von Richthofen, Manfred, *The Red Fighter Pilot: The Autobiography of the Red Baron*, Red and Black Publishers, Florida, 2007.
Wallace, Graham, *The Flying Witness*, Putnam, London, 1958.
Wilkins, George Hubert, *Flying the Arctic*, Kessinger Publishing (reprint), Whitefish, USA, 2004.
Williams, Sir Richard, *These are the Facts: The Autobiography of Air Marshall Sir Richard Williams*, Australian War Memorial and the Australian Government Publishing Service, Canberra, 1977.
Wixted, Edward P., *The Last Flight of Bert Hinkler*, Vantage Press, New York, 1992.
Wixted, Edward P., *The Life and Times of Sir Charles Kingsford Smith: An Illustrated Chronology*, private source, Queensland, 1996.
Wohl, Robert, *A Passion for Wings: Aviation and the Western Imagination, 1908–918*, Yale University Press, New Haven/London, 1994.
Wilson, Stewart, *Beaufort, Beaufighter & Mosquito in Australian Service*, Aerospace Publications Pty, Weston Creek, Australian Capital Territory, 1990.
Wilson, Stewart, *Military Aircraft of Australia*, Aerospace Publications Pty, Weston Creek, Australian Capital Territory, 1984.
Wright, Nicolas, *The Red Baron*, Sidgewick and Jackson, London, 1976.
Wright, Wilbur, *The Papers of Wilbur and Orville Wright, Including the Chanute-Wright letters and Other Papers of Octave Chanute (2 Volumes)*, Ayer Company Publishers, Manchester, 1972.
Yeates, V.M., *Winged Victory (Echoes of War)*, Buchan & Enright, London, 1985.
Young, Margaret and Gammage, Bill (eds), *Hail and Farewell: Letters From Two Brothers Killed in France in 1916*, Kangaroo Press, Sydney, 1995.

INDEX